Magill's
Bibliography
of
Literary Criticism

Magill's
Bibliography
of
Literary Criticism

SELECTED SOURCES FOR THE STUDY OF MORE THAN
2,500 OUTSTANDING WORKS OF WESTERN LITERATURE

Edited by
FRANK N. MAGILL

Associate Editors
STEPHEN L. HANSON
PATRICIA KING HANSON

Volume Three
Longus - Sexton
1223 - 1832

SALEM PRESS

Englewood Cliffs

LIBRARY OF CONGRESS CATALOG CARD NUMBER: 79-63017

Complete Set:	ISBN 0-89356-188-6
Volume 3:	ISBN 0-89356-191-6

PRINTED IN THE UNITED STATES OF AMERICA

Magill's
Bibliography
of
Literary Criticism

LIST OF AUTHORS AND TITLES—VOLUME THREE

LONGUS
(fl. Third century A.D.)

Daphnis and Chloë

Bonnard, A. "Other Escapisms: Herodas and Realistic Mime, the Novel— *Daphnis and Chloë*," in *Greek Civilization: From Euripides to Alexandria.* New York: Macmillan, 1961, pp. 246–258.

Chalk, H.H.D. "Eros and the Lesbian Pastorals of Longus," in *Journal of Hellenic Studies.* LXXX (1960), pp. 32–51.

Deligiorgis, S. "Longus' Art in Brief Lives," in *Philological Quarterly.* LIII (1974), pp. 1–9.

Haight, E.H. "Lesbian Pastorals of *Daphnis and Chloë*, by Longus," in *Essays on the Greek Romances.* New York: Longmans, 1943, pp. 119–143.

Heiserman, Arthur Ray. "Antonine Comedy," in *The Novel Before the Novel.* Chicago: University of Chicago Press, 1977, pp. 117–166.

Kestner, J. "Ehphrases as Frame in Longus' *Daphnis and Chloë*," in *Classical World.* LXVII (1973), pp. 161–171.

McCulloh, W.C. *Longus.* New York: Twayne, 1970.

Mittelstadt, M.C. "Longus, *Daphnis and Chloë* and Roman Narrative Painting," in *Latomus.* XXVI (1967), pp. 752–761.

————. "Longus, *Daphnis and Chloë* and the Pastoral Tradition," in *Classica et Medialvalia.* XXVII (1969), pp. 162–177.

Todd, F.A. "*Daphnis and Chloë*," in *Some Ancient Novels.* Freeport, N.Y.: Books for Libraries, 1968, pp. 34–64.

RICHARD LOVELACE
(1618–1658)

The Poetry of Lovelace

Allen, D.C. *Image and Meaning: Metaphoric Traditions in Renaissance Poetry.* Baltimore: Johns Hopkins University Press, 1960, pp. 80–92. Reprinted in *Ben Jonson and the Cavalier Poets.* Edited by Hugh Maclean. New York: Norton, 1974, pp. 570–577.

Brooks, C. "Literary Criticism: Poet, Poem, and Reader," in *Perspectives in Contemporary Criticism: A Collection of Recent Essays by American, English, and European Literary Critics.* Edited by Sheldon Grebstein. New York: Harper's, 1968, pp. 96–107.

King, B.A. "Green Ice and a Breast of Proof," in *Seventeenth-Century English Poetry: Modern Essays in Criticism.* Edited by William R. Keast. New York: Oxford University Press, 1971, pp. 324–332.

Lindsay, Philip. *For King or Parliament.* London: Evans, 1949, pp. 170–202.

Praz, Mario. "Richard Lovelace," in *Modern Language Review.* XXI (1926), pp. 319–322.

Skelton, Robin. *The Cavalier Poets.* London: Longmans, Green, 1960, pp. 26–33.

Walton, Geoffrey. "The Cavalier Poets," in *From Donne to Marvell.* Edited by Boris Ford. London: Penguin, 1956, pp. 169–172.

Weidhorn, Manfred. *Richard Lovelace.* New York: Twayne, 1970.

"To Lucasta, Going to the Wars"

Ciardi, John. *How Does a Poem Mean?* Boston: Houghton Mifflin, 1959, pp. 929–932.

Holland, Norman. "Literary Value: A Psychoanalytic Approach," in *Literature and Psychology.* XIV (1964), pp. 43–55, 116–127.

Jones, G.F. "Lov'd I Not Honour More: The Durability of a Literary Motif," in *Comparative Literature.* XI (1959), pp. 131–143.

Kirk, Richard Ray and Roger P. McCutcheon. *An Introduction to the Study of Poetry.* New York: American Book, 1934, pp. 12–14.

Pearson, N.H. "Lovelace's 'To Lucasta,' " in *Explicator.* VII (1949), item 58.

Richmond, H.M. "A Note on Professor Holland's Psychoanalytic Approach," in *Literature and Psychology.* XIV (1964), pp. 116–127.

Van Doren, Mark. *Introduction to Poetry.* New York: Sloane, 1951, pp. 22–26.

Walton, Geoffrey. "The Cavalier Poets," in *From Donne to Marvell.* Edited by Boris Ford. London: Penguin, 1956, pp. 61, 170.

Weidhorn, Manfred. *Richard Lovelace.* New York: Twayne, 1970, pp. 92–98.

JAMES RUSSELL LOWELL
(1819–1891)

The Biglow Papers

Beatty, Richmond Groom. *James Russell Lowell.* Nashville, Tenn.: Vanderbilt University Press, 1942, pp. 75–90, 166–176.

Brenner, Rica. *Twelve American Poets Before 1900.* New York: Harcourt, Brace, 1933, pp. 213–214.

Duberman, Martin. *James Russell Lowell.* Boston: Houghton Mifflin, 1966, pp. 101–107.

Enkvist, N.E. *"The Biglow Papers* in Nineteenth Century England," in *New England Quarterly.* XXVI (1953), pp. 219–236.

Greenslet, Ferris. *James Russell Lowell.* Boston: Houghton Mifflin, 1905.

Howard, Leon. *Victorian Knight-Errant: A Study of the Early Literary Career of James Russell Lowell.* Berkeley: University of California Press, 1952, pp. 232–260.

Kreymborg, Alfred. *Our Singing Strength: An Outline of American Poetry (1620–1930).* New York: Coward-McCann, 1929, pp. 122–125.

Onderdonk, James L. *History of American Poetry (1610–1897).* Chicago: A.C. McClurg, 1901, pp. 280–285.

Pearce, Roy Harvey. *The Continuity of American Poetry.* Princeton, N.J.: Princeton University Press, 1961, pp. 219–220.

Scudder, Horace Elisha. *James Russell Lowell: A Biography,* Volume 1. Boston: Houghton Mifflin, 1901, pp. 255–266.

Stedman, Edmund Clarence. *Poets of America.* Boston: Houghton Mifflin, 1885, pp. 321–325.

Waggoner, Hyatt H. *American Poets from the Puritans to the Present.* Boston: Houghton Mifflin, 1968, pp. 61–69.

Wells, Henry W. *The American Way of Poetry.* New York: Russell and Russell, 1964, pp. 47–48.

Wilson, Edmund. *Patriotic Gore: Studies in the Literature of the American Civil War.* New York: Oxford University Press, 1962, pp. 476–479.

Wortham, Thomas. "Introduction," in *The Biglow Papers.* By James Russell Lowell. DeKalb: Northern Illinois University Press, 1977, pp. ix–xxxiv.

A Fable for Critics

Beatty, Richmond Groom. *James Russell Lowell.* Nashville, Tenn.: Vanderbilt University Press, 1942, pp. 94–100.

Duberman, Martin.   *James Russell Lowell.* Boston: Houghton Mifflin, 1966, pp. 96–102.

Ehrlich, Heyward.   "Charles Frederick Briggs and Lowell's *Fable for Critics*," in *Modern Language Quarterly.* XXVII (1967), pp. 329–341.

Greenslet, Ferris.   *James Russell Lowell.* Boston: Houghton Mifflin, 1905, pp. 76–77, 80–81.

Howard, Leon.   *Victorian Knight-Errant: A Study of the Early Literary Career of James Russell Lowell.* Berkeley: University of California Press, 1952, pp. 260–269.

Kreymborg, Alfred.   *Our Singing Strength: An Outline of American Poetry (1620–1930).* New York: Coward-McCann, 1929, pp. 118–122.

Oggel, L.T.   "*A Fable for Critics*," in *Explicator.* XXVII (April, 1969), item 60.

Onderdonk, James L.   *History of American Poetry (1610–1897).* Chicago: A.C. McClurg, 1901, pp. 286–289.

Scudder, Horace Elisha.   *James Russell Lowell: A Biography*, Volume 1. Boston: Houghton Mifflin, 1901, pp. 238–255.

Smith, Herbert F.   "Introduction to *A Fable for Critics*," in *Literary Criticism of James Russell Lowell.* Edited by Herbert F. Smith. Lincoln: University of Nebraska Press, 1969, pp. 153–155.

ROBERT LOWELL
(1917–1977)

For the Union Dead

Axelrod, Steven. "Private and Public Worlds in Lowell's *For the Union Dead*," in *Perspectives on Contemporary Literature*. I (1975), pp. 53–73.

Bly, Robert. "Robert Lowell's *For the Union Dead*," in *Sixties*. VII (Spring, 1966), pp. 93–96. Reprinted in *Robert Lowell: A Portrait of the Artist in His Time*. Edited by Michael London and Robert Boyers. New York: David Lewis, 1970, pp. 73–76.

Bobbitt, Joan. "Lowell and Plath: Objectivity and Confessional Mode," in *Arizona Quarterly*. XXXIII (Winter, 1977), pp. 311–318.

Cooper, Philip. *The Autobiographical Myth of Robert Lowell*. Chapel Hill: University of North Carolina Press, 1970, pp. 68–117.

Cosgrave, Patrick. *The Public Poetry of Robert Lowell*. London: Victor Gollancz, 1970, pp. 149–184.

Crick, John. *Robert Lowell*. Edinburgh: Oliver and Boyd, 1974, pp. 83–99.

Curran, Mary Doyle. "Poems Public and Private," in *Massachusetts Review*. VI (1965), pp. 411–415.

Dickey, William. "Poetic Language," in *Hudson Review*. XVII (1964–1965), pp. 587–596.

Fein, Richard J. *Robert Lowell*. New York: Twayne, 1970, pp. 93–115.

Fraser, G.S. "Amid the Horror, a Song of Praise," in *New York Times Book Review*. (October 4, 1964), p. 1. Reprinted in *Profile of Robert Lowell*. Edited by Jerome Mazzaro. Columbus, Oh.: Merrill, 1971, pp. 49–52.

Hartman, Geoffrey. "The Eye of the Storm," in *Partisan Review*. XXXII (1965), pp. 277–280. Reprinted in *Robert Lowell: A Portrait of the Artist in His Time*. Edited by Michael London and Robert Boyers. New York: David Lewis, 1970, pp. 60–64.

Holbrook, David. *Lost Bearings in English Poetry*. New York: Barnes & Noble, 1977, pp. 48–57.

Mazzaro, Jerome. *The Poetic Themes of Robert Lowell*. Ann Arbor: University of Michigan Press, 1965, pp. 120–135.

Parkinson, Thomas. "*For the Union Dead*," in *Salmagundi*. I (1966–1967), pp. 87–96. Reprinted in *Robert Lowell: A Collection of Critical Essays*. Edited by Thomas Parkinson. Englewood Cliffs, N.J.: Prentice-Hall, 1968, pp. 143–151.

Poirier, Richard. "*For the Union Dead*," in *Book Week*. (October 11, 1964), pp. 1, 16. Reprinted in *Critics on Robert Lowell*. Edited by Jonathan Price. Coral Gables, Fla.: University of Miami Press, 1972, pp. 92–96.

Ramsey, Paul. "In Exasperation and Gratitude," in *Sewanee Review*. LXXIV (1966), pp. 930–945.

Ricks, Christopher. "The Three Lives of Robert Lowell," in *New Statesman*. LXIX (March 26, 1965), pp. 496–497. Reprinted in *Critics on Robert Lowell*. Edited by Jonathan Price. Coral Gables, Fla.: University of Miami Press, 1972, pp. 97–101.

Smith, Vivian. *The Poetry of Robert Lowell*. Sydney: Sydney University Press, 1974, pp. 80–100.

Yenser, Stephen. *Circle to Circle: The Poetry of Robert Lowell*. Berkeley: University of California Press, 1975, pp. 200–240.

Wain, John. "The New Robert Lowell," in *New Republic*. CLI (October 17, 1964), pp. 21–23. Reprinted in *Robert Lowell: A Portrait of the Artist in His Time*. Edited by Michael London and Robert Boyers. New York: David Lewis, 1970, pp. 65–72.

Imitations

Belitt, Ben. "*Imitations*: Translation as Personal Mode," in *Salmagundi*. I (1966–1967), pp. 44–56. Reprinted in *Robert Lowell: A Portrait of the Artist in His Time*. Edited by Michael London and Robert Boyers. New York: David Lewis, 1970, pp. 115–129.

Carne-Ross, Donald. "The Two Voices of Translation," in *Robert Lowell: A Collection of Critical Essays*. Edited by Thomas Parkinson. Englewood Cliffs, N.J.: Prentice-Hall, 1968, pp. 152–170.

Chadwick, C. "Meaning and Tone," in *Essays in Criticism*. XIII (October, 1963), pp. 432–435. Reprinted in *Critics on Robert Lowell*. Edited by Jonathan Price. Coral Gables, Fla.: University of Miami Press, 1972, pp. 89–91.

Cooper, Philip. *The Autobiographical Myth of Robert Lowell*. Chapel Hill: University of North Carolina Press, 1970, pp. 64–65, 111–112.

Cosgrave, Patrick. *The Public Poetry of Robert Lowell*. London: Victor Gollancz, 1970, pp. 185–212.

Crick, John. *Robert Lowell*. Edinburgh: Oliver and Boyd, 1974, pp. 65–70.

Fein, Richard J. *Robert Lowell*. New York: Twayne, 1970, pp. 72–92.

Gunn, Thom. "Imitations and Originals," in *Yale Review*. LI (1962), pp. 480–489.

Hill, Geoffrey. "Robert Lowell: 'Contrasts and Repetitions,' " in *Essays in Criticism*. XIII (1963), pp. 188–197. Reprinted in *Critics on Robert Lowell*. Edited by Jonathan Price. Coral Gables, Fla.: University of Miami Press, 1972, pp. 80–88.

Martin, Jay. *Robert Lowell.* Minneapolis: University of Minnesota Press, 1970, pp. 23–26. Reprinted in *American Writers: A Collection of Literary Biographies*, Volume II. Edited by Leonard Unger. New York: Scribner's, 1974, pp. 543–545.

Perloff, Marjorie G. *The Poetic Art of Robert Lowell.* Ithaca, N.Y.: Cornell University Press, 1973, pp. 55–75.

Simon, John. "Abuse of Privilege: Lowell as Translator," in *Hudson Review.* XX (Winter, 1967–1968), pp. 543–562. Reprinted in *Robert Lowell: A Portrait of the Artist in His Time.* Edited by Michael London and Robert Boyers. New York: David Lewis, 1970, pp. 130–154.

Yenser, Stephen. *Circle to Circle: The Poetry of Robert Lowell.* Berkeley: University of California Press, 1975, pp. 165–199.

Life Studies

Altieri, Charles. "Poetry in a Prose World: Robert Lowell's *Life Studies*," in *Modern Poetry Studies.* I (1970), pp. 182–199. Reprinted in *Profile of Robert Lowell.* Edited by Jerome Mazzaro. Columbus, Oh.: Merrill, 1971, pp. 19–31.

Cooper, Philip. *The Autobiographical Myth of Robert Lowell.* Chapel Hill: University of North Carolina Press, 1970, pp. 56–67.

Cosgrave, Patrick. *The Public Poetry of Robert Lowell.* London: Victor Gollancz, 1970, pp. 109–148.

Crick, John. *Robert Lowell.* Edinburgh: Oliver and Boyd, 1974, pp. 43–62.

Fein, Richard J. *Robert Lowell.* New York: Twayne, 1970, pp. 46–71.

Hollander, John. "Robert Lowell's New Book," in *Poetry.* XCV (October, 1959), pp. 41–46. Reprinted in *Critics on Robert Lowell.* Edited by Jonathan Price. Coral Gables, Fla.: University of Miami Press, 1972, pp. 66–70.

McFadden, George. "*Life Studies*: Robert Lowell's Comic Breakthrough," in *PMLA.* XC (1975), pp. 96–106.

Martin, Jay. *Robert Lowell.* Minneapolis: University of Minnesota Press, 1970, pp. 28–35. Reprinted in *American Writers: A Collection of Literary Biographies*, Volume II. Edited by Leonard Unger. New York: Scribner's, 1974, pp. 546–550.

Mazzaro, Jerome. *The Poetic Themes of Robert Lowell.* Ann Arbor: University of Michigan Press, 1965, pp. 104–121.

Perloff, Marjorie G. *The Poetic Art of Robert Lowell.* Ithaca, N.Y.: Cornell University Press, 1973, pp. 80–89, 100–109.

Rosenthal, M.L. *The Modern Poets.* New York: Oxford University Press, 1960, pp. 231–237. Reprinted in *Robert Lowell: A Portrait of the Artist in His Time.* Edited by Michael London and Robert Boyers. New York: David Lewis, 1970, pp. 44–57.

————. *The New Poets.* New York: Oxford University Press, 1967, pp. 25–66.

Smith, Vivian. *The Poetry of Robert Lowell.* Sydney: Sydney University Press, 1974, pp. 51–79.

Standerwick, De Sales. "Pieces Too Personal," in *Renascence.* XIII (1960), pp. 53–56. Reprinted in *Profile of Robert Lowell.* Edited by Jerome Mazzaro. Columbus, Oh.: Merrill, 1971, pp. 15–18.

Staples, Hugh B. *Robert Lowell: The First Twenty Years.* New York: Farrar, Straus, 1962, pp. 66–84.

Stern, Richard G. "A Poet's Self-Portrait," in *Commentary.* XXVIII (1959), pp. 272–274.

Yenser, Stephen. *Circle to Circle: The Poetry of Robert Lowell.* Berkeley: University of California Press, 1975, pp. 118–164.

Lord Weary's Castle

Berryman, John. *The Freedom of the Poet.* New York: Farrar, Straus, 1976, pp. 286–296.

Bogan, Louise. "Experiment and Post-Experiment," in *American Scholar.* XVI (1947), pp. 237–252.

Cooper, Philip. *The Autobiographical Myth of Robert Lowell.* Chapel Hill: University of North Carolina Press, 1970, pp. 44–55.

Crick, John. *Robert Lowell.* Edinburgh: Oliver and Boyd, 1974, pp. 27–36.

Eberhart, Richard. "Four Poets," in *Sewanee Review.* LV (1947), pp. 324–336. Reprinted in *Robert Lowell: A Collection of Critical Essays.* Edited by Thomas Parkinson. Englewood Cliffs, N.J.: Prentice-Hall, 1968, pp. 48–52.

Fein, Richard J. *Robert Lowell.* New York: Twayne, 1970, pp. 6–35.

Fiedler, Leslie A. "The Believing Poet and the Infidel Reader," in *New Leader.* XXX (May 10, 1947), p. 12. Reprinted in *Robert Lowell: A Portrait of the Artist in His Time.* Edited by Michael London and Robert Boyers. New York: David Lewis, 1970, pp. 14–18.

Jarrell, Randall. *Poetry and the Age.* New York: Knopf, 1953, pp. 208–219. Reprinted in *Robert Lowell: A Portrait of the Artist in His Time.* Edited by Michael London and Robert Boyers. New York: David Lewis, 1970, pp. 19–27.

Jumper, Will C. "Whom Seek Ye? A Note on Robert Lowell's Poetry," in *Hudson Review.* IX (Spring, 1956), pp. 117–125. Reprinted in *Robert Lowell: A Collection of Critical Essays.* Edited by Thomas Parkinson. Englewood Cliffs, N.J.: Prentice-Hall, 1968, pp. 53–62.

Martin, Jay. *Robert Lowell.* Minneapolis: University of Minnesota Press, 1970, pp. 13–19. Reprinted in *American Writers: A Collection of Literary Biographies,* Volume II. Edited by Leonard Unger. New York: Scribner's, 1974, pp. 538–554.

Mazzaro, Jerome. *The Poetic Themes of Robert Lowell.* Ann Arbor: University of Michigan Press, 1965, pp. 48–61.

Perloff, Marjorie G. *The Poetic Art of Robert Lowell.* Ithaca, N.Y.: Cornell University Press, 1973, pp. 115–119.

Remaley, Peter P. "The Quest for Grace in Robert Lowell's *Lord Weary's Castle*," in *Renascence.* XXVIII (Spring, 1976), pp. 115–122.

Rosenthal, M.L. *The New Poets.* New York: Oxford University Press, 1967, pp. 68–72.

Standerwick, DeSales. "Notes on Robert Lowell," in *Renascence.* VIII (1955–1956), pp. 75–83. Reprinted in *Profile of Robert Lowell.* Edited by Jerome Mazzaro. Columbus, Oh.: Merrill, 1971, pp. 3–11.

Staples, Hugh B. *Robert Lowell: The First Twenty Years.* New York: Farrar, Straus, 1962, pp. 32–44.

Wiebe, Dallas E. "Mr. Lowell and Mr. Edwards," in *Wisconsin Studies in Contemporary Literature.* III (Spring–Summer, 1962), pp. 21–31.

Yenser, Stephen. *Circle to Circle: The Poetry of Robert Lowell.* Berkeley: University of California Press, 1975, pp. 36–80.

Near the Ocean

Bach, Bert C. "*Near the Ocean*," in *Commonweal.* LXXXVI (1967), pp. 238–241.

Carruth, Hayden. "A Meaning of Robert Lowell," in *Hudson Review.* XX (Autumn, 1967), pp. 429–447.

Cooper, Philip. *The Autobiographical Myth of Robert Lowell.* Chapel Hill: University of North Carolina Press, 1970, pp. 118–139.

Cosgrave, Patrick. *The Public Poetry of Robert Lowell.* London: Victor Gollancz, 1970, pp. 185–212.

Crick, John. *Robert Lowell.* Edinburgh: Oliver and Boyd, 1974, pp. 100–117.

Fein, Richard J. *Robert Lowell.* New York: Twayne, 1970, pp. 138–150.

Garrigue, Jean. "A Study of Continuity and Change," in *New Leader.* L (March 27, 1967), pp. 23–25.

Hoffman, Daniel. "The Greatness and Horror of Empire: Robert Lowell's *Near the Ocean*," in *The Sounder Few: Essays from the Hollins Critic.* Edited by R.H.W. Dillard *et al.* Athens: University of Georgia Press, 1971, pp. 213–246.

Howard, Richard. "Fuel on the Fire," in *Poetry.* CX (1967), pp. 413–415. Reprinted in *Robert Lowell: A Portrait of the Artist in His Time.* Edited by Michael London and Robert Boyers. New York: David Lewis, 1970, pp. 98–100.

Link, Hilda. "A Tempered Triumph," in *Prairie Schooner.* XLI (1967–1968), pp. 439–442.

London, Michael. "Wading for Godot," in *Robert Lowell: A Portrait of the Artist in His Time.* Edited by Michael London and Robert Boyers. New York: David Lewis, 1970, pp. 100–105.

Mahon, Derek. "*Near the Ocean,*" in *Phoenix.* II (Summer, 1967), pp. 50–54.

Mazzaro, Jerome. "Lowell After *For the Union Dead,*" in *Robert Lowell: A Portrait of the Artist in His Time.* Edited by Michael London and Robert Boyers. New York: David Lewis, 1970, pp. 84–97.

Smith, Vivian. *The Poetry of Robert Lowell.* Sydney: Sydney University Press, 1974, pp. 101–110.

Yenser, Stephen. *Circle to Circle: The Poetry of Robert Lowell.* Berkeley: University of California Press, 1975, pp. 241–272.

Notebook 1967–1968

Boyers, Robert. "On Robert Lowell," in *Salmagundi.* XIII (Summer, 1970), pp. 36–44. Reprinted in *Profile of Robert Lowell.* Edited by Jerome Mazzaro. Columbus, Oh.: Merrill, 1971, pp. 97–104.

Connolly, Cyril. *The Evening Colonnade.* New York: Harcourt, 1975, pp. 361–364.

Cooper, Philip. *The Autobiographical Myth of Robert Lowell.* Chapel Hill: University of North Carolina Press, 1970, pp. 140–155.

Crick, John. *Robert Lowell.* Edinburgh: Oliver and Boyd, 1974, pp. 118–134.

Fein, Richard J. *Robert Lowell.* New York: Twayne, 1970, pp. 102–103.

Ferguson, Frances. "Appointments with Time: Robert Lowell's Poetry Through the *Notebooks,*" in *American Poetry Since 1960: Some Critical Perspectives.* Edited by Robert B. Shaw. Chester Springs, Pa.: Dufour, 1973, pp. 15–27.

Martz, Lewis. "*Notebook,*" in *Yale Review.* LIX (1969), pp. 252–256. Reprinted in *Critics on Robert Lowell.* Edited by Jonathan Price. Coral Gables, Fla.: University of Miami Press, 1972, pp. 114–118.

Meredith, William. "Looking Back," in *New York Times Book Review.* (June 15, 1969), pp. 1, 27. Reprinted in *Critics on Robert Lowell.* Edited by Jonathan Price. Coral Gables, Fla.: University of Miami Press, 1972, pp. 119–122.

Perloff, Marjorie G. *The Poetic Art of Robert Lowell.* Ithaca, N.Y.: Cornell University Press, 1973, pp. 123–125.

Smith, Vivian. *The Poetry of Robert Lowell.* Sydney: Sydney University Press, 1974, pp. 101–110.

Yenser, Stephen. *Circle to Circle: The Poetry of Robert Lowell.* Berkeley: University of California Press, 1975, pp. 273–297.

The Old Glory

Brustein, Robert. *Seasons of Discontent: Dramatic Opinions, 1959–1965.* New York: Simon and Schuster, 1965, pp. 225–259. Reprinted in *Robert Lowell: A Portrait of the Artist in His Time.* Edited by Michael London and Robert Boyers. New York: David Lewis, 1970, pp. 77–79.

Clurman, Harold. *The Naked Image: Observations on the Modern Theatre.* New York: Macmillan, 1966, pp. 94–97.

Cooper, Philip. *The Autobiographical Myth of Robert Lowell.* Chapel Hill: University of North Carolina Press, 1970, pp. 77–79.

Crick, John. *Robert Lowell.* Edinburgh: Oliver and Boyd, 1974, pp. 74–80.

Fein, Richard J. *Robert Lowell.* New York: Twayne, 1970, pp. 116–137.

Gilman, Richard. "Life Offers No Neat Conclusions," in *New York Times Book Review.* (May 5, 1968), pp. 1, 5. Reprinted in *Profile of Robert Lowell.* Edited by Jerome Mazzaro. Columbus, Oh.: Merrill, 1971, pp. 61–64.

Hochman, Baruch. "Robert Lowell's *The Old Glory,*" in *Tulane Drama Review.* XI (Summer, 1967), pp. 127–138.

Howard, Richard. "A Movement Outward," in *New Leader.* XLVIII (December 6, 1965), pp. 26–28.

Martin, Jay. *Robert Lowell.* Minneapolis: University of Minnesota Press, 1970, pp. 26–28. Reprinted in *American Writers: A Collection of Literary Biographies,* Volume II. Edited by Leonard Unger. New York: Scribner's, 1974, pp. 545–546.

Mazzaro, Jerome. "On *The Old Glory,*" in *Western Humanities Review.* XXIV (Autumn, 1970), pp. 347–358.

Simon, John. "Strange Devices on the Banner," in *New York Herald Tribune Book Week.* (February 20, 1966), pp. 4, 20. Reprinted in *Robert Lowell: A Portrait of the Artist in His Time.* Edited by Michael London and Robert Boyers. New York: David Lewis, 1970, pp. 80–83.

MALCOLM LOWRY
(1909–1957)

Dark as the Grave Wherein My Friend Is Laid

Bareham, Terence. "After the Volcano: An Assessment of Malcolm Lowry's Posthumous Fiction," in *Studies in the Novel*. VI (1974), pp. 349–362.

Bradbrook, M.C. *Malcolm Lowry: His Art and Early Life*. London: Cambridge University Press, 1974, pp. 64–75.

Corrigan, Matthew. "Masks and the Man: The Writer as Actor," in *Shenandoah*. XIX (Summer, 1968), pp. 89–93.

Costa, Richard Hauer. *Malcolm Lowry*. New York: Twayne, 1972, pp. 115–123.

Day, Douglas. "Preface," in *Dark as the Grave Wherein My Friend Is Laid*. New York: New American Library, 1968, pp. ix–xxiii.

Dodson, Daniel B. *Malcolm Lowry*. New York: Columbia University Press, 1970, pp. 43–46.

Miller, David. *Malcolm Lowry and the Voyage That Never Ends*. London: Enitharmon Press, 1976, pp. 37–40.

New, William H. *Malcolm Lowry*. Toronto: McClelland and Stewart, 1971, pp. 44–51.

Woodcock, George. "Art as the Writer's Mirror: Literary Solipism in *Dark as the Grave*," in *Malcolm Lowry: The Man and His Work*. Edited by George Woodcock. Vancouver: University of British Columbia Press, 1971, pp. 66–70.

Hear Us O Lord from Heaven Thy Dwelling Place

Bradbrook, M.C. *Malcolm Lowry: His Art and Early Life*. London: Cambridge University Press, 1974, pp. 35–37, 83–85.

Bradbury, Malcolm. "*Hear Us O Lord . . .*," in *Critical Quarterly*. IV (Winter, 1962), pp. 377–379.

Breit, Harvey. "Introductory Note: Lowry's 'Through the Panama,'" in *Paris Review*. XXIII (Spring, 1960), p. 84.

Costa, Richard Hauer. *Malcolm Lowry*. New York: Twayne, 1972, pp. 108–114, 130–145.

Durrant, Geoffrey. "Death in Life: Neo-Platonic Elements in 'Through the Panama,'" in *Canadian Literature*. XLIV (Spring, 1970), pp. 13–27. Reprinted in *Malcolm Lowry: The Man and His Work*. Edited by George Woodcock. Vancouver: University of British Columbia Press, 1971, pp. 42–55.

Edelstein, J.M. "Legacy of Malcolm Lowry," in *New Republic*. CXLIV (June 5, 1961), pp. 24–25.

Edmonds, Dale. "The Short Fiction of Malcolm Lowry," in *Tulane Studies in English*. XV (1967), pp. 59–80.

Thompson, John. *"Hear Us O Lord from Heaven Thy Dwelling Place,"* in *Partisan Review*. XXVIII (1961), pp. 712–715.

Woodcock, George. "Under Seymour Mountain: A Note on Lowry's Stories," in *Malcolm Lowry: The Man and His Work*. Edited by George Woodcock. Vancouver: University of British Columbia Press, 1971, pp. 38–41.

Ultramarine

Binns, Ronald. "Lowry's Anatomy of Melancholy," in *Canadian Literature*. LXIV (Spring, 1975), pp. 8–23.

Bradbrook, M.C. *Malcolm Lowry: His Art and Early Life*. London: Cambridge University Press, 1974, pp. 40–48, 125–129.

Costa, Richard Hauer. *Malcolm Lowry*. New York: Twayne, 1972, pp. 37–40.

Dahlie, Hallvard. "Malcolm Lowry's *Ultramarine*," in *Journal of Canadian Fiction*. III (1975), pp. 65–68.

Day, Douglas. *Malcolm Lowry: A Biography*. New York: Oxford University Press, 1973, pp. 161–169.

Dodson, Daniel B. *Malcolm Lowry*. New York: Columbia University Press, 1970, pp. 6–9.

Kilgallin, Tony. *Lowry*. Erin, Ontario: Porcepic, 1973, pp. 85–114.

Miller, David. *Malcolm Lowry and the Voyage That Never Ends*. London: Enitharmon Press, 1976, pp. 19–20.

New, William H. *Malcolm Lowry*. Toronto: McClelland and Stewart, 1971, pp. 20–25.

Woodcock, George. "Malcolm Lowry as Novelist," in *Queen's Quarterly*. XXIV (April, 1961), pp. 26–28.

Under the Volcano

Allen, Walter. "The Masterpiece of the Forties," in *On Contemporary Literature*. Edited by Richard Kostelanetz. New York: Avon, 1964, pp. 419–421.

Bareham, Terence. "Paradigms of Hell: Symbolic Patterning in *Under the Volcano*," in *On the Novel*. Edited by B.S. Benedikz. London: Dent, 1971, pp. 113–126.

Barnes, James. "The Myth of Sisyphus in *Under the Volcano*," in *Prairie Schooner*. XLII (Winter, 1968–1969), pp. 341–348.

Bradbrook, M.C. *Malcolm Lowry: His Art and Early Life*. London: Cambridge University Press, 1974, pp. 54–68, 133–137.

Costa, Richard Hauer. *Malcolm Lowry*. New York: Twayne, 1972, pp. 61–81.

Day, Douglas. *Malcolm Lowry: A Biography*. New York: Oxford University Press, 1973, pp. 258–274, 316–350.

Dodson, Daniel B. *Malcolm Lowry*. New York: Columbia University Press, 1970, pp. 10–34.

Doyen, Victor. "Elements Towards a Spatial Reading of Malcolm Lowry's *Under the Volcano*," in *English Studies*. L (1959), pp. 65–74.

Edelstein, J.M. "On Re-reading *Under the Volcano*," in *Prairie Schooner*. XXXVII (Winter, 1963–1964), pp. 336–339.

Edmonds, Dale. "Mescallusions or the Drinking Man's *Under the Volcano*," in *Journal of Modern Literature*. VI (April, 1977), pp. 277–288.

————. "*Under the Volcano*: A Reading of the 'Immediate Level,' " in *Tulane Studies in English*. XIV (1968), pp. 63–105.

Epstein, Perle S. *The Private Labyrinth of Malcolm Lowry*. New York: Holt, Rinehart, and Winston, 1969, pp. 3–216.

Gass, William H. "In Terms of the Toenail: Fiction and the Figures of Life," in *New American Review 10*. Edited by Theodore Solotaroff. New York: New American Library, 1970, pp. 51–68. Reprinted in *Fiction and the Figures of Life*. New York: Knopf, 1971, pp. 55–76.

Grace, Sherrill E. "*Under the Volcano*: Narrative Mode and Technique," in *Journal of Canadian Fiction*. II (1973), pp. 57–61.

Heilman, Robert B. "The Possessed Artist and the Ailing Soul," in *Canadian Literature*. VIII (Spring, 1961), pp. 7–16. Reprinted in *Malcolm Lowry: The Man and His Work*. Edited by George Woodcock. Vancouver: University of British Columbia Press, 1971, pp. 16–25.

Hirschman, Jack. "Kabbala/Lowry, etc.," in *Prairie Schooner*. XXXVII (Winter 1963–1964), pp. 347–353.

Kilgallin, Tony. *Lowry*. Erin, Ontario: Porcepic, 1973, pp. 119–211. Earlier version in *Malcolm Lowry: The Man and His Work*. Edited by George Woodcock. Vancouver: University of British Columbia Press, 1971, pp. 26–37.

McCormick, John. *Catastrophe and Imagination: An Interpretation of the Recent English and American Novel*. New York: Longmans, Green, 1957, pp. 65–66, 85–89.

Markson, David. Malcolm Lowry's Volcano: Myth, Symbol, Meaning. New York: Times Books, 1978.

Miller, David. *Malcolm Lowry and the Voyage That Never Ends*. London: Enitharmon Press, 1976, pp. 21–30.

New, William H. *Malcolm Lowry*. Toronto: McClelland and Stewart, 1971, pp. 29–41.

Spender, Stephen. "Introduction," in *Under the Volcano*. Philadelphia: Lippincott, 1965.

Widmer, Eleanor. "The Drunken Wheel: Malcolm Lowry and *Under the Volcano*," in *The Forties: Fiction, Poetry, Drama*. Edited by Warren French. Deland, Fla.: Everett/Edwards, 1968, pp. 217–266.

Woodcock, George.   "Malcolm Lowry's *Under the Volcano*," in *Modern Fiction Studies*. IV (Summer, 1948), pp. 151–156.

Wright, Terence.   "*Under the Volcano*—The Static Art of Malcolm Lowry," in *Ariel*. I (October, 1970), pp. 67–76.

LUCIAN
(c. 120–c. 200)

Satires

Allison, Francis Greenleaf. *Lucian, Satirist and Artist.* Boston: Marshall Jones, 1926.

Anderson, Graham. *Studies in Lucian's Comic Fiction.* Leiden: E.J. Brill, 1976.

Baldwin, B. "Lucian as Social Satirist," in *Classical Quarterly.* XI (1961), pp. 199–208.

————. *Studies in Lucian.* Toronto: Hakkert, 1973.

Bellinger, A.R. "Lucian's Dramatic Technique," in *Yale Classical Studies.* I (1928), pp. 3–40.

Chapman, John Jay. *Lucian, Plato and Greek Morals.* Oxford: Basil Blackwell, 1931.

Craig, Hardin. *Written Word and Other Essays.* Port Washington, N.Y.: Kennikat, 1969.

Downs, R.B. "Master of Satiric Dialogue: Lucian," in *Famous Books, Ancient and Medieval.* New York: Barnes & Noble, 1964, pp. 238–242.

Grube, G.M.A. "The Second Sophistic and Its Satirist," in *The Greek and Roman Critics.* Toronto: University of Toronto Press, 1965, pp. 333–338.

Haight, E.H. "Lucian and His Satiric Romances: The 'True History' and 'Lucius or Ass,'" in *Essays on the Greek Romances.* Port Washington, N.Y.: Kennikat, 1965, pp. 144–185.

Householder, F.W. *Literary Quotation and Allusion in Lucian.* New York: Columbia University Press, 1941.

————. "The Mock Decrees in Lucian," in *Transactions of the American Philological Association.* LXXI (1940), pp. 199–126.

McCarthy, B.P. "Lucian and Menippus," in *Yale Classical Studies.* XLIV (1934), pp. 3–55.

McLeod, M.D. "Homeric Parody in Lucian," in *Classical Review.* X (June, 1960), p. 103.

————. "Lucian's Knowledge of Theophrastus," in *Mnemosyne.* XXVII (1974), pp. 75–76, and XXX (1977), pp. 174–176.

Perry, B.E. "Who Was Lucius of Patrae?," in *Classical Journal.* LXIV (1968), pp. 97–101.

Read, H.E. "The Dialogue," in *Poetry and Experience.* New York: Horizon Press, 1967, pp. 83–103.

Walsh, P.G. "Was Lucius a Roman?," in *Classical Journal.* LXIII (1968), pp. 264–265.

LUCRETIUS
(c.98 B.C.–55 B.C.)

De rerum natura

Amory A. "Obscura de re lucida carmina: Science and Poetry in *De rerum natura*," in *Yale Classical Studies*. XXI (1969), pp. 143–168.

Cairns, H., et al. *Invitation to Learning*. New York: Random House, 1941, pp. 275–290.

Classen, C.J. "Poetry and Rhetoric in Lucretius," in *Transactions of the American Philological Association*. XCIX (1968), pp. 77–118.

Commager, Henry Steele. "Lucretius' Interpretation of the Plague," in *Harvard Studies in Classical Philology*. LXII (1957), pp. 19–31.

Downs, R.B. *Famous Books, Ancient and Medieval*. New York: Barnes & Noble, 1964, pp. 169–173.

Grant, M. *Roman Literature*. Baltimore: Penguin, 1964, pp. 142–147.

Lienhard, J.T. "The Prooemia of *De rerum natura*," in *Classical Journal*. LXIV (May, 1969), pp. 346–353.

Mendell, C.W. *Latin Poetry: The New Poets and the Augustans*. New Haven, Conn.: Yale University Press, 1965, pp. 14–27.

Minadeo, R. "The Formal Design of *De rerum natura*," in *Arion*. IV (Autumn, 1965), pp. 444–461.

Murley, C. "Lucretius and the History of Satire," in *Transactions of the American Philological Association*. LXX (1939), pp. 380–395.

————. "Lucretius *De rerum natura*, Viewed as Epic," in *Transactions of the American Philological Association*. LXXVIII (1947), pp. 336–346.

Owen, W.H. "Structural Pattern in Lucretius' *De rerum natura*," in *Classical World*. LXII (December, 1968), pp. 121–127.

Rexroth, K. "Lucretius: *On the Nature of Things*," in *Classics Revisited*. Chicago: Quadrangle, 1968, pp. 85–90.

Santayana, G. *Essays in Literary Criticism*. New York: Scribner's, 1956, pp. 10–30.

Sikes, E.E. *Lucretius, Poet and Philosopher*. New York: Russell and Russell, 1971.

Smith, M.F. "Some Lucretian Thought Processes," in *Hermatheria*. CII (Spring, 1966), pp. 73–83.

Stewart, D.J. "The Silence of Magna Mater," in *Harvard Studies in Classical Philology*. LXXIV (1970), pp. 75–84.

Strauss, Leo. *Liberalism, Ancient and Modern*. New York: Basic Books, 1968, pp. 76–139.

Van Doren, Mark. "Concerning the Nature of Things," in his *Noble Voice; A Study of Ten Great Poems*. New York: Holt, 1946, pp. 148–171.

West, D.A. *The Imagery and Poetry of Lucretius*. Edinburgh: Edinburgh University Press, 1969.

JOHN LYLY
(1554–1606)

Campaspe

Bevington, David M. "John Lyly and Queen Elizabeth: Royal Flattery in *Campaspe* and *Sappho and Phao*," in *Renaissance Papers.* (1966), pp. 37–67.

————. *Tudor Drama and Politics: A Critical Approach to Topical Meaning.* Cambridge, Mass.: Harvard University Press, 1968, pp. 171–175.

Houppert, Joseph W. *John Lyly.* Boston: Twayne, 1975, pp. 55–60, 63–73.

Hunter, G.K. *Lyly and Peele.* London: Longmans, Green, 1968, pp. 20–35.

Knight, G. Wilson. "Lyly," in *Elizabethan Drama: Modern Essays in Criticism.* Edited by R.J. Kaufmann. New York: Oxford University Press, 1961, pp. 45–48.

Mustard, W.P. "Agrippa's Shadows in Lyly's *Campaspe*," in *Modern Language Notes.* XLIII (1928), p. 325.

Price, Hereward T. "Shakespeare and His Young Contemporaries," in *Philological Quarterly.* XLI (January, 1962), pp. 40–41.

Saccio, Peter. *The Court Comedies of John Lyly: A Study in Allegorical Dramaturgy.* Princeton, N.J.: Princeton University Press, 1969, pp. 26–94.

Turner, Robert Y. "Some Dialogues of Love in Lyly's Comedies," in *ELH: Journal of English Literary History.* XXIX (1962), pp. 276–288.

Whiting, G.W. "Canary Wine and *Campaspe*," in *Modern Language Notes.* XLV (1930), pp. 148–151.

Endymion

Bennett, Josephine W. "Oxford and *Endimion*," in *PMLA.* LVII (1942), pp. 354–369.

Bevington, David. *Tudor Drama and Politics: A Critical Approach to Topical Meaning.* Cambridge, Mass.: Harvard University Press, 1968, pp. 178–186.

Bond, Sallie. "John Lyly's *Endimion*," in *Studies in English Literature, 1500–1900.* XIV (1974), pp. 189–199.

Boughner, Daniel C. "The Background of Lyly's *Tophas*," in *PMLA.* LIV (1939), pp. 967–973.

Braendel, Doris B. "The Limits of Clarity: Lyly's *Endimion*, Bronzino's *Allegory of Venus and Cupid*, Webster's *White Devil*, and Botticelli's *Primavera*," in *Hartford Studies in Literature.* IV (1972), pp. 197–215.

Bryant, J.A., Jr. "The Nature of the Allegory in Lyly's *Endymion*," in *Renaissance Papers.* (1956), pp. 4–11.

Deats, Sara. "The Disarming of the Knight: Comic Parody in Lyly's *Endymion*," in *South Atlantic Bulletin*. XL (1975), pp. 67–75.

Gannon, C.C. "Lyly's *Endimion*: From Myth to Allegory," in *English Literary Renaissance*. VI (1976), pp. 220–243.

Harrison, G.B. *Elizabethan Plays and Players*. Ann Arbor: University of Michigan Press, 1956, pp. 32–34.

Houppert, Joseph W. *John Lyly*. Boston: Twayne, 1975, pp. 94–106.

Huppe, Bernard F. "Allegory of Love in Lyly's Court Comedies," in *ELH: Journal of English Literary History*. XIV (1947), pp. 93–113.

Knapp, Robert S. "The Monarchy of Love in Lyly's *Endimion*," in *Modern Philology*. LXXIII (1976), pp. 353–367.

Lenz, Carolyn Ruth Swift. "The Allegory of Wisdom in Lyly's *Endimion*," in *Comparative Drama*. X (1976), pp. 235–257.

Long, P.W. "Lyly's *Endimion*," in *Modern Philology*. VIII (1911), pp. 509–605.

————. "Purport of Lyly's *Endimion*," in *PMLA*. XXIV (1909), pp. 164–184.

Mehl, Dieter. *The Elizabethan Dumb Show*. Cambridge, Mass.: Harvard University Press, 1966, pp. 86–87.

Saccio, Peter. *The Court Comedies of John Lyly: A Study in Allegorical Dramaturgy*. Princeton, N.J.: Princeton University Press, 1969, pp. 169–186.

————. "The Oddity of Lyly's *Endimion*," in *The Elizabethan Theater, V*. Edited by George Richard Hibbard. Hamden, Conn.: Archon, 1975, pp. 92–111.

Stevenson, David Lloyd. *The Love-Game Comedy*. New York: Columbia University Press, 1946, pp. 159–162.

Weltner, Peter. "The Antinomic Vision of Lyly's *Endymion*," in *English Literary Renaissance*. III (1973), pp. 5–29.

Euphues: The Anatomy of Wit and Euphues and His England

Croll, Morris William. "Introduction," in *Euphues: The Anatomy of Wit; Euphues and His England*. By John Lyly. Edited by Morris William Croll and Harry Clemons. New York: Russell and Russell, 1964, pp. xv–lxiv.

Gregg, Kate L. *Thomas Dekker: A Study in Economic and Social Backgrounds*. Seattle: University of Washington Press, 1924, pp. 63–64.

Harrison, G.B. *Elizabethan Plays and Players*. Ann Arbor: University of Michigan Press, 1956, pp. 27–28.

Houppert, Joseph W. *John Lyly*. Boston: Twayne, 1975, pp. 22–52.

Hunter, G.K. *Lyly and Peele*. London: Longmans, Green, 1968, pp. 14–19.

Lewis, C.S.   *English Literature in the Sixteenth Century, Excluding Drama.* London: Oxford University Press, 1954, pp. 313–316.

Saccio, Peter.   *The Court Comedies of John Lyly: A Study in Allegorical Dramaturgy.* Princeton, N.J.: Princeton University Press, 1969, pp. 40–42.

Silvette, Herbert.   *The Doctor on the Stage: Medicine and Medical Men in Seventeenth-Century England.* Knoxville: University of Tennessee Press, 1967, pp. 258–259.

THOMAS BABINGTON MACAULAY
(1800–1859)

The History of England from the Accession of James the Second

Abbott, Wilbur C. "Macaulay and the New History," in *Yale Review*. XVIII (1929), pp. 539–557.

Bagehot, Walter. "Mr. Macaulay," in *National Review* (London). II (1856), pp. 357–387.

Bensly, Edward. "Queries from Macaulay's *History of England*," in *Notes & Queries*. CLXIX (December 21, 1935), pp. 444–445.

Carleton, William. "Macaulay and the Trimmers," in *American Scholar*. XIX (1949), pp. 73–82.

Clive, John. "Macaulay, History and the Historians," in *History Today*. IX (1959), pp. 830–836.

Davies, Godfrey. "The Treatment of Constitutional History in Macaulay's *History of England*," in *Huntington Library Quarterly*. II (January, 1939), pp. 179–204.

Firth, Charles. *A Commentary on Macaulay's* History of England. London: Frank Cass, 1964.

Foxcroft, H.C. "The Limitations of Lord Macaulay," in *Fortnightly Review*. LXXII (1902), pp. 826–830.

Hamburger, Joseph. *Macaulay and the Whig Tradition*. Chicago: University of Chicago Press, 1976, pp. 73–114.

Hinton, R.W.K. "History Yesterday: Five Points Above Whig History," in *History Today*. IX (1959), pp. 720–728.

Hocking, William J. "Queries from Macaulay's *History of England*," in *Notes & Queries*. CLXIX (December 7, 1935), p. 407.

Levine, George. *Boundaries of Fiction: Carlyle, Macaulay, Newman*. Princeton, N.J.: Princeton University Press, 1968, pp. 118–163.

Levine, George and William Madden. *The Art of Victorian Prose*. New York: Oxford University Press, 1968, pp. 149–150.

Millgate, Jane. *Macaulay*. London: Routledge and Kegan Paul, 1973, pp. 124–181.

Schuyler, Robert L. "Macaulay and His *History*—A Hundred Years After," in *Political Science Quarterly*. LXIII (June, 1948), pp. 161–193.

Starzinger, Vincent E. *Middlingness: "Juste Milieu" Political Theory in France and England, 1815–48*. Charlottesville: University Press of Virginia, 1965, pp. 128–131.

Trevelyan, George Macaulay. "The Centenary of Macaulay's *History*," in *Time and Tide.* (December 4, 1948), pp. 1121–1122.

————. *Clio: A Muse, and Other Essays Literary and Pedestrian.* London: Longmans, 1913, pp. 45–46.

Trevor-Roper, Hugh. *Men and Events.* New York: Harper, 1957, pp. 249–253.

Vowles, Richard B. "Macaulay's *History* and the Lampoon," in *Notes & Queries.* CXCVI (1951), p. 320.

MARY MCCARTHY
(1912–   )

Birds of America

Adams, Phoebe. *"Birds of America,"* in *Atlantic.* CCXXVIII (July, 1971), p. 103.

Aldridge, John W. "Egalitarian Snobs," in *Saturday Review.* LIV (May 8, 1971), pp. 21–24.

Boatwright, James. "Carnival Ducks and Acute Social Criticism," in *New Republic.* CLXIV (June 19, 1971), pp. 25–26.

Davenport, Guy. "Low Seriousness and High Comedy," in *National Review.* XXIII (October 8, 1971), p. 1123.

Hayes, Carol. *"Birds of America,"* in *Critic.* XXIX (July–August, 1971), pp. 70–72.

Hirsch, Foster. *"Birds of America,"* in *Commonweal.* XCIV (September 3, 1971), pp. 459–460.

May, Derwent. *"Birds of America,"* in *Encounter.* XXXVIII (January, 1972), pp. 75–77.

A Charmed Life

Auchincloss, Louis. *Pioneers and Caretakers: A Study of Nine American Women Novelists.* Minneapolis: University of Minnesota Press, 1965, pp. 178–180.

Cass, Cashenden. "Puppets in the High Bohemia," in *New Republic.* CXXXIII (December 5, 1955), pp. 18–19.

Grumbach, Doris. *The Company She Kept.* New York: Coward-McCann, 1967, pp. 174–180.

Herbst, Josephine. "Who Is Martha?," in *Nation.* CLXXXI (November 26, 1955), pp. 463–464.

Holzhauer, Jean. "Diamond-Hard," in *Commonweal.* LXIII (November 18, 1955), p. 171.

Kelly, James. "New Faces and New Leads," in *Saturday Review.* XXXVIII (November 5, 1955), p. 17.

McKenzie, Barbara. *Mary McCarthy.* New York: Twayne, 1966, pp. 122–134.

Podhoretz, Norman. *Doings and Undoings: The Fifties and After in American Writing.* New York: Farrar, Straus and Giroux, 1964, pp. 81–87.

Rolo, Charles J. "Mary McCarthy's *A Charmed Life*," in *Atlantic.* CXCVI (December, 1955), pp. 96–97.

Schlueter, Paul. "The Dissections of Mary McCarthy," in *Contemporary American Novelists*. Edited by Harry T. Moore. Carbondale: Southern Illinois University Press, 1964, pp. 59–61.

Stock, Irvin. *Mary McCarthy*. Minneapolis: University of Minnesota Press, 1968, pp. 29–35.

The Company She Keeps

Cowley, Malcolm. "Bad Company," in *New Republic*. CVI (May 25, 1942), p. 737.

Eisinger, Chester E. *Fiction of the Forties*. Chicago: University of Chicago Press, 1963, pp. 129–131.

Fadiman, Clifton. "*The Company She Keeps*," in *New Yorker*. XVIII (May 16, 1942), p. 61.

Gay, Robert M. "*The Company She Keeps*," in *Atlantic*. CLXX (August, 1942), p. 109.

Grumbach, Doris. *The Company She Kept*. New York: Coward-McCann, 1967, pp. 91–111.

Isherwood, Christopher. "Her Name Is Legion," in *Nation*. CLIV (June 20, 1942), p. 714.

Stock, Irvin. *Mary McCarthy*. Minneapolis: University of Minnesota Press, 1968, pp. 29–35.

Wade, Mason. "*The Company She Keeps*: Mary McCarthy," in *Commonweal*. XXXVI (June 19, 1942), pp. 209–210.

The Group

Aldridge, John W. *A Time To Murder and Create: The Contemporary Novel in Crisis*. New York: David McKay, 1966, pp. 95–100, 124–132.

Auchincloss, Louis. *Pioneers and Caretakers: A Study of Nine American Women Novelists*. Minneapolis: University of Minnesota Press, 1965, pp. 181–184.

Cook, Bruce. "Mary McCarthy: One of Ours?," in *Catholic World*. CXCIX (April, 1964), pp. 34–42.

Grumbach, Doris. *The Company She Kept*. New York: Coward-McCann, 1967, pp. 189–210.

Hicks, Granville. "The Group in Second Meeting," in *Saturday Review*. XLVII (February 22, 1964), pp. 51–52.

McKenzie, Barbara. *Mary McCarthy*. New York: Twayne, 1966, pp. 134–154.

Mailer, Norman. *Cannibals and Christians*. New York: Dial, 1966, pp. 133–140.

Mathewson, Ruth. "The Vassar Joke," in *Columbia University Forum*. VI (Fall, 1963), pp. 10–16.

Ohmann, Carol B. and Richard Ohmann. "Class Notes from Vassar," in *Commonweal*. LXXIX (September 27, 1963), pp. 12–15.

Podhoretz, Norman. *Doings and Undoings: The Fifties and After in American Writing*. New York: Farrar, Straus and Giroux, 1964, pp. 87–89.

Raban, Jonathan. *The Technique of Modern Fiction: Essays in Practical Criticism*. Notre Dame, Ind.: University of Notre Dame Press, 1968, pp. 97–100.

Schlueter, Paul. "The Dissections of Mary McCarthy," in *Contemporary American Novelists*. Edited by Harry T. Moore. Carbondale: Southern Illinois University Press, 1964, pp. 61–62.

Soule, George. "Must a Novelist Be an Artist?," in *Carleton Miscellany*. V (Spring, 1964), pp. 92–98.

Stock, Irvin. *Mary McCarthy*. Minneapolis: University of Minnesota Press, 1968, pp. 35–43.

Whitehorn, Katharine. "Three Women," in *Encounter*. XXI (December, 1963), pp. 78–79.

The Groves of Academe

Auchincloss, Louis. *Pioneers and Caretakers: A Study of Nine American Women Novelists*. Minneapolis: University of Minnesota Press, 1965, pp. 176–178.

Chamberlain, John. "The Conservative Miss McCarthy," in *National Review*. XV (October 22, 1963), pp. 353–355.

Eisinger, Chester E. *Fiction of the Forties*. Chicago: University of Chicago Press, 1963, pp. 133–135.

Grumbach, Doris. *The Company She Kept*. New York: Coward-McCann, 1967, pp. 159–172.

Latham, Earl. "The Managerialization of the Campus," in *Public Administration Review*. XIX (Winter, 1959), pp. 48–57.

Lyons, John O. *The College Novel in America*. Carbondale: Southern Illinois University Press, 1962, pp. 169–174, 177–178.

McKenzie, Barbara. *Mary McCarthy*. New York: Twayne, 1966, pp. 112–121.

Millgate, Michael. *American Social Fiction: James to Cozzens*. New York: Barnes & Noble, 1965, pp. 166–168.

Schlueter, Paul. "The Dissections of Mary McCarthy," in *Contemporary American Novelists*. Edited by Harry T. Moore. Carbondale: Southern Illinois University Press, 1964, pp. 57–59.

Stock, Irvin. *Mary McCarthy.* Minneapolis: University of Minnesota Press, 1968, pp. 24–29.

Walcutt, Charles Child. *Man's Changing Mask: Modes and Methods of Characterization in Fiction.* Minneapolis: University of Minnesota Press, 1966, pp. 292–294.

Memories of a Catholic Girlhood

Eisinger, Chester E. *Fiction of the Forties.* Chicago: University of Chicago Press, 1963, p. 133.

Hoskins, Katharine. "Give a Life to Live," in *Nation.* CLXXXV (July 6, 1957), pp. 16–17.

Lange, Victor. "The Women and the Orphan Child," in *New Republic.* CXXXVI (June 24, 1957), pp. 18–19.

Logal, N.W. "*Memories of a Catholic Girlhood,*" in *Catholic World.* CLXXXVI (November, 1957), p. 157.

McGinley, Phyllis. "Mary Was an Orphan," in *Saturday Review.* XL (June 8, 1957), p. 31.

Rolo, Charles J. "Remembrance of Things Past," in *Atlantic.* CXCIX (June, 1957), pp. 90–91.

Simons, John W. "An Author of Few Pieties and Few Illusions," in *Commonweal.* LXVI (July 12, 1957), pp. 379–380.

The Oasis

Eisinger, Chester E. *Fiction of the Forties.* Chicago: University of Chicago Press, 1963, pp. 132–133.

Gottfried, Alex and Sue Davidson. "Utopia's Children: An Interpretation of Three Political Novels," in *Western Political Quarterly.* XV (March, 1962), pp. 24–32.

Grumbach, Doris. *The Company She Kept.* New York: Coward-McCann, 1967, pp. 128–147.

Hollenbeck, Don. "Satirist's Utopia," in *New Republic.* CXXI (December 5, 1949), pp. 19–20.

McKenzie, Barbara. *Mary McCarthy.* New York: Twayne, 1966, pp. 104–112.

Marshall, Margaret. "Notes by the Way," in *Nation.* CLXIX (September 17, 1949), pp. 281–282.

Munson, Gorham. "Parlor Pinks Playing Utopia," in *Saturday Review of Literature.* XXXII (August 20, 1949), p. 12.

Rago, Henry. "*The Oasis*: Mary McCarthy," in *Commonweal.* L (September 9, 1949), pp. 536–537.

Schlueter, Paul. "The Dissections of Mary McCarthy," in *Contemporary American Novelists*. Edited by Harry T. Moore. Carbondale: Southern Illinois University Press, 1964, pp. 56–57.

Stock, Irvin. *Mary McCarthy*. Minneapolis: University of Minnesota Press, 1968, pp. 20–24.

CARSON MCCULLERS
(1917–1967)

The Ballad of the Sad Café

Broughton, Panthea R. "Rejection of the Feminine in Carson McCullers' *The Ballad of the Sad Cafe*," in *Twentieth Century Literature*. XX (January, 1974), pp. 34–43.

Cook, Richard M. *Carson McCullers*. New York: Frederick Ungar, 1975, pp. 84–104.

Dodd, Wayne D. "The Development of Theme Through Symbol in the Novels of Carson McCullers," in *Georgia Review*. XVII (Summer, 1963), pp. 206–213.

Eisinger, Chester E. "Carson McCullers and the Failure of Dialogue," in *Fiction of the Forties*. Chicago: University of Chicago Press, 1963, pp. 256–258.

Evans, Oliver. *The Ballad of Carson McCullers: A Biography*. New York: Coward-McCann, 1966, pp. 126–138.

Folk, Barbara N. "The Sad Sweet Music of Carson McCullers," in *Georgia Review*. XVI (1962), pp. 200–203.

Gaillard, Dawson F. "The Presence of the Narrator in Carson McCullers' *Ballad of the Sad Cafe*," in *Mississippi Quarterly*. XXV (Fall, 1972), pp. 419–428.

Gossett, Louise Y. "Dispossessed Love: Carson McCullers," in *Violence in Recent Southern Fiction*. Durham, N.C.: Duke University Press, 1965, pp. 167–168.

Graver, Lawrence. *Carson McCullers*. Minneapolis: University of Minnesota Press, 1969, pp. 24–33. Reprinted in *American Writers: A Collection of Literary Biographies*, Volume II. Edited by Leonard Unger. New York: Scribner's, 1974, pp. 595–599.

Griffith, Albert J. "Carson McCullers' Myth of the Sad Cafe," in *Georgia Review*. XXI (Spring, 1967), pp. 46–56.

Hamilton, Alice. "Loneliness and Alienation: The Life and Work of Carson McCullers," in *Dalhousie Review*. L (Summer, 1970), pp. 225–227.

Hart, Jane. "Carson McCullers, Pilgrim of Loneliness," in *Georgia Review*. XI (Spring, 1957), pp. 53–58.

Hassan, Ihab. "Carson McCullers: The Alchemy of Love and Aesthetics of Pain," in *Modern Fiction Studies*. V (1959), pp. 311–326. Reprinted in his *Radical Innocence: Studies in the Contemporary American Novel*. Princeton, N.J.: Princeton University Press, 1961, pp. 223–227.

Hoffman, Frederick J. *The Art of Southern Fiction: A Study of Some Modern Novelists.* Carbondale: Southern Illinois University Press, 1967, pp. 68–71.

Kazin, Alfred. *Bright Book of Life: American Storytellers from Hemingway to Mailer.* Boston: Little, Brown, 1973, pp. 50–54.

Kohler, Dayton. "Carson McCullers: Variations on a Theme," in *College English.* XIII (1951), pp. 4–5.

McNally, John. "The Introspective Narrator in *The Ballad of the Sad Cafe,*" in *South Atlantic Bulletin.* XXXVIII (November, 1973), pp. 40–44.

Malin, Irving. *New American Gothic.* Carbondale: Southern Illinois University Press, 1962, pp. 25–26, 137–139.

Millichap, Joseph R. "Carson McCullers' Literary Ballad," in *Georgia Review.* XXVII (Fall, 1973), pp. 329–339.

Phillips, Robert S. "Dinesen's *Monkey* and McCullers' *Ballad*: A Study in Literary Affinity," in *Studies in Short Fiction.* I (Spring, 1964), pp. 184–190.

————. "Painful Love: Carson McCullers' Parable," in *Southwest Review.* LI (Winter, 1966), pp. 80–86.

Rechnitz, Robert M. "The Failure of Love: The Grotesque in Two Novels by Carson McCullers," in *Georgia Review.* XXII (Winter, 1968), pp. 459–463.

Robinson, W.R. "The Life of Carson McCullers' Imagination," in *Southern Humanities Review.* II (Summer, 1968), pp. 291–302.

Vickery, John B. "Carson McCullers: A Map of Love," in *Wisconsin Studies in Contemporary Literature.* I (Winter, 1960), pp. 13–24.

Clock Without Hands

Allen, Walter. *The Modern Novel in Britain and the United States.* New York: Dutton, 1964, pp. 132–137.

Auchincloss, Louis. *Pioneers and Caretakers: A Study of Nine American Women Novelists.* Minneapolis: University of Minnesota Press, 1965, pp. 167–169.

Cook, Richard M. *Carson McCullers.* New York: Frederick Ungar, 1975, pp. 106–120.

Edmonds, Dale. *Carson McCullers.* Austin, Tex.: Steck-Vaughn, 1969, pp. 30–32.

Emerson, Donald. "The Ambiguities of *Clock Without Hands,*" in *Wisconsin Studies in Contemporary Literature.* III (Fall, 1962), pp. 15–28.

Evans, Oliver. *The Ballad of Carson McCullers: A Biography.* New York: Coward-McCann, 1966, pp. 170–182.

Ford, Nick Aaron. "Search for Identity: A Critical Survey of Significant Belles-Lettres by and About Negroes Published in 1961," in *Phylon.* XXIII (Summer, 1962), pp. 130–133.

Graver, Lawrence. *Carson McCullers*. Minneapolis: University of Minnesota Press, 1969, pp. 42–45. Reprinted in *American Writers: A Collection of Literary Biographies*, Volume II. Edited by Leonard Unger. New York: Scribner's, 1974, pp. 605–606.

Grumbach, Doris. "*Clock Without Hands*," in *America*. CV (September 23, 1961), p. 809.

Hamilton, Alice. "Loneliness and Alienation: The Life and Work of Carson McCullers," in *Dalhousie Review*. L (Summer, 1970), pp. 227–228.

Hartt, J.N. "The Return of Moral Passion," in *Yale Review*. LI (Winter, 1962), pp. 300–301.

Hicks, Granville. "The Subtler Corruptions," in *Saturday Review*. XLIV (September 23, 1961), pp. 14–15, 49.

Howe, Irving. "In the Shadow of Death," in *New York Times Book Review*. (September 17, 1961), p. 5.

Hughes, Catherine. "A World of Outcasts," in *Commonweal*. LXXV (October 13, 1961), pp. 73–75.

Martin, Jean. "*Clock Without Hands*," in *Nation*. CXCIII (November 18, 1961), pp. 411–412.

Parker, Dorothy. "*Clock Without Hands* Belongs in Yesterday's Tower of Ivory," in *Esquire*. (December, 1961), pp. 72–73.

Presley, Delma Eugene. "Carson McCullers' Descent to Earth," in *Descant*. XVII (1972), pp. 54–60.

Rolo, Charles. "A Southern Drama," in *Atlantic*. CCVIII (October, 1961), pp. 126–127.

Schorer, Mark. "McCullers and Capote: Basic Patterns," in *The Creative Present: Notes on Contemporary American Fiction*. Edited by Nona Balakian and Charles Simmons. New York: Doubleday, 1963, pp. 283–285.

Sullivan, Walter. "*Clock Without Hands*," in *Georgia Review*. XV (Winter, 1961), pp. 467–469.

Tracy, Honor. "A Voice Crying in the South," in *New Republic*. CXLV (November 13, 1961), pp. 16–17.

Vidal, Gore. "The World Outside," in *Rocking the Boat*. Boston: Little, Brown, 1962, pp. 178–183.

The Heart Is a Lonely Hunter

Allen, Walter. *The Modern Novel in Britain and the United States*. New York: Dutton, 1964, pp. 132–134.

Auchincloss, Louis. *Pioneers and Caretakers: A Study of Nine American Women Novelists*. Minneapolis: University of Minnesota Press, 1965, pp. 161–163.

Bluefarb, Sam. *The Escape Motif in the American Novel: Mark Twain to Richard Wright.* Columbus: Ohio State University Press, pp. 114–132.

Cargill, Oscar. *Intellectual America: Ideas on the March.* New York: Macmillan, 1941, pp. 396–397.

Cook, Richard M. *Carson McCullers.* New York: Frederick Ungar, 1975, pp. 20–45.

Durham, Frank. "God and No God in *The Heart Is a Lonely Hunter,*" in *South Atlantic Quarterly.* LVI (1957), pp. 494–499.

Edmonds, Dale. *Carson McCullers.* Austin, Tex.: Steck-Vaughn, 1969, pp. 9–14.

Eisinger, Chester E. *Fiction of the Forties.* Chicago: University of Chicago Press, 1963, pp. 245–251.

Evans, Oliver. *The Ballad of Carson McCullers: A Biography.* New York: Coward-McCann, 1966, pp. 98–117.

Fiedler, Leslie A. *Love and Death in the American Novel.* New York: Stein and Day, 1960, pp. 449–451.

Graver, Lawrence. *Carson McCullers.* Minneapolis: University of Minnesota Press, 1969, pp. 10–20. Reprinted in *American Writers: A Collection of Literary Biographies,* Volume II. Edited by Leonard Unger. New York: Scribner's, 1974, pp. 588–593.

Hamilton, Alice. "Loneliness and Alienation: The Life and Work of Carson McCullers," in *Dalhousie Review.* L (Summer, 1970), pp. 218–223.

Hassan, Ihab H. "Carson McCullers: The Alchemy of Love and Aesthetics of Pain," in *Modern Fiction Studies.* V (Winter, 1959–1960), pp. 315–318. Reprinted in *Radical Innocence: Studies in the Contemporary American Novel.* Princeton, N.J.: Princeton University Press, 1961, pp. 211–215.

Kazin, Alfred. *Bright Book of Life: American Storytellers from Hemingway to Mailer.* Boston: Little, Brown, 1973, pp. 50–54.

Knowles, A.S. "Six Bronze Petals and Two Red: Carson McCullers in the Forties," in *The Forties: Fiction, Poetry, Drama.* Edited by Warren French. Deland, Fla.: Everett/Edwards, 1969, pp. 87–98.

Madden, David. "The Paradox of the Need for Privacy and the Need for Understanding in Carson McCullers' *The Heart Is a Lonely Hunter,*" in *Literature and Psychology.* XVII (1967), pp. 128–140.

Malin, Irving. *New American Gothic.* Carbondale: Southern Illinois University Press, 1962, pp. 21–23, 54–55, 111–113, 133–134.

Millichap, Joseph R. "The Realistic Structure of *The Heart Is a Lonely Hunter,*" in *Twentieth Century Literature.* XVII (January, 1971), pp. 11–17.

Moore, Jack B. "Carson McCullers: The Heart Is a Timeless Hunter," in *Twentieth Century Literature.* XI (July, 1965), pp. 76–81.

Redman, Ben Ray. "Of Human Loneliness," in *Saturday Review.* XXII (June 8, 1940), p. 6.

Rubin, Louis D., Jr. "Carson McCullers: The Aesthetic of Pain," in *Virginia Quarterly Review.* LIII (Spring, 1977), pp. 265–283.

Sherrill, Roland A. "McCullers' *The Heart Is a Lonely Hunter,*" in *Kentucky Review.* II (1968), pp. 5–17.

Solomon, Louis B. "Someone to Talk To," in *Nation.* CLI (July 13, 1940), p. 36.

Taylor, Horace. "*The Heart Is a Lonely Hunter:* A Southern Wasteland," in *Studies in American Literature.* Edited by Waldo McNeir and Leo B. Levy. Baton Rouge: Louisiana State University Press, 1960, pp. 154–160.

Wright, Richard. "Inner Landscape," in *New Republic.* CIII (August 5, 1940), p. 195.

The Member of the Wedding

Allen, Walter. *The Modern Novel in Britain and the United States.* New York: Dutton, 1964, pp. 134–135.

Auchincloss, Louis. *Pioneers and Caretakers: A Study of Nine American Women Novelists.* Minneapolis: University of Minnesota Press, 1965, pp. 165–166.

Cook, Richard M. *Carson McCullers.* New York: Frederick Ungar, 1975, pp. 60–81.

Cowley, Malcolm. *The Literary Situation.* New York: Viking, 1954, p. 94.

Dusenbury, Winifred L. "An Unhappy Family," in *The Theme of Loneliness in Modern American Drama.* Gainesville: University of Florida Press, 1960, pp. 57–85.

Edmonds, Dale. *Carson McCullers.* Austin, Tex.: Steck-Vaughn, 1969, pp. 24–29.

Eisinger, Chester E. *Fiction of the Forties.* Chicago: University of Chicago Press, 1963, pp. 254–256.

Evans, Oliver. *The Ballad of Carson McCullers: A Biography.* New York: Coward-McCann, 1966, pp. 98–117.

Graver, Lawrence. *Carson McCullers.* Minneapolis: University of Minnesota Press, 1969, pp. 33–42. Reprinted in *American Writers: A Collection of Literary Biographies*, Volume II. Edited by Leonard Unger. New York: Scribner's, 1974, pp. 600–605.

Hart, Jane. "Carson McCullers, Pilgrim of Loneliness," in *Georgia Review.* XI (Spring, 1957), pp. 53–58.

Hassan, Ihab B. "Carson McCullers: The Alchemy of Love and Aesthetics of Pain," in *Modern Fiction Studies.* V (Winter, 1959–1960), pp. 320–323. Reprinted in *Radical Innocence: Studies in the Contemporary American Novel.* Princeton, N.J.: Princeton University Press, 1961, pp. 219–223.

Kazin, Alfred. "The Alone Generation," in *Contemporaries.* Boston: Little, Brown, 1962, pp. 207–216.

Malin, Irving. *New American Gothic.* Carbondale: Southern Illinois University Press, 1962, pp. 57–59, 114–116, 135–137. Reprinted in *Psychoanalysis and American Fiction.* Edited by Irving Malin. New York: Dutton, 1965, pp. 261–262.

Phillips, Robert S. "The Gothic Architecture of *The Member of the Wedding,*" in *Renascence.* XVI (Winter, 1964), pp. 59–72.

Robinson, W.R. "The Life of Carson McCullers' Imagination," in *Southern Humanities Review.* II (Summer, 1968), pp. 291–302.

Rosenfeld, Isaac. *"The Member of the Wedding,"* in *New Republic.* CXIV (April 29, 1946), pp. 633–634.

Schorer, Mark. "McCullers and Capote: Basic Patterns," in *The Creative Present: Notes on Contemporary American Fiction.* Edited by Nona Balakian and Charles Simmons. Garden City, N.Y.: Doubleday, 1963, pp. 83–107. Reprinted in *The World We Imagine.* New York: Farrar, Straus, and Giroux, 1969, pp. 274–285.

Tinkham, Charles B. "The Members of the Sideshow," in *Phylon.* XVIII (October, 1958), pp. 383–390.

Vickery, John B. "Carson McCullers: A Map of Love," in *Wisconsin Studies in Contemporary Literature.* I (Winter, 1960), pp. 21–23.

Wikborg, Eleanor. *Carson McCullers'* The Member of the Wedding: *Aspects of Structure and Style.* Göteborg, Sweden: Acta Universitatis Gothoburgensis, 1975.

Young, Marguerite. "Metaphysical Fiction," in *Kenyon Review.* IX (Winter, 1957), pp. 151–155.

The Mortgaged Heart

Adams, Phoebe. *"The Mortgaged Heart,"* in *Atlantic Monthly.* CCXXVIII (November, 1971), p. 153.

Clemons, Walter. *"The Mortgaged Heart,"* in *New York Times Book Review.* (November 7, 1971), p. 7.

Cook, Richard M. *Carson McCullers.* New York: Frederick Ungar, 1975, pp. 16–18.

Gullason, Thomas A. *"The Mortgaged Heart,"* in *Saturday Review.* LIV (November 13, 1971), p. 57.

Madden, David. "Transfixed Among the Self-Inflicted Ruins: Carson McCullers' *The Mortgaged Heart,*" in *Southern Literary Journal.* V (Fall, 1972), pp. 137–162.

Phillips, Robert. "Freaking Out: The Short Stories of Carson McCullers," in *Southwest Review.* LXIII (Winter, 1978), pp. 65–73.

Reflections in a Golden Eye

Allen, Walter. *The Modern Novel in Britain and the United States.* New York: Dutton, 1964, pp. 132–137.

Auchincloss, Louis. *Pioneers and Caretakers: A Study of Nine American Women Novelists.* Minneapolis: University of Minnesota Press, 1965, pp. 163–165.

Cook, Richard M. *Carson McCullers.* New York: Frederick Ungar, 1975, pp. 48–58.

Davenport, Basil. *"Reflections in a Golden Eye,"* in *Saturday Review.* XXIII (February 22, 1941), p. 12.

Edmonds, Dale. *Carson McCullers.* Austin, Tex.: Steck-Vaughn, 1969, pp. 14–19.

Eisinger, Chester E. *Fiction of the Forties.* Chicago: University of Chicago Press, 1963, pp. 251–254.

Evans, Oliver. *The Ballad of Carson McCullers: A Biography.* New York: Coward-McCann, 1966, pp. 60–71.

Ferguson, Otis. "Fiction: Odd and Ordinary," in *New Republic.* CIV (March 3, 1942), p. 317.

Graver, Lawrence. *Carson McCullers.* Minneapolis: University of Minnesota Press, 1969, pp. 20–24. Reprinted in *American Writers: A Collection of Literary Biographies*, Volume II. Edited by Leonard Unger. New York: Scribner's, 1974, pp. 593–595.

Hamilton, Alice. "Loneliness and Alienation: The Life and Work of Carson McCullers," in *Dalhousie Review.* L (Summer, 1970), pp. 223–225.

Hassan, Ihab H. "Carson McCullers: The Alchemy of Love and Aesthetics of Pain," in *Modern Fiction Studies.* V (Winter, 1959–1960), pp. 318–320. Reprinted in *Radical Innocence: Studies in the Contemporary American Novel.* Princeton, N.J.: Princeton University Press, 1961, pp. 216–218.

Hoffman, Frederick J. *The Art of Southern Fiction: A Study of Some Modern Novelists.* Carbondale: Southern Illinois University Press, 1967, pp. 67–68.

McPherson, Hugo. "Carson McCullers: Lonely Huntress," in *Tamarack Review.* XI (Spring, 1959), pp. 34–38.

Malin, Irving. *New American Gothic.* Carbondale: Southern Illinois University Press, 1962, pp. 23–25, 113–114, 134–135.

Rechnitz, Robert M. "The Failure of Love: The Grotesque in Two Novels by Carson McCullers," in *Georgia Review.* XXII (Winter, 1968), pp. 454–458.

Schorer, Mark. "McCullers and Capote: Basic Patterns," in *The Creative Present: Notes on Contemporary American Fiction.* Edited by Nona Balakian and Charles Simmons. Garden City, N.Y.: Doubleday, 1963, pp. 83–107. Reprinted in *The World We Imagine.* New York: Farrar, Straus, and Giroux, 1969, pp. 274–285.

Vickery, John B. "Carson McCullers: A Map of Love," in *Wisconsin Studies in Contemporary Literature.* I (Winter, 1960), pp. 18–21.

Williams, Tennessee. "Introduction," in *Reflections in a Golden Eye.* Norfolk, Conn.: New Directions, 1950, pp. i–xxi.

JOAQUIM MACHADO DE ASSÍS
(1839–1908)

Dom Casmurro

Caldwell, Helen. *Machado de Assis: Brazilian Master and His Novels.* Los Angeles: University of California Press, 1970, pp. 142–149.

————. *The Brazilian Othello of Machado de Assis.* Los Angeles: University of California Press, 1960.

Ellis, Keith. "Ambiguity and Point of View in Some Novelistic Representations of Jealousy," in *Modern Language Notes.* LXXXVI (1971), pp. 899–909.

Frank, Waldo. "Introduction," in *Dom Casmurro.* By Machado de Assis. New York: Noonday, 1953, pp. 5–13.

Machado, Jose Bettencourt. *Machado of Brazil.* New York: Bramerica, 1953, pp. 199–202.

Putnam, Samuel. *Marvelous Journey: A Survey of Four Centuries of Brazilian Writing.* New York: Knopf, 1948, pp. 182–183.

Epitaph of a Small Winner

Caldwell, Helen. *Machado de Assis: Brazilian Master and His Novels.* Los Angeles: University of California Press, 1970, pp. 74, 116.

Getlein, Frank. *"Epitaph of a Small Winner,"* in *Commonweal.* LVI (August 1, 1952), p. 417.

MacAdam, Alfred. "Machado de Assis: Satire and Madness," in *Modern Latin American Narratives.* Chicago: University of Chicago Press, 1977, pp. 11–28.

Pimentel, A. Fonseca. "Machado de Assis—Brazilian Writer," in *Journal of Inter-American Studies.* X (1968), pp. 154–158.

Webster, H.C. *"Epitaph of a Small Winner,"* in *Saturday Review.* XXXV (July 26, 1952), p. 9.

West, Anthony. "Machado de Assis," in *Principles and Persuasions.* New York: Harcourt, 1957, pp. 141–147.

NICCOLÒ MACHIAVELLI
(1469–1527)

The Prince

Adams, R.M. "Machiavelli Now and Here: An Essay for the First World," in *American Scholar*. XLIV (Summer, 1975), pp. 365–381.

Anglo, Sydney. *Machiavelli: A Dissection.* New York: Harcourt, Brace and World, 1970.

Barricelli, Jean-Pierre. The Prince: *An Analysis of Machiavelli's Treatise on Power Politics.* New York: Barron, 1975.

Bonadeo, Alfredo. *Corruption, Conflict, and Power in the Works and Times of Niccolò Machiavelli.* Los Angeles: Center for Medieval and Renaissance Studies, UCLA, 1973.

————. "The Role of the People in the Works and Times of Machiavelli," in *Bibliothèque d'Humanisme et Renaissance.* XXXII (1970), pp. 351–377.

Bondanella, Peter E. *Machiavelli and the Art of Renaissance History.* Detroit: Wayne State University Press, 1974.

Butterfield, Herbert. *The Statecraft of Machiavelli.* New York: Macmillan, 1962.

Chabod, Federico. *Machiavelli and the Renaissance.* Translated by David Moore. Cambridge, Mass.: Harvard University Press, 1960.

Christie, Richard, *et al.* *Studies in Machiavellianism.* New York: Academic Press, 1970.

Clough, Cecile H. "Niccolò Machiavelli's Political Assumptions and Objectives," in *Bulletin of the John Rylands Library.* LIII (1970), pp. 33–74.

Colish, Marcia L. "The Idea of Liberty in Machiavelli," in *Journal of the History of Ideas.* XXXII (1971), pp. 323–350.

D'Andrea, Antonio. "Machiavelli, Satan and the Gospel," in *Yearbook of Italian Studies.* I (1971), pp. 156–177.

Della Terza, Dante. "The Most Recent Image of Machiavelli: The Contribution of the Linguist and the Literary Historian," in *Italian Quarterly.* LIII (1970), pp. 91–113.

Dyer, Louis. *Machiavelli and the Modern State.* New York: Gordon Press, 1904.

Filler, L. "Machiavelli for the Millions: Some Notes on Power Structures," in *American Dreams, American Nightmares.* Edited by David Madden. Carbondale: Southern Illinois University Press, 1970, pp. 28–44.

Fleisher, Martin, Editor. *Machiavelli and the Nature of Political Thought.* New York: Atheneum, 1972.

Hale, John R.   *Machiavelli and Renaissance Italy.* Mystic, Conn.: Verry, 1961.

Hexter, J.H.   *Vision of Politics on the Eve of the Reformation: More, Machiavelli, Seyssel.* New York: Basic Books, 1973.

Major, J.R.   "The Renaissance Monarchy as Seen by Erasmus, More, Seyssel, and Machiavelli," in *Action and Conviction in Early Modern Europe; Essays in Memory of E.H. Harbison.* Edited by Theodore K. Rabb and Jerrold E. Seigel. Princeton, N.J.: Princeton University Press, 1969, pp. 17–31.

Pansini, Anthony J.   *Machiavelli and the U.S.A.* Greenvale, N.Y.: Greenvale Press, 1970.

Paul, Anthony J., Editor.   *Political Calculus: Essays on Machiavelli's Philosophy.* Toronto: University of Toronto Press, 1972.

Pocock, J.G.   *The Machiavellian Moment: Florentine Political Thought and the Atlantic Republican Tradition.* Princeton, N.J.: Princeton University Press, 1975.

Tarlton, Charles D.   "Symbolism, Redemption and Exorcism of Fortune in Machiavelli's *Prince*," in *Review of Politics.* XXX (1968), pp. 332–348.

Tsurutani, T.   "Machiavelli and the Problem of Political Development," in *Review of Politics.* XXX (1968), pp. 316–331.

ARCHIBALD MACLEISH
(1892–   )

Conquistador

Aiken, W.E.   "Poetic Form in *Conquistador*," in *Modern Language Notes*. LI (February, 1936), pp. 107–109.

Brooks, Cleanth.   *Modern Poetry and the Tradition*. New York: Oxford University Press, 1965, pp. 118–129.

Falk, Signi Lenea.   *Archibald MacLeish*. New York: Twayne, 1965, pp. 56–64.

Kirstein, Lincoln.   "Arms and Men," in *Hound and Horn*. V (April–June, 1932), pp. 484–492.

Monroe, Harriet.   "The Conqueror," in *Poetry*. XL (July, 1932), pp. 216–222.

Tate, Allen.   *Reactionary Essays on Poetry and Ideas*. New York: Scribner's, 1936, pp. 202–209.

J.B.

Abel, Lionel.   *Metatheatre: A New View of Dramatic Form*. New York: Hill and Wang, 1963, pp. 116–122.

Bond, Charels M.   "*J.B.* Is Not Job," in *Bucknell Review*. IX (1961), pp. 272–280.

Campbell, Colin C.   "The Transformation of Biblical Myth: MacLeish's Use of Adam and Job Stories," in *Myth and Symbol: Critical Approaches and Applications*. Edited by Bernice Slote. Lincoln: University of Nebraska Press, 1963, pp. 82–88.

Ciardi, John.   "The Birth of a Classic," in *The Voice Out of the Whirlwind*. Edited by Ralph E. Hone. San Francisco: Chandler, 1960, pp. 276–281.

Donoghue, Denis.   *The Third Voice: Modern British and American Verse Drama*. Princeton, N.J.: Princeton University Press, 1959, pp. 207–212.

Eberhart, Richard.   "Outer and Inner Verse Drama," in *Virginia Quarterly Review*. XXXIV (Autumn, 1958), pp. 618–623.

Falk, Signi Lenea.   *Archibald MacLeish*. New York: Twayne, 1965, pp. 138–150.

Grebstein, Sheldon Norman.   "*J.B.* and the Problems of Evil," in *University of Kansas City Review*. XXIV (Summer, 1963), pp. 253–261.

Hamilton, Kenneth.   "The Patience of *J.B.*," in *Dalhousie Review*. XLI (Spring, 1961), pp. 32–39.

Hayes, Richard.   "The Humanism of Crisis," in *Commonweal*. LXX (May 8, 1959), pp. 153–157.

Kahn, S. "The Games God Plays with Man: A Discussion of *J.B.*," in *The Fifties: Fiction, Poetry, Drama.* Edited by Warren G. French. Deland, Fla.: Everett/Edwards, 1970, pp. 249–259.

Lewis, Allan. *American Plays and Playwrights of the Contemporary Theatre.* New York: Crown, 1970, pp. 119–123, 125–128.

Montgomery, Marion. "On First Looking into Archibald MacLeish's Play in Verse, *J.B.*," in *Modern Drama.* II (December, 1959), pp. 231–242.

Sickels, Eleanor M. "MacLeish and the Fortunate Fall," in *American Literature.* LXIII (May, 1963), pp. 205–217.

Weals, Gerald C. *American Drama Since World War II.* New York: Harcourt, 1962, pp. 182–190.

Wells, Arvin R. "*J.B.*," in *Insight IV: Analyses of Modern British and American Drama.* Frankfurt, Germany: Hirschgraben, 1975, pp. 217–223.

Weiner, Herbert. "Job on Broadway: MacLeish's Man and the Bible's," in *Commentary.* XXVII (February, 1959), pp. 153–158.

White, William S. "MacLeish and the Broken Major," in *Harpers.* CCXVIII (1959), pp. 77–80.

The Poetry of MacLeish

Brenner, Rica. *Poets of Our Time.* New York: Harcourt, 1941, pp. 45–104.

Brooks, Cleanth. *Modern Poetry and the Tradition.* New York: Oxford University Press, 1965, pp. 116–125.

Ciardi, John. "The Poetry of Archibald MacLeish," in *Atlantic.* CXCI (May, 1953), pp. 67–68.

Deutsch, Babette. *This Modern Poetry.* New York: Norton, 1935, pp. 214–221.

Falk, Signi Lenea. *Archibald MacLeish.* New York: Twayne, 1965, pp. 15–78, 118–170.

Friar, Kimon. "Poet of Action," in *New Republic.* CXXVII (December 15, 1952), pp. 19–20.

Gregory, Horace, and Marya Zaturenska. *History of American Poetry, 1900–1940.* New York: Harcourt, 1946, pp. 448–457.

Lutyens, David Bulwer. *The Creative Encounter.* London: Secker and Warburg, 1960, pp. 66–97.

Mizener, Arthur. "The Poetry of Archibald MacLeish," in *Sewanee Review.* XLVI (October–December, 1938), pp. 501–519.

Smith, Grover. *Archibald MacLeish.* Minneapolis: University of Minnesota Press, 1971.

Southworth, James Granville. *Some Modern American Poets.* New York: Macmillan, 1950, pp. 122–134.

Van Ghent, Dorothy. "The Poetry of Archibald MacLeish," in *Science and Society.* II (Fall, 1938), pp. 500–511.

Waggoner, Hyatt H. *Heel of Elohim.* Norman: University of Oklahoma Press, 1950, pp. 133–154.

Whittemore, Reed. "MacLeish and the Democratic Pastoral," in *Sewanee Review.* LXI (October, 1953), pp. 700–709.

Wilson, Edmund. "The Omelet of Archibald MacLeish," in *New Yorker.* XIX (January 14, 1939), pp. 23–24.

LARRY MCMURTRY
(1936–)

All My Friends Are Going to Be Strangers

Crooks, Alan. "Larry McMurtry—A Writer in Transition: An Essay Review," in *Western American Literature.* VII (Summer, 1972), pp. 151–155.

Granzow, Barbara. "The Western Writer: A Study of Larry McMurtry's *All My Friends Are Going to Be Strangers,*" in *Southwestern American Literature.* IV (1974), pp. 37–52.

Harrison, Jim. "Women Impossible Not to Love and Impossible to Love Right," in *New York Times Book Review.* (March 19, 1972), pp. 5, 26.

Neinstein, Raymond L. *The Ghost Country: A Study of the Novels of Larry McMurtry.* Berkeley, Calif.: Creative Arts, 1976, pp. 39–48.

Peavy, Charles D. *Larry McMurtry.* Boston: Twayne, 1977, pp. 41–44.

Phillips, Billie. "McMurtry's Women: 'Eros [Libido, Caritas, and Philia] in [and out of] Archer Country,' " in *Southwestern Literature.* IV (1974), pp. 29–36.

Phillips, Raymond C., Jr. "The Ranch as Place and Symbol in the Novels of Larry McMurtry," in *South Dakota Review.* XIII (Summer, 1975), pp. 27–47.

Prigozy, Ruth. "*All My Friends Are Going to Be Strangers,*" in *Commonweal.* XCVII (October 20, 1972), pp. 70–71.

Stout, Janis P. "Journeying as a Metaphor for Cultural Loss in the Novels of Larry McMurtry," in *Western American Literature.* XI (May, 1976), pp. 37–50.

Summerlin, Tim. "Larry McMurtry and the Persistent Frontier," in *Southwestern American Literature.* IV (1974), pp. 22–28.

Whittemore, Reed. "Texas Sex," in *New Republic.* CLXVI (April 1, 1972), pp. 28–29.

Horseman, Pass By

Ahearn, Kerry. "Morte D'Urban: The Texas Novels of Larry McMurtry," in *Texas Quarterly.* XIX (Autumn, 1976), pp. 109–129.

Davis, Kenneth W. "The Theme of Initiation in the Works of Larry McMurtry and Tom Mayer," in *Arlington Quarterly.* II (Winter, 1969–1970), pp. 29–43.

Degenfelder, E. Pauline. "McMurtry and the Movies: *Hud* and *The Last Picture Show,*" in *Western Humanities Review.* XXIX (1975), pp. 81–91.

Landess, Thomas. *Larry McMurtry.* Austin, Tex.: Steck-Vaughn, 1969, pp. 5–14.

Neinstein, Raymond L. *The Ghost Country: A Study of the Novels of Larry McMurtry*. Berkeley, Calif.: Creative Arts, 1976, pp. 1–11.

Peavy, Charles D. "Coming of Age in Texas: The Novels of Larry McMurtry," in *Western American Literature*. IV (Fall, 1969), pp. 171–188.

————. *Larry McMurtry*. Boston: Twayne, 1977, pp. 28–31, 46–48.

Phillips, Raymond C., Jr. "The Ranch as Place and Symbol in the Novels of Larry McMurtry," in *South Dakota Review*. XIII (Summer, 1975), pp. 27–47.

Stout, Janis P. "Journeying as a Metaphor for Cultural Loss in the Novels of Larry McMurtry," in *Western American Literature*. XI (May, 1976), pp. 37–50.

Summerlin, Tim. "Larry McMurtry and the Persistent Frontier," in *Southwestern American Literature*. IV (1974), pp. 22–28.

The Last Picture Show

Ahearn, Kerry. "Morte D'Urban: The Texas Novels of Larry McMurtry," in *Texas Quarterly*. XIX (Autumn, 1976), pp. 109–129.

Davis, Kenneth W. "The Theme of Initiation in the Works of Larry McMurtry and Tom Mayer," in *Arlington Quarterly*. II (Winter, 1969–1970), pp. 29–43.

Degenfelder, E. Pauline. "McMurtry and the Movies: *Hud* and *The Last Picture Show*," in *Western Humanities Review*. XXIX (1975), pp. 81–91.

Landess, Thomas. *Larry McMurtry*. Austin, Tex.: Steck-Vaughn, 1969, pp. 23–30.

Neinstein, Raymond L. *The Ghost Country: A Study of the Novels of Larry McMurtry*. Berkeley, Calif.: Creative Arts, 1976, pp. 16–25.

Peavy, Charles D. "Coming of Age in Texas: The Novels of Larry McMurtry," in *Western American Literature*. IV (Fall, 1969), pp. 171–188.

————. *Larry McMurtry*. Boston: Twayne, 1977, pp. 52–56, 60–62, 93–95, 102–105.

————. "Larry McMurtry and Black Humor: A Note on *The Last Picture Show*," in *Western American Literature*. II (Fall, 1967), pp. 223–227.

Phillips, Billie. "McMurtry's Women: 'Eros [Libido, Caritas, and Philia] in [and out of] Archer Country,' " in *Southwestern Literature*. IV (1974), pp. 29–36.

Phillips, Raymond C., Jr. "The Ranch as Place and Symbol in the Novels of Larry McMurtry," in *South Dakota Review*. XIII (Summer, 1975), pp. 27–47.

Stout, Janis P. "Journeying as a Metaphor for Cultural Loss in the Novels of Larry McMurtry," in *Western American Literature*. XI (May, 1976), pp. 37–50.

Summerlin, Tim. "Larry McMurtry and the Persistent Frontier," in *Southwestern American Literature*. IV (1974), pp. 22–28.

Leaving Cheyenne

Ahearn, Kerry. "Morte D'Urban: The Texas Novels of Larry McMurtry," in *Texas Quarterly*. XIX (Autumn, 1976), pp. 109–129.

Davis, Kenneth W. "The Theme of Initiation in the Works of Larry McMurtry and Tom Mayer," in *Arlington Quarterly*. II (Winter, 1969–1970), pp. 29–43.

Giles, James R. "Larry McMurtry's *Leaving Cheyenne* and the Novels of John Rechy: Four Trips Along 'the Mythical Pecos,' " in *Forum*. X (Summer/Fall, 1972), pp. 34–40.

Landess, Thomas. *Larry McMurtry*. Austin, Tex.: Steck-Vaughn, 1969, pp. 14–22.

Neinstein, Raymond L. *The Ghost Country: A Study of the Novels of Larry McMurtry*. Berkeley, Calif.: Creative Arts, 1976, pp. 11–16.

Peavy, Charles D. "Coming of Age in Texas: The Novels of Larry McMurtry," in *Western American Literature*. IV (Fall, 1969), pp. 171–188.

————. *Larry McMurtry*. Boston: Twayne, 1977, pp. 31–34, 48–52, 63–67.

Phillips, Billie. "McMurtry's Women: 'Eros [Libido, Caritas, and Philia] in [and out of] Archer Country,' " in *Southwestern American Literature*. IV (1974), pp. 29–36.

Phillips, Raymond C., Jr. "The Ranch as Place and Symbol in the Novels of Larry McMurtry," in *South Dakota Review*. XIII (Summer, 1975), pp. 27–47.

Stout, Janis P. "Journeying as a Metaphor for Cultural Loss in the Novels of Larry McMurtry," in *Western American Literature*. XI (May, 1976), pp. 37–50.

Moving On

Ahearn, Kerry. "Morte D'Urban: The Texas Novels of Larry McMurtry," in *Texas Quarterly*. XIX (Autumn, 1976), pp. 109–129.

Crooks, Alan. "Larry McMurtry—A Writer in Transition: An Essay Review," in *Western American Literature*. VII (Summer, 1972), pp. 151–155.

Decker, William. "*Moving On*," in *Saturday Review*. LIII (October 17, 1970), p. 36.

Neinstein, Raymond L. *The Ghost Country: A Study of the Novels of Larry McMurtry*. Berkeley, Calif.: Creative Arts, 1976, pp. 27–39.

Peavy, Charles D. *Larry McMurtry*. Boston: Twayne, 1977, pp. 38–41.

Phillips, Billie. "McMurtry's Women: 'Eros [Libido, Caritas, and Philia] in [and out of] Archer Country,'" in *Southwestern Literature.* IV (1974), pp. 29–36.

Phillips, Raymond C., Jr. "The Ranch as Place and Symbol in the Novels of Larry McMurtry," in *South Dakota Review.* XIII (Summer, 1975), pp. 27–47.

Schott, Webster. "Words, Words, Sex, Sex," in *New York Times Book Review.* (July 26, 1970), p. 16.

Stout, Janis P. "Journeying as a Metaphor for Cultural Loss in the Novels of Larry McMurtry," in *Western American Literature.* XI (May, 1976), pp. 37–50.

Summerlin, Tim. "Larry McMurtry and the Persistent Frontier," in *Southwestern American Literature.* IV (1974), pp. 22–28.

LOUIS MACNEICE
(1907–1963)

"Areopagus"

Brown, Terence. *Louis MacNeice: Sceptical Vision.* New York: Barnes & Noble, 1975, pp. 189–190.

McKinnon, William T. *Apollo's Blended Dream: A Study of the Poetry of Louis MacNeice.* London: Oxford University Press, 1971, p. 89.

Moore, D.B. *The Poetry of Louis MacNeice.* Leicester, England: Leicester University Press, 1972, pp. 157–160.

Smith, Elton Edward. *Louis MacNeice.* New York: Twayne, 1970, pp. 145–148.

Autumn Journal

Brown, S.G. "Some Poems of Louis MacNeice," in *Sewanee Review.* LI (Winter, 1943), pp. 68–72.

Brown, Terence. *Louis MacNeice: Sceptical Vision.* New York: Barnes & Noble, 1975, pp. 50–55.

————. "MacNeice: Father and Son," in *Time Was Away: The World of Louis MacNeice.* Edited by Terence Brown and Alec Reid. Dublin: Dolmen Press, 1974, p. 23.

Lewis, C. Day. *The Lyric Impulse.* Cambridge, Mass.: Harvard University Press, 1965, pp. 98–99.

McKinnon, William T. *Apollo's Blended Dream: A Study of the Poetry of Louis MacNeice.* London: Oxford University Press, 1971, pp. 105–107.

Moore, D.B. *The Poetry of Louis MacNeice.* Leicester, England: Leicester University Press, 1972, pp. 67–100.

Press, John. *Louis MacNeice.* London: Longmans, Green, 1965, pp. 29–30.

Scarfe, Francis. *Auden and After: The Liberation of Poetry, 1930–1941.* London: Routledge, 1942, pp. 59–60.

Smith, Elton Edward. *Louis MacNeice.* New York: Twayne, 1970, pp. 86–87, 122–123, 156–157.

"Perseus"

Brown, Terence. *Louis MacNeice: Sceptical Vision.* New York: Barnes & Noble, 1975, p. 110.

Cope, John I. " 'Perseus,' " in *Explicator.* XXVI (February, 1968), item 48.

Drew, Elizabeth and John L. Sweeney. *Directions in Modern Poetry.* New York: Norton, 1940, pp. 87–88.

Smith, Elton Edward. *Louis MacNeice.* New York: Twayne, 1970, p. 34.

The Poetry of MacNeice

Brown, Terence. "Louis MacNeice and the 'Dark Conceit,'" in *Ariel.* III (1972), pp. 16–24.

―――. *Louis MacNeice: Sceptical Vision.* New York: Barnes & Noble, 1975.

―――. "MacNeice: Father and Son," in *Time Was Away: The World of Louis MacNeice.* Edited by Terence Brown and Alec Reid. Dublin: Dolmen Press, 1974, pp. 21–34.

Highet, Gilbert. *The Powers of Poetry.* New York: Oxford University Press, 1960, pp. 25–26.

Longley, Michael. "A Misrepresented Poet," in *Dublin Magazine.* VI (1967), pp. 68–74.

McKinnon, William T. *Apollo's Blended Dream: A Study of the Poetry of Louis MacNeice.* London: Oxford University Press, 1971, pp. 39–170.

Montague, John. "Despair and Delight," in *Time Was Away: The World of Louis MacNeice.* Edited by Terence Brown and Alec Reid. Dublin: Dolmen Press, 1974, pp. 123–127.

Moore, D.B. *The Poetry of Louis MacNeice.* Leicester, England: Leicester University Press, 1972.

Press, John. *Louis MacNeice.* London: Longmans, Green, 1965, pp. 23–44.

Scarfe, Francis. *Auden and After: The Liberation of Poetry, 1930–1941.* London: Routledge, 1942, pp. 53–67.

Skelton, Robin. "Celt and Classicist: The Versecraft of Louis MacNeice," in *Time Was Away: The World of Louis MacNeice.* Edited by Terence Brown and Alec Reid. Dublin: Dolmen Press, 1974, pp. 43–53.

Smith, Elton Edward. *Louis MacNeice.* New York: Twayne, 1970.

Smith, William J. "The Black Clock: The Poetic Achievement of Louis Mac-Neice," in *Hollins Critic.* IV (1967), pp. 1–11.

"Prayer Before Birth"

McKinnon, William T. *Apollo's Blended Dream: A Study of the Poetry of Louis MacNeice.* London: Oxford University Press, 1971, pp. 190–191.

Moore, D.B. *The Poetry of Louis MacNeice.* Leicester, England: Leicester University Press, 1972, pp. 106–112.

Press, John. *Louis MacNeice.* London: Longmans, Green, 1965, p. 35.

Smith, Elton Edward. *Louis MacNeice.* New York: Twayne, 1970, p. 111.

"Snow"

Barroff, Marie. "What a Poem Is: For Instance 'Snow,' " in *Essays in Criticism*. VIII (October, 1958), pp. 393–404.

Barry, Sister M. Martin. " 'Snow,' " in *Explicator*. XVI (November, 1957), item 10.

Brown, Terence. *Louis MacNeice: Sceptical Vision*. New York: Barnes & Noble, 1975, p. 97.

Drew, Elizabeth. *Poetry: A Modern Guide to Its Understanding and Enjoyment*. New York: Norton, 1959, pp. 226–228.

McKinnon, William T. *Apollo's Blended Dream: A Study of the Poetry of Louis MacNeice*. London: Oxford University Press, 1971, pp. 151–153, 201–202.

Moore, D.B. *The Poetry of Louis MacNeice*. Leicester, England: Leicester University Press, 1972, pp. 59–62.

"The Stygian Banks"

Brown, Terence. *Louis MacNeice: Sceptical Vision*. New York: Barnes & Noble, 1975, pp. 41–42.

McKinnon, William T. *Apollo's Blended Dream: A Study of the Poetry of Louis MacNeice*. London: Oxford University Press, 1971, pp. 66–67, 127–129, 174–175.

Moore, D.B. *The Poetry of Louis MacNeice*. Leicester, England: Leicester University Press, 1972, pp. 128–134.

Smith, Elton Edward. *Louis MacNeice*. New York: Twayne, 1970, pp. 131–133.

Visitations

Brown, Terence. *Louis MacNeice: Sceptical Vision*. New York: Barnes & Noble, 1975, pp. 104–105, 187–188.

McKinnon, William T. *Apollo's Blended Dream: A Study of the Poetry of Louis MacNeice*. London: Oxford University Press, 1971, pp. 73–74, 206–207, 215–216.

Moore, D.B. *The Poetry of Louis MacNeice*. Leicester, England: Leicester University Press, 1972, pp. 224–226.

Smith, Elton Edward. *Louis MacNeice*. New York: Twayne, 1970, pp. 169–171.

NORMAN MAILER
(1923–   )

Advertisements for Myself

Adams, Laura. *Existential Battles: The Growth of Norman Mailer.* Athens: Ohio University Press, 1976, pp. 27–64.

Bone, Robert A. "Private Mailer Re-enlists," in *Dissent.* VII (Autumn, 1961), pp. 389–394.

Bufithis, Philip H. *Norman Mailer.* New York: Frederick Ungar, 1978, pp. 56–63.

Dupee, F.W. "The American Norman Mailer," in *Commentary.* XXIX (February, 1960), pp. 128–132. Reprinted in *Norman Mailer: A Collection of Critical Essays.* Edited by Leo Braudy. Englewood Cliffs, N.J.: Prentice-Hall, 1972, pp. 96–103.

Foster, Richard. *Norman Mailer.* Minneapolis: University of Minnesota Press, 1968, pp. 21–25.

Fuller, Edmund. *Man in Modern Fiction: Some Minority Opinions of Contemporary American Writing.* New York: Random House, 1958, pp. 154–162.

Gutman, Stanley T. *Mankind in Barbary: The Individual and Society in the Novels of Norman Mailer.* Hanover, N.H.: University Press of New England, 1975, pp. 67–94.

Harper, Howard M., Jr. *Desperate Faith: A Study of Bellow, Salinger, Mailer, Baldwin and Updike.* Chapel Hill: University of North Carolina Press, 1967, pp. 115–120, 124–129.

Hoffman, Frederick J. *The Mortal No: Death and the Modern Imagination.* Princeton, N.J.: Princeton University Press, 1964, pp. 476–481.

Howe, Irvin. *A World More Attractive.* New York: Horizon Press, 1963, pp. 90–91, 123–129.

Kazin, Alfred. *Contemporaries.* Boston: Little, Brown, 1962, pp. 246–250. Reprinted in *Norman Mailer: The Man and His Work.* Edited by Robert F. Lucid. Boston: Little, Brown, 1971, pp. 89–94.

Leeds, Barry H. *The Structured Vision of Norman Mailer.* New York: New York University Press, 1969, pp. 223–236.

Poirier, Richard. *Norman Mailer.* New York: Viking, 1972, pp. 35–42.

Radford, Jean. *Norman Mailer: A Critical Study.* New York: Barnes & Noble, 1975, pp. 88–95, 140–145.

Schrader, George Alfred. "Norman Mailer and the Despair of Defiance," in *Yale Review.* LI (December, 1961), pp. 267–280. Reprinted in *Norman*

Mailer: A Collection of Critical Essays. Edited by Leo Braudy. Englewood Cliffs, N.J.: Prentice-Hall, 1972, pp. 82–95.

Solotaroff, Robert. *Down Mailer's Way*. Urbana: University of Illinois Press, 1974, pp. 55–57.

An American Dream

Adams, Laura. *Existential Battles: The Growth of Norman Mailer*. Athens: Ohio University Press, 1976, pp. 70–97.

Aldridge, James W. *Time to Murder and Create: The Contemporary Novel in Crisis*. New York: David McKay, 1966, pp. 160–163.

Bersani, Leo. "The Interpretation of Dreams," in *Partisan Review*. XXXII (Fall, 1965), pp. 603–608. Reprinted in *Norman Mailer: A Collection of Critical Essays*. Edited by Leo Braudy. Englewood Cliffs, N.J.: Prentice-Hall, 1972, pp. 120–126.

Bufithis, Philip H. *Norman Mailer*. New York: Frederick Ungar, 1978, pp. 65–74.

Corrington, John William. "An American Dreamer," in *Chicago Review*. XVIII (Spring, 1965), pp. 58–66.

Fiedler, Leslie A. "Master of Dreams," in *Partisan Review*. XXIV (Summer, 1967), pp. 352–356.

Foster, Richard. *Norman Mailer*. Minneapolis: University of Minnesota Press, 1968, pp. 18–19.

Gutman, Stanley T. *Mankind in Barbary: The Individual and Society in the Novels of Norman Mailer*. Hanover, N.H.: University Press of New England, 1975, pp. 95–132.

Hardwick, Elizabeth. "Bad Boy," in *Partisan Review*. XXXII (Spring, 1965), pp. 291–294. Reprinted in *Norman Mailer: The Man and His Work*. Edited by Robert F. Lucid. Boston: Little, Brown, 1971, pp. 145–150.

Harper, Howard M., Jr. *Desperate Faith: A Study of Bellow, Salinger, Mailer, Baldwin and Updike*. Chapel Hill: University of North Carolina Press, 1967, pp. 120–124.

Hyman, Stanley E. *Standards: A Chronicle of Books for Our Time*. New York: Horizon Press, 1966, pp. 274–278. Reprinted in *Norman Mailer: A Collection of Critical Essays*. Edited by Leo Braudy. Englewood Cliffs, N.J.: Prentice-Hall, 1972, pp. 104–108.

Kaufmann, Donald L. *Norman Mailer: The Countdown (The First Twenty Years)*. Carbondale: Southern Illinois University Press, 1969, pp. 35–50.

Langbaum, Robert. "Mailer's New Style," in *Novel*. II (Fall, 1968), pp. 69–78.

Leeds, Barry H. *The Structured Vision of Norman Mailer*. New York: New York University Press, 1969, pp. 125–177, 231–236.

McConnell, Frank D. *Four Postwar American Novelists: Bellow, Mailer, Barth, and Pynchon.* Chicago: University of Chicago Press, 1977, pp. 94–100.

Middlebrook, Jonathan. *Mailer and the Times of His Time.* San Francisco: Bay Books, 1976, pp. 105–137.

Newman, Paul B. "Mailer: The Jew as Existentialist," in *North American Review.* II (July, 1965), pp. 48–55.

Poirier, Richard. *Norman Mailer.* New York: Viking, 1972, pp. 119–130.

Radford, Jean. *Norman Mailer: A Critical Study.* New York: Barnes & Noble, 1975, pp. 33–37, 100–110, 148–155.

Rahv, Philip. *Literature and the Sixth Sense.* Boston: Houghton Mifflin, 1969, pp. 409–417.

Richler, Mordecai. "Norman Mailer," in *Encounter.* XXV (July, 1965), pp. 61–64.

Schulz, Max F. *Radical Sophistication: Studies in Contemporary Jewish-American Novelists.* Athens: Ohio University Press, 1969, pp. 91–99.

Scott, Nathan A., Jr. *Three American Moralists: Mailer, Bellow, Trilling.* Notre Dame, Ind.: University of Notre Dame Press, 1973, pp. 56–70.

Solotaroff, Robert. *Down Mailer's Way.* Urbana: University of Illinois Press, 1974, pp. 130–178.

Tanner, Tony. *City of Words: American Fiction, 1950–1970.* New York: Harper's, 1971, pp. 356–366.

Wagenheim, Allan J. "Square's Progress: *An American Dream*," in *Critique.* X (1967–1968), pp. 45–68.

Weber, Brom. "A Fear of Dying: Norman Mailer's *An American Dream*," in *Hollins Critic.* II (June, 1965), pp. 1–6, 8–11.

Weinberg, Helen. *The New Novel in America: The Kafkan Mode in Contemporary Fiction.* Ithaca, N.Y.: Cornell University Press, 1970, pp. 124–140.

Witt, Grace. "The Bad Man as Hipster: Norman Mailer's Use of Frontier Metaphor," in *Western American Literature.* IV (Fall, 1969), pp. 203–217.

The Armies of the Night

Adams, Laura. *Existential Battles: The Growth of Norman Mailer.* Athens: Ohio University Press, 1976, pp. 121–136.

Bufithis, Philip H. *Norman Mailer.* New York: Frederick Ungar, 1978, pp. 85–95.

Foster, Richard. *Norman Mailer.* Minneapolis: University of Minnesota Press, 1968, pp. 30–31.

Gilman, Richard. "What Mailer Has Done," in *New Republic.* CLVIII (June 8, 1968), pp. 27–31. Reprinted in *Norman Mailer: A Collection of Critical*

Essays. Edited by Leo Braudy. Englewood Cliffs, N.J.: Prentice-Hall, 1972, pp. 158–166.

Gutman, Stanley T. *Mankind in Barbary: The Individual and Society in the Novels of Norman Mailer.* Hanover, N.H.: University Press of New England, 1975, pp. 159–194.

Johnson, Michael L. "Journalist," in *Will the Real Norman Mailer Please Stand Up?* Port Washington, N.Y.: Kennikat, 1974, pp. 173–194.

Leeds, Barry H. *The Structured Vision of Norman Mailer.* New York: New York University Press, 1969, pp. 247–264.

McConnell, Frank D. *Four Postwar American Novelists: Bellow, Mailer, Barth, and Pynchon.* Chicago: University of Chicago Press, 1977, pp. 104–107.

Middlebrook, Jonathan. *Mailer and the Times of His Time.* San Francisco: Bay Books, 1976, pp. 158–189.

Poirier, Richard. *Norman Mailer.* New York: Viking, 1972, pp. 77–106.

Radford, Jean. *Norman Mailer: A Critical Study.* New York: Barnes & Noble, 1975, pp. 72–74, 116–121.

Schroth, Raymond A. "Mailer and His Gods," in *Commonweal.* XC (May 9, 1969), pp. 226–229.

Solotaroff, Robert. *Down Mailer's Way.* Urbana: University of Illinois Press, 1974, pp. 212–237.

Trilling, Diana. *We Must March My Darlings: A Critical Decade.* New York: Harcourt, 1977, pp. 77–153.

Barbary Shore

Adams, Laura. *Existential Battles: The Growth of Norman Mailer.* Athens: Ohio University Press, 1976, pp. 39–42.

Bufithis, Philip H. *Norman Mailer.* New York: Frederick Ungar, 1978, pp. 31–38.

Cook, Bruce A. "Norman Mailer: The Temptation to Power," in *Renascence.* XIV (Summer, 1962), pp. 210–211.

Foster, Richard. *Norman Mailer.* Minneapolis: University of Minnesota Press, 1968, pp. 12–14.

Gutman, Stanley. *Mankind in Barbary: The Individual and Society in the Novels of Norman Mailer.* Hanover, N.H.: University Press of New England, 1975, pp. 29–44.

Harper, Howard M., Jr. *Desperate Faith: A Study of Bellow, Salinger, Mailer, Baldwin and Updike.* Chapel Hill: University of North Carolina Press, 1967, pp. 103–109.

Kaufmann, Donald L. *Norman Mailer: The Countdown (The First Twenty Years).* Carbondale: Southern Illinois University Press, 1969, pp. 12–23.

Leeds, Barry H. *The Structured Vision of Norman Mailer.* New York: New York University Press, 1969, pp. 53–103.

McConnell, Frank D. *Four Postwar American Novelists: Bellow, Mailer, Barth, and Pynchon.* Chicago: University of Chicago Press, 1977, pp. 80–87.

Middlebrook, Jonathan. *Mailer and the Times of His Time.* San Francisco: Bay Books, 1976, pp. 60–81.

Podhoretz, Norman. *Doings and Undoings: The Fifties and After in American Writing.* New York: Farrar, Straus, 1964, pp. 194–200.

Poirier, Richard. *Norman Mailer.* New York: Viking, 1972, pp. 25–45.

Radford, Jean. *Norman Mailer: A Critical Study.* New York: Barnes & Noble, 1975, pp. 16–19, 50–54, 82–85.

Schulz, Max F. *Radical Sophistication: Studies in Contemporary Jewish-American Novelists.* Athens: Ohio University Press, 1969, pp. 73–81.

Scott, Nathan A., Jr. *Three American Moralists: Mailer, Bellow, Trilling.* Notre Dame, Ind.: University of Notre Dame Press, 1973, pp. 30–39.

Silverstein, Howard. "Norman Mailer: The Family Romance and the Oedipal Family," in *American Imago.* XXXIV (Fall, 1977), pp. 277–286.

Solotaroff, Robert. *Down Mailer's Way.* Urbana: University of Illinois Press, 1974, pp. 40–45.

Stark, John. "*Barbary Shore*: The Basis of Mailer's Best Work," in *Modern Fiction Studies.* XVII (1971), pp. 403–408.

Trilling, Diana. *Claremont Essays.* New York: Harcourt, 1964, pp. 190–193.

Cannibals and Christians

Adams, Laura. *Existential Battles: The Growth of Norman Mailer.* Athens: Ohio University Press, 1976, pp. 102–107.

Aldridge, John W. *The Devil in the Fire: Essays in American Literature and Culture, 1951–1971.* New York: Harper's Magazine Press, 1971, pp. 180–184.

Foster, Richard. *Norman Mailer.* Minneapolis: University of Minnesota Press, 1968, pp. 28–29.

Poirier, Richard. *Norman Mailer.* New York: Viking, 1972, pp. 11–14.

Pritchard, William H. "Norman Mailer's Extravagances," in *Massachusetts Review.* VIII (Summer, 1967), pp. 562–568.

Radford, Jean. *Norman Mailer: A Critical Study.* New York: Barnes & Noble, 1975, pp. 63–65, 95–97.

Solotaroff, Robert. *Down Mailer's Way.* Urbana: University of Illinois Press, 1974, pp. 179–180, 186–189.

Tanner, Tony. "In the Lion's Den," in *Partisan Review*. XXXIV (Summer, 1967), pp. 465–471.

Wain, John. "Mailer's America," in *New Republic*. CLV (October 1, 1966), pp. 19–20.

The Deer Park

Adams, Laura. *Existential Battles: The Growth of Norman Mailer.* Athens: Ohio University Press, 1976, pp. 47–50.

Bufithis, Philip H. *Norman Mailer.* New York: Frederick Ungar, 1978, pp. 43–51.

Bryant, Jerry H. *The Open Decision: The Contemporary Novel and Its Intellectual Background.* New York: Free Press, 1970, pp. 376–382.

Cook, Bruce A. "Norman Mailer: The Temptation to Power," in *Renascence.* XIV (Summer, 1962), pp. 212–214.

Foster, Richard. *Norman Mailer.* Minneapolis: University of Minnesota Press, 1968, pp. 14–18.

Geismar, Maxwell. *American Moderns: From Rebellion to Conformity.* New York: Hill and Wang, 1958, pp. 174–179.

Gutman, Stanley T. *Mankind in Barbary: The Individual and Society in the Novels of Norman Mailer.* Hanover, N.H.: University Press of New England, 1975, pp. 45–65.

Harper, Howard M., Jr. *Desperate Faith: A Study of Bellow, Salinger, Mailer, Baldwin and Updike.* Chapel Hill: University of North Carolina Press, 1967, pp. 109–115.

Kaufmann, Donald L. *Norman Mailer: The Countdown (The First Twenty Years).* Carbondale: Southern Illinois University Press, 1969, pp. 24–34.

Krim, Seymour. "An Open Letter to Norman Mailer," in *Evergreen Review.* XLV (February, 1967), pp. 89–96.

Leeds, Barry H. *The Structured Vision of Norman Mailer.* New York: New York University Press, 1969, pp. 105–123.

McConnell, Frank D. *Four Postwar American Novelists: Bellow, Mailer, Barth, and Pynchon.* Chicago: University of Chicago Press, 1977, pp. 87–94.

Middlebrook, Jonathan. *Mailer and the Times of His Time.* San Francisco: Bay Books, 1976, pp. 82–104.

Millgate, Michael. *American Social Fiction: James to Cozzens.* New York: Barnes & Noble, 1965, pp. 159–162.

Podhoretz, Norman. *Doings and Undoings: The Fifties and After in American Writing.* New York: Farrar, Straus, 1964, pp. 194–200.

Poirier, Richard. *Norman Mailer.* New York: Viking, 1972, pp. 32–39.

Radford, Jean. *Norman Mailer: A Critical Study.* New York: Barnes & Noble, 1975, pp. 19–27, 132–140.

Rother, James. "Mailer's 'O'Shaugnessy Chronicle': A Speculative Autopsy," in *Critique.* XIX (1978), pp. 21–39.

Schulz, Max F. *Radical Sophistication: Studies in Contemporary Jewish-American Novelists.* Athens: Ohio University Press, 1969, pp. 81–90.

Scott, Nathan A., Jr. *Three American Moralists: Mailer, Bellow, Trilling.* Notre Dame, Ind.: University of Notre Dame Press, 1973, pp. 39–70.

Solotaroff, Robert. *Down Mailer's Way.* Urbana: University of Illinois Press, 1974, pp. 53–74.

Spatz, Jonas. *Hollywood in Fiction: Some Versions of the American Myth.* The Hague: Mouton, 1969, pp. 72–75, 102–105.

Tanner, Tony. *City of Words: American Fiction, 1950–1970.* New York: Harper's, 1971, pp. 352–355.

Weinberg, Helen. *The New Novel in America: The Kafkan Mode in Contemporary Fiction.* Ithaca, N.Y.: Cornell University Press, 1970, pp. 112–124.

The Naked and the Dead

Aldridge, John. *After the Lost Generation.* New York: Noonday, 1958, pp. 133–141.

Bryant, Jerry H. "The Last of the Social Protest Writers," in *Arizona Quarterly.* XIX (Winter, 1963), pp. 315–325.

Bufithis, Philip H. *Norman Mailer.* New York: Frederick Ungar, 1978, pp. 15–29.

Burg, David F. "The Hero of *The Naked and the Dead*," in *Modern Fiction Studies.* XVII (1971), pp. 387–401.

Burgess, Anthony. *The Novel Now: A Guide to Contemporary Fiction.* New York: Norton, 1967, pp. 49–52.

Eisinger, Chester D. *Fiction of the Forties.* Chicago: University of Chicago Press, 1963, pp. 33–38.

Foster, Richard. *Norman Mailer.* Minneapolis: University of Minnesota Press, 1968, pp. 8–12.

Geismar, Maxwell. *American Moderns: From Rebellion to Conformity.* New York: Hill and Wang, 1958, pp. 171–173.

Gutman, Stanley T. *Mankind in Barbary: The Individual and Society in the Novels of Norman Mailer.* Hanover, N.H.: University Press of New England, 1975, pp. 3–28.

Harper, Howard M., Jr. *Desperate Faith: A Study of Bellow, Salinger, Mailer, Baldwin and Updike.* Chapel Hill: University of North Carolina Press, 1967, pp. 96–102.

Hassan, Ihab. *Radical Innocence: Studies in the Contemporary American Novel.* Princeton, N.J.: Princeton University Press, 1961, pp. 140–151.

Kaufmann, Donald L. *Norman Mailer: The Countdown (The First Twenty Years).* Carbondale: Southern Illinois University Press, 1969, pp. 1–12.

Leeds, Barry H. *The Structured Vision of Norman Mailer.* New York: New York University Press, 1969, pp. 9–52.

McConnell, Frank D. *Four Postwar American Novelists: Bellow, Mailer, Barth, and Pynchon.* Chicago: University of Chicago Press, 1977, pp. 65–80.

Middlebrook, Jonathan. *Mailer and the Times of His Time.* San Francisco: Bay Books, 1976, pp. 37–59.

Newman, Paul B. "Mailer: The Jew as Existentialist," in *North American Review.* II (July, 1965), pp. 48–55.

Podhoretz, Norman. *Doings and Undoings: The Fifties and After in American Writing.* New York: Farrar, Straus, 1964, pp. 180–187.

Poirier, Richard. *Norman Mailer.* New York: Viking, 1972, pp. 27–50.

Prescott, Orvill. *In My Opinion: An Inquiry into the Contemporary Novel.* New York: Bobbs-Merrill, 1952, pp. 146–164.

Radford, Jean. *Norman Mailer: A Critical Study.* New York: Barnes & Noble, 1975, pp. 7–16, 44–50, 77–82, 124–130.

Scott, Nathan A., Jr. *Three American Moralists: Mailer, Bellow, Trilling.* Notre Dame, Ind.: University of Notre Dame Press, 1973, pp. 23–30.

Solotaroff, Robert. *Down Mailer's Way.* Urbana: University of Illinois Press, 1974, pp. 3–39.

Tanner, Tony. *City of Words: American Fiction, 1950–1970.* New York: Harper's, 1971, pp. 349–351.

Waldmeir, Joseph J. *American Novels of the Second World War.* The Hague: Mouton, 1968, pp. 110–118.

Of a Fire on the Moon

Adams, Laura. *Existential Battles: The Growth of Norman Mailer.* Athens: Ohio University Press, 1976, pp. 158–163.

Bell, Pearl K. "The Power and the Vainglory," in *New Leader.* LIV (February 8, 1971), pp. 16–17.

Bufithis, Philip H. *Norman Mailer.* New York: Frederick Ungar, 1978, pp. 100–105.

DeMott, Benjamin. "Inside Apollo II with Aquarius Mailer," in *Saturday Review.* LIV (January 16, 1971), pp. 25–27, 57–58.

Kaufmann, Donald L. "Mailer's Lunar Bits and Pieces," in *Modern Fiction Studies.* XVII (1971), pp. 451–454.

Poirier, Richard. *Norman Mailer.* New York: Viking Press, 1972, pp. 90–106. Earlier version in *Norman Mailer: A Collection of Critical Essays.* Edited by Leo Braudy. Englewood Cliffs, N.J.: Prentice-Hall, 1972, pp. 167–174.

Radford, Jean. *Norman Mailer: A Critical Study.* New York: Barnes & Noble, 1975, pp. 120–122.

Schroth, Raymond A. "Mailer on the Moon," in *Commonweal.* XCIV (May 7, 1971), pp. 216–218.

Solotaroff, Robert. *Down Mailer's Way.* Urbana: University of Illinois Press, 1974, pp. 242–251.

Werge, T.A. "An Apocalyptic Voyage: God, Satan, and the American Tradition in Norman Mailer's *Of a Fire on the Moon*," in *America in Change: Reflections on the 60's and 70's.* Notre Dame, Ind.: University of Notre Dame Press, 1972, pp. 108–128.

BERNARD MALAMUD
(1914–   )

The Assistant

Baumbach, Jonathan. *The Landscape of Nightmare: Studies in the Contemporary American Novel.* New York: New York University Press, 1965, pp. 111–122.

Fiedler, Leslie. *No! In Thunder: Essays on Myth and Literature.* Boston: Beacon Press, 1960, pp. 106–110.

Francis, H.E. "Bernard Malamud's Everyman," in *Midstream.* VII (Winter, 1961), pp. 93–97.

Freedman, William. "From Bernard Malamud, with Discipline and with Love," in *The Fifties: Fiction, Poetry, Drama.* Edited by Warren French. Deland, Fla.: Everett/Edwards, 1971, pp. 133–143. Reprinted in *Bernard Malamud: A Collection of Critical Essays.* Edited by Leslie A. Field and Joyce W. Field. Englewood Cliffs, N.J.: Prentice-Hall, 1975, pp. 156–165.

Goldsmith, Arnold L. "Nature in Bernard Malamud's *The Assistant*," in *Renascence.* XXIX (Summer, 1977), pp. 211–223.

Hassan, Ihab. *Radical Innocence: Studies in the Contemporary American Novel.* Princeton, N.J.: Princeton University Press, 1961, pp. 161–168.

Hays, Peter L. "The Complex Pattern of Redemption in *The Assistant*," in *Centennial Review.* XIII (Spring, 1969), pp. 200–214. Reprinted in *Bernard Malamud and the Critics.* Edited by Leslie A. Field and Joyce W. Field. New York: New York University Press, 1970, pp. 219–234.

Kazin, Alfred. "Fantasist of the Ordinary," in *Commentary.* XXIV (July, 1957), pp. 89–92.

Klein, Marcus. *After Alienation: American Novels in Mid-Century.* Cleveland: World, 1962, pp. 267–277.

Leer, Norman. "The Double Theme in Malamud's *Assistant*: Dostoevsky with Irony," in *Mosaic.* IV (Spring, 1971), pp. 89–102.

Mandel, Ruth B. "Bernard Malamud's *The Assistant* and *A New Life*: Ironic Affirmation," in *Critique.* VII (Winter, 1964–1965), pp. 110–121. Reprinted in *Bernard Malamud and the Critics.* Edited by Leslie A. Field and Joyce W. Field. New York: New York University Press, 1970, pp. 261–274.

Meeter, Glenn. *Bernard Malamud and Philip Roth: A Critical Essay.* Grand Rapids, Mich.: William B. Eerdmans, 1968, pp. 34–39.

Mellard, James M. "Malamud's Novels: Four Versions of Pastoral," in *Critique.* IX (1967), pp. 5–19. Reprinted in *Bernard Malamud and the Critics.* Edited by Leslie A. Field and Joyce W. Field. New York: New York University Press, 1970, pp. 67–84.

————. "Malamud's *The Assistant*: The City Novel as Pastoral," in *Studies in Short Fiction*. V (1967), pp. 1–11.

Richman, Sidney. *Bernard Malamud*. New York: Twayne, 1966, pp. 50–76.

Shear, Walter. "Culture Conflict in *The Assistant*," in *Midwest Quarterly*. VII (1966), pp. 367–380. Reprinted in *Bernard Malamud and the Critics*. Edited by Leslie A. Field and Joyce W. Field. New York: New York University Press, 1970, pp. 207–218.

Tanner, Tony. *City of Words: American Fiction, 1950–1970*. New York: Harper, 1971, pp. 326–369.

The Fixer

Alter, Robert. "Malamud as a Jewish Writer," in *Commentary*. XLII (September, 1966), pp. 71–76. Revised version in his *After the Tradition: Modern Jewish Writing*. New York: Dutton, 1969, pp. 122–130.

Baumbach, Jonathan. "Malamud's Heroes," in *Commonweal*. LXXXV (October 28, 1966), pp. 97–98.

Burgess, Anthony. *Urgent Copy: Literary Studies*. New York: Norton, 1968, pp. 136–140.

Desmond, J.F. "Malamud's Fixer—Jew, Christian, or Modern?," in *Renascence*. XXVII (Winter, 1975), pp. 101–110.

Elkin, Stanley. "*The Fixer*," in *Massachusetts Review*. VIII (Spring, 1967), pp. 388–392.

Farber, Stephen. "*The Fixer*," in *Hudson Review*. XXII (1969), pp. 134–138.

Friedman, Alan Warren. "Bernard Malamud: The Hero as Schnook," in *Southern Review*. IV (October, 1968), pp. 927–944. Reprinted in *Bernard Malamud and the Critics*. Edited by Leslie A. Field and Joyce W. Field. New York: New York University Press, 1970, pp. 285–303.

Handy, William J. *Modern Fiction: A Formalist Approach*. Carbondale: Southern Illinois University Press, 1972, pp. 131–158.

Hicks, Granville. "One Man to Stand for Six Million," in *Saturday Review*. XLIX (September 10, 1966), pp. 37–39.

Horne, Lewis B. "Yakov Agonistes," in *Research Studies*. XXXVII (December, 1969), pp. 320–326.

Jacobson, Dan. "The Old Country," in *Partisan Review*. XXXIV (Spring, 1967), pp. 307–309.

Kort, Wesley A. *Shriven Selves: Religious Problems in Recent American Fiction*. Philadelphia: Fortress Press, 1972, pp. 90–115.

Meeter, Glenn. *Bernard Malamud and Philip Roth: A Critical Essay*. Grand Rapids, Mich.: Eerdmans, 1968, pp. 40–44.

Mellard, James M. "Malamud's Novels: Four Versions of Pastoral," in *Critique*. IX (1967), pp. 5–19. Reprinted in *Bernard Malamud and the Critics*. Edited by Leslie A. Field and Joyce W. Field. New York: New York University Press, 1970, pp. 67–84.

Pinsker, Sanford. *The Schlemiel as Metaphor: Studies in the Yiddish and American Jewish Novel*. Carbondale: Southern Illinois University Press, 1971, pp. 87–124. Reprinted in *Bernard Malamud: A Collection of Critical Essays*. Edited by Leslie A. Field and Joyce W. Field. Englewood Cliffs, N.J.: Prentice-Hall, 1975, pp. 45–71.

Ratner, Marc. "The Humanism of Malamud's *The Fixer*," in *Critique*. IX (1967), pp. 81–84.

Samuels, Charles Thomas. "The Fixer," in *The Critic as Artist: Essays on Books 1920–1970*. Edited by Gilbert A. Harrison. New York: Liveright, 1972, pp. 291–298.

Tanner, Tony. *City of Words: American Fiction, 1950–1970*. New York: Harper, 1971, pp. 333–338.

Idiots First

Bellman, Samuel I. "Women, Children, and Idiots First: The Transformation Psychology of Bernard Malamud," in *Critique*. VII (Winter, 1964–1965), pp. 123–138. Reprinted in *Bernard Malamud and the Critics*. Edited by Leslie A. Field and Joyce W. Field. New York: New York University Press, 1970, pp. 11–28.

Dupee, F.W. "The Power of Positive Sex," in *Partisan Review*. XXXI (Summer, 1964), pp. 425–430.

Johnson, Richard A. "*Idiots First*," in *Studies in Short Fiction*. I (1964), pp. 171–172.

Leibowitz, Herbert. "Malamud and the Anthromorphic Business," in *New Republic*. C (December 21, 1963), pp. 21–23.

Richman, Sidney. *Bernard Malamud*. New York: Twayne, 1966, pp. 123–141.

The Magic Barrel

Foff, Arthur. "*The Magic Barrel*," in *Northwest Review*. I (Fall–Winter, 1958), pp. 63–67.

Jacobson, Dan. "Magic and Morality," in *Commentary*. XXIV (October, 1958), pp. 359–361.

Miller, Theodore C. "The Minister and the Whore: An Examination of Bernard Malamud's *The Magic Barrel*," in *Studies in the Humanities*. III (October, 1972), pp. 43–44.

Pinsker, Sanford. *The Schlemiel as Metaphor: Studies in the Yiddish and American Jewish Novel*. Carbondale: Southern Illinois University Press,

1971, pp. 87–124. Reprinted in *Bernard Malamud: A Collection of Critical Essays.* Edited by Leslie A. Field and Joyce W. Field. Englewood Cliffs, N.J.: Prentice-Hall, 1975, pp. 45–71.

Popkin, Henry. "Jewish Stories," in *Kenyon Review.* XX (Autumn, 1958), pp. 637–641.

Richman, Sidney. *Bernard Malamud.* New York: Twayne, 1966, pp. 98–123. Reprinted in *Bernard Malamud and the Critics.* Edited by Leslie A. Field and Joyce W. Field. New York: New York University Press, 1970, pp. 305–332.

Siegel, Ben. "Victims in Motion: Bernard Malamud's Sad and Bitter Clowns," in *Northwest Review.* V (Spring, 1962), pp. 69–80.

The Natural

Baumbach, Jonathan. *The Landscape of Nightmare: Studies in the Contemporary American Novel.* New York: New York University Press, 1965, pp. 106–111.

Fiedler, Leslie. *No! In Thunder: Essays on Myth and Literature.* Boston: Beacon Press, 1960, pp. 101–105.

Freedman, William. "From Bernard Malamud, with Discipline and with Love," in *The Fifties: Fiction, Poetry, Drama.* Edited by Warren French. Deland, Fla.: Everett/Edwards, 1971, pp. 133–143. Reprinted in *Bernard Malamud: A Collection of Critical Essays.* Edited by Leslie A. Field and Joyce W. Field. Englewood Cliffs, N.J.: Prentice-Hall, 1975, pp. 156–165.

Graber, Ralph S. "Baseball in American Fiction," in *English Journal.* LVI (November, 1967), pp. 1107–1114.

Greiff, Louis K. "Quest and Defeat in *The Natural,*" in *Thoth.* VIII (Winter, 1967), pp. 23–34.

Klein, Marcus. *After Alienation: American Novels in Mid-Century.* Cleveland: World, 1962, pp. 255–263.

Meeter, Glenn. *Bernard Malamud and Philip Roth: A Critical Essay.* Grand Rapids, Mich.: Eerdmans, 1968, pp. 24–26.

Mellard, James M. "Malamud's Novels: Four Versions of Pastoral," in *Critique.* IX (1967), pp. 5–19. Reprinted in *Bernard Malamud and the Critics.* Edited by Leslie A. Field and Joyce W. Field. New York: New York University Press, 1970, pp. 67–84.

Podhoretz, Norman. "Achilles in Left Field," in *Commentary.* XV (March, 1953), pp. 321–326.

Richman, Sidney. *Bernard Malamud.* New York: Twayne, 1966, pp. 27–49.

Tanner, Tony. *City of Words: American Fiction, 1950–1970.* New York: Harper, 1971, pp. 322–327.

Turner, Frederick W., III. "Myth Inside and Out: Malamud's *The Natural*," in *Novel*. I (Winter, 1968), pp. 133–139. Reprinted in *Bernard Malamud and the Critics*. Edited by Leslie A. Field and Joyce W. Field. New York: New York University Press, 1970, pp. 109–119.

Wasserman, Earl R. "*The Natural*: Malamud's World Ceres," in *Centennial Review*. IX (1965), pp. 438–460. Reprinted in *Bernard Malamud and the Critics*. Edited by Leslie A. Field and Joyce W. Field. New York: New York University Press, 1970, pp. 45–65.

A New Life

Astro, Richard. "In the Heart of the Valley: Bernard Malamud's *A New Life*," in *Bernard Malamud: A Collection of Critical Essays*. Edited by Leslie A. Field and Joyce W. Field. Englewood Cliffs, N.J.: Prentice-Hall, 1975, pp. 143–155.

Barsness, John A. "*A New Life*: The Frontier Myth in Perspective," in *Western American Literature*. III (Winter, 1969), pp. 297–302.

Baumbach, Jonathan. *The Landscape of Nightmare: Studies in the Contemporary American Novel*. New York: New York University Press, 1965, pp. 102–106.

Daniels, Sally. "Flights and Evasions," in *Minnesota Review*. II (Summer, 1962), pp. 551–554.

Elman, Richard M. "Malamud on Campus," in *Commonweal*. LXXV (October 27, 1961), pp. 114–115.

Halley, Anne. "The Good Life in Recent Fiction," in *Massachusetts Review*. III (Autumn, 1961), pp. 190–196.

Hollander, John. "To Find the Westward Path," in *Partisan Review*. XXIX (Winter, 1962), pp. 137–139.

Hyman, Stanley E. *Standards: A Chronicle of Books for Our Time*. New York: Horizon Press, 1966, pp. 33–37.

Klein, Marcus. *After Alienation: American Novels in Mid-Century*. Cleveland: World, 1962, pp. 280–293. Reprinted in *Bernard Malamud and the Critics*. Edited by Leslie A. Field and Joyce W. Field. New York: New York University Press, 1970, pp. 249–260.

Lyons, John O. *The College Novel in America*. Carbondale: Southern Illinois University Press, 1962, pp. 161–162.

Mandel, Ruth B. "Bernard Malamud's *The Assistant* and *A New Life*: Ironic Affirmation," in *Critique*. VII (Winter, 1964–1965), pp. 110–121. Reprinted in *Bernard Malamud and the Critics*. Edited by Leslie A. Field and Joyce W. Field. New York: New York University Press, 1970, pp. 261–274.

Meeter, Glenn. *Bernard Malamud and Philip Roth: A Critical Essay*. Grand Rapids, Mich.: Eerdmans, 1968, pp. 27–29.

Mellard, James M.   "Malamud's Novels: Four Versions of Pastoral," in *Critique*. IX (1967), pp. 5–19. Reprinted in *Bernard Malamud and the Critics*. Edited by Leslie A. Field and Joyce W. Field. New York: New York University Press, 1970, pp. 67–84.

Pinsker, Sanford.   *The Schlemiel as Metaphor: Studies in the Yiddish and American Jewish Novel*. Carbondale: Southern Illinois University Press, 1971, pp. 87–124. Reprinted in *Bernard Malamud: A Collection of Critical Essays*. Edited by Leslie A. Field and Joyce W. Field. Englewood Cliffs, N.J.: Prentice-Hall, 1975, pp. 45–71.

Ratner, Marc L.   "Style and Humanity in Malamud's Fiction," in *Massachusetts Review*. V (Summer, 1964), pp. 670–677.

Richman, Sidney.   *Bernard Malamud*. New York: Twayne, 1966, pp. 78–97.

Schulz, Max F.   "Malamud's *A New Life*: The New Wasteland of the Fifties," in *Western Review*. VI (Summer, 1969), pp. 37–44.

Solotaroff, Theodore.   "Bernard Malamud's Fiction: The Old Life and the New," in *Commentary*. XXXIII (March, 1962), pp. 201–204.

Tanner, Tony.   *City of Words: American Fiction, 1950–1970*. New York: Harper, 1971, pp. 329–333.

Weinberg, Helen.   *The New Novel in America: The Kafkan Mode in Contemporary Fiction*. Ithaca, N.Y.: Cornell University Press, 1970, pp. 173–178.

White, Robert L.   "The English Instructor as Hero: Two Novels by Roth and Malamud," in *Forum*. IV (Winter, 1963), pp. 16–22.

Pictures of Fidelman

Ducharme, Robert.   "Structure and Content in Malamud's *Pictures of Fidelman*," in *Connecticut Review*. V (1971), pp. 26–36.

Field, Leslie A.   "Portrait of the Artist as *Schlemiel*," in *Bernard Malamud: A Collection of Critical Essays*. Edited by Leslie A. Field and Joyce W. Field. Englewood Cliffs, N.J.: Prentice-Hall, 1975, pp. 117–129.

Lefcowitz, Barbara F.   "The *Hybris* of Neurosis: Malamud's *Pictures of Fidelman*," in *Literature and Psychology*. XX (1970), pp. 115–120.

Sheed, Wilfrid.   "Bernard Malamud: *Pictures of Fidelman*," in *The Morning After: Selected Essays and Reviews*. New York: Farrar, Straus and Giroux, 1971, pp. 59–61.

Stetler, Charles.   "*Pictures of Fidelman*," in *Studies in Short Fiction*. VIII (1971), pp. 341–343.

Tanner, Tony.   *City of Words: American Fiction, 1950–1970*. New York: Harper, 1971, pp. 339–343.

Tucker, Martin.   "*Pictures of Fidelman*," in *Commonweal*. XC (1969), pp. 420–421.

The Tenants

Allen, John Alexander. "The Promised End: Bernard Malamud's *The Tenants*," in *Hollins Critic*. VIII (1971), pp. 1–15. Reprinted in *Bernard Malamud: A Collection of Critical Essays*. Edited by Leslie A. Field and Joyce W. Field. Englewood Cliffs, N.J.: Prentice-Hall, 1975, pp. 104–116.

Alter, Robert. "*The Tenants*," in *Commentary*. LIV (October, 1972), pp. 68–74.

Catinella, Joseph. "*The Tenants*," in *Saturday Review*. LIV (September 25, 1971), p. 36.

Craib, Roderick. "*The Tenants*," in *Commonweal*. XCV (1971), pp. 309, 311.

Lindberg-Seyersted, Brita. "A Reading of Bernard Malamud's *The Tenants*," in *Journal of American Studies*. IX (April, 1975), pp. 85–102.

Marcus, Mordecai. "*The Tenants*," in *Prairie Schooner*. XLVI (Fall, 1972), p. 275.

Ozick, Cynthia. "Literary Blacks and Jews," in *Midstream*. XVIII (June/ July, 1972), pp. 10–24. Reprinted in *Bernard Malamud: A Collection of Critical Essays*. Edited by Leslie A. Field and Joyce W. Field. Englewood Cliffs, N.J.: Prentice-Hall, 1975, pp. 80–98.

Richey, C.W. " 'The Woman in the Dunes': A Note on Bernard Malamud's *The Tenants*," in *Notes on Contemporary Literature*. III (January, 1973), pp. 4–5.

Weals, Gerald. "*The Tenants*," in *Hudson Review*. XXIV (Winter, 1971–1972), pp. 726–727.

STÉPHANE MALLARMÉ
(1842–1898)

The Afternoon of a Faun (L'Après-midi d'un Faune)

Balakian, Anna. *The Symbolist Movement: A Critical Appraisal.* New York: Random House, 1967, pp. 75–76.

Mossop, D.J. *Pure Poetry: Studies in French Poetic Theory and Practice, 1746–1945.* Oxford: Clarendon Press, 1971, pp. 117–128.

Musser, Frederic O. *Strange Clamor: A Guide to the Critical Reading of French Poetry.* Detroit: Wayne State University Press, 1965, pp. 35–36.

St. Aubyn, Frederic Chase. *Stéphane Mallarmé.* New York: Twayne, 1969, pp. 74–80.

Smith, Harold J. "Mallarmé's Faun: Hero or Anti-Hero?," in *Romanic Review.* LXIV (1973), pp. 111–124.

Sonnenfeld, Albert. "Eros and Poetry: Mallarmé's Disappearing Visions," in *Order and Adventure in Post-Romantic French Poetry.* Edited by E.M. Beaumont, J.M. Cocking and J. Cruickshank. Oxford: Basil Blackwell, 1973, pp. 89–98.

Williams, Thomas A. *Mallarmé and the Language of Mysticism.* Athens: University of Georgia Press, 1970, pp. 66–70.

"Herodiade"

Balakian, Anna. *The Symbolist Movement: A Critical Appraisal.* New York: Random House, 1967, pp. 76–79.

Chisholm, A.R. *Mallarmé's Grand Oeuvre.* Manchester, England: Manchester University Press, 1962, pp. 66–78.

Danahy, Michael. "The Drama of 'Herodiade': Liturgy and Irony," in *Modern Language Quarterly.* XXXIV (1973), pp. 292–311.

Lawler, James R. *The Language of French Symbolism.* Princeton, N.J.: Princeton University Press, 1969, pp. 15–16.

St. Aubyn, Frederic Chase. *Stéphane Mallarmé.* New York: Twayne, 1969, pp. 49–52, 59–71.

Smith, Harold J. "The Mirror of Art: Mallarmé's 'Herodiade' and Tennyson's 'The Lady of Shalott,' " in *Romance Notes.* XVI (1974), pp. 91–94.

William, Thomas A. *Mallarmé and the Language of Mysticism.* Athens: University of Georgia Press, 1970, pp. 60–66.

"Igitur"

Chisholm, A.R. *Mallarmé's Grand Oeuvre.* Manchester, England: Manchester University Press, 1962, pp. 79–90, 130–134.

Fowlie, Wallace. *Mallarmé as Hamlet: A Study of Igitur.* Yonkers, N.Y.: Alicat Bookshop Press, 1949.

Lawler, James R. *The Language of French Symbolism.* Princeton, N.J.: Princeton University Press, 1969, pp. 12–14.

Mossop, D.J. *Pure Poetry: Studies in French Poetic Theory and Practice, 1746–1945.* Oxford: Clarendon Press, 1971, pp. 143–145.

St. Aubyn, Frederic Chase. *Stéphane Mallarmé.* New York: Twayne, 1969, pp. 138–144.

Senior, John. *The Way Down and Out: The Occult in Symbolist Literature.* New York: Greenwood Press, 1968, pp. 140–143.

Williams, Thomas A. *Mallarmé and the Language of Mysticism.* Athens: University of Georgia Press, 1970, pp. 76–80.

The Poetry of Mallarmé

Austin, L.J. "Mallarmé's Reshaping of 'Le Pitre Chatie,' " in *Order and Adventure in Post-Romantic French Poetry.* Edited by E.M. Beaumont, J.M. Cocking and J. Cruickshank. Oxford: Basil Blackwell, 1973, pp. 56–71.

————. "Stéphane Mallarmé: 'Dans le jardin,' II: Remarks on the Poem," in *French Studies.* XXIX (1975), pp. 416–420.

Balakian, Anna. *The Symbolist Movement: A Critical Appraisal.* New York: Random House, 1967, pp. 82–100.

Brereton, Geoffrey. *An Introduction to the French Poets: Villon to the Present Day.* London: Methuen, 1973, pp. 205–219.

Broome, Peter and Graham Chesters. *The Appreciation of Modern French Poetry (1850–1950).* London: Cambridge University Press, 1976, pp. 83–88.

Chadwick, Charles. *Symbolism.* London: Methuen, 1971, pp. 32–43.

Chisholm, A.R. *Mallarmé's Grand Oeuvre.* Manchester, England: Manchester University Press, 1962.

Cornell, Kenneth. *The Symbolist Movement.* New Haven, Conn.: Yale University Press, 1951.

Franklin, Ursula. "From Premonition to 'Reminiscence': A Prose Poem by Stéphane Mallarmé," in *Nineteenth-Century French Studies.* II (1974), pp. 154–163.

————. "Poet and People: Mallarmé's *Conflit* and the Thirteen Prose Poems of *Divagations*," in *French Review.* XLVI (1973), pp. 77–86.

————. "A Reexamination of Mallarmé's 'Le demon de l'analogie,' " in *Romanic Review.* LXV (1974), pp. 266–277.

Giauque, Gerald S. "An Explication of 'Brise Marine,' " in *Romance Notes.* XVII (1976), pp. 7–12.

Gill, Austin. "Mallarmé's Use of Christian Imagery for Post-Christian Concepts," in *Order and Adventure in Post-Romantic French Poetry.* Edited by E.M. Beaumont, J.M. Cocking and J. Cruickshank. Oxford: Basil Blackwell, 1973, pp. 72–88.

Holt, Eileen. "Stéphane Mallarmé: 'Dans le jardin,' I: The Unpublished Sonnet and Its Background," in *French Studies.* XXIX (1975), pp. 411–415.

Lawler, James R. *The Language of French Symbolism.* Princeton, N.J.: Princeton University Press, 1969, pp. 3–20.

Legee, J.G. *Chanticleer: A Study of the French Muse.* Port Washington, N.Y.: Kennikat, 1969, pp. 226–233.

Lewis, Paula Gilbert. "Stéphane Mallarmé: Literature as Social Action," in *Romance Notes.* XVII (1976), pp. 13–20.

Mossop, D.J. *Pure Poetry: Studies in French Poetic Theory and Practice, 1746–1945.* Oxford: Clarendon Press, 1971, pp. 107–167.

Musser, Frederic O. *Strange Clamor: A Guide to the Critical Reading of French Poetry.* Detroit: Wayne State University Press, 1965, pp. 195–197.

Raymond, Marcel. *From Baudelaire to Surrealism.* New York: Wittenborn, Schultz, 1950, pp. 23–31.

St. Aubyn, Frederic Chase. *Stéphane Mallarmé.* New York: Twayne, 1969.

Senior, John. *The Way Down and Out: The Occult in Symbolist Literature.* New York: Greenwood Press, 1968, pp. 133–144.

Smith, Harold J. "Dilemma and Dramatic Structure in Mallarmé's Parnasse Poems," in *French Review.* XLVI (1973), pp. 66–76.

Symons, Arthur. *The Symbolist Movement in Literature.* London: Constable, 1911, pp. 112–135.

Williams, Thomas A. *Mallarmé and the Language of Mysticism.* Athens: University of Georgia Press, 1970.

"A Throw of the Dice" ("Un Coup de Des")

Balakian, Anna. *The Symbolist Movement: A Critical Appraisal.* New York: Random House, 1967, pp. 96–100.

Chadwick, Charles. *Symbolism.* London: Methuen, 1971, pp. 42–43.

Chisholm, A.R. *Mallarmé's Grand Oeuvre.* Manchester, England: Manchester University Press, 1962, pp. 91–100.

Cohn, Robert Greer. *Mallarmé's 'Un Coup de Des': An Exegesis.* New Haven, Conn.: Yale French Studies, 1949.

Mossop, D.J. *Pure Poetry: Studies in French Poetic Theory and Practice, 1746–1945.* Oxford: Clarendon Press, 1971, pp. 148–153.

Raymond, Marcel. *From Baudelaire to Surrealism.* New York: Wittenborn, Schultz, 1950, pp. 25–26.

St. Aubyn, Frederic Chase.   *Stéphane Mallarmé.* New York: Twayne, 1969, pp. 144–153.

Senior, John.   *The Way Down and Out: The Occult in Symbolist Literature.* Westport, Conn.: Greenwood Press, 1968, pp. 143–144.

Williams, Thomas A.   *Mallarmé and the Language of Mysticism.* Athens: University of Georgia Press, 1970, pp. 87–90.

EDUARDO MALLEA
(1903–   )

All Green Shall Perish

Bouise, O.A. "All Green Shall Perish *and Other Novellas*—Review," in *Best Sellers*. XXVI (June 15, 1966), p. 120.

Crow, John A. "Man Trapped by Tension," in *Saturday Review*. L (May 27, 1967), pp. 32–33.

Lewald, Herald Ernest. *Eduardo Mallea*. Boston: Twayne, 1977, pp. 76–78.

Polt, John H. "The Writings of Eduardo Mallea," in *University of California Publications in Modern Philology*. LIV (1959), pp. 1–132.

Shaw, Donald L. "Introduction," in *Todo Verdor Perecera*. By Eduardo Mallea. Oxford: Pergamon Press, 1968, pp. vii–xxxiii.

The Bay of Silence

Belloni, Manuel. "The Inner Silence of Eduardo Mallea," in *Americas*. XIX (October, 1967), pp. 20–27.

Chapman, Arnold. "Sherwood Anderson and Eduardo Mallea," in *PMLA*. LXIX (March, 1954), pp. 34–45.

Davis, Grace Norris. "Eduardo Mallea, *La Bahid de Silence*," XVII (1943), pp. 70–71.

La Driere, Craig. "*The Bay of Silence*," in *Americas*. I (1945), pp. 521–524.

Lewald, Herald Ernest. *Eduardo Mallea*. Boston: Twayne, 1977, pp. 68–77, 103–105.

Mallan, Lloyd. "Tom Wolfe of Argentina," in *Kenyon Review*. VI (1944), pp. 476–481.

Polt, John H. "The Writings of Eduardo Mallea," in *University of California Publications in Modern Philology*. LIV (1959), pp. 1–12.

Shaw, Donald L. "Narrative Technique in Mallea's *La Bahia de Silencio*," in *Symposium*. XX (1966), pp. 50–55.

Wilson, Edmund. "*The Bay of Silence*," in *New Yorker*. XX (March 18, 1944), pp. 89–92.

Fiesta in November

Belloni, Manuel. "The Inner Silence of Eduardo Mallea," in *Americas*. XIX (October, 1967), pp. 20–27.

Crow, John A. "Man Trapped by Tension," in *Saturday Review*. L (May 27, 1967), pp. 32–33.

Duran, Manuel. "Argentine and Universal," in *New York Times Book Review*. (July 10, 1966), p. 4.

Lewald, Herald Ernest. *Eduardo Mallea*. Boston: Twayne, 1977, p. 57, 70, 82.

Polt, John H. "The Writings of Eduardo Mallea," in *University of California Publications in Modern Philology*. LIV (1959), pp. 1–132.

Wolfe, Bertram D. "The Novel in Latin America," in *Antioch Review*. III (1943), pp. 191–208.

SIR THOMAS MALORY
(1400?–1471)

Le Morte d'Arthur

Baldwin, Charles Sears. *Renaissance Literary Theory and Practice: Classicism in the Rhetoric and Poetic of Italy, France, and England, 1400–1600.* Edited by D.L. Clark. New York: Columbia University Press, 1939, pp. 91–132.

Bartholomew, Barbara Gray. "The Thematic Function of Malory's Gawain," in *College English.* XXIV (1963), pp. 254–265.

Benson, Larry D. *"Le Morte d'Arthur,"* in *Critical Approaches to Six Major English Works:* Beowulf *Through* Paradise Lost. Edited by R.M. Lumiansky and Herschel Baker. Philadelphia: University of Pennsylvania Press, 1968, pp. 81–131.

Davis, Gilbert R. "Malory's Tale of Sir Lancelot and the Question of Unity in the *Morte d'Arthur*," in *Papers of the Michigan Academy of Science, Arts and Letters.* XLIX (1964), pp. 523–530.

DiPasquale, Pasquale, Jr. "Malory's Guinevere: Epic Queen, Romance Heroine and Tragic Mistress," in *Bucknell Review.* XVI (May, 1968), pp. 86–102.

Field, P.J.C. *Romance and Chronicle: A Study of Malory's Prose Style.* Bloomington: Indiana University Press, 1971, pp. 36–159.

Greaves, Margaret. *The Blazon of Honour: A Study in Renaissance Magnanimity.* New York: Barnes & Noble, 1964, pp. 46–61.

Guerin, Wilfred L. " 'The Tale of Gareth': The Chivalric Flowering," in *Malory's Originality: A Critical Study of* Le Morte d'Arthur. Edited by R.M. Lumiansky. Baltimore: Johns Hopkins University Press, 1964, pp. 99–117.

Hampsten, Elizabeth. "A Reading of Sir Thomas Malory's *Morte d'Arthur*," in *North Dakota Quarterly.* XXXV (1967), pp. 29–37.

Hartung, Albert E. "Narrative Technique, Characterization, and the Source in Malory's 'Tale of Sir Lancelot,' " in *Studies in Philology.* LXX (1973), pp. 252–268.

Lewis, C.S. *Studies in Medieval and Renaissance Literature.* Cambridge: Cambridge University Press, 1966, pp. 103–110.

Lumiansky, R.M. "Arthur's Final Companions in Malory's *Morte d'Arthur*," in *Tulane Studies in English.* XI (1961), pp. 5–19.

―――――. " 'The Tale of Lancelot and Guenevere': Suspense," in *Malory's Originality: A Critical Study of* Le Morte d'Arthur. Edited by R.M. Lumiansky. Baltimore: Johns Hopkins University Press, 1964, pp. 205–232.

Moorman, Charles. *The Book of Kyng Arthur: The Unity of Malory's* Morte d'Arthur. Lexington: University of Kentucky Press, 1965.

————. *Kings and Captains: Variations on a Heroic Theme.* Lexington: University of Kentucky Press, 1971, pp. 148–172.

Morgan, Henry Grady. "The Role of Morgan le Fay in Malory's *Morte d'Arthur*," in *Southern Quarterly.* II (1964), pp. 150–168.

Pochoda, Elizabeth T. *Arthurian Propaganda:* Le Morte d'Arthur *as an Historical Ideal of Life.* Chapel Hill: University of North Carolina Press, 1971, pp. 61–140.

Reiss, Edmund. *Sir Thomas Malory.* New York: Twayne, 1966.

Snyder, Robert L. "Malory and 'Historial' Adaptation," in *Essays in Literature.* I (1974), pp. 135–148.

Vinaver, Eugène. *The Rise of Romance.* New York: Oxford University Press, 1971, pp. 123–139.

————. "Introduction," in *The Works of Sir Thomas Malory*, Volume I. Oxford: Clarendon Press, 1948, pp. xiv–lxxxv.

Williams, Charles. "Malory and the Grail Legend," in *Image of the City and Other Essays.* London: Oxford University Press, 1958, pp. 186–194.

Wilson, Robert H. *Characterization in Malory: A Comparison with His Sources.* Chicago: University of Chicago Press, 1934.

Wright, Thomas L. " 'The Tale of King Arthur': Beginnings and Foreshadowings," in *Malory's Originality: A Critical Study of* Le Morte d'Arthur. Edited by R.M. Lumiansky. Baltimore: Johns Hopkins University Press, 1964, pp. 9–66.

ANDRÉ MALRAUX
(1901–1976)

The Conquerors

Blumenthal, Gerda. *André Malraux*. Baltimore: Johns Hopkins University Press, 1960, pp. 3–9.

Bree, Germaine and Margaret Guiton. *An Age of Fiction: The French Novel from Gide to Camus*. New Brunswick, N.J.: Rutgers University Press, 1957, pp. 182–186.

Chiaromonte, Nicola. "Malraux and the Demons of Action in *Partisan Review*. XV (July, 1948), pp. 783–784.

Frohock, W.M. *André Malraux and the Tragic Imagination*. Stanford, Calif.: Stanford University Press, 1952, pp. 36–46.

Gannon, Edward. *The Honor of Being a Man*. Chicago: Loyola University Press, 1957, pp. 7–8, 29–30.

Hatzfeld, Helmut. *Trends and Styles in Twentieth Century French Literature*. Washington, D.C.: Catholic University of America Press, 1957, pp. 33–35.

Howe, Irving. *Politics and the Novel*. New York: Meridian Books, 1957, pp. 207–210.

Langlois, Walter G. *André Malraux; The Indo-China Adventures*. New York: Praeger, 1966, pp. 224–228.

Lewis, Richard W.B., Editor. *Malraux; A Collection of Critical Essays*. New York: Prentice-Hall, 1964, pp. 12–19.

Peyre, Henri. *The Contemporary French Novel*. New York: Oxford University Press, 1955, pp. 193–195.

Reck, Rima Drell. "Malraux's Heroes: Activists and Aesthetes," in *University of Kansas City Review*. XXVIII (October, 1961), pp. 40–44.

Saisselin, Remy G. "Malraux: From Hero to the Artist," in *Journal of Aesthetics and Art Criticism*. XVI (December, 1957), pp. 256–257.

Days of Wrath

Blend, Charles D. *André Malraux: Tragic Humanist*. Columbus: Ohio State University Press, 1963, pp. 31–32.

Blumenthal, Gerda. *André Malraux*. Baltimore: Johns Hopkins University Press, 1960, pp. 59–62.

Frohock, W.M. *André Malraux and the Tragic Imagination*. Stanford, Calif.: Stanford University Press, 1952, pp. 93–104.

————. "*Le Temps Du Mepris*: A Note on Malraux as Man of Letters," in *Romanic Review*. XXXIX (April, 1948), pp. 130–139.

Gannon, Edward. *The Honor of Being a Man.* Chicago: Loyola University Press, 1957, pp. 78–84.

Hartman, Geoffrey H. *André Malraux.* London: Bowes and Bowes, 1960, pp. 53–59.

————. *Beyond Formalism; Literary Essays, 1958–1970.* New Haven, Conn.: Yale University Press, 1970, pp. 85–92.

Herz, Micheline. "Woman's Fate," in *Yale French Studies.* XVIII (Winter, 1957), pp. 17–18.

Slochower, Harry. *No Voice Is Wholly Lost.* New York: Creative Age Press, 1945, pp. 324–327.

Sonnenfeld, Albert. "Malraux and the Tyranny of Time: The Circle and the Gesture," in *Romanic Review.* LIV (October, 1963), pp. 204–208.

Man's Fate

Batchelor, R. "André Malraux and the Concept of Revolt," in *Modern Language Review.* LXVII (October, 1972), pp. 799–809.

Blend, Charles D. *André Malraux: Tragic Humanist.* Columbus: Ohio State University Press, 1963, pp. 25–30.

Boak, Denis. *André Malraux.* New York: Oxford University Press, 1968, pp. 248–250.

Bree, Germaine and Margaret Guiton. *An Age of Fiction: The French Novel from Gide to Camus.* New Brunswick, N.J.: Rutgers University Press, 1957, pp. 182–193.

Chiaromonte, Nicola. "Malraux and the Demons of Action," in *Partisan Review.* XV (July, 1948), pp. 784–787.

Cook, Albert. *The Meaning of Fiction.* Detroit: Wayne State University Press, 1960, pp. 175–177.

Frank, Joseph. "André Malraux: The Image of Man," in his *Widening Gyre: Crisis and Mastery in Modern Literature.* New Brunswick, N.J.: Rutgers University Press, 1963, pp. 105–130.

Friedman, Melvin J. "Some Notes on the Technique of *Man's Fate,*" in his *The Shaken Realist: Essays in Modern Literature in Honor of Frederick J. Hoffman.* Baton Rouge: Louisiana State University Press, 1970, pp. 128–143.

Frohock, W.M. *André Malraux and the Tragic Imagination.* Stanford, Calif.: Stanford University Press, 1952, pp. 16–18, 141–144.

————. "Notes on Malraux's Symbols," in *Romanic Review.* XLII (December, 1951), pp. 276–281.

Gannon, Edward. *The Honor of Being a Man.* Chicago: Loyola University Press, 1957, pp. 54–69, 83–86.

Glicksberg, Charles. *The Tragic Vision in Twentieth-Century Literature.* Carbondale: Southern Illinois University Press, 1963, pp. 141–146.

Gross, Harvey. "André Malraux," in his *The Contrived Corridor: History and Fatality in Modern Literature.* Ann Arbor: University of Michigan Press, 1971, pp. 124–154.

Herz, Micheline. "Woman's Fate," in *Yale French Studies.* XVIII (Winter, 1957), pp. 12–17.

Leefmans, Bert M.P. "Malraux and Tragedy: The Structure of *La Condition Humaine*," in *Romanic Review.* XLIV (October, 1953), pp. 208–214.

Lewis, R.W.B. "Introduction," in *Malraux: A Collection of Critical Essays.* Edited by R.W.B. Lewis. Englewood Cliffs, N.J.: Prentice-Hall, 1964, pp. 1–9.

Peyre, Henri. *French Novelists Today.* New York: Oxford University Press, 1967, pp. 225–229.

Reck, Rima Drell. "The Heroes in the Novels of Malraux," in *University of Kansas City Review.* XXVIII (December, 1961), pp. 151–156.

————. "Malraux's Heroes: Activists and Aesthetes," in *University of Kansas City Review.* XXVIII (October, 1961), pp. 39–45.

Rees, G.O. "Sound and Silence in Malraux's Novels," in *French Review.* XXXII (January, 1959), pp. 223–230.

Rice, Philip Blair. "Malraux and the Individual Will," in *International Journal of Ethics.* XLVIII (January, 1938), pp. 184–188.

Rosenberg, Harold. *Act and the Actor: Making the Self.* New York: New American Library, 1970, pp. 152–169.

St. Aubyn, F.C. "André Malraux: The Syntax of Greatness," in *French Review.* XXXIV (December, 1960), pp. 140–145.

Sayre, Robert. "Solitude and Solidarity: The Case of André Malraux," in *Mosaic.* IX (Fall, 1975), pp. 53–66.

Slochower, Harry. "Freud and Marx in Contemporary Literature," in *Sewanee Review.* XLIX (July–September, 1941), pp. 320–321.

————. *No Voice Is Wholly Lost.* New York: Creative Age Press, 1945, pp. 320–324.

Sonnenfeld, Albert. "Malraux and the Tyranny of Time: The Circle and the Gesture," in *Romanic Review.* LIV (October, 1963), pp. 198–212.

Winegarten, Renee. "Malraux's Fate," in *Commentary.* LI (November, 1971), pp. 69–74.

Man's Hope

Baumgartner, Paul. "Solitude and Involvement: Two Aspects of Tragedy in Malraux's Novels," in *French Review.* XXXII (January, 1959), pp. 223–230.

Blend, Charles D. *André Malraux: Tragic Humanist.* Columbus: Ohio State University Press, 1963, pp. 33–35, 106–126.

Blumenthal, Gerta. *André Malraux*. Baltimore: Johns Hopkins University Press, 1960, pp. 69–95.

Bree, Germaine and Margaret Guiton. *An Age of Fiction: The French Novel from Gide to Camus*. New Brunswick, N.J.: Rutgers University Press, 1957, pp. 186–192.

Brombert, Victor. "Malraux; Passion and Intellect," in *Yale French Studies*. XVIII (Winter, 1957), pp. 71–73.

Cordle, Thomas H. "Malraux and Nietzsche's *Birth of Tragedy*," in *Bucknell Review*. VIII (February, 1959), pp. 95–102.

Courcel, Martine Hallade de, Editor. *Malraux; Life and Work*. New York: Harcourt, 1976, pp. 40–50.

Cowley, Malcolm. *Think Back on Us: A Contemporary Chronicle of the 1930's*. Carbondale: Southern Illinois University Press, 1967, pp. 228–232.

Frohock, W.M. *André Malraux and the Tragic Imagination*. Stanford, Calif.: Stanford University Press, 1952, pp. 104–125.

Gannon, Edward. *The Honor of Being a Man*. Chicago: Loyola University Press, 1957, pp. 84–90.

Harrington, Michael. "André Malraux: Metamorphosis of the Hero," in *Partisan Review*. XXI (November–December, 1954), pp. 658–659.

Hartman, Geoffrey H. *André Malraux*. London: Bowes and Bowes, 1960, pp. 59–66.

O'Brien, Justin. *The French Literary Horizon*. New Brunswick, N.J.: Rutgers University Press, 1967, pp. 253–256.

Picon, Gaetan. "*Man's Hope*," in *Yale French Studies*. XVIII (Winter, 1957), pp. 3–6.

Reck, Rima Drell. "Malraux's Heroes: Activists and Aesthetes," in *University of Kansas City Review*. XXVIII (October, 1961), pp. 45–46.

Rees, G.O. "Sound and Silence in Malraux's Novels," in *French Review*. XXXII (January, 1959), pp. 224–230.

Slochower, Harry. "Freud and Marx in Contemporary Literature," in *Sewanee Review*. XLIX (July–September, 1941), p. 322.

————. *No Voice Is Wholly Lost*. New York: Creative Age Press, 1945, pp. 327–330.

Sonnenfeld, Albert. "Malraux and the Tyranny of Time: The Circle and the Gesture," in *Romanic Review*. LIV (October, 1963), pp. 205–212.

The Royal Way

Ball, Bertrand Logan, Jr. "Nature, Symbol of Death in *La Voie Royale*," in *French Review*. XXXV (February, 1962), pp. 390–395.

Blend, Charles D. *André Malraux: Tragic Humanist.* Columbus: Ohio State University Press, 1963, pp. 22–29.

Blumenthal, Gerda. *André Malraux.* Baltimore: Johns Hopkins University Press, 1960, pp. 9–22.

Boak, Denis. "Malraux's *La Voie Royale*," in *French Studies.* XIX (January, 1965), pp. 42–50.

Casey, Bill. "André Malraux's Heart of Darkness," in *Twentieth Century Literature.* V (April, 1959), pp. 21–26.

Chiaromonte, Nicola. "Malraux and the Demons of Action," in *Partisan Review.* XV (July, 1948), pp. 781–782.

Cordle, Thomas. "*The Royal Way*," in *Yale French Studies.* XVIII (Winter, 1957), pp. 20–26.

Frohock, W.M. *André Malraux and the Tragic Imagination.* Stanford, Calif.: Stanford University Press, 1952, pp. 47–57.

————. "Notes on Malraux's Symbols," in *Romanic Review.* XLII (December, 1951), pp. 274–276.

Gannon, Edward. *The Honor of Being a Man.* Chicago: Loyola University Press, 1957, pp. 30–33.

Hartman, Geoffrey H. *André Malraux.* London: Bowes and Bowes, 1960, pp. 38–42.

Herz, Micheline. "Woman's Fate," in *Yale French Studies.* XVIII (Winter, 1957), pp. 11–12.

Lewis, R.W.B. *The Picaresque Saint.* New York: Lippincott, 1959, pp. 279–295.

Peyre, Henri. *The Contemporary French Novel.* New York: Oxford University Press, 1955, pp. 195–197.

Rice, Philip Blair. "Malraux and the Individual Will," in *International Journal of Ethics.* XLVIII (January, 1938), p. 184.

Turnell, Martin. "Malraux's Fate," in *Commonweal.* LXXXII (June, 1965), pp. 411–412.

The Walnut Trees of Altenberg

Blend, Charles D. *André Malraux; Tragic Humanist.* Columbus: Ohio State University Press, 1963, pp. 39–41.

Bree, Germaine. "Poetry of the Novel," in *The Culture of France in Our Time.* Edited by Julian Park. Ithaca, N.Y.: Cornell University Press, 1954, pp. 23–25.

Bree, Germaine and Margaret Guiton. *An Age of Fiction: The French Novel from Gide to Camus.* New Brunswick, N.J.: Rutgers University Press, 1957, pp. 192–193.

Frank, Joseph. "André Malraux: The Image of Man," in *Hudson Review*. XIV (Spring, 1961), pp. 50–67.

_____. "Malraux and the Image of Man," in *New Republic*. CXXXI (August 30, 1954), pp. 18–19.

Frohock, W.M. *Style and Temper; Studies in French Fiction, 1925–1960.* Cambridge, Mass.: Harvard University Press, 1967, pp. 62–77.

Gannon, Edward. *The Honor of Being a Man.* Chicago: Loyola University Press, 1957, pp. 14–15.

Glicksberg, C.I. *The Literature of Nihilism.* Lewisburg, Pa.: Bucknell University Press, 1975, pp. 179–197.

Hartman, Geoffrey H. *André Malraux.* London: Bowes and Bowes, 1960, pp. 66–72.

Lewis, R.W.B. *The Picaresque Saint.* New York: Lippincott, 1959, pp. 276–277.

Matthewson, Rufus W., Jr. "Dostoevsky and Malraux," in *American Contributions to the Fourth International Congress of Slavicists.* The Hague: Mouton, 1958, pp. 221–223.

Peyre, Henri. *The Contemporary French Novel.* New York: Oxford University Press, 1955, pp. 209–212.

Reck, Rima Drell. "Malraux's Transitional Novel: *Les Noyer De L'Altenberg*," in *French Review*. XXXIV (May, 1961), pp. 537–544.

Righter, William. *The Rhetorical Hero.* London: Routledge and Kegan Paul, 1964, pp. 11–20.

Wilson, E. *Europe Without Baedecker.* New York: Farrar, Straus, 1966, pp. 80–90.

THOMAS MANN
(1875–1955)

The Black Swan

Baker, Carlos. "Facts of Life—and Death," in *Nation*. CLXXVIII (June 19, 1954), pp. 526–527.

Feuerlicht, Ignace. *Thomas Mann.* New York: Twayne, 1968, pp. 146–149.

Frank, Joseph. "Mann—Death and Transfiguration," in *New Republic*. CXXXI (July 5, 1954), pp. 18–19.

Gill, Brendan. "Lean Years," in *New Yorker*. XXX (July 10, 1954), pp. 70–71.

Highet, Gilbert. "Life and Health, Disease and Death," in *Harper's Magazine*. CCIX (July, 1954), p. 93.

Hollingdale, R.J. *Thomas Mann: A Critical Study.* Lewisburg, Pa.: Bucknell University Press, 1971, pp. 157–159.

McWilliams, James R. "Thomas Mann's *Die Betrogene*—A Study in Ambivalence," in *College Language Association Journal*. X (September, 1966), pp. 56–63.

Mertens, Gerald M. "Hemingway's *Old Man and the Sea* and Mann's *The Black Swan*," in *Literature and Psychology*. VI (August, 1956), pp. 96–99.

Mileck, Joseph. "A Comparative Study of *Die Betrogene* and *Death in Venice*," in *Modern Language Forum*. XLII (December, 1957), pp. 124–129.

Parry, Idris. "Thomas Mann's Latest Phase," in *German Life and Letters*. VIII (July, 1955), pp. 241–246.

Rahv, Philip. "The Triumph of Decay," in *Commentary*. XVIII (July, 1954), pp. 82–84.

Buddenbrooks

Boeschenstein, Hermann. *The German Novel, 1939–1944.* Toronto: University of Toronto Press, 1949, pp. 6–7.

Brennan, Joseph G. *Thomas Mann's World.* New York: Columbia University Press, 1942, pp. 1–9, 41–44, 68–69.

Brewster, Dorothy and Angus Burrell. "*Buddenbrooks*," in *Modern Fiction*. Edited by Dorothy Brewster. New York: Columbia University Press, 1934, pp. 101–109.

Burgum, Edwin Berry. "The Sense of the Present in Thomas Mann," in *Antioch Review*. II (September–October, 1942), pp. 387–406. Reprinted in *The Novel and the World's Dilemma*. By Edwin Berry Burgum. New York: Oxford University Press, 1947, pp. 47–71.

Burkhard, Arthur. "The Genealogical Novel in Scandanavia," in *PMLA*. XLIV (March, 1929), pp. 310–313.

————. "Mann's Treatment of the Marked Man," in *PMLA*. XLIII (June, 1928), pp. 563–564.

Church, Margaret. *Time and Reality*. Chapel Hill: University of North Carolina, 1963, pp. 134–137.

Clark, A.F.B. "The Dialectical Humanism of Thomas Mann," in *University of Toronto Quarterly*. VIII (October, 1938), pp. 90–93.

Cleugh, James. *Thomas Mann*. London: Martin Secker, 1933, pp. 79–97.

Eickhorst, William. *Decadence in German Fiction*. Denver: Swallow Press, 1953, pp. 48–50.

Gray, Ronald. *The German Tradition in Literature, 1871–1945*. Cambridge: Cambridge University Press, 1965, pp. 105–136.

Hatfield, Henry C. "Thomas Mann's *Buddenbrooks*: The World of the Father," in *University of Toronto Quarterly*. XX (October, 1950), pp. 33–44. Reprinted in his *Thomas Mann*. New York: New Directions, 1951, pp. 31–50.

Heller, Erich. *The Ironic German*. Boston: Little, Brown, 1958, pp. 27–67.

Kaufmann, Fritz. *Thomas Mann: The World as Will and Representation*. Boston: Beacon Press, 1957, pp. 85–94.

Lewisohn, Ludwig. *Cities and Man*. New York: Harper, 1927, pp. 133–145.

Liptzin, Sol. *Historical Survey of German Literature*. Englewood Cliffs, N.J.: Prentice-Hall, 1936, pp. 216–218.

Lovett, Robert Morss. *Preface to Fiction: A Discussion of Great Modern Novels*. New York: Rockwell, 1931, pp. 81–96. Reprinted in *The Stature of Thomas Mann*. New York: New Directions, 1947, pp. 111–118.

March, George. "Thomas Mann and the Novel of Decadence," in *Sewanee Review*. XXXVII (October, 1929), pp. 496–497.

Millett, Fred B. "In My Opinion," in *University of Chicago Magazine*. XXX (June, 1938), pp. 17–19.

Root, John G. "Stylistic Irony in Thomas Mann," in *Germanic Review*. XXXV (April, 1960), pp. 97–99.

Thomas, R. Hinton. *Thomas Mann*. Oxford: Clarendon Press, 1956, pp. 35–58.

Zucker, A.E. "The Genealogical Novel Again," in *PMLA*. XLIV (September, 1929), pp. 925–927.

Confessions of Felix Krull, Confidence Man

Baker, Carlos. "Education by Escapade," in *Nation*. CLXXXI (October 1, 1955), pp. 286–287.

Bennett, Joseph. "A Bourgeois Eros," in *Hudson Review.* VIII (Spring, 1955), pp. 617–620.

Church, Margaret. *Time and Reality.* Chapel Hill: University of North Carolina Press, 1962, pp. 168–170.

Eichner, Hans. "Aspects of Parody in the Works of Thomas Mann," in *Modern Language Review.* XLVII (January, 1952), pp. 33–34.

Fowler, Alastair. "The Confidence Man," in *Listener.* LXV (May 4, 1961), pp. 781–784.

Heilman, Robert B. "Variations of Picaresque (*Felix Krull*)," in *Sewanee Review.* LXVI (Autumn, 1958), pp. 547–577. Reprinted in *Thomas Mann: A Collection of Critical Essays.* Edited by Henry C. Hatfield. Englewood Cliffs, N.J.: Prentice-Hall, 1964, pp. 133–154.

Heller, Erich. *The Ironic German.* Boston: Little, Brown, 1958, pp. 279–285.

_____. "Parody, Tragic and Comic: Mann's *Doctor Faustus* and *Felix Krull*," in *Sewanee Review.* LXVI (1958), pp. 519–546.

Hollmann, Werner. "Thomas Mann's *Felix Krull* and *Lazarillo*," in *Modern Language Notes.* LXVI (November, 1951), pp. 445–451.

Hunt, Joel A. "The Stylistics of a Foreign Language: Thomas Mann's Use of French," in *Germanic Review.* XXXII (February, 1957), pp. 24–25.

Kaufmann, Edward. "Thomas Mann's Sunday Child," in *Chicago Review.* X (September, 1956), pp. 117–123.

Kleine, Don W. "Felix Krull as Fairy Tale Hero," in *Accent.* XIX (Summer, 1959), pp. 131–141.

Parry, Idris. "Thomas Mann's Latest Phase," in *German Life and Letters.* VIII (July, 1955), pp. 246–251.

Riley, Anthony W. "Three Cryptic Quotations in Thomas Mann's *Felix Krull*," in *Journal of English and Germanic Philology.* LXV (January, 1966), pp. 99–106.

Sands, Donald B. "The Light and Shadow of Thomas Mann's *Felix Krull*," in *Renascence.* XIII (1961), pp. 119–124.

Schiffer, Eva. "Changes in an Episode: A Note on *Felix Krull*," in *Modern Language Quarterly.* XXIV (September, 1963), pp. 257–262.

_____. "Manolescu's Memoirs: The Beginning of *Felix Krull*," in *Monatshefte.* XLI (November, 1960), pp. 283–292.

Seidin, Oskar. "Picaresque Elements in Thomas Mann's Works," in *Modern Language Quarterly.* XII (June, 1951), pp. 184–200.

Smeed, J.W. "The Role of Professor Kuckuck in *Felix Krull*," in *Modern Language Review.* LIX (July, 1964), pp. 411–412.

Stilwell, Robert L. "Mann's *Confessions of Felix Krull, Confidence Man*," in *Explicator.* XX (November, 1961), item 24.

Death in Venice

Amory, Frederic. "The Classical Style of *Der Tod in Venedig*," in *Modern Language Review*. LIX (July, 1964), pp. 399–409.

Church, Margaret. "*Death in Venice*: A Study of Creativity," in *College English*. XXIII (1962), pp. 648–651.

Cleugh, James. *Thomas Mann*. London: Martin Secker, 1933, pp. 136–145.

Frank, Bruno. "*Death in Venice*," in *The Stature of Thomas Mann*. Edited by Charles Neider. New York: New Directions, 1947, pp. 119–123.

Gray, Ronald. *The German Tradition in Literature, 1871–1945*. Cambridge: Cambridge University Press, 1965, pp. 145–156.

Gronicka, Andre von. "Myth Plus Psychology: A Style Analysis of *Death in Venice*," in *Germanic Review*. XXXI (October, 1956), pp. 206–214. Reprinted in *Thomas Mann: A Collection of Critical Essays*. Edited by Henry C. Hatfield. Englewood Cliffs, N.J.: Prentice-Hall, 1964, pp. 46–61.

Heller, Erich. *The Ironic German*. Boston: Little, Brown, 1958, pp. 97–115.

Hepworth, James B. "Tadzio-Sabazios: Notes on *Death in Venice*," in *Western Humanities Review*. XVII (1963), pp. 172–175.

Kohut, Heinz. "*Death in Venice* by Thomas Mann: A Story About the Disintegration of Artistic Sublimation," in *Psychoanalytic Quarterly*. XXVI (1957), pp. 206–228. Reprinted in *Psychoanalysis and Literature*. Edited by Hendrik M. Ruitenbeek. New York: Dutton, 1964, pp. 282–302.

Lehnert, Herbert. "Thomas Mann's Own Interpretations of *Der Tod in Venedig* and Their Reliability," in *Rice University Studies*. L (February, 1964), pp. 41–60.

Lewisohn, Ludwig. "*Death in Venice*," in *The Stature of Thomas Mann*. Edited by Charles Neider. New York: New Directions, 1947, pp. 124–128.

————. "Preface," in *Death in Venice*. By Thomas Mann. New York: Knopf, 1930, pp. v–xv.

McClain, William H. "Wagnerian Overtones in *Der Tod in Venedig*," in *Modern Language Notes*. LXXIX (December, 1964), pp. 481–495.

MacIver, R.M. *Great Moral Dilemmas*. New York: Harper, 1956, pp. 25–36.

McNamara, Eugene. "*Death in Venice*: The Disguised Self," in *College English*. XXIV (1962), pp. 233–234.

Mileck, Joseph. "A Comparative Study of *Die Betrogene* and *Der Tod in Venedig*," in *Modern Language Forum*. XLVII (December, 1957), pp. 124–129.

Rey, William H. "Tragic Aspects of the Artist in Thomas Mann's Work," in *Modern Language Quarterly*. XIX (September, 1958), pp. 195–203.

Rosenthal, Macha L. "The Corruption of Aschenbach," in *University of Kansas City Review*. XIV (Autumn, 1947), pp. 49–65.

Seyppel, Joachim H. "Two Variations on a Theme: Dying in Venice," in *Literature and Psychology.* VII (February, 1957), pp. 8–12.

Stelzmann, Rainulf A. "Thomas Mann's *Death in Venice*: Reset Imago," in *Xavier University Studies.* III (1964), pp. 160–167.

Thomas, R. Hinto. *Thomas Mann.* Oxford: Clarendon Press, 1956, pp. 59–84.

Traschen, Isadore. "The Uses of Myth in *Death in Venice*," in *Modern Fiction Studies.* XI (1965), pp. 165–179.

Urdang, Constance. "Faust in Venice: The Artist and the Legend in *Death in Venice*," in *Accent.* XV (Autumn, 1958), pp. 253–267.

Venable, Vernon. "Poetic Reason in Thomas Mann," in *Virginia Quarterly Review.* XIV (Winter, 1938), pp. 61–76.

Doctor Faustus

Blackmur, Richard P. "Parody and Critique: Notes on Thomas Mann's *Doctor Faustus*," in *Kenyon Review.* XII (Winter, 1950), pp. 20–40.

Bonwit, Marianne. "Babel in Modern Fiction," in *Comparative Literature.* II (Summer, 1950), pp. 236–247.

Butler, E.M. *The Fortunes of Faust.* London: Cambridge University Press, 1952, pp. 321–338.

————. "The Traditional Elements in Thomas Mann's *Doctor Faustus*," in *Publications of the English Goethe Society.* XVIII (1948), pp. 1–33.

Campbell, Lily B. "*Doctor Faustus*: A Case of Conscience," in *PMLA.* LXVII (1952), pp. 219–239.

Enright, D.J. "The *Doctor Faustus* of Thomas Mann," in *Scrutiny.* XVII (Summer, 1950), pp. 154–167.

Frank, Joseph. "Reaction as Progress: Thomas Mann's *Doctor Faustus*," in *Chicago Review.* XV (Autumn, 1961), pp. 19–39. Reprinted in *The Widening Gyre: Crisis and Mastery in Modern Literature.* By Joseph Frank. New Brunswick, N.J.: Rutgers University Press, 1963, pp. 131–161.

Gray, Ronald. *The German Tradition in Literature, 1871–1945.* Cambridge: Cambridge University Press, 1965, pp. 208–223.

Hatfield, Henry C. "Two Notes on Thomas Mann's *Doctor Faustus*," in *Modern Language Forum.* XXXIV (March–June, 1949), pp. 11–17.

Heller, Erich. "Parody, Tragic and Comic: Mann's *Doctor Faustus* and *Felix Krull*," in *Sewanee Review.* LXVI (1958), pp. 519–546.

Kaufmann, Fritz. *Thomas Mann: The World as Will and Representation.* Boston: Beacon Press, 1957, pp. 197–238.

Krieger, Murray. *The Tragic Vision.* New York: Holt, Rinehart and Winston, 1960, pp. 87–102.

Lindsay, J.M. *Thomas Mann.* Oxford: Blackwell, 1954, pp. 113–124.

Mann, Thomas. *The Story of a Novel.* New York: Knopf, 1961.

Nemerov, Howard. "Thomas Mann's Faust Novel," in *Graduate Journal.* III (Fall, 1960), pp. 205–217. Reprinted in *Poetry and Fiction: Essays.* By Howard Nemerov. New Brunswick, N.J.: Rutgers University Press, 1963, pp. 303–315.

Pickard, P.M. "Thomas Mann's *Doctor Faustus*: A Psychological Approach," in *German Life and Letters.* IV (1950), pp. 90–100.

Reed, Carroll E. "Thomas Mann and the Faust Tradition," in *Journal of English and Germanic Philology.* LI (January, 1952), pp. 17–34.

Rey, William H. "Return to Health? — 'Disease' in Mann's *Doctor Faustus*," in *PMLA.* LXV (March, 1960), pp. 21–26.

Rice, Philip Blair. "The Merging Parallels: Thomas Mann's *Doctor Faustus*," in *Kenyon Review.* XI (Spring, 1949), pp. 199–217.

Taubes, Jacob. "From Cult to Culture," in *Partisan Review.* XXI (July, 1954), pp. 387–400.

Thomas, R. Hinton. *Thomas Mann.* Oxford: Clarendon Press, 1956, pp. 137–167.

Tuska, Jon. "The Visions of Doktor Faustus," in *Germanic Review.* XL (November, 1965), pp. 281–299.

Van Ghent, Dorothy. "Vestiges and Premises," in *Western Review.* XIV (Autumn, 1949), pp. 67–70.

Weinstock, Herbert. "*Doctor Faustus*," in *A Pocket Guide to Thomas Mann's* Doctor Faustus. Edited by Alfred A. Knopf. New York: Knopf, 1949, pp. 2–10, 13–15.

Williams, W.D. "Thomas Mann's *Dr. Faustus*," in *German Life and Letters.* XII (July, 1959), pp. 273–281.

Witte, William. "Faust and Dr. Faustus," in *Aberdeen University Review.* XXXIII (Autumn, 1949), pp. 113–117.

The Holy Sinner

Bauer, Arnold. *Thomas Mann.* New York: Frederick Ungar, 1971, pp. 92–93.

Bercovitch, Sacvan. "Thomas Mann's 'Heavenly Alchemy': The Politics of *The Holy Sinner*," in *Symposium.* XX (Winter, 1966), pp. 293–304.

Brandt, Thomas O. "Narcissism in Thomas Mann's *Der Erwahlte*," in *German Life and Letters.* VII (July, 1954), pp. 233–241.

Church, Margaret. *Time and Reality.* Chapel Hill, N.C.: University of North Carolina Press, 1962, pp. 166–167.

Feuerlicht, Ignace. *Thomas Mann.* New York: Twayne, 1968, pp. 85–91.

Fraiberg, Selma. "Two Modern Incest Heroes," in *Partisan Review.* XXVIII (1961), pp. 651–661.

Furstenheim, E.G. "The Place of *Der Erwahlte* in the Work of Thomas Mann," in *Modern Language Review.* LI (January, 1956), pp. 55–70.

Hollingdale, R.J. *Thomas Mann: A Critical Study.* Lewisburg, Pa.: Bucknell University Press, 1971, pp. 134–136.

Honsa, William M., Jr. "Parody and Narrator in Thomas Mann's *Doctor Faustus* and *The Holy Sinner,*" in *Orbis Litterarum.* XXIX (1974), pp. 61–76.

Raleigh, John Henry. "Mann's Double Vision: *Doctor Faustus* and *The Holy Sinner,*" in *Pacific Spectator.* VII (Autumn, 1953), pp. 380–392.

Schoolfield, George C. "Thomas Mann and the Honest Pagans," in *Philological Quarterly.* XXXVI (April, 1957), pp. 280–285.

Stock, Irvin. "Mann's Christian Parable: A View of *The Holy Sinner,*" in *Accent.* XIV (Spring, 1954), pp. 98–114.

Weigand, Hermann J. "Thomas Mann's *Gregorius* I–III," in *Germanic Review.* XXVII (1952), pp. 10–30.

————. "Thomas Mann's *Gregorius* IV–V," in *Germanic Review.* XXVII (April, 1952), pp. 83–95.

West, Ray B., Jr. "Thomas Mann: Moral Precept as Psychological Truth," in *Sewanee Review.* LX (1952), pp. 310–317.

Joseph and His Brothers

Bab, Julius. "*Joseph and His Brothers,*" in *The Stature of Thomas Mann.* Edited by Charles Neider. New York: New Directions, 1947, pp. 195–210.

Bauer, Arnold. *Thomas Mann.* New York: Frederick Ungar, 1971, pp. 68–73.

Blissett, William. "Thomas Mann: The Last Wagnerite," in *Germanic Review.* XXXV (February, 1960), pp. 65–70.

Bloch, Adele. "The Archetypal Influence in Thomas Mann's *Joseph and His Brothers,*" in *Germanic Review.* XXXVIII (March, 1963), pp. 151–156.

Cather, Willa. *Not Under Forty.* New York: Knopf, 1936, pp. 96–122.

Daemmrich, Horst S. "Fertility-Sterility: A Sequence of Motifs in Thomas Mann's *Joseph* Novels," in *Modern Language Quarterly.* XXXI (1970), pp. 461–473.

Dassin, Joan. "The Dialectics of Recurrence: The Relation of the Individual to Myth and Legend in Thomas Mann's *Joseph and His Brothers,*" in *Centennial Review.* XV (1971), pp. 352–390.

Feuerlicht, Ignace. *Thomas Mann.* New York: Twayne, 1968, pp. 43–58.

Frederick, John. "Thomas Mann and *Joseph the Provider,*" in *College English.* VI (October, 1944), pp. 1–5.

Gray, Ronald. *The German Tradition in Literature, 1871–1945.* Cambridge: Cambridge University Press, 1965, pp. 185–207.

Hatfield, Henry. *Thomas Mann.* Norfolk, Conn.: New Directions, 1951, pp. 95–120.

Heller, Erich. *The Ironic German.* Boston: Little, Brown, 1958, pp. 219–258.

Heller, Peter. "Some Functions of the Leitmotiv in Thomas Mann's *Joseph* Tetralogy," in *Germanic Review.* XXII (April, 1947), pp. 126–141.

Hollingdale, R.J. *Thomas Mann: A Critical Study.* Lewisburg, Pa.: Bucknell University Press, 1971, pp. 113–117.

Kaufmann, Fritz. *Thomas Mann: The World as Will and Representation.* New York: Cooper Square, 1973, pp. 119–168.

Lindsay, J.M. *Thomas Mann.* Oxford: Blackwell, 1954, pp. 100–112.

Mann, Thomas. "The *Joseph* Novels," in *The Stature of Thomas Mann.* Edited by Charles Neider. New York: New Directions, 1947, pp. 218–232.

Rice, Philip Blair. "Thomas Mann and the Religious Revival," in *Kenyon Review.* VII (Summer, 1945), pp. 366–373.

Slochower, Harry. *No Voice Is Wholly Lost.* New York: Creative Age Press, 1945, pp. 338–355.

Stern, J.P. "Thomas Mann's Last Period," in *Critical Quarterly.* VIII (Autumn, 1966), pp. 245–249.

Thomas, R. Hinton. *Thomas Mann.* Oxford: Clarendon Press, 1956, pp. 112–136.

Van Doren, Mark. "*Joseph and His Brothers*: A Comedy in Four Parts," in *American Scholar.* XXVI (Summer, 1957), pp. 289–302.

Watts, Harold H. "Thomas Mann and the Opposites," in *South Atlantic Quarterly.* XLV (1946), pp. 102–114.

————. "The Thrice-Told Tale: Thomas Mann's Myth for His Times," in *Quarterly Review of Literature.* IV (1949), pp. 299–310.

The Magic Mountain

Beach, Joseph W. "*The Magic Mountain*," in *The Stature of Thomas Mann.* Edited by Charles Neider. New York: New Directions, 1947, pp. 142–149.

Berland, Alwyn. "In Search of Thomas Mann," in *Symposium.* XVIII (Fall, 1964), pp. 215–227.

Blackmur, R.P. "Hans Castorp, Small Lord of Counterpositions," in *Hudson Review.* I (Autumn, 1948), pp. 318–339.

Braverman, Albert S. and Larry Nachman. "Nature and the Moral Order in *The Magic Mountain*," in *Germanic Review.* LIII (January, 1978), pp. 1–12.

Brennan, Joseph G. *Thomas Mann's World.* New York: Columbia University Press, 1942, pp. 48–69, 97–108.

Burgum, Edwin Berry. "The Sense of the Present in Thomas Mann," in *Antioch Review.* II (Fall, 1942), pp. 394–400.

Church, Margaret. *Time and Reality.* Chapel Hill: University of North Carolina Press, 1962, pp. 146–154.

Cleugh, James. *Thomas Mann.* London: Martin Secker, 1933, pp. 181–197.

Gaertner, Johannes A. "Dialectic Thought in Thomas Mann's *The Magic Mountain*," in *German Quarterly.* XXXVIII (November, 1965), pp. 605–618.

Gray, Ronald. *The German Tradition in Literature, 1871–1945.* Cambridge: Cambridge University Press, pp. 157–172.

Hatfield, Henry. *Thomas Mann.* Norfolk, Conn.: New Directions, 1951, pp. 66–87.

Heller, Erich. *The Ironic German.* Boston: Little, Brown, 1958, pp. 169–214.

Kaufmann, Fritz. *Thomas Mann: The World as Will and Representation.* Boston: Beacon Press, 1957, pp. 95–118, 125–129.

Martin, John S. "Circean Seduction in Three Works by Thomas Mann," in *Modern Language Notes.* LXXVII (October, 1963), pp. 346–352.

Mumford, Lewis. "*The Magic Mountain*," in *The Stature of Thomas Mann.* Edited by Charles Neider. New York: New Directions, 1947, pp. 150–155.

Pascal, Roy. *The German Novel.* Manchester, England: Manchester University Press, 1956, pp. 76–98.

Passage, Charles E. "Hans Castorp's Musical Incantation," in *Germanic Review.* XXXVIII (May, 1963), pp. 238–256.

Rebelsky, Freda Gould. "Coming of Age in Davos: An Analysis of the Maturation of Hans Castorp in Thomas Mann's *The Magic Mountain*," in *American Imago.* XVIII (Winter, 1961), pp. 413–421.

Schmeck, Erna H. "Women in the Works of Thomas Mann," in *Monatshefte.* XXXII (April, 1940), pp. 145–164.

Schultz, H. Stefan. "On the Interpretation of Thomas Mann's *Der Zauberberg*," in *Modern Philology.* LII (November, 1954), pp. 110–122.

Slochower, Harry. *Three Ways of Modern Man.* New York: International, 1937, pp. 50–104.

Thirlwall, John C. "Orphic Influence in *Magic Mountain*," in *Germanic Review.* XXV (February, 1950), pp. 290–298.

Thomas, R. Hinton. *Thomas Mann.* Oxford: Clarendon Press, 1956, pp. 85–111.

Weigand, Hermann J. *A Study of* The Magic Mountain: *Thomas Mann's Novel Der Zauberberg.* New York: Appleton-Century, 1933.

Zinberg, Dorothy S. and Norman E. Zinberg. "Hans Castorp: Identity Crisis Without Resolution," in *American Imago.* XX (Winter, 1963), pp. 393–402.

Mario and the Magician

Bauer, Arnold. *Thomas Mann.* New York: Frederick Ungar, 1971, pp. 61–63.

Brennan, Joseph G. *Thomas Mann's World.* New York: Columbia University Press, 1942, pp. 150–152.

Feuerlicht, Ignace. *Thomas Mann.* New York: Twayne, 1968, pp. 126–129.

Gray, Ronald. *The German Tradition in Literature, 1871–1945.* Cambridge: Cambridge University Press, 1965, pp. 173–184.

Gronicka, Andre von. *Thomas Mann: Profile and Perspectives.* New York: Random House, 1970, pp. 164–166.

Hatfield, Henry C. "*Mario and the Magician,*" in *The Stature of Thomas Mann.* Edited by Charles Neider. New York: New Directions, 1947, pp. 168–173.

――――――. *Thomas Mann.* Norfolk: New Directions, 1951, pp. 90–94.

――――――. "Thomas Mann's *Mario und der Zauberer*: An Interpretation," in *Germanic Review.* XXI (December, 1946), pp. 306–312.

Hollingdale, R.J. *Thomas Mann: A Critical Study.* Lewisburg, Pa.: Bucknell University Press, 1971, pp. 40–44.

Kaufmann, Fritz. *Thomas Mann: The World as Will and Representation.* New York: Cooper Square, 1973, pp. 217–218.

McIntyre, Allan J. "Determinism in *Mario and the Magician,*" in *Germanic Review.* LII (May, 1977), pp. 205–216.

Martin, John S. "Circean Seduction in Three Works by Thomas Mann," in *Modern Language Notes.* LXXVIII (October, 1963), pp. 346–352.

Matenko, Percy. "The Prototype of Cipolla in *Mario und der Zauberer,*" in *Italica.* XXXI (September, 1954), pp. 133–135.

Schwarz, Egon. "Fascism and Society: Remarks on Thomas Mann's Novella *Mario and the Magician,*" in *Michigan Germanic Studies.* II (1976), pp. 47–67.

Slochower, Harry. *Three Ways of Modern Man.* New York: International, 1945, pp. 100–101.

Tonio Kröger

Basilius, H.A. "Thomas Mann's Use of Musical Structure and Techniques in *Tonio Kröger,*" in *Germanic Review.* XIX (December, 1944), pp. 284–308.

Bauer, Arnold. *Thomas Mann.* New York: Frederick Ungar, 1971, pp. 25–27.

Bennett, E.K. *History of the German Novelle.* Cambridge: Cambridge University Press, 1961, pp. 254–255.

Brennan, Joseph G. *Thomas Mann's World.* New York: Columbia University Press, 1942, pp. 11–13, 19–22, 115–117.

Burkhard, Arthur. "Mann's Treatment of the Marked Man," in *PMLA*. XLIII (June, 1928), pp. 562–563.

————. "Thomas Mann's Appraisal of the Poet," in *PMLA*. XLVI (1931), pp. 887–893.

Church, Margaret. *Time and Reality*. Chapel Hill: University of North Carolina Press, 1962, pp. 137–143.

Clark, A.F.B. "The Dialectical Humanism of Thomas Mann," in *University of Toronto Quarterly*. VIII (October, 1938), pp. 93–94.

Cleugh, James. *Thomas Mann: A Study*. London: Martin Secker, 1933, pp. 97–101.

Feuerlicht, Ignace. *Thomas Mann*. New York: Twayne, 1968, pp. 109–114.

Gray, Ronald. *The German Tradition, 1871–1945*. Cambridge: Cambridge University Press, 1965, pp. 137–145.

Gronicka, Andre von. *Thomas Mann: Profile and Perspectives*. New York: Random House, 1970, pp. 113–120.

Hatfield, Henry. *Thomas Mann*. Norfolk, Conn.: New Directions, 1951, pp. 52–56.

Heller, Erich. *The Ironic German*. Boston: Little, Brown, 1958, pp. 68–85.

Hollingdale, R.J. *Thomas Mann: A Critical Study*. Lewisburg, Pa.: Bucknell University Press, 1971, pp. 62–67.

Hunt, Joel A. "The Stylistics of a Foreign Language: Thomas Mann's Use of French," in *Germanic Review*. XXXII (February, 1957), pp. 21–22.

March, George. "Thomas Mann and the Novel of Decadence," in *Sewanee Review*. XXXVII (October, 1929), pp. 493–496.

Maurer, K.W. "*Tonio Kröger* and *Hamlet*," in *Modern Language Review*. XLIII (October, 1948), p. 520.

Morgan, B.Q. "On Translating *Tonio Kröger*," in *German Quarterly*. XIX (May, 1946), pp. 220–225.

O'Neill, Patrick. "Dance and Counterdance: A Note on *Tonio Kröger*," in *German Life and Letters*. XXIX (1976), pp. 291–295.

Pearson, Gabriel. "The Heroism of Thomas Mann," in *International Literary Annual*. I (1958), pp. 126–127.

Root, Winthrop H. "Grillparzer's *Sappho* and Thomas Mann's *Tonio Kröger*," in *Monatshefte*. XXIX (February, 1937), pp. 59–64.

Swales, M.W. "Punctuation and the Narrative Mode: Some Remarks on *Tonio Kröger*," in *Forum for Modern Language Studies*. VI (1970), pp. 235–242.

Wilkinson, E.M. "*Tonio Kröger*: An Interpretation," in *Thomas Mann: A Collection of Critical Essays*. Edited by Henry C. Hatfield. Englewood Cliffs, New Jersey: Prentice-Hall, 1964, pp. 22–34.

Wilson, Kenneth. "The Dance as Symbol and Leitmotiv in Thomas Mann's *Tonio Kröger*," in *Germanic Review*. XXIX (December, 1954), pp. 282–287.

KATHERINE MANSFIELD
(1888–1923)

"At the Bay"

Alpers, Antony. *Katherine Mansfield: A Biography.* New York: Knopf, 1953, pp. 316–322.

Berkman, Sylvia. *Katherine Mansfield: A Critical Study.* New Haven, Conn.: Yale University Press, 1951, pp. 168–169.

Brewster, Dorothy and Angus Burrell. *Modern Fiction.* New York: Columbia University Press, 1934.

Corin, Fernand. "Creation of Atmosphere in Katherine Mansfield's Stories," in *Revue des Langues Vivantes.* XXII (1956), pp. 65–78.

Daly, Saralyn. *Katherine Mansfield.* New York: Twayne, 1965, pp. 92–99.

Hubbell, George S. "Katherine Mansfield and Kezia," in *Sewanee Review.* XXXV (1927), pp. 332–333.

Kempton, Kenneth. *Short Stories for Study.* Cambridge, Mass.: Harvard University Press, 1953, pp. 280–282.

Kleine, Don W. "An Eden for Insiders: Katherine Mansfield's New Zealand," in *College English.* XXVII (1965), pp. 205–206.

Magalaner, Marvin. *The Fiction of Katherine Mansfield.* Carbondale: Southern Illinois University Press, 1971, pp. 38–45.

Stegner, Wallace, Richard Snowcroft and Boris Ilyin. *The Writers Art.* Boston: Heath, 1950, pp. 74–77.

Walsh, William. *A Manifold Voice: Studies in Commonwealth Literature.* London: Chatto and Windus, 1970, pp. 176–180.

"Bliss"

Armstrong, Martin. "The Art of Katherine Mansfield," in *Fortnightly Review.* CXIII (1923), p. 484–490.

Berkman, Sylvia. *Katherine Mansfield: A Critical Study.* New Haven, Conn.: Yale University Press, 1951.

Brewster, Dorothy and Angus Burrell. *Modern Fiction.* New York: Columbia University Press, 1934, pp. 374–377.

Daly, Saralyn. *Katherine Mansfield.* New York: Twayne, 1965, pp. 82–88.

Eliot, Thomas E. *After Strange Gods.* London: Faber, 1934, pp. 35–36.

Foff, Arthur and Daniel Knapp. *Story: An Introduction to Prose Fiction.* Belmont, Calif.: Wadsworth, 1964, pp. 70–75.

Heilman, Robert B. *Modern Short Stories: A Critical Anthology.* New York: Harcourt, Brace, 1950, pp. 207–209.

Lawrence, Margaret. *The School of Femininity.* New York: Stokes, 1963.

Magalaner, Marvin. *The Fiction of Katherine Mansfield.* Carbondale: Southern Illinois University Press, 1971, pp. 74–86.

Murry, John M. *Katherine Mansfield and Other Literary Portraits.* London: Peter Nevill, 1949.

Nebeker, Helen E. "The Pear Tree: Sexual Implications in Katherine Mansfield's 'Bliss,' " in *Modern Fiction Studies.* XVIII (1973), pp. 545–551.

Orvis, Mary B. *The Art of Writing Fiction.* New York: Prentice-Hall, 1948.

Van Kramendonk, A.G. "Katherine Mansfield," in *English Studies.* XII (April, 1930), pp. 56–57.

Ward, Alfred C. *Aspects of the Modern Short Story.* London: University of London Press, 1924, pp. 287–289.

Wright, Celeste T. "Katherine Mansfield's Dog Image," in *Literature and Psychology.* X (1960), pp. 80–81.

"The Doll's House"

Daly, Saralyn. *Katherine Mansfield.* New York: Twayne, 1965, pp. 100–101.

Delaney, Paul. "Short and Simple Annals of the Poor: Katherine Mansfield's 'The Doll's House,' " in *Mosaic.* X (1976), pp. 7–17.

Hubbell, George S. "Katherine Mansfield and Kezia," in *Sewanee Review.* XXXV (1927), pp. 334–335.

Kleine, Don W. "An Eden for Insiders: Katherine Mansfield's New Zealand," in *College English.* XXVII (1965), pp. 204–206.

Lawrence, Margaret. *The School of Femininity.* New York: Stokes, 1963.

Ryan, Alvan S. " 'The Doll's House,' " in *Insight II: Analyses of British Literature.* Frankfurt, Germany: Hirschgraben, 1964, pp. 247–250.

Singleton, Ralph H. *Instructor's Manual for Two and Twenty: A Collection of Short Stories.* New York: St. Martin's, 1962.

Walsh, William. *A Manifold Voice: Studies in Commonwealth Literature.* London: Chatto and Windus, 1970, pp. 164–168.

"The Fly"

Bateson, F.W. "More on 'The Fly,' " in *Essays in Criticism.* XII (October, 1962), pp. 451–452.

Bateson, F.W. and B. Shahevitch. "Katherine Mansfield's 'The Fly': A Critical Exericse," in *Essays in Criticism.* XII (January, 1962), pp. 39–53.

Berkman, Sylvia. *Katherine Mansfield: A Critical Study.* New Haven, Conn.: Yale University Press, 1951, pp. 137–140.

Boyle, Ted E. "The Death of the Boss: Another Look at Katherine Mansfield's 'The Fly,' " in *Modern Fiction Studies.* XI (Summer, 1965), pp. 183–185.

Copland, R.A. "Katherine Mansfield's 'The Fly,' " in *Essays in Criticism*. XII (July, 1962), pp. 338–341.

Daly, Saralyn. *Katherine Mansfield*. New York: Twayne, 1965, pp. 109–111.

Greenwood, E.B. "Katherine Mansfield's 'The Fly,' " in *Essays in Criticism*. XII (July, 1962), pp. 341–347.

Hagopian, John. "Capturing Mansfield's 'Fly,' " in *Modern Fiction Studies*. IX (Winter, 1963–1964), pp. 385–390.

————. " 'The Fly,' " in *Insight II: Analyses of British Literature*. Edited by John V. Hagopian and Martin Dolch. Frankfurt, Germany: Hirschgraben, 1964, pp. 240–247.

Jolly, R.A. "Katherine Mansfield's 'The Fly,' " in *Essays in Criticism*. XII (July, 1962), pp. 335–338.

Meredith, Robert C. and John D. Fitzgerald. *The Professional Story Writer and His Art*. New York: Crowell, 1963, pp. 411–420.

Michel-Michot, Paulette. "Katherine Mansfield's 'The Fly': An Attempt to Capture the Boss," in *Studies in Short Fiction*. XI (1974), pp. 85–92.

Peltzie, Bernard E. "Teaching Meaning Through Structure in the Short Story," in *English Journal*. LV (September, 1966), pp. 703–709.

Rohrberger, Mary. *Hawthorne and the Modern Short Story: A Study in Genre*. The Hague: Mouton, 1966, pp. 68–74.

Thomas, J.D. "Symbol and Parallelism in 'The Fly,' " in *College English*. XXII (January, 1961), pp. 256–262.

"The Garden Party"

Bloom, Edward A. *The Order of Fiction*. New York: Odyssey, 1964, pp. 176–179.

Brewster, Dorothy and Angus Burrell. *Modern Fiction*. New York: Columbia University Press, 1934.

Daly, Saralyn. *Katherine Mansfield*. New York: Twayne, 1965, pp. 99–100.

Davis, Robert M. "The Unity of 'The Garden Party,' " in *Studies in Short Fiction*. II (1964), pp. 61–65.

Iverson, Anders. "A Reading of Katherine Mansfield's 'The Garden Party,' " in *Orbis Litterarum*. XXIII (1968), pp. 5–34.

Kleine, Don W. "An Eden for Insiders: Katherine Mansfield's New Zealand," in *College English*. XXVII (1965), pp. 207–209.

————. " 'The Garden Party': A Portrait of the Artist," in *Criticism*. V (1963), pp. 360–371.

Lawrence, Margaret. *The School for Femininity*. New York: Stokes, 1963.

Magalaner, Marvin. *The Fiction of Katherine Mansfield*. Carbondale: Southern Illinois University Press, 1971, pp. 110–119.

O'Connor, Frank. *The Lonely Voice: A Study of the Short Story.* Cleveland: World, 1963, pp. 138–139.

Taylor, Donald S. "A Dream—A Wakening," in *Modern Fiction Studies.* IV (1958), pp. 361–362.

Walker, Warren S. "The Unresolved Conflict in 'The Garden Party,' " in *Modern Fiction Studies.* III (1957), pp. 354–358.

Walsh, William. *A Manifold Voice: Studies in Commonwealth Literature.* London: Chatto and Windus, 1970, pp. 170–171.

Weiss, Daniel A. "The Garden Party of Proserpina," in *Modern Fiction Studies.* IV (1958), pp. 363–364.

"Prelude"

Alpers, Antony. *Katherine Mansfield: A Biography.* New York: Knopf, 1953, pp. 213–219.

Berkman, Sylvia. *Katherine Mansfield: A Critical Study.* New Haven, Conn.: Yale University Press, 1951, pp. 83–86.

Daly, Saralyn. *Katherine Mansfield.* New York: Twayne, 1965, pp. 67–73.

Hale, Nancy. "Through the Looking Glass to Reality," in *Saturday Review of Literature.* XLI (November 8, 1958), pp. 39–40.

Hubbell, George S. "Katherine Mansfield and Kezia," in *Sewanee Review.* XXXV (1927), pp. 329–331.

Kleine, Don W. "An Eden for Insiders: Katherine Mansfield's New Zealand," in *College English.* XXVII (1965), pp. 205–206.

Magalaner, Marvin. *The Fiction of Katherine Mansfield.* Carbondale: Southern Illinois University Press, 1971, pp. 26–38.

Maurois, André. *Points of View from Kipling to Graham Greene.* Translated by Hamish Miles. New York: Frederick Ungar, 1968, pp. 331–332.

Murry, John M. *Katherine Mansfield and Other Literary Portraits.* London: Peter Nevill, 1949, pp. 12–14.

O'Connor, Frank. *The Lonely Voice: A Study of the Short Story.* Cleveland: World, 1963, pp. 139–140.

ALESSANDRO MANZONI
(1785–1873)

The Betrothed

Barricelli, Gian P. *Alessandro Manzoni.* New York: Twayne, 1976.

————. "Structure and Symbol in Manzoni's *I Promessi Sposi*," in *Italian Quarterly.* LXVII (1973), pp. 79–102.

Chandler, S.B. *Alessandro Manzoni: The Story of a Spiritual Quest.* Edinburgh: Edinburgh University Press, 1974.

————. "The Innominato's Perception of Time in *I Promessi Sposi*," in *Philological Quarterly.* XLII (October, 1963), pp. 548–557.

————. "The Moment in Manzoni," in *Petrarch to Pirandello.* Edited by Julius A. Molinaro. Toronto: University of Toronto Press, 1973, pp. 151–167.

————. "Point of View in the Descriptions of *I Promessi Sposi*," in *Italica.* XLIII (December, 1966), pp. 386–400.

Chase, Richard. "Notes on Manzoni's *I Promessi Sposi* and the English and European Traditions," in *English Miscellany.* VIII (1957), pp. 109–123.

Collison-Morby, Lacy. *Modern Italian Literature.* London: Pitman, 1911, pp. 199–205.

Colquhuon, Archibald. *Manzoni and His Times.* New York: Dutton, 1954, pp. 165–197.

De Simone, Joseph Francis. *Alessandro Manzoni: Esthetics and Literary Criticism.* New York: S.F. Vanni, 1946, pp. 67–86.

————. "Manzoni and the Fine Arts," in *Italica.* XXVIII (December, 1951), pp. 271–278.

Dombroski, R.S. "Seicento as Strategy: Providence and the Bourgeois in *I Promessi Sposi*," in *Modern Language Notes.* XCI (January, 1976), pp. 80–100.

Foster, Kenelm. "Alessandro Manzoni (1785–1873)," in *Italian Quarterly.* LXVII (1973), pp. 7–23.

Friedson, Marion Facinger. "The Meaning of Gertrude in *I Promessi Sposi*," in *Italica.* XXVIII (March, 1951), pp. 27–32.

Garofolo, Silvano. "Manzoni and the American Literary Scene (1830–1840)," in *Forum Italicum.* VII (1973), pp. 375–385.

Hall, Robert A., Jr. *A Short History of Italian Literature.* Ithaca, N.Y.: Linguistica, 1951, pp. 365–369.

Kennard, Joseph Spencer. *Italian Romance Writers.* New York: Brentano's, 1906, pp. 89–115.

Lansing, Richard H. "Stylistic and Structural Duality in Manzoni's *I Promessi Sposi*," in *Italica*. LIII (1976), pp. 347–361.

Meiklejohn, M.F.M. "Sir Walter Scott and Alessandro Manzoni," in *Italian Studies*. XII (1957), pp. 91–98.

Norman, Hilda L. "Renzo's Garden," in *Italica*. XVI (December, 1939), pp. 12–22.

Orne, Jerrold. "The Sources of *I Promessi Sposi*," in Modern Philology. XXXVIII (May, 1941), pp. 405–420.

Pritchett, V.S. *Books in General*. London: Chatto and Windus, 1953, pp. 13–18.

Ragusa, Olga. "The Latest Manzoni," in *Italian Quarterly*. V (Winter, 1961), pp. 107–116.

Raimondi, E. "*I Promessi Sposi*: Genesis and Structure of a 'Catholic' Novel," in *Interpretation: Theory and Practice*. Edited by Charles S. Singleton. Baltimore: Johns Hopkins University Press, 1969, pp. 123–152.

Wall, Bernard. *Alessandro Manzoni*. New Haven, Conn.: Yale University Press, 1954, pp. 23–56.

Zimmerman, Eleonore M. "Structural Patterns in *I Promessi Sposi*," in *Italica*. XXXIX (September, 1962), pp. 159–172.

MARIE DE FRANCE
(c.1150–1190)

Lais

Cottrell, Robert D. "*Le Lai du Laustic*: From Physicality to Spirituality," in *Philological Quarterly*. XLVII (1968), pp. 499–505.

Cross, Tom P. "The Celtic Elements in the Lays of *Lanval* and *Graelent*," in *Modern Philology*. XII (1914/1915), pp. 585–644.

————. "The Celtic Origin of the Lay of *Yonec*," in *Studies in Philology*. XI (1913), pp. 26–60.

Damon, S.F. "Marie de France: Psychologist of Courtly Love," in *PMLA*. XLIV (1929), pp. 968–996.

Davison, Muriel. "Marie de France's *Lai de Lanval*, 31–38," in *Explicator*. XXI (1962), item 12.

Donovan, Mortimer J. *The Breton Lay: A Guide to Varieties*. Notre Dame, Ind.: University of Notre Dame Press, 1969, pp. 8–13.

————. "*Lai du Lecheor*: A Reinterpretation," in *Romanic Review*. XLIII (1952), pp. 81–86.

Ferguson, Mary H. "Folklore in the *Lais* of Marie de France," in *Romanic Review*. LVIII (1966), pp. 3–24.

Foulet, Lucien. "English Words in the *Lais* of Marie de France," in *Modern Language Notes*. XX (1905), pp. 108–110.

Frey, John A. "Linguistic and Psychological Couplings in the Lays of Marie de France," in *Studies in Philology*. LXI (1964), pp. 3–18.

Harris, Julian. The Lays of Guigeman, Lanval, *and a Fragment of* Yonec, *with a Study of the Life and Work of an Author*. New York: Institute of French Studies, 1930.

Hatzfeld, H. "Esthetic Criticism Applied to Romance Literature," in *Romance Philology*. I (1947/1948), pp. 319–320.

Holmes, Urban T. "A Welsh Motif in Marie's *Guigemar*," in *Studies in Philology*. XXXIX (1942), pp. 11–14.

Johnston, Oliver M. "Sources of the Lay of the 'Two Lovers,' " in *Modern Language Notes*. XXI (1906), pp. 34–39.

————. "Sources of the *Lay of Yonec*," in *PMLA*. XX (1905), pp. 322–338.

Mickel, Emanuel J., Jr. "A Reconsideration of the *Lais* of Marie de France," in *Speculum*. XLVI (1971), pp. 39–65.

Ogle, M.B. "Some Theories in Irish Literary Influence and the *Lay of Yonec*," in *Romanic Review*. X (1919), pp. 123–148.

O'Sharkey, Eithne M. "The Identity of the Fairy Mistress in Marie de France's *Lai de Lanval*," in *Trivium*. VI (1971), pp. 17–25.

Robertson, D.W., Jr. "Love Conventions in Marie's *Equitan*," in *Romanic Review*. XLIV (1953), pp. 241–245.

————. "Marie de France, *Lais*, Prologue, 13–15," in *Modern Language Notes*. LXIV (1949), pp. 336–338.

Rothschild, J. "A Rapproachment Between Bisclavret and Lanval," in *Speculum*. XLVIII (1973), pp. 78–88.

Spitzer, Leo. "The Prologue to the *Lais* of Marie de France and Medieval Poetics," in *Modern Philology*. XLI (1943), pp. 96–102.

Stokoe, W. "The Sources of *Sir Launfal: Lanval* and *Graelent*," in *PMLA*. LXIII (1948), pp. 392–404.

Woods, William Sledge. "Femininity in the *Lais* of Marie de France," in *Studies in Philology*. XLVII (1950), pp. 1–19.

————. "Marie de France's *Laustic*," in *Romance Notes*. XII (1970), pp. 203–207.

KAMALA MARKANDAYA
(1924–   )

The Works of Markandaya

Caliri, Fortunata. "*A Handful of Rice,*" in *America.* CXV (August 27, 1966), p. 212.

Carter, A.H. "Possession," in *Books Abroad.* XXXIX (Autumn, 1965), p. 479.

Kumar, S.K. "Tradition and Change in the Novels of Kamala Markandaya," in *Books Abroad.* XLIII (Autumn, 1969), pp. 508–513.

Parameswaran, U. "India for the Western Reader: A Study of Kamala Markandaya's Novels," in *Texas Quarterly.* XI (Summer, 1968), pp. 231–247.

Parton, Margaret. "Cursed with Conscience," in *Saturday Review.* XLIX (August 27, 1966), p. 34.

Rao, K.S. Narayana. "Kamala Markandaya: The Novelist as Craftsman," in *Indian Writing Today.* VIII (April–June, 1969), pp. 32–40.

————. "Religious Elements in Kamala Markandaya's Novels," in *Ariel.* VIII (January, 1977), pp. 35–50.

Wendt, Allen. "Under the Hair Dryer," in *Literature East and West.* (June, 1967), p. 208.

CHRISTOPHER MARLOWE
(1564–1593)

Doctor Faustus

Baker, Donald C. "Ovid and Faustus: The *Noctis Equi*," in *Classical Journal*. LV (1959), pp. 126–128.

Barber, C.L. "The Form of Faustus' Fortunes, Good or Bad," in *Tulane Drama Review*. VIII (1964), pp. 92–119.

Briggs, William D. "Marlowe's *Faustus*, 305–18, 548–70," in *Modern Language Notes*. XXXVIII (1923), pp. 385–393.

Brooke, C.F. Tucker. "Notes on *Doctor Faustus*," in *Philological Quarterly*. XII (1933), pp. 17–23.

Brown, Beatrice D. "Christopher Marlowe, Faustus, and Simon Magus," in *PMLA*. LIV (1939), pp. 82–121.

Campbell, Lily B. "*Doctor Faustus*: A Case of Conscience," in *PMLA*. LXVII (1952), pp. 219–239.

Fabian, Bernhard. "A Note on Marlowe's *Faustus*," in *English Studies*. XLI (1960), pp. 365–369.

Frey, Leonard H. "Antithetical Balance in the Opening and Close of *Doctor Faustus*," in *Modern Language Quarterly*. XXIV (1963), pp. 350–353.

Gardner, Helen. "Milton's 'Satan' and the Theme of Damnation in Elizabethan Tragedy," in *English Studies*. I (1948), pp. 46–66.

Green, Clarence. "*Doctor Faustus*: The Tragedy of Individualism," in *Science and Society*. X (1946), pp. 275–283.

Greg, W.W. "The Damnation of Faustus," in *Modern Language Review*. XLI (1946), pp. 97–107.

Heilman, Robert B. "The Tragedy of Knowledge: Marlowe's Treatment of Faustus," in *Quarterly Review of Literature*. II (1946), pp. 316–332.

Heller, Erich. "Faust's Damnation: The Morality of Knowlege," in *Listener*. (January 11, 1961), pp. 60–62.

Homan, Sidney R., Jr. "*Doctor Faustus*, Dekker's *Old Fortunatus*, and the Morality Plays," in *Modern Language Quarterly*. XXVI (1965), pp. 497–505.

Hunter, G.K. "Five-Act Structure in *Doctor Faustus*," in *Tulane Drama Review*. VIII (1964), pp. 77–91.

Kaula, David. "Time and the Timeless in *Everyman* and *Doctor Faustus*," in *College English*. XXII (1960), pp. 9–14.

Kirschbaum, Leo. "Marlowe's *Faustus*: A Reconsideration," in *Review of English Studies*. XIX (1943), pp. 225–241.

Kocher, Paul H. "The Witchcraft Basis in Marlowe's *Faustus*," in *Modern Philology*. XXXVIII (1940), pp. 9–36.

McCloskey, J.C. "The Theme of Despair in Marlowe's *Faustus*," in *College English*. IV (1942), pp. 110–113.

Mizener, Arthur. "The Tragedy of Marlowe's *Doctor Faustus*," in *College English*. V (1943), pp. 70–75.

Ornstein, Robert. "The Comic Synthesis in *Doctor Faustus*," in *Journal of English Literary History*. XXII (1955), pp. 165–172.

Palmer, D.J. "Magic and Poetry in *Doctor Faustus*," in *Critical Quarterly*. VI (1964), pp. 56–67.

Reynolds, James A. "Faustus' Flawed Learning," in *English Studies*. LVII (August, 1976), pp. 329–336.

Sayers, Dorothy Leigh. "The Faust Legend and the Idea of the Devil," in *Publications of the English Goethe Society*. XV (1946), pp. 1–20.

Zimansky, Curt A. "Marlowe's *Faustus*: The Date Again," in *Philosophical Quarterly*. XLI (1962), pp. 181–187.

Edward the Second

Berdan, John M. "Marlowe's *Edward II*," in *Philological Quarterly*. III (1924), pp. 197–207.

Bobin, Donna. "Marlowe's Humor," in *Massachusetts Studies in English*. II (Fall, 1969), pp. 29–40.

Briggs, W.D. "The Meaning of the Word 'Lake' in *Edward II*," in *Modern Language Notes*. XXXIX (1924), pp. 437–438.

Brodwin, Leonora Leet. "*Edward II*: Marlowe's Culminating Treatment of Love," in *Journal of English Literary History*. XXXI (1964), pp. 139–155.

Craig, Hardin. "The Origin of the History Play," in *Arlington Quarterly*. I (Spring 1968), pp. 5–11.

Crundell, H.W. "The Death of Edward II in Marlowe's Play," in *Notes and Queries*. CLXXIX (1940), p. 207.

Cushner, Arnold W. "Some Observations on Marlowe's *Edward II*," in *Renaissance and Modern Essays in Honor of Edwin M. Moseley*. Edited by Murray J. Levith. Saratoga Springs, N.Y.: Skidmore College, 1976, pp. 11–20.

Empson, William. "Two Proper Crimes," in *Nation*. CLVIII (1946), pp. 444–445.

Fricker, Robert. "The Dramatic Structure of *Edward II*," in *English Studies*. XXXIV (1953), pp. 204–217.

Johnson, Samuel Frederick. "Marlowe's *Edward II*," in *Explicator*. X (1952), item 53.

Leech, Clifford. "Marlowe's *Edward II*: Power and Suffering," in *Critical Quarterly*. I (1959), pp. 181–196.

Manheim, Michael. "The Weak King History Play of the Early 1590's," in *Renaissance Drama*. II (1969), pp. 71–80.

Masinton, Charles G. "Marlowe's Artists: The Failure of Imagination," in *Ohio University Review*. XI (1969), pp. 22–35.

Mills, L.J. "The Meaning of *Edward II*," in *Modern Philology*. XXXII (1934), pp. 11–31.

Morris, Harry. "Marlowe's Poetry," in *Tulane Drama Review*. VIII (1964), pp. 134–154.

Ricks, Christopher. "English Drama to 1710," in *History of Literature in the English Language*. III (1971), pp. 143–145.

Summers, Claude J. "Isabella's Plea for Gaveston in Marlowe's *Edward II*," in *Philological Quarterly*. LII (1973), pp. 308–310.

Sunesen, Bent. "Marlowe and the Dumb Show," in *English Studies*. XXXV (1954), pp. 241–253.

Watson, R.A. "*Edward II*: A Study in Evil," in *Durham University Journal*. XXXVII (1976), pp. 162–167.

Hero and Leander

Adamson, Jane. "Marlowe, *Hero and Leander*, and the Art of Leaping in Poetry," in *Critical Review*. XVII (1974), pp. 59–81.

Banerjee, Chinmoy. "*Hero and Leander* as Erotic Comedy," in *Journal of Narrative Technique*. III (1973), pp. 40–52.

Bradbrook, M.C. "*Hero and Leander*," in *Journal of English and Germanic Philology*. LIV (1955), pp. 478–485.

Bush, Douglas. "*Hero and Leander* and *Romeo and Juliet*," in *Philological Quarterly*. IX (1930), pp. 396–399.

————. "Notes on *Hero and Leander*," in *PMLA*. LXIV (1929), pp. 760–764.

————. "The Influence of *Hero and Leander* on Early Mythological Poems," in *Modern Language Notes*. XLII (1927), pp. 211–217.

Cantelupe, Eugene B. "*Hero and Leander*, Marlowe's Tragicomedy of Love," in *College English*. XXIV (1963), pp. 295–298.

Collins, S. Ann. "Sundrie Shapes, Committing Headdie Ryots, Incest, Rapes: Functions of Myth in Determining Narrative and Tone in Marlowe's *Hero and Leander*," in *Mosaic*. IV (1970), pp. 107–122.

Cubeta, Paul M. "Marlowe's Poet in *Hero and Leander*," in *College English*. XXVI (1965), pp. 500–505.

Kostic, Veselin. "Marlowe's *Hero and Leander* and Chapman's Continuation," in *Renaissance and Modern Essays.* XLVIII (1966), pp. 25–34.

Marsh, T.N. "Marlowe's *Hero and Leander*, I, 45–50," in *Explicator.* XXI (1962), item 30.

Maxwell, J.C. "*Hero and Leander* and *Love's Labour's Lost*," in *Notes and Queries.* CXCVII (1952), pp. 334–335.

Miller, Paul W. "A Function of Myth in Marlowe's *Hero and Leander*," in *Studies in Philology.* L (1953), pp. 158–167.

————. "The Problem of Justice in Marlowe's *Hero and Leander*," in *Notes and Queries.* IV (1957), pp. 163–164.

Mills, John. "The Courtship Ritual of *Hero and Leander*," in *English Literary Renaissance.* II (1972), pp. 298–306.

Neuse, Richard. "Atheism and Some Functions of Myth in Marlowe's *Hero and Leander*," in *Modern Language Quarterly.* XXXI (1970), pp. 424–439.

Schaus, Hermann. "The Relationship of *Comus* to *Hero and Leander* and *Venus and Adonis*," in *Studies in English* (University of Texas). XXV (1945/46), pp. 129–141.

Sheidley, William E. "The Seduction of the Reader in Marlowe's *Hero and Leander*," in *Concerning Poetry.* III (1970), pp. 50–56.

Strachey, J. "*Hero and Leander*," in *Spectator.* (October 4, 1924), pp. 471–472.

Taylor, A.B. "A Note on Christopher Marlowe's *Hero and Leander*," in *Notes and Queries.* XVI (January, 1969), pp. 20–21.

Turner, Myron. "Pastoral and Hermaphrodite: A Study in the Naturalism of Marlowe's *Hero and Leander*," in *Texas Studies in Literature and Language.* XVII (1974), pp. 397–414.

Walsh, William P. "Sexual Discovery and Renaissance Morality in Marlowe's *Hero and Leander*," in *Studies in English Literature, 1500–1900.* XII (1972), pp. 33–54.

Williams, Gordon I. "Acting and Suffering in *Hero and Leander*," in *Trivium.* VIII (1973), pp. 11–26.

Williams, Martin T. "The Temptations in Marlowe's *Hero and Leander*," in *Modern Language Quarterly.* XVI (1955), pp. 226–231.

The Jew of Malta

Babb, Howard S. "Policy in Marlowe's *The Jew of Malta*," in *Journal of English Literary History.* XXIV (1957), pp. 85–97.

Bawcutt, N.W. "Machiavelli and Marlowe's *The Jew of Malta*," in *Renaissance Drama.* III (1970), pp. 3–49.

Black, Matthew. "Enter Citizens," in *Studies in the English Renaissance Drama.* (1960), pp. 16–27.

Bowers, Fredson T. "The Audience and the Poisoner of Elizabethan Tragedy," in *Journal of English and Germanic Philology*. XXXVI (1937), pp. 491–504.

Carpenter, Nan C. "Infinite Riches: A Note on Marlovian Unity," in *Notes and Queries*. CXCVI (1951), pp. 50–52.

Cole, Douglas. "The Comic Accomplice in Elizabethan Revenge Tragedy," in *Renaissance Drama*. IX (1966), pp. 125–139.

Dameron, J. Lasley. "Marlowe's 'Ship of War,'" in *American Notes and Queries*. II (1963), pp. 19–20.

D'Andrea, Antonio. "Studies on Machiavelli and His Reputation in the Sixteenth Century: I. Marlowe's Prologue to *The Jew of Malta*," in *Medieval and Renaissance Studies* (Warburg Institute). V (1961), pp. 214–248.

Dean, Leonard, Michael Bristol and Neil Kleinman. "Marlowe's *The Jew of Malta*: Grammar of Policy," in *Midwest Monographs* (University of Illinois, Urbana). II (1967), pp. 1–6.

Flosdorf, J.W. "The 'Odi et Amo' Theme in *The Jew of Malta*," in *Notes and Queries*. VII (1960), pp. 10–14.

Freeman, Arthur. "A Source for *The Jew of Malta*," in *Notes and Queries*. IX (1962), pp. 139–141.

Halio, Jay L. "Perfection and Elizabethan Ideas of Conception," in *English Language Notes*. I (1964), pp. 179–182.

Harrison, Thomas P., Jr. "Further Background for *The Jew of Malta* and *The Massacre at Paris*," in *Philological Quarterly*. XXVII (1948), pp. 52–56.

———. "The Literary Background of Renaissance Poisons," in *Studies in English*. XXVII (1948), pp. 35–67.

Hunter, G.K. "The Theology of Marlowe's *The Jew of Malta*," in *Journal of the Warburg and Courtauld Institutes*. XXVII (1964), pp. 211–240.

Kay, Donald. "The Appearance–Reality Theme in *The Jew of Malta*," in *Studies in English Literature*. (1972), pp. 200–201.

Kocher, Paul H. "English Legal History in Marlowe's *Jew of Malta*," in *Huntington Library Quarterly*. XXVI (1962), pp. 155–163.

Kreisman, Arthur. "The Jews of Marlowe and Shakespeare," in *Shakespeare Newsletter*. VIII (1958), p. 29.

Pearce, T.M. "Marlowe's *The Jew of Malta*, IV, vi, 7–10," in *Explicator*. IX (1961), item 40.

Peavy, Charles E. "*The Jew of Malta*: Anti-Semitic or Anti-Catholic?," in *McNeese Review*. XI (1959/60), pp. 51–60.

Ribner, Irving. "The Significance of Gentillets' *Contre-Machiavel*," in *Modern Language Quarterly*. X (1949), pp. 153–157.

Rusche, H.G. "Two Proverbial Images in Whitney's *A Choice of Emblemes* and Marlowe's *The Jew of Malta*," in *Notes and Queries*. XI (1964), p. 261.

Wright, Celeste T. "The Usurer's Sin in Elizabethan Literature," in *Studies in Philology*. XXXV (1938), pp. 178–194.

Tamburlaine the Great

Battenhouse, Roy Wesley. *Marlowe's Tamburlaine, A Study in Renaissance Moral Philosophy*. Nashville, Tenn.: Vanderbilt University Press, 1964.

————. "Tamburlaine, the 'Scourge of God,' " in *PMLA*. LVI (1941), pp. 377–398.

Blau, Herbert. "Language and Structure in Poetic Drama," in *Modern Language Quarterly*. XVIII (1957), pp. 27–34.

Boas, Guy. "*Tamburlaine* and the Horrific," in *English*. XIII (1951), pp. 275–277.

Brereton, John LeGay. "Marlowe's Dramatic Art Studied in His *Tamburlaine*," in *Writings on Elizabethan Drama*. Edited by R.G. Howarth. Carlton, Australia: Melbourne University Press, 1948, pp. 67–80.

Brooks, Charles. "*Tamburlaine* and Attitudes Toward Women," in *Journal of English Literary History*. XXIV (1957), pp. 1–11.

Cutts, John. "Tamburlaine 'As Fierce Achilles Was,' " in *Comparative Drama*. I (1967), pp. 105–109.

Dick, Hugh G. "*Tamburlaine* Sources Once More," in *Studies in Philology*. XLVI (1949), pp. 154–166.

Duthie, G.I. "The Dramatic Structure of Marlowe's *Tamburlaine the Great, Parts I and II*," in *English Studies*. I (1948), pp. 101–126.

Gardner, Helen L. "The Second Part of *Tamburlaine the Great*," in *Modern Language Review*. XXXVII (1942), pp. 18–24.

Izard, T.C. "The Principal Source for Marlowe's *Tamburlaine*," in *Modern Language Notes*. LVIII (1943), pp. 411–417.

Kocher, Paul. "Marlowe's Art of War," in *Studies in Philology*," XXXIX (1942), pp. 207–225.

Leech, Clifford. "The Structure of *Tamburlaine*," in *Tulane Drama Review*. VIII (1964), pp. 32–46.

LePage, Peter V. "The Search for Godhead in Marlowe's *Tamburlaine*," in *College English*. XXVI (1964/65), pp. 604–609.

Nathanson, Leonard. "*Tamburlaine*'s 'Pampered Jades' and Gascoigne," in *Notes and Queries*. V (1958), pp. 53–54.

Nosworthy, J.M. "The Shakespearean Heroic Vaunt," in *Review of English Studies*. II (1951), pp. 259–261.

Pearce, T.M.   "Tamburlaine's 'Discipline to His Three Sonnes': An Interpretation of *Tamburlaine, Part II*," in *Modern Language Quarterly*. XV (1954), pp. 18–27.

Quinn, Michael.   "The Freedom of *Tamburlaine*," in *Modern Language Quarterly*. XXI (1960), pp. 315–320.

Ribner, Irving.   "The Idea of History in Marlowe's *Tamburlaine*," in *Journal of English Literary History*. XX (1954), pp. 251–266.

Smith, Hallett D.   "Tamburlaine and the Renaissance," in *Elizabethan Studies in Honor of George F. Reynolds. University of Colorado Studies, Series B: Studies in the Humanities*. II (1945), pp. 126–131.

Sternlicht, Sanford.   "*Tamburlaine* and the Iterative Sun-Image," in *English Record*. XVI (1966), pp. 23–29.

Taylor, Robert T.   "Maximinus and *Tamburlaine*," in *Notes and Queries*. IV (1957), pp. 417–418.

Thorp, Willard.   "The Ethical Problem in Marlowe's *Tamburlaine*," in *Journal of English and Germanic Philology*. XXIX (1930), pp. 385–389.

Van Dam, B.A.P.   "Marlowe's *Tamburlaine*," in *English Studies*. XVI (1934), pp. 1–17, 49–58.

Wekling, Mary Mellen.   "Marlowe's Mnemonic Nominology, with Especial Reference to *Tamburlaine*," in *Modern Language Notes*. LXXIII (1958), pp. 243–247.

JOHN P. MARQUAND
(1893–1960)

H.M. Pulham, Esq.

Greene, George. "A Tunnel from Persepolis: The Legacy of John Marquand," in *Queen's Quarterly*. LXXIII (Autumn, 1966), pp. 350–351.

Gross, John J. *John P. Marquand*. New York: Twayne, 1963, pp. 64–83.

Holman, C. Hugh. *John P. Marquand*. Minneapolis: University of Minnesota Press, 1965.

Johnson, Robert O. "Mr. Marquand and Lord Tennyson," in *Research Studies*. XXXII (1964), pp. 29–32.

MacLean, Hugh. "Conservatism in Modern American Fiction," in *College English*. XV (March, 1954), pp. 315–325.

Marquand, John P. "*Apley*, *Wickford Point*, and *Pelham*: My Early Struggles," in *Atlantic*. CXCVIII (September, 1956), pp. 73–74.

Oppenheimer, Franz. "Lament for Unbought Grace: The Novels of John P. Marquand," in *Antioch Review*. XVIII (Spring, 1958), pp. 46–48.

The Late George Apley

Beach, Joseph Warren. *American Fiction, 1920–1940*. New York: Russell and Russell, 1960, pp. 259–270.

Goodwin, George. "The Last Hurrahs: George Apley and Frank Skeffington," in *Massachusetts Review*. I (May, 1960), pp. 461–471.

Gordon, Edward J. "What's Happened to Humor?," in *English Journal*. XLVII (1958), pp. 127–133.

Greene, George. "A Tunnel from Persepolis: The Legacy of John Marquand," in *Queen's Quarterly*. LXXIII (Autumn, 1966), pp. 343–349.

Gross, John J. *John P. Marquand*. New York: Twayne, 1963, pp. 31–50.

Holman, C. Hugh. *John P. Marquand*. Minneapolis: University of Minnesota Press, 1965.

Johnson, Robert O. "Mary Monahan: Marquand's Sentimental Slip?," in *Research Studies*. XXXIII (December, 1965), pp. 208–213.

Macauley, Robie. "Let Me Tell You About the Rich . . . ," in *Kenyon Review*. XXVII (Autumn, 1965), pp. 664–666.

Oppenheimer, Franz. "Lament for Unbought Grace: The Novels of John P. Marquand," in *Antioch Review*. XVIII (Spring, 1958), pp. 41–45.

Stuckey, W.J. *The Pulitzer Prize Novels: A Critical Backward Look*. Norman: University of Oklahoma Press, 1966, pp. 112–116.

Warren, Austin.   "The Last Puritan," in his *The New England Conscience.*
Ann Arbor: University of Michigan Press, 1966, pp. 195–201.

Melville Goodwin, U.S.A.

Geisman, Maxwell.   *American Moderns: From Rebellion to Conformity.*
New York: Hill and Wang, 1958.

Gross, John J.   *John P. Marquand.* New York: Twayne, 1963, pp. 127–140.

Holman, C. Hugh.   *John P. Marquand.* Minneapolis: University of Minnesota
Press, 1965.

Johnson, Robert O.   "Mr. Marquand and Mr. Tennyson," in *Research Studies.*
XXXII (1964), pp. 35–38.

Oppenheimer, Franz.   "Lament for Unbought Grace: The Novels of John P.
Marquand," in *Antioch Review.* XVIII (Spring, 1958), pp. 58–60.

The Point of No Return

Geisman, Maxwell.   *American Moderns: From Rebellion to Conformity.*
New York: Hill and Wang, 1958, pp. 156–159.

Greene, George.   "A Tunnel from Persepolis: The Legacy of John Marquand,"
in *Queen's Quarterly.* LXXIII (Autumn, 1966), pp. 351–352.

Gross, John J.   *John P. Marquand.* New York: Twayne, 1963, pp. 111–126.

Haugh, Robert F.   "The Dilemma of John P. Marquand," in *Michigan Alumnus Quarterly Review.* LIX (December 6, 1952), pp. 19–24.

Hicks, Granville.   "John Marquand of Newburyport," in *Harper's.* CC (April,
1950), pp. 101–108.

Holman, C. Hugh.   *John P. Marquand.* Minneapolis: University of Minnesota
Press, 1965.

Johnson, Robert O.   "Mr. Marquand and Mr. Tennyson," in *Research Studies.*
XXXII (1964), pp. 35–38.

Oppenheimer, Franz.   "Lament for Unbought Grace: The Novels of John P.
Marquand," in *Antioch Review.* XVIII (Spring, 1958), pp. 52–57.

Van Nostrand, Albert D.   "After Marquand, the Deluge," in *English Journal.*
XLVIII (February, 1959), pp. 55–65.

————.   "Fiction's Flagging Man of Commerce," in *English Journal.*
XLVIII (January, 1959), pp. 1–11.

Wickford Point

Beach, Joseph Warren.   *American Fiction, 1920–1940.* New York: Russell and
Russell, 1960, pp. 254–259.

Gray, James.   *On Second Thought.* Minneapolis: University of Minnesota
Press, 1946, pp. 88–90.

Greene, George. "A Tunnel from Persepolis: The Legacy of John Marquand," in *Queen's Quarterly.* LXXIII (Autumn, 1966), pp. 349–350.

Gross, John J. *John P. Marquand.* New York: Twayne, 1963, pp. 51–63.

Holman, C. Hugh. *John P. Marquand.* Minneapolis: University of Minnesota Press, 1964.

Marquand, John P. "*Apley, Wickford Point,* and *Pelham:* My Early Struggles," in *Atlantic.* CXCVIII (September, 1956), pp. 72–73.

Oppenheimer, Franz. "Lament for Unbought Grace: The Novels of John P. Marquand," in *Antioch Review.* XVIII (Spring, 1958), pp. 48–50.

Van Gelder, Robert. "Marquand Unburdens Himself," in *New York Times Book Review.* (April 7, 1940), pp. 20–21.

Women and Thomas Harrow

Gardiner, H.C. "Hero as Yo-Yo," in *America.* C (October 11, 1958), p. 51.

Greene, George. "A Tunnel from Persepolis: The Legacy of John Marquand," in *Queen's Quarterly.* LXXIII (Autumn, 1966), pp. 352–356.

Gross, John J. *John P. Marquand.* New York: Twayne, 1963, pp. 158–175.

Holman, C. Hugh. *John P. Marquand.* Minneapolis: University of Minnesota Press, 1965.

Kazin, Alfred. *Contemporaries.* Boston: Little, Brown, 1962, pp. 122–130.

————. "John P. Marquand and the American Failure," in *Atlantic.* CCII (November, 1958), pp. 152–156.

Smith, William J. "J.P. Marquand, Esq.," in *Commonweal.* LXIX (November 7, 1958), pp. 148–150.

MARTIAL
(c.40–c.104)

Epigrams of Martial

Allen, W., et al. "Martial, Knight, Publisher and Poet," in *Classical Journal.* LXV (1970), pp. 345–357.

Anderson, W.S. "Lascivia vs. Ira. Martial and Juvenal," in *California Studies in Classical Antiquity.* III (1970), pp. 1–34.

Bovie, P. "Introduction," in *The Epigrams of Martial.* New York: New American Library, 1970.

Carrington, A.G. *Aspects of Martial's* Epigrams. Sydney: Shakespeare Head Press, 1960.

Chaney, V.M. "Women, According to Martial," in *Classical Bulletin.* XLVIII (1971), pp. 21–25.

Colton, R.E. "Martial in Juvenal's Tenth Satire," in *Studies in Philology.* LXXIV (October, 1977), pp. 341–353.

Downs, R.B. "Creator of the Epigram: Marcus Valerius Martialis," in *Famous Books, Ancient and Medieval.* New York: Barnes & Noble, 1964, pp. 217–220.

Fuller, J. "Pope and Martial," in *Notes and Queries.* XV (June, 1968), pp. 334–342.

Marino, P.A. "Women, Poorly Inferior or Richly Superior," in *Classical Bulletin.* XLVIII (1971), pp. 17–21.

Nixon, Paul. *Martial and the Modern Epigram.* New York: Cooper Square Press, 1963.

Porter, Peter. *After Martial.* London: Oxford University Press, 1972.

Rothberg, I.P. "Covarrubias, Graciás, and the Greek Anthology (Similarity Between the Anthology and Martial)," in *Studies in Philology.* LIII (October, 1956), pp. 540–552.

White, P. "Presentation and Dedication of *The Silvae* and the *Epigrams*," in *Journal of Roman Studies.* LXIV (1974), pp. 40–61.

Whipple, Thomas K. *Martial and English Epigrams from Sir Thomas Wyatt to Ben Jonson.* New York: Phaeton, 1970.

ROGER MARTIN DU GARD
(1881–1958)

Jean Barois

Boak, Denis. *Roger Martin du Gard.* Oxford: Clarendon Press, 1963, pp. 29–56.

Bree, Germaine. "Roger Martin du Gard: The Corneille of the Bourgeois Novel," in her *An Age of Fiction: French Novel from Gide to Camus.* New Brunswick, N.J.: Rutgers University Press, 1957, pp. 76–79.

Brombert, Victor H. "Martin du Gard's *Jean Barois* and the Challenge of History," in his *The Intellectual Hero.* New York: Lippincott, 1961, pp. 94–118.

Gibson, Robert. *Roger Martin du Gard.* London: Bowes and Bowes, 1961, pp. 28–48.

Hatzfeld, Helmut. *Trends and Styles in Twentieth Century French Literature.* Washington, D.C.: Catholic University of America Press, 1957, pp. 30–31.

Kaiser, Grant. "Roger Martin du Gard's *Jean Barois*, an Experiment in Novelistic Form," in *Symposium.* XIV (Summer, 1960), pp. 135–141.

Peyre, Henri. *The Contemporary French Novel.* New York: Oxford University Press, 1955, pp. 38–44.

Roudiez, Leon S. "The Function of Irony in Roger Martin du Gard," in *Romanic Review.* XLVIII (December, 1957), pp. 277–280.

Savage, Catharine. *Roger Martin du Gard.* New York: Twayne, 1968, pp. 41–64.

Schalk, David L. *Roger Martin du Gard: The Novelist and History.* Ithaca, N.Y.: Cornell University Press, 1967, pp. 34–55.

Weber, Eugen. "The Secret World of *Jean Barois*," in *The Origins of Modern Consciousness.* Edited by John Weiss. Detroit: Wayne State University Press, 1965, pp. 79–109.

Wood, John S. "Roger Martin du Gard," in *French Studies.* XIV (April, 1960), pp. 130–133.

The Postman

Boak, Denis. *Roger Martin du Gard.* Oxford: Clarendon Press, 1963, pp. 106–124.

Gibson, Robert. *Roger Martin du Gard.* London: Bowes and Bowes, 1961, pp. 99–108.

Savage, Catharine. *Roger Martin du Gard.* New York: Twayne, 1968, pp. 152–158.

Schalk, David L. *Roger Martin du Gard: The Novelist and History.* Ithaca, N.Y.: Cornell University Press, 1967, pp. 191–198.

Williams, E.F. "Roger Martin du Gard," in *Contemporary Review.* CXCIV (December, 1958), pp. 329–331.

The World of the Thibaults

Boak, Denis. *Roger Martin du Gard.* Oxford: Clarendon Press, 1963, pp. 57–105.

Bree, Germaine. "Roger Martin du Gard: The Corneille of the Bourgeois," in her *Age of Fiction: French Novel from Gide to Camus.* New Brunswick, N.J.: Rutgers University Press, 1975, pp. 79–84.

Cowley, Malcolm. "Roger Martin du Gard: The Next to Longest Novelist," in his *Think Back on Us.* Carbondale: Southern Illinois University Press, 1967, pp. 364–368.

Gibson, Robert. *Roger Martin du Gard.* London: Bowes and Bowes, 1961, pp. 49–88.

Gilbert, J. "Symbols of Continuity and the Unity of *Les Thibaults*," in *Image and Theme.* Edited by W.M. Frohock. Cambridge, Mass.: Harvard University Press, 1969, pp. 124–148.

Guerard, Albert. "The Leading French Novelists of the Present Moment," in *College English.* XII (April, 1951), p. 365.

Hall, Thomas White. "A Note on the So-Called Change in Technique in *Les Thibault* of Roger Martin du Gard," in *French Review.* XXVII (December, 1953), pp. 108–113.

Hatzfeld, Helmut. *Trends and Styles in Twentieth Century French Literature.* Washington, D.C.: Catholic University of America Press, 1957, pp. 28–30.

Howe, Irving. "Martin du Gard: The Novelty of Goodness," in *Decline of the New.* New York: Harcourt, 1970, pp. 43–53.

Moore-Renvolucri, Mina J. "*Les Thibault* and Their Creator," in *Modern Languages.* XXXIII (September, 1952), pp. 85–89.

O'Brien, J. "Martin du Gard: *The World of the Thibaults*," in his *The French Literary Horizon.* New Brunswick, N.J.: Rutgers University Press, 1967, pp. 245–250.

Peyre, Henri. *The Contemporary French Novel.* New York: Oxford University Press, 1955, pp. 38–44.

Roudiez, Leon S. "The Function of Irony in Roger Martin du Gard," in *Romanic Review.* XLVIII (December, 1957), pp. 280–284.

Savage, Catharine. *Roger Martin du Gard.* New York: Twayne, 1968, pp. 65–74.

Schalk, David L.   *Roger Martin du Gard: The Novelist and History.* Ithaca, N.Y.: Cornell University Press, 1967, pp. 83–86, 112–117, 160–162.

Spurdle, S.M.   "Roger Martin du Gard's Debt to Ibsen in *L'une de Nous* and *Les Thibault*," in *Modern Language Review.* LXV (January, 1970), pp. 54–64.

————.   "Tolstoy and Martin du Gard's *Les Thibault*," in *Contemporary Literature.* XXIII (Fall, 1971), pp. 325–345.

Wood, John S.   "Roger Martin du Gard," in *French Studies.* XIV (April, 1960), pp. 134–140.

ANDREW MARVELL
(1621–1678)

"The Bermudas"

Berthoff, Ann E. *The Resolved Soul: A Study of Marvell's Major Poems.* Princeton, N.J.: Princeton University Press, 1970, pp. 52–54.

Colie, Rosalie L. "Marvell's 'Bermudas' and the Puritan Paradise," in *Renaissance News.* X (1957), pp. 75–79.

Cummings, R.M. "The Difficulty of Marvell's 'Bermudas,' " in *Modern Philology.* LXVII (May, 1970), pp. 331–340.

Fizdale, Tay. "Irony in Marvell's 'Bermudas,' " in *Journal of English Literary History.* XLII (1975), pp. 203–213.

Hartwig, Joan. "Double Time in Andrew Marvell's 'Bermudas,' " in *Renaissance Papers.* (1974), pp. 51–59.

Hyman, Lawrence W. *Andrew Marvell.* New York: Twayne, 1964, pp. 39–41.

Kawasaki, Toshihiko. "Marvell's 'Bermudas': A Little World or a New World?," in *Journal of English Literary History.* XLIII (1976), pp. 38–52.

Leishman, J.B. *The Art of Marvell's Poetry.* London: Hutchinson's, 1966, pp. 278–282.

Toliver, Harold E. *Marvell's Ironic Vision.* New Haven, Conn.: Yale University Press, 1965, pp. 101–103.

Wilding, Michael. " 'Apples' in Marvell's 'Bermudas,' " in *English Language Notes.* VI (1969), pp. 254–257.

"The Garden"

Berthoff, Ann E. *The Resolved Soul: A Study of Marvell's Major Poems.* Princeton, N.J.: Princeton University Press, 1970, pp. 145–162.

Bradbrook, M.C. and M.G. Floyd Thomas. "Marvell and the Concept of Metamorphosis," in *Criterion.* XVIII (January, 1939), pp. 236–244.

Carpenter, Margaret Ann. "Marvell's 'Garden,' " in *Studies in English Literature.* X (Winter, 1970), pp. 155–169.

Colie, Rosalie L. *"My Echoing Song": Andrew Marvell's Poetry of Criticism.* Princeton, N.J.: Princeton University Press, 1970, pp. 141–177.

Daniels, Earl. *The Art of Reading Poetry.* New York: Farrar and Rinehart, 1941, pp. 261–264.

Douglas, Wallace, Roy Lamson and Hallett Smith. *The Critical Reader.* New York: Norton, 1949, pp. 68–72.

Empson, William. *Some Versions of the Pastoral.* London: Chatto and Windus, 1935, pp. 119–120, 123–128, 130–132. Reprinted in *The Garden.* Edited by Thomas O. Calhoun and John M. Potter. Columbus, Oh.: Merrill, 1970, pp. 18–23.

Friedman, Donald M. *Marvell's Pastoral Art.* Berkeley: University of California Press, 1970, pp. 149–175.

Godshalk, William Leigh. "Marvell's 'Garden' and the Theologians," in *Studies in Philology.* LXVI (July, 1969), pp. 639–653.

Hecht, Anthony. "Shades of Keats and Marvell," in *Hudson Review.* XV (Spring, 1962), pp. 50–71.

Hyman, Lawrence W. *Andrew Marvell.* New York: Twayne, 1964, pp. 63–72.

Kermode, Frank. "The Argument of Marvell's 'Garden,' " in *Essays in Criticism.* II (July, 1952), pp. 225–241. Reprinted in *The Garden.* Edited by Thomas O. Calhoun and John M. Potter. Columbus, Oh.: Merrill, 1970, pp. 52–66.

Klonsky, Milton. "A Guide Through the Garden," in *Sewanee Review.* LVIII (Winter, 1950), pp. 16–35. Reprinted in *The Garden.* Edited by Thomas O. Calhoun and John M. Potter. Columbus, Oh.: Merrill, 1970, pp. 41–50.

Legouis, Pierre. "Marvell and the New Critics," in *Review of English Studies.* VIII (November, 1957), pp. 382–389. Reprinted in *The Garden.* Edited by Thomas O. Calhoun and John M. Potter. Columbus, Oh.: Merrill, 1970, pp. 68–74.

Leishman, J.B. *The Art of Marvell's Poetry.* London: Hutchinson's, 1966, pp. 292–318. Reprinted in *The Garden.* Edited by Thomas O. Calhoun and John M. Potter. Columbus, Oh.: Merrill, 1970, pp. 118–132.

Rostvig, Maren-Sofie. "Andrew Marvell's 'The Garden': A Hermetic Poem," in *English Studies.* XL (April, 1959), pp. 65–77. Reprinted in *The Garden.* Edited by Thomas O. Calhoun and John M. Potter. Columbus, Oh.: Merrill, 1970, pp. 75–90.

Salerno, Nicholas A. "Andrew Marvell and the *Furor Hortensis*," in *Studies in English Literature.* VIII (Winter, 1968), pp. 103–120.

Stewart, Stanley N. *The Enclosed Garden.* Madison: University of Wisconsin Press, 1966, pp. 152–171, 176–181. Reprinted in *The Garden.* Edited by Thomas O. Calhoun and John M. Potter. Columbus, Oh.: Merrill, 1970, pp. 92–116.

Toliver, Harold E. *Marvell's Ironic Vision.* New Haven, Conn.: Yale University Press, 1965, pp. 138–151.

Unger, Leonard. *The Man in the Name: Essays on the Experience of Poetry.* Minneapolis: University of Minnesota Press, 1956, pp. 126–128.

Van Doren, Mark. *Introduction to Poetry.* New York: William Sloane, 1951, pp. 61–65.

Wallerstein, Ruth. *Studies in Seventeenth-Century Poetic.* Madison: University of Wisconsin Press, 1950, pp. 318–335. Reprinted in *The Garden.* Edited by Thomas O. Calhoun and John M. Potter. Columbus, Oh.: Merrill, 1970, pp. 25–39.

Williamson, George. "The Context of Marvell's 'Hortus' and 'Garden,' " in *Modern Language Notes.* LXXVI (November, 1961), pp. 590–598.

"An Horatian Ode upon Cromwell's Return from Ireland"

Berthoff, Ann E. *The Resolved Soul: A Study of Marvell's Major Poems.* Princeton, N.J.: Princeton University Press, 1970, pp. 60–64.

Brooks, Cleanth. "Criticism and Literary History: Marvell's 'Horatian Ode,' " in *Sewanee Review.* LV (April–June, 1947), pp. 199–222.

Brooks, Cleanth and Robert Penn Warren. *Understanding Poetry.* New York: Holt, 1950, pp. 667–682.

Bush, Douglas. "Marvell's 'Horatian Ode,' " in *Sewanee Review.* LX (1952), pp. 363–376.

Carens, James F. "Andrew Marvell's Cromwell Poems," in *Bucknell Review.* VII (1957), pp. 41–70.

Coolidge, John S. "Marvell and Horace," in *Modern Philology.* LXIII (November, 1965), pp. 111–120. Reprinted in *Andrew Marvell: A Collection of Critical Essays.* Edited by George DeF. Lord. Englewood Cliffs, N.J.: Prentice-Hall, 1968, pp. 85–100.

Friedman, Donald M. *Marvell's Pastoral Art.* Berkeley: University of California Press, 1970, pp. 253–274.

Hyman, Lawrence W. *Andrew Marvell.* New York: Twayne, 1964, pp. 76–82.

Lerner, L.D. "Marvell: 'An Horatian Ode,' " in *Interpretations: Essays on Twelve English Poems.* Edited by John Wain. London: Routledge and Kegan Paul, 1972, pp. 59–74.

Mazzeo, Joseph A. "Cromwell as Machiavellian Prince in Marvell's 'An Horatian Ode,' " in *Journal of the History of Ideas.* XXI (1960), pp. 1–17.

Nevo, Ruth. *The Dial of Virtue: A Study of Poems on Affairs of State in the Seventeenth Century.* Princeton, N.J.: Princeton University Press, 1967, pp. 97–109.

Syfret, R.H. "Marvell's 'Horatian Ode,' " in *Review of English Studies.* XII (1961), pp. 160–172.

Toliver, Harold E. *Marvell's Ironic Vision.* New Haven, Conn.: Yale University Press, 1965, pp. 183–191.

Wallace, John M. *Destiny His Choice: The Loyalism of Andrew Marvell.* Cambridge: Cambridge University Press, 1968, pp. 69–105.

———. "Marvell's 'Horation Ode,' " in *PMLA.* LXXVII (1962), pp. 33–45.

Wilson, A.J.N. "Andrew Marvell: 'An Horation Ode upon Cromwell's Return from Ireland': The Thread of the Poem and Its Use of Classical Allusion," in *Critical Quarterly.* XI (1969), pp. 325–341.

The Poetry of Marvell

Beer, Patricia. *An Introduction to the Metaphysical Poets.* London: Macmillan, 1972, pp. 85–98.

Bennett, Joan. *Five Metaphysical Poets.* London: Cambridge University Press, 1964, pp. 109–133.

Berthoff, Ann E. *The Resolved Soul: A Study of Marvell's Major Poems.* Princeton, N.J.: Princeton University Press, 1970.

Bradbrook, F.W. "The Poetry of Andrew Marvell," in *From Donne to Marvell.* Edited by Boris Ford. London: Penguin, 1956, pp. 193–204.

Bradbrook, M.C. and M.G. Lloyd Thomas. *Andrew Marvell.* London: Cambridge University Press, 1961.

Cullen, Patrick. *Spenser, Marvell, and Renaissance Pastoral.* Cambridge, Mass.: Harvard University Press, 1970, pp. 151–202.

Davison, Dennis. *The Poetry of Andrew Marvell.* London: E. Arnold, 1964.

Eliot, T.S. "Andrew Marvell," in his *Selected Essays.* New York: Harcourt, Brace, 1950, pp. 251–263. Reprinted in *Andrew Marvell: A Collection of Critical Essays.* Edited by George DeF. Lord. Englewood Cliffs, N.J.: Prentice-Hall, 1968, pp. 18–28.

Hyman, Lawrence W. *Andrew Marvell.* New York: Twayne, 1964.

Lord, George DeF. "From Contemplation to Action: Marvell's Poetical Career," in *Philological Quarterly.* XLVI (April, 1967), pp. 207–224. Reprinted in *Andrew Marvell: A Collection of Critical Essays.* Edited by George DeF. Lord. Englewood Cliffs, N.J.: Prentice-Hall, 1968, pp. 55–73.

Press, John. *Andrew Marvell.* London: Longmans, Green, 1958.

Toliver, Harold E. *Marvell's Ironic Vision.* New Haven, Conn.: Yale University Press, 1965.

"To His Coy Mistress"

Baumann, Michael. "Marvell's 'To His Coy Mistress,' " in *Explicator.* XXI (1973), item 72.

Berthoff, Ann E. *The Resolved Soul: A Study of Marvell's Major Poems.* Princeton, N.J.: Princeton University Press, 1970, pp. 110–114.

Brooks, Cleanth, John Thibaut Purser and Robert Penn Warren. *An Approach to Literature.* New York: Crofts, 1952, pp. 393–395.

Carroll, John J. "The Sun and the Lovers in 'To His Coy Mistress,' " in *Modern Language Notes.* LXXIV (January, 1959), pp. 4–7.

Colie, Rosalie L. *"My Echoing Song": Andrew Marvell's Poetry of Criticism.* Princeton, N.J.: Princeton University Press, 1970, pp. 59–61.

Friedman, Donald M. *Marvell's Pastoral Art.* Berkeley: University of California Press, 1970, pp. 183–187.

Gwynn, Frederick L.   "Marvell's 'To His Coy Mistress,' " in *Explicator*. XI (1953), item 7.

Hartwig, Joan.   "The Principle of Measure in 'To His Coy Mistress,' " in *College English*. XXV (1964), pp. 572–575.

Hogan, Patrick G., Jr.   "Marvell's 'Vegetable Love,' " in *Studies in Philology*. LX (January, 1963), pp. 1–11.

Hyman, Lawrence W.   *Andrew Marvell*. New York: Twayne, 1964, pp. 59–63.

King, Bruce.   "Irony in Marvell's 'To His Coy Mistress,' " in *Southern Review*. V (1969), pp. 689–703.

Leishman, J.B.   *The Art of Marvell's Poetry*. London: Hutchinson's, 1966, pp. 70–78.

Ransom, John Crowe.   *The New Criticism*. Norfolk, Conn.: New Directions, 1941, pp. 311–313.

Sedelow, Walter A., Jr.   "Marvell's 'To His Coy Mistress,' " in *Modern Language Notes*. LXXI (1956), pp. 6–8.

Toliver, Harold E.   *Marvell's Ironic Vision*. New Haven, Conn.: Yale University Press, 1965, pp. 154–162.

Wheelwright, Philip.   *The Burning Fountain: A Study in the Language of Symbolism*. Bloomington: Indiana University Press, 1954, pp. 112–113.

JOHN MASEFIELD
(1878–1967)

The Poetry of Masefield

Aiken, Conrad P. "Narrative Poetry and the Vestigial Lyric," in *Scepticisms.* New York: Knopf, 1933, pp. 170–177.

Berkelman, R.G. "Chaucer and Masefield," in *English Journal.* XVI (November, 1927), pp. 698–705.

Bush, Douglas. "From the Nineties to the Present," in *Mythology and the Romantic Tradition in English Poetry.* Cambridge, Mass.: Harvard University Press, 1937, pp. 457–480.

Cunliffe, John William. "Masefield and the New Georgian Poets," in *English Literature in the Twentieth Century.* New York: Macmillan, 1933, pp. 292–334.

Davidson, Donald. "John Masefield," in *The Spy Glass.* Nashville, Tenn.: Vanderbilt University Press, 1963, pp. 99–102.

Davison, E. "Poetry of John Masefield," in *English Journal.* XV (January, 1926), pp. 5–13.

Deutsch, Babette. "Farewell, Romance," in *Poetry in Our Time.* New York: Doubleday, 1963, pp. 31–58.

Drew, F.B. "Masefield's *Dauber*: Autobiography or Sailor's Tale Retold," in *Modern Language Notes.* LXXII (February, 1957), pp. 99–101.

Du Bois, A.E. "Cult of Beauty: A Study of John Masefield," in *PMLA.* XLV (December, 1930), pp. 1218–1257.

Duffin, H.C. "New Laureate: A Lyric Poet," in *Cornhill Magazine.* LXIX (July, 1930), pp. 1–9.

Fairchild, Hoxie Neale. "Realists," in *Religious Trends in English Poetry, Volume 5.* Irvington, N.Y.: Columbia University Press, 1962, pp. 222–253.

Highet, Gilbert. "Poetry and Romance: John Masefield," in his *People, Place, and Books.* New York: Oxford University Press, 1949, pp. 45–52.

Hopkins, Kenneth. "John Masefield," in his *Poets Laureate.* New York: Library Publications, 1955, pp. 185–191.

Hutchinson, R.E. "John Masefield and His Work," in *World Review.* IV (February 21, 1927), pp. 38–39.

Lamont, C. "Remembering John Masefield," in *Literary Review.* XIII (Summer, 1970), pp. 420–455.

Mims, Edwin. "Contemporary Poets: John Masefield," in his *Christ of the Poets.* Nashville, Tenn.: Abingdon Press, 1948, pp. 217–219.

Raven, A.A.   "Study in Masefield's Vocabulary," in *Modern Language Notes*. XXXVII (March, 1922), pp. 148–153.

Schelling, Felix E.   "Mr. Masefield and the Key Poetic," in his *Appraisements and Asperities*. New York: Lippincott, 1922, pp. 85–90.

Shanks, Edward B.   "Mr. Masefield: Some Characteristics," in his *First Essays on Literature*. Cleveland, Oh.: Collins, 1927, pp. 104–124.

Spanos, William V.   "The Nativity: The Humanization of the Morality," in *The Christian Tradition in Modern British Verse Drama*. New Brunswick, N.J.: Rutgers University Press, 1967, pp. 135–183.

Stevenson, L.   "Masefield and the New Universe," in *Sewanee Review*. XXXVII (July, 1929), pp. 336–348.

Swinnerton, F.A.   "Pre-War Poets," in his *Georgian Scene*. New York: Farrar, 1934, pp. 253–277.

Weals, Gerald C.   "Laurence Housman and John Masefield," in his *Religion in Modern English Drama*. Philadelphia: University of Pennsylvania Press, 1961, pp. 122–141.

Woody, L.   "Masefield's Use of Dipodic Meter," in *Philological Quarterly*. X (July, 1931), pp. 277–293.

PHILIP MASSINGER
(1583–1640)

The Bondman

Boas, Frederick S. *An Introduction to Stuart Drama*. London: Oxford University Press, 1946, pp. 311–314.

Dunn, T.A. *Philip Massinger: The Man and the Playwright*. London: Thomas Nelson, 1957, pp. 164–165.

Edwards, Philip. "Massinger the Censor," in *Essays on Shakespeare and Elizabethan Drama in Honor of Hardin Craig*. Edited by Richard Hosley. Columbia: University of Missouri Press, 1962, pp. 346–348.

————. "The Sources of Massinger's *The Bondman*," in *Review of English Studies*. XV (February, 1964), pp. 21–26.

Gross, Allen. "Contemporary Politics in Massinger," in *Studies in English Literature, 1500–1900*. VI (1966), pp. 279–290.

Spencer, Benjamin Townley. "Introduction," in *The Bondman*. By Philip Massinger. Princeton, N.J.: Princeton University Press, 1932, pp. 1–74.

The Maid of Honour

Boas, Frederick S. *An Introduction to Stuart Drama*. London: Oxford University Press, 1946, pp. 308–311.

Dunn, T.A. *Philip Massinger: The Man and the Playwright*. London: Thomas Nelson, 1957, pp. 179–184.

Edwards, Philip. "Massinger the Censor," in *Essays on Shakespeare and Elizabethan Drama in Honor of Hardin Craig*. Edited by Richard Hosley. Columbia: University of Missouri Press, 1962, pp. 344–346.

Gross, Allen. "Contemporary Politics in Massinger," in *Studies in English Literature, 1500–1900*. VI (1966), pp. 279–290.

Mullany, Peter F. "Religion in Massinger's *The Maid of Honour*," in *Renaissance Drama*. (1969), pp. 143–156.

A New Way to Pay Old Debts

Ball, Robert H. "Sir Giles Mompesson and Sir Giles Overreach," in *Essays in Dramatic Literature: The Parrott Presentation Volume*. Edited by Hardin Craig. Princeton, N.J.: Princeton University Press, 1935, pp. 277–287.

Boas, Frederick S. *An Introduction to Stuart Drama*. London: Oxford University Press, 1946, pp. 328–330.

Bowers, R.H. "A Note on Massinger's *New Way*," in *Modern Language Review*. LIII (1958), pp. 214–215.

Burelbach, Frederick M., Jr.   "*A New Way to Pay Old Debts*: Jacobean Morality," in *College Language Association Journal*. XII (1969), pp. 205–213.

Byrne, M. St. Clare.   "Introduction," in *A New Way to Pay Old Debts*. By Philip Massinger. Westport, Conn.: Greenwood Press, 1976, pp. 5–16.

Cunningham, John E.   *Elizabethan and Early Stuart Drama*. London: Evans, 1965, pp. 103–107.

Dunn, T.A.   *Philip Massinger: The Man and the Playwright*. London: Thomas Nelson, 1957, pp. 58–61, 122–125, 252–255.

Enright, D.J.   "Poetic Satire and Satire in Verse: A Consideration of Jonson and Massinger," in *Scrutiny*. XVIII (Winter, 1952), pp. 219–223.

Fothergill, Robert A.   "The Dramatic Experience of Massinger's *The City Madam* and *A New Way to Pay Old Debts*," in *University of Toronto Quarterly*. XLIII (1973), pp. 68–86.

Gross, Alan Gerald.   "Social Change and Philip Massinger," in *Studies in English Literature, 1500–1900*. VII (1967), pp. 329–342.

Knights, L.C.   *Drama and Society in the Age of Jonson*. London: Chatto and Windus, 1962, pp. 273–280.

Levin, Richard.   *The Multiple Plot in English Renaissance Drama*. Chicago: University of Chicago Press, 1971, pp. 134–136.

Reed, Robert Rentoul, Jr.   *Bedlam on the Jacobean Stage*. Cambridge, Mass.: Harvard University Press, 1952, pp. 61–63.

Thomson, Patricia.   "The Old Way and the New Way in Dekker and Massinger," in *Modern Language Review*. LI (1956), pp. 168–178.

The Roman Actor

Boas, Frederick S.   *An Introduction to Stuart Drama*. London: Oxford University Press, 1946, pp. 317–319.

Crabtree, John Henry, Jr.   "Philip Massinger's Use of Rhetoric in *The Roman Actor*," in *Furman Studies*. VII (1960), pp. 40–58.

Dunn, T.A.   *Philip Massinger: The Man and the Playwright*. London: Thomas Nelson, 1957, pp. 65–69, 113–114, 142–143, 167–169.

Gurr, Andrew.   *The Shakespearean Stage, 1574–1642*. Cambridge: University Press, 1970, pp. 17–18.

Hogan, A.P.   "Imagery of Acting, in *The Roman Actor*," in *Modern Language Review*. LXVI (1971), pp. 273–281.

EDGAR LEE MASTERS
(1869–1950)

Spoon River Anthology

Burgess, Charles E. "Edgar Lee Masters: The Lawyer as Writer," in *The Vision of This Land: Studies of Vachel Lindsay, Edgar Lee Masters, and Carl Sandburg.* Edited by John E. Hallwas and Dennis J. Reader. Macomb: Western Illinois University Press, 1976, pp. 55–73.

Crawford, John W. "A Defense of 'A One-Eyed View,' " in *The CEA Critic.* XXXI (February, 1969), pp. 14–15.

————. "Naturalistic Tendencies in *Spoon River Anthology,*" in *The CEA Critic.* XXX (June, 1968), pp. 6–8.

Earnest, Ernest. "A One-Eyed View of Spoon River," in *The CEA Critic.* XXXI (November, 1968), pp. 8–9.

————. "Spoon River Revisited," in *Western Humanities Review.* XXI (1967), pp. 59–65.

Flanagan, John T. *Edgar Lee Masters: The Spoon River Poet and His Critics.* Metuchen, N.J.: Scarecrow, 1974.

————. "The Spoon River Poet," in *Southwest Review.* XXXVIII (1953), pp. 226–237.

Gregory, Horace and Marya Zaturenska. *A History of American Poetry, 1900–1940.* New York: Harcourt, Brace, 1946, pp. 226–232.

Hallwas, John E. "Masters and the Pioneers: Four Epitaphs from *Spoon River Anthology,*" in *The Old Northwest.* II (1976), pp. 389–399.

————. "Two Autobiographical Epitaphs in *Spoon River Anthology,*" in *Great Lakes Review: A Journal of Midwest Culture.* III (1976), pp. 28–36.

Hartley, Lois. *Spoon River Revisited.* Muncie, Ind.: Ball State Teachers College, 1963.

Kreymborg, Alfred. *Our Singing Strength: An Outline of American Poetry (1620–1930).* New York: Coward-McCann, 1929, pp. 379–384.

Laning, Edward. "Spoon River Revisited," in *American Heritage.* XXII (1971), pp. 14–17, 104–107.

Lohf, Kenneth A. "Spoon River and After," in *Columbia Library Columns.* XIV (February, 1965), pp. 5–10.

Putzel, Max. *The Man in the Mirror: William Marion Reedy and His Magazine.* Cambridge, Mass.: Harvard University Press, 1963, pp. 193–216.

Waggoner, Hyatt H. *American Poets from the Puritans to the Present.* Boston: Houghton Mifflin, 1968, pp. 449–450.

Weirick, Bruce. *From Whitman to Sandburg in American Poetry: A Critical Survey.* New York: Macmillan, 1924, pp. 195–198.

Wells, Henry W. "Varieties of American Poetic Drama," in *Literary Half-Yearly.* XIV (1973), pp. 14–46.

Williams, Ellen. *Harriet Monroe and the Poetry Renaissance: The First Ten Years of Poetry, 1912–22.* Urbana: University of Illinois Press, 1977, pp. 111–117, 151–152.

Wood, Clement. *Poets of America.* New York: Dutton, 1925, pp. 165–176.

Yatron, Michael. *America's Literary Revolt.* New York: Philosophical Library, 1959, pp. 48–54, 68–70.

W. SOMERSET MAUGHAM
(1874–1965)

Cakes and Ale

Allen, Walter. "Summing Up Somerset Maugham at 90," in *New York Times Book Review*. (January 19, 1964), pp. 1–24.

Altman, W. "Somerset Maugham: An Appreciation," in *Contemporary Review*. CCVIII (February, 1966), pp. 99–104.

Amis, Kingsley. "Mr. Maugham's Notions," in *Spectator*. CCVII (July 7, 1961), pp. 23–24.

Barnes, Ronald E. *The Dramatic Comedy of William Somerset Maugham*. The Hague: Mouton, 1968.

Brander, Laurence. *Somerset Maugham: A Guide*. Edinburgh: Oliver and Boyd, 1963.

Brown, Allen B. "Substance and Shadow: The Originals of the Characters in *Cakes and Ale*," in *Papers of Michigan Academy of Science, Arts, and Letters*. XLV (1960), pp. 444–456.

Brown, Ivor. *W. Somerset Maugham*. London: International Profiles, 1970.

Calder, Robert L. *W. Somerset Maugham and the Quest for Freedom*. London: Heinemann, 1972.

Cordell, Richard A. *Somerset Maugham, A Writer for All Seasons: A Biography and Critical Study*. Bloomington: Indiana University Press, 1969.

Curtis, Anthony. *The Patterns of Maugham: A Critical Portrait*. London: Hamish Hamilton, 1974.

Jensen, Sven A. *William Somerset Maugham: Some Aspects of the Man and His Work*. Oslo, Norway: Oslo University Press, 1957.

Jonas, Klaus W., Editor. *The Maugham Enigma*. New York: Citadel Press, 1954.

————, **Editor.** *The World of Somerset Maugham*. New York: British Book Centre, 1959.

Kanin, Garson. *Remember Mr. Maugham*. New York: Atheneum, 1966.

MacCarthy, Desmond. "William Somerset Maugham: The English Maupassant, An Appreciation," in his *Memories*. London: MacGibbon and Kees, 1953, pp. 61–68.

McIver, Claude S. *William Somerset Maugham: A Study of Techniques and Literary Sources*. Upper Darby, Pa.: The Author, 1936.

Maugham, Robin. *Somerset and All the Maughams*. Westport, Conn.: Greenwood Press, 1977. Reprint of 1966 Edition.

Menard, Wilmon. *The Two Worlds of Somerset Maugham.* Los Angeles: Sherbourne Press, 1965.

Naik, M.K. *William Somerset Maugham.* Norman: University of Oklahoma Press, 1966.

Pfeiffer, Karl G. *William Somerset Maugham: A Candid Portrait.* New York: Norton, 1959.

Raphael, Frederic. *William Somerset Maugham and His World.* New York: Scribner's, 1977.

Sanders, Charles. *W. Somerset Maugham: An Annotated Bibliography of Writings About Him.* DeKalb: Northern Illinois University Press, 1970.

Toole-Stott, Raymond. *A Bibliography of the Works of W. Somerset Maugham.* Revised Edition. London: Kaye and Ward, 1973.

Towne, Charles Hanson. *W. Somerset Maugham, Essayist, Dramatist, Novelist.* Folcroft, Pa.: Folcroft Library Editions, 1976. Reprint of 1925 Edition.

Zabel, Morton D. "A Cool Hand," in *Nation.* CLII (May 3, 1941), pp. 534–536.

Liza of Lambeth

Allen, Walter. "Summing Up Somerset Maugham at 90," in *New York Times Book Review.* (January 19, 1964), pp. 1–24.

Altman, W. "Somerset Maugham: An Appreciation," in *Contemporary Review.* CCVIII (February, 1966), pp. 99–104.

Amis, Kingsley. "Mr. Maugham's Notions," in *Spectator.* CVIII (July 7, 1961), pp. 23–24.

Barnes, Ronald E. *The Dramatic Comedy of William Somerset Maugham.* The Hague: Mouton, 1968.

Brander, Laurence. *Somerset Maugham: A Guide.* Edinburgh: Oliver and Boyd, 1963.

Brown, Ivor. *W. Somerset Maugham.* London: International Profiles, 1970.

Calder, Robert L. *W. Somerset Maugham and the Quest for Freedom.* London: Heinemann, 1972.

Colburn, William E. "Dr. Maugham's Prescription for Success," in *Emory University Quarterly.* IX (Spring, 1963), pp. 14–21.

Cordell, Richard A. *Somerset Maugham, A Writer for All Seasons: A Biographical and Critical Study.* Bloomington: Indiana University Press, 1969.

Curtis, Anthony. *The Pattern of Maugham: A Critical Portrait.* London: Hamish Hamilton, 1974.

Jensen, Sven A. *William Somerset Maugham: Some Aspects of the Man and His Work.* Oslo, Norway: Oslo University Press, 1957.

Jonas, Klaus W., Editor. *The Maugham Enigma.* New York: Citadel Press, 1954.

————, **Editor.** *The World of Somerset Maugham.* New York: British Book Centre, 1959.

Kanin, Garson. *Remembering Mr. Maugham.* New York: Atheneum, 1966.

Krim, Seymour. "Somerset Maugham," in *Commonweal.* LXI (December 3, 1954), pp. 245–250.

"Liza's Jubilee," in *Times Literary Supplement* (London). (January 24, 1948), p. 52.

MacCarthy, Desmond. "William Somerset Maugham: The English Maupassant, An Appreciation," in his *Memories.* London: MacGibbon and Kees, 1953, pp. 61–68.

Maugham, Robin. *Somerset and All the Maughams.* Westport, Conn.: Greenwood Press, 1977. Reprint of 1966 Edition.

Menard, Wilmon. *The Two Worlds of Somerset Maugham.* Los Angeles: Sherbourne Press, 1965.

Naik, M.K. *William Somerset Maugham.* Norman: University of Oklahoma Press, 1966.

Pfeiffer, Karl G. *William Somerset Maugham: A Candid Portrait.* New York: Norton, 1959.

Raphael, Frederic. *William Somerset Maugham and His World.* New York: Scribner's, 1977.

Sanders, Charles. *W. Somerset Maugham: An Annotated Bibliography of Writings About Him.* DeKalb: Northern Illinois University Press, 1970.

Toole-Stott, Raymond. *A Bibliography of the Works of W. Somerset Maugham.* London: Kaye and Ward, 1973.

Towne, Charles Hanson. *W. Somerset Maugham: Novelist, Essayist, Dramatist.* Folcroft, Pa.: Folcroft Library Editions, 1976. Reprint of 1925 Edition.

The Moon and Sixpence

Allen, Walter. "Summing Up Somerset Maugham at 90," in *New York Times Book Review.* (January 19, 1964), pp. 1–24.

Altman, W. "Somerset Maugham: An Appreciation," in *Contemporary Review.* CCVIII (February, 1966), pp. 99–104.

Amis, Kingsley. "Mr. Maugham's Notions," in *Spectator.* CCVII (July 7, 1961), pp. 23–24.

Barnes, Ronald E. *The Dramatic Comedy of William Somerset Maugham.* The Hague: Mouton, 1968.

Brander, Laurence. *Somerset Maugham: A Guide.* Edinburgh: Oliver and Boyd, 1963.

Brown, Ivor. *W. Somerset Maugham.* London: International Profiles, 1970.

Calder, Robert L. *W. Somerset Maugham and the Quest for Freedom.* London: Heinemann, 1972.

Cordell, Richard A. *Somerset Maugham, A Writer for All Seasons: A Biographical and Critical Study.* Bloomington: Indiana University Press, 1969.

Curtis, Anthony. *The Pattern of Maugham: A Critical Portrait.* London: Hamish Hamilton, 1974.

Jensen, Sven A. *William Somerset Maugham: Some Aspects of the Man and His Work.* Oslo, Norway: Oslo University Press, 1957.

Jonas, Klaus W., Editor. *The Maugham Enigma.* New York: Citadel Press, 1954.

———, **Editor.** *The World of Somerset Maugham.* New York: British Book Centre, 1959.

Kanin, Garson. *Remembering Mr. Maugham.* New York: Atheneum, 1966.

MacCarthy, Desmond. "William Somerset Maugham: The English Maupassant, An Appreciation," in his *Memories.* London: MacGibbon and Kees, 1953, pp. 61–68.

Maugham, Robin. *Somerset and All the Maughams.* Westport, Conn.: Greenwood Press, 1977. Reprint of 1966 Edition.

Menard, Wilmon. *The Two Worlds of Somerset Maugham.* Los Angeles: Sherbourne Press, 1965.

Naik, M.K. *William Somerset Maugham.* Norman: University of Oklahoma Press, 1966.

Pfeiffer, Karl G. *William Somerset Maugham: A Candid Portrait.* New York: Norton, 1959.

Raphael, Frederic. *William Somerset Maugham and His World.* New York: Scribner's, 1977.

Sanders, Charles. *W. Somerset Maugham: An Annotated Bibliography of Writings About Him.* DeKalb: Northern Illinois University Press, 1970.

Toole-Stott, Raymond. *A Bibliography of the Works of W. Somerset Maugham.* London: Kaye and Ward, 1973.

Towne, Charles Hanson. *W. Somerset Maugham: Novelist, Essayist, Dramatist.* Folcroft, Pa.: Folcroft Library Editions, 1976. Reprint of 1925 Edition.

Of Human Bondage

Allen, Walter. "Summing Up Somerset Maugham at 90," in *New York Times Book Review.* (January 19, 1964), pp. 1–24.

Altman, W. "Somerset Maugham: An Appreciation," in *Contemporary Review.* CCVIII (February, 1966), pp. 99–104.

Amis, Kingsley. "Mr. Maugham's Notions," in *Spectator*. CCVII (July 7, 1961), pp. 23–24.

Barnes, Ronald E. *The Dramatic Comedy of William Somerset Maugham.* The Hague: Mouton, 1968.

Brander, Laurence. *Somerset Maugham: A Guide.* Edinburgh: Oliver and Boyd, 1963.

Brewster, Dorothy. "Time Passes," in her *Adventure or Experience: Four Essays on Certain Writers and Readers of Novels.* New York: Columbia University Press, 1930, pp. 37–75.

Calder, Robert L. *W. Somerset Maugham and the Quest for Freedom.* London: Heinemann, 1972.

Cordell, Richard A. *Somerset Maugham, A Writer for All Seasons: A Biographical and Critical Study.* Bloomington: Indiana University Press, 1969.

Curtis, Anthony. *The Pattern of Maugham: A Critical Portrait.* London: Hamish Hamilton, 1974.

Dreiser, Theodore. "Introduction," in W. Somerset Maugham's *Of Human Bondage.* New Haven, Conn.: Yale University Press, 1938, pp. iii–xiv.

Gray, James. "Obituary for the Human Race," in his *On Second Thought.* Minneapolis: University of Minnesota Press, 1946, pp. 165–183.

Jonas, Klaus W., Editor. *The Maugham Enigma.* New York: Citadel Press, 1954.

————, **Editor.** *The World of Somerset Maugham.* New York: British Book Centre, 1959.

Kanin, Garson. *Remembering Mr. Maugham.* New York: Atheneum, 1966.

Kochan, Lionel. "Somerset Maugham," in *Contemporary Review.* CLXXVII (February, 1950), pp. 94–98.

MacCarthy, Desmond. "William Somerset Maugham: The English Maupassant, An Appreciation," in his *Memories.* London: MacGibbon and Kees, 1953, pp. 61–68.

Maugham, Robin. *Somerset and All the Maughams.* Westport, Conn.: Greenwood Press, 1977. Reprint of 1966 Edition.

Menard, Wilmon. *The Two Worlds of Somerset Maugham.* Los Angeles: Sherbourne Press, 1965.

Naik, M.K. *William Somerset Maugham.* Norman: University of Oklahoma Press, 1966.

O'Connor, William Van. "Two Types of Heroes in Postwar Fiction," in *PMLA.* LXXVII (March, 1962), pp. 168–174.

Pfeiffer, Karl G. *William Somerset Maugham: A Candid Portrait.* New York: Norton, 1959.

Raphael, Frederic. *William Somerset Maugham and His World.* New York: Scribner's, 1977.

Sanders, Charles. *W. Somerset Maugham: An Annotated Bibliography of Writings About Him.* DeKalb: Northern Illinois University Press, 1970.

Swinnerton, Frank. *The Georgian Literary Scene: A Panorama.* London: Heinemann, 1935, pp. 208–215.

Zabel, Morton D. "A Cool Hand," in *Nation.* CLII (May 3, 1941), pp. 534–536.

The Summing Up

Allen, Walter. "Summing Up Somerset Maugham at 90," in *New York Times Book Review.* (January 19, 1964), pp. 1–24.

Altman, W. "Somerset Maugham: An Appreciation," in *Contemporary Review.* CCVIII (February, 1966), pp. 99–104.

Amis, Kingsley. "Mr. Maugham's Notions," in *Spectator.* CCVII (July 7, 1961), pp. 23–24.

Barnes, Ronald E. *The Dramatic Comedy of William Somerset Maugham.* The Hague: Mouton, 1968.

Brander, Laurence. *Somerset Maugham: A Guide.* Edinburgh: Oliver and Boyd, 1963.

Brown, Ivor. *W. Somerset Maugham.* London: International Profiles, 1970.

Calder, Robert L. *W. Somerset Maugham and the Quest for Freedom.* London: Heinemann, 1972.

Cordell, Richard A. *Somerset Maugham, A Writer for All Seasons: A Biographical and Critical Study.* Bloomington: Indiana University Press, 1969.

Curtis, Anthony. *The Pattern of Maugham: A Critical Portrait.* London: Hamish Hamilton, 1974.

Jensen, Sven A. *William Somerset Maugham: Some Aspects of the Man and His Work.* Oslo, Norway: Oslo University Press, 1957.

Jonas, Klaus W., Editor. *The Maugham Enigma.* New York: Citadel Press, 1954.

————, **Editor.** *The World of Somerset Maugham.* New York: British Book Centre, 1959.

Kanin, Garson. *Remembering Mr. Maugham.* New York: Atheneum, 1966.

MacCarthy, Desmond. "William Somerset Maugham: The English Maupassant, An Appreciation," in his *Memories.* London: MacGibbon and Kees, 1953, pp. 61–68.

Maugham, Robin. *Somerset and All the Maughams.* Westport, Conn.: Greenwood Press, 1977. Reprint of 1966 Edition.

Menard, Wilmon. *The Two Worlds of Somerset Maugham.* Los Angeles: Sherbourne Press, 1965.

Naik, M.K. *William Somerset Maugham.* Norman: University of Oklahoma Press, 1966.

Pfeiffer, Karl G. *William Somerset Maugham: A Candid Portrait.* New York: Norton, 1959.

Raphael, Frederic. *William Somerset Maugham and His World.* New York: Scribner's, 1977.

Sanders, Charles. *W. Somerset Maugham: An Annotated Bibliography of Writings About Him.* DeKalb: Northern Illinois University Press, 1970.

Toole-Stott, Raymond. *A Bibliography of the Works of W. Somerset Maugham.* Revised Edition. London: Kaye and Ward, 1973.

Towne, Charles Hanson. *W. Somerset Maugham: Novelist, Essayist, Dramatist.* Folcroft, Pa.: Folcroft Library Editions, 1976. Reprint of 1925 Edition.

GUY DE MAUPASSANT
(1850–1893)

Bel-Ami

Artinian, Robert W. "Chacun son egout: A Metaphoric Structure in *Bel-Ami*," in *Nassau Review*. II (1973), pp. 15–20.

Boyd, Ernest. *Guy de Maupassant*. New York: Knopf, 1926, pp. 178–181.

Chaikin, Milton. "Maupassant's *Bel-Ami* and Balzac," in *Romance Notes*. II (Spring, 1960), pp. 109–112.

Grant, Richard B. "The Function of the First Chapter of Maupassant's *Bel-Ami*," in *Modern Language Notes*. LXXVI (December, 1961), pp. 748–752.

Ignotus, Paul. *The Paradox of Maupassant*. New York: Funk & Wagnalls, 1968, pp. 150–154.

Lerner, Michael G. *Maupassant*. London: Allen & Unwin, 1975, pp. 201–206.

Smith, Maxwell A. "Maupassant as a Novelist," in *Tennessee Studies in Literature*. I (1956), p. 44.

Steegmuller, Francis. *Maupassant: A Lion in the Path*. New York: Random House, 1949, pp. 211–220, 226–231.

Sullivan, Edward. *Maupassant the Novelist*. Princeton, N.J.: Princeton University Press, 1954, pp. 72–93.

Turnell, Martin. *The Art of French Fiction*. Norfolk, Conn.: New Directions, 1959, pp. 213–218.

Wallace, A.H. *Guy de Maupassant*. New York: Twayne, 1973, pp. 57–59.

Weisstein, Ulrich. "Maupassant's *Bel-Ami* and Heinrich Mann's *Im Schlaraffenland*," in *Romance Notes*. II (Spring, 1961), pp. 124–128.

Mont-Oriol

Boyd, Ernest. *Guy de Maupassant*. New York: Knopf, 1926, pp. 191–195.

Ignotus, Paul. *The Paradox of Maupassant*. New York: Funk & Wagnalls, 1968, pp. 190–193.

Lerner, Michael G. *Maupassant*. London: Allen & Unwin, 1975, pp. 221–223.

Saintsbury, George. *A History of the French Novel (To the Close of the 19th Century)*. London: Macmillan, 1919, pp. 490–491.

Smith, Maxwell A. "Maupassant as a Novelist," in *Tennessee Studies in Literature*. I (1956), pp. 44–45.

Steegmuller, Francis. *Maupassant: A Lion in the Park*. New York: Random House, 1949, pp. 229–237.

Sullivan, Edward D. *Maupassant the Novelist*. Princeton, N.J.: Princeton University Press, 1954, pp. 94–101.

Wallace, A.H.   *Guy de Maupassant*. New York: Twayne, 1973, pp. 54–56.

Pierre et Jean

Artinian, Robert W.   " 'Then, Venom, to Thy Work': Pathological Representation in *Pierre et Jean*," in *Modern Fiction Studies*. XVII (1972), pp. 225–229.

Freimanis, Dzintars.   "More on the Meaning of *Pierre et Jean*," in *French Review*. XXXVIII (1965), pp. 326–331.

Grant, Elliott M.   "On the Meaning of Maupassant's *Pierre et Jean*," in *French Review*. XXXVI (1963), pp. 469–473.

Hainsworth, G.   "Introduction," in *Pierre et Jean*. By Guy de Maupassant. London: Goerge G. Harrap, 1966, pp. 7–31.

Ignotus, Paul.   *The Paradox of Maupassant*. New York: Funk & Wagnalls, 1968, pp. 207–209.

Lerner, Michael G.   *Maupassant*. London: Allen & Unwin, 1975, pp. 235–238.

Niess, Robert J.   *"Pierre et Jean*: Some Symbols," in *French Review*. XXXII (1959), pp. 511–519.

Sachs, Murray.   "The Meaning of Maupassant's *Pierre et Jean*," in *French Review*. XXXIV (1961), pp. 244–250.

Saintsbury, George.   *A History of the French Novel (To the Close of the 19th Century)*. London: Macmillan, 1919, pp. 493–495.

Simon, Ernest.   "Descriptive and Analytical Techniques in Maupaussant's *Pierre et Jean*," in *Romanic Review*. LI (1960), pp. 45–52.

Smith, Maxwell A.   "Maupassant as a Novelist," in *Tennessee Studies in Literature*. I (1956), pp. 45–46.

Steegmuller, Francis.   *Maupassant: A Lion in the Path*. New York: Random House, 1949, pp. 260–271, 293–297.

Sullivan, Edward D.   *Maupassant the Novelist*. Princeton, N.J.: Princeton University Press, 1954, pp. 102–119.

Turnell, Martin.   *The Art of French Fiction*. Norfolk, Conn.: New Directions, 1959, pp. 218–220.

Wallace, A.H.   *Guy de Maupassant*. New York: Twayne, 1973, pp. 84–90.

A Woman's Life

Boyd, Ernest.   *Guy de Maupassant*. New York: Knopf, 1926, pp. 132–135.

Grant, Richard B.   "Imagery as a Means of Psychological Revelation in Maupassant's *Une Vie*," in *Studies in Philology*. LX (October, 1960), pp. 669–684.

Ignotus, Paul.   *The Paradox of Maupassant*. New York: Funk & Wagnalls, 1968, pp. 50–57, 161–162.

Jaloux, Edmond. "Introduction," in *A Woman's Life*. By Guy de Maupassant. London: Nonesuch Press, 1942, pp. ix–xiv.

Lerner, Michael G. *Maupassant*. London: Allen & Unwin, 1975, pp. 149–150, 166–170.

Pritchett, V.S. *Books in General*. London: Chatto and Windus, 1953, pp. 95–99.

Saintsbury, George. *A History of the French Novel (To the Close of the 19th Century)*. London: Macmillan, 1919, pp. 489–490.

Smith, Maxwell A. "Maupassant as a Novelist," in *Tennessee Studies in Literature*. I (1956), pp. 43–44.

Steegmuller, Francis. *Maupassant: A Lion in the Path*. New York: Random House, 1949, pp. 165–171.

Sullivan, Edward D. *Maupassant the Novelist*. Princeton, N.J.: Princeton University Press, 1954, pp. 57–71.

Turnell, Martin. *The Art of French Fiction*. Norfolk, Conn.: New Directions, 1959, pp. 210–213.

Wallace, A.H. *Guy de Maupassant*. New York: Twayne, 1973, pp. 59–63, 81–84.

CLAUDE MAURIAC
(1910–   )

The Dinner Party

Engler, Winfried. *The French Novel from Eighteen Hundred to the Present.* New York: Frederick Ungar, 1969, pp. 230–231.

Johnston, Stuart L. "Structure in the Novels of Claude Mauriac," in *French Review.* XXXVIII (February, 1965), pp. 452–455.

Mercier, Vivian. *The New Novel: From Queneau to Pinget.* New York: Farrar, Straus and Giroux, 1971, pp. 327–336.

Roudiez, Leon S. *French Fiction Today: A New Direction.* New Brunswick, N.J.: Rutgers University Press, 1972, pp. 136–138.

The Marquise Went Out at Five

Johnston, Stuart L. "Structure in the Novels of Claude Mauriac," in *French Review.* XXXVIII (February, 1965), pp. 453–457.

Mercier, Vivian. *The New Novel: From Queneau to Pinget.* New York: Farrar, Straus and Giroux, 1971, pp. 336–345.

Roudiez, Leon S. *French Fiction Today: A New Direction.* New Brunswick, N.J.: Rutgers University Press, 1972, pp. 138–147.

FRANÇOIS MAURIAC
(1885–1970)

The Desert of Love

Flower, J.E. *Intention and Achievement: An Essay on the Novels of François Mauriac.* Oxford: Clarendon Press, 1969, pp. 72–73, 100–101.

Fowlie, Wallace. "The Art of François Mauriac," in *A Mauriac Reader.* By François Mauriac. New York: Farrar, Straus and Giroux, 1968, pp. xii–xiii.

———. "Mauriac's Dark Hero," in *Sewanee Review.* LVI (Winter, 1948), pp. 51–55.

Humiliata, Sister Mary. "The Theme of Isolation in Mauriac's *The Desert of Love*," in *Twentieth Century Literature.* VII (October, 1961), pp. 107–112.

Iyengar, K.R. Sprinivasa. *François Mauriac.* New York: Asia Publishing House, 1963, pp. 32–35.

Jenkins, Cecil. *Mauriac.* New York: Barnes & Noble, 1965, pp. 66–73.

Jerome, Sister M. "Human and Divine Love in Dante and Mauriac," in *Renascence.* XVIII (Summer, 1966), pp. 178–179.

Paine, Ruth Benson. *Thematic Analysis of François Mauriac's* Genitrix, Le Desert de l'Amour, *and* Le noeud de viperes. University, Miss.: Romance Monographs, 1976, pp. 65–115.

Peyre, Henri. *The Contemporary French Novel.* New York: Oxford University Press, 1955, pp. 111–113.

———. *French Novelists of Today.* New York: Oxford University Press, 1967, pp. 110–111.

Reck, Rima Drell. *Literature and Responsibility: The French Novelist in the Twentieth Century.* Baton Rouge: Louisiana State University Press, 1969, pp. 183–184.

Rubin, Louis D., Jr. François Mauriac and the Freedom of the Religious Novelist," in *Southern Review.* II (January, 1966), p. 38.

Smith, Maxwell. *François Mauriac.* New York: Twayne, 1970, pp. 91–96.

Speaight, Robert. *François Mauriac: A Study of the Writer and the Man.* London: Chatto and Windus, 1976, pp. 82–86.

Turnell, Martin. *The Art of French Fiction.* Norfolk, Conn.: New Directions, 1959, pp. 322–329.

The Frontenacs

Flower, J.E. *Intention and Achievement: An Essay on the Novels of François Mauriac.* Oxford: Clarendon Press, 1969, pp. 80–94.

Iyengar, K.R. Sprinivasa. *François Mauriac.* New York: Asia Publishing House, 1963, pp. 77–81.

Jarrett-Kerr, Martin. *François Mauriac.* New Haven, Conn.: Yale University Press, 1954, pp. 58–60.

Jenkins, Cecil. *Mauriac.* New York: Barnes & Noble, 1965, pp. 87–90.

Smith, Maxwell. *François Mauriac.* New York: Twayne, 1970, pp. 61–65.

Speaight, Robert. *François Mauriac: A Study of the Writer and the Man.* London: Chatto and Windus, 1976, pp. 116–119.

Stratford, Philip. *Faith and Fiction.* Notre Dame, Ind.: University of Notre Dame Press, 1964, pp. 244–245.

Turnell, Martin. *The Art of French Fiction.* Norfolk, Conn.: New Directions, 1959, pp. 290–291.

Genitrix

Bree, Germaine and Margaret Guiton. *An Age of Fiction: The French Novel from Gide to Camus.* New Brunswick, N.J.: Rutgers University Press, 1957, pp. 117–118.

Flower, J.E. *Intention and Achievement: An Essay on the Novels of François Mauriac.* Oxford: Clarendon Press, 1969, pp. 69–73.

Fowlie, Wallace. "Mauriac's Dark Hero," in *Sewanee Review.* LVI (Winter, 1948), pp. 47–51.

Houston, John Porter. *Fictional Technique in France, 1802–1927: An Introduction.* Baton Rouge: Louisiana State University Press, 1972, pp. 120–128.

Iyengar, K.R. Sprinivasa. *François Mauriac.* New York: Asia Publishing House, 1963, pp. 24–26.

Jenkins, Cecil. *Mauriac.* New York: Barnes & Noble, 1965, pp. 58–61.

McNab, James P. "The Mother in François Mauriac's *Genitrix*," in *Hartford Studies in Literature.* II (1970), pp. 207–213.

Murphy, Eugene F. "Mauriac's *Genitrix*," in *Explicator.* XIII (April, 1955), item 37.

Paine, Ruth Benson. *Thematic Analysis of François Mauriac's* Genitrix, Le Desert de l'Amour, *and* Le noeud de viperes. University, Miss.: Romance Monographs, 1976, pp. 25–64.

Pell, Elsie. *François Mauriac: In Search of the Infinite.* New York: Philosophical Library, 1947, pp. 46–56.

Peyre, Henri. *The Contemporary French Novel.* New York: Oxford University Press, 1955, pp. 110–111.

_____. *French Novelists of Today.* New York: Oxford University Press, 1967, pp. 109–110.

Reck, Rima Drell. *Literature and Responbibility: The French Novelist in the Twentieth Century.* Baton Rouge: Louisiana State University Press, 1969, pp. 182–183.

Rubin, Louis D., Jr. "François Mauriac and the Freedom of the Religious Novelist," in *Southern Review.* II (January, 1966), pp. 29–30.

Smith, Maxwell. *François Mauriac.* New York: Twayne, 1970, pp. 86–91.

Speaight, Robert. *François Mauriac: A Study of the Writer and the Man.* London: Chatto and Windus, 1976, pp. 78–80.

Stratford, Philip. *Faith and Fiction.* Notre Dame, Ind.: Notre Dame University Press, 1964, pp. 157–160.

Turnell, Martin. *The Art of French Fiction.* Norfolk, Conn.: New Directions, 1959, pp. 316–322.

A Kiss for the Leper

Bree, Germaine and Margaret Guiton. *An Age of Fiction: The French Novel from Gide to Camus.* New Brunswick, N.J.: Rutgers University Press, 1957, pp. 116–117.

Flower, J.E. *Intention and Achievement: An Essay on the Novels of François Mauriac.* Oxford: Clarendon Press, 1969.

Houston, John Porter. *Fictional Technique in France, 1802–1927: An Introduction.* Baton Rouge: Louisiana State University Press, 1972, pp. 120–128.

Iyengar, K.R. Sprinivasa. *François Mauriac.* New York: Asia Publishing House, 1963, pp. 21–23.

Jarrett-Kerr, Martin. *François Mauriac.* New Haven, Conn.: Yale University Press, 1954, pp. 21–24.

Jenkins, Cecil. *Mauriac.* New York: Barnes & Noble, 1965, pp. 47–49, 55–56.

Melland, James M. "The Reconstructed Reality: Mauriac's *A Kiss for the Leper*," in *Renascence.* XXV (1972), pp. 24–34.

Peyre, Henri. *The Contemporary French Novel.* New York: Oxford University Press, 1955, pp. 108–110.

————. *French Novelists of Today.* New York: Oxford University Press, 1967, pp. 108–109.

Reck, Rima Drell. *Literature and Responsibility: The French Novelist in the Twentieth Century.* Baton Rouge: Louisiana State University Press, 1969, pp. 180–182.

Rubin, Louis D., Jr. "François Mauriac and the Freedom of the Religious Novelist," in *Southern Review.* II (January, 1966), pp. 27–29.

Smith, Maxwell. *François Mauriac.* New York: Twayne, 1970, pp. 82–86.

Speaight, Robert. *François Mauriac: A Study of the Writer and the Man.* London: Chatto and Windus, 1976, pp. 76–79.

Stoker, J.T. "The Question of Grace in Mauriac's Novels," in *Culture*. XXVI (September, 1965), pp. 292–294.

Stratford, Philip. *Faith and Fiction*. Notre Dame, Ind.: University of Notre Dame Press, 1964, pp. 1–30.

Turnell, Martin. *The Art of French Fiction*. Norfolk, Conn.: New Directions, 1959, pp. 314–316.

The Lamb

Bree, Germaine and Margaret Guiton. *An Age of Fiction: The French Novel from Gide to Camus*. New Brunswick, N.J.: Rutgers University Press, 1957, pp. 114–115.

Dillistone, F.W. *The Novelist and the Passion Story*. New York: Sheed and Ward, 1960, pp. 27–44.

Flower, J.E. *Intention and Achievement: An Essay on the Novels of François Mauriac*. Oxford: Clarendon Press, 1969, pp. 98–104.

Iyengar, K.R. Sprinivasa. *François Mauriac*. New York: Asia Publishing House, 1963, pp. 112–116.

Kibbe, Lawrence H. "Mauriac's Incredible 'Priest,' " in *Catholic World*. CLXXXII (November, 1955), pp. 116–119.

Smith, Maxwell. *François Mauriac*. New York: Twayne, 1970, pp. 77–80.

Speaight, Robert. *François Mauriac: A Study of the Writer and the Man*. London: Chatto and Windus, 1976, pp. 194–197.

Questions of Precedence

Flower, J.E. *Intention and Achievement: An Essay on the Novels of François Mauriac*. Oxford: Clarendon Press, 1969, pp. 46–47, 53–54.

Iyengar, K.R. Sprinivasa. *François Mauriac*. New York: Asia Publishing House, 1963, pp. 17–20.

Jenkins, Cecil. *Mauriac*. New York: Barnes & Noble, 1965, pp. 46–47.

Smith, Maxwell A. *François Mauriac*. New York: Twayne, 1970, pp. 35–36.

Speaight, Robert. *François Mauriac: A Study of the Writer and the Man*. London: Chatto and Windus, 1976, pp. 72–73.

Stratford, Philip. *Faith and Fiction*. Notre Dame, Ind.: University of Notre Dame Press, 1964, pp. 79–85.

Thérèse Desqueyroux

Bree, Germaine and Margaret Guiton. *An Age of Fiction: The French Novel from Gide to Camus*. New Brunswick, N.J.: Rutgers University Press, 1957, pp. 118–120.

Crisafulli, Alessandro S. "The Theme of Captivity and Its Metaphorical Expression in Mauriac's *Thérèse Desqueyroux*," in *Studies in Honor of Tatiana Fotitch*. Edited by Josep M. Sola-Sole, Alessandro S. Crisafulli, and Siegfried A. Schulz. Washington, D.C.: Catholic University of America Press, 1973, pp. 29–35.

Farrell, C. Frederick, Jr. and Edith R. Farrell. "The Animal Imagery of *Thérèse Desqueyroux*," in *Kentucky Romance Quarterly*. XXI (1974), pp. 419–427.

————. "The Multiple Murders of *Thérèse Desqueyroux*," in *Hartford Studies in Literature*. II (1970), pp. 195–206.

————. "*Thérèse Desqueyroux*: A Complete Suicide," in *Language Quarterly*. XIV (1976), pp. 13–15, 18, 22.

Flower, J.E. *Intention and Achievement: An Essay on the Novels of François Mauriac*. Oxford: Clarendon Press, 1969, pp. 72–78.

Gregor, Ian and Brian Nicholas. *The Moral and the Story*. London: Faber and Faber, 1962, pp. 207–216.

Houston, John Porter. *Fictional Technique in France, 1802–1927: An Introduction*. Baton Rouge: Louisiana State University Press, 1972, pp. 128–130.

Iyengar, K.R. Sprinivasa. *François Mauriac*. New York: Asia Publishing House, 1963, pp. 36–46.

Jenkins, Cecil. *Mauriac*. New York: Barnes & Noble, 1965, pp. 73–78, 95–96.

Murray, Jack. "Three Murders in the Contemporary French Novel," in *Texas Studies in Literature and Language*. VI (Autumn, 1964), pp. 363–366.

Peyre, Henri. *French Novelists of Today*. New York: Oxford University Press, 1967, pp. 111–113.

Reck, Rima Drell. *Literature and Responsibility: The French Novelist in the Twentieth Century*. Baton Rouge: Louisiana State University Press, 1969, pp. 184–187.

Rubin, Louis D., Jr. "François Mauriac and the Freedom of the Religious Novelist," in *Southern Review*. II (January, 1966), pp. 32–38.

Smith, Maxwell. *François Mauriac*. New York: Twayne, 1970, pp. 96–104.

Speaight, Robert. *François Mauriac: A Study of the Writer and the Man*. London: Chatto and Windus, 1976, pp. 87–89, 122–125, 143–146.

Stratford, Philip. *Faith and Fiction*. Notre Dame, Ind.: Notre Dame University Press, 1964, pp. 154–160, 216–217.

Swift, Bernard C. "Structure and Meaning in *Thérèse Desqueyroux*," in *Wascana Review*. V (1970), pp. 33–44.

Turnell, Martin. *The Art of French Fiction*. Norfolk, Conn.: New Directions, 1959, pp. 329–337.

Ullmann, Stephen. *Style in the French Novel*. Oxford: Basil Blackwell, 1964, pp. 173–187.

Vipers' Tangle

Batchelor, R. "Art and Theology in Mauriac's *Le noeud de viperes*," in *Nottingham French Studies*. XII (1973), pp. 33–43.

Bree, Germaine and Margaret Guiton. *An Age of Fiction: The French Novel from Gide to Camus*. New Brunswick, N.J.: Rutgers University Press, 1957, pp. 120–122.

Flower, J.E. *Intention and Achievement: An Essay on the Novels of François Mauriac*. Oxford: Clarendon Press, 1969, pp. 74–83.

Fowlie, Wallace. "The Art of François Mauriac," in *A Mauriac Reader*. By François Mauriac. New York: Farrar, Straus and Giroux, 1968, pp. xv–xvi.

Iyengar, K.R. Sprinivasa. *François Mauriac*. New York: Asia Publishing House, 1963, pp. 68–76.

Jenkins, Cecil. *Mauriac*. New York: Barnes & Noble, 1965, pp. 81–86.

Jerome, Sister M. "Human and Divine Love in Dante and Mauriac," in *Renascence*. XVIII (Summer, 1966), pp. 179–181.

Paine, Ruth Benson. *Thematic Analysis of François Mauriac's* Genitrix, Le Desert de l'Amour, *and* Le noeud de viperes. University, Miss.: Romance Monographs, 1976, pp. 116–171.

Pell, Elsie. *François Mauriac: In Search of the Infinite*. New York: Philosophical Library, 1947, pp. 57–68.

Peyre, Henri. *The Contemporary French Novel*. New York: Oxford University Press, 1955, pp. 105–106, 113–115.

————. *French Novelists of Today*. New York: Oxford University Press, 1967, pp. 113–114.

Reck, Rima Drell. *Literature and Responsibility: The French Novelist in the Twentieth Century*. Baton Rouge: Louisiana State University Press, 1969, pp. 187–189.

Smith, Maxwell. *François Mauriac*. New York: Twayne, 1970, pp. 108–115.

Speaight, Robert. *François Mauriac: A Study of the Writer and the Man*. London: Chatto and Windus, 1976, pp. 111–113.

Stoker, J.T. "The Question of Grace in Mauriac's Novels," in *Culture*. XXVI (September, 1965), pp. 295–302.

Stratford, Philip. *Faith and Fiction*. Notre Dame, Ind.: University of Notre Dame Press, 1964, pp. 193–198.

Swift, Bernard C. "Consistency in François Mauriac's *Le noeud de viperes*," in *Western Canadian Studies in Modern Languages and Literature*. II (1970), pp. 44–57.

Tartella, Vincent P. "Thematic Imagery in Mauriac's *Vipers' Tangle*," in *Renascence*. XVII (Summer, 1965), pp. 195–200.

Turnell, Martin.   *The Art of French Fiction.* Norfolk, Conn.: New Directions, 1959, pp. 344–347.

Wentersdorf, Karl P.   "The Chronology of Mauriac's *Le noeud de viperes*," in *Kentucky Romance Quarterly.* XIII, Supplement (1967), pp. 89–100.

HERMAN MELVILLE
(1819–1891)

"The Apple Tree Table"

Browne, Roy B. *Melville's Drive to Humanism.* West Lafayette, Ind.: Purdue University Press, 1971, pp. 271–279.

Davidson, Frank. "Melville, Thoreau, and 'The Apple Tree Table,' " in *American Literature.* XXV (1954), pp. 479–488.

Fisher, Marvin. "Bug and Humbug in Melville's 'Apple Tree Table,' " in *Studies in Short Fiction.* VIII (1971), pp. 459–466.

Fogle, Richard H. *Melville's Shorter Tales.* Norman: University of Oklahoma Press, 1960, pp. 78–84.

Karcher, Carolyn L. "The Spiritual Lesson of Melville's 'The Apple Tree Table,' " in *American Quarterly.* XXIII (1971), pp. 101–109.

Magaw, Malcolm O. "Apocalyptic Imagery in Melville's 'The Apple Tree Table,' " in *Midwest Quarterly.* VIII (1967), pp. 357–369.

Rosenberry, Edward H. *Melville and the Comic Spirit.* Cambridge, Mass.: Harvard University Press, 1955, pp. 182–183.

Sackman, Douglas. "The Original of Melville's 'Apple Tree Table,' " in *American Literature.* XI (1940), pp. 448–451.

Slater, Judith. "The Domestic Adventurer in Melville's Tales," in *American Literature.* XXXVII (1965), pp. 275–277.

Bartleby the Scrivener

Abcarian, Richard. "The World of Love and the Spheres of Fright: Melville's *Bartleby the Scrivener,*" in *Studies in Short Fiction.* I (1964), pp. 207–215.

Barnett, Louise K. "Bartleby as Alienated Worker," in *Studies in Short Fiction.* XI (1974), pp. 379–385.

Bigelow, Gordon E. "The Problem of Symbolist Form in Melville's *Bartleby the Scrivener,*" in *Modern Language Quarterly.* XXXI (1970), pp. 345–358.

Bollas, Christopher. "Melville's Lost Self: Bartleby," in *American Imago.* XXXI (1974), pp. 401–411.

Chase, Richard. *Herman Melville: A Critical Study.* New York: Macmillan, 1949, pp. 143–149.

Davidson, Frank. "Bartleby: A Few Observations," in *Emerson Society Quarterly.* XXVII (1962), pp. 25–32.

Felheim, Marvin. "Meaning and Structure in *Bartleby,*" in *College English.* XXIII (February, 1962), pp. 364–370, 375–376.

Marx, Leo. "Melville's Parable of the Walls," in *Sewanee Review.* LXI (Autumn, 1953), pp. 602–627.

Spector, Robert D. "Melville's Bartleby and the Absurd," in *Nineteenth-Century Fiction.* XVI (1961), pp. 175–177.

Springer, Norman. "Bartleby and the Terror of Limitation," in *PMLA.* LXXX (1965), pp. 410–418.

Stein, Allen F. "The Motif of Voracity in *Bartleby*," in *ESQ: Journal of the American Renaissance.* XXI, i (1975), pp. 29–34.

Stein, William B. "Bartleby: The Christian Conscience," in *Melville Annual, 1965.* (1967), pp. 104–112.

Stempel, Daniel and Bruce M. Stillians. "*Bartleby the Scrivener*: A Parable of Pessimism," in *Nineteenth-Century Fiction.* XXVII (1972), pp. 268–282.

Stone, Edward. *A Certain Morbidness: A View of American Literature.* Carbondale: Southern Illinois University Press, 1969, pp. 32–42.

Vincent, Howard P., Editor. "A Symposium: *Bartleby the Scrivener*," in *Melville Annual, 1965*, pp. 1–199.

Walton, Patrick R. "Melville's *Bartleby* and the Doctrine of Necessity," in *American Literature.* XLI (1969), pp. 39–54.

Widmer, Kingsley. "Melville's Radical Resistance: The Method and Meaning of *Bartleby*," in *Studies in the Novel.* I (1969), pp. 444–458.

Zink, David D. "Bartleby and the Contemporary Search for Meaning," in *Forum.* VIII (Summer, 1970), pp. 46–50.

The Bell Tower

Baird, James. *Ishmael.* Baltimore: Johns Hopkins University Press, 1956, pp. 396–400.

Browne, Roy B. *Melville's Drive to Humanism.* West Lafayette, Ind.: Purdue University, 1971, pp. 247–259.

Chase, Richard. *Herman Melville: A Critical Study.* New York: Macmillan, 1949, pp. 122–125.

Costello, Jacqueline A. and Robert J. Kloss. "The Psychological Depth of Melville's *The Bell Tower*," in *Emerson Society Quarterly.* XIX (1973), pp. 254–261.

Fenton, C.A. "*The Bell Tower*: Melville and Technology," in *American Literature.* XXII (May, 1951), pp. 219–232.

Fisher, Marvin. "Melville's *Bell Tower*: A Double Thrust," in *American Quarterly.* XVIII (1966), pp. 200–207.

Fogle, Richard H. *Melville's Shorter Tales.* Norman: University of Oklahoma Press, 1960, pp. 63–71.

Franklin, H. Bruce.   *Future Perfect: American Science Fiction of the Nine-teenth Century*. New York: Oxford University Press, 1966, pp. 145–150.

Howard, Leon.   *Herman Melville: A Biography*. Berkeley: University of California Press, 1951, pp. 222–223.

Oliver, Egbert S., Editor.   Piazza Tales *by Herman Melville*. New York: Hendricks House, 1948, pp. 247–250.

Vernon, John.   "Melville's *The Bell Tower*," in *Studies in Short Fiction*. VII (1970), pp. 264–276.

Benito Cereno

Canaday, Nicholas, Jr.   "A New Reading of Melville's *Benito Cereno*," in *Studies in American Literature*. (1960), pp. 49–57.

✓Cardwell, Guy.   "Melville's Gray Story: Symbols and Meaning in *Benito Cereno*," in *Bucknell Review*. VIII (May, 1959), pp. 154–167.

Carlisle, E.F.   "Captain Amasa Delano: Melville's American Fool," in *Criticism*. VII (1965), pp. 349–362.

D'Azevedo, Warren.   "Revolt on the San Dominick," in *Phylon*. XVII (June, 1956), pp. 129–140.

Dew, Marjorie.   "*Benito Cereno*: Melville's Vision and Re-Vision," in *A* Benito Cereno *Handbook*. Edited by Seymour L. Gross. Belmont, Calif.: Wadsworth, 1965, pp. 178–184.

Feltenstein, Rosalie.   "Melville's *Benito Cereno*," in *American Literature*. XIX (November, 1947), pp. 245–255.

Franklin, H. Bruce.   *The Wake of the Gods: Melville's Mythology*. Stanford, Calif.: Stanford University Press, 1963, pp. 136–150.

Glicksberg, Charles J.   "Melville and the Negro Problem," in *Phylon*. XI (Autumn, 1950), pp. 207–215.

Gross, Seymour L.   *A* Benito Cereno *Handbook*. Belmont, Calif.: Wadsworth, 1965.

Guttman, Allen.   "The Enduring Innocence of Captain Amasa Delano," in *Boston University Studies in English*. V (Spring, 1961), pp. 35–45.

Jackson, Margaret Y.   "Melville's Use of a Real Slave Mutiny in *Benito Cereno*," in *CLA Journal*. IV (December, 1960), pp. 79–93.

Kaplan, Sidney.   "Herman Melville and the American National Sin," in *Journal of Negro History*. XLII (October, 1956), pp. 311–338.

✓Magowan, Robin.   "Masque and Symbol in Melville's *Benito Cereno*," in *College English*. XXIII (February, 1962), pp. 346–351.

Phillips, Barry.   " 'The Good Captain': A Reading of *Benito Cereno*," in *Texas Studies in Literature and Language*. IV (Summer, 1962), pp. 188–197.

Putzel, Max. "The Source and the Symbols of Melville's *Benito Cereno*," in *American Literature*. XXXIV (May, 1962), pp. 191–206.

Williams, Stanley. " 'Follow Your Leader': Melville's *Benito Cereno*," in *Virginia Quarterly Review*. XXII (Winter, 1947), pp. 61–76.

Billy Budd, Foretopman

Anderson, Charles R. "The Genesis of *Billy Budd*," in *American Literature*. XII (1940), pp. 328–346.

Arvin, Newton. *Herman Melville: A Critical Biography*. New York: William Sloane, 1950, pp. 292–299.

————. "A Note on the Background of *Billy Budd*," in *American Literature*. XX (1948), pp. 51–55.

Berthoff, Warner. "Certain Phenomenal Men: The Example of *Billy Budd*," in *English Literary History*. XXVII (1960), pp. 334–351.

Braswell, William. "Melville's *Billy Budd* as 'An Inside Narrative,' " in *American Literature*. XXIX (1957), pp. 133–146.

Bredahl, A. Carl. *Melville's Angles of Vision*. Gainesville: University of Florida Press, 1972, pp. 63–73.

Chase, Richard. *Herman Melville: A Critical Study*. New York: Macmillan, 1949, pp. 258–277.

Fogle, Richard H. "*Billy Budd*—Acceptance or Irony," in *Tulane Studies in English*. VIII (1958), pp. 107–113.

Franklin, H. Bruce. *The Wake of the Gods: Melville's Mythology*. Stanford, Calif.: Stanford University Press, 1963, pp. 188–202.

Glick, Wendell. "Expediency and Absolute Morality in *Billy Budd*," in *PMLA*. LXVIII (1953), pp. 103–110.

Hillway, Tyrus. "*Billy Budd*: Melville's Human Sacrifice," in *Pacific Spectator*. VI (1952), pp. 342–347.

Howard, Leon. *Herman Melville: A Biography*. Berkeley: University of California Press, 1951, pp. 324–328.

Lemon, Lee T. "*Billy Budd*: The Plot Against the Story," in *Studies in Short Fiction*. II (1964), pp. 32–43.

Lewis, R.W.B. *The American Adam: Innocence, Tragedy, and Tradition in the Nineteenth Century*. Chicago: University of Chicago Press, 1955, pp. 147–152.

McCarthy, Paul. "Character and Structure in *Billy Budd*," in *Discourse*. IX (1966), pp. 201–217.

Mason, Ronald. *The Spirit Above the Dust: A Study of Herman Melville*. London: John Lehmann, 1951, pp. 245–260.

Matthiessen, F.O. *American Renaissance.* New York: Oxford University Press, 1941, pp. 500–514.

Merrill, Robert. "The Narrative Voice of *Billy Budd*," in *Modern Language Quarterly.* XXXIV (1973), pp. 283–291.

Miller, James E. "Billy Budd: The Catastrophe of Innocence," in *Modern Language Notes.* LXXIII (1958), pp. 168–176.

Rathbun, John W. "*Billy Budd* and the Limits of Perception," in *Nineteenth-Century Fiction.* XX (1965), pp. 19–34.

Reich, Charles A. "The Tragedy of Justice in *Billy Budd*," in *Yale Review.* LVI (1967), pp. 368–389.

Rosenberry, Edward H. "The Problem of *Billy Budd*," in *PMLA.* LXXX (1965), pp. 489–498.

Schroth, Evelyn. "Melville's Judgment on Captain Vere," in *Midwest Quarterly.* X (1969), pp. 189–200.

Sten, Christopher W. "Vere's Use of Forms: Means and Ends in *Billy Budd*," in *American Literature.* XLVII (1975), pp. 37–51.

Stern, Milton R. *The Fine Hammered Steel of Herman Melville.* Urbana: University of Illinois Press, 1957, pp. 206–239.

Thompson, Lawrance. *Melville's Quarrel with God.* Princeton, N.J.: Princeton University Press, 1952, pp. 355–414.

Tindall, William Y. "The Ceremony of Innocence," in *Great Moral Dilemmas in Literature, Past and Present.* Edited by R.M. MacIvor. New York: Harper, 1956, pp. 73–81.

Watson, E.L. Grant. "Melville's Testament of Acceptance," in *New England Quarterly.* VI (1933), pp. 319–327.

Zink, Karl E. "Herman Melville and the Forms—Irony and Social Criticism in *Billy Budd*," in *Accent.* XII (1952), pp. 131–139.

Clarel

Ault, N.A. "The Sea Imagery in Herman Melville's *Clarel*," in *Research Studies of State College of Washington.* XXVII (June, 1959), pp. 72–84.

Beyanson, W.E. "Melville's *Clarel*: The Complex Passion," in *ELH.* XXI (June, 1954), pp. 146–159.

Chaffee, Patricia. "The Kedron in Melville's *Clarel*," in *College Language Association.* XVIII (1975), pp. 374–382.

Dea, Eugene M. "Evolution and Atheism in *Clarel*," in *Extracts.* XXVI (1976), pp. 3–4.

Fogle, R.H. "Melville's *Clarel*: Doubt and Belief," in *Tulane Studies in English.* X (1960), pp. 101–116.

Kenny, Vincent S.   *Herman Melville's* Clarel; *a Spiritual Autobiography.* Hamden, Conn.: Archon Books, 1973.

Parker, Hershel.   "The Ambiguous Portrait of Vine in Melville's *Clarel*," in *Extracts.* XXVI (1976), pp. 4–5.

Requa, Kenneth A.   "The Pilgrim's Problems: Melville's *Clarel*," in *Ball State University Forum.* XVI (1975), pp. 16–20.

Reynolds, Larry J.   "Vine and Clarel," in *Extracts.* XXIII (1975), p. 11.

Short, Bryan C.   " 'Betwixt the Chimes and Knell': Versification as Symbol in *Clarel*," in *Extracts.* XXVI (1976), p. 4.

Walker, Franklin Dickerson.   *Irreverent Pilgrims: Melville, Browne, and Mark Twain in the Holy Land.* Seattle: University of Washington Press, 1974.

Wasilewski, William H.   "Melville's Poetic Strategy in *Clarel*: The Satellite Poem," in *Essays in Arts and Sciences.* V (1976), pp. 149–159.

"Cock-a-Doodle-Doo"

Bernstein, John.   *Pacificism and Rebellion in the Writings of Herman Melville.* The Hague: Mouton, 1964, pp. 174–175.

Brack, Vida K. and O.M. Brack.   "Weathering Cape Horn: Survivors in Melville's Minor Short Fiction," in *Arizona Quarterly.* XXVIII (1972), pp. 64–65.

Browne, Roy B.   *Melville's Drive to Humanism.* West Lafayette, Ind.: Purdue University Press, 1971, pp. 189–200.

Chase, Richard.   *Herman Melville: A Critical Study.* New York: Macmillan, 1949, pp. 163–167.

Fogle, Richard H.   *Melville's Shorter Tales.* Norman: University of Oklahoma Press, 1960, pp. 28–35.

Hoffman, Charles G.   "The Shorter Fiction of Herman Melville," in *South Atlantic Quarterly.* LII (1953), pp. 421–422.

Howard, Leon.   *Herman Melville: A Biography.* Berkeley: University of California Press, 1951.

Lynn, Kenneth S., Editor.   *The Comic Tradition in America.* New York: Doubleday, 1958, pp. 232–235.

Miller, James A.   *A Reader's Guide to Herman Melville.* New York: Farrar, Straus and Cudahy, 1962, pp. 165–167.

Moss, Sidney P.   " 'Cock-a-Doodle-Doo!' and Some Legends in Melville Scholarship," in *American Literature.* XL (1968), pp. 192–210.

Oliver, Egbert S.   " 'Cock-a-Doodle-Doo' and Transcendental Hocus-Pocus," in *New England Quarterly.* XXI (1948), pp. 204–216.

Rosenberry, Edward H. *Melville and the Comic Spirit.* Cambridge, Mass.: Harvard University Press, 1955, pp. 162–163.

Stein, William B. "Melville Roasts Thoreau's Cock," in *Modern Language Notes.* LXXIV (1959), pp. 218–219.

————. "Melville's Cock and the Bell of Saint Paul," in *Emerson Society Quarterly.* XXVII (1962), pp. 5–10.

The Confidence Man

Cawelti, John G. "Some Notes on the Structure of *The Confidence Man*," in *American Literature.* XXIX (November, 1957), pp. 278–288.

Chase, Richard. "Melville's Confidence Man," in *Kenyon Review.* XI (Winter, 1944), pp. 122–140.

Drew, Philip. "Appearance and Reality in Melville's *The Confidence Man*," in *ELH.* XXXI (1965), pp. 418–442.

Dubler, Walter. "Theme and Structure in Melville's *The Confidence Man*," in *American Literature.* XXXIII (November, 1961), pp. 308–319.

Foster, Elizabeth. "Introduction," of *The Confidence Man* in the *Complete Works of Herman Melville.* Edited by Howard P. Vincent. New York: Hendricks House, 1954.

Hayford, Harrison. "Poe in *The Confidence Man*," in *Nineteenth-Century Fiction.* XIV (December, 1959), pp. 207–218.

Hoffman, Daniel G. "Melville's Story of China Aster," in *American Literature.* XXII (May, 1950), pp. 137–149.

Mason, Ronald. *The Spirit Above the Dust: A Study of Herman Melville.* London: John Lehmann, 1951, pp. 198–207.

Miller, James E., Jr. "The Confidence Man: His Guises," in *PMLA.* LXXIV (March, 1959), pp. 102–111.

Mumford, Lewis. *Herman Melville.* New York: Harcourt, Brace, 1924, pp. 247–255.

Oliver, Egbert S. "Melville's Goneril and Fanny Kemble," in *New England Quarterly.* XVIII (December, 1945), pp. 489–506.

————. "Melville's Picture of Emerson and Thoreau in *The Confidence Man*," in *College English.* VIII (November, 1946), pp. 61–72.

Pearce, Roy Harvey. "Melville's Indian Hater: A Note on the Meaning of *The Confidence Man*," in *PMLA.* LXVII (December, 1952), pp. 942–948.

Rosenberry, Edward H. *Melville and the Comic Spirit.* Cambridge, Mass.: Harvard University Press, 1955, pp. 146–178.

Sedgwick, William Ellery. *Herman Melville: The Tragedy of Mind.* Cambridge, Mass.: Harvard University Press, 1944, pp. 186–193.

Shroeder, John W.   "Sources and Symbols for Melville's Confidence Man," in *PMLA*. LXVI (June, 1951), pp. 363–380.

Stone, Geoffrey.   *Melville.* New York: Sheed and Ward, 1949, pp. 228–234.

Thompson, Lawrance.   *Melville's Quarrel with God.* Princeton, N.J.: Princeton University Press, 1952, pp. 297–328.

Tuveson, Ernest.   "The Creed of the Confidence Man," in *ELH*. XXXIII (1966), pp. 247–270.

Weissbuch, T.N.   "A Note on the Confidence Man's Counterfeit Detector," in *Emerson Society Quarterly*. XIX (1960), pp. 16–18.

Daniel Orme

Braswell, William.   *Melville's Religious Thought.* Durham, N.C.: Duke University Press, 1943, pp. 124–126.

Chase, Richard.   *Herman Melville: A Critical Study.* New York: Macmillan, 1949, pp. 298–301.

Freeman, F. Barron.   "The Enigma of Melville's *Daniel Orme*," in *American Literature*. XVI (1944), pp. 208–211.

The Encantadas

Albrecht, Robert C.   "The Thematic Unity of Melville's *The Encantadas*," in *Texas Studies in Literature and Language*. XIV (1972), pp. 463–477.

Bavid, James.   *Ishmael.* Baltimore: Johns Hopkins University Press, 1956, pp. 313–314.

Browne, Roy B.   *Melville's Drive to Humanism.* West Lafayette, Ind.: Purdue University Press, 1971, pp. 280–301.

Canaday, Nicholas.   "Melville's *The Encantadas*: The Deceptive Enchantment of the Absolute," in *Papers in Language and Literature*. X (1974), pp. 58–69.

Chase, Richard.   *Herman Melville: A Critical Study.* New York: Macmillan, 1949, pp. 210–213.

Fogle, Richard H.   "The Unity of *The Encantadas*," in *Nineteenth Century-Fiction*. X (1955), pp. 34–52.

Haber, Richard.   "Patience and Charity in *The Encantadas, Chola Widow* and *Cock-a-Doodle-Doo*," in *Massachusetts Studies in English*. III (1972), pp. 100–107.

Hillway, Tyrus.   *Herman Melville.* New York: Twayne, 1963.

Hoffman, Charles G.   "The Shorter Fiction of Herman Melville," in *South Atlantic Quarterly*. LII (1953), pp. 421–422.

Howard, Leon.   *Herman Melville: A Biography.* Berkeley: University of California Press, 1951, pp. 209–213.

Jackson, Arlene M. "Technique and Discovery in Melville's *Encantadas*," in *Studies in American Fiction.* I (1973), pp. 133–140.

Lacy, Patricia. "The Agatha Theme in Melville's Stories," in *University of Texas Studies in English.* XXXV (1956), pp. 102–103.

Mason, Ronald. *The Spirit Above the Dust: A Study of Herman Melville.* London: John Lehmann, 1951, pp. 188–190.

Miller, James C. *A Reader's Guide to Herman Melville.* New York: Farrar, Straus, and Cudahy, 1962.

Mumford, Lewis. *Herman Melville.* New York: Harcourt, Brace, 1929, pp. 239–240.

Newberry, J. "*The Encantadas*: Melville's Inferno," in *American Literature.* XXXVIII (1966), pp. 49–68.

Pearce, Howard D. "The Narrator of Norfolk Isle and the Chola Widow," in *Studies in Short Fiction.* III (1965), pp. 56–62.

Seelye, John. *Melville: The Ironic Diagram.* Evanston, Ill.: Northwestern University Press, 1970, pp. 101–103.

Watson, Charles N. "Melville's Agatha and Hunilla: A Literary Reincarnation," in *English Language Notes.* VI (1968), pp. 114–118.

Winters, Yvar. *In Defense of Reason.* Denver: University of Denver Press, 1947, pp. 222–223.

Yarina, Margaret. "The Dualistic Vision of Herman Melville's *The Encantadas*," in *Journal of Narrative Technique.* III (1973), pp. 141–148.

"The Fiddler"

Bier, Jesse. "Melville's 'The Fiddler' Reconsidered," in *American Transcendental Quarterly.* XIV (1972), pp. 2–4.

Brack, Vida K. and O.M. Brack. "Weathering Cape Horn: Survivors in Melville's Minor Short Fiction," in *Arizona Quarterly.* XXVIII (1972), pp. 67–68.

Browne, Roy B. *Melville's Drive to Humanism.* West Lafayette, Ind.: Purdue University Press, 1971, pp. 240–242.

Campbell, Marie A. "A Quiet Crusade: Melville's Tales of the Fifties," in *American Transcendental Quarterly.* VII (1970), p. 10.

Chase, Richard. *Herman Melville: A Critical Study.* New York: Macmillan, 1949, pp. 173–175.

Fisher, Marvin. "Melville's 'The Fiddler': Succumbing to the Drummer," in *Studies in Short Fiction.* XI (1974), pp. 153–160.

Fogle, Richard H. *Melville's Shorter Tales.* Norman: University of Oklahoma Press, 1960, pp. 59–61.

Gupta, R.K. "Hautboy and Plinlimmon: A Reinterpretation of Melville's 'The Fiddler,' " in *American Literature.* XLIII (1971), pp. 437–442.

Miller, James E. *A Reader's Guide to Herman Melville.* New York: Farrar, Straus and Cudahy, 1962, pp. 168–169.

Rosenberry, Edward H. *Melville and the Comic Spirit.* Cambridge, Mass.: Harvard University Press, 1955, pp. 144–145.

Thompson, W.R. " 'The Fiddler': A Study in Dissolution," in *Texas Studies in Literature and Language.* II (1961), pp. 492–500.

"The Gees"

Bickley, R. Bruce. "The Triple Thrust of Satire in Melville's Short Stories: Society, the Narrator, and the Reader," in *Studies in American Humor.* I (1975), pp. 173–174.

Karcher, Carolyn L. "Melville's 'The Gees': A Forgotten Satire on Scientific Racism," in *American Quarterly.* XXVII (1975), pp. 421–442.

"The Happy Failure"

Brack, Vida K. and O.M. Brack. "Weathering Cape Horn: Survivors in Melville's Minor Short Fiction," in *Arizona Quarterly.* XXVIII (1972), p. 66.

Browne, Roy B. *Melville's Drive to Humanism.* West Lafayette, Ind.: Purdue University Press, 1971, pp. 237–240.

Fogle, Richard H. *Melville's Shorter Tales.* Norman: University of Oklahoma Press, 1960, pp. 58–59.

Hoffman, Charles G. "The Shorter Fiction of Herman Melville," in *South Atlantic Quarterly.* LII (1953), pp. 423–424.

Lynde, Richard D. "Melville's Success in 'The Happy Failure': A Story of the River Hudson," in *College Language Association Journal*, XIII (1969), pp. 119–130.

Miller, James E. *A Reader's Guide to Herman Melville.* New York: Farrar, Straus, and Cudahy, 1962, pp. 167–168.

"I and My Chimney"

Bickley, R. Bruce. "The Minor Fiction of Hawthorne and Melville," in *American Transcendental Quarterly.* XIV (1972), pp. 149–150.

Brack, Vida K. and O.M. Brack. "Weathering Cape Horn: Survivors in Melville's Minor Short Fiction," in *Arizona Quarterly.* XXVIII (1972), pp. 69–70.

Browne, Roy B. *Melville's Drive to Humanism.* West Lafayette, Ind.: Purdue University Press, 1971, pp. 259–271.

Campbell, Marie A. "A Quiet Crusade: Melville's Tales of the Fifties," in *American Transcendental Quarterly.* VII (1970), pp. 10–11.

Chase, Richard. *Herman Melville: A Critical Study.* New York: Macmillan, 1949, pp. 168–171.

Chatfield, E. Hale. "Levels of Meaning in Melville's 'I and My Chimney,' " in *American Imago.* XIX (1962), pp. 163–169.

Crowley, William G. "Melville's Chimney," in *Emerson Society Quarterly.* XIV (1959), pp. 2–6.

Finkelstein, Dorothee M. *Melville's Orienda.* New Haven, Conn.: Yale University Press, 1961, pp. 139–143.

Fogle, Richard H. *Melville's Shorter Tales.* Norman: University of Oklahoma Press, 1960, pp. 72–78.

Hillway, Tyrus. *Herman Melville.* New York: Twayne, 1963.

Howard, Leon. *Herman Melville: A Biography.* Berkeley: University of California Press, 1951, pp. 224–225.

McCullagh, James C. "More Smoke from Melville's Chimney," in *American Transcendental Quarterly.* XVII (1973), pp. 17–22.

Rosenberry, Edward H. *Melville and the Comic Spirit.* Cambridge, Mass.: Harvard University Press, 1955, pp. 180–182.

Sealts, Merton M. "Herman Melville's 'I and My Chimney,' " in *American Literature.* XIII (1941), pp. 142–154.

Sedgwick, William E. *Herman Melville: The Tragedy of Mind.* Cambridge, Mass.: Harvard University Press, 1944, pp. 143–197.

Slater, Judith. "The Domestic Adventurer in Melville's Tales," in *American Literature.* XXXVII (1965), pp. 272–273.

Sowder, William J. "Melville's 'I and My Chimney': A Southern Exposure," in *Mississippi Quarterly.* XVI (1963), pp. 128–145.

Stein, William B. "Melville's Chimney Chivy," in *Emerson Society Quarterly.* XXXV (1964), pp. 63–65.

Turner, Darwin T. "Smoke from Melville's Chimney," in *College Language Association Journal.* VII (1963), pp. 107–113.

Woodruff, Stuart C. "Melville and His Chimney," in *PMLA.* LXXV (1960), pp. 283–292.

Israel Potter

Chase, Richard. *Herman Melville: A Critical Study.* New York: Macmillan, 1949, pp. 176–184.

Farnsworth, R.M. "*Israel Potter*: Pathetic Comedy," in *Bulletin of the New York Public Library.* LXV (February, 1961), pp. 125–132.

Frederick, John T. "Symbol and Theme in Melville's *Israel Potter*," in *Modern Fiction Studies.* VIII (Autumn, 1962), pp. 265–275.

Hull, Raymond. "London and Melville's *Israel Potter*," in *Emerson Society Quarterly.* XLVII (1967), pp. 78–81.

Jackson, Kenny. "*Israel Potter*: Melville's Fourth of July Story," in *College Language Association Journal*. VI (March, 1963), pp. 194–204.

Keyssar, Alexander. *Melville's* Israel Potter, *Reflections on the American Dream*. Cambridge, Mass.: Harvard University Press, 1969.

McCutcheon, Roger P. "The Technique of Melville's *Israel Potter*," in *South Atlantic Quarterly*. XXVII (April, 1928), pp. 161–174.

Rampersad, Arnold. *Melville's* Israel Potter: *A Pilgrimage and Progress*. Bowling Green, Oh.: Bowling Green University Popular Press, 1969.

Watson, Charles N., Jr. "Melville's Israel Potter: Fathers and Sons," in *Studies in the Novel*. VII (1975), pp. 563–568.

————. "Premature Burial in *Arthur Gordon Pym* and *Israel Potter*," in *American Literature*. XLVII, pp. 105–107.

Weaver, Raymond M. "Introduction in *Israel Potter* by Herman Melville. New York: A & C. Boni, 1924, p. xvii.

Yates, Norris. "An Instance of Parallel Imagery in Hawthorne, Melville, and Frost," in *Philological Quarterly*. XXXVI (April, 1957), pp. 276–280.

"Jimmy Rose"

Brack, Vida K. and O.M. Brack. "Weathering Cape Horn: Survivors in Melville's Minor Short Fiction," in *Arizona Quarterly*. XXVIII (1972), pp. 66–67.

Browne, Roy B. *Melville's Drive to Humanism*. West Lafayette, Ind.: Purdue University Press, 1971, pp. 242–247.

Campbell, Marie A. "A Quiet Crusade: Melville's Tales of the Fifties," in *American Transcendental Quarterly*. VII (1970), pp. 9–10.

Chase, Richard. *Herman Melville: A Critical Study*. New York: Macmillan, 1949, pp. 171–173.

Fisher, Marvin. "Melville's 'Jimmy Rose': Truly Risen?," in *Studies in Short Fiction*. IV (1966), pp. 1–11.

Fogle, Richard H. *Melville's Shorter Tales*. Norman: University of Oklahoma Press, 1960, pp. 61–62.

Gargano, James W. "Melville's 'Jimmy Rose,' " in *Western Humanities Review*. XVI (1962), pp. 276–280.

Miller, James E. *A Reader's Guide to Herman Melville*. New York: Farrar, Straus, and Cudahy, 1962.

Slater, Judith. "The Domestic Adventurer in Melville's Tales," in *American Literature*. XXXVII (1965), pp. 273–275.

Tutt, Ralph M. "Jimmy Rose—Melville's Displaced Noble," in *Emerson Society Quarterly*. XXXIII (1963), pp. 28–32.

"The Lightning-Rod Man"

Bickley, R. Bruce. "The Triple Thrust of Satire in Melville's Short Stories: Society, the Narrator, and the Reader," in *Studies in American Humor.* I (1975), pp. 178–179.

Brack, Vida K. and O.M. Brack. "Weathering Cape Horn: Survivors in Melville's Minor Short Fiction," in *Arizona Quarterly.* XXVIII (1972), pp. 68–69.

Browne, Roy B. *Melville's Drive to Humanism.* West Lafayette, Ind.: Purdue University Press, 1971, pp. 229–237.

Campbell, Marie A. "A Quiet Crusade: Melville's Tales of the Fifties," in *American Transcendental Quarterly.* VII (1970), p. 10.

Chase, Richard. *Herman Melville: A Critical Study.* New York: Macmillan, 1949, pp. 169–170.

Fisher, Marvin. " 'The Lightning-Rod Man': Melville's Testament of Rejection," in *Studies in Short Fiction.* VII (1970), pp. 433–438.

Fogle, Richard H. *Melville's Shorter Tales.* Norman: University of Oklahoma Press, 1960, pp. 55–58.

Hoffman, Charles G. "The Shorter Fiction of Herman Melville," in *South Atlantic Quarterly.* LII (1953), pp. 423–424.

Oliver, Egbert S. "Herman Melville's Lightning-Rod Man," in *Philadelphia Forum.* XXXV (June 1, 1956), pp. 4–5.

Shusterman, Alan. "Melville's 'The Lightning-Rod Man': A Reading," in *Studies in Short Fiction.* IX (1972), pp. 165–174.

Slater, Judith. "The Domestic Adventurer in Melville's Tales," in *American Literature.* XXXVII (1965), pp. 272–273.

Stockton, Eric W. "A Commentary on Melville's 'The Lightning-Rod Man,' " *Papers of the Michigan Academy of Science, Arts and Letters.* XL (1955), pp. 321–328.

Werge, Thomas. "Melville's Satanic Salesman: Scientism and Puritanism in 'The Lightning-Rod Man,' " in *Christianity and Literature.* XXI (1972), pp. 6–12.

Wilson, Harry B. "The Double View: Melville's 'The Lightning-Rod Man,' " in *Approaches to the Short Story.* Edited by Neil D. Isaacs and Louis H. Leiter. San Francisco: Chandler, 1963, pp. 16–29.

Mardi

Arvin, Newton. "Melville's *Mardi,*" in *American Quarterly.* II (Spring, 1950), pp. 71–81.

Bernard, Kenneth. "Melville's *Mardi* and the Second Loss of Paradise," in *Lock Haven Review.* VII (1965), pp. 23–30.

Blansett, B.N. "From Dark to Dark; *Mardi*, A Foreshadowing of *Pierre*," in *Southern Quarterly*. I (April, 1963), pp. 213–227.

Braswell, William. *Melville's Religious Thought: An Essay in Interpretation*. Durham, N.C.: Duke University Press, 1943, pp. 86–106.

Davis, Merrell R. "The Flower Symbolism in *Mardi*," in *Modern Language Quarterly*. II (December, 1941), pp. 625–638.

————. *Melville's* Mardi: *A Charter Voyage*. New Haven, Conn.: Yale University Press, 1952.

Freeman, John. *Herman Melville*. New York: Macmillan, 1926, pp. 95–108.

Graham, Philip. "The Riddle of Melville's *Mardi*: A Reinterpretation," in *Texas Studies in English*. XXXVI (1957), pp. 93–99.

Hillway, Tyrus. "Toji's Abdication in Herman Melville's *Mardi*," in *American Literature*. XVI (November, 1944), pp. 204–207.

————. "Toji's Quest for Certainty," in *American Literature*. XVIII (March, 1946), pp. 27–34.

Jaffe, David. "Some Sources of Melville's *Mardi*," in *American Literature*. IX (March, 1937), pp. 56–69.

Larrabee, Stephen A. "Melville Against the World," in *South Atlantic Quarterly*. XXXIV (October, 1935), pp. 410–418.

Mason, Ronald. *The Spirit Above the Dust: A Study of Herman Melville*. London: John Lehmann, 1951, pp. 38–65.

Miller, James E., Jr. "The Many Masks of *Mardi*," in *Journal of English and Germanic Philology*. LVIII (July, 1959), pp. 400–413.

Mills, Gordon. "The Significance of Arcturus in *Mardi*," in *American Literature*. XIV (May, 1942), pp. 158–161.

Mumford, Lewis. *Herman Melville*. New York: Harcourt, Brace, 1929, pp. 93–107.

Rosenberry, Edward H. *Melville and the Comic Spirit*. Cambridge, Mass.: Harvard University Press, 1955, pp. 57–89.

Sedgwick, William Ellery. *Herman Melville: The Tragedy of Mind*. Cambridge, Mass.: Harvard University Press, 1944, pp. 37–61.

Stern, Milton R. *The Fine Hammered Steel of Herman Melville*. Urbana: University of Illinois Press, 1957, pp. 66–149.

Stone, Geoffrey. *Melville*. New York: Sheed and Ward, 1949, pp. 86–108.

Thompson, Lawrance. *Melville's Quarrel with God*. Princeton, N.J.: Princeton University Press, 1952, pp. 59–69.

Wright, Nathalia. "The Head and the Heart in Melville's *Mardi*," in *PMLA*. LXVI (June, 1951), pp. 351–362.

Moby Dick

Anderson, Charles Robert. *Melville in the South Seas.* New York: Columbia University Press, 1939, pp. 11–65.

Arvin, Newton. *Herman Melville.* New York: William Sloane, 1950, pp. 143–193.

Austin, Allen. "The Three-Stranded Allegory of *Moby Dick*," in *College English.* XXVI (February, 1965), pp. 344–349.

Bernstein, John. *Pacifism and Rebellion in the Writings of Herman Melville.* The Hague: Newton, 1964, pp. 82–125.

Berthoff, Warner. *The Example of Melville.* Princeton, N.J.: Princeton University Press, 1962, pp. 78–98, 159–170, 175–182.

Boath, T.Y. "*Moby Dick*: Standing Up to God," in *Nineteenth-Century Fiction.* XVII (June, 1962), pp. 33–43.

Bowden, Edwin T. *The Dungeon of the Heart: Human Isolation and the American Novel.* New York: Macmillan, 1961, pp. 156–172.

Bowen, Merlin. *The Long Encounter: Self and Experience in the Writings of Herman Melville.* Chicago: University of Chicago Press, 1960, pp. 143–157, 240–252.

Braswell, William. "The Main Theme of *Moby Dick*," in *Emerson Society Quarterly.* XXVIII (October, 1962), pp. 15–17.

Chase, Richard. *Herman Melville: A Critical Study.* New York: Macmillan, 1949, pp. 43–102.

Cowan, S.A. "In Praise of Self-Reliance; The Role of Bulkington in *Moby Dick*," in *American Literature.* XXXVIII (January, 1967), pp. 547–556.

Dillingham, William B. "The Narrator of *Moby Dick*," in *English Studies.* XLIX (February, 1968), pp. 20–29.

Dryden, Edgar E. *Melville's Thematics of Form: The Great Art of Telling the Truth.* Baltimore: Johns Hopkins University Press, 1968, pp. 81–113.

Eldridge, H.G. "Careful Disorder: The Structure of *Moby Dick*," in *American Literature.* XXXIX (May, 1967), pp. 145–162.

Ellen, Sister Mary, I.H.M. "Duplicate Imagery in *Moby Dick*," in *Modern Fiction Studies.* VIII (Autumn, 1962), pp. 252–275.

Fiedler, Leslie A. *Love and Death in the American Novel.* New York: Criterion Books, 1960, pp. 520–552.

Finkelstein, Dorothee. *Melville's Orienda.* New Haven, Conn.: Yale University Press, 1961, pp. 223–234.

Franklin, H. Bruce. *The Wake of the Gods: Melville's Mythology.* Stanford, Calif.: Stanford University Press, pp. 53–98.

Frederix, Pierre. *Herman Melville.* Paris: Gallimard, 1950, pp. 185–203.

Freeman, John.   *Herman Melville.* New York: Macmillan, 1926, pp. 114–131.

Friedrich, Gerhard.   *In Pursuit of* Moby Dick. Wallingford, Pa.: Pendle Hill, 1958.

Gleim, William S.   *The Meaning of* Moby Dick. New York: Edmond Byrne Hackett, 1938.

————. "The Meaning of *Moby Dick*," in *New England Quarterly.* II (July, 1929), pp. 402–419.

Green, Martin.   *Re-Appraisals: Some Commonsense Readings in American Literature.* New York: Norton, 1963, pp. 87–108.

Hayford, Harrison and Hershel Parker, Editors.   Moby Dick: *An Authoritative Text: Reviews and Letters by Melville; Analogues and Sources; Criticism.* New York: Norton, 1967.

Hillway, Tyrus.   *Herman Melville.* New York: Twayne, 1963, pp. 83–106.

————. *Melville and the Whale.* Stonington, Conn.: Stonington, 1950.

Horsford, Howard C.   "The Design of the Argument in *Moby Dick*," in *Modern Fiction Studies.* VIII (Autumn, 1962), pp. 233–251.

Humphreys, A.R.   *Melville.* London: Oliver and Boyd, 1962, pp. 41–82.

Mason, Ronald.   *The Spirit Above the Dust: A Study of Herman Melville.* London: John Lehmann, 1951, pp. 111–157.

Matthiessen, F.O.   *American Renaissance: Art and Expression in the Age of Emerson and Whitman.* New York: Oxford University Press, 1949, pp. 282–291, 409–466.

Maxwell, D.E.S.   *Herman Melville.* New York: Humanities Press, 1968, pp. 32–53.

Mengeling, Marvin E.   "*Moby Dick*: The Fundamental Principles," in *Emerson Society Quarterly.* XXXVIII (1965), pp. 74–87.

Miller, James E., Jr.   *Quests Surd and Absurd: Essays in American Literature.* Chicago: University of Chicago Press, 1967, pp. 196–198, 206–207, 227–238.

Mumford, Lewis.   *Herman Melville.* New York: Harcourt, Brace, 1929, pp. 158–195.

————. "The Writing of *Moby Dick*," in *American Mercury.* XV (December, 1928), pp. 482–490.

Murray, Henry A.   "In Nomine Diaboli," in *New England Quarterly.* XXIV (December, 1951), pp. 435–452.

Myers, Henry Alonzo.   "Captain Ahab's Discovery: The Tragic Meaning of *Moby Dick*," in *New England Quarterly.* XV (March, 1942), pp. 15–34.

Olson, Charles.   *Call Me Ishmael.* New York: Reynad & Hitchcock, 1947.

Parke, John.   "Seven Moby Dicks," in *New England Quarterly.* XXVIII (September, 1955), pp. 319–338.

Parker, Hershel and Harrison Hayford, Editors. *Essays and Extracts:* Moby Dick *as Doubloon, 1851–1970.* New York: Norton, 1970.

Percival, M.O. *A Reading of* Moby Dick. Chicago: University of Chicago Press, 1950.

Rosenberry, Edward H. *Melville and the Comic Spirit.* Cambridge, Mass.: Harvard University Press, 1955, pp. 93–138.

Schroeder, Fred E.H. "Enter Ahab, Then All: Theatrical Elements in Melville's Fiction," in *Dalhousie Review.* XLVI (Summer, 1966), pp. 223–232.

Sedgwick, William Ellery. *Herman Melville: The Tragedy of Mind.* Cambridge, Mass.: Harvard University Press, 1944, pp. 82–136.

Sewall, Richard B. "*Moby Dick* as Tragedy," in Moby Dick: *An Authoritative Text; Reviews and Letters by Melville; Analogues and Sources; Criticism.* Edited by Harrison Hayford and Hershel Parker. New York: Norton, 1967, pp. 692–702.

Short, R.W. "Melville as Symbolist," in *University of Kansas City Review.* XV (Autumn, 1948), pp. 38–46.

Shulman, Robert. "The Serious Functions of Melville's Phallic Jokes," in *American Literature.* XXXIII (May, 1961), pp. 179–194.

Stern, Milton R., Editor. *Discussions of* Moby Dick. Boston: Heath, 1960.

————. "Melville's Tragic Imagination: The Hero Without a Home," in *Patterns of Commitment in American Literature.* Edited by Marston La France. Toronto: University of Toronto Press, 1967, pp. 42–50.

Stewart, George R. "The Two *Moby Dicks*," in *American Literature.* XXV (January, 1954), pp. 417–448.

Stone, Edward. *Voices of Despair.* Athens: Ohio University Press, 1966, pp. 93–102.

Stone, Geoffrey. *Melville.* New York: Sheed and Ward, 1944, pp. 160–186.

Thompson, Lawrance. *Melville's Quarrel with God.* Princeton, N.J.: Princeton University Press, 1952, pp. 127–243.

Vincent, Howard P. *The Trying-Out of Moby Dick.* Boston: Houghton Mifflin, 1949.

Vogel, Dan. "The Dramatic Chapters in *Moby Dick*," in *Nineteenth-Century Fiction.* XIII (December, 1958), pp. 239–247.

Walcutt, Charles Child. "The Fire Symbolism in *Moby Dick*," in *Modern Language Notes.* LIX (May, 1944), pp. 304–310.

————. *Man's Changing Mask: Modes and Methods of Characterization in Fiction.* Minneapolis: University of Minnesota Press, 1966, pp. 104–123.

Ward, J.A. "The Function of the Cetological Chapters in *Moby Dick*," in *American Literature.* XXVIII (May, 1956), pp. 164–183.

Watters, R.E. "The Meanings of the White Whale," in *University of Toronto Quarterly.* XX (January, 1951), pp. 155–168.

Woodson, Thomas. "Ahab's Greatness: Prometheus as Narcissus," in *ELH.* (September, 1966), pp. 351–369.

Young, James Dean. "The Nine Gams of the Pequod," in *American Literature.* XXV (January, 1954), pp. 449–463.

Yu, Beongcheon. "Ishmael's Equal Eye: The Source of Balance in *Moby Dick*," in *ELH.* XXXII (March, 1965), pp. 110–125.

Omoo

Anderson, Charles Roberts. "Contemporary American Opinions of *Typee* and *Omoo*," in *American Literature.* IX (March, 1937), pp. 1–25.

————. "Melville's English Debut," in *American Literature.* XI (March, 1939), pp. 23–38.

————. *Melville in the South Seas.* New York: Columbia University Press, 1939, pp. 199–345.

Bernstein, John. *Pacifism and Rebellion in the Writings of Herman Melville.* The Hague: Mouton, 1964, pp. 126–145.

Canaday, Nicholas. "The Theme of Authority in Melville's *Typee* and *Omoo*," in *Forum.* IV (Fall, 1963), pp. 38–41.

Dryden, Edgar A. *Melville's Thematics of Form: The Great Art of Telling the Truth.* Baltimore: Johns Hopkins University Press, 1968.

Eigner, Edwin M. "The Romantic Unity of Melville's *Omoo*," in *Philological Quarterly.* XLVI (January, 1967), pp. 95–108.

Forsythe, Robert S. "Herman Melville in the Marquesas," in *Philological Quarterly.* XV (January, 1936), pp. 1–15.

————. "Herman Melville in Tahiti," in *Philological Quarterly.* XVI (October, 1937), pp. 344–357.

————. "Herman Melville's Father Murphy," in *Notes and Queries.* CLXXII (April 10, 1937), pp. 254–258.

————. "More upon Herman Melville in Tahiti," in *Philological Quarterly.* XVII (January, 1938), pp. 1–17.

Frederix, Pierre. *Herman Melville.* Paris: Gallimard, 1950, pp. 132–147.

Kaplan, Sidney. "Herman Melville and the Whaling Enderbys," in *American Literature.* XXIV (May, 1952), pp. 224–230.

Lawrence, D.H. *Studies in Classic American Literature.* New York: Doubleday, 1955, pp. 142–156.

Levin, Harry. *The Power of Blackness: Hawthorne, Poe, Melville.* New York: Knopf, 1960.

Mason, Ronald. *The Spirit Above the Dust: A Study of Herman Melville.* London: John Lehmann, 1951, pp. 31–37.

Miller, James E., Jr. *A Reader's Guide to Herman Melville.* New York: Noonday, 1962, pp. 18–37.

Rosenberry, Edward. *Melville and the Comic Spirit.* Cambridge, Mass.: Harvard University Press, 1955.

"The Paradise of Bachelors and the Tartarus of Maids"

Arvin, Newton. *Herman Melville: A Critical Biography.* New York: William Sloane, 1950, pp. 236–237.

Bickley, R. Bruce. "The Triple Thrust of Satire in Melville's Short Stories: Society, the Narrator, and the Reader," in *Studies in American Humor.* I (1975), pp. 176–178.

Brack, Vida K. and O.M. Brack. "Weathering Cape Horn: Survivors in Melville's Minor Short Fiction," in *Arizona Quarterly.* XXVIII (1972), pp. 63–64.

———. "Two Views of Commitment: 'The Paradise of Bachelors and the Tartarus of Maids,' " in *American Transcendental Quarterly.* VII (Summer, 1970), pp. 43–47.

Browne, Ray B. *Melville's Drive to Humanism.* West Lafayette, Ind.: Purdue University Press, 1971, pp. 219–229.

Chase, Richard. *Herman Melville: A Critical Study.* New York: Macmillan, 1949, pp. 159–163.

Eby, E.H. "Herman Melville's 'Tartarus of Maids,' " in *Modern Language Quarterly.* I (1940), pp. 95–100.

Fiedler, Leslie. *Love and Death and the American Novel.* New York: Criterion Books, 1960.

Fisher, Marvin. "Melville's Tartarus: The Deflowering of New England," in *American Quarterly.* XXIII (1971), pp. 79–100.

Fogle, Richard H. *Melville's Shorter Tales.* Norman: University of Oklahoma Press, 1960, pp. 45–54.

Hoffman, Charles G. "The Shorter Fiction of Herman Melville," in *South Atlantic Quarterly.* LII (1953), p. 424.

Kaul, A.N. *The American Vision: Actual and Ideal Society in Nineteenth-Century Fiction.* New Haven, Conn.: Yale University Press, 1963, pp. 275–276.

Mayoux, Jean-Jacques. *Melville.* New York: Grove, 1960.

Rowland, Beryl. "Melville's Bachelors and Maids: Interpretation Through Symbol and Metaphor," in *American Literature.* LII (1969), pp. 389–405.

Sandberg, Alvin. "Erotic Patterns in 'The Paradise of Bachelors and the Tartarus of Maids,' " in *Literature and Psychology.* XVIII (1968), pp. 2–8.

Stein, William B. "Melville's Eros," in *Texas Studies in Literature and Language.* III (1961), pp. 297–308.

Thompson, W.R. " 'The Paradise of Bachelors and the Tartarus of Maids': A Reinterpretation," in *American Quarterly.* IX (1957), pp. 34–45.

Piazza Tales

Breinig, Helmbrecht. "The Destruction of Fairyland: Melville's Piazza in the Tradition of the American Imagination," in *English Literary History.* XXXV (1968), pp. 254–283.

Donaldson, Scott. "The Dark Truth of *The Piazza Tales,*" in *PMLA.* LXXXV (1970), pp. 1082–1083.

Fisher, Marvin. "Prospect and Perspective in Melville's 'Piazza,' " in *Criticism.* XVI (1974), pp. 203–216.

Fogle, Richard H. *Melville's Shorter Tales.* Norman: University of Oklahoma Press, 1960, pp. 85–91.

Howard, Leon. *Herman Melville: A Biography.* Berkeley: University of California Press, 1951.

Mason, Ronald. *The Spirit Above the Dust: A Study of Herman Melville.* London: John Lehmann, 1951, pp. 182–184.

Poenicke, Klaus. "A View from the Piazza: Herman Melville and the Legacy of the European Sublime," in *Comparative Literature Studies.* IV (1967), pp. 267–281.

Porte, Joel. *The Romance in America.* Middletown, Conn.: Wesleyan University Press, 1969, pp. 152–155.

Slater, Judith. "The Domestic Adventurer in Melville's Tales," in *American Literature.* XXXVII (1965), pp. 277–279.

Stein, William B. "Melville's Comedy of Faith," in *English Literary History.* XXVII (1960), pp. 315–333.

Turner, Darwin T. "A View of Melville's Piazza," in *College Language Association Journal.* VII (1963), pp. 56–62.

Pierre

Bernstein, John. *Pacifism and Rebellion in the Writings of Herman Melville.* The Hague: Mouton, 1964, pp. 126–145.

Berthoff, Warner. *The Example of Melville.* Princeton, N.J.: Princeton University Press, 1962, pp. 47–54.

Braswell, William. "Melville's Opinion of *Pierre,*" in *American Literature.* XXIII (May, 1951), pp. 246–250.

_____. *Melville's Religious Thought: An Essay in Interpretation.* Durham, N.C.: Duke University Press, 1943, pp. 75–106.

_____. "The Satirical Temper of Melville's *Pierre*," in *American Literature.* VII (January, 1936), pp. 424–438.

Chase, Richard. *Herman Melville: A Critical Study.* New York: Macmillan, 1949, pp. 103–141.

Dryden, Edgar E. *Melville's Thematics of Form: The Great Art of Telling the Truth.* Baltimore: Johns Hopkins University Press, 1968, pp. 115–148.

Fiedler, Leslie A. *Love and Death in the American Novel.* New York: Criterion Books, 1960, pp. 403–408.

Franklin, H. Bruce. *The Wake of the Gods: Melville's Mythology.* Stanford, Calif.: Stanford University Press, 1963, pp. 99–125.

Frederix, Pierre. *Herman Melville.* Paris: Gallimard, 1950, pp. 204–213.

Freeman, John. *Herman Melville.* New York: Macmillan, 1926, pp. 108–113.

Fussell, Edwin. "Herman Melville," in *Frontier: American Literature and the American West.* Princeton, N.J.: Princeton University Press, 1965.

Gupta, R.K. "Melville's Use of Non-Novelistic Conventions in *Pierre*," in *Emerson Society Quarterly.* XLVIII (1967), pp. 141–145.

Hillway, Tyrus. *Herman Melville.* New York: Twayne, 1963.

_____. "Pierre, the Fool of Virtue," in *American Literature.* XXI (May, 1949), pp. 201–211.

Howard, Leon. "Herman Melville," in *Six American Novelists of the Nineteenth Century: An Introduction.* Edited by Richard Foster. Minneapolis: University of Minnesota Press, 1968, pp. 101–105.

Humphreys, A.R. *Melville.* London: Oliver and Boyd, 1962, pp. 83–92.

Kissane, James. "Imagery, Myth, and Melville's *Pierre*," in *American Literature.* XXVI (January, 1955), pp. 564–572.

Mason, Ronald. *The Spirit Above the Dust: A Study of Herman Melville.* London: John Lehmann, 1951, pp. 158–178.

Mayoux, Jean-Jacques. *Melville.* London: Evergreen Books, 1960, pp. 100–111.

Miller, James E., Jr. *A Reader's Guide to Herman Melville.* New York: Noonday, 1962, pp. 118–139.

Mogan, Joseph J., Jr. "Pierre and Manfred: Melville's Study of the Byronic Hero," in *Papers on English Language and Literature.* I (Summer, 1965), pp. 230–240.

Moorman, Charles. "Melville's Pierre in the City," in *American Literature.* XXVII (January, 1956), pp. 571–577.

————. "Melville's Pierre and the Fortunate Fall," in *American Literature*. XXV (March, 1953), pp. 13–30.

Mumford, Lewis. *Herman Melville.* New York: Harcourt, Brace, 1929, pp. 203–222.

Sedgwick, William Ellery. *Herman Melville: The Tragedy of Mind.* Cambridge, Mass.: Harvard University Press, 1944, pp. 137–172.

Stern, Milton R. *The Fine Hammered Steel of Herman Melville.* Urbana: University of Illinois Press, 1957, pp. 150–205.

Stone, Geoffrey. *Melville.* New York: Sheed and Ward, 1949, pp. 187–210.

Thompson, Lawrance. *Melville's Quarrel with God.* Princeton, N.J.: Princeton University Press, 1952, pp. 247–294.

Watson, E.L. Grant. "Melville's *Pierre*," in *New England Quarterly*. III (April, 1930), pp. 195–234.

Wright, Nathalia. "*Pierre*: Herman Melville's Inferno," in *American Literature*. XXXII (May, 1960), pp. 167–181.

Yaggy, Elinor. "Shakespeare and Melville's *Pierre*," in *Boston Public Library Quarterly*. VI (January, 1954), pp. 43–51.

The Poetry of Melville

Barrett, Lawrence. "The Differences in Melville's Poetry," in *PMLA*. LXX (September, 1955), pp. 606–623.

Bezanson, W.E. "Melville's Reading of Arnold's Poetry," in *PMLA*. LXIX (June, 1954), pp. 365–391.

Cannon, Agnes D. "Melville's Concepts of the Poet and Poetry," in *Arizona Quarterly*. XXXI (1975), pp. 315–339.

Dillingham, W.B. " 'Neither Believer Nor Infidel': Theme of Melville's Poetry," in *Personalist*. XLVI (Fall, 1965), pp. 501–516.

Fogle, R.H. "Melville's Poetry," in *Tulane Studies in English*. XII (1962), pp. 81–86.

————. "The Themes of Melville's Later Poetry," in *Tulane Studies in English*. XI (1961), pp. 65–86.

Hand, H.E. " 'And War Be Done': Battle-Pieces and Other Civil War Poetry of Herman Melville," in *Journal of Human Relations*. XI (1963), pp. 326–340.

Mathieu, Bertrand. " 'Plain Mechanic Power': Melville's *Earliest Poems, Battle-Pieces and Aspects of the War*," in *Essays in Arts and Sciences*. V (1976), pp. 113–128.

Montague, G.B. "Melville's *Battle-Pieces*," in *University of Texas Studies in English*. XXXV (1956), pp. 106–115.

Perrine, Lawrence. "The Nature of Proof in the Interpretation of Poetry," in *English Journal*. LI (September, 1962), pp. 393–398.

Robillard, Douglas, Editor. "Symposium: Melville the Poet," in *Essays in Arts and Sciences.* V (1976), p. ii.

Shaw, R.O. "The Civil War Poems of Herman Melville," in *Lincoln Herald.* LXVIII (Spring, 1966), pp. 44–49.

Stein, W.B. "Melville's Poetry: Its Symbols of Individuation," in *Literature and Poetry.* VII (May, 1957), pp. 21–26.

————. "Melville's Poetry: Two Rising Notes," in *Emerson Society Quarterly.* XXVII (1962), pp. 10–13.

————. "Time, History and Religion: A Glimpse of Melville's Lute Poetry," in *Arizona Quarterly.* XXII (Summer, 1966), pp. 136–145.

Warren, R.P. "Melville's Poems," in *Southern Review.* ns 3 (August, 1967), pp. 799–855.

"Poor Man's Pudding and Rich Man's Crumbs"

Bickley, R. Bruce. "The Triple Thrust of Satire in Melville's Short Stories: Society, the Narrator, and the Reader," in *Studies in American Humor.* I (1975), pp. 174–176.

Brack, Vida K. and O.M. Brack. "Weathering Cape Horn: Survivors in Melville's Minor Short Fiction," in *Arizona Quarterly.* XXVIII (1972), p. 63.

Browne, Roy B. *Melville's Drive to Humanism.* West Lafayette, Ind.: Purdue University Press, 1971, pp. 209–219.

Fisher, Marvin. " 'Poor Man's Pudding': Melville's Meditation on Grace," in *American Transcendental Quarterly.* XIII (1972), pp. 32–36.

Fogle, Richard H. *Melville's Shorter Tales.* Norman: University of Oklahoma Press, 1960, pp. 40–45.

Hoffman, Charles G. "The Shorter Fiction of Herman Melville," in *South Atlantic Quarterly.* LII (1953), pp. 423–424.

Rowland, Beryl. "Melville's Waterloo in 'Rich Man's Crumbs,' " in *Nineteenth-Century Fiction.* XXV (1970), pp. 216–221.

————. "Sitting Up with a Corpse: Malthus According to Melville in 'Poor Man's Pudding and Rich Man's Crumbs,' " in *Journal of American Studies.* VI (1972), pp. 69–83.

Redburn

Bell, Michael D. "Melville's Redburn: Initiation and Authority," in *New England Quarterly.* XLVI (1973), pp. 558–572.

Bercovitch, Sacvan. "Melville's Search for National Identity: Son and Father in *Redburn, Pierre* and *Billy Budd,*" in *College Language Association Journal.* X (March, 1967), pp. 217–228.

Bernstein, Warner. *Pacifism and Rebellion in the Writings of Herman Melville.* The Hague: Mouton, 1964, pp. 57–67.

Berthoff, Warner. *The Example of Melville.* Princeton, N.J.: Princeton University Press, 1962, pp. 30–36.

Davison, R.A. "Redburn, Pierre, and Robin: Melville's Debt to Hawthorne?," in *Emerson Society Quarterly.* XLVII (1967), pp. 32–34.

Dryden, Edgar A. *Melville's Thematics of Form: The Great Art of Telling the Truth.* Baltimore: Johns Hopkins University Press, 1968, pp. 58–67.

Fiess, Edward. "Byron's Dark Blue Ocean and Melville's Rolling Sea," in *English Language Notes.* III (June, 1966), pp. 274–278.

Franklin, H. Bruce. "Redburn's Wicked End," in *Nineteenth-Century Fiction.* XX (September, 1965), pp. 140–194.

Freeman, John. *Herman Melville.* New York: Macmillan, 1926, pp. 84–88.

Gilman, William H. *Melville's Early Life and* Redburn. New York: New York University Press, 1951.

————. "Melville's Liverpool Trip," in *Modern Language Notes.* LXI (December, 1946), pp. 543–547.

Gozzi, Raymond D. "Melville's *Redburn*: Civilization and Its Discontents," in *Literature and Psychology.* XIII (Fall, 1963), p. 104.

Gross, John J. "The Rehearsal of Ishmael: Melville's *Redburn*," in *Virginia Quarterly Review.* XXVII (Summer, 1951), pp. 581–600.

Humphreys, A.R. *Melville.* London: Oliver and Boyd, 1962, pp. 28–40.

Huntress, Keith. "A Note on Melville's *Redburn*," in *New England Quarterly.* XVIII (June, 1945), pp. 259–260.

Kosak, Heinz. "Redburn's Image of Childhood," in *Emerson Society Quarterly.* XXXIX (1965), pp. 40–42.

Lisk, T.G. "Melville's Redburn: A Study in Dualism," in *English Language Notes.* V (December, 1967), pp. 113–120.

Mason, Ronald. *The Spirit Above the Dust: A Study of Herman Melville.* London: John Lehmann, 1951, pp. 67–79.

Miller, James E. "Redburn and White Jacket: Initiation and Baptism," in *Nineteenth-Century Fiction.* XIII (March, 1959), pp. 273–293.

Schweter, James. "Redburn and the Failure of Mythic Criticism," in *American Literature.* XXXIX (November, 1967), pp. 274–297.

Sedgwick, William Ellery. *Herman Melville: The Tragedy of Mind.* Cambridge, Mass.: Harvard University Press, 1944, pp. 62–81.

Thompson, Lawrance. *Melville's Quarrel with God.* Princeton, N.J.: Princeton University Press, 1952, pp. 73–89.

Thorp, Willard. "Redburn's Prosy Old Guidebook," in *PMLA.* LIII (1938), pp. 1146–1156.

"The Two Temples"

Asals, Frederick. "Satire and Skepticism in 'The Two Temples,' " in *Books at Brown.* XXIV (1971), pp. 7–18.

Bickley, R. Bruce. "The Triple Thrust of Satire in Melville's Short Stories: Society, the Narrator, and the Reader," in *Studies in American Humor.* I (1975), pp. 173–174.

Browne, Roy B. *Melville's Drive to Humanism.* West Lafayette, Ind.: Purdue University Press, 1971, pp. 200–208.

Fisher, Marvin. "Focus on Herman Melville's 'The Two Temples': The Denigration of the American Dream," in *American Dreams, American Nightmares.* Edited by David Madden. Carbondale: Southern Illinois University Press, 1970, pp. 76–86.

Fogle, Richard H. *Melville's Shorter Tales.* Norman: University of Oklahoma Press, 1960, pp. 36–40.

Rowland, Beryl. "Melville Answers the Theologian: The Ladder of Charity in "The Two Temples," in *Mosaic.* VII (1974), pp. 1–13.

Typee

Anderson, Charles Roberts. "Contemporary American Opinions of *Typee* and *Omoo,*" in *American Literature.* IX (March, 1937), pp. 1–25.

————. "Melville's English Debut," in *American Literature.* XI (March, 1939), pp. 23–38.

————. *Melville in the South Seas.* New York: Columbia University Press, 1939, pp. 69–195.

Bernstein, John. *Pacificism and Rebellion in the Writings of Herman Melville.* The Hague: Mouton, 1964.

Birss, John H. "The Story of Toby, A Sequel to *Typee,*" in *Harvard Library Bulletin.* I (Winter, 1947), pp. 118–119.

Canaday, Nicholas. "The Theme of Authority in Melville's *Typee* and *Omoo,*" in *Forum.* IV (Fall, 1963), pp. 38–41.

Dryden, Edgar A. *Melville's Thematics of Form: The Great Art of Telling the Truth.* Baltimore: Johns Hopkins University Press, 1968, pp. 37–46.

Firebaugh, J.J. "Humanist as Rebel: The Melville of *Typee,*" in *Nineteenth-Century Fiction.* IX (September, 1954), pp. 108–120.

Forsythe, Robert S. "Herman Melville in the Marquesas," in *Philological Quarterly.* XV (January, 1936), pp. 1–15.

Frederix, Pierre. *Herman Melville.* Paris: Gallimard, 1950, pp. 132–147.

Freeman, John. *Herman Melville.* New York: Macmillan, 1926, pp. 74–80.

Gobdes, Clarence. "Gossip About Melville in the South Seas," in *New England Quarterly.* X (September, 1937), pp. 526–531.

_____. "Melville's Friend Toby," in *Modern Language Notes.* LIX (January, 1944), pp. 52–55.

Houghton, D.E. "The Incredible Ending of Melville's *Typee,*" in *Emerson Society Quarterly.* XXII (1961), pp. 28–31.

Ishoy, Saada. *The American Novel: Two Studies.* Emporia: Kansas State Teachers College, 1965, pp. 7–13.

Jones, B.C. "American Frontier Humor in Melville's *Typee,*" in *New York Folklore Quarterly.* XV (Winter, 1950), pp. 283–288.

Lawrence, D.H. *Studies in Classic American Literature.* New York: Doubleday, 1955, pp. 142–156.

Mason, Ronald. *The Spirit Above the Dust: A Study of Herman Melville.* London: John Lehmann, 1951, pp. 21–30.

Mayoux, Jean-Jacques. *Melville.* London: Evergreen Books, 1960, pp. 36–42.

Miller, James E., Jr. *A Reader's Guide to Herman Melville.* New York: Noonday, 1962, pp. 18–37.

Petrullo, H.B. "The Neurotic Hero of *Typee,*" in *American Imago.* XII (Winter, 1955), pp. 317–323.

Ruland, Richard. "Melville and the Fortunate Fall: Typee as Eden," in *Nineteenth-Century Fiction.* XXIII (December, 1968), pp. 312–323.

Sedgwick, William Ellery. *Herman Melville: The Tragedy of Mind.* Cambridge, Mass.: Harvard University Press, 1944, pp. 19–35.

Stern, Milton R. *The Fine Hammered Steel of Herman Melville.* Urbana: University of Illinois Press, 1957, pp. 29–65.

Thomas, Russell. "Yarn for Melville's *Typee,*" in *Philological Quarterly.* XV (January, 1936), pp. 16–29.

Thompson, Lawrance. *Melville's Quarrel with God.* Princeton, N.J.: Princeton University Press, 1952, pp. 45–55.

Weathers, Winston. "Melville and the Comedy of Communications," in *ETC.* XX (December, 1963), pp. 411–420.

White-Jacket

Allen, Priscilla. "*White-Jacket* and the Man-of-War Microcosm," in *American Quarterly.* XXV (1973), pp. 32–47.

Anderson, Charles Roberts. *Melville in the South Seas.* New York: Columbia University Press, 1939, pp. 349–434.

_____. "A Reply to Herman Melville's *White-Jacket* by Rear-Admiral Thomas O. Selfridge, Sr.," in *American Literature.* VII (May, 1935), pp. 123–144.

Bernstein, John. *Pacifism and Rebellion in the Writings of Herman Melville.* The Hague: Mouton, 1964, pp. 68–81.

Dryden, Edgar A. *Melville's Thematics of Form: The Great Art of Telling the Truth.* Baltimore: Johns Hopkins University Press, 1968, pp. 67–79.

Freeman, John. *Herman Melville.* New York: Macmillan, 1926.

Hayford, Harrison. "The Sailor Poet of *White-Jacket*," in *Boston Public Library Quarterly.* III (July, 1951), pp. 221–228.

Humphreys, A.R. *Melville.* London: Oliver and Boyd, 1962, pp. 28–40.

Huntress, Keith. "Melville's Use of a Source for *White-Jacket*," in *American Literature.* XVII (March, 1945), pp. 66–74.

McCarthy, Paul. "Symbolic Elements in *White-Jacket*," in *Midwest Quarterly.* VII (Summer, 1966), pp. 309–329.

Mason, Ronald. *The Spirit Above the Dust: A Study of Herman Melville.* London: John Lehmann, 1951, pp. 80–95.

Miller, James E. "*Redburn* and *White-Jacket*: Initiation and Baptism," in *Nineteenth-Century Fiction.* XIII (March, 1959), pp. 273–293.

Mordell, Albert. "Melville and *White-Jacket*," in *Saturday Review of Literature.* VII (July 4, 1931), p. 946.

Nichol, John W. "Melville's Soiled Fish of the Sea," in *American Literature.* XXI (November, 1949), pp. 338–339.

Philbrick, Thomas L. "Another Source for *White-Jacket*," in *American Literature.* XXIX (January, 1958), pp. 431–439.

————. "Melville's Best Authorities," in *Nineteenth-Century Fiction.* XV (September, 1960), pp. 171–179.

Procter, Page S. "A Source for the Flogging Incident in *White-Jacket*," in *American Literature.* XXII (May, 1958), pp. 176–182.

Regan, Charles L. "Melville's Horned Woman," in *English Language Notes.* V (September, 1967), pp. 34–39.

Sedgwick, William Ellery. *Herman Melville: The Tragedy of Mind.* Cambridge, Mass.: Harvard University Press, 1944.

Seelye, John D. " 'Spontaneous Impress of Truth': Melville's Jack Chase: A Source, an Analogue, a Conjecture," in *Nineteenth-Century Fiction.* XX (March, 1966), pp. 367–376.

Stone, Geoffrey. *Melville.* New York: Sheed and Ward, 1949, pp. 125–135.

Thompson, Lawrance. *Melville's Quarrel with God.* Princeton, N.J.: Princeton University Press, 1952, pp. 93–124.

Vincent, Howard P. "*White-Jacket*: An Essay in Interpretation," in *New England Quarterly.* XXII (September, 1949), pp. 304–315.

Walker, Warren S. "A Note on Nathaniel Ames," in *American Literature.* XXVI (May, 1954), pp. 239–241.

Zirker, Priscilla. "Evidence of the Slavery Dilemma in *White-Jacket*," in *American Quarterly.* XVIII (Fall, 1966), pp. 477–492.

MENANDER
(342 B.C.–291 B.C.)

Dyskolos

Arnott, W. Geoffrey. *Menander, Plautus, Terence.* Oxford: Clarendon Press, 1975.

————. "The Modernity of Menander," in *Greece and Rome.* XXII (October, 1975), pp. 140–155.

————. "Young Lovers and Confidence Tricksters, the Rebirth of Menander," in *University of Leeds Review.* XIII (1970), pp. 1–18.

Blake, W.E. "Menander's *Dyskolos*: Restorations and Emendations," in *Classical Philology.* LV (1960), pp. 174–176.

Downs, R.B. "Father of Modern Comedy: Menander," in *Famous Books, Ancient and Medieval.* New York: Barnes & Noble, 1964, pp. 135–139.

Fantham, E. "Adaptation and Survival: a Genre Study of Roman Comedy in Relation to Its Greek Sources," in *Versions of Medieval Comedy.* Edited by Paul G. Ruggiers. Norman: University of Oklahoma Press, 1977, pp. 19–49.

Gomme, Arnold Wycombe and F.H. Sandback. *Menander, A Commentary.* Oxford: Oxford University Press, 1973.

Griffin, J.G. "The Distribution of Parts in Menander's *Dyskolos*," in *Classical Quarterly.* X (1960), pp. 113–117.

Keuls, E. "Mystery Elements in Menander's *Dyskolus*," in *Transactions of the American Philological Association.* C (1969), pp. 209–220.

Lever, K. "The *Dyskolos* and Menander's Reputation," in *Classical Journal.* LV (April, 1960), pp. 321–326.

MacCary, W.T. "Menander's Characters; Their Names, Roles and Masks," in *Transactions of the American Philological Association.* CI (1970), pp. 277–290.

————. "Menander's Slaves; The Names, Roles and Masks," in *Transactions of the American Philological Association.* C (1969), pp. 277–294.

Moulton, Carroll. "Introduction," in *The Dyskolos.* By Menander. New York: American Library, 1977.

Nicoll, Allardyce. "From Menander to the Mimes," in *World Drama; From Aeschylus to Anouilh.* New York: Barnes & Noble, 1976, pp. 74–99.

Pack, R.A. "On the Plot of Menander's *Dyskolos*," in *Classical Philology.* XXX (1935), pp. 151–160.

Photiades, P.J. "Pan's Prologue to the *Dyskolos* of Menander," in *Greece and Rome.* V (October, 1958), pp. 108–122.

Post, L.A. "Some Subtleties in Menander's *Dyskolus*, in *American Journal of Philology*. LXXXIV (January, 1963), pp. 36–51.

_____. "Virtue Promoted in Menander's *Dyskolus*," in *Transactions of the American Philological Association*. XCI (1960), pp. 152–161.

Quincey, J.H. *Notes on the* Dyskolos *of Menander*. Adelaide, Australia: Griffin Press, 1959.

Reckford, K.J. "*Dyskolos* of Menander with Synopsis of Play," in *Studies in Philology*. LVIII (January, 1961), pp. 1–24.

Sandbach, F.H. "Menander," in *The Comic Theatre of Greece and Rome*. New York: Norton, 1977, pp. 76–102.

Ussher, R.G. "Old Comedy and Character: Some Comments," in *Greece and Rome*. XXIV (April, 1977), pp. 71–79.

Webster, Thomas B.L. "The Comedy of Menander," in *Roman Drama*. Edited by T.A. Dorey and D.R. Dudley. New York: Basic Books, 1965, pp. 1–20.

_____. *An Introduction to Menander*. New York: Barnes & Noble, 1974.

_____. *Studies in Menander*. Manchester, England: Manchester University Press, 1950.

GEORGE MEREDITH
(1828–1909)

The Adventures of Harry Richmond

Bailey, Elmer James. *The Novels of George Meredith: A Study.* New York: Haskell House, 1971, pp. 106–115.

Baker, Ernest A. *The History of the English Novel,* Volume VIII. New York: Barnes & Noble, 1950, pp. 350–355.

Beach, Joseph Warren. *The Comic Spirit in George Meredith: An Interpretation.* New York: Longmans, Green, 1911, pp. 77–82.

Beer, Gillian. *Meredith: A Change of Masks, A Study of the Novels.* London: Athlone, 1970, pp. 35–69.

Buckley, Jerome Hamilton. *Season of Youth: The Bildungsroman from Dickens to Golding.* Cambridge, Mass.: Harvard University Press, 1974, pp. 82–91.

Crees, J.H.E. *George Meredith: A Study of His Works and Personality.* Oxford: B.H. Blackwell, 1928, pp. 57–60.

Eaker, J. Gordon. "Meredith's Human Comedy," in *Nineteenth-Century Fiction.* V (March, 1951), pp. 257–258.

Edgar, Pelham. *The Art of the Novel from 1700 to the Present Time.* New York: Macmillan, 1933, pp. 154–156.

Gretton, Mary Sturge. *The Writings and Life of George Meredith, A Centenary Study.* London: Oxford University Press, 1926, pp. 100–106.

Hardy, Barbara and Bernard A. Brunner. " 'A Way to Your Hearts Through Fire and Water': The Structure of Imagery in *Harry Richmond,*" in *Essays in Criticism.* X (April, 1960), pp. 163–180. Reprinted in their *The Appropriate Form: An Essay on the Novel.* London: Athlone, 1964, pp. 83–104.

Hergenhan, L.T. "Introduction," in *The Adventures of Harry Richmond.* Lincoln: University of Nebraska Press, 1970, pp. xi–xxxiv.

————. "Meredith's Attempts to Win Popularity: Contemporary Reactions," in *Studies in English Literature, 1500–1900.* IV (Autumn, 1964), pp. 637–651.

Hudson, Richard B. "Meredith's Autobiography and *The Adventures of Harry Richmond,*" in *Nineteenth-Century Fiction.* IX (June, 1954), pp. 38–49.

Kelvin, Norman. *A Troubled Eden: Nature and Society in the Works of George Meredith.* Stanford, Calif.: Stanford University Press, 1961, pp. 56–57, 73–83.

Lindsay, Jack. *George Meredith: His Life and Work.* London: Bodley Head, 1956, pp. 319–326.

Mannheimer, Monica. *The Generations in Meredith's Novels.* Stockholm: Almquist and Wiksell, 1972, pp. 90–105, 143–147.

Moffatt, James. *George Meredith: A Primer to the Novels.* Port Washington, N.Y.: Kennikat, 1969, pp. 193–208.

Pritchett, V.S. *George Meredith and English Comedy.* New York: Random House, 1969, pp. 79–96.

Stevenson, Lionel. *The Ordeal of George Meredith, A Biography.* New York: Scribner's, 1953, pp. 178–185.

Tarratt, Margaret. "*The Adventures of Harry Richmond*: Bildungsroman and Historical Novel," in *Meredith Now: Some Critical Essays.* Edited by Ian Fletcher. New York: Barnes & Noble, 1971, pp. 165–187.

Weygandt, Cornelius. "George Meredith and His Reading of Life," in *A Century of the English Novel.* New York: Century, 1925, pp. 205–206.

Williams, David. *George Meredith: His Life and Lost Love.* London: Hamish Hamilton, 1977, pp. 123–127.

Williams, Ioan. *The Realist Novel in England: A Study in Development.* London: Macmillan, 1974, pp. 193–196.

Wright, Walter F. *Art and Substance in George Meredith, A Study in Narrative.* Lincoln: University of Nebraska Press, 1953, pp. 94–99.

The Amazing Marriage

Bailey, Elmer James. *The Novels of George Meredith: A Study.* New York: Haskell House, 1971, pp. 176–181.

Baker, Ernest A. *The History of the English Novel,* Volume VIII. New York: Barnes & Noble, 1950, pp. 378–379.

Beach, Joseph Warren. *The Comic Spirit in George Meredith: An Interpretation.* New York: Longmans, Green, 1911, pp. 142–156.

Beer, Gillian. "*The Amazing Marriage*: A Study in Contraries," in *Review of English Literature.* VII (1966), pp. 92–105. Reprinted in her *Meredith: A Change of Masks, A Study of the Novels.* London: Athlone, 1970, pp. 168–181.

DeGraaff, Robert M. "The Double Narrator in *The Amazing Marriage*," in *Victorian Newsletter.* XLIX (1976), pp. 24–26.

Eaker, J. Gordon. "Meredith's Human Comedy," in *Nineteenth-Century Fiction.* V (March, 1951), pp. 266–267.

Gretton, Mary Sturge. *The Writings and Life of George Meredith, A Centenary Study.* London: Oxford University Press, 1926, pp. 216–232.

Hardy, Barbara. "*Lord Ormont and His Aminta* and *The Amazing Marriage*," in *Meredith Now: Some Critical Essays.* Edited by Ian Fletcher. New York: Barnes & Noble, 1971, pp. 295–312.

Kelvin, Norman. *A Troubled Eden: Nature and Society in the Works of George Meredith.* Stanford, Calif.: Stanford University Press, 1961, pp. 188–197.

Kruppa, Joseph E. "Meredith's Late Novels: Suggestions for a Critical Approach," in *Nineteenth-Century Fiction.* XIX (December, 1964), pp. 271–286.

Lawrence, F.B. "Lyric and Romance: Meredith's Poetic Fiction," in *Victorian Essays: A Symposium.* Edited by Warren D. Anderson and Thomas D. Clareson. Kent, Ohio: Kent State University Press, 1967, pp. 87–106.

Lindsay, Jack. *George Meredith: His Life and Work.* London: Bodley Head, 1956, pp. 319–326.

McCullen, M.L. "Handsome Heroes and Healthy Heroines: Patterns of the Ideal in George Meredith's Later Novels," in *Cithara.* XIV (1974), pp. 95–106.

Moffatt, James. *George Meredith: A Primer to the Novels.* Port Washington, N.Y.: Kennikat, 1969, pp. 355–399.

Sassoon, Siegfried. *Meredith.* New York: Viking, 1948, pp. 233–238.

Stevenson, Lionel. *The Ordeal of Geroge Meredith, A Biography.* New York: Scribner's, 1953, pp. 319–322.

Williams, David. *George Meredith: His Life and Lost Love.* London: Hamish Hamilton, 1977, pp. 162–165.

Wright, Walter F. *Art and Substance in George Meredith, A Study in Narrative.* Lincoln: University of Nebraska Press, 1953, pp. 99–100, 182–185.

Beauchamp's Career

Bailey, Elmer James. *The Novels of George Meredith: A Study.* New York: Haskell House, 1971, pp. 115–128.

Baker, Ernest A. *The History of the English Novel,* Volume VIII. New York: Barnes & Noble, 1950, pp. 356–363.

Bartlett, Phyllis. "The Novels of George Meredith," in *Review of English Literature.* III (1962), pp. 31–46.

Beer, Gillian. *Meredith: A Change of Masks, A Study of the Novels.* London: Athlone, 1970, pp. 70–107.

Crees, J.H.E. *George Meredith: A Study of His Works and Personality.* Oxford: B.H. Blackwell, 1928, pp. 55–57.

Eaker, J. Gordon. "Meredith's Human Comedy," in *Nineteenth-Century Fiction.* V (March, 1951), pp. 258–269.

Edgar, Pelham. *The Art of the Novel From 1700 to the Present Time.* New York: Macmillan, 1933, pp. 162–163.

Gretton, Mary Sturge. *The Writings and Life of George Meredith, A Centenary Study.* London: Oxford University Press, 1926, pp. 113–126.

Howard, David. "George Meredith: 'Delicate' and 'Epical' Fiction," in *Literature and Politics in the Nineteenth Century*. Edited by John Lucas. London: Methuen, 1971, pp. 160–171.

Karl, Frederick R. "*Beauchamp's Career*: An English Ordeal," in *Nineteenth-Century Fiction*. XVI (September, 1961), pp. 117–131.

Kelvin, Norman. *A Troubled Eden: Nature and Society in the Works of George Meredith*. Stanford, Calif.: Stanford University Press, 1961, pp. 83–100.

Kettle, Arnold. "*Beauchamp's Career*," in *Meredith Now: Some Critical Essays*. Edited by Ian Fletcher. New York: Barnes & Noble, 1971, pp. 188–204.

Lindsay, Jack. *George Meredith: His Life and Work*. London: Bodley Head, 1956, pp. 203–223.

Mannheimer, Monica. *The Generations in Meredith's Novels*. Stockholm, Sweden: Almquist and Wiksell, 1972, pp. 105–119, 147–155.

Moffat, James. *George Meredith: A Primer to the Novels*. Port Washington, N.Y.: Kennikat, 1969, pp. 211–229.

Poole, Adrian. *Gissing in Context*. Totowa, N.J.: Rowman and Littlefield, 1975, pp. 17–18.

Pritchett, V.S. *George Meredith and English Comedy*. New York: Random House, 1969, pp. 99–112.

Sassoon, Siegfried. *Meredith*. New York: Viking, 1948, pp. 123–129.

Speare, Morris Edmund. "George Meredith—'Beauchampism,' The Idealist in Politics," in his *The Political Novel: Its Development in England and in America*. New York: Oxford University Press, 1924, pp. 237–254.

Stevenson, Lionel. *The Ordeal of George Meredith, A Biography*. New York: Scribner's, 1953, pp. 198–206.

Weygandt, Cornelius. "George Meredith and His Reading of Life," in his *A Century of the English Novel*. New York: Century, 1925, p. 206.

Williams, David. *George Meredith: His Life and Lost Love*. London: Hamish Hamilton, 1977, pp. 128–135.

Williams, Ioan. *The Realist Novel in England: A Study in Development*. London: Macmillan, 1974, pp. 196–200.

Wright, Walter F. *Art and Substance in George Meredith, A Study in Narrative*. Lincoln: University of Nebraska Press, 1953, pp. 102–126.

Diana of the Crossways

Bailey, Elmer James. *The Novels of George Meredith: A Study*. New York: Haskell House, 1971, pp. 149–158.

Baker, Ernest A. *The History of the English Novel*, Volume VIII. New York: Barnes & Noble, 1950, pp. 374–376.

Baker, Robert S. "Sanctuary and Dungeon: The Imagery of Sentimentalism in Meredith's *Diana of the Crossways*," in *Texas Studies in Literature and Language*. XVIII (1976), pp. 63–81.

Beach, Joseph Warren. *The Comic Spirit in George Meredith: An Interpretation*. New York: Longmans, Green, 1911, pp. 169–175.

Beer, Gillian. *Meredith: A Change of Masks, A Study of the Novels*. London: Athlone, 1970, pp. 140–167.

Booth, Thornton Y. *Mastering the Event: Commitment to Fact in George Meredith's Fiction*. Logan: Utah State University Press, 1967, pp. 42–46.

Conrow, Margaret. "Coming to Terms with George Meredith's Fiction," in her *The English Novel in the Nineteenth Century: Essays on the Literary Mediation of Human Values*. Urbana: University of Illinois Press, 1972, pp. 191–193.

Eaker, J. Gordon. "Meredith's Human Comedy," in *Nineteenth-Century Fiction*. V (March, 1951), pp. 265–266.

Edgar, Pelham. *The Art of the Novel From 1700 to the Present Time*. New York: Macmillan, 1933, pp. 158–161.

Fowler, Lois Josephs. "*Diana of the Crossways*: A Prophecy for Feminism," in *In Honor of Austin Wright*. Edited by Joseph Baim. Pittsburgh: Carnegie-Mellon University, 1972, pp. 32–36.

Gindin, James. *Harvest of a Quiet Eye: The Novel of Compassion*. Bloomington: Indiana University Press, 1971, pp. 63–76.

Gordon, Jan B. "*Diana of the Crossways*: Internal History and the Brainstuff of Fiction," in *Meredith Now: Some Critical Essays*. Edited by Ian Fletcher. New York: Barnes & Noble, 1971, pp. 246–264.

Gretton, Mary Sturge. *The Writings and Life of George Meredith, A Centenary Study*. London: Oxford University Press, 1926, pp. 161–173.

Kelvin, Norman. *A Troubled Eden: Nature and Society in the Works of George Meredith*. Stanford, Calif.: Stanford University Press, 1961, pp. 58–61.

Kerpneck, Harvey. "George Meredith, Sunworshipper and Diana's Redworth," in *Nineteenth-Century Fiction*. XVIII (June, 1963), pp. 77–82.

Lindsay, Jack. *George Meredith: His Life and Work*. London: Bodley Head, 1956, pp. 262–268.

Marcus, Jane. " 'Clio in Calliope': History and Myth in Meredith's *Diana of the Crossways*," in *Bulletin of the New York Public Library*. LXXIX (1976), pp. 167–192.

Moffatt, James. *George Meredith: A Primer to the Novels*. Port Washington, N.Y.: Kennikat, 1969, pp. 291–308.

Sassoon, Siegfried. *Meredith.* New York: Viking, 1948, pp. 183–190.

Skilton, David. "New Approaches: Meredith, Hardy and Butler," in his *The English Novel: Defoe to the Victorians.* New York: Barnes & Noble, 1977, pp. 167–168.

Stevenson, Lionel. *The Ordeal of George Meredith, A Biography.* New York: Scribner's, 1953, pp. 253–261.

Weygandt, Cornelius. "George Meredith and His Reading of Life," in his *A Century of the English Novel.* New York: Century, 1925, pp. 207–208.

Wilt, Judith. "Meredith's Diana: Freedom, Fiction, and the Female," in *Texas Studies in Literature and Language.* XVIII (1976), pp. 42–62.

Wright, Walter F. *Art and Substance in George Meredith, A Study in Narrative.* Lincoln: University of Nebraska Press, 1953, pp. 140–146.

The Egoist

Bailey, Elmer James. *The Novels of George Meredith: A Study.* New York: Haskell House, 1971, pp. 133–142.

Baker, Robert S. "Faun and Satyr: Meredith's Theory of Comedy and *The Egoist*," in *Mosaic.* IX (1976), pp. 173–193.

Beach, Joseph Warren. *The Comic Spirit in George Meredith: An Interpretation.* New York: Longmans, Green, 1911, pp. 123–141.

Beer, Gillian. *Meredith: A Change of Masks, A Study of the Novels.* London: Athlone, 1970, pp. 122–137.

Buchen, Irving H. "The Egoists in *The Egoist*: The Sensualists and the Ascetics," in *Nineteenth-Century Fiction.* XIX (1964), pp. 255–269.

————. "Science, Society and Individuality," in *University Review.* XXX (1964), pp. 185–192.

Gindin, James. *Harvest of a Quiet Eye: The Novel of Compassion.* Bloomington: Indiana University Press, 1971, pp. 58–61, 63–70, 74–76.

Goode, John. "*The Egoist*: Anatomy or Striptease?," in *Meredith Now: Some Critical Essays.* Edited by Ian Fletcher. New York: Barnes & Noble, 1971, pp. 205–230.

Gretton, Mary Sturge. *The Writings and Life of George Meredith, A Centenary Study.* London: Oxford University Press, 1926, pp. 131–141.

Halperin, John. *The Language of Meditation: Four Studies in Nineteenth Century Fiction.* Elms Court, England: Stockwell, 1973, pp. 98–114.

Hill, Charles J. "Theme and Image in *The Egoist*," in *University of Kansas City Review.* XX (Summer, 1954), pp. 281–285.

Hudson, Richard B. "The Meaning of Egoism in George Meredith's *The Egoist*," in *Trollopian.* III (December, 1948), pp. 163–176.

Kelvin, Norman. *A Troubled Eden: Nature and Society in the Works of George Meredith.* Stanford, Calif.: Stanford University Press, 1961, pp. 104–113.

Lindsay, Jack. *George Meredith: His Life and Work.* London: Bodley Head, 1956, pp. 238–244.

McCullough, Bruce W. *Representative English Novelists: Defoe to Conrad.* New York: Harper, 1946, pp. 221–230.

Mannheimer, Monica. *The Generations in Meredith's Novels.* Stockholm: Almquist and Wiksell, 1972, pp. 155–164.

Sassoon, Siegfried. *Meredith.* New York: Viking, 1948, pp. 143–154.

Stevenson, Lionel. *The Ordeal of George Meredith, A Biography.* New York: Scribner's, 1953, pp. 224–233.

Stevenson, Richard C. "Laetitia Dale and the Comic Spirit in *The Egoist*," in *Nineteenth-Century Fiction.* XXVI (1972), pp. 406–418.

Stone, Donald David. *Novelists in a Changing World: Meredith, James and the Transformation of English Fiction in the 1880's.* Cambridge, Mass.: Harvard University Press, 1972, pp. 116–137.

Van Ghent, Dorothy. "On *The Egoist*," in *The English Novel: Form and Function.* New York: Rinehart, 1953, pp. 183–194.

Wilkenfeld, R.B. "Hands Around: Image and Theme in *The Egoist*," in *Journal of English Literary History.* XXXIV (September, 1967), pp. 367–379.

Williams, David. *George Meredith: His Life and Lost Love.* London: Hamish Hamilton, 1977, pp. 149–159.

Williams, Orlo. "*The Egoist*," in his *Some Great English Novels: Studies in the Art of Fiction.* London: Macmillan, 1926, pp. 84–119.

Wright, Walter F. *Art and Substance in George Meredith, A Study in Narrative.* Lincoln: University of Nebraska Press, 1953, pp. 60–78.

Evan Harrington

Bailey, Elmer James. *The Novels of George Meredith: A Study.* New York: Haskell House, 1971, pp. 64–75.

Baker, Ernest A. *The History of the English Novel*, Volume VIII. New York: Barnes & Noble, 1950, pp. 326–331.

Beach, Joseph Warren. *The Comic Spirit in George Meredith: An Interpretation.* New York: Longmans, Green, 1911, pp. 61–77.

Beer, Gillian. *Meredith: A Change of Masks, A Study of the Novels.* London: Athlone, 1970, pp. 41–43.

Booth, Thornton Y. *Mastering the Event: Commitment to Fact in George Meredith's Fiction.* Logan: Utah State University Press, 1967, pp. 7–29.

Crees, J.H.E. *George Meredith: A Study of His Works and Personality.* Oxford: B.H. Blackwell, 1928, pp. 60–66.

Eaker, J. Gordon. "Meredith's Human Comedy," in *Nineteenth-Century Fiction.* V (March, 1951), pp. 256–257.

Gretton, Mary Sturge. *The Writings and Life of George Meredith, A Centenary Study.* London: Oxford University Press, 1926, pp. 44–50.

Kelvin, Norman. *A Troubled Eden: Nature and Society in the Works of George Meredith.* Stanford, Calif.: Stanford University Press, 1961, pp. 16–25.

Lindsay, Jack. *George Meredith: His Life and Work.* London: Bodley Head, 1956, pp. 105–110.

Mannheimer, Monica. *The Generations in Meredith's Novels.* Stockholm: Almquist and Wiksell, 1972, pp. 80–90.

Moffatt, James. *George Meredith: A Primer to the Novels.* Port Washington, N.Y.: Kennikat, 1969, pp. 119–136.

Pritchett, V.S. *George Meredith and English Comedy.* New York: Random House, 1969, pp. 75–79.

Sassoon, Siegfried. *Meredith.* New York: Viking, 1948, pp. 31–40.

Stevenson, Lionel. *The Ordeal of George Meredith, A Biography.* New York: Scribner's, 1953, pp. 81–84.

Stevenson, Richard C. "Innovations of Comic Method in George Meredith's *Evan Harrington,*" in *Texas Studies in Literature and Language.* XV (1973), pp. 311–323.

Tarratt, Margaret. " 'Snips,' 'Snobs' and the 'True Gentleman' in *Evan Harrington,*" in *Meredith Now: Some Critical Essays.* Edited by Ian Fletcher. New York: Barnes & Noble, 1971, pp. 95–113.

Tompkins, J.M.S. "On Re-reading *Evan Harrington,*" in *Meredith Now: Some Critical Essays.* Edited by Ian Fletcher. New York: Barnes & Noble, 1971, pp. 114–129.

Weygandt, Cornelius. "George Meredith and His Reading of Life," in *A Century of the English Novel.* New York: Century, 1925, pp. 199–200.

Williams, David. *George Meredith: His Life and Lost Love.* London: Hamish Hamilton, 1977, pp. 114–116.

Wright, Walter F. *Art and Substance in George Meredith, A Study in Narrative.* Lincoln: University of Nebraska Press, 1953, pp. 88–89.

Lord Ormont and His Aminta

Bailey, Elmer James. *The Novels of George Meredith: A Study.* New York: Haskell House, 1971, pp. 172–175.

Baker, Ernest A. *The History of the English Novel*, Volume VIII. New York: Barnes & Noble, 1950, pp. 377–378.

Brunner, Bernard A. "Meredith's Symbolism: *Lord Ormont and His Aminta*," in *Nineteenth-Century Fiction.* VIII (September, 1953), pp. 124–133.

Crees, J.H.E. *George Meredith: A Study of His Works and Personality.* Oxford: Blackwell, 1928, pp. 92–93.

Eaker, J. Gordon. "Meredith's Human Comedy," in *Nineteenth-Century Fiction.* V (March, 1951), pp. 263–264.

Gretton, Mary Sturge. *The Writings and Life of George Meredith, A Centenary Study.* London: Oxford University Press, 1926, pp. 207–216.

Hardy, Barbara. "*Lord Ormont and His Aminta* and *The Amazing Marriage*," in *Meredith Now: Some Critical Essays.* Edited by Ian Fletcher. New York: Barnes & Noble, 1971, pp. 295–312.

Kelvin, Norman. *A Troubled Eden: Nature and Society in the Works of George Meredith.* Stanford, Calif.: Stanford University Press, 1961, pp. 112–113, 180–189.

Kruppa, Joseph E. "Meredith's Late Novels: Suggestions for a Critical Approach," in *Nineteenth-Century Fiction.* XIX (December, 1964), pp. 271–286.

Lindsay, Jack. *George Meredith: His Life and Work.* London: Bodley Head, 1956, pp. 313–318.

McCullen, M.L. "Handsome Heroes and Healthy Heroines: Patterns of the Ideal in George Meredith's Later Novels," in *Cithara.* XIV (December, 1974), pp. 95–106.

Moffatt, James. *George Meredith: A Primer to the Novels.* Port Washington, N.Y.: Kennikat, 1969, pp. 311–333.

Sassoon, Siegfried. *Meredith.* New York: Viking, 1948, pp. 230–233.

Stevenson, Lionel. *The Ordeal of George Meredith, A Biography.* New York: Scribner's, 1953, pp. 312–316.

Wright, Walter F. *Art and Substance in George Meredith, A Study in Narrative.* Lincoln: University of Nebraska Press, 1953, pp. 100–101, 131–132, 181–182.

Modern Love

Baker, Ernest A. *The History of the English Novel*, Volume VIII. New York: Barnes & Noble, 1950, pp. 280–283.

Ball, Patricia M. " 'If I be Dear to someone else,' " in her *The Heart's Events: The Victorian Poetry of Relationships.* London: Athlone Press, 1976, pp. 105–166.

Chambers, Edmund Kerchever. "Meredith's *Modern Love*," in *A Sheaf of Studies*. London: Oxford University Press, 1942, pp. 71–83.

Evans, B. Ifor. *English Poetry in the Later Nineteenth Century*. London: Methuen, 1933, pp. 167–169.

Faverty, F.E. "Browning's Debt to Meredith in James Lee's Wife," in *Essays in American and English Literature Presented to Bruce Robert McElderry, Jr.* Edited by Max F. Schulz. Columbus: Ohio University Press, 1968, pp. 290–305.

Friedman, Norman. "The Jangled Harp: Symbolic Structure in *Modern Love*," in *Modern Language Quarterly*. XVIII (1957), pp. 9–26.

Going, William T. "A Note on 'My Lady' of *Modern Love*," in *Modern Language Quarterly*. VII (1946), pp. 311–314.

Golden, Arline. " 'The Game of Sentiment': Tradition and Innovation in Meredith's *Modern Love*," in *Journal of English Literary History*. XL (1973), pp. 264–284.

Gretton, Mary Sturge. *The Writings and Life of George Meredith, A Centenary Study*. London: Oxford University Press, 1926, pp. 54–67.

Kowalczyk, Richard L. "Moral Relativism and the Cult of Love in Meredith's *Modern Love*," in *Research Studies*. XXXVII (1969), pp. 38–53.

Kwinn, David. "Meredith's Psychological Insight in *Modern Love* XXIII," in *Victorian Poetry*. VII (1969), pp. 151–153.

LeGallienne, Richard. *George Meredith: Some Characteristics*. London: John Lane, 1905, pp. 112–133.

Lucas, John. "Meredith as Poet," in *Meredith Now: Some Critical Essays*. Edited by Ian Fletcher. New York: Barnes & Noble, 1971, pp. 14–33.

Mermin, Dorothy M. "Poetry as Fiction: Meredith's *Modern Love*," in *Journal of English Literary History*. XLIII (1976), pp. 100–119.

Reader, Willie D. "The Autobiographical Author as Fictional Character: Point of View in Meredith's *Modern Love*," in *Victorian Poetry*. X (1972), pp. 131–143.

————. "Stanza Form in Meredith's *Modern Love*," in *Victorian Newsletter*. XXXVIII (1970), pp. 26–27.

Sassoon, Siegfried. *Meredith*. New York: Viking, 1948, pp. 47–53.

Simpson, Arthur L., Jr. "Meredith's Pessimistic Humanism: A New Reading of *Modern Love*," in *Modern Philology*. LXXVII (1970), pp. 341–356.

Stevenson, Lionel. *The Ordeal of George Meredith, A Biography*. New York: Scribner's, 1953, pp. 103–105.

Trevelyan, George Macaulay. *The Poetry and Philosophy of George Meredith*. London: Archibald Constable, 1907, pp. 18–35.

Williams, David. *George Meredith: His Life and Lost Love.* London: Hamish Hamilton, 1977, pp. 104–109.

Wright, Elizabeth Cox. "The Significance of Image Patterns in Meredith's *Modern Love*," in *Victorian Newsletter.* XIII (1958), pp. 1–9.

Wright, Walter F. *Art and Substance in George Meredith, A Study in Narrative.* Lincoln: University of Nebraska Press, 1953, pp. 164–168.

One of Our Conquerors

Bailey, Elmer James. *The Novels of George Meredith: A Study.* New York: Haskell House, 1971, pp. 162–171.

Baker, Ernest A. *The History of the English Novel,* Volume VIII. New York: Barnes & Noble, 1950, pp. 376–377.

Baker, Robert S. "Victorian Conventions and Imagery in George Meredith's *One of Our Conquerors*," in *Criticism.* XVIII (1976), pp. 317–333.

Beach, Joseph Warren. *The Comic Spirit in George Meredith: An Interpretation.* New York: Longmans, Green, 1911, pp. 109–122.

Beer, Gillian. *Meredith: A Change of Masks, A Study of the Novels.* London: Athlone, 1970, pp. 111–112, 184–186.

————. "*One of Our Conquerors*: Language and Music," in *Meredith Now: Some Critical Essays.* Edited by Ian Fletcher. New York: Barnes & Noble, 1971, pp. 265–280.

Crees, J.H.E. *George Meredith: A Study of His Works and Personality.* Oxford: Blackwell, 1928, pp. 93–98.

Gretton, Mary Sturge. *The Writings and Life of George Meredith, A Centenary Study.* London: Oxford University Press, 1926, pp. 192–199.

Gudas, Fabian. "George Meredith's *One of Our Conquerors*," in *From Jane Austen to Joseph Conrad: Essays Collected in Memory of James T. Hillhouse.* Edited by Robert C. Rathburn and Martin Steinmann, Jr. Minneapolis: University of Minnesota Press, 1958, pp. 222–233.

Johnson, Lionel Pigot. "*One of Our Conquerors*, by George Meredith," in *Reviews and Critical Papers.* Freeport, N.Y.: Books for Libraries Press, 1966, pp. 66–70.

Kelvin, Norman. *A Troubled Eden: Nature and Society in the Works of George Meredith.* Stanford, Calif.: Stanford University Press, 1961, pp. 167–180.

Kruppa, Joseph E. "Meredith's Late Novels: Suggestions for a Critical Approach," in *Nineteenth-Century Fiction.* XIX (December, 1964), pp. 271–286.

Lindsay, Jack. *George Meredith: His Life and Work.* London: Bodley Head, 1956, pp. 282–292.

Mannheimer, Monica. *The Generations in Meredith's Novels.* Stockholm: Almquist and Wiksell, 1972, pp. 165–181.

Poole, Adrian. *Gissing in Context.* Totowa, N.J.: Rowman and Littlefield, 1975, pp. 18–20.

Richards, Bernard A. "*One of Our Conquerors* and the Country of the Blue," in *Meredith Now: Some Critical Essays.* Edited by Ian Fletcher. New York: Barnes & Noble, 1971, pp. 281–294.

Sassoon, Siegfried. *Meredith.* New York: Viking, 1948, pp. 207–210.

Stevenson, Lionel. *The Ordeal of George Meredith, A Biography.* New York: Scribner's, 1953, pp. 290–294.

Thomson, Fred C. "The Design of *One of Our Conquerors*," in *Studies in English Literature.* II (1962), pp. 463–480.

————. "Symbolic Characterization in *One of Our Conquerors*," in *Victorian Newsletter.* XXVI (Fall, 1964), pp. 12–14.

Wright, Walter F. *Art and Substance in George Meredith, A Study in Narrative.* Lincoln: University of Nebraska Press, 1953, pp. 186–201.

The Ordeal of Richard Feverel

Bailey, Elmer James. *The Novels of George Meredith: A Study.* New York: Haskell House, 1971, pp. 49–63.

Baker, Robert S. "*The Ordeal of Richard Feverel*: A Psychological Approach to Structure," in *Studies in the Novel.* VI (1974), pp. 200–217.

Bartlett, Phyllis. "The Novels of George Meredith," in *Review of English Literature.* III (1962), pp. 31–46.

Beach, Joseph Warren. *The Comic Spirit in George Meredith: An Interpretation.* New York: Longmans, Green, 1911, pp. 34–55.

Beer, Gillian. *Meredith: A Change of Masks, A Study of the Novels.* London: Athlone, 1970, pp. 6–34.

Buchen, Irving H. "The Importance of the Minor Characters in *The Ordeal of Richard Feverel*," in *Boston University Studies in English.* V (Autumn, 1961), pp. 154–166.

Buckley, Jerome Hamilton. *Season of Youth: The Bildungsroman from Dickens to Golding.* Cambridge, Mass.: Harvard University Press, 1974, pp. 68–82.

Curtin, Frank D. "Adrian Harley: The Limits of Meredith's Comedy," in *Nineteenth-Century Fiction.* VII (March, 1953), pp. 272–282.

Ekeberg, Gladys W. "*The Ordeal of Richard Feverel* as Tragedy," in *College English.* VII (April, 1946), pp. 387–393.

Erskine, John. "*The Ordeal of Richard Feverel*," in *The Delight of Great Books.* Indianapolis, Ind.: Bobbs-Merrill, 1928, pp. 243–259.

Fisher, Benjamin Franklin, IV. "Sensational Fiction in a Minor Key: *The Ordeal of Richard Feverel*," in *Nineteenth-Century Literary Perspectives: Essays in Honor of Lionel Stevenson*. Edited by Clyde de L. Ryals. Durham, N.C.: Duke University Press, 1974, pp. 283–294.

Gindin, James. *Harvest of a Quiet Eye: The Novel of Compassion*. Bloomington: Indiana University Press, 1971, pp. 64–75.

Goldfarb, Russell M. *Sexual Repression and Victorian Literature*. Lewisburg, Pa.: Bucknell University Press, 1970, pp. 158–177.

Gretton, Mary Sturge. *The Writings and Life of George Meredith, A Centenary Study*. London: Oxford University Press, 1926, pp. 29–43.

Halperin, John. *Egoism and Self-Discovery in the Victorian Novel: Studies in the Ordeal of Knowledge in the Nineteenth Century*. New York: Burt Franklin, 1974, pp. 202–214.

Kelvin, Norman. *A Troubled Eden: Nature and Society in the Works of George Meredith*. Stanford, Calif.: Stanford University Press, 1961, pp. 5–14.

Knoepflmacher, Ulrich Camillus. *Laughter and Despair: Readings in Ten Novels of the Victorian Age*. Berkeley: University of California Press, 1971, pp. 109–136.

Korg, Jacob. "Expressive Styles in *The Ordeal of Richard Feverel*," in *Nineteenth-Century Fiction*. XXVII (1972), pp. 253–267.

Lawrence, F.B. "Lyric and Romance: Meredith's Poetic Fiction," in *Victorian Essays: A Symposium*. Edited by Warren D. Anderson and Thomas D. Clareson. Kent, Oh.: Kent State University Press, 1967, pp. 87–106.

Mitchell, Juliet. "*The Ordeal of Richard Feverel*: A Sentimental Education," in *Meredith Now: Some Critical Essays*. Edited by Ian Fletcher. New York: Barnes & Noble, 1971, pp. 69–94.

Poston, Lawrence, III. "Dramatic Reference and Structure in *The Ordeal of Richard Feverel*," in *Studies in English Literature, 1500–1900*. VI (1966), pp. 743–752.

Stevenson, Lionel. "Meredith and the Art of Implication," in *The Victorian Experience: The Novelists*. Edited by Richard A. Levine. Athens: Ohio University Press, 1976, pp. 177–201.

Stevenson, R.C. "Comedy, Tragedy, and the Spirit of Critical Intelligence in *Richard Feverel*," in *The Worlds of Victorian Fiction*. Edited by Jerome H. Buckley. Cambridge, Mass.: Harvard University Press, 1975, pp. 205–222.

Williams, David. *George Meredith: His Life and Lost Love*. London: Hamish Hamilton, 1977, pp. 109–114.

Wright, Walter F. *Art and Substances in George Meredith, A Study in Narrative*. Lincoln: University of Nebraska Press, 1953, pp. 147–161.

The Poetry of Meredith

Armstrong, Martin. "The Poetry of George Meredith," in *North American Review*. CCXIII (1921), pp. 354–361.

Austin, Deborah. "Meredith on the Nature of Metaphor," in *University of Toronto Quarterly*. XXVII (1957), pp. 96–102.

Baker, Ernest A. *The History of the English Novel*, Volume VIII. New York: Barnes & Noble, 1950, pp. 287–299.

Beach, Joseph Warren. *The Concept of Nature in Nineteenth-Century English Poetry*. New York: Macmillan, 1936, pp. 470–499.

Bogner, Delmar. "The Sexual Side of Meredith's Poetry," in *Victorian Poetry*. VIII (1970), pp. 107–125.

Chambers, Edmund Kerchever. "Meredith's Nature Poetry," in *A Sheaf of Studies*. London: Oxford University Press, 1942, pp. 84–91.

Clutton-Brock, Arthur. "George Meredith," in *More Essays on Books*. London: Methuen, 1921, pp. 35–46.

Crees, J.H.E. *George Meredith: A Study of His Works and Personality*. Oxford: Blackwell, 1928, pp. 70–84.

Crum, Ralph B. *Scientific Thought in Poetry*. New York: Columbia University Press, 1931, pp. 207–227.

Eaker, J. Gordon. "Meredith's Human Comedy," in *Ninteenth-Century Fiction*. V (March, 1951), pp. 267–272.

Edgar, Pelham. "The Poetry of George Meredith," in *Living Age*. CCLV (1907), pp. 744–751.

Evans, B. Ifor. *English Poetry in the Later Nineteenth Century*. London: Methuen, 1933, pp. 162–177.

Gretton, Mary Sturge. *The Writings and Life of George Meredith, A Centenary Study*. London: Oxford University Press, 1926, pp. 174–191.

Kelvin, Norman. *A Troubled Eden: Nature and Society in the Works of George Meredith*. Stanford, Calif.: Stanford University Press, 1961, pp. 114–164.

Priestley, J.B. *George Meredith*. New York: Macmillan, 1926, pp. 86–111.

Quiller-Couch, Arthur Thomas. "The Poetry of George Meredith," in his *Studies in Literature*. Cambridge: Cambridge University Press, 1937, pp. 158–177. Reprinted in his *Cambridge Lectures*. New York: Dutton, 1944, pp. 259–273.

Ridley, M.R. "Meredith's Poetry," in his *Second Thoughts: More Studies in Literature*. London: Dent, 1965, pp. 146–171.

Robertson, Leo C. "Meredith the Poet," in *English Review*. XLIV (1927), pp. 463–471.

Stuart-Young, J.M. "The Poetry of George Meredith," in *Poetry Review.* XVIII (1926), pp. 173–176.

Tinker, Chauncey Brewster. "Meredith's Poetry," in *Essays in Retrospect.* New Haven, Conn.: Yale University Press, 1948, pp. 83–89.

Trevelyan, George Macaulay. *The Poetry and Philosophy of George Meredith.* London: Archibald Constable, 1907.

Vivante, Leone. "George Meredith, 1828–1909," in *English Poetry and Its Contribution to the Knowledge of a Creative Principle.* London: Faber and Faber, 1950, pp. 248–261.

Weygandt, Cornelius. *The Time of Tennyson: English Victorian Poetry as It Affected America.* New York: Appleton-Century, 1936, pp. 181–191.

Wolf, William. "The Poetry of George Meredith," in *Poetry Review.* XLIV (1953), pp. 464–466.

Rhoda Fleming

Bailey, Elmer James. *The Novels of George Meredith: A Study.* New York: Haskell House, 1971, pp. 92–97.

Baker, Ernest A. *The History of the English Novel,* Volume VIII. New York: Barnes & Noble, 1950, pp. 336–340.

Crees, J.H.E. *George Meredith: A Study of His Works and Personality.* Oxford: Blackwell, 1928, pp. 90–92.

Gretton, Mary Sturge. *The Writings and Life of George Meredith, A Centenary Study.* London: Oxford University Press, 1926, pp. 82–88.

Hergenhan, L.T. "Meredith's Attempts to Win Popularity: Contemporary Reactions," in *Studies in English Literature, 1500–1900.* IV (Autumn, 1964), pp. 637–651.

Hill, Charles J. "George Meredith's 'Plain Story,' " in *Nineteenth-Century Fiction.* VII (September, 1952), pp. 90–102.

Howard, David. "*Rhoda Fleming*: Meredith in the Margin," in *Meredith Now: Some Critical Essays.* Edited by Ian Fletcher. New York: Barnes & Noble, 1971, pp. 130–143.

Lindsay, Jack. *George Meredith: His Life and Work.* London: Bodley Head, 1956, pp. 150–157.

Mannheimer, Monica. *The Generations in Meredith's Novels.* Stockholm: Almquist and Wiksell, 1972, pp. 132–141.

Moffatt, James. *George Meredith: A Primer to the Novels.* Port Washington, N.Y.: Kennikat, 1969, pp. 157–170.

Sassoon, Siegfried. *Meredith.* New York: Viking, 1948, pp. 71–74.

Stevenson, Lionel. "Meredith's Atypical Novel: A Study of *Rhoda Fleming*," in *English Studies.* XI (1955), pp. 89–109.

Williams, David. *George Meredith: His Life and Lost Love.* London: Hamish Hamilton, 1977, pp. 122–123.

Wright, Walter F. *Art and Substance in George Meredith, A Study in Narrative.* Lincoln: University of Nebraska Press, 1953, pp. 134–139.

Sandra Belloni, or Emilia in England

Bailey, Elmer James. *The Novels of George Meredith: A Study.* New York: Haskell House, 1971, pp. 78–87.

Baker, Ernest A. *The History of the English Novel,* Volume VIII. New York: Barnes & Noble, 1950, pp. 331–336.

Beach, Joseph Warren. *The Comic Spirit in George Meredith: An Interpretation.* New York: Longmans, Green, 1911, pp. 89–107.

Beer, Gillian. *Meredith: A Change of Masks, A Study of the Novels.* London: Athlone, 1970, pp. 43–44, 101–102.

Edgar, Pelham. *The Art of the Novel from 1700 to the Present Time.* New York: Macmillan, 1933, pp. 153–154.

Gretton, Mary Sturge. *The Writings and Life of George Meredith, A Centenary Study.* London: Oxford University Press, 1926, pp. 71–80.

Howard, David. "George Meredith: 'Delicate' and 'Epical' Fiction," in *Literature and Politics in the Nineteenth Century.* Edited by John Lucas. London: Methuen, 1971, pp. 131–151.

Lindsay, Jack. *George Meredith: His Life and Work.* London: Bodley Head, 1956, pp. 138–148.

Mannheimer, Monica. *The Generations in Meredith's Novels.* Stockholm: Almquist and Wiksell, 1972, pp. 130–132.

Moffatt, James. *George Meredith: A Primer to the Novels.* Port Washington, N.Y.: Kennikat, 1969, pp. 139–154.

Rance, Nicholas. *The Historical Novel and Popular Politics in Nineteenth-Century England.* London: Vision, 1975, pp. 155–171.

Sassoon, Siegfried. *Meredith.* New York: Viking, 1948, pp. 74–80.

Stevenson, Lionel. *The Ordeal of George Meredith, A Biography.* New York: Scribner's, 1953, pp. 132–136.

Stone, Donald David. *Novelists in a Changing World: Meredith, James and the Transformation of English Fiction in the 1880's.* Cambridge, Mass.: Harvard University Press, 1972, pp. 106–108.

Watson, Robert W. "George Meredith's *Sandra Belloni*: The 'Philosopher' on the Sentimentalists," in *Journal of English Literary History.* XXIV (December, 1957), pp. 321–335.

Williams, David. *George Meredith: His Life and Lost Love.* London: Hamish Hamilton, 1977, pp. 117–119.

Williams, Ioan. "Emilia in England and Italy," in *Meredith Now: Some Critical Essays*. Edited by Ian Fletcher. New York: Barnes & Noble, 1971, pp. 144–164.

Wright, Walter F. *Art and Substance in George Meredith, A Study in Narrative*. Lincoln: University of Nebraska Press, 1953, pp. 168–175.

The Tragic Comedians

Bailey, Elmer James. *The Novels of George Meredith: A Study*. New York: Haskell House, 1971, pp. 142–147.

Baker, Ernest A. *The History of the English Novel*, Volume VIII. New York: Barnes & Noble, 1950, pp. 373–374.

Beach, Joseph Warren. *The Comic Spirit in George Meredith: An Interpretation*. New York: Longmans, Green, 1911, pp. 158–168.

Beer, Gillian. *Meredith: A Change of Masks, A Study of the Novels*. London: Athlone, 1970, pp. 137–139.

Crees, J.H.E. *George Meredith: A Study of His Works and Personality*. Oxford: Blackwell, 1928, pp. 43–55.

Gretton, Mary Sturge. *The Writings and Life of George Meredith, A Centenary Study*. London: Oxford University Press, 1926, pp. 148–158.

Häusermann, Hans Walter. *The Genevese Background*. London: Routledge and Kegan Paul, 1952, pp. 182–198.

Lindsay, Jack. *George Meredith: His Life and Work*. London: Bodley Head, 1956, pp. 245–252.

Moffatt, James. *George Meredith: A Primer to the Novels*. Port Washington, N.Y.: Kennikat, 1969, pp. 277–287.

Ormond, Leonée. "*The Tragic Comedians*: Meredith's Use of Image Patterns," in *Meredith Now: Some Critical Essays*. Edited by Ian Fletcher. New York: Barnes & Noble, 1971, pp. 231–245.

Sassoon, Siegfried. *Meredith*. New York: Viking, 1948, pp. 155–159.

Stevenson, Lionel. *The Ordeal of George Meredith, A Biography*. New York: Scribner's, 1953, pp. 238–242.

Stone, Donald David. *Novelists in a Changing World: Meredith, James and the Transformation of English Fiction in the 1880's*. Cambridge, Mass.: Harvard University Press, 1972, pp. 137–143.

Wright, Walter F. *Art and Substance in George Meredith, A Study in Narrative*. Lincoln: University Of Nebraska Press, 1953, pp. 175–180.

JAMES A. MICHENER
(1907–   )

Tales of the South Pacific

Day, A. Grove. *James Michener.* Boston: Twayne, 1977, pp. 37–54.

Dempsey, David. "Atolls of the Sun," in *New York Times Book Review.* (February 2, 1947), p. 5.

Havighurst, W. "Michener of the South Pacific," in *English Journal.* XLI (October, 1952), pp. 397–402.

Nathan, George J. *The Magic Mirror; Selected Writings on the Theatre.* New York: Knopf, 1960, pp. 250–257.

Prescott, Orville. "Outstanding Novels," in *Yale Review.* XXXVI (Spring, 1947), p. 576.

Stuckey, W.J. *The Pulitzer Prize Novels: A Critical Backward Look.* Norman: University of Oklahoma Press, 1966, pp. 138–143.

THOMAS MIDDLETON
(1580–1627)

A Chaste Maid in Cheapside

Barber, Charles. "Critical Introduction," in *A Chaste Maid in Cheapside*. By Thomas Middleton. Berkeley: University of California Press, 1969, pp. 1–7.

Barker, Richard Hindry. *Thomas Middleton*. New York: Columbia University Press, 1958, pp. 77–85.

Brittin, Norman A. *Thomas Middleton*. New York: Twayne, 1972, pp. 50–58.

Buckingham, E.L. "Campion's *Art of English Poesie* and Middleton's *Chaste Maid in Cheapside*," in *PMLA*. XLIII (1928), pp. 784–792.

Covatta, Anthony. *Thomas Middleton's City Comedies*. Lewisburg, Pa.: Bucknell University Press, 1973, pp. 137–162.

Ellis-Fermor, U.M. *The Jacobean Drama: An Interpretation*. London: Methuen, 1936, pp. 135–138.

Hallett, Charles A. "Middleton's Allwit: The Urban Cynic," in *Modern Language Quarterly*. XXX (1969), pp. 498–507.

Holmes, David M. *The Art of Thomas Middleton: A Critical Study*. London: Oxford University Press, 1970, pp. 90–98.

Levin, Richard. "The Four Plots of *A Chaste Maid in Cheapside*," in *Review of English Studies*. XVI (1965), pp. 14–24.

————. "Middleton's Way with Names in *A Chaste Maid in Cheapside*," in *Notes and Queries*. XII (1965), pp. 102–103.

————. *The Multiple Plot in English Renaissance Drama*. Chicago: University of Chicago Press, 1971, pp. 192–202.

Marotti, Arthur F. "Fertility and Comic Form in *A Chaste Maid in Cheapside*," in *Comparative Drama*. III (Spring, 1969), pp. 65–74.

Mehl, Dieter. *The Elizabethan Dumb Show: The History of a Dramatic Convention*. London: Methuen, 1964, pp. 148–149.

Parker, R.B. "Middleton's Experiments with Comedy and Judgement," in *Stratford-Upon-Avon Studies*. I (1960), pp. 188–192.

Schoenbaum, Samuel. "*A Chaste Maid in Cheapside* and Middleton's City Comedy," in *Studies in the English Renaissance Drama in Memory of Karl Julius Holzknecht*. Edited by Josephine W. Bennett, Oscar Cargill and Vernon Hall, Jr. New York: New York University Press, 1959, pp. 288–309.

Tomlinson, Thomas Brian. *A Survey of Elizabethan and Jacobean Tragedy*. Cambridge: Cambridge University Press, 1964, pp. 158–184.

Wigler, Stephen. "Thomas Middleton's *A Chaste Maid in Cheapside*: The Delicious and the Disgusting," in *American Imago*. XXXIII (1976), pp. 197–215.

Williams, Robert L.   "Machiavelli's Mandragola, Touchwood Senior and the Comedy of Middleton's *A Chaste Maid in Cheapside*," in *Studies in English Literature, 1500–1900*. X (1970), pp. 385–396.

The Family of Love

Barker, Richard Hindry.   *Thomas Middleton*. New York: Columbia University Press, 1958, pp. 30–31, 159–161.

Brittin, Norman A.   *Thomas Middleton*. New York: Twayne, 1972, pp. 35–37.

Covatta, Anthony.   *Thomas Middleton's City Comedies*. Lewisburg, Pa.: Bucknell University Press, 1973, pp. 58–65.

Davidson, Clifford.   "Middleton and *The Family of Love*," in *English Miscellany*. XX (1969), pp. 81–92.

Eberle, Gerald J.   "Dekker's Part in *The Familie of Love*," in *Joseph Quincey Adams Memorial Studies*. Edited by James G. McManaway. Washington, D.C.: Folger Shakespeare Library, 1948, pp. 723–738.

Levin, Richard.   "The Elizabethan 'Three Level' Play," in *Renaissance Drama*. II (1969), pp. 23–37.

————.   "The Family of Lust and *The Family of Love*," in *Studies in English Literature, 1500–1900*. VI (1966), pp. 263–277.

————.   *The Multiple Plot in English Renaissance Drama*. Chicago: University of Chicago Press, 1971, pp. 58–66.

————.   "Name Puns in *The Family of Love*," in *Notes and Queries*. XII (1965), pp. 340–342.

Marotti, Arthur F.   "The Purgations of Middleton's *The Family of Love*," in *Papers on Language and Literature*. VII (1971), pp. 80–84.

Maxwell, Baldwin.   " 'Twenty Good-Nights'—*The Knight of the Burning Pestle* and Middleton's *Family of Love*," in *Modern Language Notes*. LXIII (1948), pp. 233–237.

Olive, W.J.   "Imitation of Shakespeare in Middleton's *The Family of Love*," in *Philological Quarterly*. XXIX (January, 1950), pp. 75–78.

————.   " 'Twenty Good Knights'—*The Knight of the Burning Pestle, The Family of Love*, and *Romeo and Juliet*," in *Studies in Philology*. XLVII (1950), pp. 182–189.

A Game at Chess

Bald, R.C.   "An Early Version of Middleton's *Game of Chesse*," in *Modern Language Review*. XXXVIII (1943), pp. 177–180.

————.   "Introduction," in *A Game at Chesse*. By Thomas Middleton. Cambridge: Cambridge University Press, 1929, pp. 1–43.

Barker, Richard Hindry.   *Thomas Middleton*. New York: Columbia University Press, 1958, pp. 146–150.

Brittin, Norman A. *Thomas Middleton.* New York: Twayne, 1972, pp. 70–76.

Bullough, Geoffrey. "*The Game of Chesse*: How It Struck a Contemporary," in *Modern Language Review.* XLIX (1954), pp. 156–163.

Davies, Richard A. and Alan R. Young. " 'Strange Cunning' in Thomas Middleton's *A Game at Chess,*" in *University of Toronto Quarterly.* XLV (1976), pp. 236–245.

Harper, J.W. "Introduction," in *A Game at Chess.* By Thomas Middleton. New York: Hill and Wang, 1966, pp. xi–xxvi.

Heinemann, Margot C. "Middleton's *A Game at Chess*: Parliamentary-Puritans and Opposition Drama," in *English Literary Renaissance.* V (1975), pp. 232–250.

Moore, J.R. "Contemporary Significance of Middleton's *Game at Chesse,*" in *PMLA.* L (1955), pp. 761–768.

Price, George R. "The Latin Oration in *A Game of Chesse,*" in *Huntington Library Quarterly.* XXXIII (1960), pp. 389–393.

Sargent, Roussel. "Theme and Structure in Middleton's *A Game of Chess,*" in *Modern Language Review.* LXVI (1971), pp. 721–730.

Wagner, B.M. "New Allusions to *A Game at Chesse,*" in *PMLA.* XLIV (1929), pp. 827–834.

Wells, Henry. *Elizabethan and Jacobean Playwrights.* New York: Columbia University Press, 1964, pp. 209–211.

Wilson, Edward M. and O. Turner. "The Spanish Protest Against *A Game of Chesse,*" in *Modern Language Review.* XLIV (1949), pp. 476–482.

A Mad World, My Masters

Barker, Richard Hindry. *Thomas Middleton.* New York: Columbia University Press, 1958, pp. 57–63.

Brittin, Norman A. *Thomas Middleton.* New York: Twayne, 1972, pp. 39–43.

Covatta, Anthony. *Thomas Middleton's City Comedies.* Lewisburg, Pa.: Bucknell University Press, 1973, pp. 120–136.

Hallett, Charles A. "Penitent Brothel, the Succubus and Parson's 'Resolution': A Reappraisal of Penitent's Position in Middleton's Canon," in *Studies in Philology.* LXIX (1972), pp. 72–86.

Levin, Richard. *The Multiple Plot in English Renaissance Drama.* Chicago: University of Chicago Press, 1971, pp. 168–173, 176–178.

Marotti, Arthur F. "The Method in the Madness of *A Mad World, My Masters,*" in *Tennessee Studies in Literature.* XV (1970), pp. 99–108.

Slights, William W.E. "The Trickster-Hero and Middleton's *A Mad World, My Masters,*" in *Comparative Drama.* III (1969), pp. 89–98.

Taylor, Michael. "Realism and Morality in Middleton's *A Mad World, My Masters*," in *Literature and Psychology*. XVIII (1968), pp. 166–178.

Wigler, Stephen. "Penitent Brothel Reconsidered: The Place of the Grotesque in Middleton's, *A Mad World, My Masters*," in *Literature and Psychology*. XXV (1975), pp. 17–26.

Michaelmas Term

Barker, Richard Hindry. *Thomas Middleton.* New York: Columbia University Press, 1958, pp. 47–54.

Brittin, Norman A. *Thomas Middleton.* New York: Twayne, 1972, pp. 43–45.

Chatterji, Ruby. "Unity Disparity: *Michaelmas Term*," in *Studies in English Literature, 1500–1900.* VIII (1968), pp. 349–363.

Covatta, Anthony. "Remarriage in *Michaelmas Term*," in *Notes and Queries*. XIX (1972), pp. 460–461.

――――. *Thomas Middleton's City Comedies.* Lewisburg, Pa.: Bucknell University Press, 1973, pp. 79–98.

Curry, John Vincent. *Deception in Elizabethan Comedy.* Chicago: Loyola University Press, 1955, pp. 46–52.

Ellis-Fermor, U.M. *The Jacobean Drama: An Interpretation.* London: Methuen, 1936, pp. 133–135.

Holdsworth, R.V. "Middleton's *Michaelmas Term*," in *Explicator*. XXXV (1976), pp. 13–14.

Knights, L.C. *Drama and Society in the Age of Jonson.* London: Chatto and Windus, 1947, pp. 263–265.

Levin, Richard. *The Multiple Plot in English Renaissance Drama.* Chicago: University of Chicago Press, 1971, pp. 168–170, 173–182.

――――. "Quomodo's Name in *Michaelmas Term*," in *Notes and Queries*. XX (1973), pp. 460–461.

Maxwell, Baldwin. "Middleton's *Michaelmas Term*," in *Philological Quarterly*. XXII (1943), pp. 29–35.

The Phoenix

Barker, Richard Hindry. *Thomas Middleton.* New York: Columbia University Press, 1958, pp. 31–36.

Bawcutt, N.W. "Middleton's *The Phoenix* as a Royal Play," in *Notes & Queries*. III (1956), pp. 287–288.

Brittin, Norman A. *Thomas Middleton.* New York: Twayne, 1972, pp. 31–35.

Brooks, John B. "Middleton's Stepfather and the Captain of *The Phoenix*," in *Notes and Queries*. VIII (1961), pp. 382–384.

Covatta, Anthony. *Thomas Middleton's City Comedies.* Lewisburg, Pa.: Bucknell University Press, 1973, pp. 66–72.

Davidson, Clifford. "*The Phoenix*: Middleton's Didactic Comedy," in *Papers on Language and Literature.* IV (1968), pp. 121–130.

Desser, Alan C. "Middleton's *The Phoenix* and the Allegorical Tradition," in *Studies in English Literature, 1500–1900.* VI (1966), pp. 263–277.

Dodson, Daniel B. "King James and *The Phoenix*—Again," in *Notes and Queries.* V (1958), pp. 434–437.

Ellis-Fermor, U.M. *The Jacobean Drama: An Interpretation.* London: Methuen, 1936, pp. 131–132.

Maxwell, Baldwin. "Middleton's *The Phoenix*," in *Joseph Quincey Adams Memorial Studies.* Edited by James G. McManaway. Washington, D.C.: Folger Shakespeare Library, 1948, pp. 743–753.

Parker, R.B. "Middleton's Experiments with Comedy and Judgement," in *Stratford-Upon-Avon Studies.* I (1960), pp. 179–185.

Power, William. "*The Phoenix*, Raleigh, and King James," in *Notes and Queries.* V (1958), pp. 57–61.

Williamson, Marilyn L. "*The Phoenix*: Middleton's Comedy de Regimine Principum," in *Renaissance News.* X (1957), pp. 183–187.

A Trick to Catch the Old One

Barker, Charles. "Critical Introduction," in *A Trick to Catch the Old One.* By Thomas Middleton. Berkeley: University of California Press, 1968, pp. 1–8.

Barker, Richard Hindry. *Thomas Middleton.* New York: Columbia University Press, 1958, pp. 52–57.

Brittin, Norman A. *Thomas Middleton.* New York: Twayne, 1972, pp. 46–49.

Bullock, Helene B. "Thomas Middleton and the Fashion in Playmaking," in *PMLA.* XLII (1927), pp. 766–776.

Covatta, Anthony. *Thomas Middleton's City Comedies.* Lewisburg, Pa.: Bucknell University Press, 1973, pp. 99–119.

Falk, Signi. "Plautus, Persa and Middleton's *A Trick to Catch the Old One*," in *Modern Language Notes.* LXVI (1951), pp. 19–21.

George, J. "Millipood," in *Notes and Queries.* CXCIII (1948), pp. 149–150.

Holmes, David M. *The Art of Thomas Middleton: A Critical Study.* London: Oxford University Press, 1970, pp. 80–84.

Knights, L.C. *Drama and Society in the Age of Johnson.* London: Chatto and Windus, 1947.

Levin, Richard. "The Dampit Scenes in *A Trick to Catch the Old One*," in *Modern Language Quarterly.* XXV (1964), pp. 140–152.

_____. *The Multiple Plot in English Renaissance Drama.* Chicago: University of Chicago Press, 1971, pp. 127–137.

Parker, R.B. "Middleton's Experiments with Comedy and Judgement," in *Stratford-Upon-Avon Studies.* I (1960), pp. 185–188.

Reed, Robert Rentoul, Jr. *Bedlam on the Jacobean Stage.* Cambridge, Mass.: Harvard University Press, 1952, pp. 120–121.

Women Beware Women

Barber, Charles. "Critical Introduction," in *Women Beware Women.* By Thomas Middleton. Berkeley: University of California Press, 1969, pp. 1–9.

Barker, Richard Hindry. *Thomas Middleton.* New York: Columbia University Press, 1958, pp. 131–145.

Batchelor, J.B. "The Pattern of *Women Beware Women,*" in *Yearbook of English Studies.* II (1972), pp. 78–88.

Bradford, Gamaliel. "The Women of Middleton and Webster," in *Sewanee Review.* XXIX (1921), pp. 14–29.

Brittin, Norman A. *Thomas Middleton.* New York: Twayne, 1972, pp. 118–132.

Champion, Larry S. "Tragic Vision in Middleton's *Women Beware Women,*" in *English Studies.* LVII (1976), pp. 410–424.

Core, George. "The Canker and the Muse: Imagery in *Women Beware Women,*" in *Renaissance Papers.* (1968), pp. 65–76.

Dodson, Daniel. "Middleton's Livia," in *Philological Quarterly.* XXVII (1948), pp. 376–381.

Ellis-Fermor, U.M. *The Jacobean Drama: An Interpretation.* London: Methuen, 1936, pp. 139–144.

Engleberg, E. "Tragic Blindness in *The Changeling* and *Women Beware Women,*" in *Modern Language Quarterly.* XXIII (March, 1962), pp. 20–28.

Ewbank, Inga-Stina. "Realism and Morality in *Women Beware Women,*" in *Essays and Studies by Members of the English Association.* XXII (1969), pp. 57–70.

Hallett, Charles A. "The Psychological Drama of *Women Beware Women,*" in *Studies in English Literature, 1500–1900.* XII (1972), pp. 375–389.

Hibbard, G.R. "The Tragedies of Thomas Middleton and the Decadence of Drama," in *Renaissance and Modern Studies.* I (1957), pp. 42–54.

Holmes, David M. *The Art of Thomas Middleton: A Critical Study.* London: Oxford University Press, 1970, pp. 161–171.

Kistner, A.L. and M.K. Kistner. "Will, Fate, and the Social Order in *Women Beware Women,*" in *Essays in Literature.* III (1976), pp. 17–31.

Mehl, Dieter. *The Elizabethan Dumb Show: The History of a Dramatic Convention.* London: Methuen, 1964, pp. 149–154.

Mulryne, J.R. "Introduction," in *Women Beware Women*, By Thomas Middleton. London: Methuen, 1975, pp. xix–lxxxix.

Ornstein, Robert. *The Moral Vision of Jacobean Tragedy.* Madison: University of Wisconsin Press, 1960, pp. 190–199.

Ribner, Irving. *Jacobean Tragedy.* New York: Barnes & Noble, 1962, pp. 137–152.

————. "Middleton's *Women Beware Women*: Poetic Imagery and the Moral Vision," in *Tulane Studies in English.* IX (1959), pp. 19–34.

Ricks, C. "Word-Play in *Women Beware Women*," in *Review of English Studies.* XII (1961), pp. 238–250.

Schoenbaum, Samuel. *Middleton's Tragedies: A Critical Study.* New York: Columbia University Press, 1955, pp. 102–132.

Stilling, Roger. *Love and Death in Renaissance Tragedy.* Baton Rouge: Louisiana State University Press, 1976, pp. 256–265.

Tomlinson, Thomas Brian. *A Study of Elizabethan and Jacobean Tragedy.* Cambridge: Cambridge University Press, 1964, pp. 158–184.

Your Five Gallants

Barker, Richard Hindry. *Thomas Middleton.* New York: Columbia University Press, 1958, pp. 42–47.

Brittin, Norman A. *Thomas Middleton.* New York: Twayne, 1972, pp. 37–39.

Gross, A.G. "Middleton's *Your Five Gallants*: The Fifth Act," in *Philological Quarterly.* XLIV (1965), pp. 124–129.

Holmes, David M. *The Art of Thomas Middleton: A Critical Study.* London: Oxford University Press, 1970, pp. 27–30, 54–56.

Hoole, W.S. "Thomas Middleton's Use of 'Impresse' in *Your Five Gallants*," in *Studies in Philology.* XXXI (1934), pp. 215–223.

Maxwell, Baldwin. "Thomas Middleton's *Your Five Gallants*," in *Philological Quarterly.* XXX (1951), pp. 30–39.

Mehl, Dieter. *The Elizabethan Dumb Show: The History of a Dramatic Convention.* London: Methuen, 1964, pp. 146–149.

Schoenbaum, Samuel. *Middleton's Tragedies: A Critical Study.* New York: Columbia University Press, 1955, pp. 169–176.

THOMAS MIDDLETON
(1580–1627)
AND
WILLIAM ROWLEY
(1585?–1642?)

The Changeling

Barker, Richard Hindry. *Thomas Middleton.* New York: Columbia University Press, 1958, pp. 121–131.

Bawcutt, N.W. "Introduction," in *The Changeling.* By Thomas Middleton and William Rowley. Cambridge, Mass.: Harvard University Press, 1958, pp. xv–lxviii.

Berger, Thomas L. "The Petrarchan Fortress of *The Changeling*," in *Renaissance Papers.* (1969), pp. 37–46.

Bradbrook, Muriel. "Thomas Middleton," in *Elizabethan Drama: Modern Essays in Criticism.* Edited by R.J. Kaufmann. New York: Oxford University Press, 1961, pp. 297–319.

Brittin, Norman A. *Thomas Middleton.* New York: Twayne, 1972, pp. 132–142.

Doob, Penelope B.R. "A Reading of *The Changeling*," in *English Literary Renaissance.* III (1973), pp. 183–206.

Duffy, Joseph M. "Madhouse Optics: *The Changeling*," in *Comparative Drama.* VIII (1974), pp. 184–198.

Eliot, T.S. *Essays on Elizabethan Drama.* New York: Haskell, 1964, pp. 89–95.

Ellis-Fermor, U.M. *The Jacobean Drama: An Interpretation.* London: Methuen, 1936, pp. 144–152.

Holzknecht, Karl L. "The Dramatic Structure of *The Changeling*," in *Renaissance Papers.* (1954), pp. 77–87.

Jacobs, Hinry E. "The Constancy of Change: Character and Perspective in *The Changeling*," in *Texas Studies in Literature and Language.* XVI (1975), pp. 651–674.

Levin, Richard. *The Multiple Plot in English Renaissance Drama.* Chicago: University of Chicago Press, 1971, pp. 34–48, 53–55.

Matthews, Ernst G. "The Murdered Substitute Tale," in *Modern Language Quarterly.* VI (1945), pp. 187–195.

Mehl, Dieter. *The Elizabethan Dumb Show: The History of a Dramatic Convention.* London: Methuen, 1964, pp. 152–153.

Ornstein, Robert.   *The Moral Vision of Jacobean Tragedy.* Madison: University of Wisconsin Press, 1960, pp. 179–190.

Pentzell, Raymond J.   "*The Changeling*: Notes on Mannerism in Dramatic Form," in *Comparative Drama.* IX (1975), pp. 3–28.

Reed, Robert Rentoul, Jr.   *Bedlam on the Jacobean Stage.* Cambridge, Mass.: Harvard University Press, 1952, pp. 47–50.

Ribner, Irving.   *Jacobean Tragedy.* New York: Barnes & Noble, 1962, pp. 126–137.

Ricks, Christopher.   "The Moral and Poetic Structure of *The Changeling*," in *Essays in Criticism.* X (1960), pp. 290–306.

Roy, Emil L.   "Sexual Paradox in *The Changeling*," in *Literature and Psychology.* XXV (1975), pp. 124–132.

Schoenbaum, Samuel.   *Middleton's Tragedies: A Critical Study.* New York: Columbia University Press, 1955, pp. 132–150.

Stilling, Roger.   *Love and Death in Renaissance Tragedy.* Baton Rouge: Louisiana State University Press, 1976, pp. 248–256.

Taylor, J. Chesley.   "Metaphors of the Moral World: Structure in *The Changeling*," in *Tulane Studies in English.* XX (1972), pp. 41–56.

Tomlinson, Thomas Brian.   "Poetic Naturalism—*The Changeling*," in *Journal of English and Germanic Philology.* LXIII (1964), pp. 648–659.

Williams, George Walton.   "Introduction," in *The Changeling.* By Thomas Middleton and William Rowley. Lincoln: University of Nebraska Press, 1965, pp. ix–xiv.

A Fair Quarrel

Barker, Richard Hindry.   *Thomas Middleton.* New York: Columbia University Press, 1958, pp. 105–110.

Bowers, Fredson T.   *Elizabethan Revenge Tragedy.* Princeton, N.J.: Princeton University Press, 1940, pp. 187–188.

———.   "Middleton's *Fair Quarrel* and the Duelling Code," in *Journal of English and Germanic Philology.* XXXVI (1937), pp. 40–65.

Brittin, Norman A.   *Thomas Middleton.* New York: Twayne, 1972, pp. 90–96.

Fisher, Margery.   " 'Bronstrops': A Note on *A Faire Quarrel*," in *Modern Language Review.* XXV (1940), pp. 59–62.

Holdsworth, R.V.   "The Medical Jargon in *A Fair Quarrel*," in *Review of English Studies.* XXIII (1972), pp. 448–454.

Holmes, David M.   *The Art of Thomas Middleton: A Critical Study.* London: Oxford University Press, 1970, pp. 113–121.

Levin, Richard.   "The Elizabethan 'Three Level' Play," in *Renaissance Drama.* II (1969), pp. 23–37.

————. *The Multiple Plot in English Renaissance Drama.* Chicago: University of Chicago Press, 1971, pp. 7–9, 66–75, 158–160.

————. "The Three Quarrels of *A Fair Quarrel*," in *Studies in Philology.* LXI (1964), pp. 219–231.

Price, George R. "Medical Men in *A Faire Quarrell*," in *Bulletin of the History of Medicine.* XXIV (1956), pp. 38–42.

Schoenbaum, Samuel. "Middleton's Tragi-Comedies," in *Modern Philology.* LIV (August, 1956), pp. 16–19.

The Spanish Gypsy

Barker, Richard Hindry. *Thomas Middleton.* New York: Columbia University Press, 1958, pp. 208–209.

Brittin, Norman A. *Thomas Middleton.* New York: Twayne, 1972, pp. 96–102.

Burlebach, Frederick M., Jr. "Theme and Structure in *The Spanish Gypsy*," in *Humanities Association Bulletin.* XIX (1968), pp. 37–41.

Kistner, A.L. and M.K. Kistner. "*The Spanish Gypsy*," in *Humanities Association Bulletin.* XXV (1974), pp. 211–224.

Morris, Edgar C. "Introduction," in *The Spanish Gipsie and All's Lost by Lust.* By Thomas Middleton and William Rowley. Boston: Heath, 1908, pp. xi–xlix.

Sykes, H. Dugdale. *Sidelights on Elizabethan Drama.* London: Frank Cass, 1966, pp. 183–199.

EDNA ST. VINCENT MILLAY
(1892–1950)

Aria da Capo

Atkins, Elizabeth. *Edna St. Vincent Millay and Her Times.* Chicago: University of Chicago Press, 1936, pp. 77–92.

Brittin, Norman A. *Edna St. Vincent Millay.* New York: Twayne, 1967, pp. 96–102.

Gerstenberger, Donna. "Verse Drama in America: 1916–1939," in *Modern Drama.* VI (December, 1963), pp. 309–322.

Gray, James. *Edna St. Vincent Millay.* Minneapolis: University of Minnesota Press, 1967, p. 35.

Gurko, Miriam. *Restless Spirit: The Life of Edna St. Vincent Millay.* New York: Thomas Y. Crowell, 1962, pp. 111–114.

McKee, Mary J. "Millay's *Aria da Capo:* Form and Meaning," in *Modern Drama.* IX (September, 1966), pp. 165–169.

Van Doren, Carl. "Youth and Wings: Edna St. Vincent Millay, Singer," in *Century.* CVI (June, 1923), pp. 310–316. Reprinted in *Many Minds: Critical Essays on American Writers.* New York: Knopf, 1924, pp. 105–119.

Untermeyer, Louis. "Edna St. Vincent Millay," in *American Poetry Since 1900.* New York: Holt, 1923, pp. 214–221.

The Buck in the Snow

Atkins, Elizabeth. *Edna St. Vincent Millay and Her Times.* Chicago: University of Chicago Press, 1936, pp. 175–198.

Benet, William Rose. "Introduction," in *Edna St. Vincent Millay's* Second April *and* The Buck in the Snow. New York: Harper, 1950, pp. v–xi.

Brittin, Norman. *Edna St. Vincent Millay.* New York: Twayne, 1967, pp. 118–123.

Deutsch, Babette. "Alas!," in *New Republic.* LVI (November 7, 1928), pp. 333–334.

Eastman, Max. "A Passing Fashion," in *Nation.* CXXVII (December 5, 1928), pp. 628, 630.

Gurko, Miriam. *Restless Spirit: The Life of Edna St. Vincent Millay.* New York: Thomas Y. Crowell, 1962, pp. 202–203.

Hutchison, Percy. "Miss Millay's New Lyrics Are More Deeply Serious," in *New York Times Book Review.* (October 7, 1928), p. 2.

Monroe, Harriet. "Miss Millay's New Book," in *Poetry.* XXXIII (January, 1929), pp. 210–214.

Parks, Edd Winfield. "Edna St. Vincent Millay," in *Sewanee Review.* XXXVIII (January–March, 1930), pp. 42–49.

————. "Miss Millay in Transition," in *Sewanee Review.* XXXVII (January–March, 1929), pp. 120–121.

Power, Sister Mary James. "Edna St. Vincent Millay Revels in Her Love of Earth," in *Poets at Prayer.* New York: Sheed and Ward, 1939, pp. 19–30.

Untermeyer, Louis. "Song from Thistles," in *Saturday Review of Literature.* V (October 13, 1928), p. 209.

"Euclid Alone Has Looked on Beauty Bare"

Booth, Bradford A. "Millay's 'Euclid Alone Has Looked on Beauty Bare,' " in *Explicator.* VI (October, 1947), item 5.

Brittin, Norman A. *Edna St. Vincent Millay.* New York: Twayne, 1967, pp. 114–115.

Cooper, Charles W. and John Holmes. *Preface to Poetry.* New York: Harcourt, Brace, 1936, pp. 46–53.

Dickson, Arthur. "Millay's 'Euclid Alone Has Looked on Beauty Bare,' " in *Explicator.* III (December, 1944), item 23.

————. "Millay's 'Euclid Alone Has Looked on Beauty Bare,' " in *Explicator.* VI (May, 1948), item 49.

Drew, Elizabeth and John L. Sweeney. *Directions in Modern Poetry.* New York: Norton, 1940, pp. 201–202, 207–208, 224. Reprinted in *The Critical Reader.* Edited by Wallace Douglas and Roy Lamson. New York: Norton, 1949, pp. 110–111.

Gray, James. *Edna St. Vincent Millay.* Minneapolis: University of Minnesota Press, 1967, pp. 26–27.

M., E.R. "Millay's 'Euclid Alone Has Looked on Beauty Bare,' " in *Explicator.* I (October, 1942), item Q9.

Neimeyer, Carl A. and Robert M. Gay. "Millay's 'Euclid Alone Has Looked on Beauty Bare,' " in *Explicator.* I (November, 1942), item 16.

A Few Figs from Thistles

Atkins, Elizabeth. *Edna St. Vincent Millay and Her Times.* Chicago: University of Chicago Press, 1936, pp. 64–76.

Brittin, Norman A. *Edna St. Vincent Millay.* New York: Twayne, 1967, pp. 80–83.

Colum, Padraic. "Miss Millay's Poems," in *Freeman.* IV (November 2, 1921), pp. 189–190.

Dell, Floyd. "Edna St. Vincent Millay," in *The Literary Spotlight.* Edited by John Farrar. New York: George H. Doran, 1924, pp. 77–90.

Gurko, Miriam. *Restless Spirit: The Life of Edna St. Vincent Millay.* New York: Thomas Y. Crowell, 1962, pp. 122–126.

Hill, Frank Ernest. "Edna St. Vincent Millay," in *Measure.* I (March, 1921), pp. 25–26.

Madeleva, Sister M. "Where Are You Going, My Pretty Maid?," in *Chaucer's Nuns and Other Essays.* New York: Appleton, 1925, pp. 150–152.

Perlmutter, Elizabeth P. "A Doll's Heart: The Girl in the Poetry of Edna St. Vincent Millay and Louise Bogan," in *Twentieth Century Literature.* XXIII (May, 1977), pp. 157–164.

Sprague, Rosemary. "Edna St. Vincent Millay, 1892–1950," in *Imaginary Gardens: A Study of Five American Poets.* Philadelphia: Chilton, 1969, pp. 154–155.

Taggard, Genevieve. "Classics of the Future," in *American Review.* II (November–December, 1924), pp. 620–623.

Untermeyer, Louis. "Edna St. Vincent Millay," in *American Poetry Since 1900.* New York: Holt, 1923, pp. 214–221.

Van Doren, Carl and Mark Van Doren. "Edna St. Vincent Millay," in *American and British Literature Since 1890.* New York: Century, 1926, pp. 38–43.

Wood, Clement. "Edna St. Vincent Millay: A Clever Sappho," in *Poets of America.* New York: Dutton, 1925, pp. 209–211.

The Harp-Weaver and Other Poems

Atkins, Elizabeth. *Edna St. Vincent Millay and Her Times.* Chicago: University of Chicago Press, 1936, pp. 122–148.

Brittin, Norman A. *Edna St. Vincent Millay.* New York: Twayne, 1967, pp. 110–118.

Collins, Joseph P. *Taking the Literary Pulse: Psychological Studies of Life and Letters.* New York: George H. Doran, 1924, pp. 118–120.

Converse, Florence. "*The Harp-Weaver,*" in *Atlantic Monthly.* CXXX (April, 1924), pp. 14, 16.

Eckman, Frederick. "Edna St. Vincent Millay: Notes Towards a Reappraisal," in *A Question of Quality: Popularity and Value in Modern Creative Writing.* Edited by Louis Filler. Bowling Green, Oh.: Bowling Green University Popular Press, 1976, pp. 193–203.

Gray, James. *Edna St. Vincent Millay.* Minneapolis: University of Minnesota Press, 1967, pp. 30–31.

Gurko, Miriam. *Restless Spirit: The Life of Edna St. Vincent Millay.* New York: Thomas Y. Crowell, 1962, pp. 155–156.

Hutchinson, Percy. "Poets Who Sing at the Christmas Shopping Season," in *New York Times Book Review.* (December 23, 1923), p. 11.

Madeleva, Sister M. "Where Are You Going, My Pretty Maid?," in *Chaucer's Nuns and Other Essays*. New York: Appleton, 1925, pp. 153–156.

Perlmutter, Elizabeth P. "A Doll's Heart: The Girl in the Poetry of Edna St. Vincent Millay and Louise Bogan," in *Twentieth Century Literature*. XXIII (May, 1977), pp. 157–164.

Sprague, Rosemary. "Edna St. Vincent Millay, 1892–1950," in *Imaginary Gardens: A Study of Five American Poets*. Philadelphia: Chilton, 1969, pp. 160–161.

Taggard, Genevieve. "Classics of the Future," in *American Review*. II (November–December, 1924), pp. 620–623.

Untermeyer, Louis. "*The Harp-Weaver*," in *Yale Review*. XIV (October, 1924), pp. 158–159.

Van Doren, Mark. "The Hungry Heart," in *Nation*. CXVIII (February 20, 1924), p. 210.

Wood, Clement. "Edna St. Vincent Millay: A Clever Sappho," in *Poets of America*. New York: Dutton, 1925, pp. 211–212.

Huntsman, What Quarry?

Bogan, Louise. "Verse," in *New Yorker*. XV (May 20, 1939), pp. 80–82. Reprinted as "Unofficial Feminine Laureate," in *Selected Criticism: Poetry and Prose*. New York: Noonday, 1955, pp. 154–156.

Brittin, Norman A. *Edna St. Vincent Millay*. New York: Twayne, 1967, pp. 147–151.

Cowley, Malcolm. "Episode in a Poet's Life," in *New Republic*. XC (June 7, 1939), pp. 135–136.

Deutsch, Babette. "Lady After Fox," in *Nation*. CXLVIII (May 27, 1939), p. 618.

Francis, Robert. "*Huntsman, What Quarry?*," in Virginia Quarterly Review. *XV (Autumn, 1939), pp. 646–647, 649.*

Hutchinson, Percy. "A New Book of Lyrics by Edna St. Vincent Millay," in *New York Times Book Review*. (May 21, 1939), p. 4.

Rodman, Selden. "Lyrics and Issues," in *Saturday Review of Literature*. XX (May 20, 1939), p. 5.

Rosenfield, Paul. "Under Angry Constellations," in *Poetry*. LV (October, 1939), pp. 47–50.

Swartz, Roberta Teale. "The Velvet Arras," in *Kenyon Review*. I (Autumn, 1939), pp. 465–468.

The Poetry of Millay

Atkins, Elizabeth. *Edna St. Vincent Millay and Her Times*. Chicago: University of Chicago Press, 1936, pp. 1–76, 93–260.

Cargill, Oscar. *Intellectual America: Ideas on the March.* New York: Macmillan, 1941, pp. 636–651.

Ciardi, John. "Edna St. Vincent Millay: A Figure of Passionate Living," in *Saturday Review of Literature.* XXXIII (November 11, 1950), pp. 8–9, 77. Reprinted in *Saturday Review Gallery.* Edited by Jerome Beatty, Jr. New York: Simon and Schuster, 1959, pp. 200–206. Also reprinted in his *Dialogue With an Audience.* Philadelphia: Lippincott, 1963, pp. 61–67.

Cook. Harold L. "Edna St. Vincent Millay: An Essay in Appreciation," in *A Bibliography of the Works of Edna St. Vincent Millay.* Edited by Karl Yost. New York: Harper, 1937, pp. 7–55.

Cowley, Malcolm. "Postscript: Twenty Years of American Literature," in *After the Genteel Tradition: American Writers Since 1910.* Edited by Malcolm Cowley. New York: Norton, 1937, pp. 213–234.

Dabbs, James McBride. "Edna St. Vincent Millay: Not Resigned," in *South Atlantic Quarterly.* XXXVII (January, 1938), pp. 54–66.

Davison, Edward. "Edna St. Vincent Millay," in *English Journal.* XVI (November, 1927), pp. 671–682.

Dubois, Arthur E. "Edna St. Vincent Millay," in *Sewanee Review.* XLIII (January–March, 1935), pp. 80–104.

Eckman, Frederick. "Edna St. Vincent Millay: Notes Towards a Reappraisal," in *A Question of Quality: Popularity and Value in Modern Creative Writing.* Edited by Louis Filler. Bowling Green, Oh.: Bowling Green University Popular Press, 1976, pp. 193–203.

Gray, James. *Edna St. Vincent Millay.* Minneapolis: University of Minnesota Press, 1967.

Gregory, Horace and Marya Zaturenska. *A History of American Poetry: 1900–1940.* New York: Harcourt, Brace, 1946, pp. 265–274.

Jones, Llewellyn. "The Younger Women Poets," in *English Journal.* XIII (May, 1924), pp. 301–310. Reprinted in *First Impressions: Essays on Poetry, Criticism and Prosody.* New York: Knopf, 1925, pp. 111–124.

Loggins, Vernon. "Edna St. Vincent Millay," in *I Hear America . . . : Literature in the United States Since 1900.* New York: Thomas Y. Crowell, 1937, pp. 84–90.

Madeleva, Sister M. "Where Are You Going My Pretty Maid?," in *Chaucer's Nuns and Other Essays.* New York: Appleton, 1925, pp. 141–158.

Minot, Walter S. "Millay's 'Ungrafted Tree': The Problem of the Artist as Woman," in *New England Quarterly.* XLVIII (1975), pp. 260–269.

Parks, Edd Winfield. "Edna St. Vincent Millay," in *Sewanee Review.* XXXVIII (January–March, 1930), pp. 42–49.

Power, Sister Mary James. "Edna St. Vincent Millay Revels in Her Love of Earth," in *Poets at Prayer.* New York: Sheed and Ward, 1939, pp. 19–30.

Preston, John Hyde. "Edna St. Vincent Millay," in *Virginia Quarterly Review.* III (July, 1927), pp. 342–355.

Ransom, John Crowe. "The Poet as Woman," in *Southern Review.* II (Spring, 1937), pp. 783–806. Reprinted in *The World's Body.* New York: Scribner's, 1938, pp. 76–110.

Schwartz, Delmore. "Poetry of Millay," in *Nation.* CLVII (December 19, 1943), pp. 735–736.

Scott, Nathan A.J. "Millay: A Reconsideration," in *Christian Century.* LXXIV (May 1, 1957), pp. 559–560.

Sprague, Rosemary. "Edna St. Vincent Millay, 1892–1950," in her*Imaginary Gardens: A Study of Five American Poets.* Philadelphia: Chilton, 1969, pp. 168–173.

Tate, Allen. "Miss Millay's Sonnets," in *New Republic.* LXVI (May 6, 1931), pp. 335–336. Revised and reprinted as "Edna St. Vincent Millay," in *Reactionary Essays on Poetry and Ideas.* New York: Scribner's, 1936, pp. 221–227.

Van Doren, Carl. "Youth and Wings: Edna St. Vincent Millay, Singer," in *Century.* CVI (June, 1923), pp. 310–316. Reprinted in *Many Minds: Critical Essays on American Writers.* New York: Knopf, 1924, pp. 105–119.

Wood, Clement. "Edna St. Vincent Millay: A Clever Sappho," in *Poets of America.* New York: Dutton, 1925, pp. 199–213.

Renascence and Other Poems

Atkins, Elizabeth. *Edna St. Vincent Millay and Her Times.* Chicago: University of Chicago Press, 1936, pp. 1–25.

Brittin, Norman A. *Edna St. Vincent Millay.* New York: Twayne, 1967, pp. 70–79.

Gray, James. *Edna St. Vincent Millay.* Minneapolis: University of Minnesota Press, 1967, pp. 10–12.

Gurko, Miriam. *Restless Spirit: The Life of Edna St. Vincent Millay.* New York: Thomas Y. Crowell, 1962, pp. 35–42, 45–47.

Power, Sister Mary James. "Edna St. Vincent Millay Revels in Her Love of Earth," in *Poets at Prayer.* New York: Sheed and Ward, 1939, pp. 19–30.

Stidger, William L. "Edna St. Vincent Millay," in *Flames of Faith.* New York: Abingdon Press, 1922, pp. 47–55.

Taggard, Genevieve. "Classics of the Future," in *American Review.* II (November–December, 1924), pp. 620–623.

Untermeyer, Louis. "Edna St. Vincent Millay," in *American Poetry Since 1900.* New York: Holt, 1923, pp. 214–221.

––––––. *The New Era in American Poetry.* New York: Holt, 1919, pp. 271–275.

Van Doren, Carl. "Youth and Wings: Edna St. Vincent Millay, Singer," in *Century*. CVI (June, 1923), pp. 310–316. Reprinted in *Many Minds: Critical Essays on American Writers*. New York: Knopf, 1924, pp. 105–119.

Wood, Clement. "Edna St. Vincent Millay: A Clever Sappho," in *Poets of America*. New York: Dutton, 1925, pp. 199–206.

Second April

Atkins, Elizabeth. *Edna St. Vincent Millay and Her Times*. Chicago: University of Chicago Press, 1936, pp. 93–121.

Benet, William Rose. "Introduction," in *Edna St. Vincent Millay's* Second April *and* The Buck in the Snow. New York: Harper, 1950, pp. v–xi.

Brittin, Norman A. *Edna St. Vincent Millay*. New York: Twayne, 1967, pp. 84–92.

Colum, Padraic. "Miss Millay's Poems," in *Freeman*. IV (November 2, 1921), pp. 189–190.

Gurko, Miriam. *Restless Spirit: The Life of Edna St. Vincent Millay*. New York: Thomas Y. Crowell, 1962, pp. 127–132.

Stidger, William L. "Edna St. Vincent Millay," in *Flames of Faith*. New York: Abingdon Press, 1922, pp. 47–55.

Taggard, Genevieve. "Classics of the Future," in *American Review*. II (November–December, 1924), pp. 620–623.

Untermeyer, Louis. "Edna St. Vincent Millay," in *American Poetry Since 1900*. New York: Holt, 1923, pp. 214–221.

Wood, Clement. "Edna St. Vincent Millay: A Clever Sappho," in *Poets of America*. New York: Dutton, 1925, pp. 206–209.

Wine from These Grapes

Atkins, Elizabeth. *Edna St. Vincent Millay and Her Times*. Chicago: University of Chicago Press, 1936, pp. 234–260.

Benet, William Rose. "Round About Parnassus," in *Saturday Review of Literature*. XI (November 10, 1934), p. 279.

Bogan, Louise. "Conversion into Self," in *Poetry*. XLV (February, 1935), pp. 277–279.

Brittin, Norman A. *Edna St. Vincent Millay*. New York: Twayne, 1967, pp. 128–133.

Brooks, Cleanth. "Edna Millay's Maturity," in *Southwest Review*. XX (January, 1935), Book Section, pp. 1–5.

Gurko, Miriam. *Restless Spirit: The Life of Edna St. Vincent Millay*. New York: Thomas Y. Crowell, 1962, pp. 203–204.

Rice, Philip Blair. "Edna Millay's Maturity," in *Nation*. CXXXIX (November 14, 1934), pp. 568, 570.

Tinker, Chauncey Brewster. "The Spirit of the Age," in *Yale Review*. XXIV (Winter, 1934), pp. 413–415.

ARTHUR MILLER
(1915–   )

After the Fall

Bigsby, C.W.E.   "The Fall and After: Arthur Miller's Confessions," in *Modern Drama*. X (September, 1967), pp. 124–136.

Brashear, William R.   "The Empty Bench: Morality, Tragedy, and Arthur Miller," in *Michigan Quarterly Review*. V (October, 1966), pp. 270–278.

Chiari, Joseph.   *Landmarks of Contemporary Drama*. London: Herbert Jenkins, 1965, pp. 151–157.

Ganz, Arthur.   "Arthur Miller: After the Silence," in *Drama Survey*. III (Fall, 1964), pp. 520–530.

Koppenhaver, Allen J.   "The Fall and After: Albert Camus and Arthur Miller," in *Modern Drama*. IX (September, 1966), pp. 206–209.

Lewis, Allan.   *American Plays and Playwrights of the Contemporary Theatre*. New York: Crown, 1965, pp. 35–52.

Moss, Leonard.   *Arthur Miller*. New York: Twayne, 1967, pp. 79–86.

————.   "Biographical and Literary Allusion in *After the Fall*," in *Educational Theatre Journal*. XVIII (March, 1966), pp. 34–40.

Murray, Edward.   "Point of View in *After the Fall*," in *College Language Association Journal*. X (December, 1966), pp. 135–142.

Sontag, Susan.   *Against Interpretation and Other Essays*. New York: Farrar, Straus and Giroux, 1966, pp. 140–145.

Stinson, John J.   "Structure in *After the Fall*: The Relevance of the Maggie Episodes to the Main Themes and the Christian Symbolism," in *Modern Drama*. X (December, 1967), pp. 233–240.

Weales, Gerald.   "Arthur Miller," in *The American Theater Today*. Edited by Alan S. Downer. New York: Basic Books, 1967, pp. 92–98.

All My Sons

Bigsby, C.W.E.   *Confrontation and Commitment*. Columbia: University of Missouri Press, 1968, pp. 26–32.

Boggs, W. Arthur.   "Oedipus and *All My Sons*," in *Personalist*. XLII (October, 1961), pp. 555–560.

Dillingham, William.   "Arthur Miller and the Loss of Conscience," in *Emory University Quarterly*. XVI (Spring, 1960), pp. 40–50.

Ganz, Arthur.   "The Silence of Arthur Miller," in *Drama Survey*. III (October, 1963), pp. 231–233.

Gassner, John. *The Theatre in Our Times.* New York: Crown, 1954, pp. 344–346.

Loughlin, Richard L. "Tradition and Tragedy in *All My Sons*," in *English Record.* XIV (February, 1964), pp. 23–27.

Murray, Edward. *Arthur Miller, Dramatist.* New York: Frederick Ungar, 1967, pp. 1–21.

Phillips, Elizabeth C. *Modern American Drama.* New York: Monarch Press, 1966, pp. 113–114.

Wells, Arvin R. "The Living and the Dead in *All My Sons*," in *Modern Drama.* VII (May, 1964), pp. 46–51.

Williams, Raymond. "The Realism of Arthur Miller," in *Critical Quarterly.* I (Summer, 1959), pp. 140–149.

Yorks, Samuel A. "Joe Keller and His Sons," in *Western Humanities Review.* XIII (Autumn, 1959), pp. 401–407.

The Crucible

Bentley, Eric. *The Dramatic Event: An American Chronicle.* New York: Horizon Press, 1954, pp. 90–94.

———. *The Theatre of Commitment.* New York: Atheneum, 1967, pp. 36–40.

Blau, Herbert. *The Impossible Theatre.* New York: Macmillan, 1964, pp. 188–192.

Calarco, N.J. "Production as Criticism: Miller's *The Crucible*," in *Educational Theatre Journal.* XXIX (October, 1977), pp. 354–361.

Curtis, Penelope. "*The Crucible*," in *Critical Review.* VIII (1965), pp. 45–58.

Douglas, James W. "Miller's *The Crucible*: Which Witch Is Which?," in *Renascence.* XV (Spring, 1953), pp. 145–151.

Fender, Stephen. "Precision and Pseudo Precision in *The Crucible*," in *Journal of American Studies.* I (April, 1967), pp. 87–98.

Ganz, Arthur. "The Silence of Arthur Miller," in *Drama Survey.* III (October, 1963), pp. 233–235.

Gilman, Richard. *Common and Uncommon Masks; Writings on Theatre, 1961–1970.* New York: Random House, 1971, pp. 152–155.

Hill, Philip F. "*The Crucible*: A Structural View," in *Modern Drama.* X (December, 1967), pp. 312–317.

Hughes, Catherine. *Plays, Politics, and Polemics.* New York: Drama Book Specialist Publishers, 1973, pp. 15–25.

Kauffmann, Stanley. *Persons of the Drama: Theater Criticism and Comment.* New York: Harper & Row, 1976, pp. 139–142.

Moss, Leonard. *Arthur Miller.* New York: Twayne, 1967, pp. 59–66.

Murray, Edward. *Arthur Miller, Dramatist.* New York: Frederick Ungar, 1967, pp. 52–75.

Nathan, George Jean. "*The Crucible,*" in *Theatre Arts.* XXXVII (April, 1953), pp. 24–26.

Popkin, Henry. "Arthur Miller's *The Crucible,*" in *College English.* XXVI (November, 1964), pp. 139–146.

Porter, Thomas E. *Myth and Modern American Drama.* Detroit: Wayne State University Press, 1966, pp. 177–199.

Warshow, Robert. *The Immediate Experience.* Garden City, N.Y.: Doubleday, 1962, pp. 189–203.

————. "The Liberal Conscience in *The Crucible,*" in *Essays in the Modern Drama.* Edited by Morris Freedman. Boston, Mass.: Heath, 1964, pp. 195–205.

Death of a Salesman

Bates, Barclay W. "The Lost Past in *Death of a Salesman,*" in *Modern Drama.* XI (September, 1968), pp. 164–172.

Bettina, Sister M. "Willy Loman's Brother Ben: Tragic Insight in *Death of a Salesman,*" in *Modern Drama.* IV (February, 1962), pp. 409–412.

Bliquez, Guerin. "Linda's Role in *Death of a Salesman,*" in *Modern Drama.* X (February, 1968), pp. 383–386.

De Schweinitz, George. "*Death of a Salesman*: A Note on Epic and *Tragedy,*" in *Western Humanities Review.* XIV (Winter, 1960), pp. 91–96.

Dusenbury, Winifred L. *The Theme of Loneliness in Modern American Drama.* Gainesville: University of Florida Press, 1960, pp. 16–26.

Eisinger, C.E. "Focus on Arthur Miller's *Death of a Salesman*: The Wrong Dreams," in *American Dreams, American Nightmares.* Edited by David Madden. Carbondale: Southern Illinois University Press, 1970, pp. 165–174.

Gross, Barry Edward. "Peddler and Pioneer in *Death of a Salesman,*" in *Modern Drama.* VII (Fall, 1965), pp. 405–410.

Hagopian, John V. "Arthur Miller: The Salesman's Two Cases," in *Modern Drama.* VI (October, 1963), pp. 117–125.

Hubbard, E.D. and Patricia Truelson. Death of a Salesman: *A Critical Commentary.* New York: American R.D.M. Cororation, 1967.

Huftel, Sheila. *Arthur Miller: The Burning Glass.* New York: Citadel Press, 1965, pp. 103–123.

Inserillo, Charles R. "Wish and Desire: Two Poles of the Imagination in the Drama of Arthur Miller and T.S. Eliot," in *Xavier University Studies.* I (Summer–Fall, 1962), pp. 247–258.

Jackson, Esther Merle. "*Death of a Salesman*: Tragic Myth in the Modern Theatre," in *College Language Association Journal*. VII (September, 1963), pp. 63–76.

Jacobson, Irving. "Family Dreams in *Death of a Salesman*," in *American Literature*. XLVII (May, 1975), pp. 247–258.

Kauffmann, Stanley. *Persons of the Drama: Theater Criticism and Comment*. New York: Harper & Row, 1976.

Kernodle, George R. "The Death of the Little Man," in *Tulane Drama Review*. I (January, 1956), pp. 47–60.

Lawrence, Stephen A. "The Right Dream in Miller's *Death of a Salesman*," in *College English*. XXV (April, 1964), pp. 547–549.

McAnany, Emile G. "The Tragic Commitment: Some Notes on Arthur Miller," in *Modern Drama*. V (May, 1962), pp. 11–20.

Moss, Leonard. *Arthur Miller*. New York: Twayne, 1967, pp. 45–59.

————. "Arthur Miller and the Common Man's Language," in *Modern Drama*. VII (May, 1964), pp. 52–59.

Otten, Charlotte F. "Who am I? A Re-investigation of Arthur Miller's *Death of a Salesman*," in *Cresset*. XXVI (February, 1963), pp. 11–13.

Parker, Brian. "Point of View in Arthur Miller's *Death of a Salesman*," in *University of Toronto Quarterly*. XXXV (1966), pp. 144–157.

Porter, Thomas E. *Myth and Modern American Drama*. Detroit: Wayne State University Press, 1969, pp. 127–152.

Schneider, Daniel E. "Play of Dreams," in *Theatre Arts*. XXXIII (1949), pp. 18–21.

Weales, Gerald, Editor. *Arthur Miller, Death of a Salesman: Text and Criticism*. New York: Viking, 1967.

Incident at Vichy

Bigsby, C.W.E. *Confrontation and Commitment*. Columbia: University of Missouri Press, 1968, pp. 47–49.

Brustein, Robert. *Seasons of Discontent*. New York: Simon and Schuster, 1965, pp. 259–263.

Huftel, Sheila. *Arthur Miller: The Burning Glass*. New York: Citadel, 1965, pp. 217–236.

Moss, Leonard. *Arthur Miller*. New York: Twayne, 1967, pp. 96–99.

Mottram, Eric. "Arthur Miller: The Development of a Political Dramatist in America," in *American Theatre*. Edited by John Russell Brown and Bernard Harris. London: Edward Arnold, 1967, pp. 156–161.

Murray, Edward. *Arthur Miller, Dramatist*. New York: Frederick Ungar, 1967, pp. 158–178.

Rahv, Philip. *The Myth and the Power-House.* New York: Farrar, Straus and Giroux, 1965, pp. 225–233.

Weales, Gerald. "Arthur Miller," in *The American Theatre Today.* Edited by Alan S. Downer. New York: Basic Books, 1967, pp. 92–95.

A View from the Bridge

Bigsby, C.W.E. *Confrontation and Commitment.* Columbia: University of Missouri Press, 1968, pp. 36–47.

————. "The Fall and After: Arthur Miller's Confessions," in *Modern Drama.* X (September, 1967), pp. 124–136.

Chiari, Joseph. *Landmarks of Contemporary Drama.* London: Herbert Jenkins, 1965, pp. 151–157.

Cubeta, Paul M. *Modern Drama for Analysis.* New York: Holt, Rinehart and Winston, 1962, pp. 382–390.

Dillingham, William. "Arthur Miller and the Loss of Conscience," in *Emory University Quarterly.* XVI (Spring, 1960), pp. 40–50.

Epstein, Arthur. "A Look at *A View from the Bridge,*" in *Texas Studies in Literature and Language.* VII (Spring, 1965), pp. 109–122.

Findlater, Richard. "No Time for Tragedy?," in *Twentieth Century.* CLXI (January, 1957), pp. 56–62.

Ganz, Arthur. "Arthur Miller After the Silence," in *Drama Survey.* III (Fall, 1964), pp. 520–530.

Huftel, Sheila. *Arthur Miller: The Burning Glass.* New York: Citadel, 1965, pp. 103–123.

Koppenhaver, Allen J. "The Fall and After: Albert Camus and Arthur Miller," in *Modern Drama.* IX (September, 1966), pp. 206–209.

Lewis, Allan. *American Plays and Playwrights of the Contemporary Theatre.* New York: Crown, 1965, pp. 35–52.

Miller, Arthur. "On Social Plays," in his *A View from the Bridge.* New York: Viking, 1955, pp. 1–15.

Moss, Leonard. *Arthur Miller.* New York: Twayne, 1967, pp. 79–86.

————. "Biographical and Literary Allusion in *After the Fall,*" in *Educational Theatre Journal.* XVIII (March, 1966), pp. 34–40.

Murray, Edward. "Point of View in *After the Fall,*" in *College Language Association Journal.* X (December, 1966), pp. 135–142.

Sontag, Susan. *Against Interpretation and Other Essays.* New York: Farrar, Straus and Giroux, 1966, pp. 140–145.

Stinson, John J. "Structure in *After the Fall*: The Relevance of the Maggie Episodes to the Main Themes and the Christian Symbolism," in *Modern Drama.* X (December, 1967), pp. 233–240.

HENRY MILLER
(1891–   )

Tropic of Cancer

Brophy, Brigid. *Don't Never Forget; Collected Views and Reviews.* New York: Holt, Rinehart and Winston, 1967, pp. 231–238.

Connolly, Cyril. *The Evening Colonade.* New York: Harcourt, 1975, pp. 293–295.

Foster, Steven. "A Critical Appraisal of Henry Miller's *Tropic of Cancer*," in *Twentieth Century Literature.* IX (January, 1964), pp. 196–208.

Fraenkal, Michael. *The Genesis of the* Tropic of Cancer. Berkeley, Calif.: Packard Press, 1946, pp. 38–56.

Friedman, Alan. "The Pitching of Love's Mansion in the Tropics of Henry Miller," in *Seven Contemporary Authors.* Edited by Thomas B. Whitbread. Austin: University of Texas Press, 1966, pp. 25–48.

Gordon, William A. *The Mind and Art of Henry Miller.* Baton Rouge: Louisiana State University Press, 1967, pp. 85–109.

Hassan, Ihab. *The Literature of Silence: Henry Miller and Samuel Beckett.* New York: Knopf, 1967, pp. 59–67.

Highet, Gilbert. *Explorations.* New York: Oxford University Press, 1971, pp. 209–215.

————. "Henry Miller's Stream of Consciousness," in *Horizon.* IV (November, 1961), pp. 104–105.

Hyman, Stanley E. *Standards: A Chronicle of Books for Our Times.* New York: Horizon Press, 1966, pp. 12–16.

Jackson, Paul R. "The Balconies of Henry Miller," in *University Review.* XXXVI (December, 1969), pp. 155–160. (Spring, 1970), pp. 221–225.

Kaufmann, Stanley. "*Tropic of Cancer*," in *The Critic as Artist.* Edited by Gilbert A. Harrison. New York: Liveright, 1972, pp. 211–216.

Littlejohn, David. *Interruptions.* New York: Grossman, 1970, pp. 37–44.

JOHN MILTON
(1608–1674)

Areopagitica

Barker, Arthur E., Editor. *Milton: Modern Essays in Criticism.* New York: Oxford University Press, 1965.

Evans, B.I. "The Lessons of the *Areopagitica*," in *Contemporary Review.* CLXVI (1944), pp. 342–346.

Fletcher, Harris F. *The Intellectual Development of John Milton.* Urbana: University of Illinois Press, 1956–1961.

Flory, Ancilla M. "Free Movement and Baroque Perspective in Milton's *Areopagitica*," in *Xavier University Studies.* VI (1967), pp. 93–98.

Huckabay, Calvin. *John Milton: An Annotated Bibliography, 1929–1968.* Pittsburgh: Duquesne University Press, 1969.

Hunter, G.K. "The Structure of Milton's *Areopagitica*," in *English Studies.* XXXIX (1958), pp. 117–119.

Johnson, C.O. "Note on Milton's Use of Gamut in *Areopagitica*," in *English Language Notes.* XIV (March, 1977), pp. 187–189.

Keeton, G.W. "The Tercentenary of the *Areopagitica*," in *Contemporary Review.* CLXVI (1944), pp. 280–286.

Kendall, Willmoore. "How to Read Milton's *Areopagitica*," in *Journal of Politics.* XXII (1960), pp. 439–473.

Lieb, Michael. "Milton and the Metaphysics of Form," in *Studies in Philology.* LXXI (April, 1974), pp. 206–224.

Macaulay, Rose. *Milton.* New York: Macmillan, 1957.

Parker, William R. *Milton: A Biography.* Oxford: Clarendon Press, 1968.

Patrick, J. Max, Editor. *SAMLA Studies in Milton: Essays on John Milton and His Works.* Gainesville: University of Florida Press, 1953.

Price, Alan F. "Incidental Imagery in *Areopagitica*," in *Modern Philology.* XLIX (1952), pp. 217–222.

Rice, Warner G. "A Note on *Areopagitica*," in *Journal of English and Germanic Philology.* XL (1941), pp. 474–481.

Richmond, Hugh M. *The Christian Revolutionary: John Milton.* Berkeley: University of California Press, 1974.

Shawcross, John T., Editor. *Milton: The Critical Heritage.* New York: Barnes & Noble, 1970.

Sirluck, Ernest. "*Areopagitica* and a Forgotten Licensing Controversy," in *Review of English Studies.* XI (1960), pp. 260–274.

Spitz, David. "Milton's *Areopagitica*: Testament for Our Times," in his *Essays in the Liberal Idea of Freedom*. Tucson: University of Arizona Press, 1964, pp. 100–110.

Tillyard, E.M.W. *Milton*. New York: Collier Macmillan, 1967.

Trevelyan, George Macaulay. "Milton's *Areopagitica*," in his *An Autobiography and Other Essays*. London: Longmans, 1949, pp. 179–182.

Wagenknecht, Edward. *The Personality of Milton*. Norman: University of Oklahoma Press, 1970.

Comus

Allen, Don Cameron. *The Harmonious Vision: Studies in Milton's Poetry*. Baltimore: Johns Hopkins University Press, 1954.

Arthos, John. "The Realms of Being in the Epilogue of *Comus*," in *Modern Language Notes*. LXXVI (1961), pp. 321–324.

Christopher, G.B. "Virginity of Faith: *Comus* as a Reformation Conceit," in *ELH*. XLIII (Winter, 1976), pp. 479–499.

Demaray, John G. *Milton and the Masque Tradition: The Early Poems, Arcades, and* Comus. Cambridge, Mass.: Harvard University Press, 1968.

Diekhoff, John S., Editor. *A Maske at Ludlow: Essays on Milton's* Comus. Cleveland, Oh.: Case Western Reserve University Press, 1968.

Fletcher, Angus John. *The Transcendental Masque: An Essay on Milton's* Comus. Ithaca, N.Y.: Cornell University Press, 1972.

Fletcher, Harris F. *The Intellectual Development of John Milton*. Urbana: University of Illinois Press, 1956–1961.

Huckabay, Calvin. *John Milton: An Annotated Bibliography, 1929–1968*. Pittsburgh: Duquesne University Press, 1969.

Kell, R. "Thesis and Action in Milton's *Comus*," in *Essays in Criticism*. XXIV (January, 1974), pp. 48–54.

Lawry, Jon S. *The Shadow of Heaven: Matter and Stance in Milton's Poetry*. Ithaca, N.Y.: Cornell University Press, 1968.

Macaulay, Rose. *Milton*. New York: Macmillan, 1957.

Major, John M. "*Comus* and *The Tempest*," in *Shakespeare Quarterly*. X (1959), pp. 177–183.

Mundhenk, R.K. "Dark Scandal and the Sun-Clad Power of Chastity: The Historical Milieu of Milton's *Comus*," in *Studies in English Literature*. XV (Winter, 1975), pp. 141–152.

Neuse, Richard. "Metamorphosis and Symbolic Action in *Comus*," in *ELH*. XXXIV (1967), pp. 49–64.

Parker, William R. *Milton: A Biography*. Oxford: Clarendon Press, 1968.

Patrick, J. Max, Editor. *SAMLA Studies in Milton: Essays on John Milton and His Works.* Gainesville: University of Florida Press, 1953.

Richmond, Hugh M. *The Christian Revolutionary: John Milton.* Berkeley: University of California Press, 1974.

Rudrum, Alan. *A Critical Commentary on Milton's* Comus *and Shorter Poems.* London: Macmillan, 1967.

Shawcross, John T., Editor. *Milton: The Critical Heritage.* New York: Barnes & Noble, 1970.

Tillyard, E.M.W. *Milton.* New York: Collier Macmillan, 1967.

Wagenknecht, Edward. *The Personality of Milton.* Norman: University of Oklahoma Press, 1970.

Wain, John. "Reflections on the First Night of *Comus*," in *Encounter.* XLVIII (March, 1977), pp. 33–42.

Wheeler, Thomas. "Magic and Morality in *Comus*," in *Studies in Honor of John C. Hodges and Alwin Thaler.* Edited by Richard B. Davis and John L. Lievsay. Knoxville: University of Tennessee Press, 1961, pp. 43–47.

Wilkenfeld, Roger B. "The Seat at the Center: An Interpretation of *Comus*," in *ELH.* XXXIII (1966), pp. 170–197.

Williamson, George. "The Context of *Comus*," in his *Milton and Others.* Chicago: University of Chicago Press, 1965, pp. 26–41.

"L'Allegro" and "Il Penseroso"

Babb, Lawrence. "The Background of 'Il Penseroso,' " in *Studies in Philology.* XXXVII (April, 1940), pp. 257–273.

Brooks, Cleanth, Jr. *The Well Wrought Urn.* New York: Reynal and Hitchcock, 1947, pp. 47–61.

Carpenter, Nan Cooke. "The Place of Music in 'L'Allegro' and 'Il Penseroso,' " in *The University of Toronto Quarterly.* XXII (July, 1953), pp. 354–367.

Eliot, T.S. "A Note on the Verse of John Milton," in *Essays and Studies.* XXI (1935), pp. 34–35.

Knight, G. Wilson. *The Burning Oracle: Studies in the Poetry of Action.* London: Oxford University Press, 1939.

MacKenzie, Phyllis. "Milton's Visual Imagination: An Answer to T.S. Eliot," in *The University of Toronto Quarterly.* XV (October, 1946), pp. 18–20.

"Lycidas"

Adams, Richard P. "The Archetypal Pattern of Death and Rebirth in Milton's 'Lycidas,' " in *PMLA.* LXIV (March, 1949), pp. 183–188.

Broadbent, J.B. "Milton's Rhetoric," in *Modern Philology.* LVI (May, 1959), pp. 224–242.

Daiches, David. *A Study of Literature for Readers and Critics.* Ithaca, N.Y.: Cornell University Press, 1948, pp. 170–195.

French, J. Milton. "The Digressions in Milton's 'Lycidas,' " in *Studies in Philology.* L (July, 1953), pp. 485–490.

Hardy, John Edward. "Reconsideration, I: 'Lycidas,' " in *Kenyon Review.* VII (Winter, 1945), pp. 99–113.

Mayerson, Caroline W. "The Orpheus Image in 'Lycidas,' " in *PMLA.* LXIV (March, 1949), pp. 189–207.

More, Paul Elmer. "How to Read 'Lycidas,' " in *The American Review.* VII (May, 1936), pp. 140–158.

Ransom, John Crowe. "A Poem Nearly Anonymous," in *The American Review.* I (May–September, 1933), pp. 179–203, 444–467.

————. *The World's Body.* New York: Scribner's, 1938, pp. 1–54.

Shumaker, Wayne. "Flowerets and Sounding Seas: A Study of the Affective Structure of 'Lycidas,' " in *PMLA.* LXVI (June, 1951), pp. 485–494.

Tillyard, E.M.W. *Poetry Direct and Oblique.* London: Chatto and Windus, 1934, pp. 208–213.

Turner, W. Arthur. "Milton's Two Handed Engine," in *Journal of English and Germanic Philology.* XLIX (October, 1950), pp. 562–565.

Wagenknecht, Edward. "Milton in 'Lycidas,' " in *College English.* VII (April, 1946), pp. 393–397.

"On His Blindness"

Cooper, Charles W. and John Holmes. *Preface to Poetry.* New York: Harcourt, Brace, 1946, pp. 231–234.

Daniels, Earl. *The Art of Reading Poetry.* New York: Farrar and Rinehart, 1941, pp. 34–36.

Goodman, Paul. *The Structure of Literature.* Chicago: University of Chicago Press, 1954, pp. 204–215.

Jackson, J.L. and W.E. Weese. " '. . . Who Only Stand and Wait': Milton's Sonnet 'On His Blindness,' " in *Modern Language Notes.* LXXII (February, 1957), pp. 91–93.

Kemp, Lysander. "On a Sonnet by Milton," in *Hopkins Review.* VI (Fall, 1952), pp. 80–83.

Parker, William R. "The Dates of Milton's Sonnet 'On His Blindness,' " in *PMLA.* LXXIII (June, 1958), pp. 199–200.

Robins, Harry R. "Milton's First Sonnet 'On His Blindness," in *Review of English Studies.* VII (October, 1956), pp. 362–366.

"On the Morning of Christ's Nativity"

Daiches, David and William Charvat. *Poems in English, 1930–1940.* New York: Ronald Press, 1950, pp. 661–667.

Knight, G. Wilson. *The Burning Oracle; Studies in the Poetry of Action.* London: Oxford University Press, 1939, pp. 59–61.

Ross, Malcolm. "Milton and the Protestant Aesthetic: The Early Poems," in *The University of Toronto Quarterly.* XVII (July, 1948), pp. 349–352.

Stapleton, Lawrence. "Milton and the New Music," in *The University of Toronto Quarterly.* XXIII (April, 1954), pp. 217–236.

Paradise Lost

Babb, Lawrence. *The Moral Cosmos of* Paradise Lost. East Lansing: Michigan State University Press, 1970.

Berry, Boyd M. *Process of Speech: Puritan Religious Writings and* Paradise Lost. Baltimore: Johns Hopkins University Press, 1976.

Berthold, D. "The Concept of Merit in *Paradise Lost,*" in *Studies in English Literature.* XV (Winter, 1975), pp. 153–167.

Blamires, Harry. *Milton's Creation: A Guide Through* Paradise Lost. London: Methuen, 1971.

Evans, J.M. Paradise Lost *and the Genesis Tradition.* Oxford: Clarendon Press, 1968.

Fish, Stanley E. *Surprised by Sin: The Reader in* Paradise Lost. Berkeley: University of California Press, 1971.

Fletcher, Harris F. *The Intellectual Developent of John Milton.* Urbana: University of Illinois Press, 1956–1961.

Grose, Christopher. *Milton's Epic Process:* Paradise Lost *and Its Miltonic Background.* New Haven, Conn.: Yale University Press, 1973.

Huckabay, Calvin. *John Milton: An Annotated Bibliography, 1929–1968.* Pittsburgh: Duquesne University Press, 1969.

Kuby, L. "The World Is Half the Devil's: Cold Warmth in *Paradise Lost,*" in *ELH.* XLI (Summer, 1974), pp. 182–191.

Lieb, Michael, Editor. *Achievements of the Left Hand: Essays on the Prose of John Milton.* Amherst: University of Massachusetts Press, 1974.

Macaulay, Rose. *Milton.* New York: Macmillan, 1957.

Norford, D.P. "My Other Half: The Coincidence of Opposites in *Paradise Lost,*" in *Modern Language Quarterly.* XXXVI (March, 1975), pp. 21–53.

Parker, William R. *Milton: A Biography.* Oxford: Clarendon Press, 1968.

Richmond, Hugh M. *The Christian Revolutionary: John Milton.* Berkeley: University of California Press, 1974.

Ryken, Leland.   *The Apocalyptic Vision in* Paradise Lost. Ithaca, N.Y.: Cornell University Press, 1970.

Savage, J.B.   "Freedom and Necessity in *Paradise Lost*," in *ELH*. XLIV (Summer, 1977), pp. 286–311.

Shawcross, John T., Editor.   *Milton: The Critical Heritage.* New York: Barnes & Noble, 1970.

Smith, G.W.   "Iterative Rhetoric in *Paradise Lost*," in *Modern Philology*. LXXIV (August, 1976), pp. 1–19.

Steadman, John M.   *Epic and Tragic Structure in* Paradise Lost. Chicago: University of Chicago Press, 1976.

Stein, Arnold S.   *The Art of Presence: The Poet and* Paradise Lost. Berkeley: University of California Press, 1977.

Tillyard, E.M.W.   *Milton.* New York: Collier Macmillan, 1967.

Wagenknecht, Edward.   *The Personality of Milton.* Norman: University of Oklahoma Press, 1970.

Wheeler, Thomas.   *Paradise Lost and the Modern Reader.* Athens: University of Georgia Press, 1974.

Woods, Mary A.   *The Characters of* Paradise Lost. Folcroft, Pa.: Folcroft Library Editions, 1972.

Paradise Regained

Allen, Don Cameron.   *The Harmonious Vision: Studies in Milton's Poetry.* Baltimore: Johns Hopkins University Press, 1954.

Barker, Arthur E., Editor.   *Milton: Modern Essays in Criticism.* New York: Oxford University Press, 1965.

Cleveland, Edward.   "On the Identity Motive in *Paradise Regained*," in *Modern Language Notes*. LXXIV (1959), pp. 232–236.

Cox, Lee Sheridan.   "Food-Word Imagery in *Paradise Regained*," in *ELH*. XVIII (1961), pp. 225–243.

Fields, Albert W.   "Milton and Self-Knowledge," in *PMLA*. LXXXIII (1968), pp. 392–399.

Fletcher, Harris F.   *The Intellectual Development of John Milton.* Urbana: University of Illinois Press, 1956–1961.

Frye, Northrop.   *The Return of Eden: Five Essays on Milton's Epics.* London: Routledge and Kegan Paul, 1965.

Huckabay, Calvin.   *John Milton: An Annotated Bibliography, 1929–1968.* Pittsburgh: Duquesne University Press, 1969.

Lawry, Jon S.   *The Shadow of Heaven: Matter and Stance in Milton's Poetry.* Ithaca, N.Y.: Cornell University Press, 1968.

Lewalski, Barbara K.   *Milton's Brief Epic: the Genre, Meaning and Art of* Paradise Regained. Providence, R.I.: Brown University Press, 1966.

Macaulay, Rose.   *Milton.* New York: Macmillan, 1957.

Marilla, Esmond L.   *"Paradise Regained:* Observations on Its Meaning," in *Milton and Modern Man: Selected Essays.* University: University of Alabama Press, 1968, pp. 56–67.

Martz, Louis L.   *"Paradise Regained:* The Meditative Combat," in *ELH.* XXVII (1960), pp. 223–247.

Parker, William R.   *Milton: A Biography.* Oxford: Clarendon Press, 1968.

Patrides, C.A., Editor.   *Milton's Epic Poetry: Essays on* Paradise Lost *and* Paradise Regained. Harmondsworth, England: Penguin, 1967.

Pope, Elizabeth M.   Paradise Regained: *The Tradition and the Poem.* New York: Russell and Russell, 1961.

Rajan, Balachandra, Editor.   *The Prison and the Pinnacle: Papers to Commemorate the Tercentenary of* Paradise Regained *and* Samson Agonistes. London: Routledge and Kegan Paul, 1973.

Richmond, Hugh M.   *The Christian Revolutionary: John Milton.* Berkeley: University of California Press, 1974.

Schultz, Howard.   "A Fairer Paradise? Some Recent Studies of *Paradise Regained,*" in *ELH.* XXXII (1965), pp. 275–302.

Shawcross, John T., Editor.   *Milton: The Critical Heritage.* New York: Barnes & Noble, 1970.

Stein, Arnold S.   *Heroic Knowledge: An Interpretation of* Paradise Regained *and* Samson Agonistes. Minneapolis: University of Minnesota Press, 1957.

Tillyard, E.M.W.   *Milton.* New York: Collier Macmillan, 1967.

Wagenknecht, Edward.   *The Personality of Milton.* Norman: University of Oklahoma Press, 1970.

Weber, Burton J.   *Wedges and Wings: The Patterning of* Paradise Regained. Carbondale: Southern Illinois University Press, 1975.

Wittreich, Joseph A., Editor.   *Calm of Mind: Tercentenary Essays on* Paradise Regained *and* Samson Agonistes *in Honor of J.S. Diekhoff.* Cleveland: Press of Case Western Reserve University, 1971.

The Poetry of Milton

Allen, Don Cameron.   *The Harmonious Vision: Studies in Milton's Poetry.* Baltimore: Johns Hopkins University Press, 1954.

Barker, Arthur E., Editor.   *Milton: Modern Essays in Criticism.* New York: Oxford University Press, 1965.

Condee, Ralph W.   *Structure in Milton's Poetry: From the Foundation to the Pinnacles.* University Park: Pennsylvania State University Press, 1974.

Demaray, John G. *Milton and the Masque Tradition: The Early Poems, Arcades, and* Comus. Cambridge, Mass.: Harvard University Press, 1968.

Fletcher, Harris F. *The Intellectual Development of John Milton.* Urbana: University of Illinois Press, 1956–1961.

Hardy, John P. *Reinterpretations: Essays on Poems.* London: Routledge and Kegan Paul, 1971.

Harrington, David V. "Feeling and Form in Milton's Sonnets," in *Western Humanities Review.* XX (1966), pp. 317–328.

Huckabay, Calvin. *John Milton: An Annotated Bibliography, 1929–1968.* Pittsburgh: Duquesne University Press, 1969.

Lawry, Jon S. *The Shadow of Heaven: Matter and Stance in Milton's Poetry.* Ithaca, N.Y.: Cornell University Press, 1968.

Macaulay, Rose. *Milton.* New York: Macmillan, 1957.

McCarthy, W. "Continuity of Milton's Sonnets," in *PMLA.* XCII (January, 1977), pp. 96–109.

Nicolson, Majorie H. *John Milton: A Reader's Guide to His Poetry.* New York: Octagon Books, 1971.

Parker, William R. *Milton: A Biography.* Oxford: Clarendon Press, 1968.

Patrick, J. Max, Editor. *SAMLA Studies in Milton: Essays on John Milton and His Works.* Gainesville: University of Florida Press, 1953.

Patrides, C.A., Editor. *Milton's "Lycidas": The Tradition and the Poem.* New York: Holt, Rinehart, and Winston, 1961.

Rajan, Balachandra. *The Lofty Rhyme: A Study of Milton's Major Poetry.* London: Routledge and Kegan Paul, 1970.

Reesing, John. *Milton's Poetic Art: A Mask, "Lycidas," and* Paradise Lost. Cambridge, Mass.: Harvard University Press, 1968.

Richmond, Hugh M. *The Christian Revolutionary: John Milton.* Berkeley: University of California Press, 1974.

Rudrum, Alan. *A Critical Commentary on Milton's* Comus *and Shorter Poems.* London: Macmillan, 1967.

Samuel, I. "Development of Milton's Poetics," in *PMLA.* XCII (March, 1977), pp. 231–240.

Shawcross, John T., Editor. *Milton: The Critical Heritage.* New York: Barnes & Noble, 1970.

Stroup, Thomas B. *Religious Rite and Ceremony in Milton's Poetry.* Lexington: University of Kentucky Press, 1968.

Tillyard, E.M.W. *Milton.* New York: Collier Macmillan, 1967.

Tuve, Rosemond. *Images and Themes in Five Poems by Milton.* Cambridge, Mass.: Harvard University Press, 1957.

Wagenknecht, Edward. *The Personality of Milton.* Norman: University of Oklahoma Press, 1970.

Whiting, George W. *Milton and This Pendant World.* Austin: University of Texas Press, 1958.

Samson Agonistes

Allen, Don Cameron. *The Harmonious Vision: Studies in Milton's Poetry.* Baltimore: Johns Hopkins University Press, 1954.

Barker, Arthur E., Editor. *Milton: Modern Essays in Criticism.* New York: Oxford University Press, 1965.

Carey, John. "Sea, Snake, Flower, and Flame in *Samson Agonistes*," in *Modern Language Review.* LXII (1967), pp. 395–399.

Chambers, A.B. "Wisdom and Fortitude in *Samson Agonistes*," in *PMLA.* LXXVIII (1963), pp. 315–320.

Cox, Lee Sheridan. "Natural Science and Figurative Design in *Samson Agonistes*," in *ELH.* XXXV (1968), pp. 51–74.

Crump, Galbraith M., Editor. *Twentieth Century Interpretations of* Samson Agonistes*: A Collection of Critical Essays.* Englewood Cliffs, N.J.: Prentice-Hall, 1968.

Ferry, Anne Davidson. "*Samson Agonistes*," in her *Milton and the Miltonic Dryden.* Cambridge, Mass.: Harvard University Press, 1968, pp. 127–218.

Fletcher, Harris F. *The Intellectual Development of John Milton.* Urbana: University of Illinois Press, 1956–1961.

Hone, Ralph E., Editor. *John Milton's* Samson Agonistes*: The Poem and Materials for Analysis.* San Francisco: Chandler, 1966.

Huckabay, Calvin. *John Milton: An Annotated Bibliography, 1929–1968.* Pittsburgh: Duquesne University Press, 1969.

Hyman, Lawrence W. "Milton's *Samson Agonistes* and the Modern Reader," in *College English.* XXVIII (1966), pp. 39–43.

Krouse, F. Michael. *Milton's Samson and the Christian Tradition.* New York: Octagon Books, 1974.

Lawry, Jon S. *The Shadow of Heaven: Matter and Stance in Milton's Poetry.* Ithaca, N.Y.: Cornell University Press, 1968.

Low, Anthony. *The Blaze of Noon: A Reading of* Samson Agonistes. New York: Columbia University Press, 1974.

Macaulay, Rose. *Milton.* New York: Macmillan, 1957.

Marilla, Esmond L. "*Samson Agonistes*: An Interpretation," in his *Milton and Modern Man: Selected Essays.* University: University of Alabama Press, 1968, pp. 68–77.

Parker, William R.   *Milton: A Biography.* Oxford: Clarendon Press, 1968.

———.   *Milton's Debt to Greek Tragedy in* Samson Agonistes. New York: Barnes & Noble, 1968.

Richmond, Hugh M.   *The Christian Revolutionary: John Milton.* Berkeley: University of California Press, 1974.

Shawcross, John T., Editor.   *Milton: The Critical Heritage.* New York: Barnes & Noble, 1970.

Slights, C.W.   "Hero of Conscience: *Samson Agonistes* and Casuistry," in *PMLA.* XC (May, 1975), pp. 395–413.

Steadman, John M.   "Milton's Summa Epitasis: The End of the Middle of *Samson Agonistes*," in *Modern Language Review.* LXIX (October, 1974), pp. 730–744.

Stein, Arnold S.   *Heroic Knowledge: An Interpretation of* Paradise Regained *and* Samson Agonistes. Minneapolis: University of Minnesota Press, 1957.

Tillyard, E.M.W.   *Milton.* New York: Collier Macmillan, 1967.

Wagenknecht, Edward.   *The Personality of Milton.* Norman: University of Oklahoma Press, 1970.

YUKIO MISHIMA
(1925–1970)

Confessions of a Mask

Dana, Robert. "Stutter of Eternity," in *Critique*. XXII (1970), pp. 87–102.

Keene, Donald. "Mishima Yukio," in *Landscapes and Portraits: Appreciations of Japanese Culture*. Tokyo: Kodansha International, 1971, pp. 204–207.

McClellan, Edwin. "Mishima," in *Yale Review*. LXIV (Summer, 1975), pp. 579–583.

Nathan, John. *Mishima: A Biography*. Boston: Little Brown, 1974, pp. 94–99.

Richie, Donald. "The Last True Samurai," in *Harper's*. L (September, 1972), pp. 105–107.

Scott-Stokes, Henry. *The Life and Death of Yukio Mishima*. New York: Farrar, Straus and Giroux, 1974, pp. 100–110, 116–121.

Ueda, Makoto. "Mishima Yukio," in *Modern Japanese Writers and the Nature of Literature*. Stanford, Calif.: Stanford University Press, 1976, p. 221.

The Decay of the Angels

Heath, Susan. *"Decay of the Angels,"* in *Saturday Review/World*. I (June 1, 1974), p. 1.

Morrow, Lance. *"Decay of the Angels,"* in *Time*. CIII (June 10, 1974), pp. 92–94.

Nathan, John. *Mishima: A Biography*. Boston, Mass.: Little, Brown, 1974, pp. 265–266.

Scott-Stokes, Henry. *The Life and Death of Yukio Mishima*. New York: Farrar, Straus and Giroux, 1974, pp. 291–297, 300–302.

Ueda, Makoto. "Mishima Yukio," in *Modern Japanese Writers and the Nature of Literature*. Stanford, Calif.: Stanford University Press, 1976, pp. 230–231.

Runaway Horses

Driver, Christopher. "The Inkbrush Is Mightier," in *The Listener*. XLV (February 14, 1974), pp. 215–216.

Jordan, Clive. "Last Rite," in *New Statesman*. XC (November 30, 1973), pp. 828–829.

Keene, Donald. "Mishima Yukio," in *Landscapes and Portraits: Appreciations of Japanese Culture*. Tokyo: Kodansha International, 1971, p. 208.

Nathan, John. *Mishima: A Biography*. Boston, Mass.: Little, Brown, 1974, pp. 214, 251.

Scott-Stokes, Henry. *The Life and Death of Yukio Mishima.* New York: Farrar, Straus and Giroux, 1974, pp. 182–190.

Ueda, Makoto. "Mishima Yukio," in *Modern Japanese Writers and the Nature of Literature.* Stanford, Calif.: Stanford University Press, 1976, p. 225.

White, Edmund. "Runaway Horses," in *New York Times Book Review.* (June 24, 1973), p. 3.

Sailor Who Fell from Grace with the Sea

Dana, Robert. "Stutter of Eternity," in *Critique.* XII (1970), pp. 87–102.

Keene, Donald. "Mishima Yukio," in *Landscapes and Portraits: Appreciations of Japanese Culture.* Tokyo: Kodansha International, 1971, pp. 220–221.

Nathan, John. *Mishima: A Biography.* Boston: Little Brown, 1974, pp. 190–192.

Scott-Stokes, Henry. *The Life and Death of Yukio Mishima.* New York: Farrar, Straus and Giroux, 1974, p. 164.

Ueda, Makoto. "Mishima Yukio," in *Modern Japanese Writers and the Nature of Literature.* Stanford, Calif.: Stanford University Press, 1976, pp. 227, 247.

The Sound of Waves

Boardman, Gwen R. "Greek Hero and Japanese Samurai," in *Critique.* XII (November 1, 1970), pp. 103–113.

Keene, Donald. "Mishima Yukio," in *Landscapes and Portraits: Appreciations of Japanese Culture.* Tokyo: Kodansha International, 1971, p. 212.

Nathan, John. *Mishima: A Biography.* Boston, Mass.: Little, Brown, 1974, pp. 120–122.

Scott-Stokes, Henry. *The Life and Death of Yukio Mishima.* New York: Farrar, Straus and Giroux, 1974, pp. 136–137.

Ueda, Makoto. "Mishima Yukio," in *Modern Japanese Writers and the Nature of Literature.* Stanford, Calif.: Stanford University Press, 1976, pp. 244–245.

The Temple of Dawn

Capitanchik, Maurice. "Means to an End," in *Books and Bookmen.* (December 1974), pp. 59–60.

Cunningham, Valentine. "Bags of Tricks," in *New Statesman.* (July 19, 1974), p. 90.

Keene, Donald. "Mishima Yukio," in *Landscapes and Portraits: Appreciations of Japanese Culture.* Tokyo: Kodansha International, 1971, pp. 223–224.

Nathan, John. *Mishima: A Biography.* Boston, Mass.: Little, Brown, 1974, pp. 202, 251.

Scott-Stokes, Henry. *The Life and Death of Yukio Mishima.* New York: Farrar, Straus and Giroux, 1974, pp. 196–211.

Theroux, Paul. "*Temple of Dawn*," in *New York Times Book Review.* (October 14, 1973), pp. 6–7.

The Temple of the Golden Pavilion

Dana, Robert. "Stutter of Eternity," in *Critique.* XII (1970), pp. 87–102.

Dures, L. "Novel as Koan: Mishima's the *Temple of the Golden Pavilion*," in *Critique.* X (1968), pp. 120–129.

Enright, D.J. "Mishima's Way," in *Man Is an Onion: Review and Essays.* Chatto and Windus, 1972, pp. 195–203.

Keene, Donald. "Mishima Yukio," in *Landscapes and Portraits; Appreciations of Japanese Culture.* Tokyo: Kodansha International, 1971, pp. 207–215.

McClellan, Edwin. "Mishima," in *Yale Review.* LXIV (Summer, 1975), pp. 579–583.

Miyoshi, M. "Mishima Yukio: *Confessions of a Mask* and *the Temple of the Golden Pavilion*," in *Accomplices of Silence.* Los Angeles: University of California Press, 1974, pp. 141–180.

Ross, Nancy Wilson. "Introduction," in *The Temple of the Golden Pavilion.* By Yukio Mishima. New York: Knopf, 1972, pp. v–xix.

Scott-Stokes, Henry. *The Life and Death of Yukio Mishima.* New York: Farrar, Straus and Giroux, 1974, pp. 141–145.

Ueda, Makoto. "Mishima Yukio," in *Modern Japanese Writers and the Nature of Literature.* Stanford, Calif.: Stanford University Press, 1976, pp. 219–223, 232–240.

MOLIÈRE
(1622–1673)

Amphitryon

Burgess, G.S. "Molière and the Pursuit of Criteria," in *Symposium*. XXII (Spring, 1969), pp. 5–15.

Cornett, Patricia L. "Doubling in *Amphytrion*," in *Essays in French Literature*. IX (1972), pp. 6–29.

Forehand, W.E. "Adaptation and Comic Intent: Plautus' *Amphituro* and Molière's *Amphytrion*," in *Comparative Literature Studies*. XI (1974), pp. 204–217.

Gossman, Lionel. *Men and Masks; A Study of Molière*. Baltimore: Johns Hopkins University Press, 1963, pp. 1–35.

————. "Molière's *Amphitryon*," in *PMLA*. LXXVIII (1963), pp. 201–213.

Hebert, Rodolphe-Louis. "An Episode in Molière's *Amphitryon* and Cartesian Epistemology," in *Modern Language Notes*. LXX (1955), pp. 416–422.

Howarth, W.D. and Merlin Thomas, Editors. *Molière's Stage and Study; Essays in Honor of W.G. Moore*. Oxford: Clarendon Press, 1973, pp. 185–197.

Johnson, Roger B., et al. *Molière and the Commonwealth of Letters: Patrimony and Posterity*. Jackson, Miss.: University Press of Mississippi, 1975, pp. 327–333.

Phelps, Ruth S. "*Amphitryon* and Montespan," in *Modern Philology*. XXIV (1927), pp. 443–461.

Walker, Hallam. *Molière*. New York: Twayne, 1971, pp. 137–142.

The Bourgeois Gentleman

DeSelincourt, Aubrey. *Six Great Playwrights*. London: Hamilton, 1960, pp. 94–95.

Falk, Eugene H. "Molière the Indignant Satirist: *Le Bourgeois Gentilhomme*," in *Tulane Drama Review*. V (1960), pp. 73–88.

Fraser, R.D. and S.F. Rendall. "The Recognition Scene in Molière's Theater," in *Romanic Review*. LXIV (1973), pp. 16–31.

Girard, Rene. "Perilous Balance: A Comic Hypothesis," in *Modern Language Notes*. LXXXVII (1972), pp. 811–826.

Howarth, W.D. and Merlin Thomas, Editors. *Molière's Stage and Study; Essays in Honor of W.G. Moore*. Oxford: Clarendon Press, 1973, pp. 170–184.

Maxfield-Miller, Elisabeth. "The Real Monsieur Jourdain of the *Bourgeois Gentilhomme*," in *Studies in Philology*. LVI (1959), pp. 62–73.

Nicolich, Robert N.   "Classicism and Baroque in *Le Bourgeois Gentilhomme*," in *French Review*. XLV (1972), pp. 21–30.

Oliver, T.E.   "Notes on the *Bourgeois Gentilhomme*," in *Modern Philology*. X (1913), pp. 407–412.

Rouillard, C.D.   "The Background of the Turkish Ceremony in Molière's *Le Bourgeois Gentilhomme*," in *University of Toronto Quarterly*. XXXIX (1969), pp. 33–52.

Walker, Hallam.   "Strength and Style in *Le Bourgeois Gentilhomme*," in *French Review*. XXXVII (1964), pp. 282–287.

Don Juan

Brody, Jules.   "*Don Juan* and *Le Misanthrope* or the Esthetics of Individualism in Molière," in *PMLA*. LXXXIV (1969), pp. 559–576.

Burgess, G.S.   "Molière and the Pursuit of Criteria," in *Symposium*. XXII (Spring, 1969), pp. 5–15.

Coquelin, C.   "*Don Juan* of Molière," in *International Quarterly*. VIII (September, 1903), pp. 60–92.

Doolittle, J.   "The Humanity of Molière's *Don Juan*," in *PMLA*. LXVIII (1953), pp. 509–534.

Goode, William.   "*Don Juan* and Heaven's Spokesman," in *French Review*. XLV (1972), pp. 3–12.

Gossman, Lionel.   *Men and Masks; A Study of Molière*. Baltimore: Johns Hopkins University Press, 1963, pp. 36–65.

Gross, Nathan.   "The Dialectic of Obligation in Molière's *Don Juan*," in *Romanic Review*. LXV (May, 1974), pp. 175–200.

Guicharnaud, Jacques, Editor.   *Molière; A Collection of Critical Essays*. New York: Prentice-Hall, 1964, pp. 79–102.

Hall, H.G.   "Comic *Don Juan*," in *Yale French Studies*. XXIII (1959), pp. 77–84.

Lawrence, Francis L.   "*Don Juan* and the Manifest God: Molière's Anti-tragic Hero," in *PMLA*. XCVIII (January, 1978), pp. 86–94.

Matthews, B.   Molière's *Don Juan*," in *Sewanee Review*. XVIII (1910), pp. 257–267.

Moore, W.G.   "*Don Juan* Reconsidered," in *Modern Language Review*. LII (1957), pp. 510–517.

Nelson, Robert J.   "The Unreconstructed Heroes of Molière," in *Tulane Drama Review*. IV (1959–1960), pp. 14–37.

Nurse, Peter H., Editor.   *The Art of Criticism; Essays in French Literary Analysis*. Edinburgh: Edinburgh University Press, 1969, pp. 69–87.

Singer, I. "Molière's *Don Juan*," in *Hudson Review*. XXIV (Autumn, 1971), pp. 447–460.

————. "Shadow of *Don Juan* in Molière," in *Modern Language Notes*. LXXXV (1970), pp. 838–857.

Stewart, Philip. "An Analysis of the Plot in *Don Juan*," in *French Review*. XLV (1972), pp. 13–20.

Turnell, Martin. *Classical Moment; Studies of Corneille, Molière and Racine.* London: Hamilton, 1947, pp. 78–90.

Walker, Hallam. *Molière.* New York: Twayne, 1971, pp. 98–111.

————. "The Self-Creating Hero in *Don Juan*," in *French Review*. XXXVI (1962), pp. 167–174.

Young, B.E. "Defense and Illustration of the *Don Juan* of Molière," in *South Atlantic Quarterly*. XI (July, 1912), pp. 251–258.

The Hypochondriac (Le Malade Imaginaire)

Berk, Philip R. "The Therapy of Art in *Le Malade Imaginaire*," in *French Review*. XLV (1972), pp. 39–48.

Guicharnaud, Jacques, Editor. *Molière; A Collection of Critical Essays.* New York: Prentice-Hall, 1964, pp. 160–169.

Stoker, J.T. "Argon's Sickness in Molière's *Le Malade Imaginaire*," in *Culture*. XXX (1969), pp. 122–128.

Tynan, Kenneth. *Curtains; Selections from the Drama, Criticism and Related Writings.* New York: Atheneum, 1961, pp. 3–6, 391–392.

Walker, Hallam. *Molière.* New York: Twayne, 1971, pp. 167–173.

Zdanowicz, C.D. "From *Le Misanthrope* to *Le Malade Imaginaire*," in *Modern Philology*. XIX (1921), pp. 17–32.

The Misanthrope

Burgess, G.S. "Molière and the Pursuit of Criteria," in *Symposium*. XXII (Spring, 1969), pp. 5–15.

Goodman, Randolph. *Drama on Stage.* New York: Holt, Rinehart, 1961, pp. 198–207, 230–232.

Gossman, Lionel. *Men and Masks; A Study of Molière.* Baltimore: Johns Hopkins University Press, 1963, pp. 66–99.

Hope, Q.M. "Society in *Le Misanthrope*," in *French Review*. XXXII (1959), pp. 329–336.

Johnson, Roger B., et al. *Molière and the Commonwealth of Letters: Patrimony and Posterity.* Jackson: University Press of Mississippi, 1975, pp. 82–89, 100–108, 457–461.

Moore, W.G. "Reflections on *Le Misanthrope*," in *Australian Journal of French Studies.* IV (1967), pp. 198–203.

Nelson, Robert J. "The Unreconstructed Heroes of Molière," in *Tulane Drama Review.* IV (1959–1960), pp. 14–37.

Regosin, R.L. "Ambiguity and Truth in *Le Misanthrope*," in *Romanic Review.* LX (December, 1969), pp. 265–272.

Rudin, Seymour. "Molière and *The Misanthrope*," in *Educational Theatre Journal.* XVII (1965), pp. 308–313.

Siedel, M.A. and E. Mendelson, Editors. *Homer to Brecht; the European Epic and Dramatic Traditions.* New Haven, Conn.: Yale University Press, 1977, pp. 255–272.

Shaw, David C. "*Le Misanthrope* and Classicism," in *Modern Languages.* LV (1974), pp. 16–26.

Simon, John. "Laughter in the Soul in Molière's *Misanthrope*," in *Hudson Review.* XXVIII (1975), pp. 404–412.

Sullivan, E.D. "The Actor's Alceste: Evolution of *The Misanthrope*," in *Modern Language Quarterly.* IX (1948), pp. 492–496.

Turnell, Martin. *Classical Moment; Studies of Corneille, Molière and Racine.* London: Hamilton, 1947, pp. 90–120.

Tynan, Kenneth. *Curtains; Selections from the Drama, Criticism and Related Writings.* New York: Atheneum, 1961, pp. 391–392.

Wadsworth, P.A. "Recollections of Cicognini's 'Gelosie Fortunate' in *Le Misanthrope*," in *PMLA.* LXXXIX (1974), pp. 1099–1105.

Walker, Hallam. "Action and Illusion in *Le Misanthrope*," in *Kentucky Foreign Language Quarterly.* IX (1962), pp. 150–161.

————. *Molière.* New York: Twayne, 1971, pp. 111–125.

Yarrow, P.J. "A Reconsideration of Alceste," in *French Studies.* XIII (1959), pp. 314–331.

Zolbrod, Paul G. "Coriolanus and Alceste; a Study in Misanthropy," in *Shakespeare Quarterly.* XXIII (1972), pp. 51–62.

The Miser (L'Avare)

Gilman, Richard. *Common and Uncommon Masks; Writings on the Theatre, 1961–1970.* New York: Random House, 1971, pp. 274–276.

Goode, William O. "The Comic Recognition Scenes in *L'Avare*," in *Romance Notes.* XIV (1972), pp. 122–127.

Guicharnaud, Jacques, Editor. *Molière; A Collection of Critical Essays.* Englewood Cliffs, N.J.: Prentice-Hall, 1964, pp. 155–159.

Gutwirth, M. "The Unity of Molière's *L'Avare*," in *PMLA.* LXXVI (1961), pp. 359–366.

Herrick, I.A. "Shylock and Harpagon, Two Specialists in Avarice," in *Education*. XIV (1894), pp. 633–637.

Hubert, Judd D. "Theme and Structure in *L'Avare*," in *PMLA*. LXXV (1960), pp. 31–36.

Walker, Hallam. "Action and Ending of *L'Avare*," in *French Review*. XXXIV (1961), pp. 531–536.

―――――. *Molière*. New York: Twayne, 1971, pp. 531–536.

Wells, David J. "The Structure of Laughter in Molière's *L'Avare*," in *South Central Bulletin*. XXXII (1972), pp. 242–245.

The School for Wives (L' Ecole des Femmes)

Fraser, R.D. and S.F. Rendall. "The Recognition Scene in Molière's Theater," in *Romanic Review*. LXIV (1973), pp. 16–31.

McBride, Robert. "The Sceptical View of Marriage and the Comic Vision in Molière," in *Forum for Modern Language Studies*. V (1969), pp. 26–46.

Nurse, P.H. "Role of Chrysalde in *L'Ecole des Femmes*," in *Modern Language Review*. LVI (1961), pp. 167–171.

Shepherd, James L., III. "Molière and Wycherley's 'Plain Dealer,' " in *South Central Bulletin*. XXIII (1963), pp. 37–40.

Turnell, Martin. *Classical Moment; Studies of Corneille, Molière and Racine*. London: Hamilton, 1947, pp. 53–58.

Walker, Hallam. *Molière*. New York: Twayne, 1971, pp. 62–70.

Zwillenberg, Myrna K. "Arnolphe, Fate's Fool," in *Modern Language Review*. LXVIII (1973), pp. 292–308.

Tartuffe

Brustein, R.S. *Seasons of Discontent; Dramatic Opinions 1959–1965*. New York: Simon and Schuster, 1967, pp. 263–269.

Chill, Emanuel. "*Tartuffe*, Religion and Courtly Culture," in *French Historical Studies*. III (1963), pp. 151–183.

DeSelincourt, Aubrey. *Six Great Playwrights*. London: Hamilton, n.d. pp. 96–101.

Gossman, Lionel. *Men and Masks; A Study of Molière*. Baltimore: Johns Hopkins University Press, 1963, pp. 100–145.

―――――. "Molière and *Tartuffe*: Law and Order in the 17th Century," in *French Review*. XLIX (1970), pp. 901–912.

Grant, E.M. "*Tartuffe* Again," in *Philological Quarterly*. VI (1927), pp. 67–74.

Gutwirth, M. "*Tartuffe* and the Mysteries," in *PMLA*. XCII (January, 1977), pp. 33–40.

Hall, H. Gaston. "Some Background to Molière's *Tartuffe*," in *Australian Journal of French Studies.* X (1973), pp. 119–129.

Hope, Quentin. "Place and Setting in *Tartuffe*," in *PMLA.* LXXXIX (January, 1974), pp. 42–49.

McCollom, William G. *The Divine Average; A View of Comedy.* Cleveland: Case Western Reserve University Press, 1971, pp. 165–179.

Montgomery, E.D. "*Tartuffe*: The History and Sense of a Name," in *Modern Language Notes.* LXXXVIII (May, 1973), pp. 838–840.

Orwin, Gifford. "*Tartuffe* Reconsidered," in *French Review.* XLI (1968), pp. 611–617.

Shelton, L. "*Tartuffe*," in *Educational Theatre Journal.* XXVII (March, 1975), pp. 122–123.

Simmonds, P.M. "Molière's Satiric Use of the *deus ex Machina* in *Tartuffe*," in *Educational Theatre Journal.* XXIX (March, 1977), pp. 85–93.

Turnell, Martin. *Classical Moment; Studies of Corneille, Molière and Racine.* London: Hamilton, 1947, pp. 58–78.

Walker, Hallam. *Molière.* New York: Twayne, 1971, pp. 81–98.

Zwillenberg, Myrna K. "Dramatic Justice in *Tartuffe*," in *Modern Language Notes.* XC (1975), pp. 583–590.

N. SCOTT MOMADAY
(1934–   )

House Made of Dawn

Evers, Lawrence J. "Words and Place: A Reading of *House Made of Dawn*," in *Western American Literature*. XI (February, 1977), pp. 297–320.

Hylton, M.W. "On a Trail of Pollen: Momaday's *House Made of Dawn*," in *Critique*. XIV (1972), pp. 60–69.

Oaks, Priscilla. "A Review of N. Scott Momaday," in *Western American Literature*. IX (February, 1975), pp. 312–314.

Smith, W.J. "*House Made of Dawn*," in *Commonweal*. LXXXVIII (September 20, 1968), p. 636.

Sprague, Marshall. "*House Made of Dawn*—Review," in *New York Times Book Review*. (June 9, 1968), p. 5.

Watkins, Floyd C. "Culture Versus Anonymity in *House Made of Dawn*," in his *In Time and Place*. Athens: University of Georgia Press, 1977, pp. 133–171.

Wood, C.L. "Momaday's *House Made of Dawn*," in *Explicator*. XXXVI (Winter, 1978), pp. 27–28.

BRIAN MOORE
(1921–   )

An Answer from Limbo

Adams, Phoebe. "Humanity and the Writer," in *Atlantic*. CCX (November, 1962), pp. 143–144.

Allen, Walter. "All for Art," in *New Statesman*. LXV (March 29, 1963), pp. 465–466.

Dahlie, Hallvard. *Brian Moore*. Toronto: Copp, Clark, 1969.

Flood, Jeanne. *Brian Moore*. Lewisburg, Pa.: Bucknell University Press, 1974, pp. 49–63.

Foster, John Wilson. "Passage Through Limbo: Brian Moore's North American Novels," in *Critique*. XIII (1970), pp. 5–18.

Gilman, Richard. "*An Answer from Limbo*," in *Commentary*. XXXVI (August, 1963), pp. 176–177.

Hicks, Granville. "Asphalt Is Bitter Soil," in *Saturday Review*. XLV (October 13, 1962), pp. 20, 47.

Hornyansky, Michael. "Countries of the Mind," in *Tamarack Review*. XXVI (Winter, 1963), pp. 63–67.

Kersnowski, Frank L. "Exit the Anti-Hero," in *Critique*. X (1967–1968), pp. 60–71.

McSweeney, Kerry. "Brian Moore: Past and Present," in *Critical Quarterly*. XVIII (Summer, 1976), pp. 60–61.

Mayhew, Alice Ellen. "Life in Neither-Heaven-Nor-Hell Land," in *Commonweal*. LXXVII (November, 9, 1962), p. 179.

Ricks, Christopher. "The Simple Excellence of Brian Moore," in *New Statesman*. (February 18, 1966), pp. 227–228.

Sale, Roger. "Gossips and Storytellers," in *Hudson Review*. XVI (Spring, 1963), pp. 141–149.

Woodcock, George. "A Close Shave," in *Canadian Literature*. (Spring, 1962), pp. 70–72.

Catholics

Flood, Jeanne. *Brian Moore*. Lewisburg, Pa.: Bucknell University Press, 1974, pp. 93–96.

Garvey, John. "*Catholics*," in *Critic*. XXXII (September–October, 1973), pp. 78–79.

McSweeney, Kerry. "Brian Moore: Past and Present," in *Critical Quarterly*. XVIII (Summer, 1976), pp. 57–58.

_____. "Brian Moore's New Novel," in *Queen's Quarterly*. LXXIX (Winter, 1972), pp. 581–583.

Mudrick, Marvin. "Old Pros with News from Nowhere," in *Hudson Review*. XXVI (Autumn, 1973), pp. 545–561.

Porter, Raymond J. "Miracle, Mystery, and Faith in Brian Moore's *Catholics*," in *Eire-Ireland*. X (1975), pp. 79–88.

Price, Martin. "Believers: Some Recent Novels," in *Yale Review*. LXIII (Autumn, 1973), pp. 80–91.

Quillin, Michael. "Since Blue Died: American Catholic Novels Since 1961," in *Critic*. XXXIV (Fall, 1975), pp. 27–28.

The Emperor of Ice-Cream

Buckeye, Robert. "*The Emperor of Ice-Cream*," in *Dalhousie Review*. XLVI (Spring, 1966), pp. 135–139.

Dahlie, Hallvard. *Brian Moore*. Toronto: Copp, Clark, 1969.

_____. "Brian Moore's Broader Vision: *The Emperor of Ice-Cream*," in *Critique*. IX (1966), pp. 43–55.

Flood, Jeanne. *Brian Moore*. Lewisburg, Pa.: Bucknell University Press, 1974, pp. 64–71.

Foster, John W. "Crisis and Ritual in Brian Moore's Belfast Novels," in *Eire-Ireland*. III (Autumn, 1968), pp. 66–74.

Hicks, Granville. "An Invitation to Live," in *Saturday Review*. XLVIII (September 18, 1965), pp. 97–98.

McSweeney, Kerry. "Brian Moore: Past and Present," in *Critical Quarterly*. XVIII (Summer, 1976), pp. 56–57.

Murray, J.G. "*The Emperor of Ice-Cream*," in *Critic*. XXIV (December, 1965–January, 1966), p. 70.

Raban, Jonathan. *The Techniques of Modern Fiction: Essays in Practical Criticism*. Notre Dame, Ind.: University of Notre Dame Press, 1968, pp. 64–66.

Ricks, Christopher. "The Simple Excellence of Brian Moore," in *New Statesman*. LXXI (February 18, 1966), pp. 227–228.

Sale, Roger. "High Mass and Low Requiem," in *Hudson Review*. XIX (Spring, 1966), pp. 124–134.

Smith, Marion B. "Existential Morality," in *Canadian Literature*. (Spring, 1966), pp. 68–70.

The Feast of Lupercal

Dahlie, Hallvard. *Brian Moore*. Toronto: Copp, Clark, 1969.

Flood, Jeanne. *Brian Moore*. Lewisburg, Pa.: Bucknell University Press, 1974, pp. 24–34.

Foster, John W.   "Crisis and Ritual in Brian Moore's Belfast Novels," in *Eire-Ireland*. III (Autumn, 1968), pp. 66–74.

Horchler, Richard.   "A Wrench of Pity," in *Commonweal*. LXVI (July 12, 1957), pp. 380–381.

La Farge, Oliver.   "Defeat in a Church School," in *Saturday Review*. XL (April 27, 1957), pp. 15, 27.

Ludwig, Jack.   "Brian Moore: Ireland's Loss, Canada's Novelist," in *Critique*. V (Spring–Summer, 1962), pp. 5–14.

Fergus

Flood, Jeanne.   *Brian Moore*. Lewisburg, Pa.: Bucknell University Press, 1974, pp. 81–88.

Gordon, David J.   "Some Recent Novels: Connoisseurs of Chaos," in *Yale Review*. LX (Spring, 1971), pp. 430–431.

McSweeney, Kerry.   "Brian Moore: Past and Present," in *Critical Quarterly*. XVIII (Summer, 1976), pp. 62–64.

Magid, Nora L.   "These, These Our Players," in *Commonweal*. XCIII (February 12, 1971), pp. 477–478.

Sale, Richard B.   "Irish Ghosts," in *Nation*. CCXI (October 12, 1970), pp. 346–347.

Woodcock, George.   "A Matter of Loyalty," in *Canadian Literature*. XLIX (Summer, 1971), pp. 81–83.

I Am Mary Dunne

Brady, Charles A.   "*I Am Mary Dunne*, by Brian Moore," in *Eire*. III (1968), pp. 136–140.

Dahlie, Hallvard.   *Brian Moore*. Toronto: Copp, Clark, 1969.

————.   "Moore's New Perspective," in *Canadian Literature*. XXXVIII (Autumn, 1968), pp. 81–84.

Flood, Jeanne.   *Brian Moore*. Lewisburg, Pa.: Bucknell University Press, 1974, pp. 71–81.

Foster, John Wilson.   "Passage Through Limbo: Brian Moore's North American Novels," in *Critique*. XIII (1970), pp. 5–18.

Hicks, Granville.   "Mary and Her Mad Twin," in *Saturday Review*. LI (June 15, 1968), pp. 23–24.

Jackson, Katherine Gauss.   "*I Am Mary Dunne*," in *Harper's*. CCCXXXVII (July, 1968), pp. 104–105.

McSweeney, Kerry.   "Brian Moore: Past and Present," in *Critical Quarterly*. XVIII (Summer, 1976), pp. 59–60.

Magid, Nora L. "*I Am Mary Dunne*," in *Commonweal*. LXXXVIII (September 27, 1968), pp. 662–664.

Sale, Richard B. "Total Recall," in *Nation*. CCVI (June 24, 1968), p. 832.

The Lonely Passion of Judith Hearne

Dahlie, Hallvard. *Brian Moore*. Toronto: Copp, Clark, 1969.

Flood, Jeanne. *Brian Moore*. Lewisburg, Pa.: Bucknell University Press, 1974, pp. 15–24.

Foster, John W. "Crisis and Ritual in Brian Moore's Belfast Novels," in *Eire-Ireland*. III (Autumn, 1968), pp. 66–74.

Kersnowski, Frank L. "Exit the Anti-Hero," in *Critique*. X (1967–1968), pp. 60–71.

Levin, Martin. "Futility and a Furnished Room," in *Saturday Review*. XXXIX (July 7, 1956), p. 9.

Ludwig, Jack. "Brian Moore: Ireland's Loss, Canada's Novelist," in *Critique*. V (Spring–Summer, 1962), pp. 5–13.

Stedmond, John. "Introduction," in *Judith Hearne*. Toronto: McClelland and Stewart, 1964, pp. v–viii.

The Luck of Ginger Coffey

Dahlie, Hallvard. *Brian Moore*. Toronto: Copp, Clark, 1969.

Flood, Jeanne. *Brian Moore*. Lewisburg, Pa.: Bucknell University Press, 1974, pp. 35–49.

Foster, John Wilson. "Passage Through Limbo: Brian Moore's North American Novels," in *Critique*. XIII (1970), pp. 5–18.

Fraser, Keath. "Introduction," in *The Luck of Ginger Coffey*. Toronto: McClelland and Stewart, 1972, pp. iii–ix.

Hicks, Granville. "The Unsuccessful Gamblers," in *Saturday Review*. XLIII (August 27, 1960), p. 12.

Kersnowski, Frank L. "Exit the Anti-Hero," in *Critique*. X (1967–1968), pp. 60–71.

Lanning, George. "Silverfish in the Plumbing," in *Kenyon Review*. XXIII (Winter, 1961), pp. 173–181.

Ludwig, Jack. "A Mirror of Moore," in *Tamarack Review*. XVII (Winter, 1961), pp. 19–23.

McSweeney, Kerry. "Brian Moore: Past and Present," in *Critical Quarterly*. XVIII (Summer, 1976), p. 58.

Magid, Nora L. "On Loneliness," in *Commonweal*. LXXIII (September 30, 1960), pp. 20–21.

Pickrel, Paul. "*The Luck of Ginger Coffey*," in *Harper's*. CCXXI (October, 1960), pp. 107–108.

Tallman, Warren. "Irishman's Luck," in *Canadian Literature*. (Autumn, 1960), pp. 69–70.

GEORGE MOORE
(1852–1933)

The Brook Kerith

Baker, Ernest A. *The History of the English Novel*, Volume IX. New York: Barnes & Noble, 1950, pp. 191–195.

Brown, Malcolm. *George Moore: A Reconsideration.* Seattle: University of Washington Press, 1955, pp. 177–178, 188–189.

Chew, Samuel C. "The Novel: Naturalism and Romance," in *A Literary History of England.* Edited by Albert C. Baugh. New York: Appleton-Century-Crofts, 1948, pp. 1493–1498.

Clutton-Brock, Arthur. "Mr. George Moore," in *Essays on Literature and Life.* London: Methuen, 1926, pp. 171–173.

Collins, Norman. *The Facts of Fiction.* London: Gollancz, 1932, pp. 249–257.

Dobrée, Bonamy. "George Moore's Final Works," in *The Man of Wax: Critical Essays on George Moore.* Edited by Douglas A. Hughes. New York: New York University Press, 1971, pp. 289–301.

Dunleavy, Janet Egleson. *George Moore: The Artist's Vision, the Storyteller's Art.* Lewisburg, Pa.: Bucknell University Press, 1973, pp. 130–136.

Ervine, St. John G. *Some Impressions of My Elders.* London: George Allen, 1923, pp. 98–111.

Freeman, John. *A Portrait of George Moore in a Study of His Work.* New York: Appleton, 1922, pp. 185–198.

Graves, Robert. "Don't Fidget, Young Man," in *Five Pens in Hand.* Garden City, N.Y.: Doubleday, 1958, pp. 123–128.

Howarth, Herbert. "George Augustus Moore," in *The Irish Writers, 1880–1940.* New York: Hill and Wang, 1958, pp. 72–76.

Hughes, Douglas A. "Introduction," in *The Man of Wax: Critical Essays on George Moore.* Edited by Douglas A. Hughes. New York: New York University Press, 1971, pp. xxi–xxiii.

Huneker, James G. "The Reformation of George Moore," in *Unicorns.* New York: Scribner's, 1921, pp. 261–276.

Noël, Jean C. "*The Brook Kerith*: Heretical Romance," in *The Man of Wax: Critical Essays on George Moore.* Edited by Douglas A. Hughes. New York: New York University Press, 1971, pp. 267–287.

Richards, I.A. "Jesus' Other Life," in *Complementarities: Uncollected Essays.* Edited by John Paul Russo. Cambridge, Mass.: Harvard University Press, 1976, pp. 209–214.

Shawe-Taylor, Desmond. "The Achievement of George Moore," in *The Life of George Moore*. By Joseph Hone. London: Gollancz, 1936, pp. 474–477.

Sherman, Stuart P. "The Aesthetic Naturalism of George Moore," in *On Contemporary Literature*. New York: Holt, 1917, pp. 159–166.

Ward, A.C. *Foundations of English Prose*. London: Bell, 1931, pp. 89–91.

Wolfe, Humbert. *George Moore*. London: Harold Schaylor, 1932, pp. 143–152.

A Drama in Muslin

Baker, Ernest A. *The History of the English Novel*, Volume IX. New York: Barnes & Noble, 1950, pp. 170–171.

Brown, Malcolm. *George Moore: A Reconsideration*. Seattle: University of Washington Press, 1955, pp. 98–99, 101–102.

Chaikin, Milton. "George Moore's Early Fiction," in *George Moore's Mind and Art*. Edited by Graham Owens. New York: Barnes & Noble, 1970, pp. 31–33.

Dunleavy, Janet Egleson. *George Moore: The Artist's Vision, the Storyteller's Art*. Lewisburg, Pa.: Bucknell University Press, 1973, pp. 76–85.

Freeman, John. *A Portrait of George Moore in a Study of His Work*. New York: Appleton, 1922, pp. 85–90.

Frierson, William C. "George Moore: Naturalist," in *The English Novel in Transition, 1885–1940*. Norman: University of Oklahoma Press, 1942, pp. 67–70.

Howarth, Herbert. "George Augustus Moore," in *The Irish Writers, 1880–1940*. New York: Hill and Wang, 1958, pp. 51–56.

Jeffares, A. Norman. "*A Drama in Muslin*," in *Essays Presented to Amy G. Stock, Professor of English, Rajasthan University, 1961–1965*. Edited by R.K. Kaul. Jaipur, India: Rajasthan University Press, 1965, pp. 137–154. Revised and reprinted in *George Moore's Mind and Art*. Edited by Graham Owens. New York: Barnes & Noble, 1970, pp. 1–20.

Nejdefors-Frisk, Sonja. *George Moore's Naturalistic Prose*. Cambridge, Mass.: Harvard University Press, 1952, pp. 86–108.

Reid, Forrest. "The Novels of George Moore," in *Westminster Review*. CLXXII (August, 1909), pp. 200–208.

Sherman, Stuart P. "The Aesthetic Naturalism of George Moore," in *On Contemporary Literature*. New York: Holt, 1917, pp. 136–145.

Sporn, Paul. "Marriage and Class Conflict: The Subversive Link in George Moore's *A Drama in Muslin*," in *Clio*. III (1973), pp. 7–20.

Starkie, Enid. *From Gautier to Eliot*. London: Hutchinson's, 1960, pp. 70–80, 100–102.

Swinnerton, Frank. *The Georgian Scene: A Literary Panorama.* New York: Farrar and Rinehart, 1934, pp. 172–182.

Ure, Peter. "George Moore as Historian of Consciences," in *The Man of Wax: Critical Essays on George Moore.* Edited by Douglas A. Hughes. New York: New York University Press, 1971, pp. 95–99, 106–108.

Esther Waters

Baker, Ernest A. *The History of the English Novel,* Volume IX. New York: Barnes & Noble, 1950, pp. 171–176.

Brown, Malcolm. *George Moore: A Reconsideration.* Seattle: University of Washington Press, 1955, pp. 125–139.

Cargill, Oscar. *Intellectual America.* New York: Macmillan, 1941, pp. 77–82.

Chew, Samuel C. "The Novel: Naturalism and Romance," in *A Literary History of England.* Edited by Albert C. Baugh. New York: Appleton-Century-Crofts, 1948, pp. 1493–1498.

Collins, Norman. *The Facts of Fiction.* London: Gollancz, 1932, pp. 249–257.

Cunliffe, John W. *Leaders of the Victorian Revolution.* New York: Appleton-Century, 1934, pp. 280–283.

Dunleavy, Janet Egleson. *George Moore: The Artist's Vision, the Storyteller's Art.* Lewisburg, Pa.: Bucknell University Press, 1973, pp. 96–110.

Freeman, John. *A Portrait of George Moore in a Study of His Work.* New York. Appleton, 1922, pp. 110–117.

Hicks, Granville. "The Miracle of *Esther Waters,*" in *The Man of Wax: Critical Essays on George Moore.* Edited by Douglas A. Hughes. New York: New York University Press, 1971, pp. 141–150.

Howarth, Herbert. "George Augustus Moore," in *The Irish Writers, 1880–1940.* New York: Hill and Wang, 1958, pp. 39–48.

Hughes, Douglas A. "Introduction," in *The Man of Wax: Critical Essays on George Moore.* Edited by Douglas A. Hughes. New York: New York University Press, 1971, pp. xii–xv.

Lovett, Robert M. and Helen S. Hughes. *The History of the Novel in England.* New York: Houghton Mifflin, 1932, pp. 369–373.

McCullough, Bruce W. *Representative English Novelists: Defoe to Conrad.* New York: Harper, 1946, pp. 266–273.

McGreevy, T. "George Moore," in *Scrutinies: By Various Writers,* Volume I. Edited by Edgell Rickword. London: Wishart, 1928, pp. 110–130.

Mansfield, Katherine. "*Esther Waters* Revisited," in *Novels and Novelists.* Edited by John Middleton Murry. New York: Knopf, 1930, pp. 242–246.

Morton, Donald E. "Lyrical Form and the World of *Esther Waters,*" in *Studies in English Literature, 1500–1900.* XIII (1973), pp. 688–700.

Muller, Herbert J. *Modern Fiction: A Study of Values.* New York: Funk and Wagnalls, 1937, pp. 196–198.

Nejdefors-Frisk, Sonja. *George Moore's Naturalistic Prose.* Cambridge, Mass.: Harvard University Press, 1952, pp. 109–129.

Nicholas, Brian. "The Case of *Esther Waters,*" in *The Man of Wax: Critical Essays on George Moore.* Edited by Douglas A. Hughes. New York: New York University Press, 1971, pp. 151–183.

Ohmann, Carol. "George Moore's *Esther Waters,*" in *Nineteenth-Century Fiction.* XXV (1970), pp. 174–187.

Reid, Forrest. "The Novels of George Moore," in *Westminster Review.* CLXXII (August, 1909), pp. 200–208.

Routh, H.V. *Toward the Twentieth Century.* New York: Macmillan, 1937, pp. 339–345.

Ure, Peter. "George Moore as Historian of Consciences," in *The Man of Wax: Critical Essays on George Moore.* Edited by Douglas A. Hughes. New York: New York University Press, 1971, pp. 99–106.

Wagenknecht, Edward. "George Moore, the Man of Wax," in *Cavalcade of the English Novel.* New York: Holt, 1954, pp. 411–416.

Weygandt, Cornelius. *A Century of the English Novel.* New York: Century, 1925, pp. 253–262.

A Modern Lover

Baker, Ernest A. "George Moore," in *The History of the English Novel,* Volume IX. New York: Barnes & Noble, 1950, pp. 166–168.

Brown, Malcolm. *George Moore: A Reconsideration.* Seattle: University of Washington Press, 1955, pp. 89–93.

Chaiken, Milton. "The Composition of George Moore's *A Modern Lover,*" in *Comparative Literature.* VII (1955), pp. 259–264.

Dunleavy, Janet Egleson. *George Moore: The Artist's Vision, the Storyteller's Art.* Lewisburg, Pa.: Bucknell University Press, 1973, pp. 50–62.

Freeman, John. *A Portrait of George Moore in a Study of His Work.* New York: Appleton, 1922, pp. 79–81.

Frierson, William C. "George Moore: Naturalist," in *The English Novel in Transition, 1885–1940.* Norman: University of Oklahoma Press, 1942, pp. 63–64.

Hicks, Granville. *Figures in Transition.* New York: Macmillan, 1939, pp. 204–205.

Howarth, Herbert. "George Augustus Moore," in *The Irish Writers, 1880–1940.* New York: Hill and Wang, 1958, pp. 36–39.

Nejdefors-Frisk, Sonja. *George Moore's Naturalistic Prose.* Cambridge, Mass.: Harvard University Press, 1952, pp. 38–56.

Reid, Forrest. "The Novels of George Moore," in *Westminster Review.* CLXXII (August, 1909), pp. 200–208.

Sherman, Stuart P. "The Aesthetic Naturalism of George Moore," in *On Contemporary Literature.* New York: Holt, 1917, pp. 132–134.

Skilton, David. "Late-Victorian Choices: James, Wilde, Gissing, and Moore," in *The English Novel: Defoe to the Victorians.* New York: Barnes & Noble, 1977, pp. 189–190.

Starkie, Enid. *From Gautier to Eliot.* London: Hutchinson's, 1960, pp. 70–80, 100–102.

Swinnerton, Frank. *The Georgian Scene: A Literary Panorama.* New York: Farrar and Rinehart, 1934, pp. 172–182.

Williams, Harold E. *Modern English Writers.* London: Sidgwick and Jackson, 1918, pp. 284–294.

A Mummer's Wife

Baker, Ernest A. *The History of the English Novel*, Volume IX. New York: Barnes & Noble, 1950, pp. 168–170.

Brown, Malcolm. *George Moore: A Reconsideration.* Seattle: University of Washington Press, 1955, pp. 91–96, 104–105.

Chaikin, Milton. "George Moore's Early Fiction," in *George Moore's Mind and Art.* Edited by Graham Owens. New York: Barnes & Noble, 1970, pp. 29–31.

Chew, Samuel C. "The Novel: Naturalism and Romance," in *A Literary History of England.* Edited by Albert C. Baugh. New York: Appleton-Century-Crofts, 1948, pp. 1493–1498.

Cunliffe, John W. *Leaders of the Victorian Revolution.* New York: Appleton-Century, 1934, pp. 279–280.

Dunleavy, Janet Egleson. *George Moore: The Artist's Vision, the Storyteller's Art.* Lewisburg, Pa.: Bucknell University Press, 1973, pp. 63–76.

Ervine, St. John G. *Some Impressions of My Elders.* London: George Allen, 1923, pp. 98–111.

Freeman, John. *A Portrait of George Moore in a Study of His Work.* New York: Appleton, 1922, pp. 71–76, 82–85.

Frierson, William C. "George Moore: Naturalist," in *The English Novel in Transition, 1885–1940.* Norman: University of Oklahoma Press, 1942, pp. 64–67.

Hicks, Granville. *Figures in Transition.* New York: Macmillan, 1939, pp. 205–207.

Howarth, Herbert. "George Augustus Moore," in *The Irish Writers, 1880–1940*. New York: Hill and Wang, 1958, pp. 51–52.

Hughes, Douglas A. "Introduction," in *The Man of Wax: Critical Essays on George Moore*. Edited by Douglas A. Hughes. New York: New York University Press, 1971, pp. x–xii.

Knight, Grant C. "The Most Pitiful," in *Superlatives*. New York: Knopf, 1925, pp. 153–166.

Nejdefors-Frisk, Sonja. *George Moore's Naturalistic Prose.* Cambridge, Mass.: Harvard University Press, 1952, pp. 57–86.

Peck, Harry Thurston. *The Personal Equation.* New York: Harper, 1898, pp. 89–132.

Poole, Adrian. *Gissing in Context.* Totowa, N.J.: Rowman and Littlefield, 1975, pp. 56–58.

Reid, Forrest. "The Novels of George Moore," in *Westminster Review.* CLXXII (August, 1909), pp. 200–208.

Sherman, Stuart P. "The Aesthetic Naturalism of George Moore," in *On Contemporary Literature*. New York: Holt, 1917, pp. 134–136.

Starkie, Enid. *From Gautier to Eliot.* London: Hutchinson's, 1960, pp. 70–80, 100–102.

Swinnerton, Frank. *The Georgian Scene: A Literary Panorama.* New York: Farrar and Rinehart, 1934, pp. 172–182.

Ure, Peter. "George Moore as Historian of Consciences," in *The Man of Wax: Critical Essays on George Moore*. Edited by Douglas A. Hughes. New York: New York University Press, 1971, pp. 88–95.

Wagenknecht, Edward. "George Moore, the Man of Wax," in *Cavalcade of the English Novel*. New York: Holt, 1954, pp. 411–416.

Weygandt, Cornelius. *A Century of the English Novel.* New York: Century, 1925, pp. 253–262.

Williams, Harold E. *Modern English Writers.* London: Sidgwick and Jackson, 1918, pp. 284–294.

MARIANNE MOORE
(1887–1972)

"Bird-Witted"

Frankenberg, Lloyd. "The Imaginary Garden," in *Quarterly Review of Literature.* IV (Fall, 1944) pp. 210–212.

————. *Pleasure Dome: On Reading Modern Poetry.* Boston: Houghton Mifflin, 1949, pp. 137–141.

Kenner, Hugh. "Meditation and Enactment," in *Poetry.* CII (May, 1963), pp. 111–113.

Nitchie, George W. *Marianne Moore: An Introduction to the Poetry.* New York: Columbia University Press, 1969, pp. 19–22, 33–34.

"The Fish"

Garrigue, Jean. *Marianne Moore.* Minneapolis: University of Minnesota Press, 1965, pp. 9–10.

Kenner, Hugh. "The Experience of the Eye: Marianne Moore's Tradition," in *Southern Review.* I (Autumn, 1963), pp. 761–763.

Koch, Vivienne. "The Peaceable Kingdom of Marianne Moore," in *Quarterly Review of Literature.* IV (Fall, 1944), pp. 163–164.

Nitchie, George W. *Marianne Moore: An Introduction to the Poetry.* New York: Columbia University Press, 1969, pp. 10–11, 29–30, 86–88.

Renick, Sue. " 'The Fish,' " in *Explicator.* XXI (September, 1962), item 7.

Sutton, Walter. *American Free Verse: The Modern Revolution in Poetry.* New York: New Directions, 1973, pp. 111–113.

Sylvester, William A. " 'The Fish,' " in *Explicator.* VII (February, 1949), item 30.

Weatherhead, A. Kingsley. *The Edge of the Image: Marianne Moore, William Carlos Williams and Some Other Poets.* Seattle: University of Washington Press, 1967, pp. 92–93.

Zabel, M.D. *Literary Opinion in America.* New York: Harper, 1937, pp. 433–434.

"He 'Digesteth Harde Yron' "

Ransom, John Crowe. "On Being Modern with Distinction," in *Quarterly Review of Literature.* IV (Fall, 1944), pp. 140–141.

Stevens, Wallace. "About One of Marianne Moore's Poems," in *Quarterly Review of Literature.* IV (Fall, 1944), pp. 143–147.

————. *The Necessary Angel.* New York: Knopf, 1951, pp. 93–103.

Sutton, Walter. *American Free Verse: The Modern Revolution in Poetry.* New York: New Directions, 1973, pp. 105–106.

Weatherhead, A. Kingsley. *The Edge of the Image: Marianne Moore, William Carlos Williams and Some Other Poets.* Seattle: University of Washington Press, 1967, p. 64.

"In Distrust of Merits"

Allentuck, Marcia Epstein. " 'In Distrust of Merits,' " in *Explicator.* X (April, 1952), item 42.

Fowlie, Wallace. "Under the Equanimity of Language," in *Quarterly Review of Literature.* IV (Fall, 1944), pp. 176–177.

Frankenberg, Lloyd. "The Imaginary Garden," in *Quarterly Review of Literature.* IV (Fall, 1944), pp. 221–222.

————. *Pleasure Dome: On Reading Modern Poetry.* Boston: Houghton Mifflin, 1949, pp. 153–155.

Nitchie, George W. *Marianne Moore: An Introduction to the Poetry.* New York: Columbia University Press, 1969, pp. 10–11, 133–138.

Therese, Sister M. *Marianne Moore: A Critical Essay.* Grand Rapids, Mich.: Eerdmans, 1969, pp. 29–30.

Weatherhead, A. Kingsley. *The Edge of the Image: Marianne Moore, William Carlos Williams and Some Other Poets.* Seattle: University of Washington Press, 1967, pp. 80–82.

"The Jerboa"

Brooks, Cleanth. "Miss Marianne Moore's Zoo," in *Quarterly Review of Literature.* IV (Fall, 1944), pp. 182–183.

Frankenberg, Lloyd. "The Imaginary Garden," in *Quarterly Review of Literature.* IV (Fall, 1944), pp. 202–203.

————. *Pleasure Dome: On Reading Modern Poetry.* Boston: Houghton Mifflin, 1949, pp. 132–133.

Garrigue, Jean. *Marianne Moore.* Minneapolis: University of Minnesota Press, 1965, pp. 31–32.

Legler, Philip. "Marianne Moore and the Idea of Freedom," in *Poetry.* LXXXIII (December, 1953), pp. 158–167.

Nitchie, George W. *Marianne Moore: An Introduction to the Poetry.* New York: Columbia University Press, 1969, pp. 114–115.

Therese, Sister M. *Marianne Moore: A Critical Essay.* Grand Rapids, Mich.: Eerdmans, 1969, p. 14.

Weatherhead, A. Kingsley. *The Edge of the Image: Marianne Moore, William Carlos Williams and Some Other Poets.* Seattle: University of Washington Press, 1967, pp. 87–89.

The Poetry of Marianne Moore

Bar-Yaacov, Lois. "Marianne Moore: An 'In-Patriot,' " in *Hebrew University Studies in Literature.* III (1975), pp. 165–195.

Brumbaugh, Thomas B. "In Pursuit of Miss Moore," in *Mississippi Quarterly.* XV (Spring, 1962), pp. 74–80.

Cecilia, Sister Mary. "The Poetry of Marianne Moore," in *Thought.* XXXVIII (1963), pp. 354–374.

Dickey, James. *Babel to Byzantium: Poets & Poetry Now.* New York: Farrar, Straus and Giroux, 1968, pp. 156–164.

Durso, J. "Marianne Moore, Baseball Fan," in *Saturday Review.* LII (July 12, 1969), pp. 51–52.

Edsal, Constance H. "Values and the Poems of Marianne Moore," in *English Journal.* LVIII (April, 1969), pp. 516–518.

Engel, Bernard F. "Moore's 'A Face,' " in *Explicator.* XXXIV (1975), item 29.

Garrigue, Jean. *Marianne Moore.* Minneapolis: University of Minnesota Press, 1965.

Glatstein, Jacob. "The Poetry of Marianne Moore," in *Prairie Schooner.* XLVII (1973), pp. 133–141.

Hall, Donald. *Marianne Moore: The Cage and the Animal.* New York: Pegasus, 1970.

Kenner, Hugh. "The Experience of the Eye: Marianne Moore's Tradition," in *Modern American Poetry: Essays in Criticism.* Edited by Jerome Mazzaro. New York: David McKay, 1970, pp. 204–221.

Nitchie, George W. *Marianne Moore: An Introduction to the Poetry.* New York: Columbia University Press, 1969.

O'Sullivan, Maurice J., Jr. "Native Genius for Disunion: Marianne Moore's 'Spenser's Ireland,' " in *Concerning Poetry.* VII (1974), pp. 42–47.

Replogle, Justin. "Marianne Moore and the Art of Intonation," in *Contemporary Literature.* XII (1971), pp. 1–17.

Sprague, Rosemary. *Imaginary Gardens: A Study of Five Poets.* Philadelphia: Chilton, 1969, pp. 185–207.

Sutton, Walter. *American Free Verse: The Modern Revolution in Poetry.* New York: New Directions, 1973, pp. 103–117.

Therese, Sister M. *Marianne Moore; A Critical Essay.* Grand Rapids, Mich.: Eerdmans, 1968.

Waggoner, Hyatt H. *American Poets from the Puritans to the Present.* Boston: Houghton Mifflin, 1968, pp. 364–368.

Wand, David Hsin-Fu. "The Dragon and the Kylin: The Use of Chinese Symbols and Myths in Marianne Moore's Poetry," in *Literature East and West.* XV (1971), pp. 470–484.

Weatherhead, A. Kingsley. *The Edge of the Image: Marianne Moore, William Carlos Williams and Some Other Poets.* Seattle: University of Washington Press, 1967, pp. 58–95.

"The Steeple-Jack"

Bogan, Louise. "Reading Contemporary Poetry," in *College English.* XIV (February, 1953), pp. 257–260.

Garrigue, Jean. *Marianne Moore.* Minneapolis: University of Minnesota Press, 1965, pp. 41–42.

Nitchie, George W. *Marianne Moore: An Introduction to the Poetry.* New York: Columbia University Press, 1969, pp. 109–112.

Sutton, Walter. *American Free Verse: The Modern Revolution in Poetry.* New York: New Directions, 1973, pp. 110–111.

Therese, Sister M. *Marianne Moore: A Critical Essay.* Grand Rapids, Mich.: Eerdmans, 1969, pp. 40–41.

Tomlinson, Charles. "Abundance, Not Too Much: The Poetry of Marianne Moore," in *Sewanee Review.* LXV (Autumn, 1957), pp. 677–682.

Weatherhead, A. Kingsley. *The Edge of the Image: Marianne Moore, William Carlos Williams and Some Other Poets.* Seattle: University of Washington Press, 1967, pp. 59–61.

ALBERTO MORAVIA
(1907–   )

Two Women

Cottrell, Jane E. *Alberto Moravia.* New York: Frederick Ungar, 1974, pp. 28–29, 66–67, 72–77.

Dego, Giuliano. *Moravia.* New York: Barnes & Noble, 1966, pp. 99–106.

Heiney, Donald. "Moravia's America," in *Western Humanities Review.* XVIII (Autumn, 1964), pp. 323–329.

Ross, Joan and Donald Freed. *The Existentialism of Alberto Moravia.* Carbondale: Southern Illinois University Press, 1972, pp. 89–92, 139–144.

Varnai, Ugo. "Italian Letters in 1957," in *International Literary Annual.* I (1958), pp. 186–187.

The Woman of Rome

Baldanza, Frank. "The Classicism of Alberto Moravia," in *Modern Fiction Studies.* III (Winter, 1957–1958), p. 314.

Cottrell, Jane E. *Alberto Moravia.* New York: Frederick Ungar, 1974, pp. 13–14, 58–59, 66–72.

Dego, Giuliano. *Moravia.* New York: Barnes & Noble, 1966, pp. 69–76.

Golino, Carlo J. "Alberto Moravia," in *Modern Language Journal.* XXXVI (November, 1952), pp. 337–338.

Mitchell, Bonner. "Moravia's Proletarian Roman Intellectuals," in *Modern Language Journal.* XLIV (November, 1960), p. 303.

Rolo, Charles J. "Alberto Moravia," in *Atlantic.* CXCV (February, 1955), p. 71.

Ross, Joan and Donald Freed. *The Existentialism of Alberto Moravia.* Carbondale: Southern Illinois University Press, 1972, pp. 66–68.

SIR THOMAS MORE
(1478–1535)

Utopia

Abrash, M. "Missing the Point in More's *Utopia*," in *Extrapolation*. XIX (December, 1977), pp. 27–38.

Allen, Peter R. "*Utopia* and European Humanism: The Function of the Prefatory Letters and Verses," in *Studies in the Renaissance*. X (1963), pp. 91–107.

Ames, Russell. *Citizen Thomas More and His* Utopia. New York: Russell, 1969.

Bevington, David M. "The Dialogue in *Utopia*: Two Sides to the Question," in *Studies in Philology*. LVIII (1961), pp. 496–509.

Bridgett, Thomas E. *Life and Writings of Sir Thomas More*. New York: Scholarly Press, 1976.

Chambers, R.W. *The Place of Saint Thomas More in English Literature and History*. Brooklyn, N.Y.: Haskell, 1969.

Donner, Henry W. *Introduction to* Utopia. Freeport, N.Y.: Books for Libraries Press, 1969.

Elliott, Robert C. "The Shape of *Utopia*," in *ELH*. XXX (1963), pp. 317–334.

Fleisher, Martin. *Radical Reform and Political Persuasion in the Life and Writings of Thomas More*. Geneva: Droz, 1973.

Gallagher, Ligeia, Editor. *More's* Utopia *and Its Critics*. Glenview, Ill.: Scott, Foresman, 1964.

Heiserman, A.R. "Satire in the *Utopia*," in *PMLA*. LXXVIII (1963), pp. 163–174.

Hexter, J.H. "Intention, Words, and Meaning: The Case of More's *Utopia*," in *New Literary History*. VI (1974), pp. 529–541.

————. *More's* Utopia: *The Biography of an Idea*. Westport, Conn.: Greenwood, 1976.

————. "Utopia and Geneva," in *Action and Conviction in Early Modern Europe; Essays in Memory of E.H. Harbison*. Edited by Theodore K. Rabb and Jerrold E. Segal. Princeton, N.J.: Princeton University Press, 1969, pp. 77–89.

————. *Vision of Politics on the Eve of the Reformation: More, Machiavelli, Seyssel*. New York: Basic Books, 1973, pp. 19–137.

Johnson, Robbin S. *More's* Utopia: *Ideal and Illusion*. New Haven, Conn.: Yale University Press, 1969.

Kautsky, Karl. *Thomas More and His* Utopia. Translated by H.J. Stenning. New York: Russell, 1959.

Kinney, A.F. "Rhetoric as Poetic: Humanist Fiction in the Renaissance," in *ELH*. XLIII (Winter, 1976), pp. 413–443.

Miles, Leland. "The Literary Artistry of Thomas More," in *Studies in English Literature*. VI (1966), pp. 7–33.

Rebhorn, W.A. "Thomas More's Enclosed Garden: Utopia and Renaissance Humanism," in *English Literary Renaissance*. VI (1976), pp. 140–155.

Sanderlin, George. "The Meaning of Thomas More's *Utopia*," in *College English*. XII (1950), pp. 74–77.

Sawada, Paul A. "Toward a Definition of *Utopia*," in *Moreana*. XXXI–XXXII (1971), pp. 135–146.

Schoeck, R.J. "More, Plutarch, and King Agis: Spartan History and the Meaning of *Utopia*," in *Philological Quarterly*. XXXV (1956), pp. 366–375.

Skinner, Quentin. "More's *Utopia*," in *Past and Present*. XXXVIII (1967), pp. 153–168.

Surtz, Edward, S.J. *The Praise of Pleasure: Philosophy, Education, and Communism in More's* Utopia. Cambridge, Mass.: Harvard University Press, 1957.

Sylvester, Richard S., Editor. *St. Thomas More—Action and Contemplation*. New Haven, Conn.: Yale University Press, 1972.

WILLIAM MORRIS
(1834–1896)

The Poetry of Morris

Berneri, Marie Louise. "Utopias of the Nineteenth Century," in *Journey Through Utopia.* Boston: Beacon Press, 1951, pp. 207–292.

Calhoun, Blue. *The Pastoral Vision of William Morris.* Athens: University of Georgia Press, 1975.

Clutton-Brock, Arthur. *William Morris: His Work and Influence.* New York: Holt, n.d.

Dahl, Curtis. "Morris's *The Chapel in Lyoness*, an Interpretation," in *Studies in Philology.* LX (July, 1954), pp. 482–491.

Faulkner, Peter. *William Morris and W.B. Yeats.* Dublin: Dolmen Press, 1962.

————. *William Morris: The Critical Heritage.* London: Routledge and Kegan Paul, 1973.

Grigson, Geoffrey. "William Morris," in his *The Contrary View.* London: Rowman and Littlefield, 1974, pp. 77–97.

Henderson, Philip. *William Morris.* London: Longmans, Green, 1952.

McAlindon, T. "The Idea of Byzantium in William Morris and W.B. Yeats," in *Modern Philology.* LXIV (May, 1967), pp. 307–319.

Noyes, Alfred. *William Morris.* London: Macmillan, 1908.

Parrott, Thomas M. "William Morris," in his *Companion to Victorian Literature.* New York: Scribner's, 1955, pp. 222–227.

Pater, Walter H. "Aesthetic Poetry," in his *Essays on Literature and Art.* London: Rowman and Littlefield, 1973, pp. 95–102.

Perrine, Laurence. "Morris's Guenevere: An Interpretation," in *Philological Quarterly.* XXXIX (1960), pp. 234–241.

Robson, W.W. "Pre-Raphaelite Poetry," in *British Victorian Literature.* Edited by S.K. Kumar. New York: New York University Press, 1969, pp. 172–191.

Saintsbury, George E. "Notes on Six Poets," in his *Last Vintage.* New York: Methuen, 1950, pp. 239–241.

Thompson, Francis. "Pre-Raphaelite Morris," in his *Literary Criticism.* New York: Dutton, 1948, pp. 198–203.

Tinker, Chauncey. "William Morris as Poet," in his *Essays in Retrospect.* New Haven, Conn.: Yale University Press, 1948, pp. 62–74.

Yeats, William Butler. "The Happiest of the Poets," in his *Essays and Introductions*. New York: Macmillan, 1961, pp. 53–64.

Young, George M. *Daylight and Champagne*. Chester Springs, Pa.: Dufour, 1948, pp. 60–66.

WRIGHT MORRIS
(1910–   )

Ceremony in Lone Tree

Baumbach, Jonathan. "Wake Before Bomb: *Ceremony in Lone Tree*," in *Critique: Studies in Modern Fiction*. IV (Winter, 1961–1962), pp. 56–71. Reprinted in *The Landscape of Nightmare: Studies in the Contemporary American Novel*. New York: New York University Press, 1965, pp. 152–169.

Harper, Robert D. "Wright Morris' *Ceremony in Lone Tree*: A Picture of Life in Middle America," in *Western American Literature*. XI (1976), pp. 199–213.

Howard, Leon. *Wright Morris*. Minneapolis: University of Minnesota Press, 1968, pp. 26–28.

Klein, Marcus. *After Alienation: American Novels in Mid-Century*. Cleveland: World, 1962, pp. 238–242.

Madden, David. "The Great Plains in the Novels of Wright Morris," in *Critique: Studies in Modern Fiction*. IV (Winter, 1961–1962), pp. 5–22.

————. *Wright Morris*. New York: Twayne, 1964, pp. 131–155.

Tornquist, Elizabeth. "The New Parochialism," in *Commentary*. XXXI (May, 1961), pp. 449–452.

Waterman, Arthur E. "The Novels of Wright Morris: An Escape from Nostalgia," in *Critique: Studies in Modern Fiction*. IV (Winter, 1961–1962), pp. 37–39.

The Field of Vision

Booth, Wayne C. "The Two Worlds in the Fiction of Wright Morris," in *Sewanee Review*. LXV (1957), pp. 375–399.

Hartman, Carl. "Mr. Morris and Some Others," in *Western Review*. XXI (Summer, 1957), pp. 307–313.

Howard, Leon. *Wright Morris*. Minneapolis: University of Minnesota Press, 1968, pp. 21–23.

Klein, Marcus. *After Alienation: American Novels in Mid-Century*. Cleveland: World, 1962, pp. 238–242.

Leer, Norman. "Three American Novels and Contemporary Society: A Search for Commitment," in *Wisconsin Studies in Contemporary Literature*. III (Fall, 1962), pp. 76–81.

Madden, David. "The Great Plains in the Novels of Wright Morris," in *Critique: Studies in Modern Fiction*. IV (Winter, 1961–1962), pp. 5–22.

————. "The Hero and the Witness in Wright Morris' *Field of Vision*," in *Prairie Schooner*. XXXIV (1960), pp. 263–278.

_____. *Wright Morris.* New York: Twayne, 1964, pp. 132–135.

Trachtenberg, Alan. "The Craft of Vision," in *Critique: Studies in Modern Fiction.* IV (Winter, 1961–1962), pp. 47–55.

Waterman, Arthur E. "The Novels of Wright Morris: An Escape from Nostalgia," in *Critique: Studies in Modern Fiction.* IV (Winter, 1961–1962), pp. 35–37.

The Huge Season

Allen, Walter. *The Modern Novel in Britain and the United States.* New York: Dutton, 1964, pp. 316–317.

Booth, Wayne C. "The Two Worlds in the Fiction of Wright Morris," in *Sewanee Review.* LXV (1957), pp. 375–399.

Howard, Leon. *Wright Morris.* Minneapolis: University of Minnesota Press, 1968, pp. 19–21.

Klein, Marcus. *After Alienation: American Novels in Mid-Century.* Cleveland: World, 1962, pp. 226–229.

Madden, David. *Wright Morris.* New York: Twayne, 1964, pp. 101–111.

Waterman, Arthur E. "The Novels of Wright Morris: An Escape from Nostalgia," in *Critique: Studies in Modern Fiction.* IV (Winter, 1961–1962), pp. 33–35.

Love Among the Cannibals

Hartman, Carl. "An Expense of Flesh," in *Western Review.* XXII (Winter, 1958), pp. 152–154.

Howard, Leon. *Wright Morris.* Minneapolis: University of Minnesota Press, 1968, pp. 24–25.

Klein, Marcus. *After Alienation: American Novels in Mid-Century.* Cleveland: World, 1962, pp. 230–234.

Madden, David. *Wright Morris.* New York: Twayne, 1964, pp. 112–130.

Oliphant, Robert. "Public Voices and Wise Guys," in *Virginia Quarterly Review.* XXXVII (Autumn, 1961), pp. 528–537.

My Uncle Dudley

Eisinger, Chester E. *Fiction of the Forties.* Chicago: University of Chicago Press, 1963, pp. 331–333.

Howard, Leon. *Wright Morris.* Minneapolis: University of Minnesota Press, 1968, pp. 7–9.

Hunt, John W., Jr. "The Journey Back: The Early Novels of Wright Morris," in *Critique: Studies in Modern Fiction.* V (Spring–Summer, 1962), pp. 41–46.

Klein, Marcus. *After Alienation: American Novels in Mid-Century.* Cleveland: World, 1962, pp. 198–200.

Madden, David. *Wright Morris.* New York: Twayne, 1964, pp. 32–41.

TONI MORRISON
(1931–   )

The Bluest Eye

Bischoff, Joan. "The Novels of Toni Morrison's Studies in Thwarted Sensitivity," in *Studies in Black Literature*. VI (1975), pp. 21–23.

Dee, Ruby. "Black Family Search for Identity," in *Freedomways*. XI (1971), pp. 319–320.

Frankel, Haskel. "Toni Morrison's *The Bluest Eye*," in *New York Times Book Review*. (November 1, 1970), p. 46.

Grant, Liz. "*The Bluest Eye*," in *Black World*. XX (May, 1971), pp. 51–52.

Loftin, Elouise. "Toni Morrison's *Bluest Eye*," in *Black Creation*. III (Fall, 1971), p. 48.

Ogunyemi, C.O. "Order and Disorder in Toni Morrison's *The Bluest Eye*," in *Critique*. XIX (1977), pp. 112–120.

Sissman, L.E. "Beginner's Luck," in *The New Yorker*. XXIII (January, 1971), pp. 92–94.

Wilder, Charles M. "Novels by Two Friends," in *College Language Association Journal*. XV (December, 1971), pp. 253–255.

Sula

Bischoff, Joan. "The Novels of Toni Morrison: Studies in Thwarted Sensitivity," in *Studies in Black Literature*. VI (1975), pp. 21–23.

Blackburn, Sara. "*Sula*," in *The New York Times Book Review*. (December 30, 1973), p. 3.

Bryant, J.H. "*Sula*," in *Nation*. CCXIX (July 6, 1974), p. 23.

Francis, W.A.C. "*Sula*," in *Best Sellers*. XXXIII (January 15, 1974), p. 469.

Jefferson, Margo. "Toni Morrison: Passionate and Precise," in *Ms*. III (December, 1974), pp. 34–38.

McClain, Ruth Rambo. "Toni Morrison's *Sula*," in *Black World*. XXIII (June, 1974), pp. 51–53.

O'Connor, Douglas. "*Sula*," in *Black Creation Annual*. VI (1974–1975), pp. 65–66.

Smith, Barbara. "Beautiful Needed Mysterious," in *Freedomways*. XIV (1974), pp. 69–72.

WILLARD MOTLEY
(1912–1965)

Knock on Any Door

Bone, Robert. *The Negro Novel in America.* New Haven, Conn.: Yale University Press, 1958, pp. 178–180.

Breit, H. "James Baldwin and Two Footnotes," in *The Creative Present.* Edited by Nona Balakian. New York: Doubleday, 1963, pp. 5–23.

Ford, Nick. "Four Popular Negro Novelists," in *Phylon.* XV (1954), pp. 32–34.

French, Warren. *The Fifties: Fiction, Poetry, Drama.* Deland, Fla.: Everett/Edwards, 1970, pp. 221–222.

Gelfand, Blanche. *American City Novel.* Norman: University of Oklahoma Press, 1954, pp. 248–252.

Hughes, John. "Common Denominator: Man," in his *Negro Novelist.* Secaucus, N.J.: Citadel Press, 1953, pp. 147–193.

Rideout, Walter. *Radical Novel in the United States.* Cambridge, Mass.: Harvard University Press, 1956, pp. 261–263.

Weissgarber, Alfred. "Willard Motley and the Sociological Novel," in *Studi Americani.* VII (1961), pp. 300–304.

Let No Man Write My Epitaph

Dempsey, David. "*Let No Man Write My Epitaph,*" in *New York Times Review of Books.* (August 10, 1958), p. 18.

French, Warren. *The Fifties: Fiction, Poetry, Drama.* Deland, Fla.: Everett/Edwards, 1970, pp. 221–222.

Hicks, Granville. "Art and Reality," in *Saturday Review.* XLI (August 9, 1958), p. 11.

Light, James F. "*Let No Man Write My Epitaph,*" in *Prairie Schooner.* XXXIII (1959), pp. 190–192.

————. "The Wire Recorder Ear," in *Time.* LXXII (August 11, 1958), p. 74.

IRIS MURDOCH
(1919-   )

The Bell

Allen, Walter. *Reading a Novel.* London: Phoenix House, 1963, pp. 61–64.

Baldanza, Frank. *Iris Murdoch.* New York: Twayne, 1974, pp. 70–83.

Byatt, A.S. *Degrees of Freedom: The Novels of Iris Murdoch.* New York: Barnes & Noble, 1965, pp. 73–104.

Dick, Bernard F. "The Novels of Iris Murdoch: A Formula for Enchantment," in *Bucknell Review.* XIV (May, 1966), pp. 72–75.

Felheim, Marvin. "Symbolic Characterization in the Novels of Iris Murdoch," in *Texas Studies in Literature and Language.* II (1960), pp. 194–196.

Gerstenberger, Donna. *Iris Murdoch.* Lewisburg, Pa.: Bucknell University Press, 1975, pp. 31–33.

Hall, James. "Blurring of the Will: The Growth of Irish Murdoch," in *Journal of English Literary History.* XXXII (June, 1965), pp. 266–273. Reprinted in his *The Lunatic Giant in the Drawing Room: The British and American Novel Since 1930.* Bloomington: Indiana University Press, 1968, pp. 190–199.

Hoffman, Frederick J. "Iris Murdoch: The Reality of Persons," in *Critique.* VII (Spring, 1964), pp. 48–57.

Howe, Irving. "Realities and Fictions," in *Partisan Review.* XXVI (Winter, 1959), pp. 132–133.

Jones, Dorothy. "Love and Morality in Iris Murdoch's *The Bell*," in *Meanjin Quarterly.* XXVI (1967), pp. 85–90.

Kaehele, Sharon and Howard German. "The Discovery of Reality in Iris Murdoch's *The Bell*," in *PMLA.* LXXXII (December, 1967), pp. 554–563.

Karl, Frederick R. *The Contemporary English Novel.* New York: Farrar, Straus, 1962, pp. 261–264.

Kriegel, Leonard. "Iris Murdoch: Everybody Through the Looking-Glass," in his *Contemporary British Novelists.* Edited by Charles Shapiro. Carbondale: Southern Illinois University Press, 1965, pp. 69–72.

McCarthy, Margot. "Dualities in *The Bell*," in *Contemporary Review.* CCXIII (December, 1968), pp. 313–317.

Majdiak, Daniel. "Romanticism in the Aesthetics of Iris Murdoch," in *Texas Studies in Literature and Language.* XIV (1972), pp. 370–372.

Meidner, Olga M. "The Progress of Iris Murdoch," in *English Studies in Africa.* IV (March, 1961), pp. 25–31.

Morrell, Roy. "Iris Murdoch: The Early Novels," in *Critical Quarterly.* IX (Autumn, 1967), pp. 277–281.

O'Connor, William Van. "Iris Murdoch: The Formal and the Contingent," in *Critique.* III (Winter–Spring, 1960), pp. 42–43. Reprinted in his *The New University Wits and the End of Modernism.* Carbondale: Southern Illinois University Press, 1963, pp. 65–66.

Pearson, Gabriel. "Iris Murdoch and the Romantic Novel," in *New Left Review.* (January–April, 1962), pp. 137–145.

Rabinovitz, Rubin. *Iris Murdoch.* New York: Columbia University Press, 1968, pp. 24–28.

Souvage, Jacques. "Symbol as Narrative Device: An Interpretation of Iris Murdoch's *The Bell,*" in *English Studies.* XLIII (April, 1962), pp. 81–96.

Toye, William. "*The Bell,*" in *Tamarack Review.* X (Winter, 1959), pp. 106–107.

Wall, Stephen. "The Bell in *The Bell,*" in *Essays in Criticism.* XIII (July, 1963), pp. 265–273.

Whiteside, George. "The Novels of Iris Murdoch," in *Critique.* VII (Spring, 1964), pp. 37–39.

Wolfe, Peter. *The Disciplined Heart: Iris Murdoch and Her Novels.* Columbia: University of Missouri Press, 1966, pp. 113–138.

The Black Prince

Amis, Martin. "Alas, Poor Bradley," in *New Statesman.* LXXXV (February 23, 1973), pp. 278–279.

Baldanza, Frank. *Iris Murdoch.* New York: Twayne, 1974, pp. 168–173.

Byatt, A.S. *Iris Murdoch.* Harlow, England: Longmans, 1976, pp. 35–38.

Fraser, Kennedy. "Ordinary Human Jumble," in *New Yorker.* XLIX (July 30, 1973), pp. 69–71.

Hill, William B. "*The Black Prince,*" in *America.* CXXIX (November 17, 1973), p. 382.

Lindroth, James R. "*The Black Prince,*" in *America.* CXXIX (September 1, 1973), p. 130.

Lurie, Alison. "Wise-Women," in *New York Review of Books.* XX (June 14, 1973), pp. 18–19.

Raban, Jonathan. "On Losing the Rabbit," in *Encounter.* XL (May, 1973), pp. 80–85.

Waugh, Auberon. "A Source of Wonder and Delight," in *Spectator.* CCXXX (February 24, 1973), pp. 235–236.

Bruno's Dream

Baldanza, Frank. *Iris Murdoch.* New York: Twayne, 1974, pp. 148–159.

Byatt, A.S. "The Spider's Web," in *New Statesman*. LXXVII (January 17, 1969), p. 86.

Davenport, Guy. "Tables of Transformation," in *National Review*. XXI (February 11, 1969), pp. 131–132.

Gerstenberger, Donna. *Iris Murdoch*. Lewisburg, Pa.: Bucknell University Press, 1975, pp. 45–49.

Hall, William F. "*Bruno's Dream*: Technique and Meaning in the Novels of Iris Murdoch," in *Modern Fiction Studies*. XV (Autumn, 1969), pp. 429–443.

Hicks, Granville. "Hanging by a Thread," in *Saturday Review*. LII (January 18, 1969), p. 32.

Kaye, H. "Delight and Instruction," in *New Republic*. CLX (February 8, 1969), pp. 19–20.

Martz, Louis L. "Iris Murdoch: The London Novels," in *Twentieth Century Literature in Retrospect*. Edited by Reuben A. Brower. Cambridge, Mass.: Harvard University Press, 1971, pp. 69–71.

Swinden, Patrick. *Unofficial Selves: Character in the Novel from Dickens to the Present Day*. London: Macmillan, 1973, pp. 1–4.

Thomson, P.W. "Iris Murdoch's Honest Puppetry—the Characters of *Bruno's Dream*," in *Critical Quarterly*. XI (Autumn, 1969), pp. 277–283.

Wain, John. "Women's Work," in *New York Review of Books*. XII (April 24, 1969), pp. 38–40.

The Flight from the Enchanter

Allsop, Kenneth. *The Angry Decade: A Survey of the Cultural Revolt of the Nineteen-Fifties*. London: P. Owen, 1958, pp. 90–91.

Baldanza, Frank. *Iris Murdoch*. New York: Twayne, 1974, pp. 43–56.

Byatt, A.S. *Degrees of Freedom: The Novels of Iris Murdoch*. New York: Barnes & Noble, 1965, pp. 40–60.

Corke, Hilary. "Conscientious Violence," in *Encounter*. VI (June, 1956), pp. 88–89.

Dick, Bernard F. "The Novels of Iris Murdoch: A Formula for Enchantment," in *Bucknell Review*. XIV (May, 1966), pp. 70–71.

Felheim, Marvin. "Symbolic Characterization in the Novels of Iris Murdoch," in *Texas Studies in Literature and Language*. II (1960), pp. 191–193.

Fiedler, Leslie A. "The Novel in the Post-Political World," in *Partisan Review*. XXIII (Summer, 1956), pp. 363–365.

German, Howard. "Allusions in the Early Novels of Iris Murdoch," in *Modern Fiction Studies*. XV (Autumn, 1969), pp. 361–377.

Gerstenberger, Donna. *Iris Murdoch.* Lewisburg, Pa.: Bucknell University Press, 1975, pp. 25–29.

Hoffman, Frederick J. "Iris Murdoch: The Reality of Persons," in *Critique.* VII (Spring, 1964), pp. 48–57.

Kriegel, Leonard. "Iris Murdoch: Everybody Through the Looking-Glass," in *Contemporary British Novelists.* Edited by Charles Shapiro. Carbondale: Southern Illinois University Press, 1965, pp. 65–67.

Kuehl, Linda. "Iris Murdoch: The Novelist as Magician/The Magician as Artist," in *Modern Fiction Studies.* XV (Autumn, 1969), pp. 347–360.

Meidner, Olga M. "Reviewer's Bane: A Study of Iris Murdoch's *The Flight from the Enchanter*," in *Essays in Criticism.* XI (October, 1961), pp. 435–447.

O'Connor, William Van. "Iris Murdoch: The Formal and the Contingent," in *Critique.* III (Winter–Spring, 1960), pp. 38–40. Reprinted in his *The New University Wits and the End of Modernism.* Carbondale: Southern Illinois University Press, 1963, pp. 59–62.

Rabinovitz, Rubin. *Iris Murdoch.* New York: Columbia University Press, 1968, pp. 13–18.

Rippier, Joseph S. *Some Postwar English Novelists.* Frankfurt, Germany: Diesterweg, 1965, pp. 74–79.

Sullivan, Zohreh Tawakuli. "Enchantment and the Demonic in Iris Murdoch: *The Flight from the Enchanter*," in *Midwest Quarterly.* XVI (Spring, 1975), pp. 276–297.

Van Ghent, Dorothy. "*The Flight from the Enchanter*," in *Yale Review.* XLVI (Autumn, 1956), pp. 153–155.

Webster, Harvey Curtis. "*The Flight from the Enchanter*," in *Saturday Review.* XXXIX (April 21, 1956), p. 14.

Whiteside, George. "The Novels of Iris Murdoch," in *Critique.* VII (Spring, 1964), pp. 32–35.

Wolfe, Peter. *The Disciplined Heart: Iris Murdoch and Her Novels.* Columbia: University of Missouri Press, 1966, pp. 68–88.

The Italian Girl

Baldanza, Frank. *Iris Murdoch.* New York: Twayne, 1974, pp. 116–125.

Davenport, Guy. "Turn the Other Face," in *National Review.* XVI (November 3, 1964), pp. 978–979.

Dick, Bernard F. "The Novels of Iris Murdoch: A Formula for Enchantment," in *Bucknell Review.* XIV (May, 1966), pp. 79–80.

Furbank, P.N. "Gowned Mortality," in *Encounter.* XXIII (November, 1964), pp. 88–90.

German, Howard. "The Range of Allusions in the Novels of Iris Murdoch," in *Journal of Modern Literature.* II (1971), pp. 69–75.

Hoffman, Frederick J. "The Miracle of Contingency: The Novels of Iris Murdoch," in *Shenandoah.* XVII (Autumn, 1965), pp. 49–56.

Janeway, Elizabeth. "But Nobody Understands," in *New York Times Book Review.* (September 13, 1964), p. 5.

Kriegel, Leonard. "Iris Murdoch: Everybody Through the Looking-Glass," in *Contemporary British Novelists.* Edited by Charles Shapiro. Carbondale: Southern Illinois University Press, 1965, pp. 76–78.

Kuehn, Robert E. "Ficition Chronicle," in *Wisconsin Studies in Contemporary Literature.* VI (1965), pp. 135–137.

Pagones, Dorrie. "Wanton Waifs and a Roman Woman," in *Saturday Review.* XLVII (September 19, 1964), pp. 48–49.

Rabinovitz, Rubin. *Iris Murdoch.* New York: Columbia University Press, 1968, pp. 36–38.

Tracy, Honor. "Misgivings About Miss Murdoch," in *New Republic.* CLI (October 10, 1964), pp. 21–22.

Tucker, Martin. "More Iris Murdoch," in *Commonweal.* LXXXI (October 30, 1964), pp. 173–174.

Wolfe, Peter. *The Disciplined Heart: Iris Murdoch and Her Novels.* Columbia: University of Missouri Press, 1966, pp. 203–208.

The Nice and the Good

Baldanza, Frank. *Iris Murdoch.* New York: Twayne, 1974, pp. 138–147.

Bergonzi, Bernard. "Nice but Not Good," in *New York Review of Books.* X (April 11, 1968), pp. 36–38.

Davenport, Guy. "Fruitfully Good, I'm Sure," in *National Review.* XX (April 9, 1968), p. 350.

Fremantle, Anne. "The Probable and the Possible," in *Reporter.* XXXVIII (January 25, 1968), pp. 47–49.

Gerstenberger, Donna. *Iris Murdoch.* Lewisburg, Pa.: Bucknell University Press, 1975, pp. 36–37.

Hicks, Granville. "Love Runs Rampant," in *Saturday Review.* LI (January 6, 1968), pp. 27–28.

Janeway, Elizabeth. "Everyone Is Involved," in *New York Times Book Review.* (January 14, 1968), p. 4.

Palmer, Tony. "Artistic Privilege," in *London Magazine.* VIII (May, 1968), pp. 47–52.

Rabinovitz, Rubin. *Iris Murdoch.* New York: Columbia University Press, 1968, pp. 42–45.

Thompson, John. "Old Friends," in *Commentary*. XLV (January, 1968), pp. 65–67.

The Red and the Green

Baldanza, Frank. *Iris Murdoch*. New York: Twayne, 1974, pp. 126–130.

Berthoff, Warner. *Fictions and Events: Essays in Criticism and Literary History*. New York: Dutton, 1971, pp. 130–143.

Davenport, Guy. "Messages from the Lost," in *National Review*. XVIII (February 8, 1966), pp. 119–120.

German, Howard. "The Range of Allusions in the Novels of Iris Murdoch," in *Journal of Modern Literature*. II (1971), pp. 75–79.

Gerstenberger, Donna. *Iris Murdoch*. Lewisburg, Pa.: Bucknell University Press, 1975, pp. 51–69.

Hicks, Granville. "Easter Monday Insights," in *Saturday Review*. XLVIII (October 30, 1965), pp. 41–42.

Kemp, Peter. "The Fight Against Fantasy: Iris Murdoch's *The Red and the Green*," in *Modern Fiction Studies*. XV (Autumn, 1969), pp. 403–415.

Kiely, Benedict. "England and Ireland," in *New York Times Book Review*. (June 5, 1966), p. 5.

Rabinovitz, Rubin. *Iris Murdoch*. New York: Columbia University Press, 1968, pp. 38–39.

Ricks, Christopher. "A Sort of Mystery Novel," in *New Statesman*. LXX (October 22, 1965), pp. 604–605.

Rome, Joy. "A Respect for the Contingent: A Study of Iris Murdoch's Novel *The Red and the Green*," in *English Studies in Africa*. XIV (March, 1971), pp. 87–98.

Sale, Roger. "Provincial Champions and Grandmasters," in *Hudson Review*. XVII (Winter, 1964–1965), pp. 608, 612–613.

Salvesen, Christopher. "A Hieroglyph," in *New Statesman*. LXVIII (September 11, 1964), pp. 365–366.

Sheed, Wilfrid. *The Morning After: Selected Essays and Reviews*. New York: Farrar, Straus and Giroux, 1971, pp. 296–298.

Sullivan, Richard. "Millicent the Magnificent," in *Critic*. XXIV (December, 1965–January, 1966), p. 63.

Tucker, Martin. "The Odd Fish in Iris Murdoch's Kettle," in *New Republic*. CLIV (February 5, 1966), pp. 26–28.

Trachtenberg, Stanley. "Accomodation and Protest," in *Yale Review*. LV (Spring, 1966), pp. 448–449.

The Sandcastle

Allsop, Kenneth.   *The Angry Decade: A Survey of the Cultural Revolt of the Nineteen-Fifties.* Birkenhead, England: Willmer Brothers and Haram, 1958, pp. 91, 94–95.

Baldanza, Frank.   *Iris Murdoch.* New York: Twayne, 1974, pp. 57–69.

Byatt, A.S.   *Degrees of Freedom: The Novels of Iris Murdoch.* New York: Barnes & Noble, 1965, pp. 61–72.

Dick, Bernard F.   "The Novels of Iris Murdoch: A Formula for Enchantment," in *Bucknell Review.* XIV (May, 1966), pp. 71–72.

Felheim, Marvin.   "Symbolic Characterization in the Novels of Iris Murdoch," in *Texas Studies in Literature and Language.* II (1960), pp. 193–194.

German, Howard.   "Allusions in the Early Novels of Iris Murdoch," in *Modern Fiction Studies.* XV (Autumn, 1969), pp. 361–377.

Gerstenberger, Donna.   *Iris Murdoch.* Lewisburg, Pa.: Bucknell University Press, 1975, pp. 29–31.

Gray, James.   "Lost Enchantment," in *Saturday Review.* XL (May 18, 1957), p. 41.

Hall, James.   "Blurring the Will: The Growth of Iris Murdoch," in *Journal of English Literary History.* XXXII (June, 1965), pp. 262–266. Reprinted in his *The Lunatic Giant in the Drawing Room: The British and American Novel Since 1930.* Bloomington: Indiana University Press, 1968, pp. 186–190.

Hoffman, Frederick J.   "Iris Murdoch: The Reality of Persons," in *Critique.* VII (Spring, 1964), pp. 48–57.

Kriegel, Leonard.   "Iris Murdoch: Everybody Through the Looking-Glass," in *Contemporary British Novelists.* Edited by Charles Shapiro. Carbondale: Southern Illinois University Press, 1965, pp. 68–69.

Morrell, Roy.   "Iris Murdoch: The Early Novels," in *Critical Quarterly.* IX (Autumn, 1967), pp. 271–274.

O'Connor, William Van.   "Iris Murdoch: The Formal and the Contingent," in *Critique.* III (Winter–Spring, 1960), pp. 40–42. Reprinted in his *The New University Wits and the End of Modernism.* Carbondale: Southern Illinois University Press, 1963, pp. 62–64.

Pearson, Gabriel.   "Iris Murdoch and the Romantic Novel," in *New Left Review.* (January–April, 1962), pp. 137–145.

Price, Martin.   "*The Sandcastle,*" in *Yale Review.* XLVII (Autumn, 1957), pp. 146–148.

Raban, Jonathan.   "Character and Symbolism," in *Techniques of Modern Fiction: Essays in Practical Criticism.* Notre Dame, Ind.: University of Notre Dame Press, 1968, pp. 108–111.

Rabinovitz, Rubin. *Iris Murdoch.* New York: Columbia University Press, 1968, pp. 18–22.

Rippier, Joseph S. *Some Postwar English Novelists.* Frankfurt, Germany: Diesterweg, 1965, pp. 78–82.

Sisk, John P. "A Sea Change," in *Commonweal.* LXVI (May 31, 1957), pp. 236–237.

Taylor, Griffin. " 'What Doth it Profit a Man. . . ?,' " in *Sewanee Review.* LXVI (January–March, 1958), pp. 137–141.

Tracy, Honor. "Passion in the Groves of Academe," in *New Republic.* CXXXVI (June 10, 1957), p. 17.

Whiteside, George. "The Novels of Iris Murdoch," in *Critique.* VII (Spring, 1964), pp. 35–37.

Wolfe, Peter. *The Disciplined Heart: Iris Murdoch and Her Novels.* Columbia: University of Missouri Press, 1966, pp. 89–112.

A Severed Head

Baldanza, Frank. *Iris Murdoch.* New York: Twayne, 1974, pp. 84–95.

Byatt, A.S. *Degrees of Freedom: The Novels of Iris Murdoch.* New York: Barnes & Noble, 1965, pp. 105–121.

Dick, Bernard F. "The Novels of Iris Murdoch: A Formula for Enchantment," in *Bucknell Review.* XIV (May, 1966), pp. 75–76.

Everett, Barbara. "*A Severed Head*," in *Critical Quarterly.* III (Autumn, 1961), pp. 270–271.

German, Howard. "Allusions in the Early Novels of Iris Murdoch," in *Modern Fiction Studies.* XV (Autumn, 1969), pp. 373–377.

Gerstenberger, Donna. *Iris Murdoch.* Lewisburg, Pa.: Bucknell University Press, 1975, pp. 33–35.

Gindin, James. *Postwar British Fiction: New Attitudes and Accents.* Berkeley: University of California Press, 1962, pp. 189–195.

Gregor, Ian. "Towards a Christian Literary Criticism," in *The Month.* XXXIII (1965), pp. 245–249.

Hall, James. *The Lunatic Giant in the Drawing Room: The British and American Novel Since 1930.* Bloomington: Indiana University Press, 1968, pp. 199–200.

Hoffman, Frederick J. "Iris Murdoch: The Reality of Persons," in *Critique.* VII (Spring, 1964), pp. 48–57.

Kane, Patricia. "The Furnishings of a Marriage: An Aspect of Characterization in Iris Murdoch's *A Severed Head*," in *Notes on Contemporary Literature.* II (November, 1972), pp. 4–5.

Karl, Frederick R. *The Contemporary English Novel.* New York: Noonday, 1962, pp. 264–265.

Kenney, Alice P. "The Mythic History of *A Severed Head*," in *Modern Fiction Studies.* XV (Autumn, 1969), pp. 387–401.

Kriegel, Leonard. "Iris Murdoch: Everybody Through the Looking-Glass," in *Contemporary British Novelists.* Edited by Charles Shapiro. Carbondale: Southern Illinois University Press, 1965, pp. 72–73.

Kuehl, Linda. "Iris Murdoch: The Novelist as Magician/The Magician as Artist," in *Modern Fiction Studies.* XV (Autumn, 1969), pp. 347–360.

Malcolm, Donald. "To Everyone with Love," in *New Yorker.* XXXVII (May 6, 1961), pp. 172–176.

Miner, Earl. "Iris Murdoch: The Uses of Love," in *Nation.* CXCIV (June 2, 1962), pp. 498–499.

Moody, Philippa. "In the Lavatory of the Athenaeum—Postwar English Novels," in *Melbourne Critical Review.* VI (1963), pp. 83–92.

O'Connor, William Van. "Iris Murdoch: *A Severed Head*," in *Critique.* V (Spring–Summer, 1962), pp. 74–77. Reprinted in *The New University Wits and the End of Modernism.* Carbondale: Southern Illinois University Press, 1963, pp. 70–74.

Pearson, Gabriel. "Iris Murdoch and the Romantic Novel," in *New Left Review.* (January–April, 1962), pp. 137–145.

Rabinovitz, Rubin. *Iris Murdoch.* New York: Columbia University Press, 1968, pp. 28–31.

Rippier, Joseph S. *Some Postwar English Novelists.* Frankfurt, Germany: Diesterweg, 1965, pp. 88–92.

Warnke, F.J. "*A Severed Head*," in *Yale Review.* L (June, 1961), pp. 632–633.

Whiteside, George. "The Novels of Iris Murdoch," in *Critique.* VII (Spring, 1964), pp. 39–41.

Wolfe, Peter. *The Disciplined Heart: Iris Murdoch and Her Novels.* Columbia: University of Missouri Press, 1966, pp. 139–160.

The Time of the Angels

Allen, Walter. "Anything Goes," in *New York Times Book Review.* (September 25, 1966), p. 5.

Baldanza, Frank. *Iris Murdoch.* New York: Twayne, 1974, pp. 130–137.

Berthoff, Warner. *Fictions and Events: Essays in Criticism and Literary History.* New York: Dutton, 1971, pp. 147–152.

Davenport, Guy. "History with Its Eyes Wide Open," in *National Review.* XVIII (November 29, 1966), p. 1227.

Donoghue, Denis. "Magic Defeated," in *New York Review of Books*. VII (November 17, 1966), pp. 22–23.

Eimerl, Sarel. "Choreography of Despair," in *Reporter*. XXXV (November 3, 1966), pp. 45–46.

Garis, Robert. "Playing Games," in *Commentary*. XLIII (March, 1967), pp. 97–100.

German, Howard. "The Range of Allusions in the Novels of Iris Murdoch," in *Journal of Modern Literature*. II (1971), pp. 79–84.

Hicks, Granville. "Rector for a Dead God," in *Saturday Review*. XLIX (October 29, 1966), pp. 25–26.

Majdiak, Daniel. "Romanticism in the Aesthetics of Iris Murdoch," in *Texas Studies in Literature and Language*. XIV (1972), pp. 370–372.

Rabinovitz, Rubin. *Iris Murdoch*. New York: Columbia University Press, 1968, pp. 39–42.

Sullivan, Zohreh T. "Iris Murdoch's Self-Conscious Gothicism: *The Time of the Angels*," in *Arizona Quarterly*. XXXIII (Spring, 1977), pp. 47–60.

Taubman, Robert. "Uncle's War," in *New Statesman*. LXXII (September 16, 1966), pp. 401–402.

Toynbee, Philip. "Miss Murdoch's Monster Rally," in *New Republic*. CLV (October 22, 1966), p. 24.

Under the Net

Allsop, Kenneth. *The Angry Decade: A Survey of the Cultural Revolt of the Nineteen-Fifties*. London: P. Owen, 1958, pp. 88–90, 93–94.

Baldanza, Frank. *Iris Murdoch*. New York: Twayne, 1974, pp. 30–42.

Bradbury, Malcolm. "Iris Murdoch's *Under the Net*," in *Critical Quarterly*. IV (Spring, 1962), pp. 47–54. Reprinted in *Possibilities: Essays on the State of the Novel*. London: Oxford University Press, 1973, pp. 231–246.

Byatt, A.S. *Degrees of Freedom: The Novels of Iris Murdoch*. New York: Barnes & Noble, 1965, pp. 14–39.

DeMott, Benjamin. "Dirty Words?," in *Hudson Review*. XVIII (Spring, 1965), pp. 37–40.

Dick, Bernard F. "The Novels of Iris Murdoch: A Formula for Enchantment," in *Bucknell Review*. XIV (May, 1966), pp. 68–70.

Felheim, Marvin. "Symbolic Characterization in the Novels of Iris Murdoch," in *Texas Studies in Literature and Language*. II (1960), pp. 190–191.

German, Howard. "Allusions in the Early Novels of Iris Murdoch," in *Modern Fiction Studies*. XV (Autumn, 1969), pp. 361–364.

Gerstenberger, Donna. *Iris Murdoch*. Lewisburg, Pa.: Bucknell University Press, 1975, pp. 21–24.

Goldberg, Gerald. "The Search for the Artist in Some Recent British Fiction," in *South Atlantic Quarterly*. LXII (Summer, 1963), pp. 394–396.

Hall, James. "Blurring the Will: The Growth of Iris Murdoch," in *Journal of English Literary History*. XXXII (June, 1965), pp. 259–262. Reprinted in his *The Lunatic Giant in the Drawing Room: The British and American Novel Since 1930*. Bloomington: Indiana University Press, 1968, pp. 183–186.

Hoffman, Frederick J. "Iris Murdoch: The Reality of Persons," in *Critique*. VII (Spring, 1964), pp. 48–57.

Kriegel, Leonard. "Iris Murdoch: Everybody Through the Looking-Glass," in *Contemporary British Novelists*. Edited by Charles Shapiro. Carbondale: Southern Illinois University Press, 1965, pp. 64–65.

Martz, Louis L. "Iris Murdoch: The London Novels," in *Twentieth Century Literature in Retrospect*. Edited by Reuben A. Brower. Cambridge, Mass.: Harvard University Press, 1971, pp. 71–75.

Meidner, Olga McDonald. "The Progress of Iris Murdoch," in *English Studies in Africa*. IV (March, 1961), pp. 17–38.

Morrell, Roy. "Iris Murdoch: The Early Novels," in *Critical Quarterly*. XI (Autumn, 1967), pp. 274–277.

O'Connor, William Van. "Iris Murdoch: The Formal and the Contingent," in *Critique*. III (Winter–Spring, 1960), pp. 40–42. Reprinted in his *The New University Wits and the End of Modernism*. Carbondale: Southern Illinois University Press, 1963, pp. 54–59.

Porter, Raymond J. " 'Leitmotif' in Iris Murdoch's *Under the Net*," in *Modern Fiction Studies*. XV (Autumn, 1969), pp. 379–385.

Rabinovitz, Rubin. *Iris Murdoch*. New York: Columbia University Press, 1968, pp. 8–13.

Rippier, Joseph S. *Some Postwar British Novelists*. Frankfurt, Germany: Diesterweg, 1965, pp. 71–74.

Swinden, Patrick. *Unofficial Selves: Character in the Novel from Dickens to the Present Day*. London: Macmillan, 1973, pp. 237–247.

Whiteside, George. "The Novels of Iris Murdoch," in *Critique*. VII (Spring, 1964), pp. 29–32.

Widmann, R.L. "Murdoch's *Under the Net*: Theory and Practice of Fiction," in *Critique*. X (1968), pp. 5–16.

Wolfe, Peter. *The Disciplined Heart: Iris Murdoch and Her Novels*. Columbia: University of Missouri Press, 1966, pp. 46–67.

The Unicorn

Auchincloss, Eve. "Oxford Gothic," in *New York Review of Books*. I (1963), pp. 38–39.

Baldanza, Frank. *Iris Murdoch.* New York: Twayne, 1974, pp. 105–116.

Byatt, A.S. *Degrees of Freedom: The Novels of Iris Murdoch.* New York: Barnes & Noble, 1965, pp. 146–180.

Cook, Eleanor. "Mythical Beasts," in *Canadian Forum.* XLIII (August, 1963), pp. 113–114.

Detweiler, Robert. *Iris Murdoch's* The Unicorn. New York: Seabury, 1969.

Dick, Bernard F. "The Novels of Iris Murdoch: A Formula for Enchantment," in *Bucknell Review.* XIV (May, 1966), pp. 78–79.

German, Howard. "The Range of Allusions in the Novels of Iris Murdoch," in *Journal of Modern Literature.* II (1971), pp. 65–68.

Gerstenberger, Donna. *Iris Murdoch.* Lewisburg, Pa.: Bucknell University Press, 1975, pp. 40–44.

Grigson, Geoffrey. "A Captured Unicorn," in *The Contrary View: Glimpses of Fudge and Gold.* Totowa, N.J.: Rowman and Littlefield, 1974, pp. 30–33.

Hall, James. *The Lunatic Giant in the Drawing Room: The British and American Novel Since 1930.* Bloomington: Indiana University Press, 1968, pp. 206–211.

Hebblethwaite, Peter. "Out Hunting Unicorn," in *Month.* (October, 1963), pp. 224–228.

Hicks, Granville. "Entrance to Enchantment," in *Saturday Review.* XLVI (May 11, 1963), pp. 27–28.

Hoffman, Frederick J. "Iris Murdoch: The Reality of Persons," in *Critique.* VII (Spring, 1964), pp. 42–57.

Kriegel, Leonard. "Iris Murdoch: Everybody Through the Looking-Glass," in *Contemporary British Novelists.* Edited by Charles Shapiro. Carbondale: Southern Illinois University Press, 1965, pp. 74–76.

Kuehl, Linda. "Iris Murdoch: The Novelist as Magician/The Magician as Artist," in *Modern Fiction Studies.* XV (Autumn, 1969), pp. 347–360.

McDowell, Frederick P.W. " 'The Devious Involutions of Human Character and Emotions': Reflections on Some Recent British Novels," in *Wisconsin Studies in Contemporary Literature.* IV (Autumn, 1963), pp. 355–359.

McKay, A.G. "*The Unicorn,*" in *Tamarack Review.* XXVIII (Summer, 1963), p. 91.

Pondrom, Cyrena Norman. "Iris Murdoch: *The Unicorn,*" in *Critique.* VI (Winter, 1963–1964), pp. 177–180.

Rabinovitz, Rubin. *Iris Murdoch.* New York: Columbia University Press, 1968, pp. 34–36.

Rippier, Joseph S. *Some Postwar English Novelists.* Frankfurt, Germany: Diesterweg, 1965, pp. 96–103.

Scholes, Robert. *The Fabulators.* New York: Oxford University Press, 1967, pp. 106–132.

Tucker, Martin. "Love and Freedom: Golden and Hard Words," in *Commonweal.* LXXVII (June 21, 1963), pp. 357–358.

Whitehorn, Katherine. "Three Women," in *Encounter.* XXI (December, 1963), pp. 78–82.

Whiteside, George. "The Novels of Iris Murdoch," in *Critique.* VII (Spring, 1964), pp. 43–46.

Wolfe, Peter. *The Disciplined Heart: Iris Murdoch and Her Novels.* Columbia: University of Missouri Press, 1966, pp. 183–202.

An Unofficial Rose

Baldanza, Frank. *Iris Murdoch.* New York: Twayne, 1974, pp. 96–104.

Byatt, A.S. *Degrees of Freedom: The Novels of Iris Murdoch.* New York: Barnes and Noble, 1965, pp. 122–145.

Dick, Bernard F. "The Novels of Iris Murdoch: A Formula for Enchantment," in *Bucknell Review.* XIV (May, 1966), p. 77.

Eimerl, Sarel. "Thorns Without a Rose," in *Reporter.* XXVI (June 7, 1962), pp. 45–46.

German, Howard. "The Range of Allusions in the Novels of Iris Murdoch," in *Journal of Modern Literature.* II (1971), pp. 58–64.

Gerstenberger, Donna. *Iris Murdoch.* Lewisburg, Pa.: Bucknell University Press, 1975, pp. 35–36.

Hall, James. *The Lunatic Giant in the Drawing Room: The British and American Novel Since 1930.* Bloomington: Indiana University Press, 1968, pp. 200–206.

Hicks, Granville. "The Operations of Love," in *Saturday Review.* XLV (May 19, 1962), p. 32.

Hoffman, Frederick J. "Iris Murdoch: The Reality of Persons," in *Critique.* VII (Spring, 1964), pp. 48–57.

Kriegel, Leonard. "Iris Murdoch: Everybody Through the Looking-Glass," in *Contemporary British Novelists.* Edited by Charles Shapiro. Carbondale: Southern Illinois University Press, 1965, pp. 73–74.

McDowell, Frederick P.W. " 'The Devious Involutions of Human Character and Emotions': Reflections on Some Recent British Novels," in *Wisconsin Studies in Contemporary Literature.* IV (Autumn, 1963), pp. 352–355.

Miller, Vincent. "Unofficial Roses," in *National Review.* XIII (September 11, 1962), pp. 194–196.

Miner, Earl. "Iris Murdoch: The Uses of Love," in *Nation.* CXCIV (June 2, 1962), pp. 498–499.

Pondrom, Cyrena Norman. "Iris Murdoch: An Existentialist," in *Comparative Literature Studies.* V (December, 1968), pp. 403–419.

Rabinovitz, Rubin. *Iris Murdoch.* New York: Columbia University Press, 1968, pp. 31–34.

Rippier, Joseph S. *Some Postwar English Novelists.* Frankfurt, Germany: Diesterweg, 1965, pp. 92–96.

Ryan, Marjorie. "Iris Murdoch: *An Unofficial Rose*," in *Critique.* V (Winter, 1962), pp. 117–121.

Whiteside, George. "The Novels of Iris Murdoch," in *Critique.* VII (Spring, 1964), pp. 41–43.

Wolfe, Peter. *The Disciplined Heart: Iris Murdoch and Her Novels.* Columbia: University of Missouri Press, 1966, pp. 161–182.

VLADIMIR NABOKOV
(1899–1977)

Ada or Ardor: A Family Chronicle

Appel, Alfred, Jr. "*Ada* Described," in *Nabokov: Criticism, Reminiscences, Translations and Tributes*. Edited by Alfred Appel, Jr., and Charles Newman. Evanston, Ill.: Northwestern University Press, 1970, pp. 160–186.

Fowler, Douglas. *Reading Nabokov*. Ithaca, N.Y.: Cornell University Press, 1974, pp. 176–201.

Johnson, Donald B. "Nabokov's *Ada* and Pushkin's *Eugene Onegin*," in *Slavic and East European Journal*. XV (1971), pp. 316–323.

Leonard, Jeffrey. "In Place of Lost Time: *Ada*," in *Nabokov: Criticism, Reminiscences, Translations and Tributes*. Edited by Alfred Appel, Jr., and Charles Newman. Evanston, Ill.: Northwestern University Press, 1970, pp. 136–146.

Mason, Bobbie Ann. *Nabokov's Garden: A Guide to Ada*. Ann Arbor, Mich.: Ardis, 1974.

Proffer, Carl R. "*Ada* as Wonderland: A Glossary of Allusions to Russian Literature," in *A Book of Things About Vladimir Nabokov*. Edited by Carl R. Proffer. Ann Arbor, Mich.: Ardis, 1974, pp. 249–279.

Swanson, Roy A. "Nabokov's *Ada* as Science Fiction," in *Science-Fiction Studies*. II (1975), pp. 76–87.

Zeller, Nancy Anne. "The Spiral of Time in *Ada*," in *A Book of Things About Vladimir Nabokov*. Edited by Carl R. Proffer. Ann Arbor, Mich.: Ardis, 1974, pp. 280–290.

Bend Sinister

Field, Andrew. *Nabokov: His Life in Art*. Boston: Little, Brown, 1967, pp. 198–203.

Fowler, Douglas. *Reading Nabokov*. Ithaca, N.Y.: Cornell University Press, 1974, pp. 21–60.

Hyman, Stanley E. "The Handle: *Invitation to a Beheading* and *Bend Sinister*," in *Nabokov: Criticism, Reminiscences, Translations and Tributes*. Edited by Alfred Appel, Jr., and Charles Newman. Evanston, Ill.: Northwestern University Press, 1970, pp. 64–71.

Kermode, Frank. *Puzzles and Epiphanies: Essays and Reviews, 1958–1961*. New York: Chilmark Press, 1962, pp. 228–233.

Lee, L.L. "*Bend Sinister*: Nabokov's Political Dream," in *Wisconsin Studies in Contemporary Literature*. VIII (Spring, 1967), pp. 193–203. Reprinted in *Nabokov: The Man and His Work*. Edited by L.S. Dembo. Madison: University of Wisconsin Press, 1967.

Moynahan, Julian. *Vladimir Nabokov.* Minneapolis: University of Minnesota Press, 1971, pp. 22–25.

Nabokov, Vladimir. "Introduction to *Bend Sinister*," in *Nabokov's Congeries.* By Vladimir Nabokov. New York: Viking, 1968, pp. 239–246.

Patteson, Richard R. "Nabokov's *Bend Sinister*: The Narrator as God," in *Studies in American Fiction.* V (Autumn, 1977), pp. 241–253.

Schaeffer, Susan F. "*Bend Sinister* and the Novelist as Anthropomorphic Deity," in *The Centennial Review.* XVII (1973), pp. 115–151.

Stegner, Page. *Escape into Aesthetics: The Art of Vladimir Nabokov.* New York: Dial, 1966, pp. 76–89.

The Defense

Dembo, L.S. "Vladimir Nabokov, an Introduction," in *Nabokov: The Man and His Work.* Edited by L.S. Dembo. Madison: University of Wisconsin Press, 1967, pp. 6–8.

Field, Andrew. *Nabokov: His Life in Art.* Boston: Little, Brown, 1967, pp. 175–179.

Furbank, P.N. "Chess and Jigsaw," in *Encounter.* XXIV (January, 1965), pp. 83–86.

Moody, Fred. "Nabokov's Gambit," in *Russian Literature Triquarterly.* XIV (1976), pp. 67–70.

Moynahan, Julian. *Vladimir Nabokov.* Minneapolis: University of Minnesota Press, 1971, pp. 19–20.

Purdy, Struther B. "Solus Rex: Nabokov and the Chess Novel," in *Modern Fiction Studies.* XIV (Winter, 1968–1969), pp. 382–384.

Struve, Glenn. "Nabokov as a Russian Writer," in *Nabokov: The Man and His Work.* Edited by L.S. Dembo. Milwaukee: University of Wisconsin Press, 1967, pp. 53–56.

Despair

Anderson, Quentin. "Nabokov in Time," in *New Republic.* CLIV (June 4, 1966), pp. 23–28.

Grayson, Jane. *Nabokov Translated: A Comparison of Nabokov's Russian and English Prose.* London: Oxford University Press, 1977, pp. 59–82.

Rosenfield, Clair. "*Despair* and the Lust for Immortality," in *Wisconsin Studies in Contemporary Literature.* VIII (Spring, 1967), pp. 174–192. Reprinted in *Nabokov: The Man and His Work.* Edited by L.S. Dembo. Milwaukee: University of Wisconsin Press, 1967, pp. 66–84.

Stuart, Dabney. "Nabokov's *Despair*: Tinker to Evers to Chance," in *Georgia Review.* XXX (1976), pp. 432–446.

Suagee, Stephen. "An Artist's Memory Beats All Other Kinds: An Essay on *Despair*," in *A Book of Things About Vladimir Nabokov*. Edited by Carl R. Proffer. Ann Arbor, Mich.: Ardis, 1974, pp. 54–62.

The Gift

Dembo, L.S. "Vladimir Nabokov, an Introduction," in *Nabokov: The Man and His Work*. Edited by L.S. Dembo. Madison: University of Wisconsin Press, 1967, pp. 13–16.

Dupee, Frederick Wilcox. *The King of the Cats and Other Remarks on Writers and Writing*. New York: Farrar, Straus and Giroux, 1965, pp. 134–138.

Field, Andrew. *Nabokov: His Life in Art*. Boston: Little, Brown, 1967, pp. 15–26, 29–32, 241–249.

Hyman, Stanley Edgar. *Standards: A Chronicle of Books for Our Time*. New York: Horizon Press, 1966, pp. 184–188.

Karlinsky, Simon. "Vladimir Nabokov's Novel *Dar* as a Work of Literary Criticism: A Structural Analysis," in *Slavic and East European Journal*. VII (Fall, 1963), pp. 284–290.

Malcolm, Donald. "A Retrospect," in *New Yorker*. XL (April 25, 1964), pp. 198–205.

Moynahan, Julian. *Vladimir Nabokov*. Minneapolis: University of Minnesota Press, 1971, pp. 37–40.

Salehar, Anna Maria. "Nabokov's *Gift*: An Appreciation in Creativity," in *A Book of Things About Vladimir Nabokov*. Edited by Carl Proffer. Ann Arbor, Mich.: Ardis, 1974, pp. 70–83.

Lolita

Appel, Alfred, Jr. "The Art of Nabokov's Artifice," in *University of Denver Quarterly*. III (Summer, 1968), pp. 25–37.

————. "*Lolita*: The Springboard of Parody," in *Wisconsin Studies in Contemporary Literature*. VIII (Spring, 1967), pp. 204–241. Reprinted in *Nabokov: The Man and His Work*. Edited by L.S. Dembo. Madison: University of Wisconsin Press, 1967, pp. 106–143.

————. "The Road to *Lolita*, or the Americanization of an Emigre," in *Journal of Modern Literature*. IV (1974), pp. 3–31.

Butler, Diana. "Lolita Lepidoptera," in *New World Writing*. No. 16 (1960), pp. 58–84.

Campbell, Felicia C. "A Princedom by the Sea," in *Lock Haven Review*. X (1968), pp. 39–46.

Dupee, Frederick Wilcox. "A Preface to *Lolita*," in *Anchor Review*. No. 2 (1957), pp. 1–13. Reprinted in *The King of the Cats and Other Remarks on*

Writers and Writing. By Frederick Wilcox Dupee. New York: Farrar, Straus and Giroux, 1965, pp. 117–131.

Field, Andrew. *Nabokov: His Life in Art.* Boston: Little, Brown, 1967, pp. 323–350.

Fowler, Douglas. *Reading Nabokov.* Ithaca, N.Y.: Cornell University Press, 1974, pp. 147–175.

Green, Martin. "The Morality of *Lolita*," in *Kenyon Review.* XXVIII (June, 1966), pp. 352–377.

Harold, Brent. "*Lolita*: Nabokov's Critique of Aloofness," in *Papers on Language and Literature.* XI (1975), pp. 71–82.

Harris, Harold J. "*Lolita* and the Sly Forward," in *Mad River Review.* I (1965), pp. 29–38.

Hiatt, L.R. "Nabokov's *Lolita*: A 'Freudian' Cryptic Crossword," in *American Imago.* XXIV (Winter, 1967), pp. 360–370.

Josipovici, G.D. "*Lolita*: Parody and the Pursuit of Beauty," in *Critical Quarterly.* VI (Spring, 1964), pp. 35–48.

King, Bruce. "*Lolita*—Sense and Sensibility at Mid-century," in *Geste.* IV (March 12, 1959), pp. 3–9.

Mitchell, Charles. "Mythic Seriousness in *Lolita*," in *Texas Studies in Literature and Language.* V (Autumn, 1963), pp. 329–343.

Nabokov, Vladimir. "On a Book Entitled *Lolita*," in *Encounter.* XII (April, 1959), pp. 4–21.

Nemerov, Howard. "The Morality of Art," in *Kenyon Review.* XXVIII (Spring, 1957), pp. 313–321. Reprinted in *Poetry and Fiction: Essays.* By Howard Nemerov. New Brunswick, N.J.: Rutgers University Press, 1963, pp. 260–266.

Phillips, Elizabeth. "The Hocus-Pocus of *Lolita*," in *Literature & Psychology.* X (Summer, 1960), pp. 97–101.

Prioleau, Elizabeth. "Humbert Humbert *Through the Looking Glass*," in *Twentieth Century Literature.* XXI (1975), pp. 428–437.

Roth, Phyllis A. "In Search of Aesthetic Bliss: A Rereading of *Lolita*," in *College Literature.* II (1975), pp. 28–49.

Rougemont, Denis de. *Love Declared: Essays on the Myths of Love.* New York: Pantheon, 1963, pp. 48–54.

Rubenstein, E. "Approaching *Lolita*," in *Minnesota Review.* VI (Winter, 1966), pp. 361–367.

Seiden, Melvin. "Nabokov and Dostoevsky," in *Contemporary Literature.* XIII (1972), pp. 423–444.

Stegner, Page. *Escape into Aesthetics: The Art of Vladimir Nabokov.* New York: Dial, 1966, pp. 102–115.

Trilling, Lionel. "The Last Lover: Vladimir Nabokov's *Lolita*," in *Encounter*. XI (October, 1958), pp. 9–19.

Pale Fire

Chester, Alfred. "Nabokov's Anti-Novel," in *Commentary*. XXXIV (November, 1962), pp. 449–451.

Field, Andrew. *Nabokov: His Life in Art*. Boston: Little, Brown, 1967, pp. 291–322.

——————. "*Pale Fire*: The Labyrinth of a Great Novel," in *Tri-Quarterly*. VIII (Winter, 1967), pp. 13–36.

Flower, Timothy F. "The Scientific Art of Nabokov's *Pale Fire*," in *Criticism*. XVII (1975), pp. 223–233.

Fowler, Douglas. *Reading Nabokov*. Ithaca, N.Y.: Cornell University Press, 1974, pp. 91–121.

Handley, Jack. "To Die in English," in *Northwest Review*. VI (Spring, 1963), pp. 23–40.

Kermode, Frank. *Continuities*. New York: Random House, 1968, pp. 176–180.

Kostelanetz, Richard. "Nabokov's Obtuse Fool," in *On Contemporary Literature*. Edited by Richard Kostelanetz. New York: Avon, 1964, pp. 481–485.

Krueger, John R. "Nabokov's Zemblan: A Constructed Language of Fiction," in *Linguistics*. XXXI (May, 1967), pp. 44–49.

Lee, L.L. "Vladimir Nabokov's Great Spiral of Being," in *Western Humanities Review*. XVIII (Summer, 1964), pp. 225–236.

Lyons, John O. "*Pale Fire* and the Fine Art of Annotation," in *Wisconsin Studies in Contemporary Literature*. VIII (Spring, 1967), pp. 242–249. Reprinted in *Nabokov: The Man and His Work*. Edited by L.S. Dembo. Madison: University of Wisconsin Press, 1967, pp. 66–84.

McCarthy, Mary. "Vladimir Nabokov's *Pale Fire*," in *Encounter*. XIX (October, 1962), pp. 71–84.

Macdonald, Dwight. "Virtuosity Rewarded, or Dr. Kinbote's Revenge," in *Partisan Review*. XXIX (Summer, 1962), pp. 437–442.

Pilon, Kevin. "A Chronology of *Pale Fire*," in *A Book of Things About Vladimir Nabokov*. Edited by Carl R. Proffer. Ann Arbor, Mich.: Ardis, 1974, pp. 218–225.

Purdy, Struther B. "Solus Rex: Nabokov and the Chess Novel," in *Modern Fiction Studies*. XIV (Winter, 1968–1969), pp. 391–395.

Raban, Jonathan. *The Technique of Modern Fiction: Essays in Practical Criticism*. Notre Dame, Ind.: University of Notre Dame Press, 1968, pp. 154–157.

Riemer, Andrew. "Dim Glow, Faint Blaze—The Meaning of *Pale Fire*," in *Balcony*. VI (1967), pp. 41–48.

Roth, Phyllis A. "The Psychology of the Double in Nabokov's *Pale Fire*," in *Essays in Literature*. II (1975), pp. 209–229.

Sprowles, Alden. "Preliminary Annotation to Charles Kinbote's Commentary on *Pale Fire*," in *A Book of Things About Vladimir Nabokov*. Edited by Carl R. Proffer. Ann Arbor, Mich.: Ardis, 1974, pp. 226–247.

Stark, John. "Borges' 'Tlon, Uqbar, Orbis Tertius' and Nabokov's *Pale Fire*: Literature of Exhaustion," in *Texas Studies in Literature and Language*. XIV (1972), pp. 139–145.

Stegner, Page. *Escape into Aesthetics: The Art of Vladimir Nabokov*. New York: Dial, 1966, pp. 116–132.

Walker, David. " 'The Viewer and the View': Chance and Choice in *Pale Fire*," in *Studies in American Fiction*. IV (1976), pp. 203–221.

Webster, W.G. "Narrative Technique in *Pale Fire*," in *The Bulletin of the West Virginia Association of College English Teachers*. I (1974), pp. 38–43.

Williams, Carol T. " 'Web of Sense': *Pale Fire* in the Nabokov Canon," in *Critique: Studies in Modern Fiction*. VI (Winter, 1963–1964), pp. 29–45.

Pnin

Field, Andrew. *Nabokov: His Life in Art*. Boston: Little, Brown, 1967, pp. 129–140.

Fowler, Douglas. *Reading Nabokov*. Ithaca, N.Y.: Cornell University Press, 1974, pp. 122–146.

Gordon, Ambrose, Jr. "The Double *Pnin*," in *Nabokov: The Man and His Work*. Edited by L.S. Dembo. Madison: University of Wisconsin Press, 1967, pp. 144–156.

Grams, Paul. "*Pnin*: The Biographer as Meddler," in *A Book of Things About Vladimir Nabokov*. Edited by Carl R. Proffer. Ann Arbor, Mich.: Ardis, 1974, pp. 193–202.

High, Roger. "*Pnin*—A Preposterous Little Explosion," in *Geste*. IV (March 12, 1959), pp. 16–18.

Lyons, John O. *The College Novel in America*. Carbondale: Southern Illinois University Press, 1962, pp. 117–119.

Mizener, Arthur. "The Seriousness of Vladimir Nabokov," in *Sewanee Review*. LXXVI (Autumn, 1968), pp. 655–664.

Moody, Fred. "At *Pnin*'s Center," in *Russian Literature Triquarterly*. XIV (1976), pp. 70–83.

Rowe, William W. "Pnin's Uncanny Looking Glass," in *A Book of Things About Vladimir Nabokov*. Edited by Carl R. Proffer. Ann Arbor, Mich.: Ardis, 1974, pp. 182–192.

Stegner, Page. *Escape into Aesthetics: The Art of Vladimir Nabokov.* New York: Dial, 1966, pp. 76–89.

Stern, Richard G. "*Pnin* and the Dust-Jacket," in *Prairie Schooner.* XXXI (Summer, 1957), pp. 161–164.

The Real Life of Sebastian Knight

Bruffee, K.A. "Form and Meaning in Nabokov's *Real Life of Sebastian Knight*: An Example of Elegiac Romance," in *Modern Language Quarterly.* XXXIV (1973), pp. 180–190.

Field, Andrew. *Nabokov: His Life in Art.* Boston: Little, Brown, 1967, pp. 26–32.

Fromberg, Susan. "The Unwritten Chapters in *The Real Life of Sebastian Knight*," in *Modern Fiction Studies.* XIII (Winter, 1967–1968), pp. 427–442.

Johnson, W.R. "*The Real Life of Sebastian Knight* by Vladimir Nabokov," in *Carleton Miscellany.* IV (Fall, 1963), pp. 111–114.

Nicol, Charles. "The Mirrors of Sebastian Knight," in *Nabokov: The Man and His Work.* Edited by L.S. Dembo. Madison: University of Wisconsin Press, 1967, pp. 85–94.

Olcott, Anthony. "The Author's Special Intention: A Study of *The Real Life of Sebastian Knight*," in *A Book of Things About Vladimir Nabokov.* Edited by Carl R. Proffer. Ann Arbor, Mich.: Ardis, 1974, pp. 104–121.

Purdy, Struther B. "Solus Rex: Nabokov and the Chess Novel," in *Modern Fiction Studies.* XIV (Winter, 1968–1969), pp. 384–387.

Stegner, Page. "The Immortality of Art: Vladimir Nobokov's *The Real Life of Sebastian Knight*," in *Southern Review.* II (April, 1966), pp. 286–296. Reprinted in *Escape into Aesthetics: The Art of Vladimir Nabokov.* By Page Stegner. New York: Dial, 1966, pp. 63–75.

Stuart, Dabney. "*The Real Life of Sebastian Knight*: Angles of Perception," in *Modern Language Quarterly.* XXIX (September, 1968), pp. 312–328.

THOMAS NASH
(1567–1601)

The Unfortunate Traveller

Broron, L. "The Unfortunate Traveller," in *Journal of Jewish Lore and Philosophy*. I (January, 1919), pp. 244–254.

Chandler, F.W. *"The Unfortunate Traveller,"* in his *The Literature of Roguery*. Boston: Franklin, 1907, pp. 192–198.

Croston, A.K. "The Use of Imagery in Nashe's *The Unfortunate Traveller*," in *Review of English Studies*. XXIV (April, 1948), pp. 90–101.

De Beer, E.S. "Thomas Nashe: The Notices of Rome in *The Unfortunate Traveller*," in *Notes and Queries*. CLXXXV (July, 1943), pp. 67–70.

Gibbon, Marina. "Polemic, the Rhetorical Tradition and *The Unfortunate Traveller*," in *Journal of English and Germanic Philology*. LXIII (1964), pp. 408–421.

Gohlke, Madelon S. "Wits Wantonness: *The Unfortunate Traveller* as Picaresque," in *Studies in Philology*. LXXIII (1976), pp. 397–413.

Hibbard, G.R. *Thomas Nashe: A Critical Introduction*. London: Routledge and Kegan Paul, 1962, pp. 145–179.

Jusserand, J.J. "Account of Jack Wilton," in his *The English Novel in the Time of Shakespeare*. London: 1890, pp. 308–321.

Kettle, Arnold. *An Introduction to the English Novel*, Volume I. London: Hutchinson's, 1951, p. 25.

Latham, Agnes C. "Satire on Literary Themes and Modes in Nashe's *Unfortunate Traveller*," in *English Studies*. XXIX (1948), pp. 85–100.

HOWARD NEMEROV
(1920–   )

The Homecoming Game

Crane, Milton. "Flunked Halfback," in *Saturday Review*. XL (April 27, 1957), pp. 27–28.

Lyons, John O. *The College Novel in America*. Carbondale: Southern Illinois University Press, 1962, pp. 112–113.

Lytle, Andrew. *The Hero with the Private Parts*. Baton Rouge: Louisiana State University Press, 1966, pp. 82–89.

Meinke, Peter. *Howard Nemerov*. Minneapolis: University of Minnesota Press, 1968, pp. 38–40.

Reagen, Michael D. "Organization Gothic," in *Nation*. CLXXXIV (May 4, 1957), p. 396.

Rolo, Charles J. "*The Homecoming Game*," in *Atlantic*. CXCIX (May, 1957), p. 86.

Umphlett, Wiley Lee. *The Sporting Myth and the American Experience: Studies in Contemporary Fiction*. Lewisburg, Pa.: Bucknell University Press, 1975, pp. 118–119.

White, Robert L. "The Trying-Out of *The Homecoming Game*," in *Colorado Quarterly*. X (Summer, 1961), pp. 84–96.

The Poetry of Nemerov

Bartholomay, Julia A. *The Shield of Perseus: The Vision and Imagination of Howard Nemerov*. Gainsville: University of Florida Press, 1972.

Dickey, James. *Babel to Byzantium: Poets & Poetry Now*. New York: Farrar, Straus and Giroux, 1968, pp. 35–41.

Dobie, Ann B. "The Poet as Critic," in *Southern Review*. XII (1976), pp. 891–894.

Harvey, Robert D. "A Prophet Armed: An Introduction to the Poetry of Howard Nemerov," in *Poets in Progress*. Edited by Edward Hungerford. Evanston, Ill.: Northwestern University Press, 1967, pp. 116–133.

Kiehl, James M. "On Howard Nemerov," in *Contemporary Poetry in America: Essays and Interviews*. Edited by Robert Boyers. New York: Schocken Books, 1974, pp. 279–302.

————. "The Poems of Howard Nemerov: Where Loveliness Adorns Intelligible Things," in *Salmagundi*. XXII–XXIII (1973), pp. 234–257.

Malkoff, Karl. *Crowell's Handbook of Contemporary American Poetry*. New York: Thomas Y. Crowell, 1973, pp. 220–222.

Meinke, Peter.   *Howard Nemerov.* Minneapolis, Tenn.: University of Minnesota Press, 1968, pp. 8–32.

Mills, William.   *The Stillness in Moving Things: The World of Howard Nemerov.* Memphis, Tenn.: Memphis State University Press, 1975.

Olsen, Douglas H.   "Such Stuff as Dreams: The Poetry of Howard Nemerov," in *Imagination and the Spirit.* Edited by Charles A. Huttar. Grand Rapids, Mich.: Eerdmans, 1971, pp. 365–385.

Ramsey, Paul.   "To Speak, or Else to Sing," in *Parnassus.* IV (1976), pp. 130–138.

Rosenthal, M.L.   *The New Poets: American and British Poetry Since World War II.* New York: Oxford University Press, 1967, pp. 310–312.

Smith, Raymond.   "Nemerov and Nature: 'The Stillness in Moving Things,' " in *Southern Review.* X (1974), pp. 153–169.

Waggoner, Hyatt H.   *American Poets from the Puritans to the Present.* Boston: Houghton Mifflin, 1968, pp. 610–614.

PABLO NERUDA
(1904–1973)

The Poetry of Neruda

Belitt, Ben. "The Burning Sarcophagus: A Revolution of Pablo Neruda," in *Southern Review*. IV (Summer, 1968), pp. 598–615.

————. "The Mourning Neruda," in *Mundus Artium*. I (Winter, 1967), pp. 14–23.

————. "Pablo Neruda and the 'gigantesque,'" in *Poetry*. LXXX (May, 1952), pp. 116–118.

Bly, Robert. "The Surprise of Neruda," in *Sixties*. (Winter, 1964), pp. 18–19.

Costa, Rene de. "Pablo Neruda's *Tentativa del Hombre Infinito*: Notes for a Reappraisal," in *Modern Philology*. LXXIII (1975), pp. 136–147.

Cramer, Mark. "Neruda and Vallejo in Contemporary United States Poetry," in *Romance Notes*. XIV (1973), pp. 455–459.

Ellis, Keith. "*Poema Veinte*: A Structural Approach," in *Romance Notes*. XI (1970), pp. 507–517.

Engler, Kay. "Image and Structure in Neruda's *Las Alturas de Macchu Picchu*," in *Symposium*. XXVIII (1974), pp. 130–145.

Eshleman, Clayton. "Neruda: An Elemental Response," in *Tri-Quarterly*. XV (Spring, 1969), pp. 228–237.

Gallagher, David P. *Modern Latin American Literature*. Oxford: Oxford University Press, 1973, pp. 39–66.

McGrath, Thomas. "The Poetry of Pablo Neruda," in *Mainstream*. XV (June, 1962), pp. 43–47.

Paseyro, Ricardo. "The Dead World of Pablo Neruda," in *Tri-Quarterly*. XV (Spring, 1969), pp. 203–227.

Riess, Frank. *The Word and the Stone: Language and Imagery in Neruda's Canto General*. Oxford: Oxford University Press, 1972.

Tolman, Jon M. "Death and Alien Environment in Pablo Neruda's *Residencia en la Tierra*," in *Hispania*. LI (March, 1968), pp. 79–85.

Willard, Nancy. *Testimony of the Invisible Man; William Carlos Williams, Francis Ponge, Rainer Maria Rilke, Pablo Neruda*. Columbia: University of Missouri Press, 1970, pp. 83–109.

P.H. NEWBY
(1918–   )

A Guest and His Going

Bufkin, E.C.   *P.H. Newby*. Boston: Twayne, 1975, pp. 92–97.

Fraser, G.S.   *P.H. Newby*. London: Longmans, 1974, pp. 23–31.

Gutwilling, Robert.   "Newby's Precise and Limited Talent," in *Commonweal*. LXXI (January 15, 1960), pp. 448–449.

Mathew, F.X.   "Newby on the Nile," in *Twentieth Century Literature*. XIV (April, 1968), pp. 12–15.

Poss, S.   "Manners and Myths in the Novels of P.H. Newby," in *Critique*. XII (1970), pp. 5–19.

Journey to the Interior

Bufkin, E.C.   *P.H. Newby*. Boston: Twayne, 1975, pp. 21–26.

————.   "Quest in the Novels of P.H. Newby," in *Critique*. VIII (1965), pp. 51–62.

Fraser, G.S.   *P.H. Newby*. London: Longmans, 1974, pp. 13–16.

Karl, Frederick.   *The Contemporary English Novel*. New York: Farrar, Straus and Cudahy, 1962, pp. 269–271.

Poss, S.   "Manners and Myths in the Novels of P.H. Newby," in *Critique*. XII (1970), pp. 5–19.

The Picnic at Sakkara

Bufkin, E.C.   *P.H. Newby*. Boston: Twayne, 1975, pp. 82–87.

Fraser, G.S.   *P.H. Newby*. London: Longmans, 1974, pp. 25–27.

Halpern, Ben.   "The Wisdom of Blindness." in *Midstream*. III (Winter, 1957), pp. 104–107.

Karl, Frederick.   *The Contemporary English Novel*. New York: Farrar, Straus and Cudahy, 1962, pp. 271–272.

Mathews, F.X.   "Newby on the Nile," in *Twentieth Century Literature*. XIV (April, 1968), pp. 12–15.

Poss, S.   "Manners and Myths in the Novels of P.H. Newby," in *Critique*. XII (1970), pp. 5–19.

The Retreat

Allen, Walter.   *Modern Novel in Britain and the United States*. New York: Dutton, 1964, pp. 266–267.

Balakian, Nona. "Three English Novels," in *Kenyon Review*. XV (Summer, 1953), pp. 490–494.

Bufkin, E.C. *P.H. Newby*. Boston: Twayne, 1975, pp. 66–67, 72–79.

————. "Quest in the Novels of P.H. Newby," in *Critique*. VIII (Fall, 1965), pp. 56–58.

Fraser, G.S. *P.H. Newby*. London: Longmans, 1974, pp. 19–23.

Karl, Frederick. *The Contemporary English Novel*. New York: Farrar, Straus and Cudahy, 1962, p. 16.

Pickrel, Paul. "*The Retreat*," in *Yale Review*. XLII (Summer, 1953), p. vi.

Poss, S. "Manners and Myths in the Novels of P.H. Newby," in *Critique*. XII (1970), pp. 5–19.

FRIEDRICH WILHELM NIETZSCHE
(1844–1900)

Beyond Good and Evil

Common, Thomas. "Introduction to the Translation," in *Beyond Good and Evil.* By Friedrich Nietzsche. New York: Russell & Russell, 1964, pp. vii–xv.

Foster, George Burman. *Friedrich Nietzsche.* New York: Macmillan, 1931, pp. 155–168.

Halevy, Daniel. *The Life of Friederich Nietzsche.* New York: Macmillan, 1911, pp. 305–329.

Helm, Robert M. "Plato in the Thought of Nietzsche and Augustine," in *Studies in Nietzsche and the Classical Tradition.* Edited by James C. O'Flaherty, Timothy F. Sellner and Robert M. Helm. Chapel Hill: University of North Carolina Press, 1976, pp. 16–32.

Hollingdale, R.J. *Nietzsche: The Man and His Philosophy.* Baton Rouge: Louisiana State University Press, 1965, pp. 216–230.

Kennedy, J.M. *The Quintessence of Nietzsche.* London: T. Werner Laurie, 1909, pp. 320–326.

Ludovici, Anthony M. *Who Is to Be Master of the World?* Edinburgh: T.N. Foulis, 1914, pp. 1–51.

Manthey-Zorn, Otto. *Dionysus: The Tragedy of Nietzsche.* Westport, Conn.: Greenwood Press, 1975, pp. 107–126.

Mencken, H.L. *The Philosophy of Friederich Nietzsche.* Boston: Luce, 1913, pp. 88–99.

Mugge, Maximilian A. *Friederich Nietzsche.* Port Washington, N.Y.: Kennikat, 1970, pp. 36–55.

Reyburn, H.A. *Nietzsche: The Story of a Human Philosopher.* London: Macmillan, 1948, pp. 404–433.

Strong, Tracy B. *Friederich Nietzsche and the Politics of Transfiguration.* Berkeley: University of California Press, 1975, pp. 87–107.

Williams, W.D. *Nietzsche and the French.* Oxford: Basil Blackwell, 1952, pp. 114–137.

Wright, Willard Huntington. *What Nietzsche Taught.* New York: B.W. Heubsch, 1915, pp. 173–185.

The Birth of Tragedy

Forster-Nietzsche, Elizabeth. "Introduction," in *The Birth of Tragedy.* By Friedrich Nietzsche. New York: Russell & Russell, 1964, pp. vii–xxix.

Foster, George Burman. *Friedrich Nietzsche.* New York: Macmillan, 1931, pp. 16–50, 136–154.

Frenzel, Ivo. *Friedrich Nietzsche.* New York: Pegasus, 1967, pp. 39–48.

Hollingdale, R.J. *Nietzsche: The Man and His Philosophy.* Baton Rouge: Louisiana State University Press, 1965, pp. 96–104.

Kaufmann, Walter. "Nietzsche and the Death of Tragedy: A Critique," in *Studies in Nietzsche and the Classical Tradition.* Edited by James O'Flaherty, Timothy F. Sellner and Robert M. Helm. Chapel Hill: University of North Carolina Press, 1976, pp. 234–254.

————. *Nietzsche: Philosopher, Psychologist, Antichrist.* Princeton, N.J.: Princeton University Press, 1974, pp. 128–134, 391–395.

————. "Translator's Introduction," in The Birth of Tragedy *and* The Case of Wagner. By Friederich Nietzsche. New York: Vintage, 1967, pp. 3–13.

Kennedy, J.M. *The Quintessence of Nietzsche.* London: T. Werner Laurie, 1909, pp. 121–141.

Knight, A.H.J. *Some Aspects of the Life and Work of Nietzsche, and Particularly of His Connection with Greek Literature and Thought.* New York: Russell & Russell, 1967, pp. 52–92.

Kofman, Sarah. "Metaphor, Symbol, Metamorphosis," in *The New Nietzsche: Contemporary Styles of Interpretation.* Edited by David B. Allison. New York: Delta, 1977, pp. 206–208.

Lea, F.A. *The Tragic Philosopher: A Study of Friederich Nietzsche.* New York: Philosophical Library, 1957, pp. 33–48.

Manthey-Zorn, Otto. *Dionysus: The Tragedy of Nietzsche.* Westport, Conn.: Greenwood Press, 1975, pp. 22–29.

Mencken, H.L. *The Philosophy of Friederich Nietzsche.* Boston: Luce, 1913, pp. 24–26, 63–73.

Mugge, Maximilian A. *Friederich Nietzsche.* Port Washington, N.Y.: Kennikat Press, 1970, pp. 19–20.

O'Flaherty, James C. "Eros and Creativity in Nietzsche's *Birth of Tragedy,*" in *Studies in German Literature of the Nineteenth and Twentieth Centuries.* Edited by Siegfried Mews. Chapel Hill: University of North Carolina Press, 1970, pp. 83–104.

————. "Socrates in Hamann's *Socratic Memorabilia* and Nietzsche's *Birth of Tragedy,*" in *Studies in Nietzsche and the Classical Tradition.* Edited by James C. O'Flaherty, Timothy F. Sellner and Robert M. Helm. Chapel Hill: University of North Carolina Press, 1976, pp. 114–143.

Pfeffer, Rose. *Nietzsche: Disciple of Dionysus.* Lewisburg, Pa.: Bucknell University Press, 1972, pp. 33–35, 221–223.

Reyburn, H.A. *Nietzsche: The Story of a Human Philosopher.* London: Macmillan, 1948, pp. 119–147.

Strong, Tracy B. *Friederich Nietzsche and the Politics of Transfiguration.* Berkeley: University of California Press, 1975, pp. 34–36, 120–122.

Thatcher, David S. *Nietzsche in England, 1890–1914: The Growth of a Reputation.* Toronto: University of Toronto Press, 1970, pp. 124–126.

————. "A Scholar's Departure: Nietzsche's *Birth of Tragedy,*" in *Malahat Review.* XXIV (1972), pp. 30–44.

Weinberg, Kurt. "Nietzsche's Paradox of Tragedy," in *Yale French Studies.* XXXVIII (1967), pp. 251–266.

Wells, George A. *"The Birth of Tragedy*: An Analysis and Assessment of Nietzsche's Essay," in *Trivium.* III (1968), pp. 59–75.

Williams, W.D. *Nietzsche and the French.* Oxford: Basil Blackwell, 1952, pp. 5–16.

Zuckerman, Elliott. "Nietzsche and Music: *The Birth of Tragedy* and *Nietzsche Contra Wagner,*" in *Symposium.* XXVIII (1974), pp. 17–32.

Thus Spake Zarathustra

Aiken, Henry David. "Introduction," in *Thus Spake Zarathustra.* By Friederich Nietzsche. New York: Heritage Press, 1967, pp. v–xvi.

Biser, Eugene. "Between *Inferno* and *Purgatorio*: Thoughts on a Structural Comparison of Nietzsche and Dante," in *Studies in Nietzsche and the Classical Tradition.* Edited by James C. O'Flaherty, Timothy F. Sellner and Robert M. Helm. Chapel Hill: University of North Carolina Press, 1976, pp. 55–70.

Carus, Paul. *Nietzsche and Other Exponents of Individualism.* New York: Haskell House, 1972, pp. 40–59.

Fischer, Kurt Rudolph. "The Existentialism of Nietzsche's *Zarathustra,*" in *Daedalus.* XCII (1964), pp. 998–1016.

Forster-Nietzsche, Elizabeth. "Introduction," in *Thus Spake Zarathustra.* By Friedrich Nietzsche. New York: Russell & Russell, 1964, pp. ix–xxvi.

Halevy, Daniel. *The Life of Friederich Nietzsche.* New York: Macmillan, 1911, pp. 229–297.

Heidegger, Martin. "Who Is Nietzsche's Zarathustra?," in *The New Nietzsche: Contemporary Styles of Interpretation.* Edited by David B. Allison. New York: Delta, 1977, pp. 64–79.

Hollingdale, R.J. *Nietzsche: The Man and His Philosophy.* Baton Rouge: Louisiana State University Press, 1965, pp. 191–202.

Kaufmann, Walter. *Nietzsche: Philosopher, Psychologist, Antichrist.* Princeton, N.J.: Princeton University Press, 1974, pp. 200–207.

Kennedy, J.M. *The Quintessence of Nietzsche.* London: T. Werner Laurie, 1909, pp. 294–319.

Knight, A.H.J. *Some Aspects of the Life and Work of Nietzsche, and Particularly of His Connection with Greek Literature and Thought.* New York: Russell & Russell, 1967, pp. 38–44, 93–117.

Knight, G. Wilson. *Christ and Nietzsche: An Essay in Poetic Wisdom.* London: Staples Press, 1948, pp. 158–218.

Lea, F.A. *The Tragic Philosopher: A Study of Friederich Nietzsche.* New York: Philosophical Library, 1957, pp. 180–226.

Ludovici, Anthony M. *Who Is to Be Master of the World?* Edinburgh: T.N. Foulis, 1914, pp. 52–104.

Manthey-Zorn, Otto. *Dionysus: The Tragedy of Nietzsche.* Westport, Conn.: Greenwood Press, 1975, pp. 82–106.

Mugge, Maximilian A. *Friederich Nietzsche.* Port Washington: N.Y.: Kennikat Press, 1970, pp. 27–30.

Nelson, Donald F. "Nietzsche, Zarathustra, and Jesus Redivivus: The Unholy Trinity," in *Germanic Review.* XLVIII (1973), pp. 175–188.

Reyburn, H.A. *Nietzsche: The Story of a Human Philosopher.* London: Macmillan, 1948, pp. 302–345.

Roy, Emil. "Friederich Nietzsche's *Thus Spake Zarathustra* as Romance," in *Genre.* III (1970), pp. 72–84.

Stambaugh, Joan. *Nietzsche's Thought of Eternal Return.* Baltimore: Johns Hopkins University Press, 1972, pp. 33–45.

Valadier, Paul. "Dionysus Versus the Crucified," in *The New Nietzsche: Contemporary Styles of Interpretation.* Edited by David B. Allison. New York: Delta, 1977, pp. 247–261.

Williams, W.D. *Nietzsche and the French.* Oxford: Basil Blackwell, 1952, pp. 97–113.

Wolfe, Peter. "Image and Meaning in *Also sprach Zarathustra*," in *Modern Language Notes.* LXXIX (1964), pp. 546–552.

Wright, Willard Huntington. *What Nietzsche Taught.* New York: B.W. Heubsch, 1915, pp. 133–142.

IPPOLITO NIEVO
(1831–1861)

The Castle of Fratta

Alberico, Alfred F. "Nievo's Disquieting Pisana," in *Italica*. XXXVII (March, 1960), pp. 13–21.

Edwards, Lovett F. "Translator's Foreword," in *The Castle of Fratta*. By Ippolito Nievo. Westport, Conn.: Greenwood Press, 1974, pp. ix–xv.

Iliescu, Nicolae. "The Position of Ippolito Nievo in the Nineteenth-Century Italian Novel," in *PMLA*. LXXV (June, 1960), pp. 275–282.

Ragusa, Olga. "Nievo, the Writer: Tendencies in Criticism," in *Italian Quarterly*. II (Summer, 1958), pp. 20–34.

ANAÏS NIN
(1913–   )

Children of the Albatross

Evans, Oliver. *Anaïs Nin.* Carbondale: Southern Illinois University Press, 1968, pp. 113–128.

McLaughlin, Richard. "Shadow Dance," in *Saturday Review of Literature.* XXX (December 20, 1947), p. 16.

Schneider, Duane. "The Art of Anaïs Nin," in *A Casebook on Anaïs Nin.* Edited by Robert Zaller. New York: New American Library, 1974, pp. 43–50.

Spencer, Sharon. "Anaïs Nin's 'Continuous Novel': *Cities of the Interior*," in *A Casebook on Anaïs Nin.* Edited by Robert Zaller. New York: New American Library, 1974, pp. 65–75.

_____. "*Cities of the Interior*—Femininity and Freedom," in her *Under the Sign of Pisces: Anaïs Nin and Her Circle.* VII (Summer, 1976), pp. 9–16.

_____. *Collage of Dreams: The Writings of Anaïs Nin.* Chicago: Swallow Press, 1977, pp. 29–31, 76–78.

_____. "Introduction," in *Cities of the Interior.* By Anaïs Nin. Chicago: Swallow Press, 1974, pp. x–xx.

Collages

Balakian, Anna. "Introduction," in *Anaïs Nin Reader.* Edited by Philip K. Jason. Chicago: Swallow Press, 1973, pp. 28–30.

Evans, Oliver. *Anaïs Nin.* Carbondale: Southern Illinois University Press, 1968, pp. 178–190.

Spencer, Sharon. *Collage of Dreams: The Writings of Anaïs Nin.* Chicago: Swallow Press, 1977, pp. 9–11, 114–116.

Zinnes, Harriet. "The Fiction of Anaïs Nin," in *A Casebook on Anaïs Nin.* Edited by Robert Zaller. New York: New American Library, 1974, pp. 37–38.

The Diary of Anaïs Nin

Centing, Richard R. "Emotional Algebra: The Symbolic Level of *The Diary of Anaïs Nin*," in *A Casebook on Anaïs Nin.* Edited by Robert Zaller. New York: New American Library, 1974, pp. 169–176.

Clark, Orville. "Anaïs Nin: Studies in the New Erotology," in *A Casebook on Anaïs Nin.* Edited by Robert Zaller. New York: New American Library, 1974, pp. 101–111.

Hinz, Evelyn J. *The Mirror and the Garden.* Columbus: Ohio State University Libraries, 1971, pp. 97–112.

Metzger, Deena.   "*The Diary of Anaïs Nin:* The Ceremony of Knowing," in *A Casebook on Anaïs Nin.* Edited by Robert Zaller. New York: New American Library, 1974, pp. 133–143.

Rainer, Tristine.   "Anaïs Nin's *Diary* I: The Birth of the Young Woman as an Artist," in *A Casebook on Anaïs Nin.* Edited by Robert Zaller. New York: New American Library, 1974, pp. 161–168.

Spencer, Sharon.   *Collage of Dreams: The Writings of Anaïs Nin.* Chicago: Swallow Press, 1977, pp. 124–140.

Stern, Daniel.   "The Novel of Her Life: *The Diary of Anaïs Nin,* Volume IV, 1944–1947," in *A Casebook on Anaïs Nin.* Edited by Robert Zaller. New York: New American Library, 1974, pp. 153–156.

Stuhlmann, Gunther.   "Introduction," in *The Diary of Anaïs Nin: 1931–1934.* By Anaïs Nin. New York: Swallow Press, 1966, pp. v–xii.

————.   "Preface," in *The Diary of Anaïs Nin: 1939–1944.* By Anaïs Nin. New York: Harcourt, Brace, Jovanovich, 1969, pp. v–xiv.

Sukerick, Lynn.   "*The Diary of Anaïs Nin,*" in *Shenandoah.* XXVII (1976), pp. 96–103.

The Four-Chambered Heart

Evans, Oliver.   *Anaïs Nin.* Carbondale: Southern Illinois University Press, 1968, pp. 129–143.

Hinz, Evelyn J.   *The Mirror and the Garden.* Columbus: Ohio State University Libraries, 1971, pp. 7–8, 38–39, 45–47.

Rolo, Charles J.   "The Life of the Heart," in *Atlantic.* CLXXXV (February, 1950), pp. 86–87.

Schneider, Duane.   "The Art on Anaïs Nin," in *A Casebook on Anaïs Nin.* Edited by Robert Zaller. New York: New American Library, 1974, pp. 43–50.

Scholar, Nancy.   "*Cities of the Interior* Revisited," in *Under the Sign of Pisces: Anaïs Nin and Her Circle.* VI (Fall, 1975), pp. 9–12.

Spencer, Sharon.   "Anaïs Nin's 'Continuous Novel': *Cities of the Interior,*" in *A Casebook on Anaïs Nin.* Edited by Robert Zaller. New York: New American Library, 1974, pp. 65–75.

————.   "*Cities of the Interior*—Femininity and Freedom," in *Under the Sign of Pisces: Anaïs Nin and Her Circle.* VII (Summer, 1976), pp. 9–16.

————.   *Collage of Dreams: The Writings of Anaïs Nin.* Chicago: Swallow Press, 1977, pp. 34–36, 78–80, 83–84.

————.   "Introduction," in *Cities of the Interior.* By Anaïs Nin. Chicago: Swallow Press, 1974, pp. x–xx.

The House of Incest

Balakian, Anna. "Introduction," in *Anaïs Nin Reader*. Edited by Philip K. Jason. Chicago: Swallow Press, 1973, pp. 15–18.

————. "The Poetic Reality of Anaïs Nin," in *A Casebook on Anaïs Nin*. Edited by Robert Zaller. New York: New American Library, 1974, pp. 118–120.

Evans, Oliver. *Anaïs Nin*. Carbondale: Southern Illinois University Press, 1968, pp. 26–43.

Hinz, Evelyn J. *The Mirror and the Garden*. Columbus: Ohio State University Libraries, 1971, pp. 36–39, 77–78.

Jason, Philip K. "Foreword," in *Anaïs Nin Reader*. Edited by Philip K. Jason. Chicago: Swallow Press, 1973, pp. 4–5.

Spencer, Sharon. *Collage of Dreams: The Writings of Anaïs Nin*. Chicago: Swallow Press, 1977, pp. 80–82.

Ladders to Fire

Balakian, Anna. "Introduction," in *Anaïs Nin Reader*. Edited by Philip K. Jason. Chicago: Swallow Press, 1973, pp. 23–25.

Evans, Oliver. *Anaïs Nin*. Carbondale: Southern Illinois University Press, 1968, pp. 88–112.

Henke, Suzette A. "Anaïs Nin: Bread and the Wafer," in *Under the Sign of Pisces: Anaïs Nin and Her Circle*. VII (Spring, 1976), pp. 7–17.

Hinz, Evelyn J. *The Mirror and the Garden*. Columbus: Ohio State University Libraries, 1971, pp. 51–56, 69–74.

Schneider, Duane. "The Art of Anaïs Nin," in *A Casebook on Anaïs Nin*. Edited by Robert Zaller. New York: New American Library, 1974, pp. 43–50.

Scholar, Nancy. "*Cities of the Interior* Revisited," in *Under the Sign of Pisces: Anaïs Nin and Her Circle*. VI (Fall, 1975), pp. 9–12.

Spencer, Sharon. "Anaïs Nin's 'Continuous Novel': *Cities of the Interior*," in *A Casebook on Anaïs Nin*. Edited by Robert Zaller. New York: New American Library, 1974, pp. 65–75.

————. "*Cities of the Interior*—Femininity and Freedom," in *Under the Sign of Pisces: Anaïs Nin and Her Circle*. VII (Summer, 1976), pp. 9–16.

————. *Collage of Dreams: The Writings of Anaïs Nin*. Chicago: Swallow Press, 1977, pp. 31–32, 74–75, 82–83, 129–130.

————. "Introduction," in *Cities of the Interior*. By Anaïs Nin. Chicago: Swallow Press, 1974, pp. x–xx.

Seduction of the Minotaur

Balakian, Anna. "Introduction," in *Anaïs Nin Reader*. Edited by Philip K. Jason. Chicago: Swallow Press, 1973, pp. 21–22, 25–27.

————. "The Poetic Reality of Anaïs Nin," in *A Casebook on Anaïs Nin.* Edited by Robert Zaller. New York: New American Library, 1974, pp. 126–131.

Evans, Oliver. *Anaïs Nin.* Carbondale: Southern Illinois University Press, 1968, pp. 162–177.

Hinz, Evelyn J. *The Mirror and the Garden.* Columbus: Ohio State University Libraries, 1971, pp. 56–57, 72–74.

McEvilly, Wayne. "The Two Faces of Death in Anaïs Nin's *Seduction of the Minotaur,*" in *A Casebook on Anaïs Nin.* Edited by Robert Zaller. New York: New American Library, 1974, pp. 51–64.

Scholar, Nancy. "*Cities of the Interior* Revisited," in *Under the Sign of Pisces: Anaïs Nin and Her Circle.* VI (Fall, 1975), pp. 9–12.

Spencer, Sharon. "Anaïs Nin's 'Continuous Novel': *Cities of the Interior,*" in *A Casebook on Anaïs Nin.* Edited by Robert Zaller. New York: New American Library, 1974, pp. 65–75.

————. "*Cities of the Interior*—Femininity and Freedom," in *Under the Sign of Pisces: Anaïs Nin and Her Circle.* VII (Summer, 1976), pp. 9–16.

————. *Collage of Dreams: The Writings of Anaïs Nin.* Chicago: Swallow Press, 1977, pp. 28–29, 62–65, 74–76.

————. "Introduction," in *Cities of the Interior.* By Anaïs Nin. Chicago: Swallow Press, 1974, pp. x–xx.

Zinnes, Harriet. "The Fiction of Anaïs Nin," in *A Casebook on Anaïs Nin.* Edited by Robert Zaller. New York: New American Library, 1974, pp. 38–40.

A Spy in the House of Love

Evans, Oliver. *Anaïs Nin.* Carbondale: Southern Illinois University Press, 1968, pp. 145–162.

Hinz, Evelyn J. *The Mirror and the Garden.* Columbus: Ohio State University Libraries, 1971, pp. 57–60.

Jason, Philip K. "Teaching *A Spy in the House of Love,*" in *Under the Sign of Pisces: Anaïs Nin and Her Circle.* II (Summer, 1971), pp. 7–15.

Schneider, Duane. "The Art of Anaïs Nin," in *A Casebook on Anaïs Nin.* Edited by Robert Zaller. New York: New American Library, 1974, pp. 43–50.

Scholar, Nancy. "*Cities of the Interior* Revisited," in *Under the Sign of Pisces: Anaïs Nin and Her Circle.* VI (Fall, 1975), pp. 9–12.

Spencer, Sharon. "Anaïs Nin's 'Continuous Novel': *Cities of the Interior,*" in *A Casebook on Anaïs Nin.* Edited by Robert Zaller. New York: New American Library, 1974, pp. 65–75.

————. "*Cities of the Interior*—Femininity and Freedom," in *Under the Sign of Pisces: Anaïs Nin and Her Circle.* VII (Summer, 1976), pp. 9–16.

_____. *Collage of Dreams: The Writings of Anaïs Nin.* Chicago: Swallow Press, 1977, pp. 33–34, 39–41, 51–52, 84–85.

_____. "Introduction," in *Cities of the Interior.* By Anaïs Nin. Chicago: Swallow Press, 1974, pp. x–xx.

The Winter of Artifice

Balakian, Anna. "Introduction," in *Anaïs Nin Reader.* Edited by Philip K. Jason. Chicago: Swallow Press, 1973, pp. 19–21.

_____. "The Poetic Reality of Anaïs Nin," in *A Casebook on Anaïs Nin.* Edited by Robert Zaller. New York: New American Library, 1974, pp. 121–122.

Evans, Oliver. *Anaïs Nin.* Carbondale: Southern Illinois University Press, 1968, pp. 44–62.

Hinz, Evelyn J. *The Mirror and the Garden.* Columbus: Ohio State University Libraries, 1971, pp. 37–38, 43–45, 54–55.

Rosenfeld, Paul. "Refinements on a Journal," in *Nation.* CLV (September 26, 1942), pp. 276–277.

Spencer, Sharon. *Collage of Dreams: The Writings of Anaïs Nin.* Chicago: Swallow Press, 1977, pp. 26–28, 72–73.

FRANK NORRIS
(1870–1902)

Blix

French, Warren. *Frank Norris.* New York: Twayne, 1962, pp. 78–84.

Frohock, W.M. *Frank Norris.* Minneapolis: University of Minnesota Press, 1968, pp. 31–32.

Geismar, Maxwell. *Rebels and Ancestors.* Boston: Houghton Mifflin, 1953, pp. 11–14.

Morgan, H. Wayne. *American Writers in Rebellion from Twain to Dreiser.* New York: Hill and Wang, 1965, pp. 129–131.

Pizer, Donald. *The Novels of Frank Norris.* Bloomington: Indiana University Press, 1966, pp. 96–102, 110–112.

McTeague

Brooks, Van Wyck. "Introduction," in *McTeague, A Story of San Francisco.* Greenwich, Conn.: Fawcett, 1960.

Chase, Richard. *The American Novel and Its Tradition.* Garden City, New York: Doubleday, 1957, pp. 188–192. Reprinted in *McTeague, A Story of San Francisco.* Edited by Donald Pizer. New York: Norton, 1977, pp. 341–344.

Collins, Carvel. "Introduction," in *McTeague, A Story of San Francisco.* New York: Rinehart, 1955. Reprinted in *The American Novel from James Fenimore Cooper to William Faulkner.* Edited by Wallace Stegner. New York: Basic Books, 1965, pp. 97–105.

Cooperman, Stanley. "Frank Norris and the Werewolf of Guilt," in *Modern Language Quarterly.* XX (September, 1959), pp. 252–258.

Dillingham, William B. *Frank Norris: Instinct and Art.* Lincoln: University of Nebraska Press, 1969, pp. 104–109, 115–119. Reprinted in *McTeague, A Story of San Francisco.* Edited by Donald Pizer. New York: Norton, 1977, pp. 354–361.

————. "The Old Folks of *McTeague*," in *Nineteenth-Century Fiction.* XVI (September, 1961), pp. 169–173. Reprinted in *McTeague, A Story of San Francisco.* Edited by Donald Pizer. New York: Norton, 1977, pp. 344–348.

Dreiser, Theodore. "Introduction," in *The Argonaut Manuscript Limited Edition of Frank Norris' Works*, Volume VIII. Garden City, N.Y.: Doubleday, 1928, pp. vii–xi.

French, Warren. *Frank Norris.* New York: Twayne, 1962, pp. 62–75.

Frohock, W.M. *Frank Norris.* Minneapolis: University of Minnesota Press, 1968, pp. 9–16.

Geismar, Maxwell. *Rebels and Ancestors: The American Novel, 1890–1915.* Boston: Houghton Mifflin, 1953, pp. 14–21. Reprinted in *McTeague, A Story of San Francisco.* Edited by Donald Pizer. New York: Norton, 1977, pp. 332–337.

Goldman, Suzy B. "*McTeague* and the Imagistic Network," in *Western American Literature.* VII (Summer, 1972), pp. 83–99.

Hill, John S. "Trina Sieppe: First Lady of American Literary Naturalism," in *University of Kansas City Review.* XXIX (Autumn, 1962), pp. 77–80.

Howells, William Dean. "A Case in Point," in *Literature.* I (March 24, 1899), pp. 241–242. Reprinted in *McTeague, A Story of San Francisco.* Edited by Donald Pizer. New York: Norton, 1977, pp. 325–327.

Johnson, George W. "Frank Norris and Romance," in *American Literature.* XXXIII (March, 1961), pp. 57–60.

Kazin, Alfred. "American Naturalism: Reflections from Another Era," in *The American Writer and the European Tradition.* Edited by Margaret Denny and William H. Gilman. Minneapolis: University of Minnesota Press, 1950, pp. 121–131.

Marchand, Ernest. *Frank Norris: A Study.* New York: Octagon Books, 1964, pp. 56–67.

Martin, Jay. *Harvests of Change: American Literature, 1865–1914.* Englewood Cliffs, N.J.: Prentice-Hall, 1967, pp. 249–252.

Morgan, H. Wayne. *American Writers in Rebellion from Twain to Dreiser.* New York: Hill and Wang, 1965, pp. 114–120.

Pizer, Donald. "Evolutionary Ethical Dualism in Frank Norris's *Vandover and the Brute* and *McTeague*," in *PMLA.* LXXVI (December, 1961), pp. 552–560.

————. *The Novels of Frank Norris.* Bloomington: Indiana University Press, 1966, pp. 23–31, 63–85.

Powell, Lawrence Clark. *California Classics: The Creative Literature of the Golden State.* Los Angeles: Ward Ritchie, 1971, pp. 175–184.

Rexroth, Kenneth. "Afterword," in *McTeague, A Story of San Francisco.* New York: New American Library, 1964, pp. 341–348.

Walcutt, Charles C. *American Literary Naturalism, A Divided Stream.* Minneapolis: University of Minnesota Press, 1956, pp. 125, 128–132. Reprinted in *McTeague, A Story of San Francisco.* Edited by Donald Pizer. New York: Norton, 1977, pp. 337–341.

The Octopus

Ahnebrink, Lars. *The Beginnings of Naturalism in American Fiction.* New York: Russell and Russell, 1961, pp. 104–124. Reprinted in *The Merrill Studies in* The Octopus. Edited by Richard Allan Davison. Columbus, Oh.: Merrill, 1969, pp. 82–83.

Cargill, Oscar. "Afterword," in *The Octopus.* New York: New American Library, 1964, pp. 459–469. Reprinted in *Toward a Pluralistic Criticism.* Carbondale: Southern Illinois University Press, 1965, pp. 118–130.

Chase, Richard Volney. *The American Novel and Its Tradition.* Garden City, N.Y.: Doubleday Books, 1957, pp. 193–198.

Dillingham, William B. *Frank Norris: Instinct and Art.* Lincoln: University of Nebraska Press, 1969, pp. 60–65, 93–96, 119–121.

Farrell, James T. "Social Themes in American Realism," in *English Journal.* XXXV (June, 1946), pp. 309–315.

Folsom, James K. "Social Darwinism or Social Protest? The 'Philosophy' of *The Octopus*," in *Modern Fiction Studies.* VIII (Winter, 1962–1963), pp. 393–400. Reprinted in *The Merrill Studies in* The Octopus. Edited by Richard Allan Davison. Columbus, Oh.: Merrill, 1969, pp. 132–140.

French, Warren. *Frank Norris.* New York: Twayne, 1962, pp. 89–106. Reprinted in *The Merrill Studies in* The Octopus. Edited by Richard Allan Davison. Columbus, Oh.: Merrill, 1969, pp. 114–131.

Frohock, W.M. *Frank Norris.* Minneapolis: University of Minnesota Press, 1968, pp. 20–27.

Geismar, Maxwell. *Rebels and Ancestors.* Boston: Houghton Mifflin, 1953, pp. 25–37. Reprinted in *The Merrill Studies in* The Octopus. Edited by Richard Allan Davison. Columbus, Oh.: Merrill, 1969, pp. 84–87.

Lundy, Robert D. "Introduction," in *The Octopus.* By Frank Norris. New York: Hill and Wang, 1957.

Lutwack, Leonard. *Heroic Fiction: The Epic Tradition and American Novels of the Twentieth Century.* Carbondale: Southern Illinois University Press, 1971, pp. 23–46.

Lynn, Kenneth S. "Introduction," in *The Octopus.* By Frank Norris. Boston: Houghton Mifflin, 1958, pp. v–xxv.

Marchand, Ernest. *Frank Norris: A Study.* New York: Octagon Books, 1964, pp. 72–82. Reprinted in *The Merrill Studies in* The Octopus. Edited by Richard Allan Davison. Columbus, Oh.: Merrill, 1969, pp. 52–63.

Martin, Jay. *Harvests of Change: American Literature, 1865–1914.* Englewood Cliffs, N.J.: Prentice-Hall, 1967, pp. 75–77.

Marx, Leo. "Two Kingdoms of Force," in *Massachusetts Review.* I (October, 1959), pp. 62–95. Revised version in *The Machine in the Garden: Technol-*

ogy and the Pastoral Ideal in America. New York: Oxford University Press, 1964, pp. 16, 343–344.

Meyer, George W.   "A New Interpretation of *The Octopus*," in *College English.* IV (March, 1943), pp. 351–359. Reprinted in *The Merrill Studies in* The Octopus. Edited by Richard Allan Davison. Columbus, Oh.: Merrill, 1969, pp. 68–81.

Morgan, H. Wayne.   *American Writers in Rebellion from Twain to Dreiser.* New York: Hill and Wang, 1965, pp. 134–140.

Pizer, Donald.   "Another Look at *The Octopus*," in *Nineteenth-Century Fiction.* X (December, 1955), pp. 217–224. Reprinted in *The Merrill Studies in* The Octopus. Edited by Richard Allan Davison. Columbus, Oh.: Merrill, 1969, pp. 88–95.

————.   "The Concept of Nature in Frank Norris' *The Octopus*," in *American Quarterly.* XIV (Spring, 1962), pp. 73–80. Reprinted in *The Merrill Studies in* The Octopus. Edited by Richard Allan Davison. Columbus, Oh.: Merrill, 1969, pp. 105–113.

————.   *The Novels of Frank Norris.* Bloomington: Indiana University Press, 1966, pp. 113–162.

Reninger, H. Willard.   "Norris Explains *The Octopus*: A Correlation of His Theory and Practice," in *American Literature.* XII (May, 1940), pp. 218–227. Reprinted in *The Merrill Studies in* The Octopus. Edited by Richard Allan Davison. Columbus, Oh.: Merrill, 1969, pp. 41–51.

Stone, Edward.   *Voices of Despair.* Athens: Ohio University Press, 1966, pp. 57–62.

Taylor, Walter F.   *The Economic Novel in America.* New York: Octagon, 1964, pp. 294–300. Reprinted in *The Merrill Studies in* The Octopus. Edited by Richard Allan Davison. Columbus, Oh.: Merrill, 1969, pp. 64–67.

Vance, William L.   "Romance in *The Octopus*," in *Genre.* III (June, 1970), pp. 111–136.

Walcutt, Charles C.   *American Literary Naturalism, A Divided Stream.* Minneapolis: University of Minnesota Press, 1956, pp. 136–151. Reprinted in *The Merrill Studies in* The Octopus. Edited by Richard Allan Davison. Columbus, Oh.: Merrill, 1969, pp. 96–100.

The Pit

Dillingham, William B.   *Frank Norris: Instinct and Art.* Lincoln: University of Nebraska Press, 1969, pp. 121–125.

French, Warren.   *Frank Norris.* New York: Twayne, 1962, pp. 107–118, 123–127.

Frohock, W.M.   *Frank Norris.* Minneapolis: University of Minnesota Press, 1968, pp. 27–29.

Geismar, Maxwell.   *Rebels and Ancestors.* Boston: Houghton Mifflin, 1953, pp. 38–43.

Hart, James D.   "Introduction," in *The Pit.* By Frank Norris. Columbus, Oh.: Merrill, 1970, pp. v–xv.

Lynn, Kenneth S.   "Frank Norris: Mama's Boy," in his *Dream of Success: A Study of the Modern American Imagination.* Boston: Little, Brown, 1955, pp. 201–207.

Marchand, Ernest.   *Frank Norris: A Study.* New York: Octagon Books, 1964, pp. 82–87.

Millgate, Michael.   *American Social Fiction: James to Cozzens.* New York: Barnes & Noble, 1964, pp. 38–47.

Morgan, H. Wayne.   *American Writers in Rebellion from Twain to Dreiser.* New York: Hill and Wang, 1965, pp. 140–143.

Pizer, Donald.   *The Novels of Frank Norris.* Bloomington: Indiana University Press, 1966, pp. 162–178.

Taylor, Walter F.   *The Economic Novel in America.* New York: Octagon, 1964, pp. 300–304.

Walcutt, Charles C.   *American Literary Naturalism, A Divided Stream.* Minneapolis: University of Minnesota Press, 1956, pp. 151–155.

Ziff, Larzer.   *The American 1890's: Life and Times of a Lost Generation.* New York: Viking, 1966, pp. 270–273, 275.

The Responsibilities of the Novelist

French, Warren.   *Frank Norris.* New York: Twayne, 1962, pp. 36–48.

Geismar, Maxwell.   *Rebels and Ancestors.* Boston: Houghton Mifflin, 1953, pp. 44–46.

Hoffman, Charles G.   "Norris and the Responsibility of the Novelist," in *South Atlantic Quarterly.* LIV (October, 1955), pp. 508–515.

Johnson, George W.   "Frank Norris and Romance," in *American Literature.* XXXIII (March, 1961), pp. 52–54.

Millgate, Michael.   *American Social Fiction: James to Cozzens.* New York: Barnes & Noble, 1964, pp. 41–42, 50–52.

Walcutt, Charles C.   "Frank Norris on Realism and Naturalism," in *American Literature.* XIII (March, 1941), pp. 61–63.

Vandover and the Brute

Cooperman, Stanley.   "Frank Norris and the Werewolf of Guilt," in *Modern Language Quarterly.* XX (September, 1959), pp. 252–258.

Dillingham, William B.   *Frank Norris: Instinct and Art.* Lincoln: University of Nebraska Press, 1969, pp. 11–13, 68–74.

French, Warren. *Frank Norris*. New York: Twayne, 1962, pp. 52–61.

Frohock, W.M. *Frank Norris*. Minneapolis: University of Minnesota Press, 1968, pp. 16–20.

Geismar, Maxwell. *Rebels and Ancestors*. Boston: Houghton Mifflin, 1953, pp. 52–63.

Johnson, George W. "Frank Norris and Romance," in *American Literature*. XXXIII (March, 1961), pp. 54–57.

Lynn, Kenneth S. "Frank Norris: Mama's Boy," in *Dream of Success: A Study of the Modern American Imagination*. Boston: Little, Brown, 1955, pp. 168–173.

Marchand, Ernest. *Frank Norris: A Study*. New York: Octagon, 1964, pp. 67–72.

Morgan, H. Wayne. *American Writers in Rebellion from Twain to Dreiser*. New York: Hill and Wang, 1965, pp. 111–114.

Pizer, Donald. "Evolutionary Ethical Dualism in Frank Norris's *Vandover and the Brute* and *McTeague*," in *PMLA*. LXXVI (December, 1961), pp. 552–560.

_____. *The Novels of Frank Norris*. Bloomington: Indiana University Press, 1966, pp. 33–52.

Walcutt, Charles C. *American Literary Naturalism, A Divided Stream*. Minneapolis: University of Minnesota Press, 1956, pp. 118–125.

_____. "The Naturalism of *Vandover and the Brute*," in *Forms of Modern Fiction*. Edited by William Van O'Connor. Minneapolis: University of Minnesota Press, 1948, pp. 254–268.

THOMAS NORTON
(1532–1584)
AND
THOMAS SACKVILLE
(1536–1608)

Gorboduc

Babula, William. *"Gorboduc* as Apology and Critique," in *Tennessee Studies in Literature.* XVII (1972), pp. 37–43.

Baker, Howard. *Introduction to Tragedy: A Study in a Development of Form in* Gorboduc, The Spanish Tragedy, *and* Titus Andronicus. New York: Russell and Russell, 1965, pp. 9–47.

Berlin, Norman. *Thomas Sackville.* New York: Twayne, 1974, pp. 33–39, 44–59, 80–119.

Clemen, Wolfgang. *English Tragedy Before Shakespeare.* London: Methuen, 1961, pp. 56–74, 253–257.

Farnham, Willard. *The Medieval Heritage of Elizabethan Tragedy.* Berkeley: University of California Press, 1936, pp. 352–356.

Herrick, Marvin T. "Senecan Influence in *Gorboduc,*" in *Studies in Speech and Drama in Honor of Alexander M. Drummond.* Ithaca, N.Y.: Cornell University Press, 1944, pp. 78–104.

Johnson, S.F. "The Tragic Hero in Early Elizabethan Drama," in *Studies in the English Renaissance Drama in Memory of Karl Julius Holzknecht.* Edited by Josephine W. Bennett, Oscar Cargill and Vernon Hall, Jr. New York: New York University Press, 1959, pp. 157–171.

McDonald, Charles Osborne. *The Rhetoric of Tragedy: Form in Stuart Drama.* Amherst: University of Massachusetts Press, 1966, pp. 116–118.

McDonnell, R.F. *The Aspiring Mind.* Ann Arbor: University of Michigan Press, 1958, pp. 70–86.

Mehl, Dieter. *The Elizabethan Dumb Show: The History of a Dramatic Convention.* London: Methuen, 1964, pp. 29–45.

Mendonca, Barbara Heliodora Carniero de. "The Influence of *Gorboduc* on *King Lear,*" in *Shakespeare Survey.* XIII (1960), pp. 41–48.

Prior, Moody E. *The Language of Tragedy.* New York: Columbia University Press, 1947, pp. 31–33.

Ribner, Irving. *The English History Play in the Age of Shakespeare.* Princeton, N.J.: Princeton University Press, 1957, pp. 41–52.

Turner, Robert Y. "Pathos and the *Gorboduc* Tradition, 1560–1590," in *Huntington Library Quarterly.* XXV (1962), pp. 97–120.

Watson, Sarah Ruth.   "*Gorboduc* and the Theory of Tyrannicide," in *Modern Language Review.* XXXIV (July, 1939), pp. 355–366.

JOYCE CAROL OATES
(1938–   )

The Assassins

Allen, Mary. *The Necessary Blankness: Women in Major American Fiction of the Sixties.* Urbana: University of Illinois Press, 1976, pp. 133–159.

Cooke, M.G. "*The Assassins,*" in *Yale Review.* LXVI (Autumn, 1976), pp. 146–150.

Kramer, H. "Naipaul's *Guerrillas* and Oates' *Assassins,*" in *Commentary.* LXI (March, 1976), pp. 54–57.

O'Hara, J.D. "*The Assassins,*" in *New York Times Book Review.* (November 23, 1975), p. 10.

Do with Me What You Will

Allen, Mary. *The Necessary Blankness: Women in Major American Fiction of the Sixties.* Urbana: University of Illinois Press, 1976, pp. 133–159.

Bedient, Calvin. "*Do with Me What You Will,*" in *New York Times Book Review.* (October 14, 1973), pp. 1 & 18.

Burwell, Rose M. "The Process of Individuation as Narrative Structure: Joyce Carol Oates's *Do with Me What You Will,*" in *Critique: Studies in Modern Fiction.* XVII (1975), pp. 93–106.

Grant, Mary. *The Tragic Vision of Joyce Carol Oates.* Durham, N.C.: Duke University Press, 1978, pp. 67–72.

Shapiro, Charles. "Law and Love," in *New Republic.* CLXIX (October 27, 1973), pp. 26–27.

Expensive People

Allen, Mary. *The Necessary Blankness: Women in Major American Fiction of the Sixties.* Urbana: University of Illinois Press, 1976, pp. 133–159.

Grant, Mary K. *The Tragic Vision of Joyce Carol Oates.* Durham, N.C.: Duke University Press, 1978, pp. 48–51, 108–112.

Hicks, Granville. "What Is Reality?," in *Saturday Review of Literature.* LI (October 26, 1968), pp. 33–34.

Knowles, John. "Nada at the Core," in *New York Times Book Review.* (November 3, 1968), p. 5.

Pinkster, S. "Suburban Molesters: Joyce Carol Oates' *Expensive People,*" in *Midwest Quarterly.* XIX (October, 1977), pp. 89–103.

Price, Martin. "*Expensive People,*" in *Yale Review.* LVIII (March, 1969), pp. 468–471.

A Garden of Earthly Delights

Allen, Mary. *The Necessary Blankness: Women in Major American Fiction of the Sixties.* Urbana: University of Illinois Press, 1976, pp. 133–159.

Burwell, Rose M. "Joyce Carol Oates and an Old Master," in *Critique: Studies in Modern Fiction.* XV (1973), pp. 48–58.

Grant, Mary K. *The Tragic Vision of Joyce Carol Oates.* Durham, N.C.: Duke University Press, 1978, pp. 45–48, 81–83.

Hicks, Granville. "Fiction That Grows from the Ground," in *Saturday Review of Literature.* L (August 5, 1967), p. 23.

Janeway, Elizabeth. "Clara the Climber," in *New York Times Book Review.* (September 10, 1967), pp. 5, 63.

Marriages and Infidelities

Abrahams, William. "Stories of a Visionary," in *Saturday Review of Literature.* LV (September 23, 1972), pp. 76–80.

Allen, Mary. *The Necessary Blankness: Women in Major American Fiction of the Sixties.* Urbana: University of Illinois Press, 1976, pp. 133–159.

Bender, Eileen. "Autonomy and Influence: Joyce Carol Oates' *Marriages and Infidelities*," in *Soundings.* LVIII (Fall, 1975), pp. 390–406.

Markmann, C.L. "The Puzzle of People," in *Nation.* CCXV (December 4, 1972), pp. 566–568.

Pickering, Samuel F., Jr. "The Short Stories of Joyce Carol Oates," in *Georgia Review.* XXVIII (Summer, 1974), pp. 218–226.

Wood, Michael. "*Marriages and Infidelities*," in *New York Times Book Review.* (October 1, 1972), pp. 6, 43.

them

Adams, R.M. "*them*," in *New York Times Book Review.* (September 28, 1969), p. 4.

Allen, Mary. *The Necessary Blankness: Women in Major American Fiction of the Sixties.* Urbana: University of Illinois Press, 1976, pp. 133–159.

Bedient, Calvin. "Vivid and Dazzling," in *Nation.* CCIX (December 1, 1969), pp. 609–611.

DeMott, Benjamin. "The Necessity in Art of a Reflective Audience," in *Saturday Review of Literature.* LII (November 22, 1969), p. 71.

Giles, James R. "Suffering, Transcendence, and Artistic 'Form': Joyce Carol Oates's *them*," in *Arizona Quarterly.* XXXII (Autumn, 1976), pp. 213–226.

Grant, Mary K. *The Tragic Vision of Joyce Carol Oates.* Durham, N.C.: Duke University Press, 1978, pp. 51–55, 133–134.

L'Heureux, John.   "Mirage-Seekers," in *Atlantic Monthly*. CCXXIV (October, 1969), pp. 128–129.

Wonderland

Allen, Mary.   *The Necessary Blankness: Women in Major American Fiction of the Sixties*. Urbana: University of Illinois Press, 1976, pp. 133–159.

Gordon, J.B.   *"Wonderland,"* in *Commonweal*. XCV (February 11, 1972), pp. 449–450.

Grant, Mary K.   *The Tragic Vision of Joyce Carol Oates*. Durham, N.C.: Duke University Press, 1978, pp. 55–59, 77–80.

Hayes, B.P.   *"Wonderland,"* in *Saturday Review of Literature*. LIV (October 9, 1971), p. 38.

Waller, G.F.   "Joyce Carol Oates' *Wonderland*: An Introduction," in *Dalhousie Review*. LIV (Autumn, 1974), pp. 480–490.

Wolff, Geoffrey.   *"Wonderland,"* in *New York Times Book Review*. (October 24, 1971), p. 5.

SEAN O'CASEY
(1884–1964)

Cock-a-Doodle Dandy

Benstock, Bernard. *Paycocks and Others: Sean O'Casey's World.* New York: Barnes & Noble, 1976, pp. 53–58.

Cowasjee, Saros. *Sean O'Casey: The Man Behind the Play.* Edinburgh: Oliver and Boyd, 1963, pp. 205–214.

Daniel, Walter C. "The False Paradise Pattern in Sean O'Casey's *Cock-a-Doodle Dandy*," in *College Language Association Journal.* XIII (1969), pp. 137–143.

daRin, Doris. *Sean O'Casey.* New York: Frederick Ungar, 1976, pp. 124–143.

Frayne, John P. *Sean O'Casey.* New York: Columbia University Press, 1969, pp. 37–39.

Koslow, Jules. *The Green and the Red: Sean O'Casey—the Man and His Plays.* New York: Golden Griffin, 1950, pp. 113–119.

Krause, David. *Sean O'Casey: The Man and His Work.* New York: Macmillan, 1975, pp. 187–202.

Malone, Maureen. *The Plays of Sean O'Casey.* Carbondale: Southern Illinois University Press, 1969, pp. 118–149.

O'Casey, Eileen. *Sean.* New York: Coward, McCann and Geoghegan, 1972, pp. 200–202.

Rollins, Ronald G. "Clerical Blackness in the Green Garden: Heroine as Scapegoat in *Cock-a-Doodle Dandy*," in *James Joyce Quarterly.* VIII (1970), pp. 64–72.

————. "Dramatic Symbolism in Sean O'Casey's Dublin Trilogy," in *Philological Papers.* XV (1966), pp. 49–56.

————. "From Ritual to Romance in *Within the Gates* and *Cock-a-Doodle Dandy*," in *Modern Drama.* XVII (1974), pp. 11–18.

————. "O'Casey's *Cock-a-Doodle Dandy*," in *Explicator.* XXIII (1964), item 8.

Roy, Emil. *British Drama Since Shaw.* Carbondale: Southern Illinois University Press, 1972, pp. 79–81.

Smith, Bobby L. "Satire in O'Casey's *Cock-a-Doodle Dandy*," in *Renascence.* XIX (1967), pp. 64–73.

Worth, Katharine J. "O'Casey's Dramatic Symbolism," in *Modern Drama.* IV (1961), pp. 260–267.

Juno and the Paycock

Agate, James. "*Juno and the Paycock* and *The Plough and the Stars*," in *Sean O'Casey: Modern Judgements*. Edited by Ronald Ayling. London: Macmillan, 1969, pp. 76–81.

Armstrong, William A. "The Integrity of *Juno and the Paycock*," in *Modern Drama*. XVII (1974), pp. 1–9.

―――――. *Sean O'Casey*. London: Longmans, Green, 1967, pp. 13–15, 17.

Ayling, Ronald F. "*Juno and the Paycock*: A Textual Study," in *Modernist Studies: Literature & Culture 1920–1940*. II (1976), pp. 15–26.

―――――. "Popular Tradition and Individual Talent in Sean O'Casey's Dublin Trilogy," in *Journal of Modern Literature*. II (1972), pp. 491–504.

Benstock, Bernard. *Paycocks and Others: Sean O'Casey's World*. New York: Barnes & Noble, 1976, pp. 10–16.

Cowasjee, Saros. *O'Casey*. New York: Barnes & Noble, 1966, pp. 21–27.

―――――. *Sean O'Casey: The Man Behind the Play*. Edinburgh: Oliver and Boyd, 1963, pp. 43–60.

daRin, Doris. *Sean O'Casey*. New York: Frederick Ungar, 1976, pp. 38–55.

Durbach, Errol. "Peacocks and Mothers: Theme and Dramatic Metaphor in O'Casey's *Juno and the Paycock*," in *Modern Drama*. XV (1972), pp. 15–25.

Fallon, Gabriel. "The Man in the Plays," in *The World of Sean O'Casey*. Edited by Sean McCann. London: New English Library, 1966, pp. 206–208.

Frayne, John P. *Sean O'Casey*. New York: Columbia University Press, 1969, pp. 14–19.

Kaufman, Michael W. "O'Casey's Structural Design in *Juno and the Paycock*," in *Quarterly Journal of Speech*. LVIII (1972), pp. 191–198.

Koslow, Jules. *Sean O'Casey: The Man and His Plays*. New York: Citadel Press, 1966, pp. 23–25, 30–32.

Krause, David. *Sean O'Casey: The Man and His Work*. New York: Macmillan, 1975, pp. 68–79.

Mabley, Edward. *Dramatic Construction: An Outline of Basic Principles*. Philadelphia: Chilton, 1972, pp. 173–186.

Malone, Andrew. *The Irish Drama*. Bronx, N.Y.: Benjamin Blom, 1965, pp. 209–219.

Malone, Maureen. *The Plays of Sean O'Casey*. Carbondale: Southern Illinois University Press, 1969, pp. 29–37.

O'Casey, Eileen. *Sean*. New York: Coward, McCann and Geoghegan, 1972, pp. 16–18.

Rollins, Ronald G. "Dramatic Symbolism in Sean O'Casey's Dublin Trilogy," in *Philological Papers*. XV (1966), pp. 49–56.

_____. "Form and Content in Sean O'Casey's Dublin Trilogy," in *Modern Drama*. VIII (1966), pp. 419–425.

Roy, Emil. *British Drama Since Shaw.* Carbondale: Southern Illinois University Press, 1972, pp. 72–78.

Worth, Katharine J. "O'Casey's Dramatic Symbolism," in *Modern Drama*. IV (1961), pp. 260–267.

Wyatt, Euphemia V.R. "*Juno and the Paycock*," in *Catholic World*. CL (1940), pp. 730–731.

The Plough and the Stars

Agate, James. "*Juno and the Paycock* and *The Plough and the Stars*," in *Sean O'Casey: Modern Judgements*. Edited by Ronald Ayling. London: Macmillan, 1969, pp. 76–81.

Armstrong, William A. *Sean O'Casey*. London: Longmans, Green, 1967, pp. 15–17.

_____. "The Sources and Themes of *The Plough and the Stars*," in *Modern Drama*. IV (December, 1961), pp. 234–242.

Ayling, Ronald. "Character Control and 'Alienation' in *The Plough and the Stars*," in *James Joyce Quarterly*. VIII (1970), pp. 29–47.

_____. "Ideas and Ideology in *The Plough and the Stars*," in *The Sean O'Casey Review*. II (1976), pp. 115–136.

Benstock, Bernard. *Paycocks and Others: Sean O'Casey's World*. New York: Barnes & Noble, 1976, pp. 25–34.

Cowasjee, Saros. *O'Casey*. New York: Barnes & Noble, 1966, pp. 27–39.

_____. *Sean O'Casey: The Man Behind the Play*. Edinburgh: Oliver and Boyd, 1963, pp. 61–84.

daRin, Doris. *Sean O'Casey*. New York: Frederick Ungar, 1976, pp. 56–77.

DeBaun, Vincent C. "Sean O'Casey and the Road to Expressionism," in *Modern Drama*. IV (December, 1961), pp. 254–259.

Dorcey, Donal. "The Great Occasions," in *The World of Sean O'Casey*. Edited by Sean McCann. London: New English Library, 1966, pp. 58–72.

Fallon, Gabriel. "The Man in the Plays," in *The World of Sean O'Casey*. Edited by Sean McCann. London: New English Library, 1966, pp. 208–209.

Frayne, John P. *Sean O'Casey*. New York: Columbia University Press, 1969, pp. 19–25.

Freedman, Morris. *The Moral Impulse: Modern Drama from Ibsen to the Present*. Carbondale: Southern Illinois University Press, 1967, pp. 67–73.

Humbert, Michel. "Some Loved the Plough, Others Preferred the Stars," in *The Sean O'Casey Review*. II (1976), pp. 14–15.

Kaufman, Michael W. "The Position of *The Plough and the Stars* in O'Casey's Dublin Trilogy," in *James Joyce Quarterly*. VIII (1970), pp. 48–63.

Koslow, Jules. *Sean O'Casey: The Man and His Plays*. New York: Citadel Press, 1966, pp. 25–30, 33–36.

Krause, David. *Sean O'Casey: The Man and His Work*. New York: Macmillan, 1975, pp. 69–75.

Lindsay, Jack. "*The Plough and the Stars* Reconsidered," in *The Sean O'Casey Review*. II (1976), pp. 187–195.

Malone, Maureen. *The Plays of Sean O'Casey*. Carbondale: Southern Illinois University Press, 1969, pp. 11–15.

O'Casey, Sean. "*The Plough and the Stars* in Retrospect," in *The Sean O'Casey Review*. II (1976), pp. 157–163.

O'Riordan, John. "O'Casey, the Peerless Ploughman," in *The Sean O'Casey Review*. II (1976), pp. 177–186.

Pixley, Edward E. "*The Plough and the Stars*—The Destructive Consequences of Human Folly," in *Educational Theatre Journal*. XXIII (1971), pp. 75–82.

Reiter, Seymour. *World Theatre: Structure and Meaning of Drama*. New York: Horizon Press, 1973, pp. 195–213.

Smith, Bobby L. "Satire in *The Plough and the Stars*: A Tragedy in Four Acts," in *Ball State University Forum*. X (1969), pp. 3–11.

Purple Dust

Armstrong, William A. *Sean O'Casey*. London: Longmans, Green, 1967, pp. 21–22.

Benstock, Bernard. *Paycocks and Others: Sean O'Casey's World*. New York: Barnes & Noble, 1976, pp. 34–43.

Casey, Kevin. "The Excitements and the Disappointments," in *The World of Sean O'Casey*. Edited by Sean McCann. London: New English Library, 1966, pp. 222–225.

Cowasjee, Saros. *O'Casey*. New York: Barnes & Noble, 1966, pp. 87–90.

————. *Sean O'Casey: The Man Behind the Play*. Edinburgh: Oliver and Boyd, 1963, pp. 61–84.

Daniel, Walter C. "Patterns of Greek Comedy in O'Casey's *Purple Dust*," in *Bulletin of the New York Public Library*. LXVI (November, 1962), pp. 603–612.

daRin, Doris. *Sean O'Casey*. New York: Frederick Ungar, 1976, pp. 78–98.

Frayne, John P. *Sean O'Casey*. New York: Columbia University Press, 1976, pp. 32–34.

Hogan, Robert. *After the Irish Renaissance.* Minneapolis: University of Minnesota Press, 1967, pp. 239–241.

Koslow, Jules. *The Green and the Red: Sean O'Casey—the Man and His Plays.* New York: Golden Griffin, 1950, pp. 77–84.

————. *Sean O'Casey: The Man and His Plays.* New York: Citadel Press, 1966, pp. 69–75.

Krause, David. *Sean O'Casey: The Man and His Work.* New York: Macmillan, 1975, pp. 177–187.

McLaughlin, John J. "Political Allegory in O'Casey's *Purple Dust*," in *Modern Drama.* XIII (1970), pp. 47–53.

Malone, Maureen. *The Plays of Sean O'Casey.* Carbondale: Southern Illinois University Press, 1969, pp. 92–94.

O'Casey, Eileen. *Sean.* New York: Coward, McCann and Geoghegan, 1972, pp. 213–217.

Rollins, Ronald G. "O'Casey's *Purple Dust*," in *Explicator.* XXVI (October, 1967), item 19.

————. "Shaw and O'Casey: John Bull and His Other Island," in *Shaw Review.* X (1967), pp. 60–69.

Red Roses for Me

Armstrong, William A. *Sean O'Casey.* London: Longmans, Green, 1967, pp. 23–24.

Benstock, Bernard. *Paycocks and Others: Sean O'Casey's World.* New York: Barnes & Noble, 1976, pp. 67–73.

Casey, Kevin. "The Excitements and the Disappointments," in *The World of Sean O'Casey.* Edited by Sean McCann. London: New English Library, 1966, pp. 225–227.

Clurman, Harold. *Lies Like Truth.* New York: Macmillan, 1958, pp. 122–124.

Cowasjee, Saros. *O'Casey.* New York: Barnes & Noble, 1966, pp. 75–82.

————. *Sean O'Casey: The Man Behind the Play.* Edinburgh: Oliver and Boyd, 1963, pp. 180–194.

daRin, Doris. *Sean O'Casey.* New York: Frederick Ungar, 1976, pp. 99–123.

Esslinger, Pat M. "Sean O'Casey and the Lockout of 1913: 'Materia Poetica' of the Two Red Plays," in *Modern Drama.* VI (1963), pp. 53–63.

Frayne, John P. *Sean O'Casey.* New York: Columbia University Press, 1976, pp. 34–36.

Koslow, Jules. *The Green and the Red: Sean O'Casey—the Man and His Plays.* New York: Golden Griffin, 1950, pp. 95–104.

————. *Sean O'Casey: The Man and His Plays.* New York: Citadel Press, 1966, pp. 85–94.

Krause, David. *Sean O'Casey: The Man and His Work.* New York: Macmillan, 1975, pp. 164–174.

Lewis, Allan. *The Contemporary Theatre.* New York: Crown, 1962, pp. 169–191.

————. "*Red Roses for Me,*" in *America.* XCIV (January 21, 1956), pp. 459–460.

Malone, Maureen. *The Plays of Sean O'Casey.* Carbondale: Southern Illinois University Press, 1969, pp. 103–109.

————. "*Red Roses for Me*: Fact and Symbol," in *Modern Drama.* IX (1966), pp. 147–152.

Stock, A.G. "The Heroic Image: *Red Roses for Me,*" in *Sean O'Casey: Modern Judgements.* Edited by Ronald Ayling. London: Macmillan, 1969, pp. 126–130.

The Shadow of a Gunman

Armstrong, William A. "History, Autobiography and *The Shadow of a Gunman,*" in *Modern Drama.* II (February, 1960), pp. 417–424.

Ayling, Ronald. "Popular Tradition and Individual Talent in Sean O'Casey's Dublin Trilogy," in *Journal of Modern Literature.* II (1972), pp. 491–504.

Benstock, Bernard. *Paycocks and Others: Sean O'Casey's World.* New York: Barnes & Noble, 1976, pp. 19–25.

Cowasjee, Saros. *O'Casey.* New York: Barnes & Noble, 1966, pp. 15–31.

————. *Sean O'Casey: The Man Behind the Play.* Edinburgh: Oliver and Boyd, 1963, pp. 28–39.

daRin, Doris. *Sean O'Casey.* New York: Frederick Ungar, 1976, pp. 24–37.

Dorcey, Donal. "The Great Occasions," in *The World of Sean O'Casey.* Edited by Sean McCann. London: New English Library, 1966, pp. 50–52.

Fallon, Gabriel. "The Man in the Plays," in *The World of Sean O'Casey.* Edited by Sean McCann. London: New English Library, 1966, pp. 199–205.

Fitzgerald, John J. "Sean O'Casey's Dramatic Slums," in *Descant.* X (Fall, 1965), pp. 26–34.

Frayne, John P. *Sean O'Casey.* New York: Columbia University Press, 1976, pp. 12–14.

Freedman, Morris. "The Modern Tragicomedy of Wilde and O'Casey," in *College English.* XXV (April, 1964), pp. 518–527.

Koslow, Jules. *The Green and the Red: Sean O'Casey—the Man and His Plays.* New York: Golden Griffin, 1950, pp. 49–58.

————. *Sean O'Casey: The Man and His Plays.* New York: Citadel Press, 1966, pp. 22–23, 42–43.

Krause, David   *Sean O'Casey: The Man and His Work.* New York: Macmillan, 1975, pp. 66–68, 88–91.

McHugh, Roger.   "The Legacy of Sean O'Casey," in *Texas Quarterly.* VIII (1965), pp. 123–137.

Malone, Maureen.   *The Plays of Sean O'Casey.* Carbondale: Southern Illinois University Press, 1969, pp. 22–24.

O'Donovan, John.   "The Big Three," in *The World of Sean O'Casey.* Edited by Sean McCann. London: New English Library, 1966, pp. 186–189.

O'Donovan, Michael.   *A Short History of Irish Literature.* New York: Putnam's, 1967, pp. 217–219.

Rollins, Ronald G.   "Form and Content in Sean O'Casey's Dublin Trilogy," in *Modern Drama.* VIII (1966), pp. 419–425.

————.   "O'Casey and Synge: The Irish Hero as Playboy and Gunman," in *Arizona Quarterly.* XXII (1966), pp. 217–222.

Snowden, J.A.   "Dialect in the Plays of Sean O'Casey," in *Modern Drama.* XIV (1971), pp. 387–391.

Tynan, Kenneth.   *Curtains: Selections from the Drama Criticism and Related Writings.* New York: Atheneum, 1961, pp. 285–288.

The Silver Tassie

Armstrong, William A.   *Sean O'Casey.* London: Longmans, Green, 1967, pp. 18–20.

Ayling, Ronald.   "Feathers Finely Aflutter," in *Modern Drama.* VII (1964), pp. 135–147.

Benstock, Bernard.   *Paycocks and Others: Sean O'Casey's World.* New York: Barnes & Noble, 1976, pp. 15–19, 98–104.

Cowasjee, Saros.   *O'Casey.* New York: Barnes & Noble, 1966, pp. 42–56.

————.   *Sean O'Casey: The Man Behind the Play.* Edinburgh: Oliver and Boyd, 1963, pp. 102–136.

daRin, Doris.   *Sean O'Casey.* New York: Frederick Ungar, 1976, pp. 152–157.

DeBaun, Vincent C.   "Sean O'Casey and the Road to Expressionism," in *Modern Drama.* IV (1961), pp. 254–259.

Frayne, John P.   *Sean O'Casey.* New York: Columbia University Press, 1969, pp. 25–30.

Henn, T.R.   *The Harvest of Tragedy.* London: Methuen, 1956, pp. 213–214.

Hughes, Catharine.   *Plays, Politics and Polemics.* New York: Drama Book Specialists, 1973, pp. 69–76.

Kavanagh, Peter.   *The Story of the Abbey Theatre from Its Origins to the Present.* New York: Devin-Adair, 1950, pp. 139–143.

Koslow, Jules. *The Green and the Red: Sean O'Casey—the Man and His Plays.* New York: Golden Griffin, 1950, pp. 49–58.

————. *Sean O'Casey: The Man and His Plays.* New York: Citadel Press, 1966, pp. 45–54.

Krause, David. "Playwright's Not for Burning," in *Virginia Quarterly Review.* XXXIV (1958), pp. 60–76.

————. *Sean O'Casey: The Man and His Work.* New York: Macmillan, 1975, pp. 109–122.

McHugh, Roger. "The Legacy of Sean O'Casey," in *Texas Quarterly.* VIII (1965), pp. 123–137.

Malone, Maureen. *The Plays of Sean O'Casey.* Carbondale: Southern Illinois University Press, 1969, pp. 43–52.

Morgan, Charles. *"The Silver Tassie,"* in *Sean O'Casey: Modern Judgements.* Edited by Ronald Ayling. London: Macmillan, 1969, pp. 88–90.

O'Casey, Eileen. *Sean.* New York: Coward, McCann and Geoghegan, 1972, pp. 83–103.

O'Casey, Sean. *Blasts and Benedictions.* London: Macmillan, 1967, pp. 99–110.

Rollins, Ronald G. "O'Casey, O'Neill and Expressionism in *The Silver Tassie,*" in *Bucknell Review.* X (1962), pp. 64–69.

————. "O'Casey's *The Silver Tassie,*" in *Explicator.* XX (1962), item 62.

Smith, B.L. "From Athlete to Statue: Satire in Sean O'Casey's *The Silver Tassie,*" in *Arizona Quarterly.* XXVII (1971), pp. 347–361.

Smith, Winifred. "The Dying God in the Modern Theatre," in *Review of Religion.* V (March,1941), pp. 269–273.

Williams, Raymond. *Drama from Ibsen to Brecht.* London: Chatto and Windus, 1968, pp. 151–153.

Within the Gates

Armstrong, William A. *Sean O'Casey.* London: Longmans, Green, 1967, p. 20.

Ayling, Ronald. "Ritual Patterns in Sean O'Casey's *Within the Gates,*" in *Theoria: A Journal of Studies in the Arts, Humanities and Social Sciences.* XLIII (1974), pp. 19–27.

Benstock, Bernard. *Paycocks and Others: Sean O'Casey's World.* New York: Barnes & Noble, 1976, pp. 233–237.

Brown, John Mason. *Two on the Aisle.* New York: Norton, 1938, pp. 126–130.

Casey, Kevin. "The Excitements and the Disappointments," in *The World of Sean O'Casey.* Edited by Sean McCann. London: New English Library, 1966, pp. 218–222.

Cowasjee, Saros. *O'Casey.* New York: Barnes & Noble, 1966, pp. 56–65.

————. *Sean O'Casey: The Man Behind the Play.* Edinburgh: Oliver and Boyd, 1963, pp. 137–153.

daRin, Doris. *Sean O'Casey.* New York: Frederick Ungar, 1976, pp. 158–160.

Frayne, John P. *Sean O'Casey.* New York: Columbia University Press, 1969, pp. 31–32.

Goldstone, Herbert. "The Unevenness of O'Casey: A Study of *Within the Gates,*" in *Forum.* IV (Winter–Spring, 1965), pp. 37–42.

Harman, Bill J. and Ronald G. Rollins. "Mythical Dimensions in O'Casey's *Within the Gates,*" in *West Virginia University Philological Papers.* XVI (1967), pp. 72–78.

Knight, G. Wilson. *The Golden Labyrinth: A Study of British Drama.* New York: Norton, 1962, pp. 376–378.

Koslow, Jules. *The Green and the Red: Sean O'Casey—the Man and His Plays.* New York: Golden Griffin, 1950, pp. 87–95.

————. *Sean O'Casey: The Man and His Plays.* New York: Citadel Press, 1966, pp. 55–68.

Krause, David. *Sean O'Casey: The Man and His Work.* New York: Macmillan, 1975, pp. 144–158.

MacCarthy, Desmond. *Drama.* London: Putnam, 1940, pp. 349–354.

Malone, Maureen. *The Plays of Sean O'Casey.* Carbondale: Southern Illinois University Press, 1969, pp. 54–59.

O'Casey, Eileen. *Sean.* New York: Coward, McCann and Geoghegan, 1972, pp. 128–144.

O'Casey, Sean. *Blasts and Benedictions.* London: Macmillan, 1967, pp. 111–131.

Rollins, Ronald G. "Desire versus Damnation in O'Casey's *Within the Gates* and Donleavy's *The Ginger Man,*" in *The Sean O'Casey Review.* I (1975), pp. 41–47.

————. "From Ritual to Romance in *Within the Gates* and *Cock-a-Doodle Dandy,*" in *Modern Drama.* XVII (1974), pp. 11–18.

————. "O'Casey's *Within the Gates,*" in *Explicator.* XXIX (1970), item 8.

Todd, R. Mary. "The Two Published Versions of Sean O'Casey's *Within the Gates,*" in *Modern Drama.* X (1968), pp. 346–355.

Washburn, A.M. "Form and Effect: Mr. O'Casey's *Within the Gates,*" in *Harvard Advocate.* CXXI (Christmas, 1934), pp. 73–76.

Worth, Katharine J. "O'Casey's Dramatic Symbolism," in *Modern Drama.* IV (1961), pp. 260–267.

EDWIN O'CONNOR
(1918–1968)

All in the Family

Darack, Arthur. "Politics and Patriarchs," in *Saturday Review of Literature.* XLIX (October 1, 1966), p. 64.

Jones, Howard M. "Politics, Mr. O'Connor, and the Family Novel," in *Atlantic Monthly.* CCXVIII (October, 1966), pp. 117–120.

Kenny, Herbert. "Boston as Barchester," in *New York Times Book Review.* (September 25, 1966), p. 4.

Oliver, Edith. "The Unconquering Hero Comes," in *New Yorker.* XLII (October 15, 1966), pp. 241–242.

Rank, Hugh. *Edwin O'Connor.* New York: Twayne, 1974, pp. 151–178.

The Edge of Sadness

Galbraith, John K. "Sadness in Boston," in *New Yorker.* XXXVII (June 24, 1961), pp. 87–94.

Hicks, Granville. "Behind the Lace Curtains," in *Saturday Review of Literature.* XLIV (June 10, 1961), p. 20.

Kelleher, J.V. "Curious Indeed the Way God Works," in *New York Times Book Review.* (June 4, 1961), pp. 1, 33.

Rank, Hugh. *Edwin O'Connor.* New York: Twayne, 1974, pp. 103–128.

————. "O'Connor's Image of the Priest," in *New England Quarterly.* XLI (March, 1968), pp. 3–29.

Sandra, Sister Mary. "The Priest-Hero in Modern Fiction," in *Personalist.* XLVI (October, 1965), pp. 527–542.

Stuckey, W.J. *The Pulitzer Prize Novels: A Critical Backward Look.* Norman: University of Oklahoma Press, 1966, pp. 197–204.

The Last Hurrah

Blotner, Joseph. *The Modern American Political Novel.* Austin: University of Texas Press, 1966, pp. 82–85.

Boulger, James D. "Puritan Allegory in Four Modern Novels," in *Thought.* XLIV (Autumn, 1969), pp. 413–432.

Goodwin, George, Jr. "The Last Hurrahs: George Apley and Frank Skeffington," in *Massachusetts Review.* I (May, 1960), pp. 461–471.

Haslam, Gerald. "*The Last Hurrah* and American Bossism," in *Rendezvous: Journal of Arts and Letters.* VIII (1973), pp. 33–44.

Milne, Gordon. *The American Political Novel.* Norman: University of Oklahoma Press, 1966, pp. 82–85.

O'Connor, Edwin. "James Michael Curley and *The Last Hurrah*," in *Atlantic Monthly.* CCVIII (September, 1961), pp. 48–50.

Rank, Hugh. *Edwin O'Connor.* New York: Twayne, 1974, pp. 57–95, 160–163.

West, Anthony. *Principles and Persuasions; the Literary Essays of Anthony West.* New York: Harcourt, Brace, 1957, pp. 219–224.

FLANNERY O'CONNOR
(1925–1964)

"The Artificial Nigger"

Browning, Preston M., Jr. *Flannery O'Connor.* Carbondale: Southern Illinois University Press, 1974, pp. 60–69.

Byrd, Turner F. "Ironic Dimension in Flannery O'Connor's 'The Artificial Nigger,' " in *Mississippi Quarterly.* XXI (1968), pp. 243–251.

Drake, Robert. *Flannery O'Connor: A Critical Essay.* Grand Rapids, Mich.: Eerdmans, 1966, pp. 28–29.

Eggenschwiler, David. *The Christian Humanism of Flannery O'Connor.* Detroit: Wayne State University Press, 1972, pp. 85–91.

Feeley, Sister Kathleen. *Flannery O'Connor: Voice of the Peacock.* New Brunswick, N.J.: Rutgers University Press, 1972, pp. 120–124.

Frakes, James R. and Isadore Traschen. *Short Fiction: A Critical Collection.* Englewood Cliffs, N.J.: Prentice-Hall, 1969, pp. 126–129.

Hays, Peter L. "Dante, Tobit, and 'The Artificial Nigger,' " in *Studies in Short Fiction.* V (1968), pp. 263–268.

Malin, Irving. "Flannery O'Connor and the Grotesque," in *The Added Dimension: The Art and Mind of Flannery O'Connor.* Edited by Melvin J. Friedman and Lewis A. Lawson. New York: Fordham University Press, 1966, pp. 115–117.

Martin, Carter W. *The True Country: Themes in the Fiction of Flannery O'Connor.* Nashville, Tenn.: Vanderbilt University Press, 1969, pp. 112–116, 148–151.

May, John R. *The Pruning Word: The Parables of Flannery O'Connor.* Notre Dame, Ind.: Notre Dame University Press, 1976, pp. 76–80.

Muller, Gilbert H. *Nightmares and Visions: Flannery O'Connor and the Catholic Grotesque.* Athens: University of Georgia Press, 1972, pp. 71–75.

Nance, William L. "Flannery O'Connor: The Trouble with Being a Prophet," in *University Review.* XXXVI (1969), pp. 101–108.

Orvell, Miles. *Invisible Parade: The Fiction of Flannery O'Connor.* Philadelphia: Temple University Press, 1972, pp. 152–160.

Stephens, Martha. *The Question of Flannery O'Connor.* Baton Rouge: Louisiana State University Press, 1973, pp. 165–167.

Taylor, Henry. "The Halt Shall be Gathered Together: Physical Deformity in the Fiction of Flannery O'Connor," in *Western Humanities Review.* XXII (1968), pp. 329–331.

Walters, Dorothy. *Flannery O'Connor.* New York: Twayne, 1973, pp. 118–121.

"The Displaced Person"

Drake, Robert. *Flannery O'Connor: A Critical Essay.* Grand Rapids, Mich.: Eerdmans, 1966, pp. 26–28.

Eggenschwiler, David. *The Christian Humanism of Flannery O'Connor.* Detroit: Wayne State University Press, 1972, pp. 78–80, 95–97.

Feeley, Sister Kathleen. *Flannery O'Connor: Voice of the Peacock.* New Brunswick, N.J.: Rutgers University Press, 1972, pp. 172–176.

Fitzgerald, Robert. "The Countryside and the True Country," in *Sewanee Review.* LXX (1962), pp. 380–394. Reprinted in *Flannery O'Connor.* Edited by Robert E. Reiter. St. Louis, Mo.: B. Herder, 1968, pp. 69–82.

Hyman, Stanley Edgar. *Flannery O'Connor.* Minneapolis: University of Minnesota Press, 1966, pp. 17–18.

Joselyn, Sister M. "Thematic Centers in 'The Displaced Person,' " in *Studies in Short Fiction.* I (1964), pp. 85–92. Reprinted in *Flannery O'Connor.* Edited by Robert E. Reiter. St. Louis, Mo.: B. Herder, 1968, pp. 83–92.

Klevar, Harvey. "Image and Imagination: Flannery O'Connor's Front Page Fiction," in *Journal of Modern Literature.* IV (1974), pp. 126–132.

McFarland, Dorothy Tuck. *Flannery O'Connor.* New York: Frederick Ungar, 1976, pp. 30–35.

Malin, Irving. *New American Gothic.* Carbondale: Southern Illinois University Press, 1962, pp. 95–97.

Martin, Carter W. *The True Country: Themes in the Fiction of Flannery O'Connor.* Nashville, Tenn.: Vanderbilt University Press, 1969, pp. 93–98.

May, John R. *The Pruning Word: The Parables of Flannery O'Connor.* Notre Dame, Ind.: Notre Dame University Press, 1976, pp. 89–94.

Mooney, Harry J. "Moments of Eternity: A Study of the Short Stories of Flannery O'Connor," in *The Shapeless God: Essays on Modern Fiction.* Edited by Harry J. Mooney, Jr. and Thomas F. Staley. Pittsburgh: University of Pittsburgh Press, 1968, pp. 122–125.

Orvell, Miles. *Invisible Parade: The Fiction of Flannery O'Connor.* Philadelphia: Temple University Press, 1972, pp. 141–152.

Walters, Dorothy. *Flannery O'Connor.* New York: Twayne, 1973, pp. 121–124.

"Everything That Rises Must Converge"

Browning, Preston M., Jr. *Flannery O'Connor.* Carbondale: Southern Illinois University Press, 1974, pp. 99–107.

Esch, Robert M. "O'Connor's 'Everything That Rises Must Converge,'" in *Explicator*. XXVII (1969), item 58.

Feeley, Sister Kathleen. *Flannery O'Connor: Voice of the Peacock*. New Brunswick, N.J.: Rutgers University Press, 1972, pp. 101–105.

Hendin, Josephine. *The World of Flannery O'Connor*. Bloomington: Indiana University Press, 1970, pp. 102–108.

Hyman, Stanley Edgar. *Flannery O'Connor*. Minneapolis: University of Minnesota Press, 1966, pp. 27–28.

Kane, Patricia. "Flannery O'Connor's 'Everything That Rises Must Converge,'" in *Critique*. VIII (1965), pp. 85–91.

Keller, Jane C. "The Figures of the Empiricist and the Rationalist in the Fiction of Flannery O'Connor," in *Arizona Quarterly*. XXVIII (1972), pp. 263–273.

McDermott, John V. "Julian's Journey into Hell: Flannery O'Connor's Allegory of Pride," in *Mississippi Quarterly*. XXVIII (1975), pp. 171–179.

McFarland, Dorothy Tuck. *Flannery O'Connor*. New York: Frederick Ungar, 1976, pp. 44–46.

Maida, Patricia Dineen. " 'Convergence' in Flannery O'Connor's 'Everything That Rises Must Converge,'" in *Studies in Short Fiction*. VII (1970), pp. 549–555.

May, John R. *The Pruning Word: The Parables of Flannery O'Connor*. Notre Dame, Ind.: Notre Dame University Press, 1976, pp. 94–97.

Montgomery, Marion. "On Flannery O'Connor's 'Everything That Rises Must Converge,'" in *Critique*. XIII (1971), pp. 15–29.

Orvell, Miles. *Invisible Parade: The Fiction of Flannery O'Connor*. Philadelphia: Temple University Press, 1972, pp. 6–10.

Stephens, Martha. *The Question of Flannery O'Connor*. Baton Rouge: Louisiana State University Press, 1973, pp. 16–17.

Walters, Dorothy. *Flannery O'Connor*. New York: Twayne, 1973, pp. 126–130.

"Good Country People"

Browning, Preston M., Jr. *Flannery O'Connor*. Carbondale: Southern Illinois University Press, 1974, pp. 42–51.

Eggenschwiler, David. *The Christian Humanism of Flannery O'Connor*. Detroit: Wayne State University Press, 1972, pp. 52–57.

Feeley, Sister Kathleen. *Flannery O'Connor: Voice of the Peacock*. New Brunswick, N.J.: Rutgers University Press, 1972, pp. 23–28.

Hendin, Josephine. *The World of Flannery O'Connor*. Bloomington: Indiana University Press, 1970, pp. 69–75.

Hyman, Stanley Edgar. *Flannery O'Connor.* Minneapolis: University of Minnesota Press, 1966, pp. 16–17.

Jones, Bartlett C. "Depth Psychology and Literary Study," in *Midcontinent American Studies Journal.* V (Fall, 1964), pp. 50–56.

McFarland, Dorothy Tuck. *Flannery O'Connor.* New York: Frederick Ungar, 1976, pp. 35–40.

Martin, Carter W. *The True Country: Themes in the Fiction of Flannery O'Connor.* Nashville, Tenn.: Vanderbilt University Press, 1969, pp. 62–65.

May, John R. *The Pruning Word: The Parables of Flannery O'Connor.* Notre Dame, Ind.: Notre Dame University Press, 1976, pp. 86–89.

Mooney, Harry J. "Moments of Eternity: A Study of the Short Stories of Flannery O'Connor," in *The Shapeless God: Essays on Modern Fiction.* Edited by Harry J. Mooney, Jr. and Thomas F. Staley. Pittsburgh: University of Pittsburgh Press, 1968, pp. 131–132.

Orvell, Miles. *Invisible Parade: The Fiction of Flannery O'Connor.* Philadelphia: Temple University Press, 1972, pp. 136–141.

Walters, Dorothy. *Flannery O'Connor.* New York: Twayne, 1973, pp. 64–67.

Wynne, Judith F. "The Sacramental Irony of Flannery O'Connor," in *Southern Literary Journal.* VII (Spring, 1975), pp. 33–49.

"A Good Man Is Hard to Find"

Browning, Preston M., Jr. *Flannery O'Connor.* Carbondale: Southern Illinois University Press, 1974, pp. 54–59.

Doxey, William S. "A Dissenting Opinion of Flannery O'Connor's 'A Good Man Is Hard to Find,' " in *Studies in Short Fiction.* X (1973), pp. 199–204.

Eggenschwiler, David. *The Christian Humanism of Flannery O'Connor.* Detroit: Wayne State University Press, 1972, pp. 46–52.

Feeley, Sister Kathleen. *Flannery O'Connor: Voice of the Peacock.* New Brunswick, N.J.: Rutgers University Press, 1972, pp. 69–76.

Frieling, Kenneth. "Flannery O'Connor's Vision: The Violence of Revelation," in *The Fifties: Fiction, Poetry, Drama.* Edited by Warren French. Deland, Fla.: Everett/Edward, 1970, pp. 111–120.

Gordon, Caroline and Allen Tate. *The House of Fiction: An Anthology of the Short Story with Commentary.* New York: Scribner's, 1960, pp. 384–386.

Hamblen, Abigail A. "Flannery O'Connor's Study of Innocence and Evil," in *University Review.* XXXIV (1968), pp. 295–297.

Hendin, Josephine. *The World of Flannery O'Connor.* Bloomington: Indiana University Press, 1970, pp. 148–151.

Kropf, C.R. "Theme and Setting in 'A Good Man Is Hard to Find,' " in *Renascence.* XXIV (1972), pp. 177–180, 206.

McFarland, Dorothy Tuck. *Flannery O'Connor.* New York: Frederick Ungar, 1976, pp. 17–22.

Marks, W.S., III. "Advertisements for Grace: Flannery O'Connor's 'A Good Man Is Hard to Find,' " in *Studies in Short Fiction.* IV (1966), pp. 19–27.

Martin, Carter W. *The True Country: Themes in the Fiction of Flannery O'Connor.* Nashville, Tenn.: Vanderbilt University Press, 1969, pp. 163–167.

Martin, Sister M. "O'Connor's 'A Good Man Is Hard to Find,' " in *Explicator.* XXIV (1965), item 19.

May, John R. *The Pruning Word: The Parables of Flannery O'Connor.* Notre Dame, Ind.: Notre Dame University Press, 1976, pp. 60–64.

Mellard, James M. *Four Modes: A Rhetoric of Modern Fiction.* New York: Macmillan, 1973, pp. 39–42.

Montgomery, Marion. "Miss Flannery's 'A Good Man,' " in *Denver Quarterly.* III (Autumn, 1968), pp. 1–19.

Orvell, Miles. *Invisible Parade: The Fiction of Flannery O'Connor.* Philadelphia: Temple University Press, 1972, pp. 130–136.

Quinn, John J. "A Reading of Flannery O'Connor," in *Thought.* XLVIII (1973), pp. 520–531.

Stephens, Martha. *The Question of Flannery O'Connor.* Baton Rouge: Louisiana State University Press, 1973, pp. 17–36.

Walters, Dorothy. *Flannery O'Connor.* New York: Twayne, 1973, pp. 70–73.

Woodward, Robert H. "A Good Route Is Hard to Find: Place Names and Setting in O'Connor's 'A Good Man Is Hard to Find,' " in *Notes on Contemporary Literature.* III (1973), pp. 2–6.

Wynne, Judith F. "The Sacramental Irony of Flannery O'Connor," in *Southern Literary Journal.* VII (Spring, 1975), pp. 33–49.

Mystery and Manners

Driskell, Leon V. and Joan T. Brittain. *The Eternal Crossroads: The Art of Flannery O'Connor.* Lexington: University Press of Kentucky, 1971, pp. 7–9.

Friedman, Melvin J. "By and About Flannery O'Connor," in *Journal of Modern Literature.* I (1970), pp. 288–292.

McDowell, Frederick P. "Toward the Luminous and the Numinous: The Art of Flannery O'Connor," in *Southern Review.* IX (1973), pp. 998–1013.

Maloff, Saul. "On Flannery O'Connor," in *Commonweal.* XC (August 8, 1969), pp. 490–491.

Mano, D. Keith. "*Mystery and Manners,*" in *New York Times Book Review.* (May 25, 1969), pp. 6–7, 20.

May, John R. *The Pruning Word: The Parables of Flannery O'Connor.* Notre Dame, Ind.: Notre Dame University Press, 1976, pp. 6–10.

Oates, Joyce Carol. "Realism and Distance and Realism of Immediacy," in *Southern Review.* VII (1971), pp. 295–313.

Sessions, William A. *"Mystery and Manners,"* in *Studies in Short Fiction.* VIII (1971), pp. 491–494.

The Violent Bear It Away

Balliff, Algene. "A Southern Allegory," in *Commentary.* XXX (October, 1960), pp. 358–362.

Browning, Preston M., Jr. *Flannery O'Connor.* Carbondale: Southern Illinois University Press, 1974, pp. 72–98.

Burns, Stuart L. "Flannery O'Connor's *The Violent Bear It Away:* Apotheosis in Failure," in *Sewanee Review.* LXXVI (1968), pp. 319–336.

Drake, Robert. *Flannery O'Connor: A Critical Essay.* Grand Rapids, Mich.: Eerdmans, 1966, pp. 33–37.

Driskell, Leon V. and Joan T. Brittain. *The Eternal Crossroads: The Art of Flannery O'Connor.* Lexington: University Press of Kentucky, 1971, pp. 83–91.

Duhamel, P. Albert. "The Novelist as Prophet," in *The Added Dimension: The Art and Mind of Flannery O'Connor.* Edited by Melvin J. Friedman and Lewis A. Lawson. New York: Fordham University Press, 1966, pp. 88–107.

Eggenschwiler, David. *The Christian Humanism of Flannery O'Connor.* Detroit: Wayne State University Press, 1972, pp. 114–139.

Fahey, William A. "Out of the Eater: Flannery O'Connor's Appetite for Truth," in *Renascence.* XX (1967), pp. 22–29.

Feeley, Sister Kathleen. *Flannery O'Connor: Voice of the Peacock.* New Brunswick, N.J.: Rutgers University Press, 1972, pp. 154–171.

Ferris, Sumner J. "The Outside and the Inside: Flannery O'Connor's *The Violent Bear It Away,"* in *Critique.* III (1960), pp. 11–19.

Hawkes, John. "Flannery O'Connor's Devil," in *Sewanee Review.* LXX (1962), pp. 395–407. Reprinted in *Flannery O'Connor.* Edited by Robert E. Reiter. St. Louis, Mo.: B. Herder, 1968, pp. 25–37.

Hoffman, Frederick J. "The Search for Redemption: Flannery O'Connor's Fiction," in *The Added Dimension: The Art and Mind of Flannery O'Connor.* Edited by Melvin J. Friedman and Lewis A. Lawson. New York: Fordham University Press, 1966, pp. 32–48.

Hyman, Stanley Edgar. *Flannery O'Connor.* Minneapolis: University of Minnesota Press, 1966, pp. 19–25.

Jeremy, Sister. *"The Violent Bear It Away:* A Linguistic Education," in *Renascence.* XVII (1964), pp. 11–16. Reprinted in *Flannery O'Connor.* Edited by Robert E. Reiter. St. Louis, Mo.: B. Herder, 1968, pp. 103–110.

McFarland, Dorothy Tuck. *Flannery O'Connor.* New York: Frederick Ungar, 1976, pp. 91–111.

Martin, Carter W. *The True Country: Themes in the Fiction of Flannery O'Connor.* Nashville, Tenn.: Vanderbilt University Press, 1969, pp. 55–61, 77–82, 100–103, 125–129.

May, John R. *The Pruning Word: The Parables of Flannery O'Connor.* Notre Dame, Ind.: Notre Dame University Press, 1976, pp. 137–150.

Muller, Gilbert H. "*The Violent Bear It Away*: Moral and Dramatic Sense," in *Renascence.* XXII (1969), pp. 17–25.

Orvell, Miles. *Invisible Parade: The Fiction of Flannery O'Connor.* Philadelphia: Temple University Press, 1972, pp. 96–125.

Rubin, Louis D., Jr. "Flannery O'Connor and the Bible Belt," in *The Added Dimension: The Art and Mind of Flannery O'Connor.* Edited by Melvin J. Friedman and Lewis A. Lawson. New York: Fordham University Press, 1966, pp. 49–72.

Scott, Nathan A., Jr. "Flannery O'Connor's Testimony: The Pressure of Glory," in *The Added Dimension: The Art and Mind of Flannery O'Connor.* Edited by Melvin J. Friedman and Lewis A. Lawson. New York: Fordham University Press, 1966, pp. 138–156. Reprinted in *Craters of the Spirit: Studies in the Modern Novel.* Washington, D.C.: Corpus Books, 1968, pp. 267–285.

Smith, J. Oates. "Ritual and Violence in Flannery O'Connor," in *Thought.* XLI (1966), pp. 545–560.

Stephens, Martha. *The Question of Flannery O'Connor.* Baton Rouge: Louisiana State University Press, 1973, pp. 98–143.

Trowbridge, Clinton W. "The Symbolic Vision of Flannery O'Connor: Patterns of Imagery in *The Violent Bear It Away*," in *Sewanee Review.* LXXVI (1968), pp. 298–318.

Walters, Dorothy. *Flannery O'Connor.* New York: Twayne, 1973, pp. 90–103.

Wise Blood

Baumbach, Jonathan. *The Landscape of Nightmare: Studies in the Contemporary American Novel.* New York: New York University Press, 1965, pp. 87–100.

Browning, Preston M., Jr. *Flannery O'Connor.* Carbondale: Southern Illinois University Press, 1974, pp. 25–39.

Davis, Joe Lee. "Outraged, or Embarrassed," in *Kenyon Review.* XV (1953), pp. 320–326.

Drake, Robert. *Flannery O'Connor: A Critical Essay.* Grand Rapids, Mich.: Eerdmans, 1966, pp. 18–23.

Driskell, Leon V. and John T. Brittain.   *The Eternal Crossroads: The Art of Flannery O'Connor.* Lexington: University Press of Kentucky, 1971, pp. 38–58.

Eggenschwiler, David.   *The Christian Humanism of Flannery O'Connor.* Detroit: Wayne State University Press, 1972, pp. 101–114.

Feeley, Sister Kathleen.   *Flannery O'Connor: Voice of the Peacock.* New Brunswick, N.J.: Rutgers University Press, 1972, pp. 56–59.

Gordon, Caroline.   "Flannery O'Connor's *Wise Blood,*" in *Critique.* II (1958), pp. 3–10.

Hoffman, Frederick J.   "The Search for Redemption: Flannery O'Connor's Fiction," in *The Added Dimension: The Art and Mind of Flannery O'Connor.* Edited by Melvin J. Friedman and Lewis A. Lawson. New York: Fordham University Press, 1966, pp. 32–48.

Hyman, Stanley Edgar.   *Flannery O'Connor.* Minneapolis: University of Minnesota Press, 1966, pp. 9–15.

Kunkel, Francis L.   *Passion and the Passion: Sex and Religion in Modern Literature.* Philadelphia: Westminster Press, 1975, pp. 129–156.

Lawson, Lewis A.   "Flannery O'Connor and the Grotesque: *Wise Blood,*" in *Renascence.* XVII (1965), pp. 137–147. Reprinted in *Flannery O'Connor.* Edited by Robert E. Reiter. St. Louis, Mo.: B. Herder, 1968, pp. 51–67.

LeClair, Thomas.   "Flannery O'Connor's *Wise Blood*: The Oedipal Theme," in *Mississippi Quarterly.* XXIX (1976), pp. 197–205.

Littlefield, Daniel F.   "Flannery O'Connor's *Wise Blood*: 'Unparalleled Prosperity and Spiritual Chaos,' " in *Mississippi Quarterly.* XXIII (1970), pp. 121–133.

Lorch, Thomas M.   "Flannery O'Connor: Christian Allegorist," in *Critique.* X (1968), pp. 69–80.

McFarland, Dorothy Tuck.   *Flannery O'Connor.* New York: Frederick Ungar, 1976, pp. 73–89.

Martin, Carter W.   *The True Country: Themes in the Fiction of Flannery O'Connor.* Nashville, Tenn.: Vanderbilt University Press, 1969, pp. 47–55, 66–71, 117–125.

May, John R.   *The Pruning Word: The Parables of Flannery O'Connor.* Notre Dame: Notre Dame University Press, 1976, pp. 125–137.

Orvell, Miles.   *Invisible Parade: The Fiction of Flannery O'Connor.* Philadelphia: Temple University Press, 1972, pp. 66–95.

Rechnitz, Robert M.   "Passionate Pilgrim: Flannery O'Connor's *Wise Blood,*" in *Georgia Review.* XIX (1965), pp. 310–316.

Rubin, Louis D., Jr.   "Flannery O'Connor and the Bible Belt," in *The Added Dimension: The Art and Mind of Flannery O'Connor.* Edited by Melvin J.

Friedman and Lewis A. Lawson. New York: Fordham University Press, 1966, pp. 49–72.

Scott, Nathan A., Jr. "Flannery O'Connor's Testimony: The Pressure of Glory," in *The Added Dimension: The Art and Mind of Flannery O'Connor.* Edited by Melvin J. Friedman and Lewis A. Lawson. New York: Fordham University Press, 1966, pp. 138–156. Reprinted in *Craters of the Spirit: Studies in the Modern Novel.* Washington, D.C.: Corpus Books, 1968, pp. 267–285.

Smith, J. Oates. "Ritual and Violence in Flannery O'Connor," in *Thought.* XLI (Winter, 1966), pp. 545–560.

Stephens, Martha. *The Question of Flannery O'Connor.* Baton Rouge: Louisiana State University Press, 1973, pp. 43–97.

Walters, Dorothy. *Flannery O'Connor.* New York: Twayne, 1973, pp. 42–63.

CLIFFORD ODETS
(1906–1963)

Awake and Sing!

Block, Anita. *The Changing World in Plays and Theatre.* Boston: Little, Brown, 1939, pp. 286–290.

Brown, John Mason. *Broadway in Review.* New York: Norton, 1940, pp. 176–184.

————. *Dramatis Personae; A Retrospective Show.* New York: Viking, 1963, pp. 69–72.

————. *Two on the Aisle.* New York: Norton, 1938, pp. 217–219.

Burt, David J. "Odets' *Awake and Sing!*" in *Explicator.* XXVII (December, 1968), item 29.

Cohn, Ruby. *Twentieth-Century Drama.* New York: Random House, 1966, pp. 221–222.

Clurman, Harold. *The Fervent Years.* New York: Hill and Wang, 1957, pp. 135–136, 139–141.

Downer, Alan Seymour. *Fifty Years of American Drama 1900–1950.* Chicago: Regnery, 1951, pp. 61–63.

Flexner, Eleanor. *American Playwrights: 1918–1938.* New York: Simon and Schuster, 1938, pp. 296–299.

Freedman, Morris. *The Moral Impulse; Modern Drama from Ibsen to the Present.* Carbondale: Southern Illinois University Press, 1967, pp. 105–107.

Gassner, John. *The Theatre in Our Times.* New York: Crown, 1954, pp. 303–307.

Griffin, Robert J. "On the Love Songs of Clifford Odets," in *The Thirties: Fiction, Poetry, Drama.* Edited by Warren G. French. Deland, Fla.: Everett/Edwards, 1976, pp. 196–199.

Haslam, Gerald W. "Odets' Use of Yiddish-English in *Awake and Sing!*" in *Research Studies.* XXXIV (September, 1966), pp. 161–164.

Kaplan, Charles. "Two Depression Plays and Broadway's Popular Idealism," in *American Quarterly.* XV (Winter, 1963), pp. 579–585.

Krutch, Joseph W. *The American Drama Since 1918.* New York: George Braziller, 1957, pp. 267–271.

Meister, Charles W. "Comparative Drama: Chekhov, Shaw, Odets," in *Poet Lore.* LV (Autumn, 1950), pp. 255–257.

Mersand, Joseph. *The American Drama Since 1930.* New York: Modern Chapbooks, 1949, pp. 63–66, 76–80.

Murray, Edward. *Clifford Odets: The Thirties and After.* New York: Frederick Ungar, 1968, pp. 33–52.

O'Hara, Frank Hurburt. *Today in American Drama.* Chicago: University of Chicago Press, 1939, pp. 68–75, 247–248.

Rabkin, Gerald. *Drama and Commitment.* Bloomington: Indiana University Press, 1964, pp. 182–186.

Sargeant, E.N. *"Awake and Sing!"* in *New Directions in Prose and Poetry.* XVI (1957), pp. 54–59.

Sievers, W.D. *Freud on Broadway.* New York: Hermitage House, 1955, pp. 262–264.

Warshow, Robert. *The Immediate Experience.* New York: Doubleday, 1962, pp. 55–67.

————. "Poet of the Jewish Middle Class," in *Commentary.* I (May, 1946), pp. 17–22.

Weales, Gerald. *Clifford Odets, Playwright.* New York: Pegasus, 1971, pp. 56–82.

Golden Boy

Block, Anita. *The Changing World in Plays and Theatre.* Boston: Little, Brown, 1939, pp. 295–300.

Brown, John Mason. *Two on the Aisle.* New York: Norton, 1938, pp. 220–222.

Burke, Kenneth. *The Philosophy of Literary Form.* New York: Vintage, 1957, pp. 28–31, 58–59.

Clurman, Harold. *The Fervent Years.* New York: Hill and Wang, 1957, pp. 195–200, 216–217.

Downer, Alan Seymour. *American Drama and Its Critics.* Chicago: University of Chicago Press, 1965, pp. 140–141.

Flexner, Eleanor. *American Playwrights: 1918–1938.* New York: Simon and Schuster, 1938, pp. 299–302, 313–314.

Gassner, John. *Theatre in Our Times.* New York: Crown, 1954, pp. 433–437.

Goldstein, Malcolm. "The Playwrights of the 1930's," in *The American Theater Today.* Edited by Alan Seymour Downer. New York: Basic Books, 1967, pp. 33–34.

Himelstein, Morgan Y. *Drama as a Weapon, the Left-Wing Theatre in New York 1929–1941.* New Brunswick, N.J.: Rutgers University Press, 1963, pp. 174–176.

Knox, George. *Critical Moments.* Seattle: University of Washington Press, 1957, pp. 9–12.

Krutch, Joseph Wood. *The American Drama Since 1918.* New York: George Braziller, 1957, pp. 271–274.

McCarthy, Mary Therese. *Sights and Spectacles 1937–1956.* New York: Farrar, Straus, 1956, pp. 9–12.

Mendelsohn, Michael J. *Clifford Odets: Humane Dramatist.* Deland, Fla.: Everett/Edwards, 1969, pp. 43–47, 71–74.

————. "Clifford Odets: The Artist's Commitment," in *Literature and Society.* Edited by Bernice Slote. Lincoln: University of Nebraska Press, 1964, pp. 148–150.

Mersand, Joseph. *The American Drama Since 1930.* New York: Modern Chapbooks, 1949, pp. 86–88.

Murray, Edward. *Clifford Odets: The Thirties and After.* New York: Frederick Ungar, 1968, pp. 53–71.

Rabkin, Gerald. *Drama and Commitment.* Bloomington: Indiana University Press, 1964, pp. 192–196.

Shuman, R.B. *Clifford Odets.* New York: Twayne, 1962, pp. 80–88.

Sievers, W.D. *Freud on Broadway.* New York: Hermitage House, 1955, pp. 265–267.

Weales, Gerald. *Clifford Odets, Playwright.* New York: Pegasus, 1971, pp. 123–129.

Waiting for Lefty

Block, Anita. *The Changing World in Plays and Theatre.* Boston: Little, Brown, 1939, pp. 280–286.

Brown, John Mason. *Dramatis Personae; A Retrospective Show.* New York: Viking, 1963, pp. 69–72.

Flexner, Eleanor. *American Playwrights: 1918–1938.* New York: Simon and Schuster, 1938, pp. 290–295.

Goldstein, Malcolm. "The Playwrights of the 1930's," in *The American Theater Today.* Edited by Alan Seymour Downer. New York: Basic Books, 1967, p. 31.

Griffin, Robert J. "On the Love Songs of Clifford Odets," in *The Thirties: Fiction, Poetry, Drama.* Edited by Warren French. Deland, Fla.: Everett/Edwards, 1976, pp. 193–197.

Himelstein, Morgan Y. *Drama as a Weapon, the Left-Wing Theatre in New York 1929–1941.* New Brunswick, N.J.: Rutgers University Press, 1963, pp. 37–43.

Krutch, Joseph Wood. "Mr. Odets Speaks His Mind," in *Nation.* CXL (April 10, 1935), pp. 427–428.

————. *The American Drama Since 1918.* New York: George Braziller, 1957, pp. 264–267.

Mendelsohn, Michael J. *Clifford Odets: Humane Dramatist.* Deland, Fla.: Everett/Edwards, 1969, pp. 21–28.

Rabkin, Gerald. *Drama and Commitment.* Bloomington: University of Indiana Press, 1964, pp. 169–176.

Shuman, R. Baird. *Clifford Odets.* New York: Twayne, 1962, pp. 44–55.

Weales, Gerald. *Clifford Odets, Playwright.* New York: Pegasus, 1971, pp. 35–55.

Willett, Ralph. "Clifford Odets and Popular Culture," in *South Atlantic Quarterly.* LXIX (Winter, 1970), pp. 68–78.

SEÁN O'FAOLÁIN
(1900–   )

I Remember! I Remember!

Barrett, William. "A Good Irish Tenor," in *Atlantic*. CCIX (February, 1962), pp. 119–120.

Dempsey, David. "The Sleeping Dogs of Memory," in *Saturday Review*. XLV (January 6, 1962), pp. 66–67.

Doyle, Paul A. *Seán O'Faoláin*. New York: Twayne, 1968, pp. 108–110.

Harmon, Maurice. *Seán O'Faoláin: A Critical Introduction*. Notre Dame, Ind.: Notre Dame University Press, 1966, pp. 134–136.

Murray, Michele. "O'Faoláin Remembers," in *Commonweal*. LXXV (January 19, 1962), pp. 441–442.

"The Man Who Invented Sin"

Doyle, Paul A. *Seán O'Faoláin*. New York: Twayne, 1968, pp. 86–88.

Felheim, Marvin, Franklin Newman and William Steinhoff. *Study Aids for Teachers for Modern Short Stories*. New York: Oxford University Press, 1951, pp. 57–59.

Hall, James and Joseph Langland. *The Short Story*. New York: Macmillan, 1956, pp. 78–79.

Harmon, Maurice. *Seán O'Faoláin: A Critical Introduction*. Notre Dame, Ind.: University of Notre Dame Press, 1966, pp. 95–100.

Havighurst, Walter. *Instructor's Manual for Masters of the Modern Short Story*. New York: Harcourt, Brace, 1955, pp. 39–40.

The Short Stories of O'Faoláin

Bloom, Edward A. *The Order of Fiction*. New York: Odyssey, 1964, pp. 36–40.

Doyle, Paul A. *Seán O'Faoláin*. New York: Twayne, 1968.

Fallis, Richard. *The Irish Renaissance*. Syracuse, N.Y.: Syracuse University Press, 1977, pp. 228–232.

Garfitt, Roger. "Constants in Contemporary Irish Fiction," in *Two Decades of Irish Writing: A Critical Survey*. Edited by Douglas Dunn. Chester Springs, Pa.: Dufour, 1975, pp. 152–154.

Hanley, Katharine. "The Short Stories of Seán O'Faoláin: Theory and Practice," in *Eire*. VI (1971), pp. 3–11.

Harmon, Maurice. *Seán O'Faoláin: A Critical Introduction*. Notre Dame, Ind.: University of Notre Dame Press, 1966.

Hopkins, Robert H. "The Pastoral Mode of Seán O'Faoláin's 'The Silence of the Valley,'" in *Studies in Short Fiction*. I (1964), pp. 93–98.

Kenny, Herbert A. *Literary Dublin: A History*. New York: Taplinger, 1974, pp. 261–263.

McMahon, Sean. "O My Youth, O My Country," in *Eire*. VI (1971), pp. 145–155.

O'Donnell, Donat. "The Parnellism of Seán O'Faoláin," in *Irish Writing*. V (July, 1948), pp. 67–68.

Rideout, Walter B. *Instructor's Manual for the Experience of Prose*. New York: Crowell, 1960, pp. 22–23.

Steinmann, Martin and Gerald Willen. *Literature for Writing*. Belmont, Calif.: Wadsworth, 1962, pp. 213–214.

Vive Moi!

Barrett, William. "Man of Parts," in *Atlantic*. CCXIV (November, 1964), pp. 202–203.

Colum, Padraic. "An Autobiography of One Who Was 'Reborn of the Uprising,'" in *Commonweal*. LXXXI (January 8, 1965), pp. 489–490.

Dooley, Roger B. "When the Dawn Came Up in Erin," in *Saturday Review*. XLVII (September 26, 1964), p. 44.

Ryan, Stephen P. "*Vive Moi*," in *America*. CXI (December 12, 1964), pp. 782–783.

LIAM O'FLAHERTY
(1896–   )

Famine

Broderick, John. "Liam O'Flaherty: A Partial View," in *Hibernia*. (December 19, 1969), p. 17.

Doyle, Paul A. *Liam O'Flaherty*. N.Y.: Twayne, 1971, pp. 96–106.

Freyer, Grattan. "The Irish Contribution," in *The Modern Age*. Edited by Boris Ford. Baltimore: Penguin, 1961, pp. 197, 205–207.

Hynes, Frank J. "Troubles in Ireland," in *Saturday Review of Literature*. XXIX (May 25, 1946), p. 12.

Kelleher, John V. "Irish Literature Today," in *Atlantic Monthly*. CLXXV (March, 1945), pp. 70–76.

Kiely, Benedict. "Liam O'Flaherty, a Study of Discontent," in *The Month*. II (September, 1949), pp. 183–193.

Mercier, Vivian. "Man Against Nature: The Novels of Liam O'Flaherty," in *Wascana Review*. I (November 2, 1966), pp. 37–46.

O'Brien, James. *Liam O'Flaherty*. Cranbury, N.J.: Associated University Presses, 1973, pp. 39–44.

Zneimer, John. *Literary Vision of Liam O'Flaherty*. Syracuse, N.Y.: Syracuse University Press, 1970, pp. 122–128.

The Informer

Broderick, John. "Liam O'Flaherty: A Partial View," in *Hibernia*. (December 19, 1969), p. 17.

Doyle, Paul A. *Liam O'Flaherty*. N.Y.: Twayne, 1971, pp. 35–45.

Freyer, Grattan. "The Irish Contribution," in *The Modern Age*. Edited by Boris Ford. Baltimore: Penguin, 1961, pp. 197, 205–207.

MacDonagh, Donagh. "Afterword," in *The Informer*. By Liam O'Flaherty. N.Y.: New American Library, 1961, p. 184.

Mercier, Vivian. "Man Against Nature: The Novels of Liam O'Flaherty," in *Wascana Review*. I (November 2, 1966), pp. 37–46.

Moseley, Maboth. "Humanity of Liam O'Flaherty," in *The Humanist*. IV (May, 1927), p. 223.

O'Brien, James. *Liam O'Flaherty*. Cranbury, N.J.: Associated University Presses, 1973, pp. 61–63.

————. "O'Flaherty's Real View of *The Informer*," in *Dublin Magazine*. VIII (Spring, 1970), pp. 57–70.

O'Keeffe, Timothy. "Introduction," in *Irish Portraits: 14 Short Stories*. London: Sphere Books, 1970, pp. 9–12.

Yeats, William Butler. *The Letters of William Butler Yeats*. Edited by Allan Wade. N.Y.: Macmillan, 1955, pp. 722, 801, 809.

Zneimer, John. *Literary Vision of Liam O'Flaherty*. Syracuse, N.Y.: Syracuse University Press, 1970, pp. 67–71.

The Puritan

Doyle, Paul A. *Liam O'Flaherty*. N.Y.: Twayne, 1971, pp. 75–80.

Freyer, Grattan. "The Irish Contribution," in *The Modern Age*. Edited by Boris Ford. Baltimore: Penguin, 1961, pp. 197, 205–207.

Mercier, Vivian. "Man Against Nature: The Novels of Liam O'Flaherty," in *Wascana Review*. I (1966), pp. 37–46.

O'Brien, James. *Liam O'Flaherty*. Cranbury, N.J.: Associated University Presses, 1973, pp. 86–88.

Zneimer, John. *Literary Vision of Liam O'Flaherty*. Syracuse, N.Y.: Syracuse University Press, 1970, pp. 84–88.

The Short Stories of O'Flaherty

Doyle, Paul A. *Liam O'Flaherty*. N.Y.: Twayne, 1971, pp. 111–112.

Hampton, A.A. "Liam O'Flaherty's Short Stories—Visual and Aural Effects," in *English Studies*. LV (October, 1974), pp. 440–447.

Murray, Michael H. "Liam O'Flaherty and the Speaking Voice," in *Studies in Short Fiction*. V (Winter, 1968), pp. 154–162.

O'Brien, James. *Liam O'Flaherty*. Cranbury, N.J.: Associated University Presses, 1973, pp. 92–117.

O'Connor, Frank. *The Lonely Voice: A Study of the Short Story*. N.Y.: World, 1963, p. 27.

Saul, George Brandon. "A Wild Sowing: Short Stories of Liam O'Flaherty," in *Review of English Literature*. IV (July, 1963), pp. 108–113.

Zneimer, John. *Literary Vision of Liam O'Flaherty*. Syracuse, N.Y.: Syracuse University Press, 1970, pp. 146–181.

JOHN O'HARA
(1905–1970)

Appointment in Samarra

Allen, Walter. *The Modern Novel in Britain and the United States.* New York: Dutton, 1964, pp. 182–183.

Bier, Jesse. "O'Hara's *Appointment in Samarra*: His First and Only Real Novel," in *College English.* XXV (November, 1963), pp. 135–141.

Blackmur, R.P. "A Morality of Pointlessness," in *Nation.* CXXXIX (August 22, 1934), pp. 220–221.

Bruccoli, Matthew J. "Focus on *Appointment in Samarra*: The Importance of Knowing What You Are Talking About," in *Tough Guy Writers of the Thirties.* Edited by David Madden. Carbondale: Southern Illinois University Press, 1968, pp. 129–136.

_____. *The O'Hara Concern.* New York: Random House, 1975.

Canley, Henry S. "Mr. O'Hara and the Vulgar School," in *Saturday Review of Literature.* XI (August 18, 1934), p. 53.

Carson, Edward R. *The Fiction of John O'Hara.* Pittsburgh: University of Pittsburgh Press, 1961, pp. 9–14.

Donaldson, Scott. "Appointment with the Dentist: O'Hara's 'Naturalistic Novel,'" in *Modern Fiction Studies.* XIV (Winter, 1968–1969), pp. 435–442.

Grebstein, Sheldon Norman. *John O'Hara.* New York: Twayne, 1966, pp. 34–45.

Gurko, Leo. *Angry Decade.* New York: Dodd, Mead, 1947, pp. 113–115.

Hierth, Harrison E. "The Class Novel," in *CEA Critic.* XXVII (December, 1964), pp. 1–4.

Walcutt, Charles Child. *John O'Hara.* Minneapolis: University of Minnesota Press, 1969, pp. 13–17.

Weaver, Robert. "Twilight Area of Fiction: The Novels of John O'Hara," in *Queen's Quarterly.* LXVI (1959), pp. 322–323.

From the Terrace

Bazelton, David. "O'Hara and America," in *New Leader.* LXI (December 29, 1958), pp. 18–19.

Bruccolli, Matthew J. *The O'Hara Concern.* New York: Random House, 1975.

Carson, Edward R. *The Fiction of John O'Hara.* Pittsburgh: University of Pittsburgh Press, 1961, pp. 29–40.

Gardiner, Harold C. "A Terrace Bounded by Curbstones," in *America*. C (December 13, 1958), pp. 347–348.

Grebstein, Sheldon Norman. *John O'Hara*. New York: Twayne, 1966, pp. 63–69.

Hicks, Granville. "The Problem of O'Hara," in *Saturday Review of Literature*. XLI (November 29, 1958), pp. 14–15.

Kazin, Alfred. *Contemporaries*. Boston: Little, Brown, 1962, pp. 161–168.

Maloff, Saul. "*From the Terrace*," in *New Republic*. CXL (January 5, 1959), pp. 20–21.

Mizener, Arthur. "Something Went Seriously Wrong," in *New York Times Book Review*. (November 23, 1958), p. 1.

Wain, John. "Snowed Under," in *New Yorker*. XXXIV (January 10, 1959), pp. 112–114.

Walcutt, Charles Child. *Man's Changing Mask: Modes and Method of Characterization in Fiction*. Minneapolis: University of Minnesota Press, 1966, pp. 314–316.

Weaver, Robert. "Twilight Area of Fiction: The Novels of John O'Hara," in *Queen's Quarterly*. LXVI (1959), pp. 320, 325.

Ourselves to Know

Adams, Phoebe. "Lolita in Pa.," in *Atlantic*. CCV (March, 1969) pp. 120–121.

Boroff, David. "A Desperate Detour to Destruction," in *Saturday Review of Literature*. XLIII (February 27, 1960), p. 23.

Bruccoli, Matthew J. *The O'Hara Concern*. New York: Random House, 1975.

Carson, Edward R. *The Fiction of John O'Hara*. Pittsburgh: University of Pittsburgh Press, 1961, pp. 40–45.

Grebstein, Sheldon N. *John O'Hara*. New York: Twayne, 1966, pp. 69–75.

Mizener, Arthur. "Some Kinds of Modern Novel," in *Saturday Review of Literature*. LXIX (Winter, 1961), pp. 156–158.

Moore, Harry T. "The Murderer Tells His Story," in *New York Times Book Review*. (February 28, 1960), p. 5.

A Rage to Live

Bruccoli, Matthew J. *The O'Hara Concern*. New York: Random House, 1975.

Carson, Edward R. *The Fiction of John O'Hara*. Pittsburgh: University of Pittsburgh Press, 1961, pp. 14–21.

Gill, Brendan. "The O'Hara Report and the Wit of Miss McCarthy," in *New Yorker*. XXV (August 20, 1949), pp. 64–65.

Grebstein, Sheldon N. *John O'Hara*. New York: Twayne, 1966, pp. 45–54.

Pickrel, Paul. "Outstanding Novels," in *Yale Review*. XXXIX (Fall, 1949), pp. 191–192.

Prescott, Orville. *In My Opinion; An Inquiry into the Contemporary Novel.* Indianapolis, Ind.: Bobbs-Merrill, 1952, pp. 72–74.

Spectorsky, A.C. "Portrait of a Woman," in *New York Times Book Review.* (August 21, 1949), p. 4.

Walcutt, Charles C. *John O'Hara*. Minneapolis: University of Minnesota Press, 1969.

Ten North Frederick

Alexander, Sidney. "Another Visit to O'Haraville," in *Reporter*. XIV (January 26, 1956), pp. 44–47.

Bruccolli, Matthew J. *The O'Hara Concern*. New York: Random House, 1975.

Carson, Edward R. *The Fiction of John O'Hara*. Pittsburgh: University of Pittsburgh Press, 1961, pp. 21–29.

Davis, Robert G. "O'Hara's World of Secret Lives," in *New York Times Book Review*. (November 27, 1955), p. 1.

Fiedler, Leslie. "Old Pro at Work," in *New Republic*. CXXXIV (January 9, 1956), pp. 16–17.

Gardiner, Harold C. "Drained of Drama," in *America*. XCIV (December 10, 1955), pp. 307–308.

Grebstein, Sheldon N. *John O'Hara*. New York: Twayne, 1966, pp. 54–63.

McKelway, St. Clair. "And Nothing but the Truth," in *New Yorker*. XXXI (December 17, 1955), p. 162.

EUGENE O'NEILL
(1888–1953)

Ah, Wilderness!

Adler, Jacob H. "The Worth of *Ah, Wilderness*," in *Modern Drama*. III (Winter, 1960), pp. 280–288.

Bogard, Travis. *Contour in Time: The Plays of Eugene O'Neill*. New York: Oxford University Press, 1972, pp. 354–362.

Brustein, Robert. *The Theater of Revolt*. Boston: Little, Brown, 1964, pp. 336–339.

Carpenter, Frederic I. *Eugene O'Neill*. New York: Twayne, 1964, pp. 145–147.

Chabrowe, Leonard. *Ritual and Pathos—The Theater of O'Neill*. Lewisburg, Pa.: Bucknell University Press, 1976, pp. 66–67.

Cronin, Harry. *Eugene O'Neill: Irish and American: A Study in Cultural Context*. New York: Arno, 1976, pp. 90–97.

Engle, Edwin A. *The Haunted Heroes of Eugene O'Neill*. Cambridge, Mass.: Harvard University Press, 1953, pp. 270–271.

Langer, Lawrence. *The Magic Curtain*. New York: Dutton, 1951, pp. 275–287.

Moses, Montrose J. "The 'New' Eugene O'Neill," in *North American Review*. CCXXXVI (December, 1933), pp. 543–549.

Shawcross, John T. "The Road to Ruin: The Beginning of O'Neill's Long Day's Journey," in *Modern Drama*. III (Winter, 1960), pp. 289–296.

Skinner, Richard Dana. *Eugene O'Neill: A Poet's Quest*. New York: Longmans, Green, 1935, pp. 227–233.

Tiusanen, Timo. *O'Neill's Scenic Images*. Princeton, N.J.: Princeton University Press, 1968, pp. 241–245.

Anna Christie

Bogard, Travis. *Contour in Time: The Plays of Eugene O'Neill*. New York: Oxford University Press, 1972, pp. 151–165. Earlier version in *O'Neill: A Collection of Critical Essays*. Edited by John Gassner. Englewood Cliffs, N.J.: Prentice-Hall, 1964, pp. 62–71.

Carpenter, Frederic I. *Eugene O'Neill*. New York: Twayne, 1964, pp. 93–96.

Dusenbury, Winifred L. *The Theme of Loneliness in Modern American Drama*. Gainesville: University of Florida Press, 1960, pp. 50–56.

Engle, Edwin A. *The Haunted Heroes of Eugene O'Neill*. Cambridge, Mass.: Harvard University Press, 1953, pp. 39–45.

Falk, Doris V.   *Eugene O'Neill and the Tragic Tension.* New Brunswick, N.J.: Rutgers University Press, 1958, pp. 48–52.

Frazer, Winifred L.   "Chris and Poseidon: Man Versus God in *Anna Christie*," in *Modern Drama.* XII (December, 1969), pp. 279–285.

Leech, Clifford.   "Eugene O'Neill and His Plays," in *Critical Quarterly.* III (Autumn, 1961), pp. 246–248.

McAleer, John J.   "Christ Symbolism in *Anna Christie*," in *Modern Drama.* IV (February, 1962), pp. 389–396.

Mickle, Alan D.   *Six Plays of Eugene O'Neill.* New York: Liveright, 1929, pp. 13–32.

Skinner, Richard Dana.   *Eugene O'Neill: A Poet's Quest.* New York: Longmans, Green, 1935, pp. 76–84.

Tiusanen, Timo.   *O'Neill's Scenic Images.* Princeton, N.J.: Princeton University Press, 1968, pp. 86–89.

Desire Under the Elms

Asselineau, Roger.   "*Desire Under the Elms*: A Phase of Eugene O'Neill's Philosophy," in *Eugene O'Neill: A Collection of Criticism.* Edited by Ernest G. Griffin. New York: McGraw-Hill, 1976, pp. 59–66.

Bogard, Travis.   *Contour in Time: The Plays of Eugene O'Neill.* New York: Oxford University Press, 1972, pp. 199–225.

Carpenter, Frederic I.   *Eugene O'Neill.* New York: Twayne, 1964, pp. 105–110.

Chabrowe, Leonard.   *Ritual and Pathos—The Theater of O'Neill.* Lewisburg, Pa.: Bucknell University Press, 1976, pp. 128–134.

Cubeta, Paul M.   *Modern Drama for Analysis, Third Edition.* New York: Holt, Rinehart, 1963, pp. 143–150.

Engle, Edwin A.   *The Haunted Heroes of Eugene O'Neill.* Cambridge, Mass.: Harvard University Press, 1953, pp. 126–134.

Falk, Doris V.   *Eugene O'Neill and the Tragic Tension.* New Brunswick, N.J.: Rutgers University Press, 1958, pp. 93–99.

Hartman, Murray.   "*Desire Under the Elms* in the Light of Strindberg's Influence," in *American Literature.* XXXIII (November, 1961), pp. 360–369.

Hays, Peter L.   "Biblical Perversions in *Desire Under the Elms*," in *Modern Drama.* XI (February, 1969), pp. 423–428.

Leaska, Mitchell.   *The Voice of Tragedy.* New York: Speller, 1963, pp. 264–268.

Long, Chester Clayton.   *The Role of Nemesis in the Structure of Selected Plays by Eugene O'Neill.* The Hague: Mouton, 1968, pp. 97–116.

Racey, Edgar F., Jr. "Myth as Tragic Structure in *Desire Under the Elms*," in *Modern Drama*. V (May, 1962), pp. 42–46. Reprinted in *O'Neill: A Collection of Critical Essays*. Edited by John Gassner. Englewood Cliffs, N.J.: Prentice-Hall, 1964, pp. 57–61.

Skinner, Richard Dana. *Eugene O'Neill: A Poet's Quest*. New York: Longmans, Green, 1935, pp. 143–156.

Tiusanen, Timo. *O'Neill's Scenic Images*. Princeton, N.J.: Princeton University Press, 1968, pp. 151–162.

Weissman, Philip. "Conscious and Unconscious Autobiographical Dramas of Eugene O'Neill," in *Journal of the Psychoanalytic Association*. V (1957), pp. 432–460.

Winther, Sophus Keith. "*Desire Under the Elms*: A Modern Tragedy," in *Modern Drama*. III (December, 1960), pp. 326–332.

The Emperor Jones

Blackburn, Clara. "Continental Influences on Eugene O'Neill's Expressionistic Dramas," in *American Literature*. XIII (May, 1941), pp. 109–116.

Bogard, Travis. *Contour in Time: The Plays of Eugene O'Neill*. New York: Oxford University Press, 1972, pp. 134–144.

Carpenter, Frederic I. *Eugene O'Neill*. New York: Twayne, 1964, pp. 89–93.

Chabrowe, Leonard. *Ritual and Pathos—The Theater of O'Neill*. Lewisburg, Pa.: Bucknell University Press, 1976, pp. 120–123.

Cronin, Harry. *Eugene O'Neill: Irish and American: A Study in Cultural Context*. New York: Arno, 1976, pp. 65–73.

Engle, Edwin A. *The Haunted Heroes of Eugene O'Neill*. Cambridge, Mass.: Harvard University Press, 1953, pp. 48–53.

Falk, Doris V. *Eugene O'Neill and the Tragic Tension*. New Brunswick, N.J.: Rutgers University Press, 1958, pp. 66–71.

Roy, Emil. "Eugene O'Neill's *The Emperor Jones* and *The Hairy Ape* as Mirror Plays," in *Comparative Drama*. II (Spring, 1968), pp. 21–31.

Skinner, Richard Dana. *Eugene O'Neill: A Poet's Quest*. New York: Longmans, Green, 1935, pp. 85–95.

Tiusanen, Timo. *O'Neill's Scenic Images*. Princeton, N.J.: Princeton University Press, 1968, pp. 97–112.

The Hairy Ape

Alexander, Doris M. "Eugene O'Neill as Social Critic," in *American Quarterly*. VI (Winter, 1954), pp. 349–356.

Andreach, Robert J. "O'Neill's Use of Dante in *The Fountain* and *The Hairy Ape*," in *Modern Drama*. X (May, 1967), pp. 48–56.

Baum, B. "*Tempest* and *Hairy Ape*: The Literary Incarnation of Mythos," in *Modern Language Quarterly*. XIV (September, 1953), pp. 258–273.

Blackburn, Clara. "Continental Influences on Eugene O'Neill's Expressionistic Dramas," in *American Literature*. XIII (May, 1941), pp. 116–122.

Bogard, Travis. *Contour in Time: The Plays of Eugene O'Neill*. New York: Oxford University Press, 1972, pp. 239–252.

Carpenter, Frederic I. *Eugene O'Neill*. New York: Twayne, 1964, pp. 99–101.

Chabrowe, Leonard. *Ritual and Pathos—The Theater of O'Neill*. Lewisburg, Pa.: Bucknell University Press, 1976, pp. 16–18, 123–125.

Clark, Marden J. "Tragic Effect in *The Hairy Ape*," in *Modern Drama*. X (February, 1968), pp. 372–382.

Dusenbury, Winifred L. *The Theme of Loneliness in Modern American Drama*. Gainesville: University of Florida Press, 1960, pp. 125–134.

Engle, Edwin A. *The Haunted Heroes of Eugene O'Neill*. Cambridge, Mass.: Harvard University Press, 1953, pp. 54–60.

Falk, Doris V. *Eugene O'Neill and the Tragic Tension*. New Brunswick, N.J.: Rutgers University Press, 1958, pp. 27–35.

Long, Chester Clayton. *The Role of Nemesis in the Structure of Selected Plays by Eugene O'Neill*. The Hague: Mouton, 1968, pp. 75–96.

Mickle, Alan D. *Six Plays of Eugene O'Neill*. New York: Liveright, 1929, pp. 33–58.

Ross, J.L. *Philosophy in Literature*. Syracuse, N.Y.: Syracuse University Press, 1949, pp. 218–222.

Roy, Emil. "Eugene O'Neill's *The Emperor Jones* and *The Hairy Ape* as Mirror Plays," in *Comparative Drama*. II (Spring, 1968), pp. 21–31.

Skinner, Richard Dana. *Eugene O'Neill: A Poet's Quest*. New York: Longmans, Green, 1935, pp. 103–113.

Tiusanen, Timo. *O'Neill's Scenic Images*. Princeton, N.J.: Princeton University Press, 1968, pp. 113–128.

The Iceman Cometh

Alexander, Doris M. "Hugo of *The Iceman Cometh*: Realism and O'Neill," in *American Quarterly*. V (Winter, 1953), pp. 357–366. Reprinted in *Twentieth Century Interpretations of* The Iceman Cometh: *A Collection of Critical Essays*. Edited by John Henry Raleigh. Englewood Cliffs, N.J.: Prentice-Hall, 1968, pp. 63–71.

Andreach, Robert J. "O'Neill's Women in *The Iceman Cometh*," in *Renascence*. XVIII (Winter, 1966), pp. 89–98. Reprinted in *Eugene O'Neill: A Collection of Criticism*. Edited by Ernest G. Griffin. New York: McGraw-Hill, 1976, pp. 103–113.

Bogard, Travis. *Contour in Time: The Plays of Eugene O'Neill.* New York: Oxford University Press, 1972, pp. 407–418. Reprinted in *Eugene O'Neill: A Collection of Criticism.* Edited by Ernest G. Griffin. New York: McGraw-Hill, 1976, pp. 92–102.

Brashear, William R. "The Wisdom of Silenus in O'Neill's *Iceman,*" in *American Literature.* XXXVI (May, 1964), pp. 180–188.

Brustein, Robert. *The Theatre of Revolt.* Boston: Little, Brown, 1964, pp. 339–348. Reprinted in *Twentieth Century Interpretations of* The Iceman Cometh: *A Collection of Critical Essays.* Edited by John Henry Raleigh. Englewood Cliffs, N.J.: Prentice-Hall, 1968, pp. 92–102.

Carpenter, Frederic I. *Eugene O'Neill.* New York: Twayne, 1964, pp. 153–158.

Chabrowe, Leonard. "Dionysus in *The Iceman Cometh,*" in *Modern Drama.* IV (Spring, 1962), pp. 377–388.

————. *Ritual and Pathos—The Theater of O'Neill.* Lewisburg, Pa.: Bucknell University Press, 1976, pp. 73–99.

Day, Cyrus. "The Iceman and the Bridegroom," in *Modern Drama.* I (May, 1958), pp. 3–9.

Dobrée, Bonamy. "Mr. O'Neill's Latest Play," in *Sewanee Review.* LVI (Winter, 1948), pp. 118–126.

Dusenbury, Winifred L. *The Theme of Loneliness in Modern American Drama.* Gainesville: University of Florida Press, 1960, pp. 26–37.

Engle, Edwin A. *The Haunted Heroes of Eugene O'Neill.* Cambridge, Mass.: Harvard University Press, 1953, pp. 281–296.

Falk, Doris V. *Eugene O'Neill and the Tragic Tension.* New Brunswick, N.J.: Rutgers University Press, 1958, pp. 156–165. Reprinted in *Twentieth Century Interpretations of* The Iceman Cometh: *A Collection of Critical Essays.* Edited by John Henry Raleigh. Englewood Cliffs, N.J.: Prentice-Hall, 1968, pp. 87–91.

Frazer, Winifred D. *Love as Death in* The Iceman Cometh: *A Modern Treatment of an Ancient Theme.* Gainesville: University of Florida Press, 1967.

Hopkins, Vivian C. "The *Iceman* Seen Through 'The Lower Depths,' " in *College English.* XI (November, 1949), pp. 81–87.

Long, Chester Clayton. *The Role of Nemesis in the Structure of Selected Plays by Eugene O'Neill.* The Hague: Mouton, 1968, pp. 175–197.

McCarthy, Mary. *Sights and Spectacles.* New York: Farrar, Straus, 1956, pp. 81–85. Reprinted in *Twentieth Century Interpretations of* The Iceman Cometh: *A Collection of Critical Essays.* Edited by John Henry Raleigh. Englewood Cliffs, N.J.: Prentice-Hall, 1968, pp. 50–53.

Muchnic, Helen. "Circe's Swine: Plays by Gorky and O'Neill," in *Comparative Literature*. III (Spring, 1951), pp. 119–128. Reprinted in *O'Neill: A Collection of Critical Essays*. Edited by John Gassner. Englewood Cliffs, N.J.: Prentice-Hall, 1964, pp. 99–109.

Myers, Henry Alonzo. "*Macbeth* and *The Iceman Cometh*: Equivalence and Ambivalence in Tragedy," in *Tragedy: A View of Life*. Ithaca, N.Y.: Cornell University Press, 1956, pp. 98–109.

Raleigh, John H. *The Plays of Eugene O'Neill*. Carbondale: Southern Illinois University Press, 1965, pp. 66–75. Reprinted in *Twentieth Century Interpretations of* The Iceman Cometh: *A Collection of Critical Essays*. Edited by John Henry Raleigh. Englewood Cliffs, N.J.: Prentice-Hall, 1968, pp. 54–62.

Reinhardt, Nancy. "Formal Patterns in *The Iceman Cometh*," in *Modern Drama*. XVI (September, 1973), pp. 119–128.

Tiusanen, Timo. *O'Neill's Scenic Images*. Princeton, N.J.: Princeton University Press, 1968, pp. 264–284.

Winther, Sophus Keith. "*The Iceman Cometh*: A Study in Technique," in *Arizona Quarterly*. III (Winter, 1947), pp. 293–300. Reprinted in *Twentieth Century Interpretations of* The Iceman Cometh: *A Collection of Critical Essays*. Edited by John Henry Raleigh. Englewood Cliffs, N.J.: Prentice-Hall, 1968, pp. 72–78.

Wright, Robert C. "O'Neill's Universalizing Technique in *The Iceman Cometh*," in *Modern Drama*. VIII (May, 1965), pp. 1–11.

Young, Stark. *Immortal Shadows*. New York: Scribner's, 1948, pp. 271–274.

Long Day's Journey into Night

Bogard, Travis. *Contour in Time: The Plays of Eugene O'Neill*. New York: Oxford University Press, 1972, pp. 421–445.

Brustein, Robert. *The Theater of Revolt*. Boston: Little, Brown, 1964, pp. 28–31, 348–358.

Carpenter, Frederic I. *Eugene O'Neill*. New York: Twayne, 1964, pp. 158–163.

Cerf, Walter. "Psychoanalysis and the Realistic Drama," in *Journal of Aesthetics and Art Criticism*. XVI (March, 1958), pp. 328–330, 333–336.

Chabrowe, Leonard. *Ritual and Pathos—The Theater of O'Neill*. Lewisburg, Pa.: Bucknell University Press, 1976, pp. 169–187.

Clurman, Harold. *Lies Like Truth*. New York: Macmillan, 1958, pp. 28–33.

Falk, Doris V. *Eugene O'Neill and the Tragic Tension*. New Brunswick, N.J.: Rutgers University Press, 1958, pp. 179–195.

Langford, Richard. "Eugene O'Neill: The Mask of Illusion," in *Essays in Modern American Literature*. Edited by Richard E. Langford. Deland, Fla.: Stetson University Press, 1963, pp. 71–75.

Long, Chester Clayton. *The Role of Nemesis in the Structure of Selected Plays by Eugene O'Neill*. The Hague: Mouton, 1968, pp. 198–215.

Raleigh, John Henry. "O'Neill's *Long Day's Journey into Night* and New England Irish-Catholicism," in *Partisan Review*. XXVI (Fall, 1959), pp. 573–592. Reprinted in *O'Neill: A Collection of Critical Essays*. Edited by John Gassner. Englewood Cliffs, N.J.: Prentice-Hall, 1964, pp. 124–141.

Redford, Grant H. "Dramatic Art vs. Autobiography: A Look at *Long Day's Journey into Night*," in *College English*. XXV (April, 1964), pp. 527–535.

Stamm, Rudolf. " 'Faithful Realism': Eugene O'Neill and the Problem of Style," in *English Studies*. XL (August, 1959), pp. 242–250.

Tiusanen, Timo. *O'Neill's Scenic Images*. Princeton, N.J.: Princeton University Press, 1968, pp. 285–303. Reprinted in *Eugene O'Neill: A Collection of Criticism*. Edited by Ernest G. Griffin. New York: McGraw-Hill, 1976, pp. 114–129.

Törnqvist, Egil. *A Drama of Souls: Studies in O'Neill's Supernaturalistic Technique*. New Haven, Conn.: Yale University Press, 1969, pp. 115–118, 239–244. Reprinted in *Eugene O'Neill: A Collection of Criticism*. Edited by Ernest G. Griffin. New York: McGraw-Hill, 1976, pp. 130–135.

Weissman, Philip. "Conscious and Unconscious Autobiographical Dramas of Eugene O'Neill," in *Journal of the Psychoanalytic Association*. V (1957), pp. 432–460.

Winther, Sophus Keith. "O'Neill's Tragic Themes: *Long Day's Journey into Night*," in *Arizona Quarterly*. XIII (Winter, 1957), pp. 295–307.

Mourning Becomes Electra

Alexander, Doris. "Psychological Fate in *Mourning Becomes Electra*," in *PMLA*. LXVIII (December, 1953), pp. 923–934.

Asselineau, Roger. "*Mourning Becomes Electra* as a Tragedy," in *Modern Drama*. I (December, 1958), pp. 143–150.

Bogard, Travis. *Contour in Time: The Plays of Eugene O'Neill*. New York: Oxford University Press, 1972, pp. 334–354.

Carpenter, Frederic I. *Eugene O'Neill*. New York: Twayne, 1964, pp. 127–133.

Chabrowe, Leonard. *Ritual and Pathos—The Theater of O'Neill*. Lewisburg, Pa.: Bucknell University Press, 1976, pp. 142–166.

Dusenbury, Winifred L. *The Theme of Loneliness in Modern American Drama*. Gainesville: University of Florida Press, 1960, pp. 74–85.

Eastman, Fred. *Christ in the Drama.* New York: Macmillan, 1947, pp. 93–97.

Engle, Edwin A. *The Haunted Heroes of Eugene O'Neill.* Cambridge, Mass.: Harvard University Press, 1953, pp. 241–259.

Frenz, Horst and Martin Mueller. "More Shakespeare and Less Aeschylus in Eugene O'Neill's *Mourning Becomes Electra,*" in *American Literature.* XXXVIII (March, 1966), pp. 85–100.

Knickerbocker, F.W. "A New England House of Atreus," in *Sewanee Review.* XL (April–June, 1932), pp. 249–254.

Lecky, Eleazer. "*Ghosts* and *Mourning Becomes Electra*: Two Versions of Fate," in *Arizona Quarterly.* XXII (Winter, 1957), pp. 320–338.

Long, Chester Clayton. *The Role of Nemesis in the Structure of Selected Plays by Eugene O'Neill.* The Hague: Mouton, 1968, pp. 117–174.

McDonough, Carole and Brian McDonough. "*Mourning Becomes Electra*: A Study of the Conflict Between Puritanism and Paganism," in *English Review.* III (1975), pp. 6–19.

Olson, Elder. "Modern Drama and Tragedy: A View of *Mourning Becomes Electra,*" in *Eugene O'Neill: A Collection of Criticism.* Edited by Ernest G. Griffin. New York: McGraw-Hill, 1976, pp. 87–91.

O'Neill, Joseph P. "The Tragic Theory of Eugene O'Neill," in *Texas Studies in Literature and Language.* IV (Winter, 1963), pp. 482–498.

Porter, Thomas E. *Myth and Modern American Drama.* Detroit: Wayne State University Press, 1969, pp. 26–52.

Skinner, Richard Dana. *Eugene O'Neill: A Poet's Quest.* New York: Longmans, Green, 1935, pp. 211–226.

Stafford, John. "Mourning Becomes America," in *Texas Studies in Literature and Language,* III (Winter, 1962), pp. 549–556.

Tiusanen, Timo. *O'Neill's Scenic Images.* Princeton, N.J.: Princeton University Press, 1968, pp. 225–240.

Young, Stark. *Immortal Shadows.* New York: Scribner's, 1948, pp. 61–66. Reprinted in *O'Neill: A Collection of Critical Essays.* Edited by John Gassner. Englewood Cliffs, N.J.: Prentice-Hall, 1964, pp. 82–88.

Strange Interlude

Alexander, Doris M. "*Strange Interlude* and Schopenhauer," in *American Literature.* XXV (May, 1953), pp. 213–228.

Blackburn, Clara. "Continental Influences on Eugene O'Neill's Expressionistic Dramas," in *American Literature.* XIII (1941), pp. 126–131.

Bogard, Travis. *Contour in Time: The Plays of Eugene O'Neill.* New York: Oxford University Press, 1972, pp. 294–315.

Carpenter, Frederic I. *Eugene O'Neill.* New York: Twayne, 1964, pp. 121–127.

Chabrowe, Leonard. *Ritual and Pathos—The Theater of O'Neill.* Lewisburg, Pa.: Bucknell University Press, 1976, pp. 134–141.

Dusenbury, Winifred L. *The Theme of Loneliness in Modern American Drama.* Gainsville: University of Florida Press, 1960, pp. 101–112.

Engle, Edwin A. *The Haunted Heroes of Eugene O'Neill.* Cambridge, Mass.: Harvard University Press, 1953, pp. 199–229.

Falk, Doris V. *Eugene O'Neill and the Tragic Tension.* New Brunswick, N.J.: Rutgers University Press, 1958, pp. 121–126.

Langer, Lawrence. *The Magic Curtain.* New York: Dutton, 1951, pp. 228–242.

Mickle, Alan D. *Six Plays of Eugene O'Neill.* New York: Liveright, 1929, pp. 139–166.

Skinner, Richard Dana. *Eugene O'Neill: A Poet's Quest.* New York: Longmans, Green, 1935, pp. 191–202.

Tiusanen, Timo. *O'Neill's Scenic Images.* Princeton, N.J.: Princeton University Press, 1968, pp. 212–224.

Winchester, Otis W. "Eugene O'Neill's *Strange Interlude* as a Transcript of America in the 1920's," in *Literature and History.* Edited by I.E. Cadenhead, Jr. Tulsa: University of Tulsa, 1970, pp. 43–58. Reprinted in *Eugene O'Neill: A Collection of Criticism.* Edited by Ernest G. Griffin. New York: McGraw-Hill, 1976, pp. 67–80.

A Touch of the Poet

Alexander, Doris. "Eugene O'Neill and Charles Lever," in *Modern Drama.* V (February, 1963), pp. 415–420.

Bogard, Travis. *Contour in Time: The Plays of Eugene O'Neill.* New York: Oxford University Press, 1972, pp. 368–407.

Carpenter, Frederic I. *Eugene O'Neill.* New York: Twayne, 1964, pp. 147–150.

Chabrowe, Leonard. *Ritual and Pathos—The Theater of O'Neill.* Lewisburg, Pa.: Bucknell University Press, 1976, pp. 193–195.

Driver, Tom F. "On the Late Plays of Eugene O'Neill," in *Tulane Drama Review.* III (December, 1958), pp. 8–10, 16–20. Reprinted in *O'Neill: A Collection of Critical Essays.* Edited by John Gassner. Englewood Cliffs, N.J.: Prentice-Hall, 1964, pp. 110–123.

Falk, Doris V. *Eugene O'Neill and the Tragic Tension.* New Brunswick, N.J.: Rutgers University Press, 1958, pp. 165–170.

Fiet, Lowell A. "O'Neill's Modification of Traditional American Themes in *A Touch of the Poet*," in *Educational Theater Journal.* XXVII (1975), pp. 508–515.

McCarthy, Mary. *Theater Chronicle.* New York: Noonday, 1963, pp. 199–208.

Marcus, Mordecai. "Eugene O'Neill's Debt to Thoreau in *A Touch of the Poet*," in *Journal of English and Germanic Philology.* LXII (April, 1963), pp. 270–279.

Pallette, Drew B. "O'Neill's *A Touch of the Poet* and His Other Last Plays," in *Arizona Quarterly.* XIII (Winter, 1957), pp. 308–319.

Raleigh, John H. *The Plays of Eugene O'Neill.* Carbondale: Southern Illinois University Press, 1965. Reprinted in *Eugene O'Neill: A Collection of Criticism.* Edited by Ernest G. Griffin. New York: McGraw-Hill, 1976, pp. 81–86.

Tiusanen, Timo. *O'Neill's Scenic Images.* Princeton, N.J.: Princeton University Press, 1968, pp. 321–330.

Winther, Sophus Keith. "O'Neill's Posthumous Play: *A Touch of the Poet*," in *Prairie Schooner.* XXXII (Spring, 1958), pp. 7–12.

JOSÉ ORTEGA Y GASSET
(1883–1955)

The Modern Theme

Binesse, Harry Lorin. *"The Modern Theme,"* in *American Review.* I (April, 1933), pp. 104–110.

Ferratur Mora, José. *Ortega y Gasset: An Outline of His Philosophy.* New Haven, Conn.: Yale University Press, 1957, pp. 31–37.

Hazlitt, Henry. "Culture vs. 'Life,' " in *Nation.* CXXXVI (February 22, 1933), p. 209.

McClintock, Robert. *Man and His Circumstances: Ortega as Educator.* New York: Teacher's College Press, 1971, pp. 397–421.

Marias, Julian. *José Ortega y Gasset: Circumstance and Vocation.* Norman: University of Oklahoma Press, 1970, pp. 380–412.

Niedermayer, Franz. *José Ortega y Gasset.* New York: Frederick Ungar, 1973, pp. 46–50.

Pell, Orlie. *"The Modern Theme,"* in *Journal of Philosophy.* XXX (August 17, 1933), pp. 470–472.

Raley, Harold C. *José Ortega y Gasset: Philosopher of European Unity.* University: University of Alabama Press, 1971, pp. 85–123.

Sanchez Villasenor, José. *Ortega y Gasset, Existentialist: A Critical Study of His Thought and Its Sources.* Chicago: Regnery, 1949, pp. 37–46.

Sands, William Franklin. "Meta-History," in *Commonweal.* XVII (March 29, 1933), pp. 611–612.

The Revolt of the Masses

Campbell, Brenton. "Perez de Ayala and Ortega y Gasset," in *Hispanic Review.* XXXVII (July, 1969), pp. 375–382.

Ceplecha, Christian. *The Historical Thought of José Ortega y Gasset.* Washington, D.C.: Catholic University of America Press, 1958, p. 21.

Clive, G. *"Revolt of the Masses,"* in *Daedalus.* CIII (Winter, 1974), pp. 75–82.

Hesse, Hermann. "José Ortega y Gasset," in *My Belief.* New York: Farrar, 1974, pp. 371–372.

Holmes, Oliver W. *Human Reality and the Social World: Ortega's Philosophy of History.* Amherst: University of Massachusetts Press, 1975, pp. 65–67.

Maldonado-Denis, M. "Ortega y Gasset and the Theory of the Masses," in *Western Political Quarterly.* XIV (September, 1961), pp. 676–690.

Marias, Julian. *José Ortega y Gasset: Circumstance and Vocation.* Norman: University of Oklahoma Press, 1970, pp. 210–211.

Niedermayer, Franz. *José Ortega y Gasset.* Translated by Peter Tirner. New York: Frederick Ungar, 1973, pp. 51–53.

Raley, Harold. *José Ortega y Gasset: Philosopher of European Unity.* University: University of Alabama Press, 1971, pp. 103–123.

Weintraub, K.J. "Ortega y Gasset," in *Visions of Culture.* Chicago: University of Chicago Press, 1966, pp. 247–287.

GEORGE ORWELL
(1903–1950)

Animal Farm: A Fairy Story

Animal Farm, *A Critical Commentary*. New York: American R.D.M. Corp., 1963.

Baker, Isadore L. *George Orwell:* Animal Farm. London: Brodie, 1961.

Brown, Spencer. "Stange Doings on *Animal Farm*," in *Commentary*. XIX (February, 1955), pp. 155–161.

Carter, Thomas. "Group Psychology Phenomena of a Political System as Satirized in *Animal Farm*: An Application of the Theories of W.R. Bion," in *Human Relations*. XXVII (June, 1974), pp. 525–546.

Colquitt, Betsey F. "Orwell; Traditionalist in Wonderland," in *Discourse*. VIII (Autumn, 1965), pp. 370–383.

Cook, Richard. "Rudyard Kipling and George Orwell," in *Modern Fiction Studies*. VII (Summer, 1961), pp. 125–135.

Cooper, Nancy. "*Animal Farm*: An Explication for Teachers of Orwell's Novel," in *California English Journal*. IV (1968), pp. 59–69.

Gulbin, Suzanne. "Parallels and Contrasts in *Lord of the Flies* and *Animal Farm*," in *English Journal*. LV (1966), pp. 86–90.

Harward, Timothy B. *European Patterns; Contemporary Patterns in European Writing*. Chester Springs, Pa.: DuFour, 1967, pp. 44–48.

Hoggart, Richard. *Speaking to Each Other; Essays*. New York: Oxford University Press, 1970, vol. 2, pp. 106–110.

Hopkinson, Tom. "*Animal Farm*," in *World Review*. XVI (June, 1950), pp. 54–57.

Kubal, David L. *Outside the Whale: George Orwell's Art and Politics*. Notre Dame, Ind.: Notre Dame University Press, 1972, pp. 37–40, 122–130.

Lee, Robert. *Orwell's Fiction*. Notre Dame, Ind.: Notre Dame University Press, 1969, pp. 105–127.

_____. "The Uses of Form: A Reading of *Animal Farm*," in *Studies in Short Fiction*. VI (1969), pp. 557–573.

Meyers, Jeffrey. "Orwell's Bestiary: The Political Allegory of *Animal Farm*," in *Studies in the Twentieth Century*. VIII (1971), pp. 65–84.

_____. *A Readers Guide to George Orwell*. London: Thames and Hudson, 1975, pp. 130–143.

Oxley, B.T. *George Orwell*. New York: Arco, 1969, pp. 75–82.

Schlesinger, Arthur, Jr. "Mr. Orwell and the Communists," in *New York Times Book Review*. (August 25, 1946), pp. 1, 28.

Zwerdling, Alex. *Orwell and the New Left.* New Haven, Conn.: Yale University Press, 1974, pp. 88–96, 198–199, 203–207.

Nineteen Eighty-Four

Alldritt, Keith. *The Making of George Orwell: An Essay in Literary History.* New York: St. Martin's, 1969, pp. 150–178.

Atkins, John A. *George Orwell: A Literary Study.* London: J. Calder, 1954, pp. 237–254.

Barr, Alan. "The Paradise Behind *1984*," in *English Miscellany.* XIX (1968), pp. 197–203.

Calder, Jenni. *Chronicles of Conscience: A Study of George Orwell and Arthur Koestler.* Pittsburgh: University of Pittsburgh Press, 1968, pp. 229–253.

Connors, J. " 'Do It to Julia': Thoughts on Orwell's *1984*," in *Modern Fiction Studies.* XVI (Winter, 1970–1971), pp. 463–473.

Dyson, Anthony E. *The Crazy Fabric; Essays in Irony.* New York: St. Martin's, 1965, pp. 197–219.

Elsbree, Langdon. "The Structured Nightmare of *1984*," in *Twentieth Century Literature.* V (October, 1959), pp. 135–141.

Fink, Howard. "Newspeak: The Epitome of Parody Techniques in *Nineteen Eighty-Four*," in *Critical Survey.* V (1971), pp. 155–163.

Harris, Harold J. "Orwell's Essays and *1984*," in *Twentieth Century Literature.* IV (January, 1959), pp. 154–161.

Howe, Irving. *Orwell's Nineteen Eighty-Four: Text, Sources, Criticism.* New York: Harcourt Brace, 1963.

Hynes, Samuel L. *Twentieth Century Interpretations of 1984: A Collection of Critical Essays.* Englewood Cliffs, N.J.: Prentice-Hall, 1971.

Karl, Frederick R. "George Orwell: The White Man's Burden," in *A Reader's Guide to the Contemporary English Novel.* Edited by Frederick R. Karl. New York: Octagon, 1972, pp. 159–161, 163–165.

Kessler, Martin. "Power and the Perfect State: A Study in Disillusionment as Reflected in Orwell's *Nineteen Eighty-Four* and Huxley's *Brave New World*," in *Political Science Quarterly.* LXXII (December, 1957), pp. 565–577.

Knox, George. "The Divine Comedy in *1984*," in *Western Humanities Review.* IX (Autumn, 1955), pp. 371–372.

Kubal, David L. *Outside the Whale: George Orwell's Art and Politics.* Notre Dame, Ind.: Notre Dame University Press, 1972, pp. 43–47, 130–141.

Lee, Robert E. *Orwell's Fiction.* Notre Dame, Ind.: Notre Dame University Press, 1969, pp. 128–157.

Lief, Ruth Ann.   *Homage to Oceania: The Prophetic Vision of George Orwell.* Columbus: Ohio State University Press, 1969.

Maddison, Michael.   "*1984*: A Burnhamite Fantasy?," in *Political Quarterly.* XXXII (January–March, 1961), pp. 71–79.

Malkin, Lawrence.   "Halfway to *1984*," in *Horizon.* XII (Spring, 1970), pp. 33–39.

Oxley, B.T.   *George Orwell.* New York: Arco, 1969, pp. 112–125.

Ranald, Ralph A.   "George Orwell and the Mad World: The Anti-Universe of *1984*," in *South Atlantic Quarterly.* LXVI (Autumn, 1967), pp. 544–553.

Rankin, David.   "Orwell's Intention in *1984*," in *English Language Notes.* XII (1975), pp. 188–192.

Smith, Marcus.   "The Wall of Blackness: A Psychological Approach to *1984*," in *Modern Fiction Studies.* XIV (Winter, 1968–1969), pp. 423–433.

Steinhoff, William.   *George Orwell and the Origins of 1984.* Ann Arbor: University of Michigan Press, 1975.

Thale, Jerome.   "Orwell's Modest Proposal," in *Critical Quarterly.* IV (Winter, 1962), pp. 365–368.

JOHN JAMES OSBORNE
(1929–   )

The Entertainer

Allsop, Kenneth. *The Angry Decade.* London: Peter Owen, 1958, pp. 114–122.

Anderson, Michael. *Anger and Detachment: A Study of Arden, Osborne, and Pinter.* London: Pitman, 1976, pp. 37–41.

Baxter, K.M. *Speak What We Feel: A Christian Looks at the Contemporary Theatre.* London: SCM Press, 1964, pp. 62–71.

Brown, John Russell. *Theatre Language: A Study of Arden, Osborne, Pinter, and Wesker.* New York: Taplinger, 1972, pp. 118–157.

Carter, Alan. *John Osborne.* Edinburgh: Oliver and Boyd, 1969, pp. 63–71.

Deming, Barbara. "John Osborne's Man Against the Philistines," in *Hudson Review.* XI (1959), pp. 411–419.

Hayman, Ronald. *John Osborne.* London: Heineman, 1969, pp. 23–31.

Kennedy, Andrew K. *Six Dramatists in Search of a Language.* London: Cambridge University Press, 1975, pp. 206–212.

Lahr, John. *Up Against the Fourth Wall.* New York: Grove, 1970, pp. 231–245.

Lucas, Barbara. "Looking Back at *The Entertainer*," in *Twentieth Century.* CLXI (June, 1957), pp. 583–585.

Lumley, Frederick. *New Trends in Twentieth Century Drama.* London: Barrie and Rockliff, 1967, pp. 221–232.

Rillie, John A.M. "*The Entertainer*," in *Insight IV: Analyses of Modern British and American Drama.* Edited by Hermann J. Weiand. Frankfurt, Germany: Hirschgraben, 1975, pp. 94–102.

Sundrann, Jean. "The Necessary Illusion," in *Antioch Review.* XVIII (Summer, 1958), pp. 236–244.

Taylor, John Russell. *The Angry Theatre: New British Drama.* New York: Hill and Wang, 1969, pp. 47–50.

Trussler, Simon. *The Plays of John Osborne: An Assessment.* London: Gollancz, 1969, pp. 56–75.

Inadmissible Evidence

Anderson, Michael. *Anger and Detachment: A Study of Arden, Osborne and Pinter.* London: Pitman, 1976, pp. 14–20.

Brown, John Russell. *Theatre Language: A Study of Arden, Osborne, Pinter and Wesker.* New York: Taplinger, 1972, pp. 118–157.

Carter, Alan. *John Osborne.* Edinburgh: Oliver and Boyd, 1969, pp. 87–92.

Clurman, Harold. *The Naked Image.* New York: Macmillan, 1966, pp. 101–104.

Hayman, Ronald. *John Osborne.* London: Heineman, 1969, pp. 65–72.

Kerr, Walter. *Thirty Plays Hath November: Pain and Pleasure in the Contemporary Theater.* New York: Simon and Schuster, 1969, pp. 46–49.

Lahr, John. *Up Against the Fourth Wall.* New York: Grove, 1970, pp. 232–245.

Lumley, Frederick. *New Trends in Twentieth Century Drama.* London: Barrie and Rockliff, 1967, pp. 221–232.

Roy, Emil. *British Drama Since Shaw.* Carbondale: Southern Illinois University Press, 1972, pp. 104–106.

Simon, John. "Theatre Chronicle," in *Hudson Review.* XIX (Spring, 1966), pp. 112–113.

Taylor, John Russell. *The Angry Theatre: New British Drama.* New York: Hill and Wang, 1969, pp. 60–63.

Trussler, Simon. *The Plays of John Osborne: An Assessment.* London: Gollancz, 1969, pp. 120–138.

Look Back in Anger

Allsop, Kenneth. *The Angry Decade.* London: Peter Owen, 1958, pp. 104–113.

Anderson, Michael. *Anger and Detachment: A Study of Arden, Osborne, and Pinter.* London: Pitman, 1976, pp. 36–37.

Bierhaus, E.G., Jr. "No World of Its Own: *Look Back in Anger* Twenty Years Later," in *Modern Drama.* XIX (1976), pp. 47–56.

Brown, John Russell. *Theatre Language: A Study of Arden, Osborne, Pinter, and Wesker.* New York: Taplinger, 1972, pp. 118–157.

Carter, Alan. *John Osborne.* Edinburgh: Oliver and Boyd, 1969, pp. 51–62.

Deming, Barbara. "John Osborne's Man Against the Philistines," in *Hudson Review.* XI (1959), pp. 411–419.

Dyson, A.E. "*Look Back in Anger*," in *Critical Quarterly.* I (1959), pp. 318–326. Reprinted in *Modern British Dramatists: A Collection of Critical Essays.* Edited by John Russell Brown. Englewood Cliffs, N.J.: Prentice-Hall, 1968, pp. 47–57.

Faber, M.D. "The Character of Jimmy Porter: An Approach to *Look Back in Anger*," in *Modern Drama.* XIII (1970), pp. 67–77.

Freedman, Morris. *The Moral Impulse: Modern Drama from Ibsen to the Present.* Carbondale: Southern Illinois University Press, 1967, pp. 115–120.

Hayman, Ronald. *John Osborne.* London: Heineman, 1969, pp. 17–22.

Huss, Roy. "John Osborne's Backward Half-Way Look," in *Modern Drama.* VI (1963), pp. 20–25.

Karrfalt, David H. "The Social Theme in Osborne's Plays," in *Modern Drama.* XIII (May, 1970), pp. 78–82.

Kershaw, John. *The Present Stage.* London: Fontana, 1966, pp. 21–41.

Lahr, John. *Up Against the Fourth Wall.* New York: Grove, 1970, pp. 231–245.

Lumley, Frederick. *New Trends in Twentieth Century Drama.* London: Barrie and Rockliff, 1967, pp. 221–232.

McCarthy, Mary. *Sights and Spectacles.* London: Heineman, 1959, pp. 184–196.

Murphy, Brian. "Jimmy Porter and the Logic of Rage in *Look Back in Anger*," in *Midwest Quarterly.* XVIII (July, 1977), pp. 361–373.

Roy, Emil. *British Drama Since Shaw.* Carbondale: Southern Illinois University Press, 1972, pp. 100–103.

Taylor, John Russell. *The Angry Theatre: New British Drama.* New York: Hill and Wang, 1969, pp. 31–36, 39–45.

Trilling, Ossia. "The New English Realism," in *Tulane Drama Review.* VII (1962), pp. 184–193.

Trussler, Simon. *The Plays of John Osborne: An Assessment.* London: Gollancz, 1969, pp. 40–55.

Weiss, Samuel A. "Osborne's Angry Young Play," in *Educational Theatre Journal.* XII (December, 1960), pp. 285–288.

Williams, Raymond. *Drama from Ibsen to Brecht.* London: Chatto and Windus, 1968, pp. 318–325.

Wolfe, Bernard. "Angry at What?," in *Nation.* CLXXXVII (1958), pp. 316–322.

Young, Wayland. "London Letter," in *Kenyon Review.* XVII (Autumn, 1956), pp. 642–647.

Luther

Brown, John Russell. *Theatre Language: A Study of Arden, Osborne, Pinter, and Wesker.* New York: Taplinger, 1972, pp. 118–157.

Brustein, Robert. *Seasons of Discontent.* New York: Simon and Schuster, 1965, pp. 196–200.

Carter, Alan. *John Osborne.* Edinburgh: Oliver and Boyd, 1969, pp. 76–87.

Gilman, Richard. "John Osborne's *Luther*," in *Commonweal.* LXXXIX (October 18, 1963), pp. 103–104.

Hayman, Ronald. *John Osborne.* London: Heineman, 1969, pp. 42–52.

Karrfalb, David H. "The Social Theme in Osborne's Plays," in *Modern Drama.* XIII (May, 1970), pp. 78–82.

Kennedy, Andrew K. *Six Dramatists in Search of a Language.* London: Cambridge University Press, 1975, pp. 202–204.

Lumley, Frederick. *New Trends in Twentieth Century Drama.* London: Barrie and Rockliff, 1967, pp. 221–232.

Marowitz, Charles. "The Ascension of John Osborne," in *Tulane Drama Review.* VII (1962), pp. 175–179.

O'Brien, Charles H. "Osborne's *Luther* and the Humanistic Tradition," in *Renascence.* XXI (1969), pp. 59–63.

Taylor, John Russell. *The Angry Theatre: New British Drama.* New York: Hill and Wang, 1969, pp. 55–57.

Trussler, Simon. *The Plays of John Osborne: An Assessment.* London: Gollancz, 1969, pp. 95–107.

Waugh, Evelyn. "*Luther*, John Osborne's New Play," in *Critic.* XX (1962), pp. 53–55.

OVID
(43 B.C.–18 A.D.)

Amores

Berman, K. "Some Propertian Imitations in Ovid's *Amores*," in *Classical Philology*. LXVII (July, 1972), pp. 170–177.

Brooks, Otis. *Ovid as an Epic Poet.* Cambridge: Cambridge University Press, 1970.

Cameron, A. "The First Edition of Ovid's *Amores*," in *Classical Quarterly*. XVIII (1968), pp. 320–333.

Dickson, T.W. "Borrowed Themes in Ovid's *Amores*," in *Classical Journal*. LIX (January, 1964), pp. 175–180.

Graves, Robert. "Ovid and the Libertines," in his *Difficult Questions, Easy Answers*. New York: Doubleday, 1973, pp. 129–138.

Kenney, E.J. "On the Somnium Attributed to Ovid," in *Agon*. III (1969), pp. 1–14.

————. "Tradition of Avid's *Amores*," in *Classical Review*. V (March, 1955), pp. 13–14, and VIII (March, 1957), p. 16.

Lee, A.G. " 'Tenerorum Lusor Amorum,' " in *Critical Essays on Roman Literature: Elegy and Lyric*. Edited by J.P. Sullivan. Cambridge, Mass.: Harvard University Press, 1962, pp. 149–179.

Oliver, R.P. "The Text of Ovid's *Amores*," in *Classical Studies Presented to Ben Edwin Perry*. Urbana: University of Illinois Press, 1969, pp. 138–164.

Parker, D. "Ovidian Coda," in *Arion*. VIII (Spring, 1969), pp. 80–97.

Singer, L. "Love in Ovid and Lucretius," in *Hudson Review*. XVIII (Winter, 1965–1966), pp. 537–559.

Thomas, E. "Variations on a Military Theme in Ovid's *Amores*," in *Greece and Rome*. XI (October, 1964), pp. 151–165.

Ars Amatoria

Alexander, W.H. "The Culpa of Ovid," in *Classical Journal*. LIII (April, 1958), pp. 319–325.

Brooks, Otis. *Ovid as an Epic Poet.* Cambridge: Cambridge University Press, 1970.

Courtney, E. "Two Cruces in the *Ars Amatoria*," in *Classical Review*. XX (March, 1970), pp. 10–11.

Crossland, J. "Ovid's Contribution to the Conception of Love Known as 'l'Amour Courtois,' " in *Modern Language Review*. XLII (April, 1947), pp. 199–206.

Leach, E.W. "Georgic Imagery in the *Ars Amatoria*," in *Transactions of the American Philological Association*. XCV (1964), pp. 142–154.

Rudd, Niall. "History: Ovid and the Augustan Myth," in his *Lines of Enquiry; Studies in Latin Poetry*. New York: Cambridge University Press, 1976, pp. 1–31.

Wardman, A.E. "The Rape of the Sabines," in *Classical Quarterly*. XV (1965), pp. 101–113.

Heroides

Courtney, E. "Problems in Ovid's *Heroides*," in *Mnemosyne*. XXVII (1974), pp. 298–299.

Cunningham, M.P. "The Novelty of Ovid's *Heroides*," in *Classical Philology*. XLIV (1949), pp. 100–106.

Dean, N. "Chaucer's Complaint, a Genre Descended from the *Heroides*," in *Comparative Literature*. XIX (Winter, 1967), pp. 1–27.

Fisher, E.A. "Two Notes on the *Heroides*," in *Harvard Studies in Classical Philology*. LXXIX (1975), pp. 193–205.

Jacobson, Howard. *Ovid's* Heroides. Princeton, N.J.: Princeton University Press, 1974, pp. 3–11.

Trowbridge, Frederich Hoyt. "Pope's Eloisa and the *Heroides* of Ovid," in his *From Dryden to Jane Austen*. Albuquerque: University of New Mexico Press, 1977, pp. 135–153.

The Metamorphoses

Anderson, W.S. "Multiple Change in *The Metamorphoses*," in *Transactions of the American Philological Association*. XCIV (1963), pp. 1–29.

Baver, D.F. "The Function of Pygmalion in the *Metamorphoses* of Ovid," in *Transactions of the American Philological Association*. XCIII (1962), pp. 1–21.

Benns, J.W. *Ovid*. London: Routledge and Kegan Paul, 1973.

Bowra, C.M. "Orpheus and Eurydice," in *Classical Quarterly*. II (1952), pp. 113–126.

Coleman, R. "Structure and Intention in the *Metamorphoses*," in *Classical Quarterly*. XXI (1971), pp. 461–477.

Frankel, H. "Ovid," in *Sather Classical Lectures*. XVIII (1945), pp. 72–110.

————. *Ovid; A Poet Between 2 Worlds*. Berkeley: University of California Press, 1945.

Galinsky, Gotthard Karl. *Ovid's* Metamorphoses: *An Introduction to the Basic Aspects*. Berkeley: University of California Press, 1975.

Grant, Michael. "The New Elegy and the *Metamorphoses* of Ovid," in *Roman Literature*. Baltimore: Penguin, 1964, pp. 207–218.

Griffin, A.H.F. "Ovid's *Metamorphoses*," in *Greece and Rome*. XXIV (April, 1977), pp. 57–70.

Highet, G. "Ovid's *Metamorphoses*: The Book of Miracles," in his *Powers of Poetry*. New York: Oxford University Press, 1960, pp. 264–270.

Hoffman, Richard Lester. *Ovid and* The Canterbury Tales. Philadelphia: University of Pennsylvania Press, 1966.

Norwood, F. "Unity in the Diversity of Ovid's *Metamorphoses*," in *Classical Journal*. LIX (January, 1964), pp. 170–174.

Otis, Brooks. *Ovid as an Epic Poet*. Cambridge: Cambridge University Press, 1970.

Parry, H. "Ovid's *Metamorphoses*: Violence in a Pastoral Language," in *Transactions of the American Philological Association*. XCV (1964), pp. 268–282.

Rand, Edward Kennard. *Ovid and His Influence*. Boston: Marshall Jones, 1925.

Segal, C. *Landscape in Ovid's* Metamorphoses. *A Study in the Transformations of a Literary Symbol*. Wiesbaden, Germany: F. Steiner, 1969.

_____. "Narrative Art in the *Metamorphoses*," in *Classical Journal*. LXVI (1971), pp. 331–337.

Shannon, Edgar Finley. *Chaucer and the Roman Poets*. Cambridge, Mass.: Harvard University Press, 1929.

Stephens, W.C. "Descent to the Underworld in Ovid's *Metamorphoses*," in *Classical Journal*. LIII (January, 1958), pp. 177–183.

Stirrup, B.E. "Technique of Rape: Variety of Wit in Ovid's *Metamorphoses*," in *Greece and Rome*. XXIV (October, 1977), pp. 170–184.

Sullivan, J.P. "Ovid and Epic," in *Oxford Review*. IV (1967), pp. 72–80.

Wilkinson, Lancelot Patrick. *Ovid Surveyed*. Cambridge: Cambridge University Press, 1962.

Wright, Frederich A. *Three Roman Poets; Plautus, Catullus, Ovid; Their Lives, Times and Works*. New York: Dutton, 1938.

THOMAS PAINE
(1737–1809)

The Age of Reason

Aldridge, Alfred Owen. *Man of Reason: The Life of Thomas Paine.* London: Cresset Press, 1960, pp. 229–237.

Best, Mary Agnes. *Thomas Paine: Prophet and Martyr of Democracy.* London: Allen and Unwin, 1927, pp. 307–321.

Conway, Moncure Daniel. *The Life of Thomas Paine.* New York: Putnam's, 1909, pp. 181–222.

Del Veccio, Thomas. *Tom Paine: American.* New York: Whittier Books, 1956, pp. 163–165.

Edwards, Samuel. *Rebel! A Biography of Tom Paine.* New York: Praeger, 1974, pp. 186–194, 284–287.

Foner, Eric. *Tom Paine and Revolutionary America.* New York: Oxford University Press, 1976, pp. 245–257.

Hawke, David Freeman. *Paine.* New York: Harper & Row, 1974, pp. 292–295.

Leffman, Henry. "The Real Thomas Paine, Patriot and Publicist, A Philosopher Misunderstood," in *Pennsylvania Magazine of History and Biography.* XLVI (1922), pp. 81–99.

McCloy, Shelby T. "Rationalists and Religion in the Eighteenth Century," in *South Atlantic Quarterly.* XLVI (1947), pp. 468–482.

Nicholson, Marjorie. "Thomas Paine, Edward Nares, and Mrs. Piozzi's Marginalia," in *Huntington Library Bulletin.* No. 10 (1936), pp. 103–133.

Prochaska, Franklyn K. "Thomas Paine's *The Age of Reason* Revisited," in *Journal of the History of Ideas.* XXXIII (1972), pp. 561–576.

Smith, Frank. *Thomas Paine: Liberator.* New York: Frederick A. Stokes, 1938, pp. 213–229.

Smylie, James H. "Clerical Perspectives on Deism: Paine's *The Age of Reason* in Virginia," in *Eighteenth-Century Studies.* VI (1972–1973), pp. 203–220.

Wilson, Jerome D. and William F. Ricketson. *Thomas Paine.* Boston: Twayne, 1978, pp. 103–125.

Wilson, Rufus Rockwell. "Foreign Authors in America," in *Bookman.* XII (1901), pp. 498–500.

Woodward, W.E. *Tom Paine: America's Godfather, 1737–1809.* New York: Dutton, 1945, pp. 254–274.

Common Sense

Alden, John R. *The American Revolution, 1775–1783.* New York: Harper Torchbooks, 1962, pp. 76–77.

————. *A History of the American Revolution.* New York: Knopf, 1969, pp. 236–239.

Aldridge, Alfred Owen. "The Influence of New York Newspapers on Paine's *Common Sense*," in *New York Historical Society Quarterly.* LX (1976), pp. 53–60.

————. *Man of Reason: The Life of Thomas Paine.* London: Cresset Press, 1960, pp. 35–43.

Best, Mary Agnes. *Thomas Paine: Prophet and Martyr of Democracy.* London: Allen and Unwin, 1927, pp. 70–80.

Conway, Moncure Daniel. *The Life of Thomas Paine.* New York: Putnam's, 1909, pp. 61–77.

Davidson, Philip. *Propaganda and the American Revolution, 1763–1783.* Chapel Hill: University of North Carolina Press, 1941, pp. 131–133.

Del Veccio, Thomas. *Tom Paine: American.* New York: Whittier Books, 1956, pp. 39–53.

Eastman, Max. "Tom Paine: Crusader for Common Sense," in *Reader's Digest.* XLIV (March, 1944), pp. 78–84.

Edwards, Samuel. *Rebel! A Biography of Tom Paine.* New York: Praeger, 1974, pp. 32–36.

Fleming, Thomas. *1776: Year of Illusions.* New York: Norton, 1975, pp. 122–128.

Foner, Eric. *Tom Paine and Revolutionary America.* New York: Oxford University Press, 1976, pp. 74–87.

Fulcher, J. Rodney. "*Common Sense* versus *Plain Truth*: Propaganda and Civil Society," in *Southern Quarterly.* XV (1976), pp. 57–74.

Goldman, Eric F. "Books That Changed America," in *Saturday Review.* XXXVI (July 4, 1953), pp. 7–8.

Hawke, David Freeman. *Paine.* New York: Harper & Row, 1974, pp. 41–49.

Ierley, Merritt. *The Year That Tried Men's Souls: A Journalistic Reconstruction of the World of 1776.* New York: Barnes, 1976, pp. 37–38, 49–51.

Roberts, Mary Margaret. "Introduction to Paine's *Common Sense*," in *Pamphlets and the American Revolution.* Edited by G. Jack Gravlee and James R. Irvine. Delmar, N.Y.: Scholar's Facsimiles and Reprints, 1976, pp. i–vii.

Smith, Frank. *Thomas Paine: Liberator.* New York: Frederick A. Stokes, 1938, pp. 21–35.

Smith, Page. *A New Age Now Begins.* New York: McGraw-Hill, 1976, pp. 677–684.

Stoehr, Taylor. "Tone and Voice," in *College English*. XXX (1968–1969), pp. 150–161.

Wilson, Jerome D. and William F. Ricketson. *Thomas Paine.* Boston: Twayne, 1978, pp. 30–44.

Woodward, W.E. *Tom Paine: America's Godfather, 1737–1809.* New York: Dutton, 1945, pp. 66–84.

The Crisis

Aldridge, Alfred Owen. *Man of Reason: The Life of Thomas Paine.* London: Cresset Press, 1960, pp. 48–58.

Best, Mary Agnes. *Thomas Paine: Prophet and Martyr of Democracy.* London: Allen and Unwin, 1927, pp. 99–105.

Conway, Moncure Daniel. *The Life of Thomas Paine.* New York: Putnam's, 1909, pp. 83–89.

Del Veccio, Thomas. *Tom Paine: American.* New York: Whittier Books, 1956, pp. 60–64.

Edwards, Samuel. *Rebel! A Biography of Tom Paine.* New York: Praeger, 1974, pp. 41–55.

Foner, Eric. *Tom Paine and Revolutionary America.* New York: Oxford University Press, 1976, pp. 139–140.

Hawke, David Freeman. *Paine.* New York: Harper & Row, 1974, pp. 59–76.

Smith, Frank. *Thomas Paine: Liberator.* New York: Frederick A. Stokes, 1938, pp. 36–52.

Wilson, Jerome D. and William F. Ricketson. *Thomas Paine.* Boston: Twayne, 1978, pp. 45–48.

Woodward, W.E. *Tom Paine: America's Godfather, 1737–1809.* New York: Dutton, 1945, pp. 89–94.

The Rights of Man

Aldridge, Alfred Owen. *Man of Reason: The Life of Thomas Paine.* London: Cresset Press, 1960, pp. 134–144, 156–168, 182–187.

Best, Mary Agnes. *Thomas Paine: Prophet and Martyr of Democracy.* London: Allen and Unwin, 1927, pp. 259–266.

Conway, Moncure Daniel. *The Life of Thomas Paine.* New York: Putnam's, 1909, pp. 328–346.

Edwards, Samuel. *Rebel! A Biography of Tom Paine.* New York: Praeger, 1974, pp. 119–125, 130–133, 279–283.

Foner, Eric. *Tom Paine and Revolutionary America.* New York: Oxford University Press, 1976, pp. 214–220, 228–231.

Hawke, David Freeman. *Paine.* New York: Harper & Row, 1974, pp. 219–249.

Lewis, Joseph. *Thomas Paine: Author of the Declaration of Independence.* New York: Freethought Press, 1947, pp. 187–188.

Schmulowitz, Nat. "Thou Shalt Not Read *The Rights of Man,*" in *United States Law Review.* LXXIII (1939), pp. 271–286.

Smith, Frank. *Thomas Paine: Liberator.* New York: Frederick A. Stokes, 1938, pp. 130–147.

West, E.G. "Tom Paine's Voucher Scheme for Public Education," in *Southern Economic Journal.* XXXIII (1966–1967), pp. 378–382.

Wilson, Jerome D. and William F. Ricketson. *Thomas Paine.* Boston: Twayne, 1978, pp. 72–100.

Woodward, W.E. *Tom Paine: America's Godfather, 1737–1809.* New York: Dutton, 1945, pp. 173–198.

BORIS PASTERNAK
(1890–1960)

Doctor Zhivago

Baird, Sister M. Julian. "Pasternak's Zhivago-Hamlet-Christ," in *Renascence*. XIV (1962), pp. 179–184.

Chiaromonte, Nicola. "Pasternak's Message," in *Partisan Review*. XXV (Winter, 1958), pp. 127–134.

Conquest, Robert. *The Pasternak Affair*. Philadelphia: Lippincott, 1962.

Dyck, J.W. *Boris Pasternak*. New York: Twayne, 1972.

———. "*Doktor Zivago*: A Quest for Self-Realization," in *Slavic and East European Journal*. VI (1962), pp. 117–124.

Fortin, R.E. "Home and the Uses of Creative Nostalgia in *Doctor Zhivago*," in *Modern Fiction Studies*. XX (Summer, 1974), pp. 202–209.

Frank, Victors. "A Russian Hamlet: Boris Pasternak's Novel," in *Dublin Review*. CCXXXII (Autumn, 1958), pp. 212–220.

Gibbian, George. *Interval of Freedom: Soviet Literature During the Thaw, 1954–1957*. Minneapolis: University of Minnesota Press, 1960, pp. 145–158.

Jackson, Robert L. "*Doktor Zivago* and the Living Tradition," in *Slavic and East European Journal*. IV (1960), pp. 103–118.

Kayden, Eugene M. "On Re-Reading the Poems of *Doctor Zhivago*," in *Colorado Quarterly*. XXIII (1975), pp. 396–401.

Lamont, R.C. "Yuri Zhivago Fairy Tale: A Dream Poem," in *World Literature Today*. LI (Autumn, 1977), pp. 517–521.

Lehrman, Edgar H. "*A Minority Opinion on* Doctor Zhivago," in *Emory University Quarterly*. XVI (1960), pp. 77–84.

Livingstone, Angela. "Allegory & Christianity in *Doctor Zhivago*," in *Melbourne Slavonic Studies*. I (1967), pp. 24–33.

Loose, Gerhard. "Pasternak's *Doctor Zhivago*," in *Colorado Quarterly*. VII (Winter, 1959), pp. 263–270.

Payne, Robert. *The Three Worlds of Boris Pasternak*. Bloomington: Indiana University Press, 1963.

Powers, Richard Howard. "Ideology and *Doctor Zhivago*," in *Antioch Review*. XIX (Summer, 1959), pp. 224–236.

Reeve, F.D. "*Doctor Zhivago*: From Prose to Verse," in *Kenyon Review*. XXII (1960), pp. 123–136.

Rogers, T.F. "Implications of Christ's Passion in *Doktor Zivago*," in *Slavic and East European Journal*. XVIII (Winter, 1974), pp. 384–391.

Sajkovic, Miriam A. "Notes on Boris Pasternak's *Doctor Zhivago*," in *Slavic and East European Journal*. IV (1960), pp. 319–330.

Struve, Gleb. "Sense and Nonsense About *Doctor Zhivago*," in *Studies in Russian and Polish Literature*. LVI (1962), pp. 229–250.

Wain, John. "The Meaning of *Doctor Zhivago*," in *Critical Quarterly*. X (1968), pp. 113–137.

The Poetry of Pasternak

Barnes, Joseph. "Pasternak's Poems," in *Sewanee Review*. LXVIII (1960), pp. 335–338.

Bayley, John and Donald Davie. "*Dr. Zhivago's* Poems," in *Essays in Criticism*. XVI (1966), pp. 212–219.

Bodin, Per Arne. *Nine Poems from* Doktor Zivago: *A Study of Christian Motifs in Boris Pasternak's Poetry*. Stockholm: Almquist and Wiksell, 1976.

Ford, R.A.D. "The Poetry of Boris Pasternak," in *Queen's Quarterly*. LXVII (1960), pp. 673–677.

Gifford, Henry. *Pasternak, A Critical Study*. New York: Cambridge University Press, 1977.

Hughes, Olga R. *The Poetic World of Boris Pasternak*. Princeton, N.J.: Princeton University Press, 1974.

Jennings, Elizabeth. *Seven Men of Vision: An Appreciation*. New York: Barnes & Noble, 1976.

Livingstone, Angela. "Pasternak's Last Poetry," in *Meanjin*. XXII (1963), pp. 388–396.

Mallac, Guy de. "Pasternak and Religion," in *Russian Review*. XXXII (1973), pp. 360–375.

Milosz, Czeslaw. "On Pasternak Soberly," in *Emperor of the Earth; Modes of Eccentric Vision*. Berkeley: University of California Press, 1977, pp. 62–78.

O'Hara, F. "About Zhivago and His Poems," in *On Contemporary Literature*. Edited by Richard Kostelanetz. New York: Funk & Wagnalls, 1968, pp. 486–497.

Payne, Robert. *The Three Worlds of Boris Pasternak*. New York: Coward-McCann, 1961.

Plank, Dale L. *Pasternak's Lyric; A Study of Sound and Imagery*. The Hague: Mouton, 1966.

Rowland, Mary F. and Paul Rowland. *Pasternak's* Doctor Zhivago. Carbondale: Southern Illinois University Press, 1967.

Tsvrtaeva, Marina. "Epic and Lyric in Contemporary Russia: Mayakovsky and Pasternak," in *Russian Literature Triquarterly*. XIII (1975), pp. 519–542.

ALAN PATON
(1903–   )

Cry, the Beloved Country

Baker, Sheridan. "Paton's Beloved Country and the Morality of Geography," in *College English.* XIX (November, 1957), pp. 56–61. Reprinted in *Paton's* Cry, the Beloved Country: *The Novel, the Critics, the Setting.* Edited by Sheridan Baker. New York: Scribner's, 1968, pp. 144–148.

Bruell, Edwin. "Keen Scalpel on Racial Ills," in *English Journal.* LIII (1964), pp. 658–661.

Callan, Edward. *Alan Paton.* New York: Twayne, 1968, pp. 49–66.

Collins, Harold R. *"Cry, the Beloved Country* and the Broken Tribe," in *College English.* XIV (April, 1953), pp. 379–385. Reprinted in *Paton's* Cry, the Beloved Country: *The Novel, the Critics, the Setting.* Edited by Sheridan Baker. New York: Scribner's, 1968, pp. 138–143.

Davies, Horton. "Alan Paton: Literary Artist and Anglican," in *Hibbert Journal.* L (April, 1952), pp. 262–268.

────────. *Mirror of the Ministry in Modern Novels.* New York: Oxford University Press, 1959, pp. 128–136.

Fuller, Edmund. *Books with the Men Behind Them.* New York: Random House, 1962, pp. 94–99.

Gailey, Harry A. "Sheridan Baker's 'Paton's Beloved Country'," in *College English.* XX (December, 1958), pp. 143–144. Reprinted in *Paton's* Cry, the Beloved Country: *The Novel, the Critics, the Setting.* Edited by Sheridan Baker. New York: Scribner's, 1968, pp. 149–150.

Gardiner, Harold C. *In All Conscience: Reflections on Books and Culture.* New York: Hanover House, 1959, pp. 108–109.

Hartt, Julian N. *The Lost Image of Man.* Baton Rouge: Louisiana State University Press, 1963, pp. 85–89.

Hester, Sister Mary. "Greek Tragedy and the Novels of Alan Paton," in *Wisconsin Studies in Literature.* I (1964), pp. 54–61.

Marcus, Fred. H. *"Cry, the Beloved Country* and *Strange Fruit;* Exploring Man's Inhumanity to Man," in *English Journal.* LI (December, 1962), pp. 658–661.

Prescott, Orville. *In My Opinion: An Inquiry into the Contemporary Novel.* Indianapolis, Ind.: Bobbs-Merrill, 1952, pp. 240–243.

Rooney, F. Charles. "The 'Message' of Alan Paton," in *Catholic World.* CXCIV (November, 1961), pp. 94–95. Reprinted in *Paton's* Cry, the Beloved Country: *The Novel, the Critics, the Setting.* Edited by Sheridan Baker. New York: Scribner's, 1968, pp. 152–153.

Tucker, Martin.   *Africa in Modern Literature: A Survey of Contemporary Writing in English.* New York: Frederick Ungar, 1967, pp. 223–225.

OCTAVIO PAZ
(1914–   )

The Poetry of Paz

Bliven, Naomi. "In a Style to Which One Is Not Accustomed," in *New Yorker.* XLVI (August 15, 1970), pp. 91–92.

Christ, Ronald. "*Eagle or Sun?*," in *Commonweal.* XCII (April 24, 1970), pp. 148–150.

Forster, Merlin H. "Four Contemporary Mexican Poets," in his *Tradition and Renewal: Essays on Twentieth-Century Latin American Literature and Culture.* Urbana: University of Illinois Press, 1975, pp. 139–141.

Franco, Jean. *An Introduction to Spanish-American Literature.* Cambridge: Cambridge University Press, 1969, pp. 290–296.

————. *Spanish American Literature Since Independence.* New York: Barnes & Noble, 1973, pp. 202–208.

Guibert, Rita. *Seven Voices: Seven Latin American Voices Talk to Rita Guibert.* New York: Knopf, 1973, pp. 183–275.

James, Daniel. "Neighbors with an Alien Complex," in *Saturday Review.* XLV (April 7, 1962), pp. 33–34.

SAMUEL PEPYS
(1633–1703)

Diary

Bennett, James O'Donnell. "The *Diary* of Samuel Pepys," in *Much Loved Books: Best Sellers of the Ages*. New York: Liveright, 1938, pp. 276–283.

Bradford, Gamaliel. *The Soul of Samuel Pepys*. Boston: Houghton Mifflin, 1924, pp. 9–36.

Britt, Albert. "Walton and the Diarists," in his *Great Biographers*. New York: McGraw-Hill, 1936, pp. 47–51.

Dale, D. "The Greatness of Samuel Pepys," in *Quarterly Review*. CCLXXV (October, 1940), pp. 227–238.

Drinkwater, John. *Pepys: His Life and Character*. Garden City, N.Y.: Doubleday, 1934, pp. 10–11, 41–42, 158–162, 200–201.

Hearsey, John E.N. "Introduction," in *Young Mr. Pepys*. New York: Scribner's, 1973, pp. 1–3.

Highet, Gilbert. "New Year's Day with Mr. Pepys," in *Explorations*. New York: Oxford University Press, 1971, pp. 233–243.

Hunt, Percival. *Samuel Pepys in the* Diary. Pittsburgh: University of Pittsburgh Press, 1958, pp. 1–12, 175–178.

Kelman, John. "Pepys' *Diary*," in his *Among Famous Books*. London: Hodder, 1912, pp. 157–199.

Latham, Robert. "The *Diary* as History," in *The Diary of Samuel Pepys*, Volume I. Edited by Robert Latham and William Matthews. Berkeley: University of California Press, 1970, pp. cxiv–cxxxvii.

LeGallienne, Richard. "Introduction," in *Passages from the* Diary *of Samuel Pepys*. New York: Modern Library, 1923, pp. v–xiv.

Lynd, Robert. "Mr. Pepys," in *The Art of Letters*. New York: Scribner's, 1921, pp. 9–15.

Mallery, Richard Davis. "Samuel Pepys," in his *Masterworks of Autobiography: Digests of 10 Great Classics*. Garden City, N.Y.: Doubleday, 1946, pp. 157–159.

Matthews, William. "The *Diary* as Literature," in *The Diary of Samuel Pepys*, Volume I. Edited by Robert Latham and William Matthews. Berkeley: University of California Press, 1970, pp. xcvii–cxiii.

Miner, Earl. "Pepys Revived," in *Hudson Review*. XXIV (1971), pp. 171–176.

Plumb, J.H. "The World of Samuel Pepys," in his *In the Light of History*. Boston: Houghton Mifflin, 1973, pp. 225–232.

Ponsonby, Arthur. *Samuel Pepys.* London: Macmillan, 1928, pp. 69–95.

Saunders, Beatrice. *Portraits of Genius.* London: John Murray, 1959, pp. 53–57.

Sutherland, James. *English Literature of the Late Seventeenth Century.* New York: Oxford University Press, 1969, pp. 267–270.

Tanner, J.R. *Mr. Pepys: An Introduction to the* Diary *Together with a Sketch of His Later Life.* London: Bell, 1925, pp. vii–xv, 204–211.

Taylor, Ivan E. *Samuel Pepys.* New York: Twayne, 1967.

Tinker, Chauncey Brewster. "The Great Diarist and Some Others," in his *Essays in Retrospect: Collected Articles and Addresses.* New Haven, Conn.: Yale University Press, 1948, pp. 10–22.

Wethered, Herbert N. "Pepys," in his *The Curious Art of Autobiography: From Benvenuto Cellini to Rudyard Kipling.* New York: Philosophical Library, 1956, pp. 45–51.

Winterich, John T. "Samuel Pepys and His *Diary*," in his *Books and the Man.* New York: Greenberg, 1929, pp. 310–325.

WALKER PERCY
(1916–   )

The Last Gentleman

Blouin, Michael. "The Novels of Walker Percy: An Attempt at Synthesis," in *Xavier University Studies*. VI (February, 1967), pp. 29–42.

Coles, Robert. *Walker Percy: An American Search*. Boston: Little, Brown, 1978.

Douglas, Ellen. *Walker Percy's* The Last Gentleman: *Introduction and Commentary*. New York: Seabury, 1969.

Dowie, William. "Walker Percy: Sensualist-Thinker," in *Novel*. VI (1972), pp. 52–66.

Hoffman, Frederick J. *The Art of Southern Fiction: A Study of Some Modern Novelists*. Carbondale: Southern Illinois University Press, 1967, pp. 133–137.

Lehan, Richard. "The Way Back: Redemption in the Novels of Walker Percy," in *Southern Review*. IV (Spring, 1968), pp. 306–319.

Luschei, Martin. *The Sovereign Wayfarer: Walker Percy's Diagnosis of the Malaise*. Baton Rouge: Louisiana State University Press, 1972, pp. 111–168.

Sheed, Wilfrid. *The Morning After; Selected Essays and Reviews*. New York: Farrar, Straus, 1971, pp. 18–21.

Tanner, Tony. *City of Words; American Fiction 1950–1970*. New York: Harper, 1971, pp. 260–262.

Tenenbaum, Ruth B. "Walker Percy's 'Consumer-Self' in *The Last Gentleman*," in *Louisiana Studies*. XV (1976), pp. 304–309.

The Moviegoer

Atkins, Anselm. "Walker Percy and the Post-Christian Search," in *Centennial Review*. XII (Winter, 1968), pp. 73–95.

Blouin, Michael. "The Novels of Walker Percy: An Attempt at Synthesis," in *Xavier University Studies*. VI (1968), pp. 29–42.

Bryant, Jerry H. *The Open Decision: The Contemporary American Novel and Its Intellectual Background*. New York: Free Press, 1970, pp. 273–277.

Byrd, Scott. "Mysteries and Movies: Walker Percy's College Articles and *The Moviegoer*," in *Mississippi Quarterly*. XXV (Spring, 1972), pp. 165–181.

Cheney, Brainard. "To Restore a Fragmented Image," in *Sewanee Review*. LXIX (1961), pp. 691–700.

Coles, Robert. *Walker Percy: An American Search*. Boston: Little, Brown, 1978.

Dowie, William. "Walker Percy: Sensualist-Thinker," in *Novel*. VI (1972), pp. 52–66.

Henisey, Sarah. "Intersubjectivity in Symbolization," in *Renascence*. XX (Summer, 1968), pp. 208–214.

Hoffman, Frederick J. *The Art of Southern Fiction: A Study of Some Modern Novelists*. Carbondale: Southern Illinois University Press, 1967, pp. 129–133.

Hoggard, James. "Death of the Vicarious," in *Southwest Review*. XLIX (Autumn, 1964), pp. 366–374.

Hyman, S.E. *Standards: A Chronicle of Books for Our Time*. New York: Horizon, 1966, pp. 63–67.

Kostelanetz, Richard. *New American Arts*. New York: Horizon, 1965, pp. 224–225.

Lehan, Richard. "The Way Back: Redemption in the Novels of Walker Percy," in *Southern Review*. IV (Spring, 1968), pp. 306–319.

Luschei, Martin. *The Sovereign Wayfarer: Walker Percy's Diagnosis of the Malaise*. Baton Rouge: Louisiana State University Press, 1972, pp. 64–110.

Pindell, Richard. "Basking in the Eye of the Storm: The Esthetics of Loss in Walker Percy's *The Moviegoer*," in *Boundary*. IV (1975), pp. 219–230.

Sheperd, Allen. "Percy's *The Moviegoer* and Warren's *All the King's Men*," in *Notes on Mississippi Writers*. IV (1971), pp. 2–14.

Tanner, Tony. *The Reign of Wonder: Naïvety and Reality in American Literature*. Cambridge: Cambridge University Press, 1965, pp. 349–356.

Thale, Mary. "The Moviegoer of the 1950's," in *Twentieth Century Literature*. XIV (July, 1968), pp. 84–89.

Vauthier, Simone. "Narrative Triangle and Triple Alliance: A Look at *The Moviegoer*," in *Les Amèricanistes; New French Criticism on Modern American Fiction*. Edited by Ira D. Johnson and Christiane Johnson. Port Washington, N.Y.: Kennikat, 1978.

————. "Title as Microtext: The Example of *The Moviegoer*," in *Journal of Narrative Technique*. V (1975), pp. 219–229.

BENITO PÉREZ GALDÓS
(1843–1920)

El Amigo Manso

Berkowitz, H. Chonon. "Galdós and Giner, a Literary Friendship," in *Spanish Review.* I (1934), pp. 64–68.

Davies, G.A. "Galdós' *El Amigo Manso*: An Experiment in Didactic Method," in *Bulletin of Hispanic Studies.* XXXIX (1962), pp. 16–30.

Eoff, Sherman H. *The Novels of Pérez Galdós: The Concept of Life as Dynamic Process.* St. Louis, Mo.: Washington University Studies, 1954, pp. 134–136.

Gillet, J.E. "The Autonomous Character in Spanish and European Literature," in *Hispanic Review.* XXIV (1956), pp. 179–190.

Hafter, Monroe Z. "Ironic Reprise in Galdós' Novels," in *PMLA.* LXXVI (1961), pp. 233–239.

_____. "*Le Crime de Sylvestre Bonnard*, a Possible Source for *El Amigo Manso*," in *Symposium.* XVII (1963), pp. 123–129.

Livingstone, L. "Interior Duplication and the Problem of Form in the Modern Spanish Novel," in *PMLA.* LXXIII (1958), pp. 393–406.

Nimetz, Michael. *Humor in Galdós; A Study of the Novelas Contemporaneas.* New Haven, Conn.: Yale University Press, 1968, pp. 44–46, 97–98.

Pattison, Walter T. *Benito Pérez Galdós.* Boston: Twayne, 1975, pp. 67–69.

Penuel, Arnold M. "Some Aesthetic Implications of Galdós' *El Amigo Manso*," in *Anales Galdosianos.* IX (1974), pp. 145–148.

Price, R.M. "The Five Padrotes in Pérez Galdós' *El Amigo Manso*," in *Philological Quarterly.* XLVIII (1969), pp. 234–246.

Russell, Robert H. "*El Amigo Manso*: Galdós with a Mirror," in *Modern Language Notes.* LXXVIII (1963), pp. 161–168.

Rutherford, John. "Story, Character, Setting, and Narrative Mode in Galdós' *El Amigo Manso*," in *Style and Structure in Literature: Essays in the New Stylistics.* Edited by Roger Fowler. Ithaca, N.Y.: Cornell University Press, 1975, pp. 177–212.

Ángel Guerra

Eoff, Sherman H. *The Novels of Pérez Galdós: The Concept of Life as Dynamic Process.* St. Louis, Mo.: Washington University Studies, 1954, pp. 73–83, 140–141.

Fedorchek, Robert Marion. "The Ideal of Christian Poverty in Galdós' Novels," in *Romance Notes.* XI (1969), pp. 76–81.

Gillespie, Gerald. "Reality and Fiction in the Novels of Galdós," in *Anales Galdosianos*. I (1966), pp. 11–31.

Nimetz, Michael. *Humor in Galdós: A Study of the Novelas Contemporaneas.* New Haven, Conn.: Yale University Press, 1968, pp. 26–29, 134–135, 152–153.

Pattison, Walter T. *Benito Pérez Galdós.* Boston: Twayne, 1975, pp. 117–124.

Penuel, Arnold M. *Charity in the Novels of Galdós.* Athens: University of Georgia Press, 1972, pp. 18–19, 65–67.

Scanlon, Geraldine M. "Religion and Art in *Ángel Guerra*," in *Anales Galdosianos*. VIII (1973), pp. 99–105.

La desheredada

Berkowitz, H. Chonon. "Galdós and Giner, a Literary Friendship," in *Spanish Review*. I (1934), pp. 64–68.

Davies, G.A. "Galdós' *El Amigo Manso*: An Experiment in Didactic Method," in *Bulletin of Hispanic Studies*. XXXIX (1962), pp. 16–30.

Durand, Frank. "The Reality of Illusion: *La desheredada*," in *Modern Language Notes*. LXXXIX (1974), pp. 191–201.

Engler, Kay. "Linguistic Determination of Point of View: *La desheredada*," in *Anales Galdosianos*. V (1970), pp. 67–73.

Eoff, Sherman H. *The Novels of Pérez Galdós; The Concept of Life as Dynamic Process.* St. Louis, Mo.: Washington University Studies, 1954, pp. 12–13, 34–39.

Fedorchek, Robert M. "Social Reprehension in *La desheredada*," in *Revista de Estudios Hispanicos* (University of Alabama). VIII (1974), pp. 43–59.

Hafter, Monroe Z. "Galdós' Presentation of Isidora in *La desheredada*," in *Modern Philology*. LX (1962), pp. 22–30.

Lowe, Jennifer. "Galdos' Skill in *La desheredada*," in *Ibero-romania*. III (1971), pp. 142–151.

Nimetz, Michael. *Humor in Galdós; A Study of the Novelas Contemporaneas.* New Haven, Conn.: Yale University Press, 1968, pp. 111–114, 118–120.

Park, Dorothy G. and Hilario Saenz y Saenz. "Galdós' Ideas on Education," in *Hispania*. XXVII (1944), pp. 138–147.

Pattison, Walter T. *Benito Pérez Galdós.* Boston: Twayne, 1975, pp. 63–67.

Penuel, Arnold M. *Charity in the Novels of Galdós.* Athens: University of Georgia Press, 1972, pp. 40–46, 92–93.

Rodgers, Eamonn. "Galdós' *La desheredada* and Naturalism," in *Bulletin of Hispanic Studies*. XLV (1968), pp. 285–298.

Russell, Robert H. "The Structure of *La desheredada*," in *Modern Language Notes.* LXXVI (1961), pp. 794–800.

Doña Perfecta

Bishop, W.H. "A Day in Literary Madrid," in *Scribner's Magazine.* VII (February, 1890), pp. 186–201.

Brown, Donald F. "An Argentine *Doña Perfecta*: Galdós and Manuel Galvez," in *Hispania.* XLVII (1964), pp. 282–287.

Cardwell, Richard A. "Galdós' *Doña Perfecta*: Art or Argument?," in *Anales Galdosianos.* VII (1972), pp. 29–47.

Chamberlin, Vernon A. and Jack Weiner. "Galdós' *Doña Perfecta* and Turgenev's *Fathers and Sons*: Two Interpretations of Conflicts Between Generations," in *PMLA.* LXXXVI (1971), pp. 19–24.

Eoff, Sherman H. *The Novels of Pérez Galdós; The Concept of Life as Dynamic Process.* St. Louis, Mo.: Washington University Studies, 1954, pp. 7–8, 65–68.

Fitzgerald, J.D. "*Doña Perfecta*," in *Modern Language Notes.* XXI (1906), pp. 223–224.

Howells, William Dean. *Criticism and Fiction and Others Essays.* Edited by Clara Kirk and Rudolf Kirk. New York: New York University Press, 1959, pp. 130–138.

Jones, C.A. "Galdós' Second Thoughts on *Doña Perfecta*," in *Modern Language Review.* LIV (1959), pp. 570–573.

Krappe, Alexander Haggerty. "The Sources of Benito Pérez Galdós's *Doña Perfecta*," in *Philological Quarterly.* VII (1928), pp. 303–306.

Mazarra, Richard A. "Some Fresh *Perspectivas* on Galdós' *Doña Perfecta*," in *Hispania.* XL (1957), pp. 52–55.

Penuel, Arnold M. *Charity in the Novels of Galdós.* Athens: University of Georgia Press, 1972.

Sisto, David T. "Pérez Galdós' *Doña Perfecta* and Louis Bromfield's *A Good Woman*," in *Symposium.* XI (1957), pp. 273–280.

Fortunata y Jacinta

Armistead, S.G. "The Canarian Background of Pérez Galdós' 'Echar los Tiempos,' " in *Romance Philology.* VII (1953–1954), pp. 190–192.

Bacarisse, S. "The Realism of Galdós: Some Reflections on Language and the Perception of Reality," in *Bulletin of Hispanic Studies.* XLII (1965), pp. 239–250.

Blanco-Aguinaga, Carlos. "On 'The Birth of Fortunata,' " in *Anales Galdosianos.* III (1968), pp. 13–24.

Braun, Lucille V. "Galdós' Re-creation of Ernestina Manuel de Villena as Guillermina Pacheco," in *Hispanic Review*. XXXVIII (1970), pp. 32–55.

Brooks, J.L. "The Character of Doña Guillermina Pacheco in Galdós' Novel *Fortunata y Jacinta*," in *Bulletin of Hispanic Studies*. XXXVIII (1961), pp. 86–94.

Calley, Louise Nelson. "Galdós' Concept of Primitivism: A Romantic View of the Character Fortunata," in *Hispania*. XLIV (1961), pp. 663–665.

Engler, Kay. "Notes on the Narrative Structure of *Fortunata y Jacinta*," in *Symposium*. XXIV (1970), pp. 111–127.

Eoff, Sherman H. *The Novels of Pérez Galdós; The Concept of Life as Dynamic Process*. St. Louis, Mo.: Washington University Studies, 1954, pp. 24–26, 31–32, 72–73, 98–101.

————. "The Treatment of Individual Personality in *Fortunata y Jacinta*," in *Hispanic Review*. XVII (1949), pp. 269–289.

Gilman, Stephen M. "The Birth of Fortunata," in *Anales Galdosianos*. I (1966), pp. 71–83.

Hafter, Monroe Z. "Ironic Reprise in Galdós' Novels," in *PMLA*. LXXXVI (1961), pp. 233–239.

Kirsner, Robert. "Galdós' Attitude Towards Spain as Seen in the Characters of *Fortunata y Jacinta*," in *PMLA*. LXVI (1951), pp. 124–137.

Moncy Gullon, Agnes. "The Bird Motif and the Introductory Motif: Structure in *Fortunata y Jacinta*," in *Anales Galdosianos*. IX (1974), pp. 51–75.

Nimetz, Michael. *Humor in Galdós: A Study of the Novelas Contemporaneas*. New Haven, Conn.: Yale University Press, 1968, pp. 186–208.

Pattison, Walter T. *Benito Pérez Galdós*. Boston: Twayne, 1975, pp. 90–106.

Penuel, Arnold M. *Charity in the Novels of Galdós*. Athens: University of Georgia Press, 1972, pp. 39–43, 95–97, 101–105.

Randolph, E. Dale. "A Source for Maxi Rubin in *Fortunata y Jacinta*," in *Hispanica*. LI (1968), pp. 49–56.

Sinnigen, John H. "Individual, Class, and Society in *Fortunata y Jacinta*," in *Galdós Studies II*. Edited by Robert J. Weber. London: Tamesis, 1974, pp. 49–68.

Smith, Paul C. "Cervantes and Galdós: The Duques and Ido del Sagrario," in *Romance Notes*. VIII (1966), pp. 47–50.

Ullman, Joan Connelly and George H. Allison. "Galdós as Psychiatrist in *Fortunata y Jacinta*," in *Anales Galdosianos*. IX (1974), pp. 7–36.

Whiston, James. "Language and Situation in Part I of *Fortunata y Jacinta*," in *Anales Galdosianos*. VII (1972), pp. 79–91.

Zahareas, Anthony. "The Tragic Sense in *Fortunata y Jacinta*," in *Symposium*. XIX (1965), pp. 38–49.

Marianela

Blanco, Louise S. "Origin and History of the Plot of *Marianela*," in *Hispanica*. XLVIII (1965), pp. 463–467.

Bly, Peter A. "Egotism and Charity in *Marianela*," in *Anales Galdosianos*. VII (1972), pp. 49–66.

Dendle, Brian J. "Galdós, Ayguals de Izco, and the Hellenic Inspiration of *Marianela*," in *Galdós Studies II*. Edited by Robert J. Weber. London: Tamesis, 1974, pp. 1–11.

Eoff, Sherman H. *The Novels of Pérez Galdós; The Concept of Life as Dynamic Process*. St. Louis, Mo.: Washington University Studies, 1954, pp. 10–11, 132–133.

Green, Otis. "Two Deaths: Don Quijote and *Marianela*," in *Anales Galdosianos*. II (1967), pp. 131–133.

Jones, Cyril A. "Galdós' *Marianela* and the Approach to Reality," in *Modern Language Review*. LVI (1961), pp. 515–519.

Lister, John Thomas. "Symbolism in *Marianela*," in *Hispania*. XIV (1931), pp. 247–250.

Pattison, Walter T. *Benito Pérez Galdós*. Boston: Twayne, 1975, pp. 57–58.

————. *Benito Pérez Galdós and the Creative Process*. Minneapolis: University of Minnesota Press, 1954, pp. 114–136.

Penuel, Arnold M. *Charity in the Novels of Galdós*. Athens: University of Georgia Press, 1972, pp. 33–36.

Misericordia

Chamberlin, Vernon A. "The Significance of the Name 'Almudena' in Galdós' *Misericordia*," in *Hispanica*. XLVII (1964), pp. 491–496.

Cohen, Sara E. "Almudena and the Jewish Theme in *Misericordia*," in *Anales Galdosianos*. VIII (1973), pp. 51–61.

Eoff, Sherman H. *The Novels of Pérez Galdós; The Concept of Life as Dynamic Process*. St. Louis, Mo.: Washington University Studies, 1954, pp. 16–23, 92–96, 152–155.

Livingstone, L. "Interior Duplication and the Problem of Form in the Modern Spanish Novel," in *PMLA*. LXXIII (1958), pp. 393–406.

Pattison, Walter T. *Benito Pérez Galdós*. Boston: Twayne, 1975, pp. 134–137.

Penuel, Arnold M. *Charity in the Novels of Galdós*. Athens: University of Georgia Press, 1972, pp. 78–87.

————. "Galdós, Freud and Humanistic Psychology," in *Hispania*. LV (1972), pp. 65–75.

Russell, Robert H. "The Christ Figure in *Misericordia*: A Monograph," in *Anales Galdosianos*. II (1967), pp. 103–130.

Realidad

Eoff, Sherman H. *The Novels of Pérez Galdós; The Concept of Life as Dynamic Process.* St. Louis, Mo.: Washington University Studies, 1954, pp. 15–16, 142–147.

Gillespie, Gerald. "Reality and Fiction in the Novels of Galdós," in *Anales Galdosianos.* I (1966), pp. 11–31.

Pattison, Walter T. *Benito Pérez Galdós.* Boston: Twayne, 1975, pp. 111–115.

Penuel, Arnold M. *Charity in the Novels of Galdós.* Athens: University of Georgia Press, 1972, pp. 71–76.

Portnoff, G. "The Influence of Tolstoy's *Ana Karenina* on Galdós' *Realidad*," in *Hispania.* XV (1932), pp. 203–214.

Starkie, Walter. "Galdós and the Modern Spanish Drama," in *Bulletin of Spanish Studies.* III (1925–1926), pp. 111–117.

ST.-JOHN PERSE
(1887–   )

Anabasis (Anabase)

Bogan, Louise. "Asian Exoticism," in *Selected Criticism: Prose, Poetry*. New York: Noonday, 1955, pp. 81–82.

Cocking, J.M. "Migrant Muse," in *Encounter*. XLVI (March, 1976), pp. 62–68.

Emmanuel, Pierre. *Saint-John Perse: Praise and Presence*. Washington, D.C.: Library of Congress, 1971, pp. 12–14.

Galand, Rene M. *Saint-John Perse*. New York: Twayne, 1972, pp. 46–65.

Knodel, Arthur. "Towards an Understanding of *Anabase*," in *PMLA*. LXXIX (June, 1964), pp. 329–343.

Little, Roger. "The Image of the Threshold in the Poetry of Saint-John Perse," in *Modern Language Review*. LXIV (October 4, 1969), pp. 777–792.

————. *Saint-John Perse*. London: Athlone Press, 1973, pp. 17–21.

Mullen, W. "Saint-John Perse," in *Arion*. II (1975), pp. 368–379.

Price, J.D. "Man, Women and the Problem of Suffering in Saint-John Perse," in *Modern Language Review*. LXXII (July, 1977), pp. 555–564.

Srinivasa-Iyengar, K.R. "St.-John Perse's *Anabase*: A Study," in *The Aryan Path*. XXXIII (January, 1962), pp. 15–18.

Weinberg, Bernard. "Saint-John Perse: *Anabase*," in *The Limits of Symbolism*. Chicago: University of Chicago Press, 1966, pp. 365–419.

Chronique

Emmanuel, Pierre. *Saint-John Perse: Praise and Presence*. Washington, D.C.: Library of Congress, 1971, pp. 2–6.

Galand, Rene M. *Saint-John Perse*. New York: Twayne, 1972, pp. 129–137.

Hemley, Cecil. "Onward and Upward," in *Hudson Review*. XV (Summer, 1962), pp. 314–317.

Little, Roger. "Image of the Threshold in the Poetry of Saint-John Perse," in *Modern Language Review*. LXIV (October, 1969), pp. 777–792.

————. *Saint-John Perse*. London: Athlone Press, 1973, pp. 53–54.

Èloges and Other Poems

Emmanuel, Pierre. *Saint-John Perse: Praise and Presence*. Washington, D.C.: Library of Congress, 1971, pp. 10–11.

Little, Roger. *Saint-John Perse*. London: Athlone Press, 1973, pp. 8–14.

Peyre, H.   "Saint-John Perse: *Èloges* 2," in *The Poem Itself.* Edited by Stanley Burnshaw. New York: Holt, 1960, pp. 92–93.

Price, J.D.   "Man, Women and the Problem of Suffering in Saint-John Perse," in *Modern Language Review.* LXXII (July, 1977), pp. 555–564.

Raine, K.   "Saint-John Perse: Poet of the Marvellous," in *Encounter.* XXIX (October, 1967), pp. 51–58.

Exil

Cocking, J.M.   "Migrant Muse," in *Encounter.* XLVI (March, 1976), pp. 62–68.

Galand, Rene M.   *Saint-John Perse.* New York: Twayne, 1972, pp. 66–87.

Little, Roger.   "Elements of the Jason-Medea Myth in *Exil* by Saint-John Perse," in *Modern Language Review.* LXI (1966), pp. 422–425.

————.   "Image of the Threshold in the Poetry of Saint-John Perse," in *Modern Language Review.* LXIV (October, 1969), pp. 777–792.

————.   *Saint-John Perse.* London: Athlone Press, 1973, pp. 21–27.

MacLeish, Archibald.   "St.-John Perse," in his *A Continuing Journey.* New York: Houghton Mifflin, 1968, pp. 313–317.

Martz, L.L.   "Paradise Lost: Princes of Exile," in *ELH.* XXXVI (March, 1969), pp. 232–249.

Price, J.D.   "Man, Women and the Problem of Suffering in Saint-John Perse," in *Modern Language Review.* LXXII (July, 1977), pp. 555–564.

"Pictures for Crusoe"

Emmanuel, Pierre.   *Saint-John Perse: Praise and Presence.* Washington, D.C.: Library of Congress, 1971, pp. 11–12.

Galand, Rene M.   *Saint-John Perse.* New York: Twayne, 1972, pp. 73–77.

Little, Roger.   *Saint-John Perse.* London: Athlone Press, 1973, pp. 12–14.

Price, J.D.   "Man, Women and the Problem of Suffering in Saint-John Perse," in *Modern Language Review.* LXXII (July, 1977), pp. 555–564.

Raine, K.   "Saint-John Perse: Poet of the Marvellous," in *Encounter.* XXIX (October, 1967), pp. 51–58.

Seamarks

Cocking, J.M.   "Migrant Muse," in *Encounter.* XLVI (March, 1976), pp. 62–68.

Emmanuel, Pierre.   *Saint-John Perse: Praise and Presence.* Washington, D.C.: Library of Congress, 1971, pp. 13, 18–20.

Fowlie, W.   "Saint-John Perse's Quest," in *Climate of Violence.* New York: Macmillan, 1967, pp. 87–101.

Galand, Rene M.   *Saint-John Perse*. New York: Twayne, 1972, pp. 108–128.

Guicharnaud, J.   "Vowels of the Sea: *Amers*," in *Yale French Studies*. XXI (1958), pp. 72–82.

Little, Roger.   "Image of the Threshold in the Poetry of Saint-John Perse," in *Modern Language Review*. LXIV (October, 1969), pp. 777–792.

Mullen, W.   "Saint-John Perse," in *Arion*. II (1975), pp. 368–379.

Nemerov, Howard.   "The Golden Compass Needle," in *Poetry and Fiction Essays*. New Brunswick, N.J.: Rutgers University Press, 1963, pp. 366–381.

Price, J.D.   "Man, Women and the Problem of Suffering in Saint-John Perse," in *Modern Language Review*. LXXII (July, 1977), pp. 555–564.

Raine, K.   "Saint-John Perse: Poet of the Marvellous," in *Encounter*. XXIX (October, 1967), pp. 51–58.

Vents

Emmanuel, Pierre.   *Saint-John Perse: Praise and Presence*. Washington, D.C.: Library of Congress, 1971, pp. 15–16.

Little, Roger.   "Image of the Threshold in the Poetry of Saint-John Perse," in *Modern Language Review*. LXIV (October, 1969), pp. 777–792.

————.   *Saint-John Perse*. London: Athlone Press, 1973, pp. 27–40.

Mullen, W.   "Saint-John Perse," in *Arion*. II (1975), pp. 368–379.

Raine, K.   "Saint-John Perse: Poet of the Marvellous," in *Encounter*. XXIX (October, 1967), pp. 51–58.

FRANCESCO PETRARCH
(1304–1374)

Le Rime of Petrarch (or Canzoniere)

Barber, J.A. "Rhyme Scheme Patterns in Petrarch's *Canzoniere*," in *Modern Language Notes*. XCII (January, 1977), pp. 139–156.

Bergin, Thomas G. *Petrarch*. New York: Twayne, 1970, pp. 154–179.

Bernardo, A.S. "The Importance of the Non-Love Poems of Petrarch's *Canzoniere*," in *Italica*. XXVII (1950), pp. 302–312.

Coogan, Robert. "Petrarch and More's Concept of Fortune," in *Italica*. XLVI (1969), pp. 167–175.

Durling, Robert M. *The Figure of the Poet in Renaissance Epic*. Cambridge, Mass.: Harvard University Press, 1965, pp. 67–87.

————. "Introduction," *Petrarch's Lyric Poems, the Rime Sparse and Other Lyrics*. Translated and Annotated by Robert M. Durling. Cambridge, Mass.: Harvard University Press, 1976.

Earl, Anthony J. "The Ambiguities of Petrarch's *Rime*," in *Modern Languages*. LV (December, 1974), pp. 161–168.

Foster, Kenelm, O.P. "Beatrice or Medusa: The Penitential Element in Petrarch's *Canzoniere*," in *Italian Studies; Presented to E.R. Vincent*. Edited by C.P. Brand *et al*. Cambridge: W. Heffer & Sons, 1962, pp. 41–56.

Merrill, R.V. "Platonism in Petrarch's *Canzoniere*," in *Modern Philology*. XXVII (1929), pp. 161–174.

Roche, T.P., Jr. "The Calendrical Structure of Petrarch's *Canzoniere*," in *Studies in Philology*. LXXI (1974), pp. 152–172.

Scaglion, Aldo, Editor. *Francis Petrarch, Six Centuries Later. A Symposium*. Chapel Hill: University of North Carolina Press, 1975, pp. 105–212.

Valency, Maurice J. *In Praise of Love; An Introduction to the Love-Poetry of the Renaissance*. New York: Macmillan, 1958.

Watkins, Renee N. "Petrarch and the Black Death: From Fear to Monuments," in *Studies in the Renaissance*. XIX (1972), pp. 196–223.

Wilkins, Ernest H. *The Making of the* Canzoniere *and Other Petrarchan Studies*. Rome: Storia e Letteratura, 1951.

————. *A History of Italian Literature*. Revised by Thomas G. Bergin. Cambridge, Mass.: Harvard University Press, 1974, pp. 80–100.

GAIUS PETRONIUS
(Unknown–c.66)

The Satyricon

Arrowsmith, W. "Luxury and Death in *Satyricon*," in *Arion*. V (Autumn, 1966), pp. 304–331.

Bagnani, Gilbert. *Arbiter of Elegance; A Study of the Life and Works of G. Petronius*. Toronto: University of Toronto Press, 1954.

Cameron, A. "The Sibylin *Satyricon*," in *Classical Journal*. LXV (May, 1970), pp. 337–379.

Connolly, C. "On Re-reading Petronius," in *Previous Convictions*. New York: Harper, 1963, pp. 105–109.

Corbett, Philip B. *Petronius*. New York: Twayne, 1970.

Dupree, F.W. "Libido Is a Latin Word," in *"The King of the Cats," and Other Remarks on Writers and Writing*. New York: Farrar, Straus and Giroux, 1965, pp. 142–148.

Fredericks, Sigmund C. "Seneca and Petronius: Menippian Satire Under Nero," in *Roman Satirists and Their Satire*. Edited by Edwin S. Ramage, David L. Sigsbee and S.C. Fredericks. Park Ridge, N.J.: Noyes Press, 1975, pp. 89–113.

George, P. "Style and Character in *The Satyricon*," in *Arion*. V (Autumn, 1966), pp. 336–358.

Haight, E.H. "Satire and the Latin Novel," in *Essays in Ancient Fiction*. London: Longmans, 1936, pp. 86–120.

Knoche, Ulrich. "Petronius' Novel," in *Roman Satire*. Bloomington: Indiana University Press, 1975, pp. 109–126.

Rexroth, Kenneth. "Petronius: *The Satyricon*," in *Classics Revisited*. Chicago: Quadrangle Books, 1968, pp. 99–103.

Rose, K.F.C. "Time and Place in *The Satyricon*," in *Transactions of The American Philological Association*. XCIII (1962), pp. 402–409.

Sandy, G. "Satire in *The Satyricon*," in *American Journal of Philology*. XC (July, 1969), pp. 293–303.

Schraidt, N.C. "Literary and Philosophical Elements in *The Satyricon* of Petronius Arbiter," in *Classical Journal*. XXXV (December, 1939), pp. 154–161.

Smith, Martin S., Editor. *Petronius: Cena Trimalchionis*. New York: Oxford University Press, 1975.

Sochatoff, A.F. "Imagery in the Poems of *The Satyricon*," in *Classical Journal*. LXV (May, 1970), pp. 340–344.

Sullivan, J.P. "Petronius, Artist or Moralist?," in *Essays on Classical Literature*. Edited by Niall Rudd. New York: Barnes & Noble, 1972, pp. 151–168.

————. The Satyricon *of Petronius, A Literary Study*. Bloomington: Indiana University Press, 1968.

Todd, F.A. "*Satyricon*," in *Some Ancient Novels*. London: Oxford University Press, 1940, pp. 65–101.

Walsh, P.G. *The Roman Novel:* The Satyricon *of Petronius and* The Metamorphoses *of Apuleius*. London: Cambridge University Press, 1970.

————. "Was Petronius a Moralist?," in *Greece and Rome*. XXI, (October, 1974), pp. 181–190.

Wright, J. "Disintegrated Assurances: The Contemporary American Response to *The Satyricon*," in *Greece and Rome*. XXIII (April, 1976), pp. 32–39.

PINDAR
(c.522 B.C.–c.443 B.C.)

The Odes

Bond, R.W. "Theban Eagle," in his *Studia Otiosa; Some Attempts at Criticism.* New York: Macmillan, 1938, pp. 133–161.

Boura, Sir Cecil Maurice. *Pindar.* Oxford: Clarendon Press, 1964.

Bundy, Elroy L. *Studia Pindarica.* Berkeley: University of California Press, 1962.

Burton, Reginald. *Pindar's Pythian Odes, Essays in Interpretation.* Oxford: Oxford University Press, 1962.

Carne-Ross, D.S. "Three Preludes for Pindar," in *Arion.* II (1975), pp. 160–193.

Farnell, Lewis Aukard. *Critical Commentary to the Works of Pindar.* Amsterdam: A.M. Hakkert, 1961.

Finley, John Huston. *Pindar and Aesckylus.* Cambridge, Mass.: Published for Oberlin College by Harvard University Press, 1855.

————. "Pindar's Beginnings," in *The Poetic Tradition.* Edited by Don Cameron Allen and Henry T. Rowell. Baltimore: Johns Hopkins University Press, 1968, pp. 3–26.

Freeman, K. "Pindar—The Function and Technique of Poetry," in *Greece and Rome.* VIII (1939), pp. 144–159.

Grant, Mary Amelia. *Folktale and Hero-Tale Motifs in the Odes of Pindar.* Lawrence: University of Kansas Press, 1968.

Grimm, R.E. "Pindar and the Beast," in *Classical Philology.* LVII (January, 1962), pp. 1–9.

Grube, G.M.A. "The Beginnings of Criticism," in his *The Greek and Roman Critics.* Toronto: University of Toronto Press, 1965, pp. 1–21.

Hamilton, E. "Pindar, the Last Greek Aristocrat," in his *Great Age of Greek Literature.* New York: Norton, 1942, pp. 85–103.

Harvey, A.E. "The Classification of Greek Lyric Poetry," in *Classical Quarterly.* V (1955), pp. 157–175.

Jaegar, W.W. *Paideia: The Ideals of Greek Culture*, Volume I. London: Oxford University Press, 1959, pp. 184–221.

Mullen, W. "Pindar and Athens: A Reading in the Aeginetan Odes," in *Arion.* I (1973–1974), pp. 446–495.

Norwood, G. *Pindar.* Berkeley: University of California Press, 1945.

Parry, H. "Poets and Athletes: Pindar and Some Modern Contrasts," in *Echos du Mode Classique.* XV (1971), pp. 64–70.

Perry, B.E.   *Babrius and Phaedrus.* Cambridge, Mass.: Harvard University Press, 1965, pp. lxxiii–cii.

Rose, H.J..   "Pindar and the Tragedians," in *Classical Review.* LXI (September, 1947), pp. 43–44.

Snell, B.   *Poetry and Society: The Role of Poetry in Ancient Greece.* Bloomington: Indiana University Press, 1961, pp. 56–71.

Sperduti, A.   "The Divine Nature of Poetry in Antiquity," in *Transactions of the American Philological Association.* LXXXI (1950), pp. 209–240.

Starr, Chester G.   "Pindar and the Greek Historical Spirit," in *Hermes.* XCV (1967), pp. 393–403.

HAROLD PINTER
(1930–   )

The Basement

Baker, William and Stephen Ely Tabachnick. *Harold Pinter.* New York: Barnes & Noble, 1973, pp. 50–51.

Dukore, Bernard F. *Where Laughter Stops: Pinter's Tragicomedy.* Columbia: University of Missouri Press, 1976, pp. 48–51.

Esslin, Martin. *The Peopled Wound: The Plays of Harold Pinter.* London: Methuen, 1970, pp. 162–167.

Gabbard, Lucina Paquet. *The Dream Structure of Pinter's Plays: A Psychoanalytic Approach.* Rutherford, N.J.: Fairleigh Dickinson University Press, 1976, pp. 164–172.

Gale, Steven H. *Butter's Going Up: A Critical Analysis of Harold Pinter's Work.* Durham, N.C.: Duke University Press, 1977, pp. 157–164.

Hayman, Ronald. *Harold Pinter.* New York: Frederick Ungar, 1973, pp. 113–120.

Hinchliffe, Arnold P. *Harold Pinter.* New York: Twayne, 1967, pp. 135–138.

Rosador, Kurt. "Pinter's Dramatic Method: *Kullus, The Examination,* and *The Basement,*" in *Modern Drama.* XIV (September, 1971), pp. 195–204.

Sykes, Alrene. *Harold Pinter.* New York: Humanities Press, 1970, pp. 2–4, 110–114.

Trussler, Simon. *The Plays of Harold Pinter.* London: Gollancz, 1974, pp. 135–180.

The Birthday Party

Baker, William and Stephen Ely Tabachnick. *Harold Pinter.* New York: Barnes & Noble, 1973, pp. 52–69.

Brown, John Russell. *Theatre Language: A Study of Arden, Osborne, Pinter, and Wesker.* New York: Taplinger, 1972, pp. 15–54.

Burghardt, Lorraine H. "Game Playing in Three by Pinter," in *Modern Drama.* XVII (1974), pp. 377–387.

Burkman, Katherine H. *The Dramatic World of Harold Pinter: Its Basis in Ritual.* Columbus: Ohio State University Press, 1971, pp. 23–36.

Carpenter, C.A. "What Have I Seen, The Scum or the Essence? Symbolic Fallout in Pinter's *Birthday Party,*" in *Modern Drama.* XVII (1974), pp. 389–402.

Cohn, Ruby. "The World of Harold Pinter," in *Tulane Drama Review.* VI (March, 1962), pp. 55–68. Reprinted in *Pinter: A Collection of Critical Es-*

says. Edited by Arthur F. Ganz. Englewood Cliffs, N.J.: Prentice-Hall, 1972, pp. 78–92.

Donoghue, Denis. "London Letter: Moral West End," in *Hudson Review.* XIV (Spring, 1961), pp. 93–103.

Dukore, Bernard F. *Where Laughter Stops: Pinter's Tragicomedy.* Columbia: University of Missouri Press, 1976, pp. 9–17.

Esslin, Martin. *The Peopled Wound: The Plays of Harold Pinter.* London: Methuen, 1970, pp. 75–86.

Gabbard, Lucina Paquet. *The Dream Structure of Pinter's Plays: A Psychoanalytic Approach.* Rutherford, N.J.: Fairleigh Dickinson University Press, 1976, pp. 42–61.

Gale, Steven H. *Butter's Going Up: A Critical Analysis of Harold Pinter's Work.* Durham, N.C.: Duke University Press, 1977, pp. 37–59.

Gordon, Lois G. *Stratagems to Uncover Nakedness: The Dramas of Harold Pinter.* Columbia: University of Missouri Press, 1969, pp. 19–29.

Hayman, Ronald. *Harold Pinter.* New York: Frederick Ungar, 1973, pp. 30–42.

Hinchliffe, Arnold P. *Harold Pinter.* New York: Twayne, 1967, pp. 48–63.

Hollis, James R. *Harold Pinter: The Poetics of Silence.* Carbondale: Southern Illinois University Press, 1970, pp. 31–43.

Kaufman, M.W. "Actions That a Man Might Play: Pinter's *The Birthday Party*," in *Modern Drama.* XVI (September, 1973), pp. 167–178.

Kerr, Walter. *Harold Pinter.* New York: Columbia University Press, 1967.

Lesser, S.O. "Reflections on Pinter's *The Birthday Party*," in *Contemporary Literature.* XIII (Winter, 1972), pp. 34–43.

Pesta, John. "Pinter's Usurpers," in *Drama Survey.* VI (Spring, 1967), pp. 54–65. Reprinted in *Pinter: A Collection of Critical Essays.* Edited by Arthur F. Ganz. Englewood Cliffs, N.J.: Prentice-Hall, 1972, pp. 123–135.

Schiff, Ellen F. "Pancakes and Soap Suds: A Study of Childishness in Pinter's Plays," in *Modern Drama.* XVI (1973), pp. 91–101.

Sykes, Alrene. *Harold Pinter.* New York: Humanities Press, 1970, pp. 2–11, 17–23, 86–93.

Taylor, John Russell. *The Angry Theatre: New British Drama.* New York: Hill and Wang, 1969, pp. 324–336.

———. *Harold Pinter.* London: Longmans, Green, 1969.

Trussler, Simon. *The Plays of Harold Pinter.* London: Gollancz, 1974, pp. 25–57.

Williams, Raymond. *Drama from Ibsen to Brecht.* London: Chatto and Windus, 1968, pp. 322–325.

The Caretaker

Baker, William and Stephen Ely Tabachnick. *Harold Pinter.* New York: Barnes & Noble, 1973, pp. 70–89.

Boulton, James T. "Harold Pinter: *The Caretaker* and Other Plays," in *Modern Drama.* VI (September, 1963), pp. 131–140. Reprinted in *Pinter: A Collection of Critical Essays.* Edited by Arthur Ganz. Englewood Cliffs, N.J.: Prentice-Hall, 1972, pp. 93–104.

Brown, John Russell. *Theatre Language: A Study of Arden, Osborne, Pinter, and Wesker.* New York: Taplinger, 1972, pp. 55–92.

Burkman, Katherine H. *The Dramatic World of Harold Pinter: Its Basis in Ritual.* Columbus: Ohio State University Press, 1971, pp. 76–87.

Cohn, Ruby. "The World of Harold Pinter," in *Tulane Drama Review.* VI (March, 1962), pp. 55–68. Reprinted in *Pinter: A Collection of Critical Essays.* Edited by Arthur F. Ganz. Englewood Cliffs, N.J.: Prentice-Hall, 1972, pp. 78–92.

Donoghue, Denis. "London Letter: Moral West End," in *Hudson Review.* XIV (Spring, 1961), pp. 93–103.

Dukore, Bernard F. *Where Laughter Stops: Pinter's Tragicomedy.* Columbia: University of Missouri Press, 1976, pp. 25–31.

Esslin, Martin. *The Peopled Wound: The Plays of Harold Pinter.* London: Methuen, 1970, pp. 94–112.

Gabbard, Lucina Paquet. *The Dream Structure of Pinter's Plays: A Psychoanalytic Approach.* Rutherford, N.J.: Fairleigh Dickinson University Press, 1976, pp. 98–116.

Gale, Steven H. *Butter's Going Up: A Critical Analysis of Harold Pinter's Work.* Durham: Duke University Press, 1977, pp. 81–95.

Gassner, John. *Dramatic Soundings.* New York: Crown, 1968, pp. 503–507.

Goodman, Florence J. "Pinter's *The Caretaker*: The Lower Depths Descended," in *Midwest Quarterly.* V (January, 1964), pp. 117–126.

Gordon, Lois G. *Stratagems to Uncover Nakedness: The Dramas of Harold Pinter.* Columbia: University of Missouri Press, 1969, pp. 40–50.

Hayman, Ronald. *Harold Pinter.* New York: Frederick Ungar, 1973, pp. 55–70.

Hinchliffe, Arnold P. *Harold Pinter.* New York: Twayne, 1967, pp. 87–107.

Hollis, James R. *Harold Pinter: The Poetics of Silence.* Carbondale: Southern Illinois University Press, 1970, pp. 77–95.

Kerr, Walter. *Harold Pinter.* New York: Columbia University Press, 1967.

Minogue, Valerie. "Taking Care of the *Caretaker*," in *Twentieth Century.* CLXVIII (September, 1960), pp. 243–248. Reprinted in *Pinter: A Collection of Critical Essays.* Edited by Arthur Ganz. Englewood Cliffs, N.J.: Prentice-Hall, 1972, pp. 72–77.

Pesta, John. "Pinter's Usurpers," in *Drama Survey.* VI (1967–1968), pp. 54–65. Reprinted in *Pinter: A Collection of Critical Essays.* Edited by Arthur Ganz. Englewood Cliffs, N.J.: Prentice-Hall, 1972, pp. 123–135.

Quigley, Austin E. *The Pinter Problem.* Princeton, N.J.: Princeton University Press, 1975, pp. 113–172.

Simon, John. "Theatre Chronicle," in *Hudson Review.* XIV (1961), pp. 586–592.

Taylor, John Russell. *The Angry Theatre: New British Drama.* New York: Hill and Wang, 1969, pp. 336–340.

————. *Harold Pinter.* London: Longmans, Green, 1969.

Trussler, Simon. *The Plays of Harold Pinter.* London: Gollancz, 1974, pp. 76–104.

Walker, Augusta. "Messages from Pinter," in *Modern Drama.* X (1967), pp. 1–10.

The Collection

Baker, William and Stephen Ely Tabachnick. *Harold Pinter.* New York: Barnes & Noble, 1973, pp. 44–48.

Burkman, Katherine H. *The Dramatic World of Harold Pinter: Its Basis in Ritual.* Columbus: Ohio State University Press, 1971, pp. 102–104.

Cohn, Ruby. "Latter Day Pinter," in *Drama Survey.* III (1964), pp. 367–377.

Dukore, Bernard F. *Where Laughter Stops: Pinter's Tragicomedy.* Columbia: University of Missouri Press, 1976, pp. 31–34.

Esslin, Martin. *The Peopled Wound: The Plays of Harold Pinter.* London: Methuen, 1970, pp. 125–130.

Gabbard, Lucina Paquet. *The Dream Structure of Pinter's Plays: A Psychoanalytic Approach.* Rutherford, N.J.: Fairleigh Dickinson University Press, 1976, pp. 145–157.

Gale, Steven H. *Butter's Going Up: A Critical Analysis of Harold Pinter's Work.* Durham, N.C.: Duke University Press, 1977, pp. 120–129.

Gordon, Lois G. *Stratagems to Uncover Nakedness: The Dramas of Harold Pinter.* Columbia: University of Missouri Press, 1969, pp. 51–52.

Hayman, Ronald. *Harold Pinter.* New York: Frederick Ungar, 1973, pp. 80–87.

Hinchliffe, Arnold P. *Harold Pinter.* New York: Twayne, 1967, pp. 114–118.

Hollis, James R. *Harold Pinter: The Poetics of Silence.* Carbondale: Southern Illinois University Press, 1970, pp. 70–77.

Kerr, Walter. *Harold Pinter.* New York: Columbia University Press, 1967.

Matthews, Honor. *The Primal Curse: The Myth of Cain and Abel in the Theatre.* New York: Schocken, 1967, pp. 198–201.

Schechner, Richard. "Puzzling Pinter," in *Tulane Drama Review*. XI (1966), pp. 176–184.

Sykes, Alrene. *Harold Pinter*. New York: Humanities Press, 1970, pp. 102–107.

Taylor, John Russell. *The Angry Theatre: New British Drama*. New York: Hill and Wang, 1969, pp. 348–352.

————. *Harold Pinter*. London: Longmans, Green, 1969.

Trussler, Simon. *The Plays of Harold Pinter*. London: Gollancz, 1974, pp. 105–134.

Walker, Augusta. "Messages from Pinter," in *Modern Drama*. X (1967), pp. 1–10.

The Dumb Waiter

Baker, William and Stephen Ely Tabachnick. *Harold Pinter*. New York: Barnes & Noble, 1973, pp. 24–38.

Burghardt, Lorraine H. "Game Playing in Three by Pinter," in *Modern Drama*. XVII (1974), pp. 377–387.

Burkman, Katherine H. *The Dramatic World of Harold Pinter: Its Basis in Ritual*. Columbus: Ohio State University Press, 1971, pp. 39–44.

Carpenter, Charles A. "The Absurdity of Dread: Pinter's *The Dumb Waiter*," in *Modern Drama*. XVI (1973), pp. 279–285.

Donoghue, Denis. "London Letter: Moral West End," in *Hudson Review*. XIV (Spring, 1961), pp. 93–103.

Dukore, Bernard F. *Where Laughter Stops: Pinter's Tragicomedy*. Columbia: University of Missouri Press, 1976, pp. 17–21.

Esslin, Martin. *The Peopled Wound: The Plays of Harold Pinter*. London: Methuen, 1970, pp. 69–74.

Gabbard, Lucina Paquet. *The Dream Structure of Pinter's Plays: A Psychoanalytic Approach*. Rutherford, N.J.: Fairleigh Dickinson University Press, 1976, pp. 61–70.

Gale, Steven H. *Butter's Going Up: A Critical Analysis of Harold Pinter's Work*. Durham, N.C.: Duke University Press, 1977, pp. 39–40, 59–63.

Gordon, Lois G. *Stratagems to Uncover Nakedness: The Dramas of Harold Pinter*. Columbia: University of Missouri Press, 1969, pp. 29–34.

Hayman, Ronald. *Harold Pinter*. New York: Frederick Ungar, 1973, pp. 25–29.

Hinchliffe, Arnold P. *Harold Pinter*. New York: Twayne, 1967, pp. 63–68.

Hollis, James R. *Harold Pinter: The Poetics of Silence*. Carbondale: Southern Illinois University Press, 1970, pp. 43–51.

Kerr, Walter. *Harold Pinter*. New York: Columbia University Press, 1967.

Quigley, Austin E.   *The Pinter Problem.* Princeton, N.J.: Princeton University Press, 1975, pp. 61–63.

Sykes, Alrene.   *Harold Pinter.* New York: Humanities Press, 1970, pp. 2–10, 13–17.

Taylor, John Russell.   *The Angry Theatre: New British Drama.* New York: Hill and Wang, 1969, pp. 324–336.

Trussler, Simon.   *The Plays of Harold Pinter.* London: Gollancz, 1974, pp. 25–57.

The Dwarfs

Baker, William and Stephen Ely Tabachnick.   *Harold Pinter.* New York: Barnes & Noble, 1973, pp. 42–44.

Brown, John Russell.   *Theatre Language: A Study of Arden, Osborne, Pinter, and Wesker.* New York: Taplinger, 1972, pp. 55–92.

Burkman, Katherine H.   *The Dramatic World of Harold Pinter: Its Basis in Ritual.* Columbus: Ohio State University Press, 1971, pp. 68–70.

Cohn, Ruby.   "Latter Day Pinter," in *Drama Survey.* III (1964), pp. 367–377.

Esslin, Martin.   *The Peopled Wound: The Plays of Harold Pinter.* London: Methuen, 1970, pp. 117–124.

Gabbard, Lucina Paquet.   *The Dream Structure of Pinter's Plays: A Psychoanalytic Approach.* Rutherford, N.J.: Fairleigh Dickinson University Press, 1976, pp. 125–140.

Gale, Steven H.   *Butter's Going Up: A Critical Analysis of Harold Pinter's Work.* Durham, N.C.: Duke University Press, 1977, pp. 110–118.

Hayman, Ronald.   *Harold Pinter.* New York: Frederick Ungar, 1973, pp. 75–79.

Hinchliffe, Arnold P.   *Harold Pinter.* New York: Twayne, 1967, pp. 78–86.

Powlick, Leonard.   "Temporality in Pinter's *The Dwarfs*," in *Modern Drama.* XX (March, 1977), pp. 67–76.

Sykes, Alrene.   *Harold Pinter.* New York: Humanities Press, 1970, pp. 37–40, 51–59.

Taylor, John Russell.   *The Angry Theatre: New British Drama.* New York: Hill and Wang, 1969, pp. 345–348.

Trussler, Simon.   *The Plays of Harold Pinter.* London: Gollancz, 1974, pp. 76–104.

The Homecoming

Aronson, Steven M.L.   "Pinter's 'Family' and Blood Knowledge," in *A Casebook on Harold Pinter's* The Homecoming. Edited by John Lahr. New York: Grove, 1971, pp. 67–86.

Baker, William and Stephen Ely Tabachnick. *Harold Pinter.* New York: Barnes & Noble, 1973, pp. 108–124.

Brown, John Russell. *Theatre Language: A Study of Arden, Osborne, Pinterand Wesker.* New York: Taplinger, 1972, pp. 93–117.

Burkman, Katherine H. *The Dramatic World of Harold Pinter: Its Basis in Ritual.* Columbus: Ohio State University Press, 1971, pp. 108–116.

Croyden, Margaret. "Pinter's Hideous Comedy," in *A Casebook on Harold Pinter's* The Homecoming. Edited by John Lahr. New York: Grove, 1971, pp. 45–56.

Dukore, Bernard F. "A Woman's Place," in *Quarterly Journal of Speech.* LII (1967), pp. 237–241. Reprinted in *A Casebook on Harold Pinter's* The Homecoming. Edited by John Lahr. New York: Grove, 1971, pp. 109–116.

Esslin, Martin. *The Peopled Wound: The Plays of Harold Pinter.* London: Methuen, 1970, pp. 137–157.

Gabbard, Lucina Paquet. *The Dream Structure of Pinter's Plays: A Psychoanalytic Approach.* Rutherford, N.J.: Fairleigh Dickinson University Press, 1976, pp. 183–208.

Gale, Steven H. *Butter's Going Up: A Critical Analysis of Harold Pinter's Work.* Durham, N.C.: Duke University Press, 1977, pp. 136–156.

Gordon, Lois G. *Stratagems to Uncover Nakedness: The Dramas of Harold Pinter.* Columbia: University of Missouri Press, 1969, pp. 53–62.

Hayman, Ronald. *Harold Pinter.* New York: Frederick Ungar, 1973, pp. 99–112.

Hewes, Henry. "Probing Pinter's Play," in *Saturday Review.* L (April 8, 1967), p. 56.

Hinchliffe, Arnold P. *Harold Pinter.* New York: Twayne, 1967, pp. 146–162.

Hollis, James R. *Harold Pinter: The Poetics of Silence.* Carbondale: Southern Illinois University Press, 1970, pp. 96–111.

Kerr, Walter. *Harold Pinter.* New York: Columbia University Press, 1967.

Lahr, John. "Pinter's Language," in *A Casebook on Harold Pinter's* The Homecoming. Edited by John Lahr. New York: Grove, 1971, pp. 123–136.

Morris, Kelly. "*The Homecoming,*" in *Tulane Drama Review.* XI (Winter, 1966), pp. 185–191.

Nelson, Hugh. "*The Homecoming*: Kith and Kin," in *Modern British Dramatists: A Collection of Critical Essays.* Edited by John Russell Brown. Englewood Cliffs, N.J.: Prentice-Hall, 1968, pp. 145–163.

Osherow, A.R. "Mother and Whore: The Role of Woman in *The Homecoming,*" in *Modern Drama.* XVII (1974), pp. 423–432.

Quigley, Austin E. *The Pinter Problem*. Princeton, N.J.: Princeton University Press, 1975, pp. 173–225.

States, Bert O. "Pinter's *Homecoming*: The Shock of Nonrecognition," in *Hudson Review*. XXI (Autumn, 1968), pp. 474–486. Reprinted in *Pinter: A Collection of Critical Essays*. Edited by Arthur Ganz. Englewood Cliffs, N.J.: Prentice-Hall, 1972, pp. 147–160.

Taylor, John Russell. *The Angry Theatre: New British Drama*. New York: Hill and Wang, 1969, pp. 353–359.

Trussler, Simon. *The Plays of Harold Pinter*. London: Gollancz, 1974, pp. 105–134.

Walker, Augusta. "Why the Lady Does It," in *A Casebook on Harold Pinter's* The Homecoming. Edited by John Lahr. New York: Grove, 1971, pp. 117–122.

Wardle, Irving. "The Territorial Struggle," in *A Casebook on Harold Pinter's* The Homecoming. Edited by John Lahr. New York: Grove, 1971, pp. 37–44.

Landscape

Anderson, Michael. *Anger and Detachment: A Study of Arden, Osborne, and Pinter*. London: Pitman, 1976, pp. 102–108.

Baker, William and Stephen Ely Tabachnick. *Harold Pinter*. New York: Barnes & Noble, 1973, pp. 125–135.

Burkman, Katherine H. *The Dramatic World of Harold Pinter: Its Basis in Ritual*. Columbus: Ohio State University Press, 1971, pp. 141–145.

Eigo, James. "Pinter's *Landscape*," in *Modern Drama*. XVI (1973), pp. 179–183.

Esslin, Martin. *The Peopled Wound: The Plays of Harold Pinter*. London: Methuen, 1970, pp. 168–175.

Gabbard, Lucina Paquet. *The Dream Structure of Pinter's Plays: A Psychoanalytic Approach*. Rutherford, N.J.: Fairleigh Dickinson University Press, 1976, pp. 211–223.

Gale, Steven H. *Butter's Going Up: A Critical Analysis of Harold Pinter's Work*. Durham, N.C.: Duke University Press, 1977, pp. 176–181.

Ganz, Arthur. "Mixing Memory and Desire: Pinter's Vision in *Landscape, Silence,* and *Old Times*," in *Pinter: A Collection of Critical Essays*. Edited by Arthur Ganz. Englewood Cliffs, N.J.: Prentice-Hall, 1972, pp. 161–178.

Hayman, Ronald. *Harold Pinter*. New York: Frederick Ungar, 1973, pp. 121–126.

Hollis, James R. *Harold Pinter: The Poetics of Silence*. Carbondale: Southern Illinois University Press, 1970, pp. 118–121.

Quigley, Austin E. *The Pinter Problem*. Princeton, N.J.: Princeton University Press, 1975, pp. 226–272.

Salmon, Eric. "Harold Pinter's Ear," in *Modern Drama.* XVII (1974), pp. 363–375.

Trussler, Simon. *The Plays of Harold Pinter.* London: Gollancz, 1974, pp. 135–180.

The Lover

Baker, William and Stephen Ely Tabachnick. *Harold Pinter.* New York: Barnes & Noble, 1973, pp. 48–49.

Brown, John Russell. *Theatre Language: A Study of Arden, Osborne, Pinterand Wesker.* New York: Taplinger, 1972, pp. 15–54.

Burkman, Katherine H. *The Dramatic World of Harold Pinter: Its Basis in Ritual.* Columbus: Ohio State University Press, 1971, pp. 104–107.

Dukore, Bernard F. *Where Laughter Stops: Pinter's Tragicomedy.* Columbia: University of Missouri Press, 1966, pp. 34–36.

Esslin, Martin. *The Peopled Wound: The Plays of Harold Pinter.* London: Methuen, 1970, pp. 131–136.

Gabbard, Lucina Paquet. *The Dream Structure of Pinter's Plays: A Psychoanalytic Approach.* Rutherford, N.J.: Fairleigh Dickinson University Press, 1976, pp. 157–164.

Gale, Steven H. *Butter's Going Up: A Critical Analysis of Harold Pinter's Work.* Durham, N.C.: Duke University Press, 1977, pp. 129–136.

Gordon, Lois G. *Stratagems to Uncover Nakedness: The Dramas of Harold Pinter.* Columbia: University of Missouri Press, 1969, pp. 52–53.

Hayman, Ronald. *Harold Pinter.* New York: Frederick Ungar, 1973, pp. 88–92.

Hinchliffe, Arnold P. *Harold Pinter.* New York: Twayne, 1967, pp. 118–124.

Hollis, James R. *Harold Pinter: The Poetics of Silence.* Carbondale: Southern Illinois University Press, 1970, pp. 62–69.

Sykes, Alrene. *Harold Pinter.* New York: Humanities Press, 1970, pp. 107–110.

Taylor, John Russell. *The Angry Theatre: New British Drama.* New York: Hill and Wang, 1969, pp. 348–352.

————. *Harold Pinter.* London: Longmans, Green, 1969.

Trussler, Simon. *The Plays of Harold Pinter.* London: Gollancz, 1974, pp. 105–134.

Wellwarth, George. *The Theatre of Protest and Paradox: Developments in the Avant-Garde Drama.* New York: New York University Press, 1971, pp. 235–238.

Old Times

Anderson, Michael. *Anger and Detachment: A Study of Arden, Osborne, and Pinter.* London: Pitman, 1976, pp. 95–100.

Baker, William and Stephen Ely Tabachnick. *Harold Pinter.* New York: Barnes & Noble, 1973, pp. 137–148.

Dukore, Bernard F. *Where Laughter Stops: Pinter's Tragicomedy.* Columbia: University of Missouri Press, 1976, pp. 51–60.

Eilenberg, Lawrence I. "Rehearsal as Critical Method: Pinter's *Old Times*," in *Modern Drama.* XVIII (December, 1975), pp. 385–392.

Gabbard, Lucina Paquet. *The Dream Structure of Pinter's Plays: A Psychoanalytic Approach.* Rutherford, N.J.: Fairleigh Dickinson University Press, 1976, pp. 234–251.

Gale, Steven H. *Butter's Going Up: A Critical Analysis of Harold Pinter's Work.* Durham, N.C.: Duke University Press, 1977, pp. 184–199.

Ganz, Arthur. "Mixing Memory and Desire: Pinter's Vision in *Landscape, Silence*, and *Old Times*," in *Pinter: A Collection of Critical Essays.* Edited by Arthur Ganz. Englewood Cliffs, N.J.: Prentice-Hall, 1972, pp. 161–178.

Hayman, Ronald. *Harold Pinter.* New York: Frederick Ungar, 1973, pp. 140–148.

Hughes, A. "They Can't Take That Away from Me: Myth and Memory in Pinter's *Old Times*," in *Modern Drama.* XVII (1974), pp. 467–476.

Kauffmann, Stanley. "Pinter and Sexuality: Notes, Mostly on *Old Times*," in *American Poetry Review.* III (1974), pp. 39–41. Reprinted in *Persons of the Drama.* New York: Harper & Row, 1976, pp. 335–348.

Martineau, Stephen. "Pinter's *Old Times*: The Memory Game," in *Modern Drama.* XVII (1973), pp. 287–297.

Trussler, Simon. *The Plays of Harold Pinter.* London: Gollancz, 1974, pp. 135–180.

The Room

Baker, William and Stephen Ely Tabachnick. *Harold Pinter.* New York: Barnes & Noble, 1973, pp. 24–38.

Burkman, Katherine H. *The Dramatic World of Harold Pinter: Its Basis in Ritual.* Columbus: Ohio State University Press, 1971, pp. 70–73.

Donoghue, Denis. "London Letter: Moral West End," in *Hudson Review.* XIV (Spring, 1961), pp. 93–103.

Dukore, Bernard F. *Where Laughter Stops: Pinter's Tragicomedy.* Columbia: University of Missouri Press, 1976, pp. 5–9.

Esslin, Martin. *The Peopled Wound: The Plays of Harold Pinter.* London: Methuen, 1970, pp. 60–68.

Gabbard, Lucina Paquet. *The Dream Structure of Pinter's Plays: A Psycho-analytic Approach.* Rutherford, N.J.: Fairleigh Dickinson University Press, 1976, pp. 17–36.

Gale, Steven H. *Butter's Going Up: A Critical Analysis of Harold Pinter's Work.* Durham, N.C.: Duke University Press, 1977, pp. 23–37.

Gordon, Lois G. *Stratagems to Uncover Nakedness: The Dramas of Harold Pinter.* Columbia: University of Missouri Press, 1969, pp. 11–19.

Hayman, Ronald. *Harold Pinter.* New York: Frederick Ungar, 1973, pp. 19–24.

Hinchliffe, Arnold P. *Harold Pinter.* New York: Twayne, 1967, pp. 41–48.

Hollis, James R. *Harold Pinter: The Poetics of Silence.* Carbondale: Southern Illinois University Press, 1970, pp. 20–31.

Kerr, Walter. *Harold Pinter.* New York: Columbia University Press, 1967.

Pesta, John. "Pinter's Usurpers," in *Drama Survey.* VI (1967–1968), pp. 54–65. Reprinted in *Pinter: A Collection of Critical Essays.* Edited by Arthur Ganz. Englewood Cliffs, N.J.: Prentice-Hall, 1972, pp. 123–135.

Quigley, Austin E. *The Pinter Problem.* Princeton, N.J.: Princeton University Press, 1975, pp. 76–112.

Sykes, Alrene. *Harold Pinter.* New York: Humanities Press, 1970, pp. 2–13.

Taylor, John Russell. *The Angry Theatre: New British Drama.* New York: Hill and Wang, 1969, pp. 324–336.

────────. *Harold Pinter.* London: Longmans, Green, 1969.

Trussler, Simon. *The Plays of Harold Pinter.* London: Gollancz, 1974, pp. 25–57.

Silence

Baker, William and Stephen Ely Tabachnick. *Harold Pinter.* New York: Barnes & Noble, 1973, pp. 125–135.

Esslin, Martin. *The Peopled Wound: The Plays of Harold Pinter.* London: Methuen, 1970, pp. 176–182.

Gabbard, Lucina Paquet. *The Dream Structure of Pinter's Plays: A Psycho-analytic Approach.* Rutherford, N.J.: Fairleigh Dickinson University Press, 1976, pp. 223–234.

Gale, Steven H. *Butter's Going Up: A Critical Analysis of Harold Pinter's Work.* Durham, N.C.: Duke University Press, 1977, pp. 181–183.

Ganz, Arthur. "Mixing Memory and Desire: Pinter's Version in *Landscape, Silence,* and *Old Times,*" in *Pinter: A Collection of Critical Essays.* Edited by Arthur Ganz. Englewood Cliffs, N.J.: Prentice-Hall, 1972, pp. 161–178.

Hayman, Ronald. *Harold Pinter.* New York: Frederick Ungar, 1973, pp. 127–135.

Hollis, James R.   *Harold Pinter: The Poetics of Silence*. Carbondale: Southern Illinois University Press, 1970, pp. 114–118.

Imhof, Rudiger.   "Pinter's *Silence*: The Impossibility of Communication," in *Modern Drama*. XVII (1974), pp. 449–459.

Kauffmann, Stanley.   *Persons of the Drama*. New York: Harper & Row, 1976, pp. 201–204.

Trussler, Simon.   *The Plays of Harold Pinter*. London: Gollancz, 1974, pp. 135–180.

A Slight Ache

Anderson, Michael.   *Anger and Detachment: A Study of Arden, Osborne and Pinter*. London: Pitman, 1976, pp. 106–108.

Baker, William and Stephen Ely Tabachnick.   *Harold Pinter*. New York: Barnes & Noble, 1973, pp. 24–38.

Burkman, Katherine H.   *The Dramatic World of Harold Pinter: Its Basis in Ritual*. Columbus: Ohio State University Press, 1971, pp. 47–64.

Clurman, Harold.   *The Naked Image: Observations of Modern Theatre*. New York: Macmillan, 1966, pp. 110–112.

Dukore, Bernard F.   *Where Laughter Stops: Pinter's Tragicomedy*. Columbia: University of Missouri Press, 1976, pp. 21–25.

Esslin, Martin.   *The Peopled Wound: The Plays of Harold Pinter*. London: Methuen, 1970, pp. 87–90.

Gabbard, Lucina Paquet.   *The Dream Structure of Pinter's Plays: A Psychoanalytic Approach*. Rutherford, N.J.: Fairleigh Dickinson University Press, 1976, pp. 70–84.

Gale, Steven H.   *Butter's Going Up: A Critical Analysis of Harold Pinter's Work*. Durham, N.C.: Duke University Press, 1977, pp. 74–81.

Gordon, Lois G.   *Stratagems to Uncover Nakedness: The Dramas of Harold Pinter*. Columbia: University of Missouri Press, 1969, pp. 34–40.

Hayman, Ronald.   *Harold Pinter*. New York: Frederick Ungar, 1973, pp. 43–48.

Hinchliffe, Arnold P.   *Harold Pinter*. New York: Twayne, 1967, pp. 68–71.

Hollis, James R.   *Harold Pinter: The Poetics of Silence*. Carbondale: Southern Illinois University Press, 1970, pp. 52–62.

Sainer, Arthur.   *The Sleepwalker and the Assassin*. New York: Bridgehead Books, 1964, pp. 99–102.

Salmon, Eric.   "Harold Pinter's Ear," in *Modern Drama*. XVII (1974), pp. 363–375.

Schiff, Ellen F.   "Pancakes and Soap Suds: A Study of Childishness in Pinter's Plays," in *Modern Drama*. XVI (1973), pp. 91–101.

Stein, Karen F. "Metaphysical Silence in Absurd Drama," in *Modern Drama*. XIII (February, 1971), pp. 423–431.

Sykes, Alrene. *Harold Pinter*. New York: Humanities Press, 1970, pp. 37–51.

Taylor, John Russell. *The Angry Theatre: New British Drama*. New York: Hill and Wang, 1969, pp. 324–336.

Trussler, Simon. *The Plays of Harold Pinter*. London: Gollancz, 1974, pp. 58–75.

Tea Party

Anderson, Michael. *Anger and Detachment: A Study of Arden, Osborne, and Pinter*. London: Pitman, 1976, pp. 9–14.

Baker, William and Stephen Ely Tabachnick. *Harold Pinter*. New York: Barnes & Noble, 1973, pp. 49–50.

Burghardt, Lorraine H. "Game Playing in Three by Pinter," in *Modern Drama*. XVII (1974), pp. 377–387.

Burkman, Katherine H. *The Dramatic World of Harold Pinter: Its Basis in Ritual*. Columbus: Ohio State University Press, 1971, pp. 98–102.

Canaday, Nicholas, Jr. "Harold Pinter's *Tea Party*: Seeing and Non-Seeing," in *Studies in Short Fiction*. VI (1969), pp. 580–585.

Dukore, Bernard F. *Where Laughter Stops: Pinter's Tragicomedy*. Columbia: University of Missouri Press, 1976, pp. 44–48.

Esslin, Martin. *The Peopled Wound: The Plays of Harold Pinter*. London: Methuen, 1970, pp. 158–161.

Gabbard, Lucina Paquet. *The Dream Structure of Pinter's Plays: A Psychoanalytic Approach*. Rutherford, N.J.: Fairleigh Dickinson University Press, 1976, pp. 172–183.

Gale, Steven H. *Butter's Going Up: A Critical Analysis of Harold Pinter's Work*. Durham, N.C.: Duke University Press, 1977, pp. 164–173.

Gillen, Francis. " '. . . Apart from the Known and the Unknown': The Unreconciled World of Harold Pinter's Characters," in *Arizona Quarterly*. XXVI (Spring, 1970), pp. 17–24.

Hayman, Ronald. *Harold Pinter*. New York: Frederick Ungar, 1973, pp. 93–98.

Hinchliffe, Arnold P. *Harold Pinter*. New York: Twayne, 1967, pp. 138–145.

Sykes, Alrene. *Harold Pinter*. New York: Humanities Press, 1970, pp. 110–113, 115–116.

Taylor, John Russell. *The Angry Theatre: New British Drama*. New York: Hill and Wang, 1969, pp. 352–353.

Trussler, Simon. *The Plays of Harold Pinter*. London: Gollancz, 1974, pp. 135–180.

LUIGI PIRANDELLO
(1867–1936)

Henry IV

Bentley, Eric Russell. *"Enrico IV,"* in *Theatre of War*. New York: Viking, 1972, pp. 32–44.

Brustein, Robert. *The Theatre of Revolt*. Boston: Little, Brown, 1964, pp. 296–301.

Costa, O. *"Six Characters, Right You Are*, and *Henry IV,"* in *World Theater*. XVI (1967), pp. 248–255.

De Casseres, B. *"Henry IV,"* in *Arts and Decoration*. XX (March, 1924), p. 32.

Kellock, H. *"Henry IV,"* in *Freeman*. VIII (February 13, 1924), pp. 544–545.

Lewis, Allan. "The Relativity of Truth—Pirandello," in *The Contemporary Theatre*. New York: Crown, 1962, pp. 127–143.

Lueders, P. "Pirandello: Reality, Illusion and the Void," in *Xavier University Studies*. I (1961/1962), pp. 158–161.

MacCarthy, Desmond. *"Henry IV,"* in *New Statesman*. XXV (June 27, 1925), pp. 309–310.

May, Frederick. "Three Major Symbols in Four Plays by Pirandello," in *Modern Drama*. VI (February, 1964), pp. 378–396.

Palmer, J. "Plays of Luigi Pirandello," in *Nineteenth Century*. XCVII (June, 1925), pp. 897–909.

————. "Pirandello and the Concept of Reality," in *Pennsylvania Literary Review*. V (1955), pp. 2–7.

Royde-Smith, N.G. *"Henry IV,"* in *Outlook*. LVI (July 25, 1925), p. 57.

Savage, E. "Masks and Mummeries in *Enrico IV* and *Caligula*," in *Modern Drama*. VI (February, 1964), pp. 397–401.

Shipp, H. *"Henry IV,"* in *English Review*. XLI (September, 1925), pp. 437–440.

Styan, J. *The Dark Comedy*. Cambridge: Cambridge University Press, 1962, pp. 168–177.

Vittorini, Domenico. *High Points in the History of Italian Literature*. New York: McKay, 1958, pp. 274–275.

Young, Stark. *Immortal Shadows; A Book of Dramatic Criticism*. New York: Scribner's, 1948, pp. 48–51.

Right You Are—If You Think So

Bentley, Eric Russell. *In Search of Theatre.* New York: Knopf, 1953, pp. 296–314.

———. *"Right You Are,"* in *Theatre of War.* New York: Viking, 1972, pp. 22–31.

Brustein, Robert. *The Theatre of Revolt.* Boston: Little, Brown, 1964, pp. 293–296.

Costa, O. *"Six Characters, Right You Are,* and *Henry IV,"* in *World Theatre.* XVI (1967), pp. 248–255.

Freedman, Morris. "Moral Perspective in Pirandello," in *Modern Drama.* VI (1963/1964), pp. 368–372.

Gascoigne, Bamber. *Twentieth Century Drama.* London: Hutchinson's, 1962, pp. 102–104.

Goldberg, Isaac. *The Drama of Transition.* Cincinnati, Ohio: Stewart Kidd Company, 1922, pp. 184–189.

Hoy, Cyrus H. *The Hyacinth Room.* New York: Knopf, 1964, pp. 81–86.

Lewis, Allan. *The Contemporary Theatre.* New York: Crown, 1962, pp. 132–134.

Nelson, Robert James. *Play Within a Play.* New Haven, Conn.: Yale University Press, 1958, pp. 122–125.

Turner, W.J. "And That's the Truth, If You Think It Is," in *New Statesman.* XXV (October 3, 1925), pp. 694–695.

Vittorini, Domenico. "Pirandello and the Concept of Reality," in *Pennsylvania Literary Review.* V (1955), pp. 2–7.

Williams, Raymond. *Modern Tragedy.* Stanford, Calif.: Stanford University Press, 1966, pp. 149–150.

———. *Drama from Ibsen to Eliot.* London: Chatto and Windus, 1954, pp. 192–193.

Young, Stark. *Immortal Shadows; A Book of Dramatic Criticism.* New York: Scribner's, 1948, pp. 84–87.

Six Characters in Search of an Author

Bentley, Eric Russell. "Father's Day," in *Drama Review.* XIII (1968), pp. 57–72.

———. *"Six Characters in Search of an Author,"* in *Theatre of War.* New York: Viking, 1972, pp. 45–63.

Brustein, Robert. *The Theater of Revolt.* Boston: Little, Brown, 1964, pp. 309–315.

Costa, O. *"Six Characters, Right You Are,* and *Henry IV,"* in *World Theatre.* XVI (1967), pp. 248–255.

Crawford, J. *"Six Characters in Search of an Author,"* in *Drama.* XIII (January, 1923), pp. 130–131.

Fergusson, Francis. *The Idea of a Theatre.* New York: Doubleday, 1957, pp. 186–193.

Gassner, John. "European Vistas: Tyrone Guthrie's or Pirandello's Six Characters," in *Theatre at the Crossroads.* New York: Holt, 1960, pp. 242–245.

Gilliatt, Penelope. "Pirandello," in *Unholy Fools.* New York: Viking, 1973, pp. 62–64.

Gilman, Richard. "Pirandello to Perfection," in *Common and Uncommon Masks.* New York: Random House, 1971, pp. 81–83.

Heffner, H. "Pirandello and the Nature of Man," in *Tulane Drama Review.* I (June, 1957), pp. 23–40.

Kennedy, A. "Six Characters: Pirandello's Last Tape," in *Modern Drama.* XXII (May, 1969), pp. 1–9.

Hudson, Lynton. *Life and the Theatre.* London: George G. Harrap, 1949, pp. 34–39.

Kernan, Alvin. "Truth and Dramatic Mode in the Modern Theater," in *Modern Drama.* I (September, 1958), pp. 107–111.

Kligerman, C.K. "A Psychoanalytic Study of Pirandello's *Six Characters in Search of an Author,"* in *Journal of American Psychoanalysis Association.* X (1962), pp. 731–744.

MacCarthy, Desmond. *Theatre.* New York: Oxford University Press, 1955, pp. 94–97.

May, Frederick. "Three Major Symbols in Four Plays by Pirandello," in *Modern Drama.* VI (February, 1964), pp. 378–396.

Newberry, Wilma. "Ramon Gomez de la Serna," in *The Pirandellian Mode in Spanish Literature from Cervantes to Sastre.* Albany: State University of New York Press, 1973, pp. 59–72.

Ongley, L. "Pirandello Confesses—Why and How He Wrote *Six Characters in Search of an Author,"* in *Virginia Quarterly Review.* I (April, 1925), pp. 36–52.

Palmer, J. "Plays of Luigi Pirandello," in *Nineteenth Century.* XCVII (June, 1925), pp. 897–909.

Pirandello, Luigi. *"Six Characters in Search of an Author,"* in *Playwrights on Playwriting.* Edited by Toby Cole. Indianapolis, Ind.: Bobbs Merrill, 1963, pp. 205–217.

Shipp, H. *"Six Characters in Search of an Author,"* in *English Review.* XLVII (July, 1928), pp. 113–114.

Sogluizzo, A. Richard. "The Uses of the Mask in *The Great God Brown* and *Six Characters in Search of an Author,"* in *Educational Theatre Journal.* XVIII (October, 1966), pp. 224–229.

Sypher, Wylie.   "Cubist Drama," in *Rococo to Cubism in Art and Literature.* New York: Random House, 1962, pp. 289–294.

Wyatt, E.   *"Six Characters in Search of an Author,"* in *Catholic World.* CXVI (January, 1923), pp. 505–507.

SYLVIA PLATH
(1932–1963)

Ariel

Aird, Eileen. *Sylvia Plath*. Edinburgh: Oliver and Boyd, 1973, pp. 70–87.

Alvarez, A. "Sylvia Plath," in *The Review*. IX (October, 1963), pp. 20–26. Reprinted in *The Art of Sylvia Plath*. Edited by Charles Newman. London: Faber and Faber, 1970, pp. 56–68.

Bierman, Larry. "The Vivid Tulips Eat My Oxygen: An Essay on Sylvia Plath's *Ariel*," in *Windless Orchard*. IV (February, 1971), pp. 44–46.

Boyers, Robert. "Sylvia Plath: The Trepanned Veteran," in *Excursions: Selected Literary Essays*. Port Washington, N.Y.: Kennikat, 1977, pp. 156–167.

Butscher, Edward. *Sylvia Plath: Method and Madness*. New York: Seabury Press, 1976, pp. 341–347.

Cooley, Peter. "Autism, Autoeroticism, Auto-da-fé: The Tragic Poetry of Sylvia Plath," in *Hollins Critic*. X (February, 1973), pp. 1–15.

Davis, Robin R. "The Honey Machine: Imagery Patterns in *Ariel*," in *New Laurel Review*. I (1972), pp. 23–31.

Davis, William V. "Sylvia Plath's *Ariel*," in *Modern Poetry Studies*. III (1972), pp. 176–184.

Drake, Barbara. "Perfection Is Terrible: It Cannot Have Children," in *Northwest Review*. IX (Summer, 1967), pp. 101–103.

Howard, Richard. *Alone with America*. New York: Atheneum, 1969, pp. 413–422.

Howe, Irving. "The Plath Celebration: A Partial Dissent," in *The Critical Point on Literature and Culture*. New York: Dell, 1975, pp. 158–169. Reprinted in *Sylvia Plath: The Woman and the Work*. Edited by Edward Butscher. New York: Dodd, Mead, 1977, pp. 225–235.

Howes, Barbara. "A Note on *Ariel*," in *Massachusetts Review*. VIII (Winter, 1967), pp. 225–226.

Hoyle, James F. "Sylvia Plath: A Poetry of Suicidal Mania," in *Literature and Psychology*. XVIII (1968), pp. 187–203.

Jones, A.R. "Necessity and Freedom: The Poetry of Robert Lowell, Sylvia Plath, and Anne Sexton," in *Critical Quarterly*. VII (Spring, 1965), pp. 11–30.

Kroll, Judith. *Chapters in a Mythology: The Poetry of Sylvia Plath*. New York: Harper & Row, 1976, pp. 129–148.

Lucie-Smith, Edward. "Sea-Imagery in the Work of Sylvia Plath," in *The Art of Sylvia Plath*. Edited by Charles Newman. London: Faber and Faber, 1970, pp. 91–99.

Nims, John Frederick. "The Poetry of Sylvia Plath: A Technical Analysis," in *The Art of Sylvia Plath.* Edited by Charles Newman. London: Faber and Faber, 1970, pp. 136–152.

Oberg, Arthur K. "Sylvia Plath and the New Decadence," in *Chicago Review.* XX (1968), pp. 66–73. Reprinted in *Sylvia Plath: The Woman and the Work.* Edited by Edward Butscher. New York: Dodd, Mead, 1977, pp. 177–185.

Ostriker, Alicia. " 'Fact' as Style: The Americanization of Sylvia," in *Language and Style.* I (Summer, 1968), pp. 201–212.

Phillips, Robert. "The Dark Funnel: A Reading of Sylvia Plath," in *Modern Poetry Studies.* III (1972), pp. 49–74. Reprinted in *Sylvia Plath: The Woman and the Work.* Edited by Edward Butscher. New York: Dodd, Mead, 1977, pp. 186–205.

Ries, Lawrence R. "Sylvia Plath: The Internalized Response," in his *Wolf Masks: Violence in Contemporary Poetry.* Port Washington, N.Y.: Kennikat, 1977, pp. 33–58.

Rosenstein, Harriet. "Reconsidering Sylvia Plath," in *Ms.* I (September, 1972), pp. 44–57, 96–98.

Scheerer, Constance. "The Deathly Paradise of Sylvia Plath," in *Antioch Review.* XXXIV (1976), pp. 469–480. Reprinted in *Sylvia Plath: The Woman and the Work.* Edited by Edward Butscher. New York: Dodd, Mead, 1977, pp. 166–176.

Smith, Pamela. "Architectonics: Sylvia Plath's *Colossus*," in *Ariel.* IV (1973), pp. 4–21. Reprinted in *Sylvia Plath: The Woman and the Work.* Edited by Edward Butscher. New York: Dodd, Mead, 1977, pp. 111–124.

Spender, Stephen. "Warnings from the Grave," in *The Art of Sylvia Plath.* Edited by Charles Newman. London: Faber and Faber, 1970, pp. 199–203.

The Bell Jar

Aird, Eileen. *Sylvia Plath.* Edinburgh: Oliver and Boyd, 1973, pp. 88–100.

Allen, Mary. "Sylvia Plath's Defiance: *The Bell Jar*," in her *The Necessary Blankness: Women in Major American Fiction of the Sixties.* Urbana: University of Illinois Press, 1976, pp. 160–178.

Butscher, Edward. *Sylvia Plath: Method and Madness.* New York: Seabury Press, 1976, pp. 306–313.

Ellmann, M. "*The Bell Jar*—An American Girlhood," in *The Art of Sylvia Plath.* Edited by Charles Newman. London: Faber and Faber, 1970, pp. 221–226.

Holbrook, David. "The Baby in the Bell Jar: The Symbolism of the Novel," in his *Sylvia Plath: Poetry and Existence.* London: Athlone Press, 1976, pp. 65–108.

Lameyer, Gordon. "The Double in Sylvia Plath's *The Bell Jar*," in *Sylvia Plath: The Woman and the Work*. Edited by Edward Butscher. New York: Dodd, Mead, 1977, pp. 143–165.

Lucie-Smith, Edward. "Sea-Imagery in the Work of Sylvia Plath," in *The Art of Sylvia Plath*. Edited by Charles Newman. London: Faber and Faber, 1970, pp. 91–99.

Maloff, Saul. "Waiting for the Voice to Crack," in *New Republic*. CLIV (May 8, 1971), pp. 33–35.

Malpezzi, Frances M. "Searching for Stephanie Daedalus," in *Research Studies*. XLVI (June, 1978), pp. 106–111.

Moss, Howard. "Dying: An Introduction," in *New Yorker*. XLVII (July 10, 1971), pp. 73–75.

Perloff, Marjorie G. " 'A Ritual for Being Born Twice': Sylvia Plath's *The Bell Jar*," in *Contemporary Literature*. XIII (1972), pp. 507–522.

Phillips, Robert. "The Dark Funnel: A Reading of Sylvia Plath," in *Modern Poetry Studies*. III (1972), pp. 49–74. Reprinted in *Sylvia Plath: The Woman and the Work*. Edited by Edward Butscher. New York: Dodd, Mead, 1977, pp. 186–205.

Rosenstein, Harriet. "Reconsidering Sylvia Plath," in *Ms*. I (September, 1972), pp. 44–57, 96–98.

Rosenthal, Lucy. "*The Bell Jar*," in *Saturday Review*. LIV (April 24, 1971), p. 42.

Schwartz, Murray M. and Christopher Bollas. "The Absence of the Center: Sylvia Plath and Suicide," in *Criticism*. XVIII (Spring, 1976), pp. 147–172.

Smith, Stan. "Attitudes Counterfeiting Life: The Irony of Artifice in Sylvia Plath's *Bell Jar*," in *Critical Quarterly*. XVII (1975), pp. 247–260.

Spacks, Patricia Meyer. *The Female Imagination*. New York: Knopf, 1975, pp. 144–150.

Tanner, Tony. *City of Words: American Fiction, 1950–1970*. New York: Harper & Row, 1971, pp. 262–264.

The Colossus and Other Poems

Aird, Eileen. *Sylvia Plath*. Edinburgh: Oliver and Boyd, 1973, pp. 15–38.

Alvarez, A. "Sylvia Plath," in *The Review*. IX (October, 1963), pp. 20–26. Reprinted in *The Art of Sylvia Plath*. Edited by Charles Newman. London: Faber and Faber, 1970, pp. 56–68.

Butscher, Edward. *Sylvia Plath: Method and Madness*. New York: Seabury Press, 1976, pp. 235–252.

Cooley, Peter. "Autism, Autoeroticism, Auto-da-fé: The Tragic Poetry of Sylvia Plath," in *Hollins Critic*. X (February, 1973), pp. 1–15.

Dearmer, Geoffrey. "Sow's Ears and Silk Purses," in *Poetry Review*. LII (July–September, 1961), p. 167.

Dickey, William. "Responsibilities," in *Kenyon Review*. XXIV (Autumn, 1962), pp. 760–764.

Hayman, Ronald. "Personal Poetry," in *Encounter*. XXIX (December, 1967), pp. 86–87.

Howard, Richard. *Alone with America*. New York: Atheneum, 1969, pp. 413–422.

Jerome, Judson. "A Poetry Chronicle—Part I," in *Antioch Review*. XXIII (Spring, 1963), pp. 110–111.

Kissick, Gary. "Plath: A Terrible Perfection," in *Nation*. CCVII (September 16, 1968), pp. 245–247.

Lucie-Smith, Edward. "Sea-Imagery in the Work of Sylvia Plath," in *The Art of Sylvia Plath*. Edited by Charles Newman. London: Faber and Faber, 1970, pp. 91–99.

Megna, Jerome. "Plath's 'Manor Garden,' " in the *Explicator*. XXX (March, 1972), item 58.

Melander, Ingrid. " 'The Disquieting Muses': A Note on a Poem by Sylvia Plath," in *Research Studies*. XXXIX (March, 1971), pp. 53–54.

Myers, E. Lucal. "The Tranquilized Fifties," in *Sewanee Review*. LXX (Spring, 1962), pp. 216–217.

Nims, John Frederick. "The Poetry of Sylvia Plath: A Technical Analysis," in *The Art of Sylvia Plath*. Edited by Charles Newman. London: Faber and Faber, 1970, pp. 136–152.

Oberg, Arthur K. "Sylvia Plath and the New Decadence," in *Chicago Review*. XX (1968), pp. 66–73. Reprinted in *Sylvia Plath: The Woman and the Work*. Edited by Edward Butscher. New York: Dodd, Mead, 1977, pp. 177–185.

Ostriker, Alicia. " 'Fact' as Style: The Americanization of Sylvia," in *Language and Style*. I (Summer, 1968), pp. 201–212.

Phillips, Robert. "The Dark Funnel: A Reading of Sylvia Plath," in *Modern Poetry Studies*. III (1972), pp. 49–74. Reprinted in *Sylvia Plath: The Woman and the Work*. Edited by Edward Butscher. New York: Dodd, Mead, 1977, pp. 186–205.

Scheerer, Constance. "The Deathly Paradise of Sylvia Plath," in *Antioch Review*. XXXIV (1976), pp. 469–480. Reprinted in *Sylvia Plath: The Woman and the Work*. Edited by Edward Butscher. New York: Dodd, Mead, 1977, pp. 166–176.

Schwartz, Murray M. and Christopher Bollas. "The Absence of the Center: Sylvia Plath and Suicide," in *Criticism*. XVIII (Spring, 1976), pp. 147–172.

Simon, John.   "More Brass than Enduring," in *Hudson Review*. XV (Autumn, 1962), p. 464.

Steiner, George.   "Dying Is an Art," in *Reporter*. XXXIII (October 7, 1965), pp. 51–54. Reprinted in *The Art of Sylvia Plath*. Edited by Charles Newman. London: Faber and Faber, 1970, pp. 211–218.

Whittemore, Reed.   "*The Colossus and Other Poems*," in *Carleton Miscellany*. III (Fall, 1962), p. 89.

Crossing the Water

Aird, Eileen.   *Sylvia Plath*. Edinburgh: Oliver and Boyd, 1973, pp. 39–50.

Boyers, Robert.   "On Sylvia Plath," in *Salmagundi*. XXI (1973), pp. 96–104.

Butscher, Edward.   *Sylvia Plath: Method and Madness*. New York: Seabury Press, 1976, pp. 279–284.

Cooley, Peter.   "Autism, Autoeroticism, Auto-da-fé: The Tragic Poetry of Sylvia Plath," in *Hollins Critic*. X (February, 1973), pp. 1–15.

Dunn, Douglas.   "Damaged Instruments," in *Encounter*. XXXVII (August, 1971), pp. 68–70.

Dyroff, Jan M.   "Sylvia Plath: Perceptions in *Crossing the Water*," in *Art and Literature Review*. I (1972), pp. 49–50.

Howe, Irving.   "The Plath Celebration: A Partial Dissent," in *The Critical Point on Literature and Culture*. New York: Dell, 1975, pp. 158–169. Reprinted in *Sylvia Plath: The Woman and the Work*. Edited by Edward Butscher. New York: Dodd, Mead, 1977, pp. 225–235.

Hughes, Ted.   "Sylvia Plath's *Crossing the Water*: Some Reflections," in *Critical Quarterly*. XIII (Summer, 1971), pp. 165–171.

Kramer, Victor.   "Life-and-Death Dialectics," in *Modern Poetry Studies*. III (1972), pp. 40–42.

Mollinger, Robert N.   "Sylvia Plath's 'Private Ground,' " in *Notes on Contemporary Literature*. V (1975), pp. 14–15.

Perloff, Marjorie G.   "On the Road to *Ariel*: The 'Transitional' Poetry of Sylvia Plath," in *Iowa Review*. IV (1973), pp. 94–110. Reprinted in *Sylvia Plath: The Woman and the Work*. Edited by Edward Butscher. New York: Dodd, Mead, 1977, pp. 125–142.

Phillips, Robert.   "The Dark Funnel: A Reading of Sylvia Plath," in *Modern Poetry Studies*. III (1972), pp. 49–74. Reprinted in *Sylvia Plath: The Woman and the Work*. Edited by Edward Butscher. New York: Dodd, Mead, 1977, pp. 186–205.

"Daddy"

Aird, Eileen.   *Sylvia Plath*. Edinburgh: Oliver and Boyd, 1973, pp. 78–82.

Blaydes, Sophie B. "Metaphors of Life and Death in the Poetry of Denise Levertov and Sylvia Plath," in *Dalhousie Review.* LVII (Autumn, 1977), pp. 494–506.

Boyers, Robert. "Sylvia Plath: The Trepanned Veteran," in *Centennial Review.* XIII (Spring, 1969), pp. 138–153.

Butscher, Edward. *Sylvia Plath: Method and Madness.* New York: Seabury Press, 1976, pp. 335–339.

Howe, Irving. "The Plath Celebration: A Partial Dissent," in his *The Critical Point on Literature and Culture.* New York: Dell, 1975, pp. 165–166. Reprinted in *Sylvia Plath: The Woman and the Work.* Edited by Edward Butscher. New York: Dodd, Mead, 1977, pp. 231–233.

Jones, A.R., and C.B. Cox. "On 'Daddy,' " in *The Art of Sylvia Plath.* Edited by Charles Newman. London: Faber and Faber, 1970, pp. 230–236.

Kroll, Judith. *Chapters in a Mythology: The Poetry of Sylvia Plath.* New York: Harper & Row, 1976, pp. 115–117, 122–126.

Mollinger, Robert N. "A Symbolic Complex: Images of Death and 'Daddy' in the Poetry of Sylvia Plath," in *Descant.* XIX (1975), pp. 44–52.

Steiner, George. "Dying Is an Art," in *Reporter.* XXXIII (October 7, 1965), pp. 51–54. Reprinted in *The Art of Sylvia Plath.* Edited by Charles Newman. London: Faber and Faber, 1970, pp. 211–218.

The Poetry of Plath

Aird, Eileen. *Sylvia Plath.* Edinburgh: Oliver and Boyd, 1973, pp. 101–111.

Bagg, Robert. "The Rise of Lady Lazarus," in *Mosaic.* II (1969), pp. 9–36.

Blodgett, E.D. "Sylvia Plath: Another View," in *Modern Poetry Studies.* II (1971), pp. 97–106.

Boyers, Robert. "Sylvia Plath: The Trepanned Veteran," in *Centennial Review.* XIII (Spring, 1969), pp. 138–153.

Claire, William F. "The Rare Random Descent: The Poetry and Pathos of Sylvia Plath," in *Antioch Review.* XXVI (Winter, 1966–1967), pp. 552–560.

Cluysenaar, Anne. "Post-Culture: Pre-Culture?," in *British Poetry Since 1960.* Edited by Michael Schmidt and Grevel Lindop. Cheadle, England: Carcanet Press, 1972, pp. 213–232.

Dyson, A.E. "On Sylvia Plath," in *Tri-Quarterly.* VII (Fall, 1966), pp. 75–80. Reprinted in *The Art of Sylvia Plath.* Edited by Charles Newman. London: Faber and Faber, 1970, pp. 204–210.

Gordon, Jan B. " 'Who Is Sylvia?' The Art of Sylvia Plath," in *Modern Poetry Studies.* I (1970), pp. 6–34.

Hardy, Barbara. "The Poetry of Sylvia Plath," in *The Survival of Poetry.* Edited by Martin Dodsworth. London: Faber and Faber, 1970, pp. 164–187.

Reprinted in her *The Advantage of Lyric: Essays on Feeling in Poetry.* Bloomington: Indiana University Press, 1977, pp. 121–140.

Kroll, Judith. *Chapters in a Mythology: The Poetry of Sylvia Plath.* New York: Harper & Row, 1976, pp. 1–6.

Lavers, Annette. "The World as Icon: On Sylvia Plath's Themes," in *The Art of Sylvia Plath.* Edited by Charles Newman. London: Faber and Faber, 1970, pp. 100–135.

Meissner, William. "The Rise of the Angel: Life Through Death in the Poetry of Sylvia Plath," in *Massachusetts Studies in English.* III (1971), pp. 34–39.

Melander, Ingrid. *The Poetry of Sylvia Plath: A Study of Themes.* Stockholm: Almquist and Wiksell, 1972.

Mollinger, Robert N. "A Symbolic Complex: Images of Death and Daddy in the Poetry of Sylvia Plath," in *Descant.* XIX (1975), pp. 44–52.

Newlin, Margaret. "The Suicide Bandwagon," in *Critical Quarterly.* XIV (1972), pp. 367–378.

Newman, Charles. "Candor Is the Only Wile: The Art of Sylvia Plath," in *Tri-Quarterly.* VII (Fall, 1966), pp. 39–64. Reprinted in *The Art of Sylvia Plath.* Edited by Charles Newman. London: Faber and Faber, 1970, pp. 21–55.

Oates, Joyce Carol. "The Death Throes of Romanticism: The Poems of Sylvia Plath," in *Southern Review.* IX (1973), pp. 501–522. Reprinted in *New Heaven, New Earth: The Visionary Experience in Literature.* New York: Vanguard, 1974, pp. 111–140. Also reprinted in *Contemporary Poetry in America: Essays and Interviews.* Edited by Robert Boyers. New York: Schocken, 1975, pp. 139–156. Also reprinted in *Sylvia Plath: The Woman and the Work.* Edited by Edward Butscher. New York: Dodd, Mead, 1977, pp. 206–224.

Oberg, Arthur. "The Modern British and American Lyric: What Will Suffice?," in *Language and Literature.* VII (Winter, 1972), pp. 70–88.

Ries, Lawrence R. "Sylvia Plath: The Internalized Response," in his *Wolf Masks: Violence in Contemporary Poetry.* Port Washington, N.Y.: Kennikat, 1977, pp. 33–58.

Rosenthal, M.L. *The New Poets: American and British Poetry Since World War II.* New York: Oxford University Press, 1967, pp. 79–89. Reprinted in *The Art of Sylvia Plath.* Edited by Charles Newman. London: Faber and Faber, 1970, pp. 69–76.

Schwartz, Murray M. and Christopher Bollas. "The Absence at the Center: Sylvia Plath and Suicide," in *Criticism.* XVIII (1976), pp. 147–172.

Sequeira, Isaac. "From Confession to Suicide: The Poetry of Sylvia Plath," in *Studies in American Literature: Essays in Honour of William Mulder.* Edited by Jagdish Chander and Narindar S. Pradhan. New York: Oxford University Press, 1976, pp. 232–242.

Smith, Pamela A.   "The Unitive Urge in the Poetry of Sylvia Plath," in *New England Quarterly*. XLV (1972), pp. 323–339.

Sumner, Nan McGowan.   "Sylvia Plath," in *Research Studies*. XXXVIII (June, 1970), pp. 112–121.

Uroff, M.D.   "Sylvia Plath's Women," in *Contemporary Poetry*. VII (1974), pp. 45–56.

Winter Trees

Aird, Eileen.   *Sylvia Plath*. Edinburgh: Oliver and Boyd, 1973, pp. 51–69.

Baumgaertner, Jill.   "Four Poets: Blood Type New," in *Cresset*. XXXVI (April, 1972), pp. 16–17.

Butscher, Edward.   *Sylvia Plath: Method and Madness*. New York: Seabury Press, 1976, pp. 326–334.

Dunn, Douglas.   "King Offa Alive and Dead," in *Encounter*. XXXVIII (January, 1972), p. 67.

Gordon, Jan B.   "Saint Sylvia," in *Modern Poetry Studies*. III (1972), pp. 282–286.

Perloff, Marjorie G.   "On the Road to *Ariel*: The 'Transitional' Poetry of Sylvia Plath," in *Iowa Review*. IV (1973), pp. 94–110. Reprinted in *Sylvia Plath: The Woman and the Work*. Edited by Edward Butscher. New York: Dodd, Mead, 1977, pp. 125–142.

Phillips, Robert.   "The Dark Funnel: A Reading of Sylvia Plath," in *Modern Poetry Studies*. III (1972), pp. 49–74. Reprinted in *Sylvia Plath: The Woman and the Work*. Edited by Edward Butscher. New York: Dodd, Mead, 1977, pp. 186–205.

Smith, Raymond.   "Late Harvest," in *Modern Poetry Studies*. III (1972), pp. 91–93.

PLATO
(427 B.C.–347 B.C.)

Republic

Annas, J. "Plato's *Republic* and Feminism," in *Philosophy*. LI (July, 1976), pp. 307–321.

Atkins, J.W.H. *Literary Criticism in Antiquity*, Volume I. Toronto: Macmillan, 1934, pp. 33–70.

Averroes. *Commentary on Plato's* Republic. Cambridge: Cambridge University Press, 1966.

Boyd, W. *An Introduction to the* Republic *of Plato*. London: Allen and Unwin, 1969.

Brumbaugh, R.S. "New Interpretation of Plato's *Republic*," in *Journal of Philosophy*. LXIV (October 26, 1967), pp. 661–670.

Cassirer, E. *Myth of the State*. New Haven, Conn.: Yale University Press, 1946, pp. 61–77.

Cross, R.C. and A.D. Woozley. *Plato's* Republic*: A Philosophical Commentary*. New York: St. Martin's, 1964.

Fireman, P. *Justice in Plato's* Republic. New York: Philosophical Library, 1957.

Hoare, F.R. *Eight Decisive Books of Antiquity*. New York: Sheed, 1952, pp. 172–213.

Jaeger, W.W. *Paideia: The Ideals of Greek Culture*, Volume II. London: Oxford University Press, 1943, pp. 198–370.

Joseph, H.W.B. *Essays in Ancient and Modern Philosophy*. Oxford: Clarendon, 1935, pp. 1–155.

Maguire, J.P. "The Individual and the Class in Plato's *Republic*," in *Classical Journal*. LX (January, 1965), pp. 145–150.

Marley, C. "Plato's *Republic*, Totalitarian or Democratic?," in *Classical Journal*. XXXVI (April, 1941), pp. 413–420.

Murphy, N.R. *Interpretations of Plato's* Republic. Oxford: Clarendon, 1951.

Notopolus, J.A. "Symbolism of the Sun and Light in the *Republic* of Plato," in *Classical Philology*. XXXIX (July, 1944), pp. 163–172, XXXIX (October, 1944), pp. 223–240.

Schiller, F.C.S. *Our Human Truths*. New York: Columbia University Press, 1939, pp. 155–167.

Sesonske, A. *Plato's* Republic*: Interpretations and Criticism*. Belmont, Calif.: Wadsworth, 1966.

Tarrant, D. "Imagery in Plato's *Republic*," in *Classical Quarterly*. XL (January, 1946), pp. 27–34.

Symposium

Cairns, H. *Invitation to Learning*. New York: Random House, 1941, pp. 35–50.

Cameron, A. "Petronius and Plato," in *Classical Quarterly*. XIX (November, 1969), pp. 367–370.

Clay, D. "The Tragic and Comic Poet of the *Symposium*," in *Arion*. II (1975), pp. 238–261.

Cornford, F.M. *Unwritten Philosophy and Other Essays*. London: Cambridge University Press, 1950, pp. 68–80.

Jaeger, W.W. *Paideia: The Ideals of Greek Culture*, Volume II. London: Oxford University Press, 1943, pp. 174–197.

Neumann, H. "Diotima's Concept of Love," in *American Journal of Philology*. LXXXVI (January, 1965), pp. 33–59.

Rosen, S. *Plato's* Symposium. New Haven, Conn.: Yale University Press, 1968.

TITUS MACCIUS PLAUTUS
(c.255 B.C.–184 B.C.)

Amphitryon

Arnott, Geoffrey. *Menander, Plautus, Terence.* Oxford: Clarendon Press, 1975.

Barnes, H.E. "The Case of Sosia Versus Sosia," in *Classical Journal.* LIII (October, 1957), pp. 19–24.

Collins, William Lucas. *Plautus and Terence.* Philadelphia: Lippincott, 1882.

Costa, C.D.N. "The Amphitryo Theme," in *Roman Drama.* Edited by T.A. Dorey and D.R. Dudley. New York: Basic Books, 1965, pp. 85–122.

Eckard, Laurence. *Prefaces to Terence's Comedies and Plautus' Comedies (1964).* Los Angeles: University of California Press, 1968.

Fantham, E. "Adaption and Survival: A Genre Study of Roman Comedy in Relation to Its Greek Sources," in *Versions of Medieval Comedy.* Edited by Paul G. Ruggiers. Norman: University of Oklahoma Press, 1977, pp. 19–49.

————. "Towards a Dramatic Reconstruction of the Fourth Act of Plautus' *Amphitruo*," in *Philologus.* CXVII (1973), pp. 197–214.

Forehand, W.E. "Adaptions and Comic Intent: Plautus' *Amphitruo* and Molière's *Amphitryon*," in *Comparative Literature Studies.* XI (September, 1974), pp. 204–217.

————. "Irony in Plautus' *Amphitryo*," in *American Journal of Philology.* XCII (1971), pp. 633–651.

Foster, Frederick Montague. *The Divisions of the Plays of Plautus and Terence.* Iowa City: University of Iowa Press, 1913.

Galinsky, G.K. "Scipionic Themes in Plautus' *Amphitruo*," in *Transactions of the American Philological Association.* XCVII (1966), pp. 203–236.

Grismer, Raymond Leonard. *The Influence of Plautus in Spain Before Lope de Vega.* New York: Hispanic Institute in the United States, 1944.

Hough, J.N. "Jupiter, Amphitruo and the Cuckoo," in *Classical Philology.* LXV (1970), pp. 95–96.

Lelievre, F.J. "Sosia and Roman Epic," in *Phoenix.* XII (1958), pp. 117–124.

Romano, A.C. "The Amphitryon Theme Again," in *Latomus.* XXXIII (1974), pp. 874–890.

Sandbach, F.H. "Plautus," in *The Comic Theatre of Greece and Rome.* New York: Norton, 1977, pp. 118–134.

Segal, Erich W. "The Business of Roman Comedy," in *Perspectives of Roman Poetry.* Edited by George Luck. Austin: University of Texas Press, 1974, pp. 93–103.

_____. *Roman Laughter; The Comedy of Plautus*. Cambridge, Mass.: Harvard University Press, 1968.

Stewart, Z. "*The Amphitruo* of Plautus and Euripides' *Bacchae*," in *Transactions of the American Philological Association*. LXXXIX (1958), pp. 348–373.

_____. "The God Nocturnus in Plautus' *Amphitruo*," in *Journal of Roman Studies*. L (1960), pp. 37–43.

The Menaechmi

Arnott, Geoffrey. *Menander, Plautus, Terence*. Oxford: Clarendon Press, 1975.

Collins, William Lucas. *Plautus and Terence*. Philadelphia: Lippincott, 1882.

Eckhard, Laurence. *Prefaces to Terence's Comedies and Plautus' Comedies (1964)*. Los Angeles: University of California Press, 1968.

Fantham, E. "Act IV of *The Menaechmi*: Plautus and His Original," in *Classical Philology*. LXIII (July, 1968), pp. 175–183.

_____. "Adaption and Survival: A Genre Study of Roman Comedy in Relation to Its Greek Sources," in *Versions of Medieval Comedy*. Edited by Paul G. Ruggiers. Norman: University of Oklahoma Press, 1977, pp. 19–49.

Foster, Frederick Montague. *The Divisions in the Plays of Plautus and Terence*. Iowa City: University of Iowa Press, 1913.

Grismer, Raymond Leonard. *The Influence of Plautus in Spain Before Lope de Vega*. New York: Hispanic Institute in the United States, 1944.

Leach, E.W. "*Meam Quom Formam Noscito*: Language and Characterization in *The Menaechmi*," in *Areth*. II (Spring, 1969), pp. 30–45.

Levin, Harry. "Two Comedies of Errors," in *Refractions; Essays in Comparative Literature*. New York: Oxford University Press, 1966, pp. 128–150.

Moorhead, P.G. "The Distribution of Roles in Plautus' *Menaechmi*," in *Classical Journal*. XLIX (December, 1953), pp. 123–126.

Sandbach, F.H. "Plautus," in *The Comic Theatre of Greece and Rome*. New York: Norton, 1977, pp. 118–134.

Segal, Erich W. "The Business of Roman Comedy," in *Perspectives of Roman Poetry*. Edited by George Luck. Austin: University of Texas Press, 1974, pp. 93–103.

_____. "*The Menaechmi*: Roman Comedy of Errors," in *Yale Classical Studies*. XXI (1969), pp. 75–93.

_____. *Roman Laughter; The Comedy of Plautus*. Cambridge, Mass.: Harvard University Press, 1968.

Westendorp, Boerma. "Plautus' *Menaechmi*," in *Hermeneus*. XXXVIII (1966), pp. 29–35.

Woodruff, J.   "Mythological Mots in *The Menaechmi*," in *Classical Bulletin.* LI (1974–1975), pp. 6–10.

GAIUS PLINIUS SECUNDUS
(23–79)

Natural History

Burns, M.A.T. "Pliny's Ideal Roman," in *Classical Journal*. LIX (March, 1964), pp. 253–258.

————. "Pliny the Elder, Some Notes," in *The Classical Bulletin*. XXXVIII (1961), pp. 17–20.

Coulson, W.D.E. "The Nature of Pliny's Remarks on Euphranor," in *The Classical Journal*. LXVII (1972), pp. 323–326.

Downs, Robert. *Famous Books: Ancient and Medieval.* New York: Barnes & Noble, 1964, pp. 206–210.

Lieberman, S. "Who Were Pliny's Blue-Eyed Chinese?," in *Classical Philology*. LII (July, 1957), pp. 174–177.

Stannard, J. "Pliny and Roman Botany," in *Isis*. LVI (Winter, 1965), pp. 420–425.

Torrey, C.C. "Magic of Lotapes (Proper Name, Appearing in the Elder Pliny's *Natural History*), in *Journal of Biblical Literature*. LXVIII (December, 1949), pp. 325–327.

Traub, H.W. "Pliny's Treatment of History in Epistolary Form," in *Transactions of the American Philological Association*. LXXXVI (1955), pp. 213–232.

Wade-Gery, H.T. "Islands of Peisistratos," in *American Journal of Philology*. LIX (October, 1938), pp. 470–475.

Wethered, H.N. *The Mind of the Ancient World: A Consideration of Pliny's Natural History.* New York: Longmans, Green, 1937.

PLUTARCH
(c.45–c.125)

Parallel Lives

Barrow, Reginald Hayes. *Plutarch and His Times.* Bloomington: Indiana University Press, 1967.

Brenk, F.E. "The Dramas of Plutarch's *Lives,*" in *Latomus.* XXXIV (1975), pp. 336–349.

Gianaharis, C.J. *Plutarch.* New York: Twayne, 1970.

Hadas, Moses. "The Religion of Plutarch," in *Review of Religion.* VI (1941–1942), pp. 270–282.

Howard, Martha Walling. *The Influence of Plutarch on the Major European Literatures of the Eighteenth Century.* Chapel Hill: University of North Carolina Press, 1970.

Johnson, V.L. "The Humanism of Plutarch," in *Classical Journal.* LXVI (1970), pp. 26–37.

Jones, Christopher Prestige. *Plutarch and Rome.* Oxford: Clarendon Press, 1971.

Lacy, Phillip de. "Biography and Tragedy in Plutarch," in *American Journal of Philology.* LXXIII (1952), pp. 159–171.

Moellering, H.A. *Plutarch on Superstition.* North Quincey, Mass.: Christopher, 1963.

Polman, G.H. "Chronology, Biography and Ahmė in Plutarch," in *Classical Philology.* LXIX (1974), pp. 169–177.

Rexroth, Kenneth. "Plutarch: *Parrallel Lives,*" in *The Classics Revisited.* Chicago: Quadrangle, 1968, pp. 108–111.

Russell, Donald Andrew. "On Reading Plutarch's *Lives,*" in *Greece and Rome.* XIII (October, 1963), pp. 139–154.

————. *Plutarch.* London: Duckworth, 1973.

Shackford, Martha Hale. *Plutarch in Renaissance England.* Folcroft, Pa.: Folcroft Library Editions, 1974.

Smith, R.E. "Plutarch's Biographical Sources in the Roman *Lives,*" in *Classical Quarterly.* XXXIV (1940), pp. 1–10.

Stadter, Ph. A. *Plutarch's Historical Methods: An Analysis of the Mulierum Virtues.* Cambridge, Mass.: Harvard University Press, 1965.

Tracy, H.L. "Notes on Plutarch's Biographical Method," in *Classical Journal.* XXXVII (1942), pp. 213–221.

Williams, M.V. "Plutarch as a Biographer," in *London Quarterly Review.* CLXV (April, 1949), pp. 207–212.

EDGAR ALLAN POE
(1809–1849)

"The Cask of Amontillado"

Altenbernd, Lynn and Leslie L. Lewis. *Introduction to Literature: Stories.* New York: Macmillan, 1963, pp. 6–9. Reprinted in their *A Handbook for the Study of Fiction.* New York: Macmillan, 1966, pp. 9–14.

Bales, Kent. "Poetic Justice in 'The Cask of Amontillado,' " in *Poe Studies.* V (1972), p. 51.

Bonaparte, Marie. *The Life and Works of Edgar Allan Poe: A Psychoanalytic Interpretation.* London: Imago, 1949, pp. 505–510.

Broussard, Louis. *The Measure of Poe.* Norman: University of Oklahoma Press, 1969, pp. 97–98.

Burns, Shannon. " 'The Cask of Amontillado': Montresor's Revenge," in *Poe Studies.* VII (1974), p. 25.

Davidson, Edward H. *Poe: A Critical Study.* Cambridge, Mass.: Harvard University Press, 1957, pp. 201–203. Reprinted in *Interpretations of American Literature.* Edited by Charles Feidelson and Paul Brodtkorb. New York: Oxford University Press, 1959, pp. 78–79.

————, **Editor.** *Selected Writings of Edgar Allan Poe.* Boston: Houghton Mifflin, 1956, pp. xix–xxi.

Foote, Dorothy N. "Poe's 'The Cask of Amontillado,' " in *Explicator.* XX (1961), item 27.

Fossum, Richard H. "Poe's 'The Cask of Amontillado,' " in *Explicator.* XVII (1958), item 16.

Gargano, James W. " 'The Cask of Amontillado': A Masquerade of Motive and Identity," in *Studies in Short Fiction.* IV (1967), 119–126.

————. "The Question of Poe's Narrators," in *College English.* XXV (1963), p. 180. Reprinted in *The Recognition of Edgar Allan Poe.* Edited by Eric W. Carlson. Ann Arbor: University of Michigan Press, 1966, pp. 313–314. Also reprinted in *Poe: A Collection of Critical Essays.* Edited by Robert Regan. Englewood Cliffs, N.J.: Prentice-Hall, 1967, pp. 168–169.

Harris, Kathryn M. "Ironic Revenge in Poe's 'The Cask of Amontillado,' " in *Studies in Short Fiction.* VI (1969), pp. 333–335.

Henninger, F.J. "The Bouquet of Poe's Amontillado," in *South Atlantic Bulletin.* XXXV (March, 1970), pp. 35–40.

Kempton, Kenneth. *The Short Story.* Cambridge, Mass.: Harvard University Press, 1947, pp. 86–91.

Levin, Harry. *The Power of Blackness.* New York: Knopf, 1958, pp. 146–147.

Levine, Stuart. *Edgar Poe: Seer and Craftsman.* Deland, Fla.: Everett/ Edwards, 1972, pp. 80–92.

Mabbott, Thomas O. "Poe's 'The Cask of Amontillado,' " in *Explicator.* XXV (1966), item 30.

Martin, Terence. "The Imagination at Play: Edgar Allan Poe," in *Kenyon Review.* XXVIII (1966), pp. 196–198.

Nevi, Charles N. "Irony and 'The Cask of Amontillado,' " in *English Journal.* LVI (1967), pp. 461–463.

Rea, J. "Poe's 'The Cask of Amontillado,' " in *Studies in Short Fiction.* IV (1966), pp. 57–69.

Rocks, James E. "Conflict and Motive in 'The Cask of Amontillado,' " in *Poe Studies.* V (1972), pp. 50–51.

Schick, Joseph S. "The Origin of 'The Cask of Amontillado,' " in *American Literature.* VI (1934), pp. 18–21.

Solomont, Susan and Ritchie Darling. *Four Stories by Poe.* Norwich, Vt.: Green Knight Press, 1965, pp. 10–13.

Steele, Charles W. "Poe's 'The Cask of Amontillado,' " in *Explicator.* XVII (1960), item 43.

Stepp, Walter. "The Ironic Double in Poe's 'The Cask of Amontillado,' " in *Studies in Short Fiction.* XIII (1976), pp. 447–453.

"The Fall of the House of Usher"

Abel, Darrel. "A Key to the House of Usher," in *University of Toronto Quarterly.* XVIII (January, 1949), pp. 176–185.

Bailey, J.O. "What Happens in 'The Fall of the House of Usher?' " in *American Literature.* XXXV (January, 1964), pp. 445–466.

Beebe, Maurice. "The Universe of Roderick Usher," in *Person.* XXXVII (Spring, 1956), pp. 147–160.

Brooks, Cleanth and Robert Penn Warren. *Understanding Fiction.* New York: Appleton-Century Croft, 1943, pp. 184–205.

Cohen, Hennig. "Roderick Usher's Tragic Struggle," in *Nineteenth-Century Fiction.* XIV (December, 1959), pp. 270–272.

Garmon, Gerald. "Roderick Usher: Portrait of the Madman as an Artist," in *Poe Studies.* V (June, 1972), pp. 11–14.

Goodwin, K.L. "Roderick Usher's Overrated Knowledge," in *Nineteenth-Century Fiction.* XVI (1961), pp. 173–175.

Hill, John. "Dual Hallucination in 'The Fall of the House of Usher,' " in *Southwest Review.* XLVIII (Autumn, 1963), pp. 396–402.

Hoffman, Michael J. "The House of Usher and Negative Romanticism," in *Studies in Romanticism.* IV (1965), pp. 158–168.

Hulfey, James. "A Tour of the House of Usher," in *Emerson Society Quarterly.* XXXI (2nd Quarter, 1963), pp. 18–20.

Kendall, Lyle. "The Vampire Motif in 'The Fall of the House of Usher,' " in *College English.* XXIV (March, 1963), pp. 450–453.

Marsh, John L. "The Psycho-Sexual Reading of 'The Fall of the House of Usher,' " in *Poe Studies.* V (June, 1972), pp. 8–9.

Martindale, Colin. "Archetype and Reality in 'The Fall of the House of Usher,' " in *Poe Studies.* V (June, 1972), pp. 9–11.

Olson, Bruce. "Poe's Strategy in 'The Fall of the House of Usher,' " in *Modern Language Notes.* LXXV (November, 1960), pp. 556–559.

Phillips, William. "Poe's 'The Fall of the House of Usher,' " in *Explicator.* IX (February, 1951), item 29.

Pittman, Diana. " 'The Fall of the House of Usher,' " in *Southern Literary Messenger.* III (November, 1941), pp. 502–509.

Porte, Joel. *The Romance in America: Studies in Cooper, Poe, Hawthorne, Melville and James.* Middletown, Conn.: Wesleyan University Press, 1969, pp. 53–94.

Robinson, E. Arthur. "Order and Sentience in 'The Fall of the House of Usher,' " in *PMLA.* LXXVI (March, 1961), pp. 68–81.

Samuels, Charles T. "Usher's Fall: Poe's Rise," in *Georgia Review.* XVIII (Summer, 1964), pp. 208–216.

Smith, Herbert F. "Usher's Madness and Poe's Organicism; a Source," in *American Literature.* XXXIX (November, 1968), pp. 379–389.

Spaulding, K.A. " 'The Fall of the House of Usher,' " in *Explicator.* X (June, 1952), item 52.

Spitzer, Leo. "A Reinterpretation of 'The Fall of the House of Usher,' " in *Comparative Literature.* IV (Autumn, 1952), pp. 351–363.

Stein, William Bysshe. "Twin Motif in 'The Fall of the House of Usher,' " in *Modern Language Notes.* LXXV (February, 1960), pp. 109–111.

Thompson, G.R. "The Face in the Pool: Reflections on the Doppelganger Motif in 'The Fall of the House of Usher,' " in *Poe Studies.* V (June, 1972), pp. 16–21.

Wilbur, Richard. "The House of Poe," in *The Recognition of Edgar Allan Poe.* Edited by Eric W. Carlson. Ann Arbor: University of Michigan Press, 1966, pp. 264–268.

"The Gold Bug"

Blanch, Robert J. "The Background of Poe's 'The Gold Bug,' " in *English Record.* XVI (April, 1966), pp. 44–48.

Bonaparte, Marie. *The Life and Works of Edgar Allan Poe: A Psychoanalytic Interpretation.* London: Imago, 1949, pp. 335–369.

Goldhurst, William. "Edgar Allan Poe and the Conquest of Death,' " in *New Orleans Review.* II (1969), pp. 316–319.

Hassell, J. Woodrow, Jr. "The Problem of Realism in 'The Gold Bug,' " in *American Literature.* XXV (May, 1953), pp. 179–192.

Laverty, Carroll. "The Death's-Head on the Gold Bug," in *American Literature.* XII (March, 1940), pp. 88–91.

Levin, Harry. *The Power of Blackness.* New York: Knopf, 1958, pp. 138–140.

Lynen, John F. *The Design of the Present: Essays on Time and Form in American Literature.* New Haven, Conn.: Yale University Press, 1969, pp. 242–245.

Ricardou, Jean. "Gold in the Bug," in *Poe Studies.* IX (1976), pp. 33–39.

St. Armand, Barton Levi. "Poe's 'Sober Mystification': The Uses of Alchemy in 'The Gold Bug,' " in *Poe Studies.* IV (June, 1971), pp. 1–7.

"Ligeia"

Askew, Melvin. "The Pseudonymic American Hero," in *Bucknell Review.* X (March, 1962), pp. 224–231.

Basler, Roy R. "The Interpretation of 'Ligeia,' " in *College English.* V (April, 1944), pp. 363–372.

———. *Sex, Symbolism and Psychology in Literature.* New Brunswick, N.J.: Rutgers University Press, 1948, pp. 177–200.

Davis, June and Jack L. Davis. "Poe's Ethereal Ligeia," in *Bulletin of the Rocky Mountain MLA.* XXIV (1970), pp. 170–176.

Gargano, James W. "Poe's 'Ligeia,' Dream and Destruction," in *College English.* XXIII (February, 1962), pp. 337–342.

Garrison, Joseph, Jr. "The Irony of 'Ligeia,' " in *Emerson Society Quarterly.* LX (Fall, 1970), pp. 13–18.

Griffith, Clark. "Poe's 'Ligeia' and the English Romantics," in *University of Toronto Quarterly.* XXIV (October, 1954), pp. 8–25.

Halio, Jay L. "The Moral Mr. Poe," in *Poe Newsletter.* I (October, 1968), pp. 23–24.

Hayter, Alethea. *Opium and Romantic Imagination.* Berkeley: University of California Press, 1968, pp. 132–151.

Hoffman, Daniel. "I Have Been Faithful to You in My Fashion: The Remarriage of Ligeia's Husband," in *Southern Review.* VIII (January, 1972), pp. 89–106.

Humma, John B. "Poe's *Ligeia*: Glanvill's Will or Blake's Will?," in *Mississippi Quarterly.* XXVI (1973), pp. 55–62.

Koster, Donald. "Poe, Romance and Reality," in *American Transcendental Quarterly.* XIX (Summer, 1973), pp. 8–13.

Lauber, John. " 'Ligeia' and Its Critics: A Plea for Literalism," in *Studies in Short Fiction*. IV (Fall, 1966), pp. 28–33.

Levine, Stuart. *Edgar Poe: Seer and Craftsman*. Deland, Fla.: Everett/ Edwards, 1972, pp. 26–37.

Morrison, Claudia. "Poe's 'Ligeia': An Analysis," in *Studies in Short Fiction*. IV (Spring, 1967), pp. 234–245.

Porte, Joel. *The Romance in America: Studies in Cooper, Poe, Hawthorne, Melville and James*. Middletown, Conn.: Wesleyan University Press, 1969, pp. 53–94.

Ramakrishna, D. "The Conclusion of Poe's 'Ligeia,' " in *Emerson Society Quarterly*. XLVII (2nd Quarter, 1967), pp. 69–70.

————. "Poe's 'Ligeia,' " in *Explicator*. XXV (October, 1966), item 19.

Rea, Joy. "Classicism and Romanticism in Poe's 'Ligeia,' " in *Ball State University Forum*. VIII (Winter, 1967), pp. 25–29.

Reed, Kenneth T. " 'Ligeia': The Story as Sermon," in *Poe Newsletter*. IV (June, 1971), p. 20.

Samuels, Charles T. "Usher's Fall: Poe's Rise," in *Georgia Review*. XVIII (Summer, 1964), pp. 208–216.

Schroeter, James. "A Misreading of Poe's 'Ligeia,' " in *PMLA*. LXXVI (September, 1961), pp. 397–406.

Stauffer, Donald B. "Style and Meaning in 'Ligeia' and 'William Wilson,' " in *Studies in Short Fiction*. II (Summer, 1965), pp. 316–331.

West, Muriel. "Poe's 'Ligeia,' " in *Explicator*. XXII (October,1963), item 15.

Zanger, Jules. "Poe and the Theme of Forbidden Knowledge," in *American Literature*. XLIX (January, 1978), pp. 533–543.

"MS. Found in a Bottle"

Feidelson, Charles. *Symbolism and American Literature*. Chicago: University of Chicago Press, 1953, pp. 35–42.

Levin, Harry. *The Power of Blackness*. New York: Knopf, 1958, p. 106.

Ljungquist, Kent. "Poe and the Sublime: His Two Short Sea Tales in the Context of an Aesthetic Tradition," in *Criticism*. XVII (1975), pp. 131–151.

Maxwell, Desmond E. *American Fiction: The Intellectual Background*. New York: Columbia University Press, 1963, pp. 76–77.

Porges, Irwin. *Edgar Allan Poe*. Philadelphia: Chilton, 1963, pp. 87–90.

Quinn, Arthur H. *Edgar Allan Poe: A Critical Biography*. New York: Appleton-Century, 1941, pp. 212–213.

Snell, George. *The Shapers of American Fiction*. New York: Dutton, 1947, pp. 49–51.

Tarbox, Raymond. "Blank Hallucinations in the Fiction of Poe and Hemingway," in *American Imago*. XXIV (1967), pp. 318–322.

Thompson, G.R. *Poe's Fiction: Romantic Irony in the Gothic Tales*. Madison: University of Wisconsin Press, 1973, pp. 167–168.

Weber, Jean-Paul. "Edgar Poe or the Theme of the Clock," in *Poe: A Collection of Critical Essays*. Edited by Robert Regan. Englewood Cliffs, N.J.: Prentice-Hall, 1967, pp. 90–92.

Zanger, Jules. "Poe and the Theme of Forbidden Knowledge," in *American Literature*. XLIX (January, 1978), pp. 533–543.

"The Masque of the Red Death"

Blair, Walter. "Poe's Conception of Incident and Tone in the Tale," in *Modern Philology*. XLI (1944), pp. 236–240. Reprinted in *Introduction to Literature*. Edited by Louis Locke, William Gibson, and George Arms. New York: Rinehart, 1948, pp. 429–433.

Bonaparte, Marie. *The Life and Works of Edgar Allan Poe: A Psychoanalytic Interpretation*. London: Imago, 1949, pp. 514–521.

Broussard, Louis. *The Measure of Poe*. Norman: University of Oklahoma Press, 1969, pp. 98–100.

Fagin, N. Bryllion. *The Histrionic Mr. Poe*. Baltimore: Johns Hopkins Press, 1949, pp. 215–216.

Levine, Stuart. *Edgar Poe: Seer and Craftsman*. Deland, Fla.: Everett/Edwards, 1972, pp. 198–203.

Mohr, F.K. "The Influence of Eichendorff's 'Ahnung und Gegenwart' on Poe's 'Masque of the Red Death,'" in *Modern Language Quarterly*. X (1949), pp. 3–15.

Pitcher, Edward William. "Horological and Chronological Time in 'Masque of the Red Death,'" in *American Transcendental Quarterly*. XXIX (1976), pp. 71–75.

Quinn, Patrick F. *The French Face of Edgar Poe*. Carbondale: Southern Illinois University Press, 1957, pp. 119–121.

Ropollo, Joseph P. "Meaning and 'The Masque of the Red Death,'" in *Tulane Studies in English*. XIII (1963), pp. 59–69. Reprinted in *Poe: A Collection of Critical Essays*. Edited by Robert Regan. Englewood Cliffs, N.J.: Prentice-Hall, 1967, pp. 134–144.

Shulman, Robert. "Poe and the Power of the Mind," in *Journal of English Literary History*. XXXVII (1970), pp. 256–259.

Solomont, Susan and Ritchie Darling. *Four Stories by Poe*. Norwich, Vt.: Green Knight Press, 1965, pp. 8–10.

Stewart, Randall and Dorothy Bethurum. *Classic American Fiction*. Chicago: Scott, Foresman, 1954, pp. 4–5.

Weber, Jean-Paul. "Edgar Poe or the Theme of the Clock," in *Poe: A Collection of Critical Essays*. Edited by Robert Regan. Englewood Cliffs, N.J.: Prentice-Hall, 1967, pp. 85–87.

Wilbur, Richard. "The House of Poe," in *Poe: A Collection of Critical Essays*. Edited by Robert Regan. Englewood Cliffs, N.J.: Prentice-Hall, 1967, pp. 118–119.

"The Murders in the Rue Morgue"

Asarch, Joel Kenneth. "A Telling Tale: Poe's Revisions in 'The Murders in the Rue Morgue,' " in *Library Chronicle*. XLI (1976), pp. 83–90.

Boll, Ernest. "The Manuscript of 'The Murders in the Rue Morgue' and Poe's Revisions," in *Modern Philology*. XL (1943), pp. 302–315.

Bonaparte, Marie. *The Life and Works of Edgar Allan Poe: A Psychoanalytic Interpretation*. London: Imago, 1949, pp. 427– 457.

Hawkins, John. "Poe's 'The Murders in the Rue Morgue,' " in *Explicator*. XXIII (1965), item 49.

Levine, Stuart. *Edgar Poe: Seer and Craftsman*. Deland, Fla.: Everett/Edwards, 1972, pp. 162–168.

Moore, John R. "Poe, Scott, and 'The Murders in the Rue Morgue,' " in *American Literature*. VIII (1936), pp. 52–57.

Porges, Irwin. *Edgar Allan Poe*. Philadelphia: Chilton, 1963, pp. 126–130.

Quinn, Arthur H. *Edgar Allan Poe: A Critical Biography*. New York: Appleton-Century, 1941, pp. 310–312.

Schwaber, Paul. "On Reading Poe," in *Literature and Psychology*. XXI (1971), pp. 81–99.

Sippel, Erich W. "Bolting the Whole Shebang Together: Poe's Predicament," in *Criticism*. XV (1973), pp. 289–308.

Smith, Allan. "The Psychological Content of Three Tales by Poe," in *Journal of American Studies*. VII (1973), pp. 279–292.

Thompson, G.R. *Poe's Fiction: Romantic Irony in the Gothic Tales*. Madison: University of Wisconsin Press, 1973, pp. 117–119.

"The Mystery of Marie Roget"

Fagin, N. Bryllion. *The Histrionic Mr. Poe*. Baltimore: Johns Hopkins University Press, 1949, pp. 172–173.

Levin, Harry. *The Power of Blackness*. New York: Knopf, 1958, p. 141.

Maxwell, Desmond E. *American Fiction: The Intellectual Background*. New York: Columbia University Press, 1963, pp. 95–96.

Porges, Irwin. *Edgar Allan Poe*. Philadelphia: Chilton, 1963, pp. 143–144.

Quinn, Arthur H. *Edgar Allan Poe: A Critical Biography.* New York: Appleton-Century, 1941, pp. 355–358.

Snow, E.R. *Mysteries and Adventure Along the Atlantic Coast.* New York: Dodd, 1948, pp. 264–265.

Thompson, G.R. *Poe's Fiction: Romantic Irony in the Gothic Tales.* Madison: University of Wisconsin Press, 1973, pp. 97–98.

Wallace, Irving. *The Fabulous Originals.* New York: Knopf, 1955, pp. 172–215.

Walsh, John. *Poe the Detective: The Curious Circumstances Behind 'The Mystery of Marie Roget.'* New Brunswick, N.J.: Rutgers University Press, 1968, pp. 39–49.

Wimsatt, William K. "Poe and the Mystery of Mary Rogers," in *PMLA.* LVI (1941), pp. 230–248.

Worthen, Samuel C. "Poe and the Beautiful Cigar Girl," in *American Literature.* XX (1948), pp. 305–312.

The Narrative of Arthur Gordon Pym

Bezanson, Walter E. "The Troubled Sleep of Arthur Gordon Pym," in *Essays in Literary History.* Edited by Rudolf Kirk and C.F. Main. New York: Russell and Russell, 1965, pp. 149–177.

Campbell, Josie P. "Deceit and Violence: Motifs in *The Narrative of Arthur Gordon Pym,*" in *English Journal.* LIV (February, 1970), pp. 206–212.

Candelaire, Cordelia. "On the Whiteness at Tsalal: A Note on *Arthur Gordon Pym,*" in *Poe Studies.* VI (June, 1973), p. 26.

Carringer, Kenneth Walter. "Circumscription of Space and the Form of Poe's *Arthur Gordon Pym,*" in *PMLA.* LXXXIX (1974), pp. 506–516.

Cecil, L. Moffitt. "Poe's Tsalal and the Virginia Springs," in *Nineteenth-Century Fiction.* XIX (March, 1965), pp. 398–402.

————. "Two Narratives of Arthur Gordon Pym," in *Texas Studies in Literature and Language.* V (Summer, 1963), pp. 232–241.

Covici, Pascal. "Toward a Reading of Poe's *The Narrative of Arthur Gordon Pym,*" in *Mississippi Quarterly.* XXI (Spring, 1968), pp. 111–118.

Fiedler, Leslie A. "The Blackness of Darkness: The Negro and the Development of American Gothic," in *Images of the Negro in American Literature.* Edited by Seymour L. Gross and John Edward Hardy. Chicago: University of Chicago Press, 1966, pp. 84–89.

————. *Love and Death in the American Novel.* New York: Criterion Books, 1960, pp. 370–382.

Fussell, Edwin. *Frontier: American Literature and the American West.* Princeton, N.J.: Princeton University Press, 1965, pp. 149–155.

Harp, Richard L. "A Note on the Harmony of Style and Theme in Poe's *Narrative of Arthur Gordon Pym*," in *CEA Critic*. XXXVI (1974), pp. 8–11.

Hinz, Evelyn J. "Tekeli-li: *The Narrative of Arthur Gordon Pym* as Satire," in *Genre*. III (1970), pp. 379–397.

Hussey, John P. " 'Mr. Pym' and 'Mr. Poe': The Two Narrators of *Arthur Gordon Pym*," in *South Atlantic Bulletin*. XXXIX (1974), pp. 22–32.

Kaplan, Sidney. "Introduction to *Pym*," in *The Narrative of Arthur Gordon Pym*. By Edgar Allan Poe. New York: Hill and Wang, 1960. Reprinted in *Poe: A Collection of Critical Essays*. Edited by Robert Regan. Englewood Cliffs, N.J.: Prentice-Hall, 1967, pp. 145–163.

La Guardia, David. "Poe, Pym, and Initiation," in *Emerson Society Quarterly*. LX (Fall, 1970), pp. 82–85.

Lee, Grace F. "The Quest of Arthur Gordon Pym," in *Southern Literary Journal*. IV (Spring, 1972), pp. 22–33.

Lee, Helen. "Possibilities of *Pym*," in *English Journal*. LV (December, 1966), pp. 1149–1154.

Maxwell, D.E.S. *American Fiction: The Intellectual Background*. New York: Columbia University Press, 1963, pp. 84–94.

Moldenhauer, J.J. "Imagination and Perversity in *The Narrative of Arthur Gordon Pym*," in *Texas Studies in Literature and Language*. XIII (Summer, 1971), pp. 267–280.

Moss, Sidney P. "*Arthur Gordon Pym*, or the Fallacy of Thematic Interpretation," in *University Review*. XXXIII (Summer, 1967), pp. 298–306.

O'Donnell, Charles. "From Earth to Ether: Poe's Flight into Space," in *PMLA*. LXXVII (March, 1962), pp. 85–89.

Porte, Joel. *The Romance in America: Studies in Cooper, Poe, Hawthorne, Melville and James*. Middletown, Conn.: Wesleyan University Press, 1969, pp. 53–94.

Quinn, Patrick F. "Poe's Imaginary Voyage," in *Hudson Review*. IV (Winter, 1952), pp. 562–585.

Ridgely, J.V. and Iola S. Haverstick. "Chartless Voyage: The Many Narratives of Arthur Gordon Pym," in *Texas Studies in Literature and Language*. VII (Spring, 1966), pp. 63–80.

Stroupe, John H. "Poe's Imaginary Voyage: Pym as Hero," in *Studies in Short Fiction*. IV (Summer, 1967), pp. 315–322.

"The Pit and the Pendulum"

Alterton, Margaret. "An Additional Source for Poe's 'The Pit and the Pendulum,' " in *Modern Language Notes*. XLVIII (1933), pp. 349–356.

Bonaparte, Marie. *The Life and Works of Edgar Allan Poe: A Psychoanalytic Interpretation.* London: Imago, 1949, pp. 575–593. Reprinted in *Psychoanalysis and Literature.* Edited by Hendrik M. Ruitenbeek. New York: Dutton, 1964, pp. 81–99.

Carter, Boyd. "Poe's Debt to Charles Brockden Brown," in *Prairie Schooner.* XXVII (1953), pp. 190–196.

Clark, D.L. "The Sources of Poe's 'The Pit and the Pendulum,' " in *Modern Language Notes.* XLIV (1929), pp. 349–356.

Engelberg, Edward. *The Unknown Distance, from Consciousness to Conscience: Goethe to Camus.* Cambridge, Mass.: Harvard University Press, 1972, pp. 124–125.

Hirsch, David H. "The Pit and the Apocalypse," in *Sewanee Review.* LXXVI (1968), pp. 632–652.

Levin, Harry. *The Power of Blackness.* New York: Knopf, 1958, pp. 152–154.

Lundquist, James. "The Moral of Averted Descent: The Failure of Sanity in 'The Pit and the Pendulum,' " in *Poe Newsletter.* II (1969), pp. 25–26.

Lynen, John F. *The Design of the Present: Essays on Time and Form in American Literature.* New Haven, Conn.: Yale University Press, 1969, pp. 215–217.

O'Brien, Edward J. *The Short Story Casebook.* New York: Farrar, Rinehart, 1935, pp. 181–211.

Sippel, Erich W. "Bolting the Whole Shebang Together: Poe's Predicament," in *Criticism.* XV (1973), pp. 289–308.

Solomont, Susan and Ritchie Darling. *Four Stories by Poe.* Norwich, Vt.: Green Knight Press, 1965, pp. 5–8.

Ward, Alfred C. *Aspects of the Modern Short Story: English and American.* New York: Dial, 1925, pp. 38–43.

Weber, Jean-Paul. "Edgar Poe or the Theme of the Clock," in *Poe: A Collection of Critical Essays.* Edited by Robert Regan. Englewood Cliffs, N.J.: Prentice-Hall, 1967, pp. 94–97.

"The Tell-Tale Heart"

Bonaparte, Marie. *The Life and Works of Edgar Allan Poe: A Psychoanalytic Interpretation.* London: Imago, 1949, pp. 491–504. Reprinted in *Psychoanalysis and Literature.* Edited by Hendrik M. Ruitenbeek. New York: Dutton, 1964, pp. 67–80.

Canario, John W. *"The Dream in 'The Tell-Tale Heart,' "* in *English Language Notes.* VII (1970), pp. 194–197.

Davidson, Edward H. *Poe: A Critical Study.* Cambridge, Mass.: Harvard University Press, 1957, pp. 189–190, 203–210.

Gargano, James W. "The Question of Poe's Narrators," in *College English.* XXV (1963), pp. 178–180. Reprinted in *The Recognition of Edgar Allan Poe.* Edited by Eric W. Carlson. Ann Arbor: University of Michigan Press, 1966, pp. 311–312. Also reprinted in *Poe: A Collection of Critical Essays.* Edited by Robert Regan. Englewood Cliffs, N.J.: Prentice-Hall, 1967, pp. 167–168.

———. "The Theme of Time in 'The Tell-Tale Heart,' " in *Studies in Short Fiction.* V (1968), pp. 378–382.

Levin, Harry. *The Power of Blackness.* New York: Knopf, 1958, pp. 145–146.

Quinn, Patrick F. *The French Face of Edgar Poe.* Carbondale: Southern Illinois University Press, 1957, pp. 232–236. Reprinted in *Psychoanalysis and American Fiction.* Edited by Irving Malin. New York: Dutton, 1965, pp. 74–77.

Reilly, John E. "The Lesser Death-Watch and 'The Tell-Tale Heart,' " in *American Transcendental Quarterly.* II (2nd Quarter, 1969), pp. 3–9.

Robinson, E. Arthur. "Poe's 'The Tell-Tale Heart,' " in *Nineteenth-Century Fiction.* XIX (1965), pp. 369–378. Reprinted in *Twentieth Century Interpretations of Poe's Tales.* Edited by William L. Howarth. Englewood Cliffs, N.J.: Prentice-Hall, 1971, pp. 94–102.

———. "Thoreau and the Deathwatch in Poe's 'The Tell-Tale Heart,' " in *Poe Studies.* IV (1971), pp. 14–16.

Senelick, Laurence. "Charles Dickens and 'The Tell-Tale Heart,' " in *Poe Studies.* VI (1973), pp. 12–14.

Shulman, Robert. "Poe and the Power of the Mind," in *Journal of English Literary History.* XXXVII (1970), pp. 259–261.

Solomont, Susan and Ritchie Darling. *Four Stories by Poe.* Norwich, Vt.: Green Knight Press, 1965, pp. 13–18.

Stone, Edward. *Voices of Despair: Four Motifs in American Literature.* Athens: Ohio University Press, 1966, pp. 183–185.

Strickland, Edward. "Dickens' 'A Madman's Manuscript' and 'The Tell-Tale Heart,' " in *Poe Studies.* IX (1976), pp. 22–23.

Ward, Alfred C. *Aspects of the Modern Short Story: English and American.* New York: Dial, 1925, pp. 35–37.

Weber, Jean-Paul. "Edgar Poe or the Theme of the Clock," in *Poe: A Collection of Critical Essays.* Edited by Robert Regan. Englewood Cliffs, N.J.: Prentice-Hall, 1967, pp. 92–94.

"William Wilson"

Bonaparte, Marie. *The Life and Works of Edgar Allan Poe: A Psychoanalytic Interpretation.* London: Imago, 1949, pp. 539–555.

Carlson, Eric W. " 'William Wilson': The Double as Primal Self," in *Topic.* XVI (1976), pp. 35–40.

Coskren, Robert. " 'William Wilson' and the Disintegration of Self," in *Studies in Short Fiction.* XII (1975), pp. 155–162.

Cox, James R. "Edgar Poe: Style as Pose," in *Virginia Quarterly Review.* XLIV (1968), pp. 81–83.

Davidson, Edward H. *Poe: A Critical Study.* Cambridge, Mass.: Harvard University Press, 1957, pp. 198–201. Reprinted in *Interpretations of American Literature.* Edited by Charles Feidelson and Paul Brodtkorb. New York: Oxford University Press, 1959, pp. 76–77.

Engelberg, Edward. *The Unknown Distance, from Consciousness to Conscience: Goethe to Camus.* Cambridge, Mass.: Harvard University Press, 1972, pp. 122–123.

Gargano, James W. "Art and Irony in 'William Wilson,' " in *English Studies Quarterly.* LX (1970), pp. 18–22.

————. "The Question of Poe's Narrators," in *College English.* XXV (1963), pp. 179–180. Reprinted in *The Recognition of Edgar Allan Poe.* Edited by Eric W. Carlson. Ann Arbor: University of Michigan Press, 1966, pp. 312–313. Also reprinted in *Poe: A Collection of Critical Essays.* Edited by Robert Regan. Englewood Cliffs, N.J.: Prentice-Hall, 1967, pp. 167–168.

————. " 'William Wilson': The Wildest Sublunary Vision," in *Washington & Jefferson Literary Journal.* I (1967), pp. 9–16.

Levin, Harry. *The Power of Blackness.* New York: Knopf, 1958, pp. 142–143.

Levine, Stuart. *Edgar Poe: Seer and Craftsman.* Deland, Fla.: Everett/ Edwards, 1972, pp. 184–193.

Quinn, Arthur H. *Edgar Allan Poe: A Critical Biography.* New York: Appleton-Century, 1941, pp. 286–287.

Quinn, Patrick F. *The French Face of Edgar Poe.* Carbondale: Southern Illinois University Press, 1957, pp. 221–223. Reprinted in *Psychoanalysis and American Fiction.* Edited by Irving Malin. New York: Dutton, 1965, pp. 65–67.

Rovner, Marc Leslie. "What William Wilson Knew: Poe's Dramatization of an Errant Mind," in *Library Chronicle.* XLI (1976), pp. 73–82.

Shanks, Edward. *Edgar Allan Poe.* New York: Macmillan, 1937, pp. 133–135.

Sippel, Erich W. "Bolting the Whole Shebang Together: Poe's Predicament," in *Criticism.* XV (1973), pp. 289–308.

Stauffer, Donald B. "Style and Meaning in 'Ligeia' and 'William Wilson,' " in *Studies in Short Fiction.* II (1965), pp. 324–330.

Sullivan, Ruth. "William Wilson's Double," in *Studies in Romanticism.* XV (1976), pp. 253–263.

HENRIK PONTOPPIDAN
(1857–1943)

The Novels of Pontoppidan

Ekman, Ernst. "Henrik Pontoppidan as a Critic of Modern Danish Society," in *Scandinavian Studies.* XXIX (November, 1957), pp. 171–183.

Jones, W. Glyn. "*Det forjaettede Land* and *Fremskridt* as Social Novels: A Comparison," in *Scandinavian Studies.* XXXVII (February, 1965), pp. 80–90.

_____. Henrik Pontoppidan (1857–1943)," in *Modern Language Review.* LII (July, 1957), pp. 380–382.

_____. "Henrik Pontoppidan, the Church and Christianity After 1900," in *Scandinavian Studies.* XXX (November, 1958), pp. 192–197.

Larsen, Hanna Astrup. "Pontoppidan of Denmark," in *American Scandinavian Review.* XXXI (September, 1943), pp. 233–237.

Robertson, J.G. *Essays and Addresses on Literature.* London: George Routledge, 1935, pp. 249–254.

ALEXANDER POPE
(1688–1744)

The Dunciad

Brower, Ruben Arthur. *Alexander Pope: The Poetry of Allusion.* Oxford: Clarendon Press, 1959, pp. 319–351.

Clark, Donald B. *Alexander Pope.* New York: Twayne, 1967, pp. 148–156.

Edwards, Thomas R., Jr. "Light and Nature: A Reading of *The Dunciad*," in *Philological Quarterly.* XXXIX (October, 1960), pp. 447–463. Reprinted in *Essential Articles for the Study of Alexander Pope.* Edited by Maynard Mack. Hamden, Conn.: Archon, 1964, pp. 704–725.

Erskine-Hill, Howard. *Pope: The Dunciad.* London: Edward Arnold, 1972.

Griffith, R.H. "*The Dunciad*," in *Philological Quarterly.* XXIV (1945), pp. 155–157. Reprinted in *Essential Articles for the Study of Alexander Pope.* Edited by Maynard Mack. Hamden, Conn.: Archon, 1964, pp. 633–665.

Johnson, Carol. "Pope's *Dunciad*: Requisitions of Verity," in *Southern Review.* I (Winter, 1965), pp. 108–116.

Jones, Emrys. "Pope and Dulness," in *Chatterton Lecture on an English Poet.* London: The British Academy, 1968, pp. 231–263. Reprinted in *Pope: A Collection of Critical Essays.* Edited by J.V. Guerinot. Englewood Cliffs, N.J.: Prentice-Hall, 1972, pp. 124–158.

Keener, Frederick M. *An Essay on Pope.* New York: Columbia University Press, 1974, pp. 96–107.

Kernan, Alvin B. "*The Dunciad* and the Plot of Satire," in *Studies in English Literature.* II (Summer, 1962), pp. 256–266. Reprinted in *Essential Articles for the Study of Alexander Pope.* Edited by Maynard Mack. Hamden, Conn.: Archon, 1964, pp. 726–738.

Knight, G. Wilson. *The Burning Oracle: Studies in the Poetry of Action.* London: Oxford University Press, 1939, pp. 174–182.

Leavis, F.R. "*The Dunciad*," in *Scrutiny.* XII (Winter, 1943), pp. 74–80.

Reichard, Hugo M. "Pope's Social Satire: Belles-Lettres and Business," in *PMLA.* LXVII (1952), pp. 420–434. Reprinted in *Essential Articles for the Study of Alexander Pope.* Edited by Maynard Mack. Hamden, Conn.: Archon, 1964, pp. 683–703.

Rogers, Pat. *An Introduction to Pope.* London: Methuen, 1975, pp. 103–130.

Rogers, Robert. *The Major Satires of Alexander Pope.* Urbana: University of Illinois Press, 1955, pp. 9–31.

Root, Robert Kilburn. *The Poetical Career of Alexander Pope.* Princeton, N.J.: Princeton University Press, 1941, pp. 125–155, 215–225.

Sitter, John E. *The Poetry of Pope's* Dunciad. Minneapolis: University of Minnesota Press, 1971.

Tanner, Tony. "Reason and the Grotesque: Pope's *Dunciad*," in *Critical Quarterly*. VII (Summer, 1965), pp. 145–160.

Williams, Aubrey L. *Pope's* Dunciad: *A Study of Its Meaning*. Baton Rouge: Louisiana State University Press, 1955.

An Essay on Criticism

Aden, John M. " 'First Follow Nature': Strategy and Stratification in *An Essay on Criticism*," in *Journal of English and Germanic Philology*. LV (October, 1956), pp. 604–617.

Brower, Reuben Arthur. *Alexander Pope: The Poetry of Allusion*. Oxford: Clarendon Press, 1959, pp. 191–206.

Clark, Donald B. *Alexander Pope*. New York: Twayne, 1967, pp. 30–37.

Empson, William. *The Structure of Complex Words*. Norfolk, Conn.: New Directions, 1951, pp. 84–100. Reprinted in *Essential Articles for the Study of Alexander Pope*. Edited by Maynard Mack. Hamden, Conn.: Archon, 1964, pp. 198–216.

Fenner, Arthur, Jr. "The Unity of Pope's *Essay on Criticism*," in *Philological Quarterly*. XXXIX (1960), pp. 435–446. Reprinted in *Essential Articles for the Study of Alexander Pope*. Edited by Maynard Mack. Hamden, Conn.: Archon, 1964, pp. 217–231.

Fisher, Alan S. "Cheerful Noonday, 'Gloomy' Twilight: Pope's *Essay on Criticism*," in *Philological Quarterly*. LI (1972), pp. 832–844.

Hooker, Edward N. "Pope on Wit: The *Essay on Criticism*," in *The Seventeenth Century: Studies in the History of English Thought and Literature from Bacon to Pope, by Richard Foster Jones and Others Writing in His Honor*. Stanford, Calif.: Stanford University Press, 1951, pp. 225–246. Reprinted in *Essential Articles for the Study of Alexander Pope*. Edited by Maynard Mack. Hamden, Conn.: Archon, 1964, pp. 175–197.

Hotch, Ripley. "Pope Surveys His Kingdom: *An Essay on Criticism*," in *Studies in English Literature*. XIII (1973), pp. 474–487.

Keener, Frederick M. *An Essay on Pope*. New York: Columbia University Press, 1974, pp. 163–169.

Marks, Emerson R. "Pope on Poetry and the Poet," in *Criticism*. XII (1970), pp. 271–280.

Parkin, Rebecca Price. "The Quality of Alexander Pope's Humor," in *College English*. XIV (January, 1953), pp. 197–199.

Ramsey, Paul. "The Watch of Judgment: Relativism and *An Essay on Criticism*," in *Studies in Criticism and Aesthetics, 1660–1800*. Edited by

Howard Anderson and John S. Shea. Minneapolis: University of Minnesota Press, 1967, pp. 128–139.

Rogers, Pat. *An Introduction to Pope.* London: Methuen, 1975, pp. 29–34.

Root, Robert Kilburn. *The Poetical Career of Alexander Pope.* Princeton, N.J.: Princeton University Press, 1941, pp. 19–30.

Tobin, James Edward. "Alexander Pope, 1744–1944," in *Thought.* XIX (June, 1944), pp. 250–261.

An Essay on Man

Brett, R.L. *Reason and Imagination: A Study of Form and Meaning in Four Poems.* London: Oxford University Press, 1960, pp. 51–77.

Brower, Reuben Arthur. *Alexander Pope: The Poetry of Allusion.* Oxford: Clarendon Press, 1959, pp. 206–239.

Cameron, J.M. *The Night Battle.* Baltimore: Helicon Press, 1962, pp. 150–168. Reprinted in *Essential Articles for the Study of Alexander Pope.* Edited by Maynard Mack. Hamden, Conn.: Archon, 1964, pp. 329–345.

Clark, Donald B. *Alexander Pope.* New York: Twayne, 1967, pp. 77–97.

Dobrée, Bonamy. *Alexander Pope.* London: Sylvan Press, 1951, pp. 99–104.

Hughes, R.E. "Pope's *Essay on Man*: The Rhetorical Structure of Epistle I," in *Modern Language Notes.* LXXX (March, 1955), pp. 177–181.

Kallich, Martin. "The Conversation and the Frame of Love: Images of Unity in Pope's *Essay on Man*," in *Papers on Language and Literature.* II (Winter, 1966), pp. 21–37.

Keener, Frederick M. *An Essay on Pope.* New York: Columbia University Press, 1974, pp. 59–69.

Knight, G. Wilson. *The Burning Oracle: Studies in the Poetry of Action.* London: Oxford University Press, 1939, pp. 159–174.

Laird, John. "Pope's *Essay on Man*," in *Review of English Studies.* XX (October, 1944), pp. 286–298.

Mack, Maynard. "1946: On Reading Pope," in *College English.* XXII (November, 1960), pp. 105–107.

Manley, Francis. "*Essay on Man*," in *Explicator.* XV (April, 1957), item 44.

Miles, Josephine. *Major Adjectives in English Poetry: From Wyatt to Auden.* Berkeley: University of California Press, 1946, pp. 340–345.

Parkin, Rebecca P. "Alexander Pope's Use of the Implied Dramatic Speaker," in *College English.* XI (December, 1949), pp. 139–140.

————. "The Quality of Alexander Pope's Humor," in *College English.* XIV (January, 1953), pp. 199–200.

Piper, William Bowman. "The Conversational Poetry of Pope," in *Studies in English Literature.* X (Summer, 1970), pp. 510–515.

Rogers, Pat. *An Introduction to Pope.* London: Methuen, 1975, pp. 62–68.

Root, Robert Kilburn. *The Poetical Career of Alexander Pope.* Princeton, N.J.: Princeton University Press, 1941, pp. 163–177.

Tuveson, Ernest. "*An Essay on Man* and 'The Way of Ideas,' " in *English Literary History.* XXVI (1959), pp. 368–386.

White, Douglas. *Pope and the Context of Controversy: The Manipulation of Ideas in* An Essay on Man. Chicago: University of Chicago Press, 1970.

The Poetry of Pope

Auden, W.H. "Alexander Pope," in *From Anne to Victoria.* Edited by Bonamy Dobrée. New York: Scribner's, 1937, pp. 89–107. Reprinted in *Pope: A Collection of Critical Essays.* Edited by J.V. Guerinot. Englewood Cliffs, N.J.: Prentice-Hall, 1972, pp. 15–29.

Brower, Reuben Arthur. *Alexander Pope: The Poetry of Allusion.* Oxford: Clarendon Press, 1959.

Clark, Donald B. *Alexander Pope.* New York: Twayne, 1967.

Edwards, Thomas R., Jr. *This Dark Estate: A Reading of Pope.* Berkeley: University of California Press, 1963.

Guerinot, J.V. "Introduction," in *Pope: A Collection of Critical Essays.* Edited by J.V. Guerinot. Englewood Cliffs, N.J.: Prentice-Hall, 1972, pp. 1–14.

Gurr, Elizabeth. *Pope.* Edinburgh: Oliver and Boyd, 1971.

Johnson, Samuel. "Alexander Pope," in *Lives of the English Poets*, Volume III. Oxford: Clarendon Press, 1905, pp. 82–276.

Keener, Frederick M. *An Essay on Pope.* New York: Columbia University Press, 1974, pp. 1–108.

Leavis, F.R. *Revaluation: Tradition and Development in English Poetry.* London: Chatto and Windus, 1935, pp. 68–91. Reprinted in *Essential Articles for the Study of Alexander Pope.* Edited by Maynard Mack. Hamden, Conn.: Archon, 1964, pp. 3–21.

Mack, Maynard. "Alexander Pope," in *Major British Writers*, Volume I. Edited by G.B. Harrison. New York: Harcourt, Brace, 1959, pp. 749–759. Reprinted in *Pope: A Collection of Critical Essays.* Edited by J.V. Guerinot. Englewood Cliffs, N.J.: Prentice-Hall, 1972, pp. 30–49.

Miller, John H. "Pope and the Principle of Reconciliation," in *Texas Studies in Literature and Language.* IX (Summer, 1967), pp. 185–192.

Moskovit, Leonard A. "Pope and the Tradition of the Neoclassical Imitation," in *Studies in English Literature.* VIII (Summer, 1968), pp. 445–462.

Rogers, Pat. *An Introduction to Pope.* London: Methuen, 1975.

Sherburn, George. "Introduction," in *The Best of Pope.* New York: Ronald Press, 1940.

Spacks, Patricia M. *An Argument of Images: The Poetry of Alexander Pope.* Cambridge, Mass.: Harvard University Press, 1971.

Tillotson, Geoffrey. *On the Poetry of Pope.* Oxford: Clarendon Press, 1950.

Warren, Austin. *Rage for Order.* Chicago: University of Chicago Press, 1948, pp. 37–51. Reprinted in *Essential Articles for the Study of Alexander Pope.* Edited by Maynard Mack. Hamden, Conn.: Archon, 1964, pp. 85–96.

Wellington, James E. "Pope and Charity," in *Philological Quarterly.* XLVI (April, 1967), pp. 225–235.

Wimsatt, William K., Jr. "Introduction," in *Alexander Pope: Selected Poetry and Prose.* New York: Rinehart, 1951, pp. vii–liv.

The Rape of the Lock

Barnes, T.R. *English Verse: Voice and Movement from Wyatt to Yeats.* Cambridge: Cambridge University Press, 1967, pp. 120–125.

Brooks, Cleanth. *The Well Wrought Urn.* New York: Harcourt, Brace, 1947, pp. 80–104. Reprinted in *Pope: A Collection of Critical Essays.* Edited by J.V. Guerinot. Englewood Cliffs, N.J.: Prentice-Hall, 1972, pp. 93–110.

Brower, Reuben Arthur. *Alexander Pope: The Poetry of Allusion.* Oxford: Clarendon Press, 1959, pp. 142–162.

Carnochan, W.B. "Pope's *The Rape of the Lock,*" in *Explicator.* XXII (1964), item 45.

Clark, Donald B. *Alexander Pope.* New York: Twayne, 1967, pp. 39–49.

Cunningham, J.S. *Pope:* The Rape of the Lock. Woodbury, N.Y.: Barron's Educational Series, 1961.

Dyson, Anthony Edward and Julian Lovelock. "In Spite of All Her Art: Pope's *The Rape of the Lock,*" in *Masterful Images: English Poetry from Metaphysicals to Romantics.* New York: Barnes & Noble, 1976, pp. 97–123.

Hyman, Stanley Edgar. "*The Rape of the Lock,*" in *Hudson Review.* XIII (Autumn, 1960), pp. 406–412. Reprinted in *The Rape of the Lock.* Edited by David Lougee and Robert McHenry, Jr. Columbus, Oh.: Merrill, 1969, pp. 112–118.

Jack, Ian. *Augustan Satire: Intention and Idiom in English Poetry 1660–1750.* Oxford: Clarendon Press, 1952, pp. 77–96. Reprinted in *Twentieth Century Interpretations of* The Rape of the Lock: *A Collection of Critical Essays.* Edited by G.S. Rousseau. Englewood Cliffs, N.J.: Prentice-Hall, 1969, pp. 38–51.

Jackson, James L. "Pope's *The Rape of the Lock* Considered as a Five Act Epic," in *PMLA.* LXV (1950), pp. 1283–1287.

Keener, Frederick M. *An Essay on Pope.* New York: Columbia University Press, 1974, pp. 39–48.

Knight, G. Wilson. *The Poetry of Pope: Laureate of Peace.* London: Routledge and Kegan Paul, 1965, pp. 22–33. Reprinted in *The Rape of the Lock.* Edited by David Lougee and Robert McHenry, Jr. Columbus, Oh.: Merrill, 1969, pp. 101–111.

Parkin, Rebecca P. "Mythopoeic Activity in *The Rape of the Lock*," in *English Literary History.* XXI (1954), pp. 30–38. Reprinted in *Twentieth Century Interpretations of* The Rape of the Lock*: A Collection of Critical Essays.* Edited by G.S. Rousseau. Englewood Cliffs, N.J.: Prentice-Hall, 1969, pp. 85–92.

Preston, John. " 'Th' Informing Soul': Creative Irony in *The Rape of the Lock*," in *Durham University Journal.* LVIII (June, 1966), pp. 125–130. Reprinted in *The Rape of the Lock.* Edited by David Lougee and Robert McHenry, Jr. Columbus, Oh.: Merrill, 1969, pp. 129–137.

Quintana, Ricardo. "*The Rape of the Lock* as a Comedy of Continuity," in *Review of English Literature.* VII (1966), pp. 9–19.

Reichard, Hugh M. "The Love Affair in Pope's *Rape of the Lock*," in *PMLA.* LXIX (September, 1954), pp. 887–902. Reprinted in *The Rape of the Lock.* Edited by David Lougee and Robert McHenry, Jr. Columbus, Oh.: Merrill, 1969, pp. 83–100.

Rogers, Pat. *An Introduction to Pope.* London: Methuen, 1975, pp. 35–41.

Root, Robert Kilburn. *The Poetical Career of Alexander Pope.* Princeton, N.J.: Princeton University Press, 1941, pp. 72–87.

Warren, Austin. "The Mask of Pope," in *Sewanee Review.* LIV (Winter, 1946), pp. 27–31. Reprinted in *Rage for Order.* Chicago: University of Chicago Press, 1948, pp. 46–49.

Wasserman, Earl R. "The Limits of Allusion in *The Rape of the Lock*," in *Journal of English and Germanic Philology.* LXV (July, 1966), pp. 425–444. Reprinted in *Twentieth Century Interpretations of* The Rape of the Lock*: A Collection of Critical Essays.* Edited by G.S. Rousseau. Englewood Cliffs, N.J.: Prentice-Hall, 1969, pp. 69–84.

Williams, Aubrey. "The 'Fall' of China and *The Rape of the Lock*," in *Philological Quarterly.* XLI (April, 1962), pp. 412–425. Reprinted in *The Rape of the Lock.* Edited by David Lougee and Robert McHenry, Jr. Columbus, Oh.: Merrill, 1969, pp. 119–128.

Wimsatt, William K., Jr. "The Game of Ombre in *The Rape of the Lock*," in *Review of English Studies.* I (1950), pp. 136–143.

KATHERINE ANNE PORTER
(1890–   )

Flowering Judas

Allen, Charles. "Southwestern Chronicle: Katherine Anne Porter," in *Arizona Quarterly*. II (Summer, 1946), pp. 90–95.

✓ **Bluefarb, Sam.** "Loss of Innocence in *Flowering Judas*," in *College Language Association Journal*. VII (March, 1964), pp. 256–262.

✓ **Bogan, Louise.** "*Flowering Judas*," in *New Republic*. LXIV (October 22, 1930), pp. 277–278.

_____. *Selected Criticisms: Prose, Poetry*. New York: Noonday, 1955, pp. 33–35.

Bradbury, John. *Renaissance in the South: A Critical History of the Literature 1920–1960*. Chapel Hill: University of North Carolina Press, 1963, pp. 70–74.

✓ **Bride, Sister Mary.** "Laura and the Unlit Lamp," in *Studies in Short Fiction*. I (Fall, 1963), pp. 61–63.

Flood, Ethelbert. "Christian Language in Modern Literature," in *Culture*. XXII (March, 1961), pp. 28–42.

Gold, Herbert and David L. Stevenson. *Stories of Modern America*. New York: St. Martin's, 1961, pp. 294, 306.

✓ **Gottfried, Leon.** "Death's Other Kingdom: Dantesque and Theological Symbolism in *Flowering Judas*," in *PMLA*. LXXXIV (1969), pp. 112–124.

Gross, Beverly. "The Poetic Narrative: A Reading of *Flowering Judas*," in *Style*. XI (Spring, 1968), pp. 129–139.

Hagopian, John V. "Katherine Anne Porter: Feeling, Form and Truth," in *Four Quarters*. XII (November, 1962), pp. 1–10.

✓ **Hartley, Lodwick.** "Katherine Anne Porter," in *Sewanee Review*. XLVII (April, 1940), pp. 206–216.

Heilman, Robert B. *Modern Short Stories*. New York: Harcourt, Brace, 1950, pp. 192–194.

Jones, Llewelyn. "Contemporary Fiction," in *American Writers on American Literature*. New York: Liveright, 1931, p. 502.

Josephson, Matthew. *Life Among the Surrealists*. New York: Holt, Rinehart and Winston, 1962, pp. 352–354.

✓ **Madden, David.** "The Charged Image in Katherine Anne Porter's *Flowering Judas*," in *Studies in Short Fiction*. VII (Spring, 1970), pp. 277–289.

✓ **Redden, Dorothy S.** "*Flowering Judas*: Two Voices," in *Studies in Short Fiction*. VI (Winter, 1969), pp. 194–204.

Steinmann, Martin and Gerald Willen.   *Literature for Writing.* Belmont, Calif.: Wadsworth, 1962, pp. 183–184.

Summers, Richard.   *The Craft of the Short Story.* New York: Rinehart, 1948, pp. 283–285.

√**Tate, Allen.**   "A New Star," in *Nation.* CXXXI (October 1, 1930), pp. 352–353.

Warren, Robert P.   "Irony with a Center: Katherine Anne Porter," in *Kenyon Review.* IV (1942), pp. 32–35. Also in his *Selected Essays.* New York: Random House, 1958, pp. 140–143.

West, Ray B.   "Katherine Anne Porter: Symbol and Theme in *Flowering Judas*," in *Accent.* VII (Spring, 1947), pp. 182–188. Also in *American Literature Readings and Critique.* Edited by Robert Stallman and Arthur Waldhorn. New York: Putnam's, 1961, pp. 767–770.

"Old Mortality"

Allen, Charles.   "The Novellas of Katherine Anne Porter," in *University of Kansas City Review.* XXIX (1962), pp. 88–90.

Baker, Howard.   "The Contemporary Short Story," in *Southern Review.* III (1938), pp. 595–596.

Bradbury, John.   *Renaissance in the South: A Critical History of the Literature 1920–1960.* Chapel Hill: University of North Carolina Press, 1963, pp. 70–74.

⤳ **Brooks, Cleanth and Robert P. Warren.**   *Understanding Fiction.* New York: Crofts, 1943, pp. 529–534.

Greene, George.   "Brimstone and Roses: Notes on Katherine Anne Porter," in *Thought.* XXXVI (1961), p. 427.

Hagopian, John V.   "Katherine Anne Porter: Feeling, Form and Truth," in *Four Quarters.* XII (November, 1962), pp. 1–10.

Hoffman, Frederick J.   *The Art of Southern Fiction: A Study of Some Modern Novels.* Carbondale: Southern Illinois University Press, 1967, pp. 41–44.

Johnson, Shirley E.   "Love Attitudes in the Fiction of Katherine Anne Porter," in *West Virginia University Philological Papers.* XIII (December, 1961), pp. 84–85.

？ **Mooney, Harry J.**   *The Fiction and Criticism of Katherine Anne Porter.* Pittsburgh: University of Pittsburgh Press, 1957, pp. 20–25.

√ **O'Connor, William Van.**   "The Novel of Experience," in *Critique.* I (Spring, 1956), pp. 37–44.

√ **Poss, S.H.**   "Variations on a Theme in Four Stories of Katherine Anne Porter," in *Twentieth Century Literature.* IV (1958), pp. 24–25.

Warren, Robert P. "Irony with a Center: Katherine Anne Porter," in *Kenyon Review.* IV (1942), pp. 35–40. Also in his *Selected Essays.* New York: Random House, 1958, pp. 149–154.

West, Ray B. "Katherine Anne Porter and 'Historic Memory,'" in *Hopkins Review.* VI (Fall, 1952), pp. 16–27.

Pale Horse, Pale Rider

Alexander, Jean. "Katherine Anne Porter's Ship in the Jungle," in *Twentieth Century Literature.* II (January, 1966), pp. 179–188.

Allen, Charles. "The Novellas of Katherine Anne Porter," in *University of Kansas City Review.* XXIX (December, 1962), pp. 87–93.

Angoff, Allen. *American Writing Today: Its Independence and Vigor.* New York: New York University Press, 1957, pp. 399–401.

Bradbury, John. *Renaissance in the South: A Critical History of the Literature 1920–1960.* Chapel Hill: University of North Carolina Press, 1963, pp. 70–74.

Crume, Paul. *Southwest Review.* XXV (January, 1940), pp. 213–218.

Fadiman, Clifton. "Katherine Anne Porter," in *New Yorker.* XV (April 1, 1939), pp. 77–78.

Hagopian, John V. "Katherine Anne Porter: Feeling, Form and Truth," in *Four Quarters.* XII (November, 1962), pp. 1–10.

Johnson, James. "The Adolescent Hero: A Trend in Modern Fiction," in *Twentieth Century Literature.* V (April, 1959), pp. 3–11.

Mooney, Harry J. *The Fiction and Criticism of Katherine Anne Porter.* Pittsburgh: University of Pittsburgh Press, 1957, pp. 25–33.

O'Connor, William Van. "The Novel of Experience," in *Critique.* I (Spring, 1956), pp. 37–44.

Poss, S.H. "Variations on a Theme in Four Stories of Katherine Anne Porter," in *Twentieth Century Literature.* IV (1958), pp. 25–27.

Schorer, Mark. "Afterword," in *Pale Horse, Pale Rider.* New York: New American Library, 1962, pp. 167–175.

Sklare, Arnold B. *The Art of the Novella.* New York: Macmillan, 1965, pp. 297–298.

Stegner, Wallace. "Conductivity in Fiction," in *Virginia Quarterly Review.* XV (Autumn, 1939), pp. 444–445.

Yannella, Philip R. "The Problems of Dislocation in *Pale Horse, Pale Rider,*" in *Studies in Short Fiction.* VI (Fall, 1969), pp. 637–642.

Youngblood, Sarah. "Structure and Imagery in Katherine Anne Porter's *Pale Horse, Pale Rider,*" in *Modern Fiction Studies.* V (Winter, 1959/1960), pp. 344–352.

Ship of Fools

Abraham, William. "Progression Through Repetition," in *Massachusetts Review*. IX (Summer, 1963), pp. 805–809.

Alexander, Jean. "Katherine Anne Porter's Ship in the Jungle," in *Twentieth Century Literature*. XI (January, 1966), pp. 179–188.

Baker, Howard. "The Upward Path: Notes on the Work of Katherine Anne Porter," in *Southern Review*. IV (Winter, 1968), pp. 1–19.

Bedford, Sybille. "Voyage to Everywhere," in *Spectator*. No. 7012 (November 16, 1962), pp. 763–764.

Curley, Daniel. "Katherine Anne Porter: The Larger Plan," in *Kenyon Review*. XXV (Autumn, 1963), pp. 671–695.

De Vries, Peter. "Nobody's Fool (A Character or Two Overlooked in Miss Katherine Anne Porter's Shipload)," in *New Yorker*. XXXVIII (June 16, 1962), pp. 28–29.

Drake, Robert. "A Modern Inferno," in *National Review*. XII (April 24, 1962), p. 290.

Finkelstein, Sidney. "*Ship of Fools*," in *Mainstream*. XV (September, 1962), pp. 42–48.

Hartley, Lodwick. "Dark Voyagers, A Study of Katherine Anne Porter's *Ship of Fools*," in *University of Kansas City Review*. XXX (December, 1963), pp. 83–94.

Heilman, Robert B. "*Ship of Fools*: Notes on Style," in *Four Quarters*. XII (November, 1962), pp. 46–55.

Hendrick, George. "Hart Crane Aboard the *Ship of Fools*: Some Speculations," in *Twentieth Century Literature*. IX (April, 1963), pp. 3–9.

Hertz, Robert N. "Sebastian Brant and Porter's *Ship of Fools*," in *Midwest Quarterly*. VI (Summer, 1965), pp. 389–401.

Josely, Sister Mary. "On the Making of *Ship of Fools*," in *South Dakota Review*. I (May, 1964), pp. 46–52.

Kirkpatrick, Smith. "*The Ship of Fools*," in *Sewanee Review*. LXXI (Winter, 1963), pp. 94–98.

Liberman, M.M. "Responsibility of the Novelists: The Critical Reception of *Ship of Fools*," in *Criticism*. VIII (Fall, 1966), pp. 377–388.

————. "The Short Story as Chapter in *Ship of Fools*," in *Criticism*. X (Winter, 1968), pp. 65–71.

McIntyre, John P. "*Ship of Fools* and Its Publicity," in *Thought*. XXXVIII (1963), pp. 211–220.

Marsden, Malcolm M. "Love as Threat in Katherine Anne Porter's Fiction," in

Twentieth Century Literature. XIII (March, 1967), pp. 29–38.

Miller, Paul W. "Katherine Anne Porter's *Ship of Fools*, A Masterpiece Manqué," in *University Review*. XXXII (December, 1965), pp. 151–157.

Ruoff, James and Del Smith. "Katherine Anne Porter on *Ship of Fools*," in *College English*. XXIV (February, 1963), pp. 396–397.

Ryan, Marjorie. "Katherine Anne Porter: *Ship of Fools* and the Short Stories," in *Bucknell Review*. XII (March, 1964), pp. 51–63.

――――. "Review of *Ship of Fools*," in *Critique*. V (1962), pp. 94–99.

Solotaroff, Theodore. "*Ship of Fools* and the Critics," in *Commentary*. XXXIV (October, 1962), pp. 277–286.

Spence, Jon. "Looking-Glass Reflections: Satirical Elements in *Ship of Fools*," in *Sewanee Review*. LXXXII (Spring, 1974), pp. 316–330.

Walton, Gerald. "Katherine Anne Porter's Use of Quakerism in *Ship of Fools*," in *University of Mississippi Studies in English*. VII (1966), pp. 15–23.

EZRA POUND
(1885–1972)

Cantos

Adams, Stephen J. "Are the *Cantos* a Fugue?," in *University of Toronto Quarterly*. XLV (1975), pp. 67–74.

Bewley, Marius. *Masks and Mirrors: Essays in Criticism*. New York: Atheneum, 1970, pp. 303–306, 321–323.

Davie, Donald. *Ezra Pound*. New York: Viking, 1975, pp. 62–98.

Dekker, George. *Sailing After Knowledge: The* Cantos *of Ezra Pound*. London: Routledge and Kegan Paul, 1963. Partially reprinted in *Critics on Ezra Pound*. Edited by E. San Juan, Jr. Coral Gables, Fla.: University of Miami Press, 1972, pp. 84–88.

Elliott, George P. "Poet of Many Voices," in *Carleton Miscellany*. II (Summer, 1961), pp. 79–103. Revised version in *Ezra Pound: A Collection of Critical Essays*. Edited by Walter Sutton. Englewood Cliffs, N.J.: Prentice-Hall, 1963, pp. 152–162.

Emery, Clark. *Ideas into Action: A Study of Pound's* Cantos. Coral Gables, Fla.: University of Miami Press, 1958.

Frohock, W.M. "The Revolt of Ezra Pound," in *Southwest Review*. XLIV (Summer, 1959), pp. 190–199. Reprinted in *Ezra Pound: A Collection of Critical Essays*. Edited by Walter Sutton. Englewood Cliffs, N.J.: Prentice-Hall, 1963, pp. 87–97.

Halperen, M. "How to Read a Canto," in *The Twenties: Fiction, Poetry, Drama*. Deland, Fla.: Everett/Edwards, 1975, pp. 335–350.

Kenner, Hugh. *The Poetry of Ezra Pound*. Norfolk, Conn.: New Directions, 1951, pp. 185–306.

————. *The Pound Era*. Berkeley: University of California Press, 1971.

Nassar, Eugene Paul. *The* Cantos *of Ezra Pound: The Lyric Mode*. Baltimore: Johns Hopkins University Press, 1975.

Pearce, Roy Harvey. *The Continuity of American Poetry*. Princeton, N.J.: Princeton University Press, 1961, pp. 85–101. Reprinted in *Ezra Pound: A Collection of Critical Essays*. Edited by Walter Sutton. Englewood Cliffs, N.J.: Prentice-Hall, 1963, pp. 163–177.

Pearlman, Daniel D. *The Barb of Time: On the Unity of Ezra Pound's* Cantos. New York: Oxford University Press, 1969. Partially reprinted in *Ezra Pound: A Collection of Criticism*. Edited by Grace Schulman. New York: McGraw-Hill, 1974, pp. 143–149.

Pevear, Richard. "Notes on the *Cantos* of Ezra Pound," in *Hudson Review.* XXV (Spring, 1972), pp. 51–70. Reprinted in *Ezra Pound: A Collection of Criticism.* Edited by Grace Schulman. New York: McGraw-Hill, 1974, pp. 132–142.

Quinn, Sister Bernetta. *Ezra Pound: An Introduction to the Poetry.* New York: Columbia University Press, 1972, pp. 101–167.

Read, Forrest. "A Man of No Fortune," in *Motive and Method in the* Cantos *of Ezra Pound.* Edited by Lewis Leary. New York: Columbia University Press, 1954, pp. 101–123. Reprinted in *Ezra Pound: A Collection of Critical Essays.* Edited by Walter Sutton. Englewood Cliffs, N.J.: Prentice-Hall, 1963, pp. 64–79.

Rosenthal, M.L. *A Primer of Ezra Pound.* New York: Grosset and Dunlap, 1960, pp. 42–51. Reprinted in *Ezra Pound: A Collection of Critical Essays.* Edited by Walter Sutton. Englewood Cliffs, N.J.: Prentice-Hall, 1963, pp. 57–63.

Stock, Noel. *Reading the* Cantos*: A Study of Meaning in Ezra Pound.* London: Routledge and Kegan Paul, 1967.

Tate, Allen. *Essays of Four Decades.* Chicago: Swallow Press, 1968, pp. 364–371. Reprinted in *Critics on Ezra Pound.* Edited by E. San Juan, Jr. Coral Gables, Fla.: University of Miami Press, 1972, pp. 23–24.

Watts, Harold H. *Ezra Pound and the* Cantos. London: Routledge and Kegan Paul, 1953. Revised and reprinted in *Ezra Pound: A Collection of Critical Essays.* Edited by Walter Sutton. Englewood Cliffs, N.J.: Prentice-Hall, 1963, pp. 98–114.

Zukofsky, Louis. "The *Cantos* of Ezra Pound," in *Criterion.* X (April, 1931), pp. 424–440.

Hugh Selwyn Mauberley

Blackmur, R.P. *Language as Gesture: Essays in Poetry.* New York: Harcourt, Brace, 1952, pp. 126–130.

David, Donald. *Ezra Pound.* New York: Viking, 1975, pp. 49–54.

————. *Ezra Pound: Poet as Sculptor.* New York: Oxford University Press, 1964, pp. 91–101.

Deutsch, Babette. *The Modern Poetry.* New York: Norton, 1935, pp. 115–118.

Drew, Elizabeth A. *Discovering Modern Poetry.* New York: Holt, Rinehart and Winston, 1961, pp. 31–34.

Espey, John J. *Ezra Pound's* Mauberley*: A Study in Composition.* Berkeley: University of California Press, 1955.

Friar, Kimon and John Malcolm Brinnin. *Modern Poetry: American and British.* New York: Appleton-Century-Crofts, 1951, pp. 527–531.

Hoffman, Frederick J.   *The Twenties: American Writing in the Postwar Decade.* New York: Free Press, 1962, pp. 55–66.

Kenner, Hugh.   *The Poetry of Ezra Pound.* Norfolk, Conn.: New Directions, 1951, pp. 164–182. Reprinted in *Ezra Pound: A Collection of Critical Essays.* Edited by Walter Sutton. Englewood Cliffs, N.J.: Prentice-Hall, 1963, pp. 41–56.

————.   *The Pound Era.* Berkeley: University of California Press, 1971, pp. 287–288.

Leavis, F.R.   *New Bearings in English Poetry.* London: Chatto and Windus, 1932, pp. 141–143. Reprinted in *Ezra Pound: A Collection of Critical Essays.* Edited by Walter Sutton. Englewood Cliffs, N.J.: Prentice-Hall, 1963, pp. 26–40.

Quinn, Sister Bernetta.   *Ezra Pound: An Introduction to the Poetry.* New York: Columbia University Press, 1972, pp. 71–74.

Rosenthal, M.L.   *A Primer of Ezra Pound.* New York: Grosset and Dunlap, 1960, pp. 29–41.

San Juan, E., Jr.   "Ezra Pound's Craftsmanship: An Interpretation of *Hugh Selwyn Mauberley*," in *Critics on Ezra Pound.* Edited by E. San Juan, Jr. Coral Gables, Fla.: University of Miami Press, 1972, pp. 106–124.

Schneidau, Herbert.   *Ezra Pound: The Image and the Real.* Baton Rouge: Louisiana State University Press, 1969, pp. 162–172.

The Pisan Cantos

Davie, Donald.   *Ezra Pound.* New York: Viking, 1975, pp. 72–74, 79–82.

————.   *Ezra Pound: Poet as Sculptor.* New York: Oxford University Press, 1964, pp. 74–84. Reprinted in *Ezra Pound: A Collection of Criticism.* Edited by Grace Schulman. New York: McGraw-Hill, 1974, pp. 114–124.

Evans, David W.   "Ezra Pound as Prison Poet," in *University of Kansas City Review.* XXIII (Spring, 1957), pp. 215–220. Reprinted in *Ezra Pound: A Collection of Critical Essays.* Edited by Walter Sutton. Englewood Cliffs, N.J.: Prentice-Hall, 1963, pp. 80–86.

Kenner, Hugh.   *The Pound Era.* Berkeley: University of California Press, 1971, pp. 474–495.

Monk, Donald.   "Intelligibility in *The Pisan Cantos*," in *Journal of American Studies.* IX (1975), pp. 213–227.

Pearlman, Daniel D.   *The Barb of Time: On the Unity of Ezra Pound's Cantos.* New York: Oxford University Press, 1969, pp. 237–292.

Quinn, Sister Bernetta.   *Ezra Pound: An Introduction to the Poetry.* New York: Columbia University Press, 1972, pp. 129–140.

Read, Forrest. "The Pattern of *The Pisan Cantos*," in *Sewanee Review*. LXV (1957), pp. 400–419. Reprinted in *Critics on Ezra Pound*. Edited by E. San Juan, Jr. Coral Gables, Fla.: University of Miami Press, 1972, pp. 49–52.

Stock, Noel. *Reading the* Cantos: *A Study of Meaning in Ezra Pound*. London: Routledge and Kegan Paul, 1967, pp. 72–90.

The Poetry of Pound

Berryman, John. "The Poetry of Ezra Pound," in *Partisan Review*. XVI (April, 1949), pp. 377–394. Reprinted in *Critics on Ezra Pound*. Edited by E. San Juan, Jr. Coral Gables, Fla.: University of Miami Press, 1972, pp. 38–43.

Blackmur, R.P. *Form and Value in Modern Poetry*. New York: Anchor Books, 1957, pp. 113–120. Reprinted in *Critics on Ezra Pound*. Edited by E. San Juan, Jr. Coral Gables, Fla.: University of Miami Press, 1972, pp. 25–30.

Brooke-Rose, Christine. *A ZBC of Ezra Pound*. Berkeley: University of California Press, 1971.

Eliot, T.S. "Ezra Pound," in *Poetry*. LXVIII (September, 1946), pp. 326–338. Reprinted in *Ezra Pound: A Collection of Critical Essays*. Edited by Walter Sutton. Englewood Cliffs, N.J.: Prentice-Hall, 1963, pp. 17–25.

Fraser, G.S. *Ezra Pound*. New York: Grove, 1961, pp. 29–85.

Kenner, Hugh. *The Poetry of Ezra Pound*. Norfolk, Conn.: New Directions, 1951.

O'Connor, William Van. *Ezra Pound*. Minneapolis: University of Minnesota Press, 1963.

Quinn, Sister Bernetta. *Ezra Pound: An Introduction to the Poetry*. New York: Columbia University Press, 1972.

Rosenthal, M.L. *A Primer of Ezra Pound*. New York: Grosset and Dunlap, 1960.

Schlauch, Margaret. "The Anti-Humanism of Ezra Pound," in *Science and Society*. XIII (Summer, 1949), pp. 258–269. Reprinted in *Critics on Ezra Pound*. Edited by E. San Juan, Jr. Coral Gables, Fla.: University of Miami Press, 1972, pp. 44–46.

Witemeyer, Hugh. *The Poetry of Ezra Pound: Forms and Renewal, 1908–1920*. Berkeley: University of California Press, 1969.

Yeats, William Butler. "Introduction," in *The Oxford Book of Modern Verse*. Edited by William Butler Yeats. London: Oxford University Press, 1936. Reprinted in *Ezra Pound: A Collection of Critical Essays*. Edited by Walter Sutton. Englewood Cliffs, N.J.: Prentice-Hall, 1963, pp. 9–10.

ANTHONY POWELL
(1905–   )

The Acceptance World

Arau, Anthony. "A Handful of Dust," in *New Republic*. CXXXIV (April 2, 1956), pp. 19–20.

Bailey, Anthony. "The Social Dance of Life," in *Commonweal*. LXIII (March 23, 1956), pp. 647–648.

Bergonzi, Bernard. *Anthony Powell*. London: Longmans, 1971, pp. 12–15.

Brennan, Neil. *Anthony Powell*. New York: Twayne, 1974, pp. 152–162.

Hall, James. "The Uses of Polite Surprise: Anthony Powell," in *Essays in Literature*. XII (April, 1962), pp. 167–183.

Hawthorne, Hazel. "Remembrance of a Recent Past," in *Nation*. CLXXXII (March 31, 1956), p. 263.

Morris, Robert K. *The Novels of Anthony Powell*. Pittsburgh: University of Pittsburgh Press, 1968, pp. 148–165.

Rolo, Charles J. "Anthony Powell," in *Atlantic*. CXCVII (April, 1956), p. 86.

Russell, John. *Anthony Powell: A Quintet, Sextet, and War*. Bloomington: Indiana University Press, 1970, pp. 129–137.

Tucker, James. *The Novels of Anthony Powell*. New York: Macmillan, 1976, pp. 141–145.

Afternoon Men

Allen, Walter. *The Modern Novel in Britain and the United States*. New York: Dutton, 1964, pp. 219–221.

Bergonzi, Bernard. *Anthony Powell*. London: Longmans, 1971, pp. 3–7.

Brennan, Neil. *Anthony Powell*. New York: Twayne, 1974, pp. 84–100.

Morris, Robert K. *The Novels of Anthony Powell*. Pittsburgh: University of Pittsburgh Press, 1968, pp. 13–31.

Russell, John. *Anthony Powell: A Quintet, Sextet, and War*. Bloomington: Indiana University Press, 1970, pp. 50–54.

————. "Quintet from the Thirties: Anthony Powell," in *Kenyon Review*. XXVII (Autumn, 1965), pp. 698–726.

Tucker, James. *The Novels of Anthony Powell*. New York: Macmillan, 1976, pp. 9–18.

Agents and Patients

Barrett, William. "Knights and Knaves," in *Atlantic*. CCXV (May, 1965), pp. 151–152.

Brennan, Neil.   *Anthony Powell.* New York: Twayne, 1974, pp. 114–120.

Moore, Harry T.   "Death in a Droshky," in *Saturday Review.* XLVIII (May 15, 1965), pp. 53–54.

Morris, Robert K.   *The Novels of Anthony Powell.* Pittsburgh: University of Pittsburgh Press, 1968, pp. 69–84.

Rolo, Charles J.   "England Made Them," in *Atlantic.* CXCI (February, 1953), p. 82.

Russell, John.   *Anthony Powell: A Quintet, Sextet, and War.* Bloomington: Indiana University Press, 1970, pp. 63–67.

_____.   "Quintet from the Thirties: Anthony Powell," in *Kenyon Review.* XXVII (Autumn, 1965), pp. 698–726.

Tucker, James.   *The Novels of Anthony Powell.* New York: Macmillan, 1976, pp. 34–36.

West, Anthony.   "Wry Humor," in *New Yorker.* XXVIII (December 13, 1952), pp. 150–158.

At Lady Molly's

Bergonzi, Bernard.   *Anthony Powell.* London: Longmans, 1971, pp. 15–17.

Brennan, Neil.   *Anthony Powell.* New York: Twayne, 1974, pp. 162–168.

Hall, James.   *The Tragic Comedians: Seven Modern British Novelists.* Bloomington: Indiana University Press, 1963, pp. 129–150.

Morris, Robert K.   *The Novels of Anthony Powell.* Pittsburgh: University of Pittsburgh Press, 1968, pp. 166–180.

Russell, John.   *Anthony Powell: A Quintet, Sextet, and War.* Bloomington: Indiana University Press, 1970, pp. 138–146.

Tucker, James.   *The Novels of Anthony Powell.* New York: Macmillan, 1976, pp. 146–150.

Books Do Furnish a Room

Bailey, Paul.   "Sniffing the Scandal," in *London Magazine.* XI (August–September, 1971), pp. 147–150.

Bergonzi, Bernard.   *Anthony Powell.* London: Longmans, 1971, pp. 18–24.

Bliven, Naomi.   "Publish and Perish," in *New Yorker.* XLVII (October 30, 1971), pp. 150–154.

Brennan, Neil.   *Anthony Powell.* New York: Twayne, 1974, pp. 192–198.

Mallet, Gina.   "*Books Do Furnish a Room,*" in *Saturday Review.* LIV (September 11, 1971), p. 43.

Mano, D. Keith.   "Uses of the Novel," in *National Review.* XXIII (September 24, 1971), pp. 1062–1063.

May, Derwent. "Heroic Curiosity," in *Encounter*. XXXVI (March, 1971), pp. 71–72.

Tucker, James. *The Novels of Anthony Powell*. New York: Macmillan, 1976, pp. 179–182.

A Buyer's Market

Bergonzi, Bernard. *Anthony Powell*. London: Longmans, 1971, pp. 12–15.

Brennan, Neil. *Anthony Powell*. New York: Twayne, 1974, pp. 147–152.

Hall, James. *The Tragic Comedians: Seven Modern British Novelists*. Bloomington: Indiana University Press, 1963, pp. 129–150.

————. "The Uses of Polite Surprise: Anthony Powell," in *Essays in Criticism*. XII (April, 1962), pp. 167–183.

Morris, Robert K. *Continuance and Change: The Contemporary British Novel Sequence*. Carbondale: Southern Illinois University Press, 1972, pp. 137–138.

————. *The Novels of Anthony Powell*. Pittsburgh: University of Pittsburgh Press, 1968, pp. 113–131.

Tucker, James. *The Novels of Anthony Powell*. New York: Macmillan, 1976, pp. 134–140.

Casanova's Chinese Restaurant

Bergonzi, Bernard. *Anthony Powell*. London: Longmans, 1971, pp. 15–17.

Bliven, Naomi. "The Marriage State," in *New Yorker*. XXXVI (December 31, 1960), pp. 53–54.

Brennan, Neil. *Anthony Powell*. New York: Twayne, 1974, pp. 168–173.

Hall, James. *The Tragic Comedians: Seven Modern British Novelists*. Bloomington: Indiana University Press, 1963, pp. 144–148.

Kermode, Frank. *Puzzles and Epiphanies: Essays and Reviews, 1958–61*. New York: Chilmark Press, 1962, pp. 127–130.

Morris, Robert K. *Continuance and Change: The Contemporary British Novel Sequence*. Carbondale: Southern Illinois University Press, 1972, pp. 141–143.

————. *The Novels of Anthony Powell*. Pittsburgh: University of Pittsburgh Press, 1968, pp. 181–199.

Pritchett, V.S. "The Bored Barbarians," in *New Statesman*. LIX (June 25, 1960), pp. 947–948.

Russell, John. *Anthony Powell: A Quintet, Sextet, and War*. Bloomington: Indiana University Press, 1970, pp. 151–163.

Tucker, James. *The Novels of Anthony Powell*. New York: Macmillan, 1976, pp. 151–156.

A Dance to the Music of Time

Allen, Walter. *The Modern Novel in Britain and the United States.* New York: Dutton, 1964, pp. 221–223.

Brennan, Neil. *Anthony Powell.* New York: Twayne, 1974, pp. 126–203.

Flory, Evelyn A. "The Imagery of Anthony Powell's *A Dance to the Music of Time,*" in *Ball State University Forum.* XVII (1976), pp. 51–59.

Gutierrez, Donald. "The Discrimination of Elegance: Anthony Powell's *A Dance to the Music of Time,*" in *Malahat Review.* XXXIV (1975), pp. 126–141.

————. "Power in *A Dance to the Music of Time,*" in *Connecticut Review.* VI (1973), pp. 50–60.

Hall, James. "The Uses of Polite Surprise: Anthony Powell," in *Essays in Criticism.* XII (April, 1962), pp. 167–183.

Herring, Anthony D. "Anthony Powell: A Reaction Against Determinism," in *Ball State University Forum.* IX (Winter, 1968), pp. 17–21.

Jones, Richard. "Anthony Powell's *Music*: Swansong of the Metropolitan Romance," in *Virginia Quarterly Review.* LII (1976), pp. 353–369.

Karl, Frederick R. *The Contemporary English Novel.* New York: Farrar, Straus and Giroux, 1962, pp. 238–244.

McCall, Raymond G. "Anthony Powell's Gallery," in *College English.* XXVII (December, 1965), pp. 227–232.

Mizener, Arthur. "*A Dance to the Music of Time*: The Novels of Anthony Powell," in *Kenyon Review.* XXII (Winter, 1960), pp. 79–92.

————. *The Sense of Life in the Modern Novel.* Boston: Houghton Mifflin, 1964, pp. 89–103.

Morris, Robert K. *The Novels of Anthony Powell.* Pittsburgh: University of Pittsburgh Press, 1968, pp. 1–10, 103–112, 247–252.

Pritchett, V.S. *The Working Novelist.* London: Chatto and Windus, 1965, pp. 172–180.

Quesenbery, W.D., Jr. "Anthony Powell: The Anatomy of Decay," in *Critique: Studies in Modern Fiction.* VII (Spring, 1964), pp. 5–26.

Radner, Sanford. "The World of Anthony Powell," in *Claremont Quarterly.* X (Winter, 1963), pp. 41–47.

Ruoff, Gene W. "Social Mobility and the Artist in *Manhattan Transfer* and *The Music of Time,*" in *Wisconsin Studies in Contemporary Literature.* V (Winter–Spring, 1964), pp. 64–76.

Shapiro, Charles. *Contemporary British Novelists.* Carbondale: Southern Illinois University Press, 1965, pp. 81–94.

Vinson, James. "Anthony Powell's *Music of Time,*" in *Perspective.* X (Summer–Autumn, 1958), pp. 146–152.

Voorhees, Richard J. *"The Music of Time*: Themes and Variation," in *Dalhousie Review.* XLII (Autumn, 1962), pp. 213–221.

Walcutt, Charles C. *Man's Changing Mask: Modes and Methods of Characterization in Fiction.* Minneapolis: University of Minnesota Press, 1966, pp. 336–339.

Zegerell, James J. "Anthony Powell's *Music of Time*: Chronicle of a Declining Establishment," in *Twentieth Century Literature.* XII (October, 1966), pp. 138–146.

From a View to a Death

Bergonzi, Bernard. *Anthony Powell.* London: Longmans, 1971, pp. 8–9.

Brennan, Neil. *Anthony Powell.* New York: Twayne, 1974, pp. 104–114.

Davenport, Guy. "Frightfully Good, I'm Sure," in *National Review.* XX (April 9, 1968), p. 350.

Morris, Robert K. *The Novels of Anthony Powell.* Pittsburgh: University of Pittsburgh Press, 1968, pp. 49–68.

Pritchett, V.S. *The Working Novelist.* London: Chatto and Windus, 1965, pp. 173–175.

Russell, John. *Anthony Powell: A Quintet, Sextet, and War.* Bloomington: Indiana University Press, 1970, pp. 59–63.

————. "Quintet from the Thirties: Anthony Powell," in *Kenyon Review.* XXVII (Autumn, 1965), pp. 698–726.

Tucker, James. *The Novels of Anthony Powell.* New York: Macmillan, 1976, pp. 27–33.

Wolfe, Peter. "Eccentric in a Closed Circle," in *Saturday Review.* LI (February 3, 1968), p. 34.

The Kindly Ones

Bergonzi, Bernard. *Anthony Powell.* London: Longmans, 1971, pp. 15–17.

Brennan, Neil. *Anthony Powell.* New York: Twayne, 1974, pp. 173–178.

Hartley, L.P. "Good Dog, Good Dog," in *Time and Tide.* XLIII (June 28, 1962), pp. 21–22.

Karl, Frederick R. "Bearers of War and Disaster," in *New Republic.* CXLVII (September 24, 1962), pp. 21–22.

McDowell, Frederick P.W. " 'The Devious Involutions of Human Characters and Emotions,' " in *Wisconsin Studies in Contemporary Literature.* IV (Autumn, 1963), pp. 362–365.

Morris, Robert K. *Continuance and Change: The Contemporary British Novel Sequence.* Carbondale: Southern Illinois University Press, 1972, pp. 143–147.

————. *The Novels of Anthony Powell.* Pittsburgh: University of Pittsburgh Press, 1968, pp. 200–217.

Symons, Julian. *Critical Occasions.* London: Hamish Hamilton, 1966, pp. 74–79.

Tucker, James. *The Novels of Anthony Powell.* New York: Macmillan, 1976, pp. 157–162.

The Military Philosophers

Beichman, Arnold. *"The Military Philosophers,"* in *Commonweal.* XC (May 30, 1969), pp. 326–327.

Bergonzi, Bernard. *Anthony Powell.* London: Longmans, 1971, pp. 17–24.

Braine, John. "The River Flows," in *National Review.* XXI (May 6, 1969), pp. 443–444.

Brennan, Neil. *Anthony Powell.* New York: Twayne, 1974, pp. 187–191.

Hicks, Granville. "Literary Horizons," in *Saturday Review.* LII (March 8, 1969), p. 28.

Karl, Frederick R. *A Reader's Guide to the Contemporary English Novel.* New York: Farrar, Straus and Giroux, 1972, pp. 315–322.

Maddocks, Melvin. "A Different Drummer," in *Atlantic.* CCXXIII (March, 1969), pp. 141–143.

Morris, Robert K. *Continuance and Change: The Contemporary British Novel Sequence.* Carbondale: Southern Illinois University Press, 1972, pp. 152–154.

Tucker, James. *The Novels of Anthony Powell.* New York: Macmillan, 1976, pp. 174–178.

A Question of Upbringing

Bergonzi, Bernard. *Anthony Powell.* London: Longmans, 1971, pp. 12–15.

Brennan, Neil. *Anthony Powell.* New York: Twayne, 1974, pp. 134–146.

Hall, James. *The Tragic Comedians: Seven Modern British Novelists.* Bloomington: Indiana University Press, 1963, pp. 134–135.

————. "The Uses of Polite Surprise: Anthony Powell," in *Essays in Criticism.* XII (April, 1962), pp. 167–183.

Karl, Frederick R. *A Reader's Guide to the Contemporary English Novel.* New York: Farrar, Straus and Giroux, 1972, pp. 315–322.

Morris, Robert K. *Continuance and Change: The Contemporary British Novel Sequence.* Carbondale: Southern Illinois University Press, 1972, pp. 127–129, 135–137.

————. *The Novels of Anthony Powell.* Pittsburgh: University of Pittsburgh Press, 1968, pp. 103–112.

Russell, John. *Anthony Powell: A Quintet, Sextet, and War.* Bloomington: Indiana University Press, 1970, pp. 112–119.

Swados, Harvey. "Anthony Powell," in *New Republic.* CXXV (August 20, 1951), p. 21.

Tucker, James. *The Novels of Anthony Powell.* New York: Macmillan, 1976, pp. 129–134.

The Soldier's Art

Bergonzi, Bernard. *Anthony Powell.* London: Longmans, 1971, pp. 17–24.

Brennan, Neil. *Anthony Powell.* New York: Twayne, 1974, pp. 182–187.

Grandsen, K.W. "Taste of the Old Time," in *Encounter.* XXVII (December, 1966), pp. 106–108.

Gravner, Lawrence. "The Virtues of Verbosity," in *New Republic.* CLVI (April 22, 1967), pp. 22–25.

Hicks, Granville. "Detour from the Darkening Path," in *Saturday Review.* L (March 18, 1967), pp. 23–24.

Jacobsen, Josephine. "*The Soldier's Art*," in *Commonweal.* LXXXVI (May 12, 1967), pp. 239–240.

Karl, Frederick R. *A Reader's Guide to the Contemporary English Novel.* New York: Farrar, Straus and Giroux, 1972, pp. 315–322.

Morris, Robert K. *Continuance and Change: The Contemporary British Novel Sequence.* Carbondale: Southern Illinois University Press, 1972, pp. 149–152.

————. "Dancing in Cadence," in *Nation.* CCIV (May 29, 1967), p. 697.

————. *The Novels of Anthony Powell.* Pittsburgh: University of Pittsburgh Press, 1968, pp. 231–246.

Russell, John. *Anthony Powell: A Quintet, Sextet, and War.* Bloomington: Indiana University Press, 1970, pp. 184–191.

Tucker, James. *The Novels of Anthony Powell.* New York: Macmillan, 1976, pp. 169–173.

Temporary Kings

Brennan, Neil. *Anthony Powell.* New York: Twayne, 1974, pp. 198–203.

De Feo, Ronald. "Dancing in the Dark," in *National Review.* XXV (December 7, 1973), pp. 1367–1368.

Morris, Robert K. "Penultimate Pavane in Venice," in *Nation.* CCXVII (December 10, 1973), pp. 632–633.

Russell, John. "More Music of Time," in *New Republic.* CLXIX (October 27, 1973), p. 30.

Starr, Roger. "The Eleventh Movement," in *Saturday Review/World*. I (November 20, 1973), pp. 18–21.

Tucker, James. *The Novels of Anthony Powell*. New York: Macmillan, 1976, pp. 183–187.

The Valley of Bones

Bergonzi, Bernard. *Anthony Powell*. London: Longmans, 1971, pp. 17–24.

Brennan, Neil. *Anthony Powell*. New York: Twayne, 1974, pp. 178–182.

Morris, Robert K. *Continuance and Change: The Contemporary British Novel Sequence*. Carbondale: Southern Illinois University Press, 1972, pp. 147–149.

————. *The Novels of Anthony Powell*. Pittsburgh: University of Pittsburgh Press, 1968, pp. 218–230.

Radner, Sanford. "Anthony Powell and *The Valley of Bones*," in *English Record*. XV (April, 1965), pp. 8–9.

Russell, John. *Anthony Powell: A Quintet, Sextet, and War*. Bloomington: Indiana University Press, 1970, pp. 184–203.

Tucker, James. *The Novels of Anthony Powell*. New York: Macmillan, 1976, pp. 163–168.

Venusberg

Barrett, William. "Knights and Knaves," in *Atlantic*. CCXV (May, 1965), pp. 151–152.

Brennan, Neil. *Anthony Powell*. New York: Twayne, 1974, pp. 100–104.

Moore, Harry T. "Death in a Droshky," in *Saturday Review*. XLVIII (May 15, 1965), pp. 53–54.

Morris, Robert K. *The Novels of Anthony Powell*. Pittsburgh: University of Pittsburgh Press, 1968, pp. 32–48.

Rolo, Charles J. "England Made Them," in *Atlantic*. CXCI (February, 1953), p. 82.

Russell, John. *Anthony Powell: A Quintet, Sextet, and War*. Bloomington: Indiana University Press, 1970, pp. 59–63.

————. "Quintet from the Thirties: Anthony Powell," in *Kenyon Review*. XXVII (Autumn, 1968), pp. 698–726.

Tucker, James. *The Novels of Anthony Powell*. New York: Macmillan, 1976, pp. 19–26.

West, Anthony. "Wry Humor," in *New Yorker*. XXVIII (December 13, 1952), pp. 150–158.

What's Become of Waring?

Barrett, William. "English Opposites," in *Atlantic.* CCXI (June, 1963), pp. 130–131.

Bergonzi, Bernard. *Anthony Powell.* London: Longmans, 1971, pp. 9–10.

Brennan, Neil. *Anthony Powell.* New York: Twayne, 1974, pp. 50–52, 120–123, 147–148.

McLaughlin, Richard. "Anthony Powell's Microscopic Lens," in *Commonweal.* LXXIX (September 27, 1963), pp. 20–22.

Morris, Robert K. *The Novels of Anthony Powell.* Pittsburgh: University of Pittsburgh Press, 1968, pp. 85–100.

Russell, John. *Anthony Powell: A Quintet, Sextet, and War.* Bloomington: Indiana University Press, 1970, pp. 67–71.

_____. "Quintet from the Thirties: Anthony Powell," in *Kenyon Review.* XXVII (Autumn, 1965), pp. 698–726.

Shapiro, Charles K. "Death of a Traveller," in *Saturday Review.* XLVI (April 27, 1963), p. 36.

Tucker, James. *The Novels of Anthony Powell.* New York: Macmillan, 1976, p. 37.

J.B. PRIESTLEY
(1894–   )

Angel Pavement

Brown, Ivor.   *J.B. Priestley*. New York: Longmans, Green, 1957, pp. 18–19.

Cooper, Susan.   *J.B. Priestley: Portrait of an Author*. New York: Harper & Row, 1970.

Hughes, David.   *J.B. Priestley*. London: R. Hart-Davis, 1958, pp. 104–112.

Orwell, G.   "Review of *Angel Pavement* by J.B. Priestley," in *The Collected Journalism and Letters of George Orwell*, Volume I. New York: Harcourt, 1968, pp. 25–27.

West, Alick.   *Mountain in the Sunlight*. London: Lawrence and Wishart, 1958, pp. 159–168.

The Good Companions

Brown, Ivor.   *J.B. Priestley*. New York: Longmans, Green, 1957, pp. 15–18.

Cooper, Susan.   *J.B. Priestley: Portrait of an Author*. New York: Harper & Row, 1970.

Evans, Gareth Lloyd.   "*Good Companions*," in *Theatre Arts*. XV (December, 1931), pp. 982–983.

————.   *J.B. Priestley—the Dramatist*. London: Heinemann, 1964, p. 20.

Sadleir, M.   "Long Novels," in *Essays of the Year, 1929–1930*. London: Argonaut, 1930–1931, pp. 229–251.

An Inspector Calls

Cooper, Susan.   *J.B. Priestley: Portrait of an Author*. New York: Harper & Row, 1970.

Evans, Gareth Lloyd.   *J.B. Priestley—the Dramatist*. London: Heinemann, 1964, pp. 206–209.

Hobson, Harold.   *Theatre*. London: Longmans, Green, 1948, pp. 18–20.

McCarthy, Mary T.   "Four Well Made Plays," in *Sights and Spectacles, 1937–1956*. New York: Farrar, Straus, 1956, pp. 121–130.

Nathan, George Jean.   "*An Inspector Calls*," in *Theatre Book of the Year, 1947–1948*. New York: Knopf, 1948–1949, pp. 113–115.

Linden Tree

Brown, Ivor.   *J.B. Priestley*. New York: Longmans, Green, 1957, p. 26.

Cooper, Susan.   *J.B. Priestley: Portrait of an Author*. New York: Harper & Row, 1970.

Evans, Gareth Lloyd. *J.B. Priestley—the Dramatist.* London: Heinemann, 1964, pp. 20, 209.

Greenwood, Ormerod. *The Playwright.* London: Pitman, 1950, pp. 204–207.

Lumley, Frederick. *New Trends in Twentieth Century Drama.* London: Barrie and Rockliff, 1960, p. 298.

Nathan, George Jean. "*Linden Tree,*" in *Theatre Book of the Year, 1947–1948.* New York: Knopf, 1948–1949, pp. 311–314.

PROPERTIUS
(c.50 B.C.–c.15 B.C.)

The Elegies

Barsby, J.A. "The Composition and Publication of the First Three Books of Propertius," in *Greece and Rome*. XXI (October, 1974), pp. 128–137.

Commager, S. *A Prolegomenon to Propertius*. Norman: University of Oklahoma Press, 1974.

Copley, F.O. "The Elegists: Tibullus, Propertius, and Ovid," in *Latin Literature from the Beginnings to the Close of the Second Century A.D.* Ann Arbor: University of Michigan Press, 1969, pp. 241–275.

Fontenrose, J. *Propertius and the Roman Career*. Berkeley: University of California Press, 1949.

Grant, Michael. "Love Lyric and Love Elegy: Catullus and Propertius," in *Roman Literature*. Baltimore: Penguin, 1964, pp. 147–162.

Griffin, J. "Propertius and Antony," in *Journal of Roman Studies*. LXVII (1977), pp. 17–26.

Hadas, Moses. "Tibullus and Propertius," in *History of Latin Literature*. New York: Columbia University Press, 1952, pp. 184–200.

Hubbard, Margaret. *Propertius*. New York: Scribner's, 1975.

Marcellino, R. "Propertius and Horace," in *Classical Journal*. L (April, 1955), pp. 34–35.

Mendell, C.W. "Propertius," in *Latin Poetry; The New Poets and the Augustans*. New Haven, Conn.: Yale University Press, 1965, pp. 194–211.

Messing, G.M. "Pound's Propertius: The Homage and the Damage," in *Poetry and Poetics from Ancient Greece to the Renaissance*. Edited by G.M. Kirkwood. Ithaca, N.Y.: Cornell University Press, 1975, pp. 105–133.

Platnauer, Maurice. *Latin Elegiae Verse; a Study of the Metrical Usages of Tibullus, Propertius and Ovid*. Hamden, Conn.: Archon, 1971.

Potts, A.F. "The Form of Elegy: Anagnorisis," in *The Elegiae Mode; Poetic Form in Wordsworth and Other Elegists*. Ithaca, N.Y.: Cornell University Press, 1967, pp. 36–66.

Ross, David O. "Propertius: From Ardoris Poeta to Romanus Collimachua," in *Backgrounds to Augustas Poetry: Gallus, Elegy and Rome*. New York: Cambridge University Press, 1975, pp. 107–130.

Shackleton, Bailey D.R. *Propertiana*. London: Cambridge University Press, 1956.

Skutsch, O. "Readings in Propertius," in *Classical Quarterly*. XXIII (1973), pp. 316–323.

_____. "The Second Book of Propertius," in *Harvard Studies in Classical Philology*. LXXIX (1976), pp. 229–233.

Solmsen, F.   "Propertius and Horace," in *Classical Philology*. XLIII (April, 1948), pp. 105–109.

Sullivan, John Patrick.   *Propertius: A Critical Introduction*. New York: Cambridge University Press, 1976.

_____. "Propertius: A Preliminary Essay," in *Arion*. V (Spring, 1966), pp. 5–22.

Thibault, J.C.   "A Difference of Metaphor Between Propertius and Ovid," in *Classical Studies Presented to Ben Edwin Perry*. Champaign-Urbana: University of Illinois Press, 1969, pp. 31–37.

Townsend, G.   "Propertius Among the Poets," in *Greece and Rome*. VIII (March, 1961), pp. 36–49.

Wilkinson, L.P.   *Golden Latin Artistry*. Cambridge: Cambridge University Press, 1963.

Yardley, J.C.   "Comic Influences in Propertius," in *Phoenix*. XXVI (1972), pp. 134–139.

_____. "Roman Elegists, Sick, and the Soteria," in *Classical Quarterly*. XXVII (1977), pp. 394–401.

MARCEL PROUST
(1871–1922)

The Captive

Barker, Richard H. *Marcel Proust: A Biography*. New York: Criterion Books, 1958, pp. 302–308.

Bell, William Stewart. *Proust's Nocturnal Muse*. New York: Columbia University Press, 1962, pp. 175–185.

Fowlie, Wallace. *A Reading of Proust*. Garden City, N.Y.: Doubleday, 1964, pp. 179–208.

Green, F.C. *The Mind of Proust*. Cambridge: Cambridge University Press, 1949, pp. 273–352.

Hewitt, James Robert. *Marcel Proust*. New York: Frederick Ungar, 1975, pp. 44–46.

Hindus, Milton. *A Reader's Guide to Marcel Proust*. New York: Noonday, 1962, pp. 125–145.

Leon, Derrick. *Introduction to Proust: His Life, His Circle and His Work*. London: Routledge and Kegan Paul, 1951, pp. 169–170.

March, Harold. *The Two Worlds of Marcel Proust*. Philadelphia: University of Pennsylvania Press, 1948, pp. 132–136, 146–149.

Mein, Margaret. *Proust's Challenge to Time*. Manchester, England: Manchester University Press, 1962, pp. 101–102, 107–109.

Miller, Milton L. *Nostalgia: A Psychoanalytic Study of Marcel Proust*. Boston: Houghton Mifflin, 1956, pp. 65–82.

Cities of the Plain

Barker, Richard H. *Marcel Proust: A Biography*. New York: Criterion Books, 1958, pp. 295–302, 327–333, 341–349.

Bell, William Stewart. *Proust's Nocturnal Muse*. New York: Columbia University Press, 1962, pp. 166–169.

Fowlie, Wallace. *A Reading of Proust*. Garden City, N.Y.: Doubleday, 1964, pp. 147–178.

Green, F.C. *The Mind of Proust*. Cambridge: Cambridge University Press, 1949, pp. 184–272.

Hewitt, James Robert. *Marcel Proust*. New York: Frederick Ungar, 1975, pp. 22–23, 49–50.

Hindus, Milton. *A Reader's Guide to Marcel Proust*. New York: Noonday, 1962, pp. 107–124.

Leon, Derrick. *Introduction to Proust: His Life, His Circle and His Work.* London: Routledge and Kegan Paul, 1951, pp. 160–163.

Levin, Harry. *The Gates of Horn: A Study of Five French Realists.* New York: Oxford University Press, 1963, pp. 406–408, 411–413.

March, Harold. *The Two Worlds of Marcel Proust.* Philadelphia: University of Pennsylvania Press, 1948, pp. 130–133, 143–147.

Miller, Milton L. *Nostalgia: A Psychoanalytic Study of Marcel Proust.* Boston: Houghton Mifflin, 1956, pp. 55–64.

The Guermantes Way

Barker, Richard H. *Marcel Proust: A Biography.* New York: Criterion Books, 1958, pp. 289–295, 321–326, 331–333.

Bell, William Stewart. *Proust's Nocturnal Muse.* New York: Columbia University Press, 1962, pp. 142–143, 162–167.

Buck, Philo M. *Directions in Contemporary Literature.* New York: Oxford University Press, 1942, pp. 115–116.

Fowlie, Wallace. *A Reading of Proust.* Garden City, N.Y.: Doubleday, 1964, pp. 114–196.

Green, F.C. *The Mind of Proust.* Cambridge: Cambridge University Press, 1949, pp. 115–183.

Hewitt, James Robert. *Marcel Proust.* New York: Frederick Ungar, 1975, pp. 17–22.

Hindus, Milton. *A Reader's Guide to Marcel Proust.* New York: Noonday, 1962, pp. 83–106.

Leon, Derrick. *Introduction to Proust: His Life, His Circle and His Work.* London: Routledge and Kegan Paul, 1951, pp. 156–157.

Levin, Harry. *The Gates of Horn: A Study of Five French Realists.* New York: Oxford University Press, 1963, pp. 403–408.

March, Harold. *The Two Worlds of Marcel Proust.* Philadelphia: University of Pennsylvania Press, 1948, pp. 146–148.

Miller, Milton L. *Nostalgia: A Psychoanalytic Study of Marcel Proust.* Boston: Houghton Mifflin, 1956, pp. 45–54.

Jean Santeuil

Alderman, Sidney S. "Young Proust's Search for Lost Time," in *South Atlantic Quarterly.* LVII (Winter, 1958), pp. 42–49.

Barker, Richard H. *Marcel Proust: A Biography.* New York: Criterion Books, 1958, pp. 93–103.

Bell, William Stewart. "The Prototype for Proust's Jean Santeuil," in *Modern Language Notes.* LXXIII (January, 1958), pp. 46–50.

————. *Proust's Nocturnal Muse.* New York: Columbia University Press, 1962, pp. 31–39.

Brée, Germaine. "*Jean Santeuil*: An Appraisal," in *L'Esprit Créateur.* V (Spring, 1965), pp. 14–25.

Cattaui, Georges. *Marcel Proust.* New York: Funk & Wagnalls, 1967, pp. 24–41.

Cocking, J.M. "Marcel Proust," in *Three Studies in Modern French Literature.* Edited by Erich Heller. New Haven, Conn.: Yale University Press, 1956, pp. 18–79, 88–127.

Cook, Gladys E. "Marcel Proust: From Analysis to Creation," in *Bucknell Review.* VIII (November, 1958), pp. 17–37.

Duthie, E.L. "The Family Circle in Proust's *Jean Santeuil*," in *Contemporary Review.* CLXXXIV (October, 1953), pp. 224–228.

Edel, Leon. *The Modern Psychological Novel.* New York: Grosset and Dunlap, 1955, pp. 109–112.

Finn, Michael R. "*Jean Santeuil* and *A la recherche du temps perdu*: Instinct and Intellect," in *Forum for Modern Language Studies.* XI (1975), pp. 122–132.

Girard, René. "Introduction," in *Proust: A Collection of Critical Essays.* Edited by René Girard. Englewood Cliffs, N.J.: Prentice-Hall, 1962, pp. 8–10.

Hindus, Milton. *The Proustian Vision.* New York: Columbia University Press, 1954, pp. 29–32.

————. *A Reader's Guide to Marcel Proust.* New York: Noonday, 1962, pp. 196–220.

Hodson, W.L. "Proust's Methods of Character Presentation in *Les plaisirs et les jours* and *Jean Santeuil*," in *Modern Language Review.* LVII (January, 1962), pp. 44–46.

Jackson, Elizabeth R. "The Genesis of the Involuntary Memory in Proust's Early Works," in *PMLA.* LXXVI (December, 1961), pp. 588–591.

Mein, Margaret. *Proust's Challenge to Time.* Manchester, England: Manchester University Press, 1962, pp. 66–69.

Miller, Milton L. *Nostalgia: A Psychoanalytic Study of Marcel Proust.* Boston: Houghton Mifflin, 1956, pp. 272–286.

O'Brien, Justin. "The Wisdom of the Young Proust," in *Romanic Review.* XLV (April, 1954), pp. 121–124.

Paul, David. "Time and the Novelist," in *Partisan Review.* XXI (November–December, 1954), pp. 645–656.

Stambolian, George. *Marcel Proust and the Creative Encounter.* Chicago: University of Chicago Press, 1972, pp. 235–240.

Strauss, Walter A. "Criticism and Creation," in *Proust: A Collection of Critical Essays.* Edited by René Girard. Englewood Cliffs, N.J.: Prentice-Hall, 1962, pp. 57–58.

Turnell, Martin. *The Art of French Fiction.* Norfolk, Conn.: New Directions, 1959, pp. 363–367.

The Past Recaptured

Barker, Richard H. *Marcel Proust: A Biography.* New York: Criterion Books, 1958, pp. 308–315.

Bell, William Stewart. *Proust's Nocturnal Muse.* New York: Columbia University Press, 1962, pp. 79–84.

Beynon, Susan E. "Life, Time and Art in Proust's *Le temps retrouve*," in *Nottingham French Studies.* XIV (1975), pp. 86–93.

Brée, Germaine and Margaret Guiton. *An Age of Fiction: The French Novel from Gide to Camus.* New Brunswick, N.J.: Rutgers University Press, 1957, pp. 42–49.

Buck, Philo M. *Directions in Contemporary Literature.* New York: Oxford University Press, 1942, pp. 116–122.

Cocking, J.M. "The Coherence of *Le temps retrouve*," in *Marcel Proust: A Critical Panorama.* Edited by Larkin B. Price. Urbana: University of Illinois Press, 1973, pp. 82–101.

————. "Marcel Proust," in *Three Studies in Modern French Literature.* Edited by Erich Heller. New Haven, Conn.: Yale University Press, 1956, pp. 44–79, 88–127.

Edel, Leon. *The Modern Psychological Novel.* New York: Grosset and Dunlap, 1955, pp. 114–115.

Fowlie, Wallace. *A Reading of Proust.* Garden City, N.Y.: Doubleday, 1964, pp. 238–270.

Green, F.C. *The Mind of Proust.* Cambridge: Cambridge University Press, 1949, pp. 442–546.

Hindus, Milton. *A Reader's Guide to Marcel Proust.* New York: Noonday, 1962, pp. 161–180.

Leon, Derrick. *Introduction to Proust: His Life, His Circle and His Work.* London: Routledge and Kegan Paul, 1951, pp. 295–298.

Levin, Harry. *The Gates of Horn: A Study of Five French Realists.* New York: Oxford University Press, 1963, pp. 431–437.

March, Harold. *The Two Worlds of Marcel Proust.* Philadelphia: University of Pennsylvania Press, 1948, pp. 147–148.

Mein, Margaret. *Proust's Challenge to Time.* Manchester, England: Manchester University Press, 1962, pp. 23–27, 31–32, 56–62.

O'Brien, Justin. "Fall and Redemption in Proust," in *Modern Language Notes.* LXXIX (May, 1964), pp. 281–283.

Rhodes, S.A. "The 'Guermantes Fete' in *Le temps retrouve*," in *Philological Quarterly.* XVII (April, 1938), pp. 144–148.

Sayce, R.A. "The Goncourt Pastiche in *Le temps retrouve*," in *Marcel Proust: A Critical Panorama.* Edited by Larkin B. Price. Urbana: University of Illinois Press, 1973, pp. 102–123.

Remembrance of Things Past

Bell, William Stewart. *Proust's Nocturnal Muse.* New York: Columbia University Press, 1962, pp. 52–185.

Black, Carl John, Jr. "Albertine as an Allegorical Figure of Time," in *Romanic Review.* LIV (October, 1963), pp. 171–186.

Brady, Patrick. *Marcel Proust.* Boston: Twayne, 1977, pp. 15–126.

Bussom, Thomas W. "Marcel Proust and Painting," in *Romanic Review.* XXXIV (February, 1943), pp. 54–70.

Clark, Charles N. "Love and Time: The Erotic Imagery of Marcel Proust," in *Yale French Studies.* XI (1959), pp. 80–90.

Cocking, J.M. "Marcel Proust," in *Three Studies in Modern French Literature.* Edited by Erich Heller. New Haven, Conn.: Yale University Press, 1956, pp. 18–79, 88–127.

Cook, Albert. *The Meaning of Fiction.* Detroit: Wayne State University Press, 1960, pp. 282–297.

Cordle, Thomas H. "The Role of Dreams in *A la recherche du temps perdu*," in *Romanic Review.* XLII (December, 1951), pp. 261–273.

Crosman, Inge K. "Metaphoric Function in *A la recherche du temps perdu*," in *Romanic Review.* LXVII (1976), pp. 290–299.

Hogan, John Arthur. "The Past Recaptured: Marcel Proust's Aesthetic Theory," in *Ethics.* XLIX (January, 1939), pp. 187–203.

Houston, J.P. "Temporal Patterns in *A la recherche du temps perdu*," in *French Studies.* XVI (January, 1962), pp. 33–44.

Jackson, Elizabeth R. "The Crystallization of *A la recherche du temps perdu*," in *French Review.* XXXVIII (December, 1964), pp. 157–166.

Johnson, Pamela Hansford. "Marcel Proust: Illusion and Reality," in *Essays by Divers Hands.* XXXII (1963), pp. 58–71.

Krutch, Joseph Wood. *Five Masters.* New York: Jonathan Cape and Harrison Smith, 1930, pp. 284–328.

Ladimer, Bethany. "The Narrator as Voyeur in *A la recherche du temps perdu*," in *Critical Quarterly.* XIX (Autumn, 1977), pp. 5–19.

Levin, Harry. *The Gates of Horn: A Study of Five French Realists.* New York: Oxford University Press, 1963, pp. 391–444.

Linn, John Gaywood. "Notes on Proust's Manipulation of Chronology," in *Romanic Review.* LII (October, 1961), pp. 210–225.

Lynes, Carlos, Jr. "Proust and Albertine: On the Limits of Autobiography and of Psychological Truth in the Novel," in *Journal of Aesthetics and Art Criticism.* X (June, 1952), pp. 328–337.

Morrow, John H. "The Comic Element in *A la recherche du temps perdu*," in *French Review.* XXVII (December, 1953), pp. 114–121.

Riva, Raymond T. "Death and Immortality in the Works of Marcel Proust," in *French Review.* XXXV (April, 1962), pp. 463–471.

Rogers, Brian G. "Narrative Tones and Perspectives in Proust's Novel," in *Modern Language Review.* LX (April, 1965), pp. 207–211.

Slochower, Harry. "Marcel Proust: Revolt Against the Tyranny of Time," in *Sewanee Review.* LI (1943), pp. 370–381.

Spagnoli, John J. "The Social Attitude of Marcel Proust," in *Marcel Proust: Reviews and Estimates.* Edited by Gladys Dudley Lindner. Stanford, Calif.: Stanford University Press, 1942, pp. 213–227.

Turnell, Martin. *The Novel in France.* New York: New Directions, 1951, pp. 336–393.

Swann's Way

Adelson, Dorothy. "Proust's Earlier and Later Styles: A Textual Comparison," in *Romanic Review.* XXXIV (April, 1943), pp. 127–138.

Barker, Richard H. *Marcel Proust: A Biography.* New York: Criterion Books, 1958, pp. 202–225.

Bell, William Stewart. *Proust's Nocturnal Muse.* New York: Columbia University Press, 1962, pp. 153–160.

Bennett, Arnold. "The Last Word," in *Marcel Proust: Reviews and Estimates.* Edited by Gladys Dudley Lindner. Stanford, Calif.: Stanford University Press, 1942, pp. 49–51.

Brée, Germaine and Margaret Guiton. *An Age of Fiction: The French Novel from Gide to Camus.* New Brunswick, N.J.: Rutgers University Press, 1957, pp. 49–53.

Buck, Philo M. *Directions in Contemporary Literature.* New York: Oxford University Press, 1942, pp. 114–115.

Cocking, J.M. *Proust.* New Haven, Conn.: Yale University Press, 1956, pp. 52–55.

Cook, Gladys E. "Marcel Proust: From Analysis to Creation," in *Bucknell Review.* VIII (November, 1958), pp. 17–37.

Edel, Leon. *The Modern Psychological Novel.* New York: Grosset and Dunlap, 1955, pp. 105–109, 116–117.

Fowlie, Wallace. *A Reading of Proust.* Garden City, N.Y.: Doubleday, 1964, pp. 51–82.

Galantiére, Lewis. "Introduction to *Swann's Way,*" in *Marcel Proust: Reviews and Estimates.* Edited by Gladys Dudley Lindner. Stanford, Calif.: Stanford University Press, 1942, pp. 112–114.

Green, F.C. *The Mind of Proust.* Cambridge: Cambridge University Press, 1949, pp. 6–60.

Hatzfeld, Helmut. *Trends and Styles in Twentieth Century French Literature.* Washington, D.C.: Catholic University of America Press, 1957, pp. 68–69.

Hewitt, James Robert. *Marcel Proust.* New York: Frederick Ungar, 1975, pp. 8–13, 29–30, 32–41.

Hindus, Milton. *A Reader's Guide to Marcel Proust.* New York: Noonday, 1962, pp. 16–62.

Jones, Louise. "Swann and the 'tubles tournantes,' " in *French Review.* XLVIII (1975), pp. 711–721.

Kolb, Philip. "An Enigmatic Proustian Metaphor," in *Romanic Review.* LIV (October, 1963), pp. 187–197.

Leon, Derrick. *Introduction to Proust: His Life, His Circle and His Work.* London: Routledge and Kegan Paul, 1951, pp. 136–138, 149–150.

March, Harold. *The Two Worlds of Marcel Proust.* Philadelphia: University of Pennsylvania Press, 1948, pp. 106–112, 135–142, 150–154.

Meyers, Jeffrey. "Proust's Aesthetic Analogies: Character and Painting in *Swann's Way,*" in *Journal of Aesthetics and Art Criticism.* XXX (1972), pp. 377–388.

Miller, Milton L. *Nostalgia: A Psychoanalytic Study of Marcel Proust.* Boston: Houghton Mifflin, 1956, pp. 24–31.

Murry, John Middleton. *Discoveries: Essays in Literary Criticism.* London: Collins, 1924, pp. 108–118.

————. "Proust and the Modern Consciousness," in *Marcel Proust: Reviews and Estimates.* Edited by Gladys Dudley Lindner. Stanford, Calif.: Stanford University Press, 1942, pp. 35–38.

Turner, W.J. "The Little Phrase," in *Marcel Proust: Reviews and Estimates.* Edited by Gladys Dudley Lindner. Stanford, Calif.: Stanford University Press, 1942, pp. 40–41.

The Sweet Cheat Gone

Barker, Richard H. *Marcel Proust: A Biography.* New York: Criterion Books, 1958, pp. 305–307.

Fowlie, Wallace. *A Reading of Proust.* Garden City, N.Y.: Doubleday, 1964, pp. 209–237.

Green, F.C. *The Mind of Proust.* Cambridge: Cambridge University Press, 1949, pp. 353–441.

Hatzfeld, Helmut. *Trends and Styles in Twentieth Century French Literature.* Washington, D.C.: Catholic University of America Press, 1957, pp. 73–74.

Hewitt, James Robert. *Marcel Proust.* New York: Frederick Ungar, 1975, pp. 46–48.

Hindus, Milton. *A Reader's Guide to Marcel Proust.* New York: Noonday, 1962, pp. 146–160.

Leon, Derrick. *Introduction to Proust: His Life, His Circle and His Work.* London: Routledge and Kegan Paul, 1951, pp. 196–210, 271–279, 300–301.

McMahon, Joseph H. "From Things to Themes," in *Yale French Studies.* XXXIV (June, 1965), pp. 5–17.

March, Harold. *The Two Worlds of Marcel Proust.* Philadelphia: University of Pennsylvania Press, 1948, pp. 116–122.

Miller, Milton L. *Nostalgia: A Psychoanalytic Study of Marcel Proust.* Boston: Houghton Mifflin, 1956, pp. 83–96.

Within a Budding Grove

Barker, Richard H. *Marcel Proust: A Biography.* New York: Criterion Books, 1958, pp. 266–288.

Bell, William Stewart. *Proust's Nocturnal Muse.* New York: Columbia University Press, 1962, pp. 54–55, 160–162.

Bersani, Leo. *Marcel Proust: The Fictions of Life and of Art.* New York: Oxford University Press, 1965, pp. 105–111.

Brody, Patrick. *Marcel Proust.* Boston: Twayne, 1977, pp. 35–37.

Fowlie, Wallace. *A Reading of Proust.* Garden City, N.Y.: Doubleday, 1964, pp. 83–113.

Green, F.C. *The Mind of Proust.* Cambridge: Cambridge University Press, 1949, pp. 61–114.

Hatzfeld, Helmut. *Trends and Styles in Twentieth Century French Literature.* Washington, D.C.: Catholic University of America Press, 1957, pp. 69–70.

Hewitt, James Robert. *Marcel Proust.* New York: Frederick Ungar, 1975, pp. 12–17.

Hindus, Milton. *A Reader's Guide to Marcel Proust.* New York: Noonday, 1962, pp. 63–82.

Leon, Derrick. *Introduction to Proust: His Life, His Circle and His Work.* London: Routledge and Kegan Paul, 1951, pp. 163–164.

Linn, John Gaywood. *The Theater in the Fiction of Marcel Proust.* Columbus: Ohio State University Press, 1966, pp. 142–144.

March, Harold. *The Two Worlds of Marcel Proust.* Philadelphia: University of Pennsylvania Press, 1948, pp. 141–143.

Miller, Milton L. *Nostalgia: A Psychoanalytic Study of Marcel Proust.* Boston: Houghton Mifflin, 1956, pp. 32–44.

ALEXANDER PUSHKIN
(1799–1837)

Boris Godunov

Bayley, John. *Pushkin: A Comparative Commentary*. Cambridge: Cambridge University Press, 1971, pp. 165–185.

Blustain, J. "*Boris Godunov*—For the Descendants of the Orthodox," in *Russian Review*. XXVII (1968), pp. 177–194.

Brasol, Boris. "Excerpt from Boris Brasol's *The Mighty Three*," in *Pushkin: The Man and the Artist*. Edited by Martha Warren Beckwith, Peter Malevsky-Malevitch and others. New York: Paisley Press, 1937, pp. 128–148.

Brody, Ervin C. "Pushkin's *Boris Godunov*: The First Modern Russian Historical Drama," in *Modern Language Review*. LXXII (October, 1977), pp. 857–875.

Cizevskij, Dmitrij. *History of Nineteenth-Century Russian Literature*. Volume I. Nashville, Tenn.: Vanderbilt University Press, 1974, pp. 56–58.

Fennel, John. "Pushkin," in *Nineteenth-Century Russian Literature: Studies of Ten Russian Writers*. Edited by John Fennel. Berkeley: University of California Press, 1973, pp. 56–67.

Lavrin, Janko. *Pushkin and Russian Literature*. London: Hodder & Stoughton, 1947, pp. 148–160.

Louria, Yvette. "The Divided Self in *Boris Godunov*," in *Language Quarterly*. XII (1974), pp. 23–28.

Magarshack, David. *Pushkin: A Biography*. New York: Grove, 1967, pp. 192–194.

Mirsky, D.S. *Pushkin*. New York: Dutton, 1926, pp. 153–162.

Nikolaneff, A.M. "*Boris Godunov* and the Oughlich Tragedy," in *Russian Review*. IX (1950), pp. 275–285.

Pushkin, Alexander. "On *Boris Godunov*," in *Pushkin on Literature*. By Tatiana Wolff. London: Methuen, 1971, pp. 220–224.

Steiner, George. *The Death of Tragedy*. New York: Knopf, 1961, pp. 159–161.

Striedter, Jurij. "Poetic Genre and the Sense of History in Pushkin," in *New Literary History*. VIII (Winter, 1977), pp. 295–300.

Troyat, Henri. *Pushkin*. Garden City, N.Y.: Doubleday, 1970, pp. 278–288.

Vickery, Walter N. *Alexander Pushkin*. New York: Twayne, 1970, pp. 58–70.

Vinokur, G.O. "Pushkin as a Playwright," in *Russian Views of Pushkin*. Edited by D.J. Richards and C.R.S. Cockrell. Oxford: Willem A. Meeuws, 1976, pp. 199–201.

Wolff, Tatiana. *Pushkin on Literature.* London: Methuen, 1971, pp. 105–109.

————. "Shakespeare's Influence on Pushkin's Dramatic Work," in *Shakespeare Survey.* V (1952), pp. 93–105.

The Bronze Horseman: A Petersburg Tale

Bayley, John. *Pushkin: A Comparative Commentary.* Cambridge: Cambridge University Press, 1971.

Brasol, Boris. "Excerpt from Boris Brasol's *The Mighty Three*," in *Pushkin: The Man and the Artist.* Edited by Martha Warren Beckwith, Peter Malevsky-Malevitch and others. New York: Paisley Press, 1937, pp. 148–154.

Call, Paul. "Pushkin's *Bronze Horseman*: A Poem of Motion," in *Slavic and East European Journal.* XI (1967), pp. 137–144.

Fennel, John. "Pushkin," in *Nineteenth-Century Russian Literature: Studies of Ten Russian Writers.* Edited by John Fennel. Berkeley: University of California Press, 1973, pp. 27–36.

Lavrin, Janko. *Pushkin and Russian Literature.* London: Hodder & Stoughton, 1947, pp. 110–114.

Lednicki, Waclaw. *Pushkin's* Bronze Horseman: *The Story of a Masterpiece.* Berkeley: University of California Press, 1955.

Magarshack, David. *Pushkin: A Biography.* New York: Grove, 1967, pp. 195–196, 268–269.

Mirsky, D.S. *Pushkin.* New York: Dutton, 1926, pp. 209–212.

Striedter, Jurij. "Poetic Genre and the Sense of History in Pushkin," in *New Literary History.* VIII (Winter, 1977), pp. 300–303.

Troyat, Henri. *Pushkin.* Garden City, N.Y.: Doubleday, 1970, pp. 462–467.

Vickery, Walter N. *Alexander Pushkin.* New York: Twayne, 1970, pp. 145–152.

The Captain's Daughter

Andersen, Roger B. "A Study of Petr Grinev as the Hero of Pushkin's *Kapitanskaja docka*," in *Canadian Slavic Studies.* V (1971), pp. 477–486.

Greene, Militsa. "Pushkin and Sir Walter Scott," in *Forum for Modern Language Studies.* I (July, 1965), pp. 212–215.

Lavrin, Janko. *Pushkin and Russian Literature.* London: Hodder & Stoughton, 1947, pp. 189–193.

Mikkelson, Gerald E. "The Mythopoetic Element in Pushkin's Historical Novel *The Captain's Daughter*," in *Canadian-American Slavic Studies.* VII (1973), pp. 296–313.

Mirsky, D.S. *Pushkin.* New York: Dutton, 1926, pp. 186–187.

Patrick, George Z. "Pushkin's Prose Writings," in *Centennial Essays for Pushkin*. Edited by Samuel H. Gross and Ernest J. Simmons. Cambridge, Mass.: Harvard University Press, 1937, pp. 122–124.

Stenbock-Fermor, Elisabeth. "Some Neglected Features of the Epigraphs in *The Captain's Daughter* and Other Stories of Pushkin," in *International Journal of Slavic Linguistics and Poetics*. VIII (1964), pp. 110–123.

Stepanov, N.L. "Paths of the Novel," in *Russian Views of Pushkin*. Edited by D.J. Richards and C.R.S. Cockrell. Oxford: Willem A. Meeuws, 1976, pp. 225–234.

Striedter, Jurij. "Poetic Genre and the Sense of History in Pushkin," in *New Literary History*. VIII (Winter, 1977), pp. 303–307.

Troyat, Henri. *Pushkin*. Garden City, N.Y.: Doubleday, 1970, pp. 510–515.

Vickery, Walter N. *Alexander Pushkin*. New York: Twayne, 1970, pp. 158–159.

Wolff, Tatiana. *Pushkin on Literature*. London: Methuen, 1971, pp. 200–203.

Eugene Onegin

Bayley, John. *Pushkin: A Comparative Commentary*. Cambridge: Cambridge University Press, 1971, pp. 236–305.

Brasol, Boris. "Excerpt from Boris Brasol's *The Mighty Three*," in *Pushkin: The Man and the Artist*. Edited by Martha Warren Beckwith, Peter Malevsky-Malevitch and others. New York: Paisley Press, 1937, pp. 172–186.

Cizevskij, Dmitrij. *History of Nineteenth-Century Russian Literature*. Volume I. Nashville, Tenn.: Vanderbilt University Press, 1974, pp. 58–63.

Clayton, J. Douglas. "Emblematic and Iconographic Patterns in Pushkin's *Eugene Onegin*: A Shakespearian Ghost?," in *Germano-Slavica*. VI (1975), pp. 53–66.

————. "The Epitaph of *Eugene Onegin*: A Hypothesis," in *Canadian Slavic Studies*. V (1971), pp. 226–233.

Dostoevsky, F.M. "Pushkin" in *Russian Views of Pushkin*. Edited by D.J. Richards and C.R.S. Cockrell. Oxford: Willem A. Meeuws, 1976, pp. 77–82.

Eidelman, Nathan. "*Evgeni Onegin*: The Puzzle of the Tenth Chapter," in *Soviet Literature*. X (1975), pp. 29–33.

Fennel, John. "Pushkin," in *Nineteenth-Century Russian Literature: Studies of Ten Russian Writers*. Berkeley: University of California Press, 1973, pp. 36–55.

Gustafson, Richard E. "The Metaphor of the Seasons in *Evgenij Onegin*," in *Slavic and East European Journal*. VI (1962), pp. 6–20.

Hoisington, Sona Stephan. "*Eugene Onegin*: An Inverted Byronic Poem," in *Comparative Literature*. XXVII (1975), pp. 136–152.

————. "*Eugene Onegin*: Product of or Challenge to *Adolphe*?," in *Comparative Literature Studies*. XIV (September, 1977), pp. 205–213.

Johnson, D. Barton. "Nabokov's *Ada* and Pushkin's *Eugene Onegin*," in *Slavic and East European Journal*. XV (1971), pp. 316–323.

Lavrin, Janko. *Pushkin and Russian Literature*. London: Hodder & Stoughton, 1947, pp. 119–139.

Manson, Joseph P. "Pushkin's *Evgenij Onegin*: A Study in Literary Counterpoint," in *Studies Presented to Professor Roman Jakobson by His Students*. Edited by Charles E. Gribble. Cambridge, Mass.: Slavica, 1968, pp. 201–206.

Matlaw, Ralph E. "The Dream in *Yevgeniy Onegin* With a Note on *Gore ot Uma*," in *Slavonic and East European Review*. XXXVII (1959), pp. 487–503.

Mirsky, D.S. *Pushkin*. New York: Dutton, 1926, pp. 137–152.

Nabokov, Vladimir. "Translator's Introduction," in *Eugene Onegin*. By Aleksandr Pushkin. Volume I. Princeton, N.J.: Princeton University Press, 1964, pp. 3–88.

Noyes, George Rapall. "Pushkin in World Literature," in *Centennial Essays for Pushkin*. Edited by Samuel H. Gross and Ernest J. Simmons. Cambridge, Mass.: Harvard University Press, 1937, pp. 176–179.

Picchio, Riccardo. "Dante and J. Malfilatre as Literary Sources for Tat'jana's Erotic Dream," in *Alexander Pushkin: A Symposium on the 175th Anniversary of His Birth*. Edited by Andrej Kodjak and Kiril Taranovsky. New York: New York University Press, 1976, pp. 42–55.

Pisarev, D.I. "Pushkin and Belinsky," in *Russian Views of Pushkin*. Edited by D.J. Richards and C.R.S. Cockrell. Oxford: Willem A. Meeuws, 1976, pp. 55–60.

Radin, Dorothea Prall. "*Eugene Onegin* Read Today," in *Centennial Essays for Pushkin*. Edited by Samuel H. Gross and Ernest J. Simmons. Cambridge, Mass.: Harvard University Press, 1937, pp. 145–163.

Troyat, Henri. *Pushkin*. Garden City, N.Y.: Doubleday, 1970, pp. 271–278, 400–407.

Vickery, Walter N. *Alexander Pushkin*. New York: Twayne, 1970, pp. 102–129.

Weil, Irwin. "Onegin's Echo," in *Russian Literature Triquarterly*. X (1974), pp. 260–273.

The Queen of Spades

Bayley, John. *Pushkin: A Comparative Commentary*. Cambridge: Cambridge University Press, 1971, pp. 316–322.

Bocharov, S.G. *"The Queen of Spades,"* in *New Literary History.* IX (Winter, 1978), pp. 315–332.

Cizevskij, Dmitrij. *History of Nineteenth-Century Russian Literature.* Volume I. Nashville, Tenn.: Vanderbilt University Press, 1974, pp. 69–70.

Gregg, Richard A. "Balzac and the Women in *The Queen of Spades,"* in *Slavic and East European Journal.* X (1966), pp. 279–282.

Kodjak, Andrej. *"The Queen of Spades* in the Context of the Faust Legend," in *Alexander Pushkin: A Symposium on the 175th Anniversary of His Birth.* Edited by Andrej Kodjak and Kiril Taranovsky. New York: New York University Press, 1976, pp. 87–118.

Mirsky, D.S. *Pushkin.* New York: Dutton, 1926, pp. 183–186.

Rosen, Nathan. "The Magic Cards in *The Queen of Spades,"* in *Slavic and East European Journal.* XIX (1975), pp. 255–275.

Schwartz, Murry M. and Albert Schwartz. *"The Queen of Spades:* A Psychoanalytic Interpretation," in *Texas Studies in Literature and Language.* XVII (1975), pp. 275–288.

Shklovsky, Viktor. "Notes on Pushkin's Prose," in *Russian Views of Pushkin.* Edited by D.J. Richards and C.R.S. Cockrell. Oxford: Willem A. Meeuws, 1976, pp. 187–195.

Stenbock-Fermor, Elisabeth. "Some Neglected Features of the Epigraphs in *The Captain's Daughter* and Other Stories of Pushkin," in *International Journal of Slavic Linguistics and Poetics.* VIII (1964), pp. 119–123.

Troyat, Henri. *Pushkin.* Garden City, N.Y.: Doubleday, 1970, pp. 467–472.

Vickery, Walter N. *Alexander Pushkin.* New York: Twayne, 1970, pp. 156–158.

Ruslan and Lyudmila

Arndt, Walter. "Introduction," in *Ruslan and Liudmila.* By Alexander Pushkin. Ann Arbor, Mich.: Ardis, 1974, pp. ix–xxi.

———. " 'Ruslan i Ljudmila': Notes from Ellis Island," in *Alexander Pushkin: A Symposium on the 175th Anniversary of His Birth.* Edited by Andrej Kodjak and Kiril Taranovsky. New York: New York University Press, 1976, pp. 155–156.

Bayley, John. *Pushkin: A Comparative Commentary.* Cambridge: Cambridge University Press, 1971, pp. 38–56.

Brasol, Boris. "Excerpt from Boris Brasol's *The Mighty Three,"* in *Pushkin: The Man and the Artist.* Edited by Martha Warren Beckwith, Peter Malevsky-Malevitch and others. New York: Paisley Press, 1937, pp. 99–105.

Cizevskij, Dmitrij. *History of Nineteenth-Century Russian Literature.* Volume I. Nashville, Tenn.: Vanderbilt University Press, 1974, pp. 49–50.

Lavrin, Janko. *Pushkin and Russian Literature.* London: Hodder & Stoughton, 1947, pp. 84–86.

Magarshack, David. *Pushkin: A Biography.* New York: Grove, 1967, pp. 87–89.

Mirsky, D.S. *Pushkin.* New York: Dutton, 1926, pp. 37–40.

Slonimsky, A.L. "The Fairy-Tales in Verse," in *Russian Views of Pushkin.* Edited by D.J. Richards and C.R.S. Cockrell. Oxford: Willem A. Meeuws, 1976, pp. 236–237.

Troyat, Henri. *Pushkin.* Garden City, N.Y.: Doubleday, 1970, pp. 138–149.

Vickery, Walter N. *Alexander Pushkin.* New York: Twayne, 1970, pp. 25–32.

THOMAS PYNCHON
(1936–   )

The Crying of Lot 49

Abernethy, Peter L. "Entropy in Pynchon's *The Crying of Lot 49*," in *Critique*. XIV (1972), pp. 18–33.

Davidson, C.N. "Oedipa as Andreoyne in Thomas Pynchon's *The Crying of Lot 49*," in *Contemporary Literature*. XVIII (Winter, 1977), pp. 38–50.

Hausdorff, Don. "Thomas Pynchon's Multiple Absurdities," in *Wisconsin Studies in Contemporary Literature*. VII (Autumn, 1966), pp. 258–269.

Hunt, John W. "Comic Escape and Anti-Vision: the Novels of Joseph Heller and Thomas Pynchon," in *Adversity and Grace*. Edited by Nathan A. Scott. Chicago: University of Chicago Press, 1968, pp. 107–110.

Hyman, Stanley. "The Goddess and the Schlemihl," in *On Contemporary Literature*. Edited by Richard Kostelanetz. New York: Avon Books, 1964, pp. 506–510.

Kazin, Alfred. *Bright Book of Life: American Novelists and Storytellers from Hemingway to Mailer*. Boston: Atlantic—Little, Brown, 1973, pp. 278–279.

Kolodny, A. "Pynchon's *The Crying of Lot 49*: The Novel as Subversive Experience," in *Modern Fiction Studies*. XIX (Spring, 1973), pp. 79–87.

Leland, J.P. "Pynchon's Linguistic Demon: *The Crying of Lot 49*," in *Critique*. XVI (1974), pp. 45–53.

McNamara, Eugene. "The Absurd Style in Contemporary Literature," in *Humanities Association Bulletin*. XIX (1968), pp. 44–49.

May, John R. "Loss of World in Barth, Pynchon, and Vonnegut: The Varieties of Humorous Apocalypse," in *Toward a New Earth: Apocalypse in the American Novel*. Notre Dame, Ind.: University of Notre Dame Press, 1972, pp. 172–200.

Mendelson, E. "The Sacred, the Profane, and *The Crying of Lot 49*," in *Individual and Community*. Edited by Kenneth H. Baldwin. Durham, N.C.: Duke University Press, 1975, pp. 182–222.

Merrill, R. "Form and Meaning of Pynchon's *The Crying of Lot 49*," in *Ariel*. VIII (January, 1977), pp. 53–71.

Sklar, Robert. "The New Novel, U.S.A.: Thomas Pynchon," in *Nation*. CCV (September 25, 1967), pp. 277–280.

Young, James D. "The Enigma Variations of Thomas Pynchon," in *Critique*. X (1968), pp. 69–77.

Vidal, Gore. *Matters of Fact and of Fiction*. New York: Random House, 1977, pp. 121–122.

Gravity's Rainbow

Adams, Robert Martin. *After Joyce: Studies in Fiction After* Ulysses. New York: Oxford University Press, 1977, pp. 175–179.

Friedman, A.J. "Science as Metaphor: Thomas Pynchon and *Gravity's Rainbow*," in *Contemporary Literature.* XV (Summer, 1974), pp. 345–359.

Krafft, J.M. "And How Far-Fallen: Puritan Themes in *Gravity's Rainbow*," in *Critique.* XVIII (1977), pp. 55–73.

Le Clair, Thomas. "*Gravity's Rainbow*," in *Critique.* XVII (1975), pp. 27–28.

Levine, George. "V-2," in *Partisan Review.* XL (Summer, 1973), pp. 517–529.

Lhamon, W.T. "Most Irresponsible Bastard," in *New Republic.* CLXVIII (April 14, 1973), pp. 24–27.

Locke, Richard. "*Gravity's Rainbow*," in *New York Times Book Review.* (March 11, 1973), p. 1.

Maddocks, Melvin. "Paleface Takeover," in *Atlantic Monthly.* CCXXXI (March, 1973), pp. 98–100.

Mendelson, Edward. "Pynchon's Gravity," in *Yale Review.* LXIII (Summer, 1973), pp. 624–631.

Ozier, L.W. "Antipointsman/Antimexico: Some Mathematical Imagery in *Gravity's Rainbow*," in *Critique.* XVI (1974), pp. 73–90.

Poirier, Richard. "Rocket Power," in *Saturday Review.* LVI (March, 1973), pp. 59–64.

Schmitz, Neil. "Describing the Demon: Appeal of Thomas Pynchon," in *Partisan Review.* XLII (1975), pp. 112–125.

Siegel, M.R. "Creative Paranoia: Understanding the System of *Gravity's Rainbow*," in *Critique.* XVIII (1977), pp. 39–54.

Simmon, S. "*Gravity's Rainbow* Described," in *Critique.* XVI (1974), pp. 54–67.

————. "Character Index: *Gravity's Rainbow*," in *Critique.* XVI (1974), pp. 68–72.

Slade, J.W. "Escaping Rationalization: Options of the Self in *Gravity's Rainbow*," in *Critique.* XVIII (1977), pp. 27–38.

Thorburn, David. "A Dissent on Pynchon," in *Commentary.* LVI (September, 1973), pp. 68–70.

Vidal, Gore. *Matters of Fact and of Fiction.* New York: Random House, 1977, pp. 122–124.

Weales, Gerald. "*Gravity's Rainbow*," in *Hudson Review.* XXVI (Winter, 1973–1974), pp. 773–775.

V

Adams, Robert Martin. *After Joyce: Studies in Fiction After* Ulysses. New York: Oxford University Press, 1977, pp. 170–175.

Bergonzi, Bernard. *The Situation of the Novel.* Pittsburgh: University of Pittsburgh Press, 1970, pp. 97–100.

Bryant, Jerry. *The Open Decision.* New York: Free Press, 1970, pp. 252–257.

Golden, Robert E. "Mass Man and Modernism: Violence in Pynchon's *V*," in *Critique.* XIV (1972), pp. 5–17.

Hausdorff, Don. "Thomas Pynchon's Multiple Absurdities," in *Wisconsin Studies in Contemporary Literature.* VII (Autumn, 1966), pp. 258–269.

Hendin, Josephine. "What Is Thomas Pynchon Telling Us?," in *Harper's.* CCXLVIII (March, 1975), pp. 82–92.

Hoffman, Frederick J. "The Questing Comedian: Thomas Pynchon's *V*," in *Critique.* VI (Winter, 1963–1964), pp. 174–177.

Hunt, John W. "Comic Escape and Anti-Vision," in *Adversity and Grace.* Edited by Nathan A. Scott. Chicago: University of Chicago Press, 1968, pp. 98–107.

Hyman, Stanley E. "The Goddess and the Schlemihl," in *Standards: A Chronicle of Books for Our Time.* New York: Horizon, 1966, pp. 138–142.

Kostelanetz, Richard. "The New American Fiction," in *New American Arts.* New York: Horizon, 1965, pp. 214–217.

Lewis, R.W.B. "Days of Wrath and Laughter," in *Trials of the World.* New Haven, Conn.: Yale University Press, 1965, pp. 228–234.

Lhamon, W.T. "Pentecost, Promiscuity and Pynchon's *V*," in *Twentieth Century Literature.* XXI (May, 1975), pp. 163–176.

McNamara, Eugene. "The Absurd Style in Contemporary American Literature," in *Humanities Association Bulletin.* XIX (1968), pp. 44–49.

Olderman, Raymond M. "The Illusion and the Possibility of Conspiracy," in *Beyond the Waste.* New Haven, Conn.: Yale University Press, 1972, pp. 123–149.

Patterson, R. "What Stencil Knew: Structure and Certitude in Pynchon's *V*," in *Critique.* XVI (1974), pp. 30–44.

Poirier, Richard. *The Performing Self: Compositions and Decompositions in the Languages of Contemporary Life.* New York: Oxford University Press, 1971, pp. 23–25.

Richter, David H. "The Failure of Completeness: Pynchon's *V*," in *Fable's End.* Chicago: University of Chicago Press, 1975, pp. 101–135.

Vidal, Gore. *Matters of Fact and of Fiction.* New York: Random House, 1977, pp. 119–121.

Young, James D. "The Enigma Variations of Thomas Pynchon," in *Critique.* X (1968), pp. 69–77.

FRANÇOIS RABELAIS
(c.1495–1553)

Gargantua and Pantagruel

Auerbach, Erich. *Mimesis; The Representation of Reality in Western Literature.* Translated by Willard R. Trask. Princeton, N.J.: Princeton University Press, 1953, pp. 229–249.

Bakhtin, M. *Rabelais and His World.* Translated by Helene Iswolsky. Cambridge, Mass.: M.I.T. Press, 1968.

Bowen, Barbara C. *Age of Bluff: Paradox and Ambiguity in Rabelais and Montaigne.* Urbana: University of Illinos Press, 1972.

Chappell, Arthur F. *The Enigma of Rabelais: An Essay in Interpretation.* Folcroft, Pa.: Folcroft Library Editions, 1973.

Coleman, D.G. *Rabelais: A Critical Study in Prose Fiction.* Cambridge: Cambridge University Press, 1971.

Frame, Donald M. *François Rabelais.* New York: Harcourt Brace Jovanovich, 1977.

Gray, Floyd. "Ambiguity and Point of View in the Prologue to *Gargantua*," in *Romanic Review.* LVI (1965), pp. 12–21.

Greene, Thomas M. *Rabelais: A Study in Comic Courage.* Englewood Cliffs, N.J.: Prentice-Hall, 1970.

Keller, Abraham C. *The Telling of Tales in Rabelais: Aspects of His Narrative Art.* Frankfurt am Main: Klostermann, 1963.

————. "Absurd and Absurdity in Rabelais," in *Kentucky Romance Quarterly.* XIX (1972), pp. 149–157.

Kleis, Charlotte C. "Structural Parallels and Thematic Unity in Rabelais," in *Modern Language Quarterly.* XXXI (1970), pp. 403–423.

Kotin, A. "Pantagruel: Language vs. Communication," in *Modern Language Notes.* LXXXVII (November, 1972), pp. 691–709.

La Charité, Raymond C. "The Unity of Rabelais' *Pantagruel*," in *French Studies.* XXVI (1972), pp. 257–265.

Lewis, Dominic B. *Doctor Rabelais.* Westport, Conn.: Greenwood, 1969.

McFarlane, I.D. *A Literary History of France: Renaissance France 1470–1589.* New York: Barnes & Noble, 1974, pp. 171–189.

Masters, Brian. *A Student's Guide to Rabelais.* London: Heinemann, 1971.

Morrison, I.R. "Ambiguity, Detachment, and Joy in *Gargantua*," in *Modern Language Review.* LXXI (July, 1976), pp. 513–522.

Muir, Edwin. "Panurge and Falstaff," in his *Essays on Literature and Society.* Cambridge, Mass.: Harvard University Press, 1965, pp. 166–181.

Rebhorn, Wayne A. "The Burdens and Joys of Freedom: An Interpretation of the Five Books of Rabelais," in *Études Rabelaisiennes*. IX (1971), pp. 71–90.

Screech, M.A. "Some Stoic Elements in Rabelais's Religious Thought (The Will-Destiny-Active Virtue)," in *Études Rabelaisiennes*. I (1956), pp. 73–87.

————. *The Rabelaisian Marriage*. London: Arnold, 1958.

Screech, M.A. and R. Calder. "Some Renaissance Attitudes to Laughter," in *Humanism in France at the End of the Middle Ages and in the Early Renaissance*. Edited by A.H.T. Levi. New York: Barnes & Noble, 1970, pp. 216–228.

Tilley, Arthur. *François Rabelais*. Port Washington, N.Y.: Kennikat, 1970.

Weinberg, Florence M. *The Wine and the Will: Rabelais's Bacchic Christianity*. Detroit: Wayne State University Press, 1972.

Wortley, W. Victor. "From Pantagruel to Gargantua: The Development of an Action Scene," in *Romance Notes*. X (1968), pp. 129–138.

JEAN BAPTISTE RACINE
(1639–1699)

Alexandre Le Grand

Abraham, Claude. *Jean Racine.* Boston: Twayne, 1977, pp. 41–45.

Adams, Henry H. and Baxter Hathaway, Editors. *Dramatic Essays of the Neo-Classic Age.* New York: Columbia University Press, 1950, pp. 102–110.

Elledge, Scott and Ronald Schier Stephens, Editors. *The Continental Model; Selected French Critical Essays of the 17th Century in English Translation.* Minneapolis: University of Minnesota Press, 1960, pp. 132–139.

Knapp, Bettina L. *Jean Racine; Mythos and Renewal in Modern Theater.* University: University of Alabama Press, 1971, pp. 46–63.

Orgel, Vera. *A New View of the Plays of Racine.* London: Macmillan, 1948, pp. 6–12.

Turnell, Martin. *Jean Racine, Dramatist.* New York: New Directions, 1972, pp. 41–52.

Andromache

Dagley, Cynthia R. "Racine's *Andromaque*; A Study of Source," in *PMLA.* LII (March, 1937), pp. 80–99.

Edwards, Michael. "Racinian Tragedy," in *Critical Quarterly.* XIII (1971), pp. 329–348.

France, Peter. "Oreste and Orestes," in *French Studies.* XXIII (April, 1969), pp. 131–137.

Hall, H. Gaston. "Pastoral, Epic, and Dynastic Denouement in Racine's *Andromaque*," in *Modern Language Review.* LXIX (January, 1974), pp. 64–78.

Han, Pierre. "Racine's Use of the Concept of Myth in *Andromaque*," in *Romance Notes.* XI (1969), pp. 339–343.

Knapp, Bettina. *Jean Racine; Mythos and Renewal in Modern Theater.* University: University of Alabama Press, 1971, pp. 68–84.

Lockert, Lacy. *Studies in French Classical Tragedy.* Nashville, Tenn.: Vanderbilt University Press, 1958, pp. 295–303.

Monaco, Marion. "Racine and the Problem of Suicide," in *PMLA.* LXX (1955), pp. 441–454.

Moravcevich, June. "Racine's *Andromaque* and the Rhetoric of Naming," in *Papers on Language and Literature.* XII (Winter, 1976), pp. 20–35.

Mould, William A. "The Innocent Stratageme of Racine's *Andromaque*," in *French Review.* XLVIII (1975), pp. 557–565.

Schweitzer, Jerome W. "Racine's *Andromaque*; Oreste, Slayer of Pyrrhus," in *Romance Notes*. III (1961), pp. 37–39.

Shaw, David. "The Function of Baroque Elements in *Andromaque*," in *Forum for Modern Language Studies*. XI (1975), pp. 205–212.
pp. 205–212.

Turnell, Martin. *Classical Moment, Studies of Corneille, Moliere and Racine*. London: Hamilton, 1947, pp. 183–187.

————. *Jean Racine, Dramatist*. New York: New Directions, 1972, pp. 53–90.

Vossler, Karl. *Jean Racine*. New York: Frederick Ungar, 1972, pp. 49–54.

Wells, B.W. "Study of Racine's *Andromaque*," in *Sewanee Review*. VI (January, 1898), pp. 51–73.

Wheatley, K.E. "*Andromaque* as the Distrest Mother," in *Romanic Review*. XXXIX (1948), pp. 3–21.

Athalie

Abel, Lionel. *Metatheatre: A New View of Dramatic Form*. New York: Hill and Wang, 1963, pp. 11–38.

Edwards, Michael. "Racinian Tragedy," in *Critical Quarterly*. XIII (1971), pp. 329–348.

Harth, Erica. "The Tragic Moment in *Athalie*," in *Modern Language Quarterly*. XXXIII (1972), pp. 382–395.

Hubert, J.D. "The Timeless Temple in *Athalie*," in *French Studies*. X (1956), pp. 140–153.

Knapp, Bettina. *Jean Racine: Mythos and Renewal in Modern Theater*. University: University of Alabama Press, 1971, pp. 218–239.

Lapp, J.C. "Athaliah's Dream," in *Studies in Philology*. LI (July, 1954), pp. 461–469.

Lockert, Lacy. *Studies in French Classical Tragedy*. Nashville, Tenn.: Vanderbilt University Press, 1958, pp. 404–414.

Orgel, Vera. "What Is Tragic in Racine?," in *Modern Language Review*. XLV (1950), pp. 312–318.

Turnell, Martin. *Classical Moment; Studies of Corneille, Moliere and Racine*. London: Hamilton, 1947, pp. 215–241.

————. *Jean Racine, Dramatist*. New York: New Directions, 1972, pp. 299–334.

Vossler, Karl. *Jean Racine*. New York: Frederick Ungar, 1972, pp. 92–101.

Williams, E.E. "*Athalie*, the Tragic Cycle and the Tragedy of Joas," in *Romanic Review*. XXVIII (February, 1937), pp. 36–45.

Bajazet

Brody, J. *"Bajazet*, or *The Tragedy of Roxane*," in *Romanic Review*. LX (December, 1969), pp. 273–290.

France, Peter. *Racine's Rhetoric*. New York: Oxford University Press, 1965, pp. 104–109.

Knapp, Bettina L. *Jean Racine; Mythos and Renewal in Modern Theater*. University: University of Alabama Press, 1971, pp. 125–136.

Lockert, Lacy. *Studies in French Classical Tragedy*. Nashville, Tenn.: Vanderbilt University Press, 1958, pp. 328–347.

Monaco, Marion. "Racine and the Problem of Suicide," in *PMLA*. LXX (1955), pp. 441–454.

Saunders, H.R. *"Bajazet* Speaks," in *Modern Languages*. XLVI (1965), pp. 51–54.

Turnell, Martin. *Jean Racine, Dramatist*. New York: New Directions, 1972, pp. 153–182.

Vossler, Karl. *Jean Racine*. New York: Frederick Ungar, 1972, pp. 57–61.

Bérénice

Cloonan, William. "Love and Gloire in *Bérénice*: A Freudian Perspective," in *Kentucky Romance Quarterly*. XXII (1975), pp. 517–525.

Dainard, J.A. "The Power of the Spoken Word in *Bérénice*," in *Romanic Review*. LXVII (May, 1976), pp. 157–171.

Evans, William M. "Does Titus Really Love Bérénice?," in *Romance Notes*. XV (1974), pp. 454–458.

Fergusson, Francis. *Idea of a Theatre; A Study of Ten Plays; The Art of Drama in Changing Perspective*. Princeton, N.J.: Princeton University Press, 1949, pp. 42–67.

France, Peter. *Racine's Rhetoric*. New York: Oxford University Press, 1965, pp. 185–196.

Knapp, Bettina L. *Jean Racine; Mythos and Renewal in Modern Theater*. University: University of Alabama Press, 1971, pp. 108–124.

Lockert, Lacy. "Racine's *Bérénice*," in *Romanic Review*. XXX (February, 1939), pp. 26–38.

————. *Studies in French Classical Tragedy*. Nashville, Tenn.: Vanderbilt University Press, 1958, pp. 310–327.

Mueller, Martin. "The Truest Daughter Dido: Racine's *Bérénice*," in *Canadian Review of Comparative Literature*. I (1974), pp. 201–207.

Soares, Sandra. "Time in *Bérénice*," in *Romance Notes*. XV (1973), pp. 104–109.

Turnell, Martin. *Classical Moment; Studies of Corneille, Moliere and Racine.* London: Hamilton, 1947, pp. 188–191.

————. *Jean Racine, Dramatist.* New York: New Directions, 1972, pp. 125–152.

Vossler, Karl. *Jean Racine.* New York: Frederick Ungar, 1972, pp. 61–71.

Whatley, J. "L'Orient Desert: *Bérénice* and Antony and Cleopatra," in *University of Toronto Quarterly.* XLIV (1975), pp. 96–114.

Britannicus

Ault, H.C. "The Tragic Protagonist and the Tragic Subject in *Britannicus*," in *French Studies.* IX (1955), pp. 18–29.

Crain, William L. "An Ambiguity in Racine's *Britannicus*," in *Romance Notes.* XVI (1974), pp. 156–159.

Kahl, Mary C. "Irony in the Tragedies of Racine," in *Harvard Library Bulletin.* XXI (1973), pp. 144–160.

Knapp, Bettina L. *Jean Racine; Mythos and Renewal in Modern Theater.* University: University of Alabama Press, 1971, pp. 85–107.

Pitou, Spire. "The Ghost of Messalina and *Britannicus*," in *Romance Notes.* XIII (1971), pp. 296–300.

Turnell, Martin. *Jean Racine, Dramatist.* New York: New Directions, 1972, pp. 279–298.

Vossler, Karl. *Jean Racine.* New York: Frederick Ungar, 1972, pp. 61–71.

Esther

Abraham, Claude. *Jean Racine.* Boston: Twayne, 1977, pp. 135–143.

Knapp, Bettina L. *Jean Racine; Mythos and Renewal in Modern Theater.* University: University of Alabama Press, 1971, pp. 193–217.

Londre, Felicia H. "The Religious Musicals of Jean Racine," in *Thought.* XLIX (1974), pp. 156–186.

Turnell, Martin. *Jean Racine, Dramatist.* New York: New Directions, 1972, pp. 279–298.

Vossler, Karl. *Jean Racine.* New York: Frederick Ungar, 1972, pp. 85–91.

Iphigénie

Edwards, Michael. "Racinian Tragedy," in *Critical Quarterly.* XIII (1971), pp. 329–348.

France, Peter. *Racine's Rhetoric.* New York: Oxford University Press, 1965, pp. 215–218.

Kahl, Mary C. "Irony in the Tragedies of Racine," in *Harvard Library Bulletin.* XXI (1973), pp. 144–160.

Knapp, Bettina L. *Jean Racine; Mythos and Renewal in Modern Theater.* University: University of Alabama Press, 1971, pp. 151–165.

Lapp, John C. "Time, Space and Symbol in *Iphigénie*," in *PMLA.* LXVI (1951), pp. 1023–1032.

Libby, Diane M. "The Double Oracle in Racine's *Iphigénie*," in *Romance Notes.* XV (1973), pp. 110–117.

Lockert, Lacy. *Studies in French Classical Tragedy.* Nashville, Tenn.: Vanderbilt University Press, 1958, pp. 366–387.

Monaco, Marion. "Racine and the Problem of Suicide," in *PMLA.* LXX (1955), pp. 441–454.

Nurse, Peter H., Editor. *The Art of Criticism: Essays in French Literary Analysis.* Edinburgh: Edinburgh University Press, 1969, pp. 89–99.

Turnell, Martin. *Jean Racine, Dramatist.* New York: New Directions, 1972, pp. 209–238.

Vossler, Karl. *Jean Racine.* New York: Frederick Ungar, 1972, pp. 71–76.

Mithridate

Cloonan, William. "Father and Sons in *Mithridate*," in *French Review.* XLIX (1976), pp. 514–521.

Knapp, Bettina L. *Jean Racine; Mythos and Renewal in Modern Theater.* University: University of Alabama Press, 1971, pp. 137–150.

Lockert, Lacy. *Studies in French Classical Tragedy.* Nashville, Tenn.: Vanderbilt University Press, 1958, pp. 348–365.

Monaco, Marion. "Racine and the Problem of Suicide," in *PMLA.* LXX (1955), pp. 441–454.

Turnell, Martin. *Jean Racine, Dramatist.* London: Hamilton, 1972, pp. 183–205.

Vossler, Karl. *Jean Racine.* New York: Frederick Ungar, 1972, pp. 71–76.

Phèdre

Brooks, Cleanth, Editor. *Tragic Themes in Western Literature.* New Haven, Conn.: Yale University Press, 1955, pp. 77–106.

Crain, William L. "A Problem in Racine's *Phèdre*: Whose Murderous Hand?," in *Romance Notes.* XIV (1973), pp. 528–535.

Edelman, Nathan. "The Central Image in *Phèdre*," in *The Eye of the Beholder; Essays in French Literature.* Edited by Jules Brody. Baltimore: Johns Hopkins University Press, 1974, pp. 130–141.

Edwards, Michael. "Racinian Tragedy," in *Critical Quarterly.* XIII (1971), pp. 329–348.

Fowlie, Wallace. *Love in Literature; Studies in Symbolic Expression.* Freeport, Conn.: Books for Libraries Press, 1972, pp. 51–57.

France, Peter. *Racine's Rhetoric.* New York: Oxford University Press, 1965, pp. 136–140.

Gassner, John. *Dramatic Soundings; Evaluations and Retractions Culled from Thirty Years of Dramatic Criticism.* New York: Crown, 1968, pp. 567–569.

Gilman, Donald. "The River of Death; Motif and Metaphor in Racine's *Phèdre,*" in *Romance Notes.* XIV (1972), pp. 326–330.

Han, Pierre. "A Baroque Marriage; Phèdre's 'Déclaration' and Théramène's Recit," in *South Atlantic Bulletin.* XXXVIII (1974), pp. 83–87.

――――. "The Symbolism of 'Lieu' in Racine's *Phèdre,*" in *South Atlantic Bulletin.* XXXVIII (1973), pp. 21–25.

Hartle, Robert W. "Racine's Hidden Metaphors," in *Modern Language Notes.* LXXVI (1961), pp. 132–139.

Kahl, Mary C. "Irony in the Tragedies of Racine," in *Harvard Library Bulletin.* XXI (1973), pp. 144–160.

Keller, Abraham C. "Death and Passion in Racine's *Phèdre,*" in *Symposium.* XVI (1962), pp. 190–192.

McCollom, William G. "The Downfall of the Tragic Hero," in *College English.* XIX (1957), pp. 51–56.

Monaco, Marion. "Racine and the Problem of Suicide," in *PMLA.* LXX (1955), pp. 441–454.

Pickens, Rupert T. "Hippolyte's Horses; A Study of a Metaphorical Action in Racine's *Phèdre,*" in *Romance Notes.* IX (1968), pp. 266–277.

Pilikian, H.I. "Racine's *Phèdre,*" in *Drama.* CXIX (Winter, 1975), pp. 30–39.

Reiss, Timothy J. "Of Time and Eternity: From *Phèdre* to History," in *Australian Journal of French Studies.* XIII (1976), pp. 225–243.

Reiter, Seymour. *World Theater: The Structure and Meaning of Drama.* New York: Horizon Press, 1973, pp. 50–56.

Rexroth, Kenneth. *The Elastic Retort; Essays in Literature and Ideas.* New York: Seabury Press, 1973, pp. 51–54.

Rogers, J. Hoyt. "The Symmetry of *Phèdre* and the Role of Aricie," in *French Review.* XLV (1972), pp. 65–74.

Turnell, Martin. *Jean Racine, Dramatist.* New York: New Directions, 1972, pp. 239–278.

Tynan, Kenneth. *Curtains; Selections from the Drama Criticism and Related Writings.* New York: Atheneum, 1961, pp. 399–401.

Vossler, Karl. *Jean Racine.* New York: Frederick Ungar, 1972, pp. 76–85.

Yarrow, P.J. "Un Temple Sacré: A Note on Racine's *Phèdre*," in *Modern Language Notes*. LXXII (March, 1957), pp. 194–199.

La Thébaïde

Brody, Jules, "Racine's *Thébaïde*; An Analysis," in *French Studies*. XIII (1959), pp. 199–213.

Hartle, Robert W. "Racine's Hidden Metaphors," in *Modern Language Notes*. LXXVI (1961), pp. 132–139.

Kahl, Mary C. "Irony in the Tragedies of Racine," in *Harvard Library Bulletin*. XXI (1973), pp. 144–160.

Knapp, Bettina L. *Jean Racine; Mythos and Renewal in Modern Theater*. University: University of Alabama Press, 1971, pp. 31–45.

Lapp, John C. "The Oracle in *La Thébaïde*," in *Modern Language Notes*. LXVI (1951), pp. 462–464.

Monaco, Marion. "Racine and the Problem of Suicide," in *PMLA*. LXX (1955), pp. 441–454.

Orgel, Vera. "What Is Tragic in Racine?," in *Modern Language Review*. XLV (1950), pp. 312–318.

Turnell, Martin. *Jean Racine, Dramatist*. New York: New Directions, 1972, pp. 29–40.

Vossler, Karl. *Jean Racine*. New York: Frederick Ungar, 1972, pp. 44–47.

Yarrow, P.J. "A Note on Racine's *Thébaïde*," in *French Studies*. X (1956), pp. 20–31.

MRS. ANN RADCLIFFE
(1764–1823)

The Mysteries of Udolpho

Allen, M.L. "The Black Veil: Three Versions of a Symbol," in *English Studies.* XLVII (1966), pp. 286–289.

Beaty, Frederick L. "Mrs. Radcliffe's Fading Gleam," in *Philological Quarterly.* XLII (January, 1963), pp. 126–129.

Christensen, Merton A. "Udolpho, Horrid Mysteries, and Coleridge's Machinery of the Imagination," in *Wordsworth Circle.* II (1971), pp. 153–159.

Grant, Aline. *Ann Radcliffe.* Denver: Swallow, 1951.

Kiely, Robert. *The Romantic Novel in England.* Cambridge, Mass.: Harvard University Press, 1972, pp. 65–80.

Kooiman-Van Middendorp, Gerarda. *The Hero in the Feminine Novel.* New York: Haskell, 1966, pp. 35–38.

McIntyre, Clara F. *Ann Radcliffe in Relation to Her Time.* New Haven, Conn.: Yale University Press, 1920.

Murray, E.B. *Ann Radcliffe.* New York: Twayne, 1972, pp. 112–134.

Scott, Sir Walter. "Ann Radcliffe," in *Sir Walter Scott on Novelists and Fiction.* Edited by Ioan Williams. New York: Barnes & Noble, 1968.

Shackford, Martha H. "*The Eve of St. Agnes* and *The Mysteries of Udolpho*," in *PMLA.* XXXVI (1921), pp. 104–118.

Smith, Nelson C. "Sense, Sensibility and Ann Radcliffe," in *Studies in English Literature, 1500–1900.* XIII (1973), pp. 577–590.

Swigert, Ford H., Jr. "Ann Radcliffe's Veil Imagery," in *Studies in the Humanities.* I (1969), pp. 55–59.

Sypher, Wylie. "Social Ambiguity in a Gothic Novel," in *Partisan Review.* XII (1945), pp. 50–60.

The Romance of the Forest

Foster, James R. *History of the Pre-Romantic Novel in England.* New York: Modern Language Association, 1949.

Grant, Aline. *Ann Radcliffe.* Denver: Swallow, 1951.

McIntyre, Clara F. *Ann Radcliffe in Relation to Her Time.* New Haven, Conn.: Yale University Press, 1920.

Mayo, Robert D. "Ann Radcliffe and Ducray—Duminil," in *Modern Language Review.* XXXVI (1941), pp. 501–505.

Murray, E.B. *Ann Radcliffe.* New York: Twayne, 1972, pp. 90–111.

Ruff, William. "Ann Radcliffe, or, The Hand of Taste," in *The Age of Johnson: Essays Presented to Chauncey Brewster Tinker*. Edited by Frederick W. Hilles. New Haven, Conn.: Yale University Press, 1949.

Scott, Sir Walter. "Ann Radcliffe," in *Sir Walter Scott on Novelists and Fiction*. Edited by Ioan Williams. New York: Barnes & Noble, 1968.

Summers, Montague. *The Gothic Quest: A History of the Gothic Novel*. London: Fortune, 1938.

Tomkins, J.M.S. *The Popular Novel in England, 1770–1800*. London: Constable, 1932.

AYN RAND
(1905–   )

Atlas Shrugged

Blackman, R.C. *"Atlas Shrugged,"* in *Christian Science Monitor.* (October 10, 1957), p. 11.

Branden, Nathaniel. "Moral Revolution in *Atlas Shrugged,"* in *Who Is Ayn Rand?* New York: Random House, 1962, pp. 3–65.

Bryant, Jerry H. *The Open Decision: The Contemporary American Novel and Its Intellectual Background.* New York: Free Press, 1970, pp. 169–171.

Cain, E. "Ayn Rand as Theorist," in *They'd Rather Be Right.* New York: Macmillan, 1963, pp. 40–42.

Rand, Ayn. *For the New Intellectual.* New York: Random House, 1961, pp. 104–242.

Rolo, Charles. *"Atlas Shrugged,"* in *Atlantic.* CC (November, 1957), p. 249.

The Fountainhead

Aaron, Daniel. "Remarks on a Bestseller," in *Partisan Review.* XIV (July–August, 1947), pp. 442–445.

Branden, Nathaniel. *Who Is Ayn Rand?* New York: Random House, 1962, pp. 78–83, 113–116.

Cain, E. "Ayn Rand as Theorist," in *They'd Rather Be Right.* New York: Macmillan, 1963, pp. 37–40.

Ephron, Nora. "A Strange Kind of Simplicity," in *New York Times Book Review.* LXXIII (May 5, 1968), pp. 8, 42.

Rand, Ayn. *For the New Intellectual.* New York: Random House, 1961, pp. 77–101.

JOHN CROWE RANSOM
(1888–1974)

"Antique Harvesters"

Buffington, Robert. *The Equilibrist: A Study of John Crowe Ransom's Poems, 1916–1963.* Nashville, Tenn.: Vanderbilt University Press, 1967, pp. 93–95, 129–130.

Koch, Vivienne. "The Achievement of John Crowe Ransom," in *Sewanee Review.* LVIII (Spring, 1950), pp. 252–255.

————. "The Poetry of John Crowe Ransom," in *Modern American Poetry.* Edited by B. Rajan. New York: Roy, 1950, pp. 58–61.

Matthiessen, F.O. "Primarily Language," in *Sewanee Review.* LVI (Summer, 1948), pp. 394–395. Reprinted in *The Responsibilities of the Critic.* Edited by John Rackliffe. New York: Oxford University Press, 1952, pp. 43–44.

Parsons, Thornton H. *John Crowe Ransom.* New York: Twayne, 1969, pp. 103–110.

Rubin, Louis D., Jr. "The Concept of Nature in Modern Poetry," in *American Quarterly.* IX (Spring, 1957), pp. 69–70.

Waggoner, Hyatt H. *American Poets from the Puritans to the Present.* Boston: Houghton Mifflin, 1968, pp. 534–535.

"Bells for John Whiteside's Daughter"

Bradford, M.E. "A Modern Elegy: Ransom's 'Bells for John Whiteside's Daughter,' " in *Mississippi Quarterly.* XXI (1968), pp. 43–47.

Buffington, Robert. *The Equilibrist: A Study of John Crowe Ransom's Poems, 1916–1963.* Nashville, Tenn.: Vanderbilt University Press, 1967, pp. 57–58.

Heilman, Robert B. "Poetic and Prosaic: Program Notes on Opposite Numbers," in *Pacific Spectator.* V (Autumn, 1951), pp. 458–460.

Hough, Graham. "John Crowe Ransom: The Poet and the Critic," in *Southern Review.* I (1965), pp. 1–21.

Koch, Vivienne. "The Achievement of John Crowe Ransom," in *John Crowe Ransom: Critical Essays and a Bibliography.* Edited by Thomas Daniel Young. Baton Rouge: Louisiana State University Press, 1968, pp. 122–123.

————. "The Poetry of John Crowe Ransom," in *Modern American Poetry.* Edited by B. Rajan. New York: Roy, 1950, pp. 43–44.

Parsons, Thornton H. *John Crowe Ransom.* New York: Twayne, 1969, pp. 53–55.

Stauffer, Donald A. "Portrait of the Critic Poet as Equilibrist," in *Sewanee Review*. LVI (Summer, 1948), p. 430.

Warren, Robert Penn. "John Crowe Ransom: A Study in Irony," in *Virginia Quarterly Review*. XI (January, 1935), p. 106. Reprinted in *John Crowe Ransom: Critical Essays and a Bibliography*. Edited by Thomas Daniel Young. Baton Rouge: Louisiana State University Press, 1968, pp. 34–35.

————. "Pure and Impure Poetry," in *Kenyon Review*. V (Spring, 1943), pp. 237–240.

"Blue Girls"

Buffington, Robert. *The Equilibrist: A Study of John Crowe Ransom's Poems, 1916–1963*. Nashville, Tenn.: Vanderbilt University Press, 1967, pp. 69–71, 113–114, 133–134.

Ciardi, John. *How Does a Poem Mean?* Boston: Houghton Mifflin, 1959, pp. 802–803.

Koch, Vivienne. "The Achievement of John Crowe Ransom," in *Sewanee Review*. LVIII (Spring, 1950), pp. 250–252.

————. "The Poetry of John Crowe Ransom," in *Modern American Poetry*. Edited by B. Rajan. New York: Roy, 1950, pp. 56–58.

Nemerov, Howard. "Summer's Flare and Winter's Flaw," in *Sewanee Review*. LVI (Summer, 1948), p. 418.

Osborn, Scott C. " 'Blue Girls,' " in *Explicator*. XXI (November, 1962), item 22.

Osborne, William R. " 'Blue Girls,' " in *Explicator*. XIX (May, 1961), item 53.

Parsons, Thornton H. *John Crowe Ransom*. New York: Twayne, 1969, pp. 97–100.

Rubin, Louis D., Jr. "Ransom's Cruel Battle," in *John Crowe Ransom: Critical Essays and a Bibliography*. Edited by Thomas Daniel Young. Baton Rouge: Louisiana State University Press, 1968, pp. 158–159.

Waggoner, Hyatt H. " 'Blue Girls,' " in *Explicator*. XVIII (October, 1959), item 6.

Williams, Miller. *The Poetry of John Crowe Ransom*. New Brunswick, N.J.: Rutgers University Press, 1972, pp. 42–43.

Young, Thomas Daniel. *Gentleman in a Dustcoat: A Biography of John Crowe Ransom*. Baton Rouge: Louisiana State University Press, 1976, pp. 367–369.

"Captain Carpenter"

Brooks, Cleanth. *Modern Poetry and the Tradition*. Chapel Hill: University of North Carolina Press, 1939, pp. 35–37.

Buffington, Robert. *The Equilibrist: A Study of John Crowe Ransom's Poems, 1916–1963.* Nashville, Tenn.: Vanderbilt University Press, 1967, pp. 90–93.

Drew, E.A. *Discovering Modern Poetry.* New York: Holt, Rinehart and Winston, 1961, pp. 81–84.

Hall, Vernon. " 'Captain Carpenter,' " in *Explicator.* XXVI (November, 1967), item 28.

Kelly, Richard. " 'Captain Carpenter,' " in *Explicator.* XXV (March, 1967), item 57.

————. "Captain Carpenter's Inverted Ancestor," in *American Notes and Queries.* VII (1968), pp. 6–7.

Parsons, Thornton H. *John Crowe Ransom.* New York: Twayne, 1969, pp. 125–128.

Riding, Laura and Robert Graves. *A Survey of Modernist Poetry.* New York: Doubleday, Doran, 1928, pp. 103–109.

Stewart, John L. *John Crowe Ransom.* Minneapolis: University of Minnesota Press, 1962, pp. 27–28.

"Dead Boy"

Buffington, Robert. *The Equilibrist: A Study of John Crowe Ransom's Poems, 1916–1963.* Nashville, Tenn.: Vanderbilt University Press, 1967, pp. 62–63, 134–135.

Hough, Graham. "John Crowe Ransom: The Poet and the Critic," in *Southern Review.* I (1965), pp. 1–21.

Knight, Karl F. *The Poetry of John Crowe Ransom.* London: Mouton, 1964, pp. 19–21.

Koch, Vivienne. "The Achievement of John Crowe Ransom," in *Sewanee Review.* LVIII (Spring, 1950), p. 239.

————. "The Poetry of John Crowe Ransom," in *Modern American Poetry.* Edited by B. Rajan. New York: Roy, 1950, p. 46.

Matthiessen, F.O. "Primarily Language," in *Sewanee Review.* LVI (Summer, 1948), pp. 398–400. Reprinted in *The Responsibilities of the Critic.* Edited by John Rackliffe. New York: Oxford University Press, 1952, pp. 47–49.

Parsons, Thornton H. *John Crowe Ransom.* New York: Twayne, 1969, pp. 50–53.

Stageberg, Norman C. and Wallace Anderson. *Poetry as Experience.* New York: American Book, 1952, pp. 26–27.

Wasserman, G.P. "The Irony of John Crowe Ransom," in *University of Kansas City Review.* XXIII (Winter, 1956), pp. 157–158. Reprinted in *John Crowe Ransom: Critical Essays and a Bibliography.* Edited by Thomas Daniel Young. Baton Rouge: Louisiana State University Press, 1968, pp. 152–153.

"The Equilibrists"

Beatty, Richmond C. "John Crowe Ransom as Poet," in *Sewanee Review*. LII (Summer, 1944), pp. 359–360.

Bergonzi, Bernard. "A Poem About the History of Love," in *Critical Quarterly*. IV (Summer, 1962), pp. 127–137.

Buffington, Robert. *The Equilibrist: A Study of John Crowe Ransom's Poems, 1916–1963*. Nashville, Tenn.: Vanderbilt University Press, 1967, pp. 49–51, 123–124, 137–138.

Drew, Elizabeth and John Sweeney. *Directions in Modern Poetry*. New York: Norton, 1940, pp. 208–211.

Knight, Karl F. "Love as Symbol in the Poetry of Ransom," in *John Crowe Ransom: Critical Essays and a Bibliography*. Edited by Thomas Daniel Young. Baton Rouge: Louisiana State University Press, 1968, pp. 184–185.

Nemerov, Howard. "Summer's Flare and Winter's Flaw," in *Sewanee Review*. LVI (Summer, 1948), pp. 419–420.

Parsons, Thornton H. *John Crowe Ransom*. New York: Twayne, 1969, pp. 69–75.

Wasserman, G.P. "The Irony of John Crowe Ransom," in *University of Kansas City Review*. XXIII (Winter, 1956), pp. 158–159. Reprinted in *John Crowe Ransom: Critical Essays and a Bibliography*. Edited by Thomas Daniel Young. Baton Rouge: Louisiana State University Press, 1968, pp. 153–154.

Williams, Miller. *The Poetry of John Crowe Ransom*. New Brunswick, N.J.: Rutgers University Press, 1972, pp. 19–23.

"Here Lies a Lady"

Bleifuss, William. " 'Here Lies a Lady,' " in *Explicator*. XI (May, 1953), item 51.

Bradbury, John M. "Ransom as Poet," in *Accent*. XI (Winter, 1951), pp. 52–54.

Buffington, Robert. *The Equilibrist: A Study of John Crowe Ransom's Poems, 1916–1963*. Nashville, Tenn.: Vanderbilt University Press, 1967, pp. 58–62.

Jarrell, Randall. "John Ransom's Poetry," in *John Crowe Ransom: Critical Essays and a Bibliography*. Edited by Thomas Daniel Young. Baton Rouge: Louisiana State University Press, 1968, pp. 72–74.

Kilby, Clyde S. *Poetry and Life: An Introduction to Poetry*. New York: Odyssey, 1953, pp. 16–17.

Parsons, Thornton H. *John Crowe Ransom*. New York: Twayne, 1969, pp. 45–47.

Stocking, F.H. and Ellsworth Mason. " 'Here Lies a Lady,' " in *Explicator.* VIII (October, 1949), item 1.

Williams, Miller. *The Poetry of John Crowe Ransom.* New Brunswick, N.J.: Rutgers University Press, 1972, pp. 64–65.

"Janet Waking"

Brooks, Cleanth. *Modern Poetry and the Tradition.* Chapel Hill: University of North Carolina Press, 1939, pp. 92–93.

Deutsch, Babette. *Poetry in Our Time.* New York: Holt, 1952, pp. 206–207.

Koch, Vivienne. "The Achievement of John Crowe Ransom," in *Sewanee Review.* LVIII (Spring, 1950), pp. 249–250.

————. "The Poetry of John Crowe Ransom," in *Modern American Poetry.* Edited by B. Rajan. New York: Roy, 1950, pp. 53–56.

O'Connor, William Van. *Sense and Sensibility in Modern Poetry.* Chicago: University of Chicago Press, 1948, pp. 140–141.

Parsons, Thornton H. *John Crowe Ransom.* New York: Twayne, 1969, pp. 44–45.

Rosenthal, M.L. and A.J.M. Smith. *Exploring Poetry.* New York: Macmillan, 1955, pp. 7–8.

Stewart, John L. *John Crowe Ransom.* Minneapolis: University of Minnesota Press, 1962, pp. 26–27.

Wasserman, G.P. "The Irony of John Crowe Ransom," in *University of Kansas City Review.* XXIII (Winter, 1956), pp. 155–156. Reprinted in *John Crowe Ransom: Critical Essays and a Bibliography.* Edited by Thomas Daniel Young. Baton Rouge: Louisiana State University Press, 1968, pp. 149–150.

"Miriam Tazewell"

Buffington, Robert. *The Equilibrist: A Study of John Crowe Ransom's Poems, 1916–1963.* Nashville, Tenn.: Vanderbilt University Press, 1967, p. 68.

Flynn, Robert. " 'Miriam Tazewell,' " in *Explicator.* XII (May, 1954), item 45.

Koch, Vivienne. "The Achievement of John Crowe Ransom," in *Sewanee Review.* LVIII (Spring, 1950), pp. 239–240.

————. "The Poetry of John Crowe Ransom," in *Modern American Poetry.* Edited by B. Rajan. New York: Roy, 1950, pp. 46–47.

Parsons, Thornton H. *John Crowe Ransom.* New York: Twayne, 1969, p. 132.

Wasserman, G.P. "The Irony of John Crowe Ransom," in *University of Kansas City Review.* XXIII (Winter, 1956), pp. 156–157. Reprinted in *John*

Crowe Ransom: Critical Essays and a Bibliography. Edited by Thomas Daniel Young. Baton Rouge: Louisiana State University Press, 1968, pp. 150–152.

Williams, Miller. *The Poetry of John Crowe Ransom*. New Brunswick, N.J.: Rutgers University Press, 1972, pp. 24–25.

The New Criticism

Buffington, Robert. *The Equilibrist: A Study of John Crowe Ransom's Poems, 1916–1963*. Nashville, Tenn.: Vanderbilt University Press, 1967, pp. 10–13, 85–86.

Jarvis, F.P. "F.H. Bradley's *Appearance and Reality* and the Critical Theory of John Crowe Ransom," in *John Crowe Ransom: Critical Essays and a Bibliography*. Edited by Thomas Daniel Young. Baton Rouge: Louisiana State University Press, 1968, pp. 208–209.

Knight, Karl F. *The Poetry of John Crowe Ransom*. London: Mouton, 1964, pp. 40–43.

Stewart, John L. *John Crowe Ransom*. Minneapolis: University of Minnesota Press, 1962, pp. 39–45.

Young, Thomas Daniel. *Gentleman in a Dustcoat: A Biography of John Crowe Ransom*. Baton Rouge: Louisiana State University Press, 1976, pp. 348–360.

————. "Introduction," in *John Crowe Ransom: Critical Essays and a Bibliography*. Edited by Thomas Daniel Young. Baton Rouge: Louisiana State University Press, 1968, pp. 18–19.

"Painted Head"

Beatty, Richmond C. "John Crowe Ransom as Poet," in *Sewanee Review*. LII (Summer, 1944), pp. 365–366.

Bradbury, John M. "Ransom as Poet," in *Accent*. XI (Winter, 1951), pp. 55–56.

Brooks, Cleanth. *Modern Poetry and the Tradition*. Chapel Hill: University of North Carolina Press, 1939, pp. 94–95.

Buffington, Robert. *The Equilibrist: A Study of John Crowe Ransom's Poems, 1916–1963*. Nashville, Tenn.: Vanderbilt University Press, 1967, pp. 124–125.

Hough, Graham. "John Crowe Ransom: The Poet and the Critic," in *John Crowe Ransom: Critical Essays and a Bibliography*. Edited by Thomas Daniel Young. Baton Rouge: Louisiana State University Press, 1968, pp. 199–200.

Koch, Vivienne. "The Poetry of John Crowe Ransom," in *Modern American Poetry*. Edited by B. Rajan. New York: Roy, 1950, pp. 62–64.

McMillan, Samuel H. "John Crowe Ransom's 'Painted Head,' " in *Georgia Review*. XXII (1968), pp. 194–197.

Moorman, Charles. " 'Painted Head,' " in *Explicator*. X (December, 1951), item 15.

Stewart, John L. *John Crowe Ransom*. Minneapolis: University of Minnesota Press, 1962, pp. 31–33.

Wallack, Virginia. " 'Painted Head,' " in *Explicator*. XIV (April, 1956), item 45.

Wasserman, G.P. "The Irony of John Crowe Ransom," in *John Crowe Ransom: Critical Essays and a Bibliography*. Edited by Thomas Daniel Young. Baton Rouge: Louisiana State University Press, 1968, pp. 140–141.

Young, Thomas Daniel. *Gentleman in a Dustcoat: A Biography of John Crowe Ransom*. Baton Rouge: Louisiana State University Press, 1976, pp. 450–451.

The Poetry of Ransom

Beatty, Richmond Croom. "John Crowe Ransom as Poet," in *Sewanee Review*. LII (1944), pp. 344–366.

Brooks, Cleanth. "The Doric Delicacy," in *Sewanee Review*. LVI (1948), pp. 402–415.

Buffington, Robert. *The Equilibrist: A Study of John Crowe Ransom's Poems, 1916–1963*. Nashville, Tenn.: Vanderbilt University Press, 1967.

_____. "Ransom's Poetics: 'Only God, My Dear,' " in *Michigan Quarterly Review*. XII (1973), pp. 353–360.

Gray, Richard. "The 'Compleat Gentleman': An Approach to John Crowe Ransom," in *Southern Review*. XII (1976), pp. 622–631.

Hough, Graham. "John Crowe Ransom: The Poet and the Critic," in *Southern Review*. I (1965), pp. 1–21.

Jarrell, Randall. "John Ransom's Poetry," in *Sewanee Review*. LVI (1948), pp. 378–390.

Knight, Karl F. *The Poetry of John Crowe Ransom*. London: Mouton, 1964.

Koch, Vivienne. "The Achievement of John Crowe Ransom," in *Sewanee Review*. LVIII (1950), pp. 227–261.

Matthiessen, F.O. "Primarily Language," in *Sewanee Review*. LVI (1948), pp. 391–401.

Parsons, Thornton H. *John Crowe Ransom*. New York: Twayne, 1969.

Rubin, Louis D., Jr. "The Wary Fugitive: John Crowe Ransom," in *Southern Review*. LXXXII (1974), pp. 583–618.

Schwartz, Delmore. "Instructed of Much Morality," in *Sewanee Review*. LIV (1946), pp. 439–448.

Stewart, John L.   *John Crowe Ransom*. Minneapolis: University of Minnesota Press, 1962.

Warren, Robert Penn.   "John Crowe Ransom: A Study in Irony," in *Virginia Quarterly Review*. XI (1935), pp. 93–112.

Wasserman, G.R.   "The Irony of John Crowe Ransom," in *University of Kansas City Review*. XXIII (1956), pp. 151–160.

Williams, Miller.   *The Poetry of John Crowe Ransom*. New Brunswick, N.J.: Rutgers University Press, 1972.

"Prelude to an Evening"

Brooks, Cleanth.   "The Doric Delicacy," in *Sewanee Review*. LVI (Summer, 1948), pp. 412–414. Reprinted in *John Crowe Ransom: Critical Essays and a Bibliography*. Edited by Thomas Daniel Young. Baton Rouge: Louisiana State University Press, 1968, pp. 67–68.

Buffington, Robert.   *The Equilibrist: A Study of John Crowe Ransom's Poems, 1916–1963*. Nashville, Tenn.: Vanderbilt University Press, 1967, pp. 106–109, 112–115.

Knight, Karl F.   "Love as Symbol in the Poetry of John Crowe Ransom," in *John Crowe Ransom: Critical Essays and a Bibliography*. Edited by Thomas Daniel Young. Baton Rouge: Louisiana State University Press, 1968, pp. 183–184.

Koch, Vivienne.   "The Poetry of John Crowe Ransom," in *Modern American Poetry*. Edited by B. Rajan. New York: Roy, 1950, pp. 62–64.

Parsons, Thornton H.   *John Crowe Ransom*. New York: Twayne, 1969, pp. 158–162.

————.   "Ransom the Revisionist," in *Southern Review*. II (Spring, 1966), pp. 460–463.

Peck, Virginia L.   " 'Prelude to an Evening,' " in *Explicator*. XX (January, 1962), item 41.

Ransom, John Crowe.   " 'Prelude to an Evening': A Poem Revised and Explicated," in *Kenyon Review*. XXV (Winter, 1963), pp. 70–80.

Schwartz, Delmore.   "Instructed of Much Mortality: A Note on the Poetry of John Crowe Ransom," in *John Crowe Ransom: Critical Essays and a Bibliography*. Edited by Thomas Daniel Young. Baton Rouge: Louisiana State University Press, 1968, pp. 56–57.

"Spectral Lovers"

Beatty, Richmond C.   "John Crowe Ransom as Poet," in *Sewanee Review*. LII (Summer, 1944), pp. 353–354.

Brooks, Cleanth.   "The Doric Delicacy," in *Sewanee Review*. LVI (Summer, 1948), pp. 410–412. Reprinted in *John Crowe Ransom: Critical Essays and a Bibliography*. Edited by Thomas Daniel Young. Baton Rouge: Louisiana State University Press, 1968, pp. 65–66.

Koch, Vivienne. "The Achievement of John Crowe Ransom," in *Sewanee Review*. LVIII (Spring, 1950), pp. 240–243.

————. "The Poetry of John Crowe Ransom," in *Modern American Poetry*. Edited by B. Rajan. New York: Roy, 1950, pp. 47–50.

Parsons, Thornton H. *John Crowe Ransom*. New York: Twayne, 1969, pp. 62–65, 130–134.

Williams, Miller. *The Poetry of John Crowe Ransom*. New Brunswick, N.J.: Rutgers University Press, 1972, pp. 48–50.

CHARLES READE
(1814–1884)

The Cloister and the Hearth

Baker, Ernest. *The History of the English Novel*, Volume VIII. New York: Barnes & Noble, 1950, pp. 206–207.

Burns, Wayne. *Charles Reade: A Study in Victorian Authorship.* New York: Bookman Associates, 1961, pp. 309–321.

Dawson, W.J. "Charles Reade," in his *Makers of English Fiction.* New York: Fleming H. Revell, 1905, pp. 164–178.

Elwin, Malcolm. *Charles Reade.* London: Jonathan Cape, 1931, pp. 150–159.

Fleishman, Avrom. *The English Historical Novel: Walter Scott to Virginia Woolf.* Baltimore: Johns Hopkins University Press, 1971, pp. 152–155.

Hornung, E.W. "Charles Reade," in *London Mercury.* VI (1921), p. 150.

Lord, Walter Frewen. "Charles Reade," in his *The Mirror of the Century.* London: John Lane, 1906, pp. 252–268.

Quiller-Couch, Arthur T. "Charles Reade," in his *Studies in Literature.* Cambridge: Cambridge University Press, 1918, pp. 274–289.

Smith, Elton E. *Charles Reade.* New York: Twayne, 1976, pp. 135–151.

Sutcliffe, Emerson Grant. "Plotting in Reade's Novels," in *PMLA.* XLVII (September, 1932), pp. 834–863.

Swinburne, Algernon Charles. "Charles Reade," in *Miscellanies.* New York: Worthington, 1886, pp. 271–302.

Turner, Albert Morton. *The Making of* The Cloister and the Hearth. Chicago: University of Chicago Press, 1938.

Wagenknecht, Edward C. "The Disciples of Dickens," in his *Cavalcade of the English Novel, from Elizabeth to George VI.* New York: Holt, 1954, pp. 243–251.

Hard Cash

Baker, Ernest. *The History of the English Novel*, Volume VIII. New York: Barnes & Noble, 1950, pp. 207–208.

Burns, Wayne. "*Hard Cash*: 'Uncomparably My Best Production,' " in *Literature and Psychology.* VIII (1958), p. 34.

Elwin, Malcolm. *Charles Reade.* London: Jonathan Cape, 1931, pp. 165–175.

Lord, Walter Frewen. "Charles Reade," in his *The Mirror of the Century.* London: John Lane, 1906, pp. 252–268.

Phillips, Walter C.   *Dickens, Reade, and Collins: Sensation Novelists: A Study in the Conditions and Theories of Novel Writing in Victorian England.* New York: Columbia University Press, 1919, pp. 201–218.

Quiller-Couch, Arthur T.   "Charles Reade," in his *Studies in Literature.* Cambridge: Cambridge University Press, 1918, pp. 274–289.

Smith, Elton E.   *Charles Reade.* New York: Twayne, 1976, pp. 117–123.

Smith, Sheila M.   "Propaganda and Hard Facts in Charles Reade's Didactic Novels: A Study of *It Is Never Too Late to Mend* and *Hard Cash*," in *Renaissance and Modern Studies.* IV (1960), pp. 135–149.

Stang, Richard.   *The Theory of the Novel in England, 1850–1870.* New York: Columbia University Press, 1959, pp. 28–29.

Sutcliffe, Emerson Grant.   "Plotting in Reade's Novels," in *PMLA.* XLVII (September, 1932), pp. 834–863.

Swinburne, Algernon Charles.   "Charles Reade," in his *Miscellanies.* New York: Worthington, 1886, pp. 271–302.

Wagenknecht, Edward C.   "The Disciples of Dickens," in his *Cavalcade of the English Novel, from Elizabeth to George VI.* New York: Holt, 1954, pp. 243–251.

It Is Never Too Late to Mend

Baker, Ernest.   *The History of the English Novel,* Volume VIII. New York: Barnes & Noble, 1950, pp. 204–205.

Burns, Wayne.   *Charles Reade: A Study in Victorian Authorship.* New York: Bookman Associates, 1961, pp. 165–171.

Dawson, W.J.   "Charles Reade," in his *Makers of English Fiction.* New York: Fleming H. Revell, 1905, pp. 164–178.

Eliot, George.   *Essays.* Edited by Thomas Pinney. New York: Columbia University Press, 1963, pp. 325–334.

Elwin, Malcolm.   *Charles Reade.* London: Jonathan Cape, 1931, pp. 111–118, 134–137.

Lord, Walter Frewen.   "Charles Reade," in his *The Mirror of the Century.* London: John Lane, 1906, pp. 252–268.

Orwell, George.   "Charles Reade," in *The Collected Essays, Journalism and Letters of George Orwell,* Volume II. Edited by Sonia Orwell and Ian Angus. New York: Harcourt, Brace and World, 1968, pp. 34–37.

Quiller-Couch, Arthur T.   "Charles Reade," in his *Studies in Literature.* Cambridge: Cambridge University Press, 1918, pp. 274–289.

Smith, Elton E.   *Charles Reade.* New York: Twayne, 1976, pp. 106–114.

Smith, Sheila M.   "Propaganda and Hard Facts in Charles Reade's Didactic Novels: A Study of *It Is Never Too Late to Mend* and *Hard Cash*," in *Renaissance and Modern Studies.* IV (1960), pp. 135–149.

Stang, Richard. *The Theory of the Novel in England, 1850–1870.* New York: Columbia University Press, 1959, pp. 28–29.

Sutcliffe, Emerson Grant. "Plotting in Reade's Novels," in *PMLA.* XLVII (September, 1932), pp. 834–863.

Swinburne, Algernon Charles. "Charles Reade," in his *Miscellanies.* New York: Worthington, 1886, pp. 271–302.

Wagenknecht, Edward C. "The Disciples of Dickens," in his *Cavalcade of the English Novel, from Elizabeth to George VI.* New York: Holt, 1954, pp. 243–251.

Peg Woffington

Baker, Ernest. *The History of the English Novel,* Volume VIII. New York: Barnes & Noble, 1950, p. 204.

Burns, Wayne. *Charles Reade: A Study in Victorian Authorship.* New York: Bookman Associates, 1961, pp. 113–118.

Elwin, Malcolm. *Charles Reade.* London: Jonathan Cape, 1931, pp. 81–86.

Smith, Elton E. *Charles Reade.* New York: Twayne, 1976, pp. 53–57.

Sutcliffe, Emerson Grant. "Plotting in Reade's Novels," in *PMLA.* XLVII (September, 1932), pp. 834–863.

ERICH MARIA REMARQUE
(1897–1970)

All Quiet on the Western Front

Bance, A.F. *"Im Westen nichts Neues: A Bestseller in Context,"* in Modern Language Review. *LXXII (April, 1977), pp. 359–373.*

Bostock, J. Knight. *Some Well-known German War Novels.* Oxford: B.H. Blackwell, 1931, pp. 3–10.

Matthews, T.S. *"All Quiet on the Western Front,"* in *The Critic as Artist: Essays on Books 1920–1970.* Edited by Gilbert A. Harrison. New York: Liveright, 1972, pp. 217–221.

Moore, Harry T. *Twentieth-Century German Literature.* New York: Basic Books, 1967, pp. 81–82.

Moseley, Edwin M. *Pseudonyms of Christ in the Modern Novel.* Pittsburgh: University of Pittsburgh Press, 1962, pp. 89–104.

Pfeiler, William K. *War and the German Mind.* New York: Columbia University Press, 1941, pp. 141–144.

Rowley, Brian A. "Journalism into Fiction: *Im Westen nichts Neues,"* in *The First World War in Fiction: A Collection of Critical Essays.* Edited by Holger Klein. London: Macmillan, 1976, pp. 101–111.

Wolle, Francis. "Novels of Two World Wars," in *Western Humanities Review.* V (Summer, 1951), pp. 285–287.

LADISLAS REYMONT
(1868–1925)

The Peasants

Borowy, Waclaw. "Reymont," in *Slavonic Review.* XVI (1938), pp. 439–448.

Boyd, Ernest. "Wladyslaw Reymont," in *Saturday Review of Literature.* I (November 29, 1924), pp. 317–319.

Hughes, Rupert. "Ladislas Reymont, Winner of the Nobel Prize," in *Literary Digest International Book Review.* III (February, 1925), p. 171.

Krzyzanowski, Jerzy Ryszard. *Wladyslaw Stanislaw Reymont.* New York: Twayne, 1972, pp. 73–93.

Zielinski, Thaddeus. "The Peasant in Polish Literature," in *Slavonic Review.* II (1923–1924), pp. 85–100.

SAMUEL RICHARDSON
(1689–1761)

Clarissa

Baker, Gerard A. "The Complacent Paragon; Exemplary Characterization in Richardson," in *Studies in English Literature, 1500–1900*. IX (Summer, 1969), pp. 503–519.

Brissenden, R.F. *Virtue in Distress: Studies in the Novel of Sentiment from Richardson to Sade*. New York: Barnes & Noble, 1974, pp. 159–186.

Browstein, Rachel M. " 'An Exemplar to Her Sex': Richardson's *Clarissa*," in *Yale Review*. LXVII (Autumn, 1977), pp. 30–47.

Carroll, John. "Lovelace as Tragic Hero," in *University of Toronto Quarterly*. XLII (1972), pp. 14–25.

Cohan, Steven M. "*Clarissa* and the Individuation of Character," in *Journal of English Literary History*. XLIII (1976), pp. 163–183.

Copeland, Edward W. "Allegory and Analogy in *Clarissa*: The 'Plan' and 'No-Plan,' " in *Journal of English Literary History*. XXXIX (1972), pp. 254–265.

Drew, E.A. "Samuel Richardson: *Clarissa*," in *The Novel: A Modern Guide to Fifteen English Masterpieces*. New York: Dell, 1963, pp. 39–58.

Dussinger, John A. "Conscience and the Pattern of Christian Perfection in *Clarissa*," in *PMLA*. LXXXI (1966), pp. 236–245.

Farrell, William J. "The Style and the Action in *Clarissa*," in *Studies in English Literature, 1500–1900*. III (1963), pp. 365–375.

Golden, Morris. *Richardson's Characters*. Ann Arbor: University of Michigan Press, 1963.

Harvey, A.D. "*Clarissa* and the Puritan Tradition," in *Essays in Criticism*. XXVIII (January, 1978), pp. 38–51.

Kaplan, F. "Our Short Story; the Narrative Devices of *Clarissa*," in *Studies in English Literature, 1500–1900*. XI (Summer, 1971), pp. 549–562.

Kinkead-Weekes, Mark. *Samuel Richardson: Dramatic Novelist*. Ithaca, N.Y.: Cornell University Press, 1973, pp. 123–276, 404–411, 433–447.

Konigsberg, Ira. *Samuel Richardson and the Dramatic Novel*. Lexington: University of Kentucky Press, 1968, pp. 28–29, 33–34, 64–65, 74–94.

————. "The Tragedy of *Clarissa*," in *Modern Language Quarterly*. XXVII (1966), pp. 285–298.

McCullough, Bruce. "The Novel of Sentiment; Samuel Richardson: *Clarissa*," in *Representative English Novelists: Defoe to Conrad*. New York: Harper, 1946, pp. 23–41.

Napier, Elizabeth R. " 'Tremble and Reform': The Inversion of Power in Richardson's *Clarissa*," in *Journal of English Literary History*. XLII (1975), pp. 214–223.

Palmer, William J. "Two Dramatists: Lovelace and Richardson in *Clarissa*," in *Studies in the Novel*. V (1973), pp. 7–21.

Park, William. "*Clarissa* as Tragedy," in *Studies in English Literature, 1500–1900*. XVI (1976), pp. 461–471.

Price, Martin. "Clarissa and Lovelace," in *To the Palace of Wisdom*. Garden City, N.Y.: Doubleday, 1964.

Sacks, Sheldon. "*Clarissa* and the Tragic Traditions," in *Studies in Eighteenth-Century Culture: Proceedings of the American Society for Eighteenth-Century Studies*. Volume II. Edited by Harold E. Pagliaro. Cleveland, Oh.: Case Western Reserve University Press, 1972, pp. 195–221.

Schmitz, Robert M. "Death and Colonel Morden in *Clarissa*," in *South Atlantic Quarterly*. LXIX (1970), pp. 346–353.

Sherbo, Arthur. "Time and Place in Richardson's *Clarissa*," in *Boston University Studies in English*. III (1957), pp. 139–146.

Smidt, Kristian. "Character and Plot in the Novels of Samuel Richardson," in *Critical Quarterly*. XVII (1975), pp. 155–166.

Winner, Anthony. "Richardson's Lovelace: Character and Prediction," in *Texas Studies in Literature and Language*. XIV (1972), pp. 53–75.

Pamela

Allentuck, Marcia. "Narration and Illustration: The Problem of Richardson's *Pamela*," in *Philological Quarterly*. LI (1972), pp. 874–886.

Barker, Gerard A. "The Complacent Paragon: Exemplary Characterization in Richardson," in *Studies in English Literature, 1500–1900*. IX (Summer, 1969), pp. 503–519.

Cowler, Rosemary, Editor. *Twentieth Century Interpretations of* Pamela: *A Collection of Critical Essays*. Englewood Cliffs, N.J.: Prentice-Hall, 1969.

Donovan, Robert A. "The Problem of Pamela or, Virtue Unrewarded," in *Studies in English Literature, 1500–1900*. III (1963), pp. 377–395.

Doody, Margaret A. *A Natural Passion: A Study of the Novels of Samuel Richardson*. Oxford: Clarendon Press, 1974, pp. 14–98.

Erickson, Robert A. "Mother Jewkes, Pamela, and the Midwives," in *Journal of English Literary History*. XLIII (1976), pp. 500–516.

Folkenflik, Robert. "A Room of Pamela's Own," in *Journal of English Literary History*. XXXIX (1972), pp. 585–596.

Golden, Morris. *Richardson's Characters*. Ann Arbor: University of Michigan Press, 1963.

Guilhamet, Leon M.   "From *Pamela* to *Grandison*: Richardson's Moral Revolution in the Novel," in *Studies in Change and Revolution: Aspects of English Intellectual History, 1640–1800*. Edited by Paul J. Dorshin. Menston, England: Scholar Press, 1972, pp. 191–210.

Kearney, Anthony M.   "Richardson's *Pamela*: The Aesthetic Case," in *Review of English Literature*. VII (1966), pp. 78–90.

Kinkead-Weekes, Mark.   *Samuel Richardson: Dramatic Novelist*. Ithaca, N.Y.: Cornell University Press, 1973, pp. 7–120.

Konigsberg, Ira.   "The Dramatic Background of Richardson's Plots and Characters," in *PMLA*. LXXXIII (March, 1968), pp. 42–53.

McIntosh, Carey.   "Pamela's Clothes," in *Journal of English Literary History*. XXXV (March, 1968), pp. 75–83.

Morton, Donald E.   "Theme and Structure in *Pamela*," in *Studies in the Novel*. III (1971), pp. 242–257.

Muecke, D.C.   "Beauty and Mr. B.," in *Studies in English Literature*. VII (1967), pp. 467–474.

Needham, Gwendolyn B.   "Richardson's Characterization of Mr. B. and the Double Purpose in *Pamela*," in *Eighteenth-Century Studies*. III (1970), pp. 433–474.

Parker, Dorothy.   "The Time Scheme of *Pamela* and the Character of B.," in *Texas Studies in Language and Literature*. XI (1969), pp. 695–704.

Reid, B.L.   "Justice to *Pamela*," in *The Long Boy and Others*. Athens: University of Georgia Press, 1969, pp. 516–533.

Roussel, Roy.   "Reflections on the Letter: The Reconciliation of Distance and Presence in *Pamela*," in *Journal of English Literary History*. XLI (1974), pp. 375–399.

Sharrock, Roger.   "Richardson's *Pamela*: The Gospel and the Novel," in *Durham University Journal*. LVIII (1966), pp. 67–74.

Smidt, Kristian.   "Character and Plot in the Novels of Samuel Richardson," in *Critical Quarterly*. XVII (1975), pp. 155–166.

Steeves, Harrison R.   *Before Jane Austen: The Shaping of the English Novel in the Eighteenth Century*. New York: Holt, Rinehart and Winston, 1965, pp. 53–87.

Ten Harmsel, Henrietta.   "The Villain-Hero in *Pamela* and *Pride and Prejudice*," in *College English*. XXIII (1961), pp. 104–108.

Wilson, Stuart.   "Richardson's *Pamela*: An Interpretation," in *PMLA*. LXXXVIII (1973), pp. 79–91.

Wolff, Cynthia G.   *Samuel Richardson and the Eighteenth-Century Puritan Character*. Hamden, Conn.: Archon, 1972, pp. 58–73.

Sir Charles Grandison

Ball, Donald. *Samuel Richardson's Theory of Fiction*. The Hague: Mouton, 1971.

Brophy, Elizabeth B. *Samuel Richardson: The Triumph of Craft*. Knoxville: University of Tennessee Press, 1974, pp. 76–90.

Cohen, Richard. "The Social-Christian and Christian-Social Doctrines of Samuel Richardson," in *Hartford Studies in Literature*. IV (1972), pp. 142–145.

Doody, Margaret A. *A Natural Passion: A Study of the Novels of Samuel Richardson*. Oxford: Clarendon Press, 1974, pp. 241–367.

Duncan-Jones, E.E. "The Misses Selby Steele," in *Times Literary Supplement (London)*. (September 10, 1964), p. 845.

Eaves, T.C. Duncan and Ben D. Kimpel. *Samuel Richardson: A Biography*. Oxford: Clarendon Press, 1971, pp. 387–400.

Golden, Morris. *Richardson's Characters*. Ann Arbor: University of Michigan Press, 1963.

Guilhamet, Leon M. "From *Pamela* to *Grandison*: Richardson's Moral Revolution in the Novel," in *Studies in Change and Revolution: Aspects of English Intellectual History, 1640–1800*. Edited by Paul J. Dorshin. Menston, England: Scolar Press, 1972, pp. 194–198.

Kinkead-Weekes, Mark. *Samuel Richardson: Dramatic Novelist*. Ithaca, N.Y.: Cornell University Press, 1973, pp. 279–391, 420–423, 447–451.

Konigsberg, Ira. "The Dramatic Background of Richardson's Plots and Characters," in *PMLA*. LXXXIII (March, 1968), pp. 42–53.

————. *Samuel Richardson and the Dramatic Novel*. Lexington: University of Kentucky Press, 1968, pp. 48, 50–52, 65–69.

Levin, Gerald. "Character and Fantasy in Richardson's *Sir Charles Grandison*," in *Connecticut Review*. VII (1973), pp. 93–99.

McKillop, Alan D. *Critical Remarks on* Sir Charles Grandison, Clarissa, *and* Pamela. Los Angeles: Clark Memorial Library, 1950.

Smidt, Kristian. "Character and Plot in the Novels of Samuel Richardson," in *Critical Quarterly*. XVII (1975), pp. 155–166.

Wolff, Cynthia G. "The Problem of Eighteenth-Century Secular Heroinism," in *Modern Language Studies*. IV (1974), pp. 37–38.

————. *Samuel Richardson and the Eighteenth-Century Puritan Character*. Hamden, Conn.: Archon, 1972, pp. 174–229.

1732

CONRAD RICHTER
(1890–1968)

The Fields

Barnard, Kenneth J. "Presentation of the West in Conrad Richter's Trilogy," in *Northwest Ohio Quarterly*. XXIX (Autumn, 1957), pp. 224–234.

Gaston, Edwin W., Jr. *Conrad Richter*. New York: Twayne, 1965, pp. 103–107.

LaHood, Marvin J. "Richter's Early America," in *University of Kansas City Review*. XXX (Summer, 1964), pp. 311–316.

Leisy, Ernest E. *The American Historical Novel*. Norman: University of Oklahoma Press, 1950, p. 124.

Prescott, Orville. "The Art of Historical Fiction," in *In My Opinion: An Inquiry into the Contemporary Novel*. Indianapolis, Ind.: Bobbs-Merrill, 1952, pp. 137–140.

Purdy, Theodore M. "Life in the Early 1800's," in *Saturday Review of Literature*. XXIX (April 13, 1946), p. 72.

Weeks, Edward. "Those Who Follow the Woods," in *Atlantic*. CLXXVII (June, 1946), p. 156.

The Lady

Barnes, Robert J. *Conrad Richter*. Austin, Tex.: Steck-Vaughn, 1968, pp. 30–36.

Flanagan, John T. "Conrad Richter, Romances of the Southwest," in *Southwest Review*. XLIII (Summer, 1958), pp. 189–196.

Gaston, Edwin W., Jr. *Conrad Richter*. New York: Twayne, 1965, pp. 89–94.

Havighurst, Walter. "*The Lady*," in *Saturday Review*. XL (May 25, 1957), pp. 14–15.

Weeks, Edward. "Family Feud in New Mexico," in *Atlantic*. CC (July, 1957), p. 84.

The Light in the Forest

Arnow, Harriette Simpson. "Code of the Tragic Encounter," in *Saturday Review*. XXXVI (May 16, 1953), pp. 12–13.

Folsom, James K. *The American Western Novel*. New Haven, Conn.: Yale University Press, 1966, pp. 159–162.

Gaston, Edwin W., Jr. *Conrad Richter*. New York: Twayne, 1965, pp. 125–131.

LaHood, Marvin J. *"The Light in the Forest*: History as Fiction," in *English Journal*. LV (March, 1966), pp. 298–304.

Weeks, Edward. "The Captive," in *Atlantic*. CXCII (July, 1953), pp. 80–81.

The Ohio Trilogy

Barnard, Kenneth J. "Presentation of the West in Conrad Richter's Trilogy," in *Northwest Ohio Quarterly*. XXIX (Autumn, 1957), pp. 224–234.

Carpenter, Frederic I. "Conrad Richter's Pioneers: Reality and Myth," in *College English*. XII (November, 1950), pp. 77–84.

Edwards, Clifford D. *Conrad Richter's Ohio Trilogy: Its Ideas, Themes and Relationship to Literary Tradition*. The Hague: Mouton, 1971, pp. 100–125, 151–166, 189–194.

Flanagan, John T. "Conrad Richter, Romancer of the Southwest," in *Southwest Review*. XLIII (Summer, 1958), pp. 189–196.

————. "Folklore in the Novels of Conrad Richter," in *Midwest Folklore*. II (Spring, 1952), pp. 5–14.

Karolides, Nicholas J. *The Pioneer in the American Novel, 1900–1950*. Norman: University of Oklahoma Press, 1967, pp. 205–206.

LaHood, Marvin J. "Richter's Early America," in *University of Kansas City Review*. XXX (Summer, 1964), pp. 311–316.

Prescott, Orville. "The Art of Historical Fiction," in *In My Opinion: An Inquiry into the Contemporary Novel*. Indianapolis, Ind.: Bobbs-Merrill, 1952, pp. 137–140.

Wagenknecht, Edward. *Cavalcade of the American Novel*. New York: Holt, 1952, p. 437.

The Sea of Grass

Barnes, Robert J. *Conrad Richter*. Austin, Tex.: Steck-Vaughn, 1968, pp. 16–25.

Carpenter, Frederic I. "Conrad Richter's Pioneers: Reality and Myth," in *College English*. XII (November, 1950), pp. 77–84.

Edwards, Clifford D. *"The Sea of Grass* and Richter's Tragic Vision," in *Conrad Richter's Ohio Trilogy: Its Ideas, Themes, and Relationship to Literary Tradition*. The Hague: Mouton, 1970, pp. 81–94.

Flanagan, John T. "Conrad Richter, Romancer of the Southwest," in *Southwest Review*. XLIII (Summer, 1958), pp. 189–196.

Folsom, James K. *The American Western Novel*. New Haven, Conn.: Yale University Press, 1966, pp. 94–98.

Gaston, Edwin W., Jr. *Conrad Richter*. New York: Twayne, 1965, pp. 74–84.

Harris, Jim R. "New Mexico History: A Transient Period in Conrad Richter's *The Sea of Grass*," in *Southwestern American Literature*. V (1975), pp. 62–67.

Kohler, Dayton. "Conrad Richter: Early Americana," in *College English*. VIII (February, 1947), pp. 223–224.

Sutherland, Bruce. "Conrad Richter's Americana," in *New Mexico Quarterly Review*. XV (Winter, 1945), pp. 418–419.

Wagenknecht, Edward. *Cavalcade of the American Novel*. New York: Holt, 1952, pp. 436–437.

A Simple Honorable Man

Dempsey, David. "In the Footsteps of the Nazarene," in *Saturday Review*. XLV (April 28, 1962), p. 19.

Edwards, Clifford D. *Conrad Richter's Ohio Trilogy: Its Ideas, Themes, and Relationship to Literary Tradition*. The Hague: Mouton, 1970, pp. 96–98.

Gaston, Edwin W., Jr. *Conrad Richter*. New York: Twayne, 1965, pp. 145–151.

LaHood, Marvin J. "Richter's Pennsylvania Trilogy," in *Susquehanna University Studies*. VIII (June, 1968), pp. 10–13.

Weeks, Edward. "The Preacher and the Naturalist," in *Atlantic*. CCX (August, 1962), p. 140.

Tacey Cromwell

Barnes, Robert J. *Conrad Richter*. Austin, Tex.: Steck-Vaughn, 1968, pp. 25–30.

Flanagan, John T. "Conrad Richter, Romancer of the Southwest," in *Southwest Review*. XLIII (Summer, 1958), pp. 189–196.

Gaston, Edwin W., Jr. *Conrad Richter*. New York: Twayne, 1965, pp. 84–89.

Sutherland, Bruce. "Conrad Richter's Americana," in *New Mexico Quarterly Review*. XV (Winter, 1945), pp. 420–421.

The Town

Arnow, Harriette Simpson. "Pioneer Woman in Americus Mansion," in *Saturday Review of Literature*. XXXIII (April 22, 1950), p. 16.

Barnard, Kenneth J. "Presentation of the West in Conrad Richter's Trilogy," in *Northwest Ohio Quarterly*. XXIX (Autumn, 1957), pp. 224–234.

Gaston, Edwin W., Jr. *Conrad Richter*. New York: Twayne, 1965, pp. 107–116.

LaHood, Marvin J. "Richter's Early America," in *University of Kansas City Review*. XXX (Summer, 1964), pp. 311–316.

Pearce, T.H.   "Conrad Richter," in *New Mexico Quarterly Review.* XX (Autumn, 1950), pp. 371–373.

Prescott, Orville.   "The Art of Historical Fiction," in *In My Opinion: An Inquiry into the Contemporary Novel.* Indianapolis, Ind.: Bobbs-Merrill, 1952, pp. 137–140.

Stuckey, W.J.   *The Pulitzer Prize Novels: A Critical Backward Look.* Norman: University of Oklahoma Press, 1966, pp. 154–157.

The Trees

Barnard, Kenneth J.   "Presentation of the West in Conrad Richter's Trilogy," in *Northwest Ohio Quarterly.* XXIX (Autumn, 1957), pp. 224–234.

Cordell, Richard A.   "Pioneer Family," in *Saturday Review of Literature.* XXI (March 2, 1940), pp. 5–6.

Gaston, Edwin W., Jr.   *Conrad Richter.* New York: Twayne, 1965, pp. 96–103.

Gessin, Max.   "The Forest Primeval," in *New Republic.* CII (March 18, 1940), p. 384.

Kohler, Dayton.   "Conrad Richter: Early Americana," in *College English.* VIII (February, 1947), pp. 224–225.

LaHood, Marvin J.   "Richter's Early America," in *University of Kansas City Review.* XXX (Summer, 1964), pp. 311–316.

Leisy, Ernest E.   *The American Historical Novel.* Norman: University of Oklahoma Press, 1950, p. 124.

Prescott, Orville.   "The Art of Historical Fiction," in *In My Opinion: An Inquiry into the Contemporary Novel.* Indianapolis, Ind.: Bobbs-Merrill, 1952, pp. 137–140.

Sutherland, Bruce.   "Conrad Richter's Americana," in *New Mexico Quarterly Review.* XV (Winter, 1945), pp. 419–420.

Weeks, Edward.   "Those Who Follow the Woods," in *Atlantic.* CLXXVII (June, 1946), p. 156.

ARTHUR RIMBAUD
(1854–1891)

The Drunken Boat

Bonnefoy, Yves. *Rimbaud.* New York: Harper & Row, 1961, pp. 41–43.

Brereton, Geoffrey. *An Introduction to the French Poets: Villon to the Present Day.* London: Methuen, 1973, pp. 190–204.

Cohn, Robert Greer. *The Poetry of Rimbaud.* Princeton, N.J.: Princeton University Press, 1973, pp. 156–172.

Fowlie, Wallace. *Rimbaud.* Chicago: University of Chicago Press, 1965, pp. 21–35, 112–115.

Frohock, W.M. *Rimbaud's Poetic Practice: Image and Theme in the Major Poems.* Cambridge, Mass.: Harvard University Press, 1963, pp. 93–114.

Houston, John Porter. *The Design of Rimbaud's Poetry.* New Haven, Conn.: Yale University Press, 1963, pp. 65–82.

St. Aubyn, Frederic Chase. *Rimbaud.* New York: Twayne, 1975, pp. 63–72.

Sewell, Elizabeth. *The Structure of Poetry.* London: Routledge and Kegan Paul, 1951, pp. 158–176.

Starkie, Enid. *Arthur Rimbaud.* New York: Norton, 1947, pp. 138–147.

Weinberg, Bernard. *"Le Bateau Ivre* or the Limits of Symbolism," in *PMLA.* LXII (March, 1959), pp. 165–193. Reprinted in *The Limits of Symbolism: Studies in Five Modern French Poets.* Chicago: University of Chicago Press, 1966, pp. 89–126.

The Illuminations

Bersani, Leo. "Rimbaud's Simplicity," in *A Future for Astyanax: Character and Desire in Literature.* Boston: Little, Brown, 1976, pp. 230–258.

Bonnefoy, Yves. *Rimbaud.* New York: Harper & Row, 1961, pp. 106–129.

Brereton, Geoffrey. *An Introduction to the French Poets: Villon to the Present Day.* London: Methuen, 1973, pp. 190–204.

Cohn, Robert Greer. *The Poetry of Rimbaud.* Princeton, N.J.: Princeton University Press, 1973, pp. 246–397.

Fowlie, Wallace. *Rimbaud.* Chicago: University of Chicago Press, 1965, pp. 70–81, 83–85, 116–224, 228–258.

Friedrich, Hugo. "Rimbaud," in *The Structure of Modern Poetry: From the Mid-Nineteenth to the Mid-Twentieth Century.* Evanston, Ill.: Northwestern University Press, 1974, pp. 39–67.

Frohock, W.M. *Rimbaud's Poetic Practice: Image and Theme in the Major Poems.* Cambridge, Mass.: Harvard University Press, 1963, pp. 178–200.

Hackett, C.A.   *Rimbaud.* New York: Hillary House, 1957, pp. 48–69.

Hanson, Elisabeth.   *My Poor Arthur: A Biography of Arthur Rimbaud.* New York: Holt, 1960, pp. 152–153, 182–184.

Houston, John Porter.   *The Design of Rimbaud's Poetry.* New Haven, Conn.: Yale University Press, 1962, pp. 201–265.

Hubert, Renée Riese.   "The Use of Reversals in Rimbaud's *Illuminations*," in *L'Esprit Créateur.* IX (Spring, 1969), pp. 9–18.

Israel, Abigail.   "The Aesthetic of Violence: Rimbaud and Genet," in *Yale French Studies.* XLVI (1971), pp. 28–40.

Peschel, Enid Rhodes.   "Rimbaud's Life and Work," in *Arthur Rimbaud:* A Season in Hell, The Illuminations. New York: Oxford University Press, 1973, pp. 29–33.

St. Aubyn, Frederic Chase.   *Arthur Rimbaud.* Boston: Twayne, 1975, pp. 112–173.

Sewell, Elizabeth.   *The Structure of Poetry.* London: Routledge and Kegan Paul, 1951, pp. 113–136.

Staples, Katherine.   "Rimbaud's *Illuminations*: Twenty-Two Translations and a Commentary," in *Denver Quarterly.* XI (Winter, 1977), pp. 49–68.

Starkie, Enid.   *Rimbaud.* New York: Norton, 1947, pp. 208–227.

Wing, Nathaniel.   *Present Appearances: Aspects of Poetic Structure in Rimbaud's* Illuminations. University: University of Mississippi Press, 1974.

The Poetry of Rimbaud

Ahearn, Edward J.   " 'Entends Comme Brame' and the Theme of Death in Nature in Rimbaud's Poetry," in *French Review.* XLIII (February, 1970), pp. 407–417.

Auden, W.H.   "Heretics," in *Literary Opinion in America.* Edited by Morton Dauwen Zabel. New York: Harper, 1951, pp. 256–259.

Bays, Gwendolyn.   *The Orphic Vision: Seer Poets from Novalis to Rimbaud.* Lincoln: University of Nebraska Press, 1964, pp. 144–247.

Bonnefoy, Yves.   *Rimbaud.* New York: Harper & Row, 1961, pp. 16–67.

Brereton, Geoffrey.   *An Introduction to French Poets: Villon to the Present Day.* London: Methuen, 1973, pp. 190–204.

Capetanakis, Demetrios.   "Rimbaud," in *The Shores of Darkness: Poems and Essays.* New York: Devin-Adair, 1949, pp. 53–71.

Carre, Jean-Marie.   *A Season in Hell: The Life of Arthur Rimbaud.* New York: Macaulay, 1931, pp. 103–112.

Cohn, Robert Greer.   *The Poetry of Rimbaud.* Princeton, N.J.: Princeton University Press, 1973, pp. 401–438.

Cournos, John. "Arthur Rimbaud—Poet and Merchant," in *Modern Plutarch*. Indianapolis, Ind.: Bobbs-Merrill, 1928, pp. 127–134.

Fay, Bernard. "Arthur Rimbaud: Initiator of a New Poetry," in *Since Victor Hugo: French Literature of Today*. Boston: Little, Brown, 1927, pp. 22–31.

Fowlie, Wallace. *Love in Literature: Studies in Symbolic Expression*. Bloomington: Indiana University Press, 1965, pp. 80–154.

————. *Rimbaud*. Chicago: University of Chicago Press, 1965, pp. 67–258.

Frohock, W.M. "Rimbaud's Internal Landscape," in *Order and Adventure in Post-Romantic French Poetry: Essays Presented to C.A. Hackett*. Edited by E.M. Beaumont, J.M. Cocking and J. Cruickshank. Oxford: Basil Blackwell, 1973, pp. 99–106.

Hackett, C.A. *Rimbaud*. New York: Hillary House, 1957, pp. 19–95.

Houston, John Porter. *The Design of Rimbaud's Poetry*. New Haven, Conn.: Yale University Press, 1963.

Lavrin, Janko. "The Riddles of Rimbaud," in *Aspects of Modernism, from Wilde to Pirandello*. New York: Nott, 1935, pp. 73–89.

Peschel, Enid R. "Arthur Rimbaud: The Aesthetics of Intoxication," in *Yale French Studies*. L (1974), pp. 65–80.

————. "Themes of Rebellion in William Blake and Rimbaud," in *French Review*. XLVI (1973), pp. 750–761.

Rexroth, Kenneth. "Rimbaud: Poems," in *Classics Revisited*. Chicago: Quadrangle, 1968, pp. 268–275.

St. Aubyn, Frederic Chase. *Arthur Rimbaud*. New York: Twayne, 1975, pp. 29–177.

Starkie, Enid. *Rimbaud*. New York: Norton, 1947, pp. 124–147, 167–227, 296–309, 411–424.

Wilson, Edmund. *Axel's Castle: A Study in the Imaginative Literature of 1870–1930*. New York: Scribner's, 1948, pp. 257–298.

Zabel, Morton Dauwen. "Rimbaud: Life and Legend," in *Partisan Review*. VII (July/August, 1940), pp. 268–282.

A Season in Hell

Bonnefoy, Yves. *Rimbaud*. New York: Harper & Row, 1961, pp. 82–105.

Brereton, Geoffrey. *An Introduction to the French Poets: Villon to the Present Day*. London: Methuen, 1973, pp. 190–204.

Carre, Jean-Marie. *A Season in Hell: The Life of Arthur Rimbaud*. New York: Macaulay, 1931, pp. 144–154.

Cohn, Robert Greer. *The Poetry of Rimbaud*. Princeton, N.J.: Princeton University Press, 1973, pp. 401–438.

Fowlie, Wallace. *Rimbaud.* Chicago: University of Chicago Press, 1965, pp. 79–83, 87–96, 119–125, 169–171, 221–258.

————. "Rimbaud's *Season,*" in *The Climate of Violence: The French Literary Tradition from Baudelaire to the Present.* New York: Macmillan, 1967, pp. 37–52.

Frohock, W.M. *Rimbaud's Poetic Practice: Image and Theme in the Major Poems.* Cambridge, Mass.: Harvard University Press, 1963, pp. 201–223.

Hackett, C.A. *Rimbaud.* New York: Hillary House, 1957, pp. 70–84.

Hanson, Elisabeth. *My Poor Arthur: A Biography of Arthur Rimbaud.* New York: Holt, 1960, pp. 145–149, 165–171.

Houston, John Porter. *The Design of Rimbaud's Poetry.* New Haven, Conn.: Yale University Press, 1962, pp. 137–200.

Peschel, Enid Rhodes. "Rimbaud's Life and Work," in *Arthur Rimbaud:* A Season in Hell, The Illuminations. New York: Oxford University Press, 1973, pp. 21–28.

St. Aubyn, Frederic Chase. *Arthur Rimbaud.* Boston: Twayne, 1975, pp. 73–111.

Schwartz, Delmore. "Rimbaud in Our Time," in *Selected Essays of Delmore Schwartz.* Edited by Donald A. Dike and David H. Zucker. Chicago: University of Chicago Press, 1970, pp. 53–57.

Starkie, Enid. *Rimbaud.* New York: Norton, 1947, pp. 248–255, 271–295.

EDWIN ARLINGTON ROBINSON
(1869–1935)

"The Book of Annandale"

Barnard, Ellsworth. *Edwin Arlington Robinson: A Critical Study*. New York: Macmillan, 1952, pp. 285–286.

Coxe, Louis. *Edwin Arlington Robinson: The Life of Poetry*. New York: Pegasus, 1969, pp. 74–75.

Davis, Charles T. "Robinson's Road to Camelot," in *Edwin Arlington Robinson: Centenary Essays*. Edited by Ellsworth Barnard. Athens: University of Georgia Press, 1969, pp. 110–111.

Hagedorn, Hermann. *Edwin Arlington Robinson: A Biography*. New York: Macmillan, 1938, pp. 177–181.

Neff, Emery. *Edwin Arlington Robinson*. New York: William Sloane, 1948, pp. 120–122.

Smith, Chard Powers. *Where the Light Falls: A Portrait of Edwin Arlington Robinson*. New York: Macmillan, 1965, pp. 190–194.

Winters, Yvor. *Edwin Arlington Robinson*. Norfolk, Conn. New Directions, 1946, p. 133.

"Captain Craig"

Anderson, Wallace. "The Young Robinson as Critic and Self-Critic," in *Edwin Arlington Robinson: Centenary Essays*. Edited by Ellsworth Barnard. Athens: University of Georgia Press, 1969, pp. 83–86.

Barnard, Ellsworth. *Edwin Arlington Robinson: A Critical Study*. New York: Macmillan, 1952, pp. 84–85.

Cestre, Charles. *An Introduction to Edwin Arlington Robinson*. New York: Macmillan, 1931, pp. 176–183.

Coxe, Louis. *Edwin Arlington Robinson: The Life of Poetry*. New York: Pegasus, 1969, pp. 68–74, 136–137.

Free, William J. "The Strategy 'Flammonde,' " in *Edwin Arlington Robinson: Centenary Essays*. Edited by Ellsworth Barnard. Athens: University of Georgia Press, 1969, pp. 21–23, 27–28.

Fussell, Edwin S. *Edwin Arlington Robinson: The Literary Background of a Traditional Poet*. Berkeley: University of California Press, 1954, pp. 22–23, 27–28, 86–87, 132–133.

Hagedorn, Hermann. *Edwin Arlington Robinson: A Biography*. New York: Macmillan, 1938, pp. 175–176, 181–187.

Kaplan, Estelle. *Philosophy in the Poetry of Edwin Arlington Robinson*. New York: Columbia University Press, 1940, pp. 43–55.

Martin, Jay. "A Crisis of Achievement: Robinson's Late Narratives," in *Edwin Arlington Robinson: Centenary Essays*. Edited by Ellsworth Barnard. Athens: University of Georgia Press, 1969, pp. 146–147.

Neff, Emery. *Edwin Arlington Robinson*. New York: William Sloane, 1948, pp. 114–119.

Smith, Chard Powers. *Where the Light Falls: A Portrait of Edwin Arlington Robinson*. New York: Macmillan, 1965, pp. 176–178, 221–222.

Waggoner, Hyatt H. *American Poets from the Puritans to the Present*. Boston: Houghton Mifflin, 1968, pp. 277–279.

Winters, Yvor. *Edwin Arlington Robinson*. Norfolk, Conn.: New Directions, 1946, pp. 8–9.

"For a Dead Lady"

Coxe, Louis. *Edwin Arlington Robinson: The Life of Poetry*. New York: Pegasus, 1969, pp. 87–91.

Crowder, Richard. " 'For a Dead Lady,' " in *Explicator*. V (December, 1946), item 19.

French, W.H. " 'For a Dead Lady,' " in *Explicator*. X (May, 1952), item 51.

Fussell, Edwin S. " 'For a Dead Lady,' " in *Explicator*. IX (March, 1951), item 33.

Super, R.H. " 'For a Dead Lady,' " in *Explicator*. III (June, 1945), item 60.

————. " 'For a Dead Lady,' " in *Explicator*. V (June, 1947), item 60.

"Luke Havergal"

Barnard, Ellsworth. *Edwin Arlington Robinson: A Critical Study*. New York: Macmillan, 1952, pp. 38–39.

Crowder, Richard. " 'Luke Havergal,' " in *Explicator*. VII (November, 1948), item 15.

Dunn, N.E. "Riddling Leaves: Robinson's 'Luke Havergal,' " in *Colby Library Quarterly*. X (1972), pp. 17–25.

Fussell, Edwin S. *Edwin Arlington Robinson: The Literary Background of a Traditional Poet*. Berkeley: University of California Press, 1954, pp. 16–17, 20–21.

Gierasch, Walter. " 'Luke Havergal,' " in *Explicator*. III (October, 1944), item 8.

McFarland, Ronald E. "Robinson's 'Luke Havergal,' " in *Colby Library Quarterly*. X (1974), pp. 365–372.

Neff, Emery. *Edwin Arlington Robinson*. New York: William Sloane, 1948, pp. 67–69.

Parlette, Mathilde M.   " 'Luke Havergal,' " in *Explicator*. III (June, 1945), item 57.

Raven, A.A.   " 'Luke Havergal,' " in *Explicator*. III (December, 1944), item 24.

Winters, Yvor.   *Edwin Arlington Robinson*. Norfolk, Conn.: New Directions, 1946, p. 35.

"The Man Against the Sky"

Barnard, Ellsworth.   *Edwin Arlington Robinson: A Critical Study*. New York: Macmillan, 1952, pp. 77–79, 113–115.

Bedell, R. Meredith.   "Perception, Action and Life in 'The Man Against the Sky,' " in *Colby Library Quarterly*. XII (1976), pp. 29–37.

Coxe, Louis.   *Edwin Arlington Robinson: The Life of Poetry*. New York: Pegasus, 1969, pp. 97–98, 106–114.

Crowder, Richard.   " 'Man Against the Sky,' " in *College English*. XIV (February, 1953), pp. 269–276.

Fish, Robert S.   "The Tempering of Faith in E.A. Robinson's 'The Man Against the Sky,' " in *Colby Library Quarterly*. IX (1972), pp. 456–468.

Fussell, Edwin S.   *Edwin Arlington Robinson: The Literary Background of a Traditional Poet*. Berkeley: University of California Press, 1954, pp. 95–96, 109–110, 160–161.

Hirsch, David H.   " 'The Man Against the Sky' and the Problem of Faith," in *Edwin Arlington Robinson: Centenary Essays*. Edited by Ellsworth Barnard. Athens: University of Georgia Press, 1969, pp. 31–42.

Kaplan, Estelle.   *Philosophy in the Poetry of Edwin Arlington Robinson*. New York: Columbia University Press, 1940, pp. 55–63.

Levenson, J.C.   "Robinson's Modernity," in *Edwin Arlington Robinson: Centenary Essays*. Edited by Ellsworth Barnard. Athens: University of Georgia Press, 1969, pp. 157–159.

Neff, Emery.   *Edwin Arlington Robinson*. New York: William Sloane, 1948, pp. 182–186.

Read, Arthur M., II.   "Robinson's 'The Man Against the Sky,' " in *Explicator*. XXVI (1968), item 49.

Robinson, W.R.   *Edwin Arlington Robinson: A Poetry of the Act*. Cleveland: Press of Western Reserve University, 1967, pp. 68–72.

Sanborn, John N.   "Juxtaposition as Structure in 'The Man Against the Sky,' " in *Colby Library Quarterly*. X (1974), pp. 486–494.

Scott, Winfield Townley.   "To See Robinson," in *New Mexico Quarterly Review*. XXVI (Summer, 1956), p. 169.

Waggoner, Hyatt H.   *The Heel of Elohim: Science and Values in Modern American Poetry.* Norman: University of Oklahoma Press, 1950, pp. 29–36.

Winters, Yvor.   *Edwin Arlington Robinson.* Norfolk, Conn.: New Directions, 1946, pp. 46–47.

————. "Religious and Social Ideas in the Didactic Work of E.A. Robinson," in *Arizona Quarterly.* I (Spring, 1945), pp. 74–75.

Merlin

Barnard, Ellsworth.   *Edwin Arlington Robinson: A Critical Study.* New York: Macmillan, 1952, pp. 91–92, 117–120, 218–219.

————. " 'Of This or That Estate': Robinson's Literary Reputation," in *Edwin Arlington Robinson: Centenary Essays.* Edited by Ellsworth Barnard. Athens: University of Georgia Press, 1969, pp. 12–13.

Cambon, Glauco.   *The Inclusive Flame: Studies in American Poetry.* Bloomington: Indiana University Press, 1963, pp. 70–76.

Cestre, Charles.   *An Introduction to Edwin Arlington Robinson.* New York: Macmillan, 1931, pp. 67–89.

Coxe, Louis.   *Edwin Arlington Robinson: The Life of Poetry.* New York: Pegasus, 1969, pp. 132–140.

Davis, Charles T.   "Robinson's Road to Camelot," in *Edwin Arlington Robinson: Centenary Essays.* Edited by Ellsworth Barnard. Athens: University of Georgia Press, 1969, pp. 97–101.

Fussell, Edwin S.   *Edwin Arlington Robinson: The Literary Background of a Traditional Poet.* Berkeley and Los Angeles: University of California Press, 1954, pp. 149–150.

Kaplan, Estelle.   *Philosophy in the Poetry of Edwin Arlington Robinson.* New York: Columbia University Press, 1940, pp. 86–95.

Levenson, J.C.   "Robinson's Modernity," in *Edwin Arlington Robinson: Centenary Essays.* Edited by Ellsworth Barnard. Athens: University of Georgia Press, 1969, pp. 169–170.

Neff, Emery.   *Edwin Arlington Robinson.* New York: William Sloane, 1948, pp. 194–197.

Smith, Chard Powers.   *Where the Light Falls: A Portrait of Edwin Arlington Robinson.* New York: Macmillan, 1965, pp. 243–250, 327–329.

Starr, Nathan Comfort.   "The Transformation of Merlin," in *Edwin Arlington Robinson: Centenary Essays.* Edited by Ellsworth Barnard. Athens: University of Georgia Press, 1969, pp. 106–119.

Stevick, Robert D.   "The Metrical Style of E.A. Robinson," in *Edwin Arlington Robinson: Centenary Essays.* Edited by Ellsworth Barnard. Athens: University of Georgia Press, 1969, pp. 64–65.

Van Doren, Mark. *Edwin Arlington Robinson.* New York: Literary Guild, 1927, pp. 67–71.

Winters, Yvor. *Edwin Arlington Robinson.* Norfolk, Conn.: New Directions, 1946, pp. 61–72.

"Mr. Flood's Party"

Baker, Carlos. " 'The Jug Makes the Paradise': New Light on Eben Flood," in *Colby Library Quarterly.* X (1974), pp. 327–336.

Barnard, Ellsworth. *Edwin Arlington Robinson: A Critical Study.* New York: Macmillan, 1952, pp. 55–56.

Brasher, Thomas L. "Robinson's 'Mr. Flood's Party,' " in *Explicator.* XXIX (1971), item 45.

Ciardi, John. *How Does a Poem Mean?* Boston: Houghton Mifflin, 1959, p. 712.

Davis, William V. " 'Enduring to the End': Edwin Arlington Robinson's 'Mr. Flood's Party,' " in *Colby Library Quarterly.* XII (1976), pp. 50–51.

Harkey, Joseph M. "Mr. Flood's Two Moons," in *Mark Twain Journal.* XV (1971), pp. 20–21.

Jacobs, Willis D. "E.A. Robinson's 'Mr. Flood's Party,' " in *College English.* XII (November, 1950), p. 110.

Levenson, J.C. "Robinson's Modernity," in *Edwin Arlington Robinson: Centenary Essays.* Edited by Ellsworth Barnard. Athens: University of Georgia Press, 1969, pp. 166–167.

Neff, Emery. *Edwin Arlington Robinson.* New York: William Sloane, 1948, pp. 198–199.

Ownbey, E. Sydnor. " 'Mr. Flood's Party,' " in *Explicator.* VIII (April, 1950), item 47.

Parish, John E. "The Rehabilitation of Eben Flood," in *English Journal.* LV (September, 1966), pp. 696–699.

The Poetry of Robinson

Baker, Carlos. "Robinson's Stoical Romanticism: 1890–1897," in *New England Quarterly.* XLVI (1973), pp. 3–16.

Barnard, Ellsworth. *Edwin Arlington Robinson: A Critical Study.* New York: Macmillan, 1952.

Cambron, Glauco. *The Inclusive Flame: Studies in American Poetry.* Bloomington: Indiana University Press, 1963, pp. 53–78.

Conner, Frederick William. *Cosmic Optimism: A Study of the Interpretation of Evolution by American Poets from Emerson to Robinson.* New York: Octagon, 1973, pp. 365–374.

Coxe, Louis. *E.A. Robinson.* Minneapolis: University of Minnesota Press, 1962.

_____. "Edwin Arlington Robinson," in *Six American Poets from Emily Dickinson to the Present: An Introduction.* Edited by Allen Tate. Minneapolis: University of Minnesota Press, 1970, pp. 45–81.

_____. *Edwin Arlington Robinson: The Life of Poetry.* New York: Pegasus, 1969.

Dickey, James. *Babel to Byzantium: Poets & Poetry Now.* New York: Farrar, Straus and Giroux, 1968, pp. 209–230.

Donaldson, Scott. "The Alien Pity: A Study of Character in Edwin Arlington Robinson's Poetry," in *American Literature.* XXXVIII (May, 1966), pp. 219–229.

Donoghue, Denis. *Connoisseurs of Chaos: Ideas of Order in Modern American Poetry.* New York: Macmillan, 1965, pp. 129–143.

Franchere, Hoyt C. *Edwin Arlington Robinson.* New York: Twayne, 1968.

Fussell, Edwin S. *Edwin Arlington Robinson: The Literary Background of a Traditional Poet.* Berkeley: University of California Press, 1954.

Kaplan, Estelle. *Philosophy in the Poetry of Edwin Arlington Robinson.* New York: Macmillan, 1940.

Morris, Celia. "E.A. Robinson and 'The Golden Horoscope of Imperfection,' " in *Colby Library Quarterly.* XI (1975), pp. 88–97.

Robinson, W.R. *Edwin Arlington Robinson: A Poetry of the Act.* Cleveland: Press of Case Western Reserve University, 1967.

Smith, Chard Powers. *Where the Light Falls: A Portrait of Edwin Arlington Robinson.* New York: Macmillan, 1965.

Untermeyer, Louis. "Edwin Arlington Robinson: A Reappraisal," in *Literary Lectures Presented at the House of Congress.* Washington, D.C.: Library of Congress, 1973, pp. 527–551.

Waggoner, Hyatt H. *American Poets from the Puritans to the Present.* Boston: Houghton Mifflin, 1968, pp. 262–292.

Winters, Yvor. *Edwin Arlington Robinson.* Norfolk, Conn.: New Directions, 1946.

"Richard Corey"

Barnard, Ellsworth. *Edwin Arlington Robinson: A Critical Study.* New York: Macmillan, 1952, pp. 98–99.

Brenner, Rica. *Ten Modern Poets.* Freeport, New York: Books for Libraries Press, 1968, pp. 97–98.

Burkhart, Charles. " 'Richard Corey,' " in *Explicator.* XIX (November, 1960), item 9.

French, Roberts W. "On Teaching 'Richard Corey,' " in *English Record.* XXIV, (1973), pp. 11–13.

Garvin, Harry R. "Poems Pickled in Anthological Brine," in *College English Association Critic.* XX (October, 1958), p. 4.

Kart, Lawrence. "Richard Corey: Artist Without an Art," in *Colby Library Quarterly.* XI (1975), pp. 160–161.

Kavka, Jerome. "Richard Corey's Suicide: A Psychoanalyst's View," in *Colby Library Quarterly.* XI (1975), pp. 150–159.

Morris, Charles R. " 'Richard Corey,' " in *Explicator.* XXXIII (March, 1965), item 52.

Stageburg, Norman C. and Wallace Anderson. *Poetry as Experience.* New York: American Book, 1952, pp. 189–192.

Turner, Steven. "Robinson's 'Richard Corey,' " in *Explicator.* XXVIII (May, 1970), item 73.

Tristram

Barnard, Ellsworth. *Edwin Arlington Robinson: A Critical Study.* New York: Macmillan, 1952, pp. 92–96, 150–152.

Cambon, Glauco. *The Inclusive Flame: Studies in American Poetry.* Bloomington: Indiana University Press, 1963, pp. 65–70.

Cestre, Charles. *An Introduction to Edwin Arlington Robinson.* New York: Macmillan, 1931, pp. 98–118.

Coxe, Louis. *Edwin Arlington Robinson: The Life of Poetry.* New York: Pegasus, 1969, pp. 123–124, 136–140.

Donoghue, Denis. *Connoisseurs of Chaos: Ideas of Order in Modern American Poetry.* New York: Macmillan, 1965, pp. 142–143.

Fussell, Edwin S. *Edwin Arlington Robinson: The Literary Background of a Traditional Poet.* Berkeley: University of California Press, 1954, pp. 144–147.

Hagedorn, Hermann. *Edwin Arlington Robinson: A Biography.* New York: Macmillan, 1938, pp. 340–342.

Neff, Emery. *Edwin Arlington Robinson.* New York: William Sloane, 1948, pp. 222–228.

Van Doren, Mark. *Edwin Arlington Robinson.* New York: Literary Guild, 1927, pp. 77–90.

Winters, Yvor. *Edwin Arlington Robinson.* Norfolk, Conn.: New Directions, 1946, pp. 86–96.

THEODORE ROETHKE
(1908–1963)

The Far Field

Alexander, Floyce M. "Roethke, Two Years Later," in *Western Humanities Review*. XX (Winter, 1966), pp. 76–78.

Bogan, Louise. "Verse," in *New Yorker*. XL (November 7, 1964), p. 243.

Brown, Dennis E. "Theodore Roethke's 'Self-World' and the Modernist Position," in *Journal of Modern Literature*. III (1974), pp. 1239–1254.

Carruth, Hayden. "Requiem for God's Gardener," in *Nation*. CXCIX (September 28, 1964), pp. 168–169.

Cookson, William. "Roethke's Last Poems," in *Agenda*. III (September, 1964), pp. 21–27.

Dickey, William. "Poetic Language," in *Hudson Review*. XVII (Winter, 1964–1965), p. 596.

Garrigue, Jean. "A Mountain on the Landscape," in *New Leader*. XLVII (December 7, 1964), pp. 33–34.

Kennedy, X.J. "Joys, Griefs and 'All Things Innocent, Hapless, Forsaken,' " in *New York Times Book Review*. (August 23, 1964), p. 5.

Kunitz, Stanley. "Roethke: Poet of Transformations," in *New Republic*. CLII (January 23, 1965), pp. 23–29. Reprinted in *Profile of Theodore Roethke*. Edited by William Heyen. Columbis, Oh.: Merrill, 1971, pp. 67–77.

Lieberman, Laurence. "Poetry Chronicle: Last Poems, Fragments, and Wholes," in *Antioch Review*. XXIV (Winter, 1964–1965), p. 537.

Lucas, John. "The Poetry of Theodore Roethke," in *Oxford Review*. VIII (1968), pp. 39–64.

McMichael, James. "The Poetry of Theodore Roethke," in *Southern Review*. V (Winter, 1969), pp. 4–25. Reprinted in *Profile of Theodore Roethke*. Edited by William Heyen. Columbus, Oh.: Merrill, 1971, pp. 78–95.

Malkoff, Karl. *Theodore Roethke: An Introduction to the Poetry*. New York: Columbia University Press, 1966, pp. 172–219.

Martz, Louis L. "A Greenhouse Eden," in *Theodore Roethke: Essays on the Poetry*. Edited by Arnold Stein. Seattle: University of Washington Press, 1965, pp. 14–35. Reprinted in his *The Poem of the Mind: Essays on Poetry— English and American*. New York: Oxford University Press, 1966, pp. 162–182.

Mills, Ralph J., Jr. "In the Way of Becoming: Roethke's Last Poems," in *Theodore Roethke: Essays on the Poetry*. Edited by Arnold Stein. Seattle: University of Washington Press, 1965, pp. 115–135. Reprinted in his *Cry of the*

Human: Essays on Contemporary American Poetry. Urbana: University of Illinois Press, 1975, pp. 47–66.

Ramsey, Paul. "A Weather of Heaven," in *Shenandoah*. XVI (Autumn, 1964), pp. 73–74.

Rosenthal, M.L. "Theodore Roethke, John Berryman, Anne Sexton," in *The New Poets: American and British Poetry Since World War Two*. New York: Oxford University Press, 1967, pp. 112–119.

Schumacher, Paul J. "The Unity of Being: A Study of Theodore Roethke's Poetry," in *Ohio University Review*. XII (1970), pp. 20–40.

Scott, Nathan A., Jr. *The Wild Prayer of Longing: Poetry and the Sacred*. New Haven, Conn.: Yale University Press, 1971, pp. 76–118.

Smith, William Jay. "Verse: Two Posthumous Volumes," in *Harper's*. CCXXIX (October, 1964), pp. 133–134.

Snodgrass, W.D. " 'That Anguish of Concreteness'—Theodore Roethke's Career," in *Theodore Roethke: Essays on the Poetry*. Edited by Arnold Stein. Seattle: University of Washington Press, 1965, pp. 78–93.

Southworth, James G. "Theodore Roethke's *The Far Field*," in *College English*. XXVII (February, 1966), pp. 413–418.

Walsh, Chad. "A Cadence for Our Time," in *Saturday Review*. XLVIII (January 2, 1966), p. 28.

"The Lost Son"

Alvarez, A. "Art and Isolation," in *Stewards of Excellence*. New York: Scribner's, 1958, pp. 186–188.

Blessing, Richard Allen. *Theodore Roethke's Dynamic Vision*. Bloomington: Indiana University Press, 1974, pp. 67–116.

Brown, Dennis E. "Theodore Roethke's 'Self-World' and the Modernistic Position," in *Journal of Modern Literature*. III (1974), pp. 1239–1254.

Burke, Kenneth. "The Vegetal Radicalism of Theodore Roethke," in *Sewanee Review*. LVII (January–March, 1950), pp. 68–108.

Deutsch, Babette. *Poetry in Our Time: A Critical Survey of Poetry in the English-Speaking World*. New York: Doubleday, 1963, pp. 197–200.

Fitzgerald, Robert. "Patter, Distraction, and Poetry," in *New Republic*. CXXI (August 8, 1949), pp. 17–18.

Galvin, Brendon. "Kenneth Burke and Theodore Roethke's 'Lost Son' Poems," in *Northwest Review*. XI (Summer, 1971), pp. 67–96.

Gibb, Hugh. "Symbols of Spiritual Growth," in *New York Times Book Review*. (August 1, 1948), p. 14.

Hamilton, Ian. "Theodore Roethke," in *Agenda*. III (April, 1964), pp. 5–10.

Heyen, William. "Theodore Roethke's Minimals," in *Minnesota Review.* VIII (1968), pp. 359–375.

Kunitz, Stanley J. *A Kind of Order, A Kind of Folly: Essays and Conversations.* Boston: Little, Brown, 1975, pp. 83–86.

La Belle, Jenijoy. "Theodore Roethke and Tradition: 'The Pure Serene of Memory in One Man,' " in *Northwest Review.* XI (Summer, 1971), pp. 1–18.

Lucas, John. "The Poetry of Theodore Roethke," in *Oxford Review.* VIII (1968), pp. 39–64.

Malkoff, Karl. *Theodore Roethke: An Introduction to the Poetry.* New York: Columbia University Press, 1966, pp. 44–62.

Martz, Louis L. "A Greenhouse Eden," in *Theodore Roethke: Essays on the Poetry.* Edited by Arnold Stein. Seattle: University of Washington Press, 1965, pp. 14–35. Reprinted in his *The Poem of the Mind: Essays on Poetry— English and American.* New York: Oxford University Press, 1966, pp. 162–182.

Mills, Ralph J., Jr. "Towards a Condition of Joy," in *Tri-Quarterly.* I (Fall, 1958), pp. 25–29.

Morgan, Frederick. "Recent Verse," in *Hudson Review.* I (Summer, 1948), pp. 261–262.

Phillips, Robert. "The Inward Journeys of Theodore Roethke," in *The Confessional Poets.* Carbondale: Southern Illinois University Press, 1973, pp. 107–127.

Ramsey, Jarold. "Roethke in the Greenhouse," in *Western Humanities Review.* XXVI (Winter, 1972), pp. 35–47.

Schumacher, Paul J. "The Unity of Being: A Study of Theodore Roethke's Poetry," in *Ohio University Review.* XII (1970), pp. 20–40.

Scott, Nathan A., Jr. *The Wild Prayer of Longing: Poetry and the Sacred.* New Haven, Conn.: Yale University Press, 1971, pp. 76–118.

Snodgrass, W.D. " 'That Anguish of Concreteness'—Theodore Roethke's Career," in *Theodore Roethke: Essays on the Poetry.* Edited by Arnold Stein. Seattle: University of Washington Press, 1965, pp. 78–93.

Spender, Stephen. "The Objective Ego," in *Theodore Roethke: Essays on the Poetry.* Edited by Arnold Stein. Seattle: University of Washington Press, 1965, pp. 3–13.

Sullivan, Rosemary. *Theodore Roethke; The Garden Master.* Seattle: University of Washington Press, 1975, pp. 37–56.

Vernon, John. "Theodore Roethke's *Praise to the End!* Poems," in *Iowa Review.* II (Fall, 1971), pp. 60–79. Slightly revised and reprinted as "Theodore Roethke," in *The Garden and the Map: Schizophrenia in Twentieth-Century Literature and Culture.* Urbana: University of Illinois Press, 1973, pp. 159–190.

"Open House"

Auden, W.H. "Verse and the Times," in *Saturday Review.* XXIII (April 5, 1941), pp. 30–31.

Baldanza, Stephen. "Books of the Week," in *Commonweal.* XXXIV (June 13, 1941), p. 188.

Belitt, Ben. "Six Poets," in *Virginia Quarterly Review.* XVII (Summer, 1941), pp. 462–463.

Blessing, Richard Allen. *Theodore Roethke's Dynamic Vision.* Bloomington: Indiana University Press, 1974, pp. 41–57.

Bonner, Amy. "The Poems of Theodore Roethke," in *New York Times Book Review.* (October 5, 1941), pp. 9, 12.

Brown, Dennis E. "Theodore Roethke's 'Self-World' and the Modernist Position," in *Journal of Modern Literature.* III (1974), pp. 1239–1254.

Ciardi, John. "Theodore Roethke: A Passion and a Maker," in *Saturday Review.* XLIV (August 31, 1963), p. 13.

Deutsch, Babette. "Three Generations in Poetry," in *Decision.* II (August, 1941), pp. 60–61.

Forster, Louis. "A Lyric Realist," in *Poetry.* LVIII (July, 1941), pp. 222–225.

Hayden, Mary H. "Open House: Poetry of the Constricted Self," in *Northwest Review.* XI (Summer, 1971), pp. 116–138.

Heyen, William. "Theodore Roethke's Minimals," in *Minnesota Review.* VIII (1968), pp. 359–375.

Humphries, Rolfe. "Inside Story," in *New Republic.* CV (July 14, 1941), p. 62.

Kunitz, Stanley. "Roethke: Poet of Transformations," in *New Republic.* CLII (January 23, 1965), pp. 23–29. Reprinted in *Profile of Theodore Roethke.* Edited by William Heyen. Columbus, Oh.: Merrill, 1971, pp. 67–77.

Malkoff, Karl. *Theodore Roethke: An Introduction to the Poetry.* New York: Columbia University Press, 1966, pp. 22–43.

Mazzaro, Jerome. "Theodore Roethke and the Failures of Language," in *Modern Poetry Studies.* I (July, 1970), pp. 73–96. Reprinted in *Profile of Theodore Roethke.* Edited by William Heyen. Columbus, Oh.: Merrill, 1971, pp. 47–64.

Mills, Ralph J., Jr. "Towards a Condition of Joy," in *Tri-Quarterly.* I (Fall, 1958), pp. 25–29.

Schumacher, Paul J. "The Unity of Being: A Study of Theodore Roethke's Poetry," in *Ohio University Review.* XII (1970), pp. 20–40.

Scott, Nathan A., Jr. *The Wild Prayer of Longing: Poetry and the Sacred.* New Haven, Conn.: Yale University Press, 1971, pp. 76–118.

Snodgrass, W.D. " 'That Anguish of Concreteness'—Theodore Roethke's Career," in *Theodore Roethke: Essays on the Poetry.* Edited by Arnold Stein. Seattle: University of Washington Press, 1965, pp. 78–93.

Sweeny, John L. "New Poetry," in *Yale Review.* XXX (June, 1941), pp. 817–818.

The Poetry of Roethke

Blessing, Richard Allen. *Theodore Roethke's Dynamic Vision.* Bloomington: Indiana University Press, 1974, pp. 40–226.

Boyd, John B. "Texture and Form in Theodore Roethke's Greenhouse Poems," in *Modern Language Quarterly.* XXXII (December, 1971), pp. 409–424.

Boyers, Robert. "A Very Separate Peace," in *The Young American Writers.* Edited by Richard Kostelanetz. New York: Funk and Wagnalls, 1967, pp. 27–34.

Deutsch, Babette. *Poetry in Our Time: A Critical Survey of Poetry in the English-Speaking World.* New York: Doubleday, 1963, pp. 197–200.

Fiedler, Leslie. "A Kind of Solution: The Situation of Poetry Now," in *Kenyon Review.* XXVI (Winter, 1964), pp. 61–64.

Galvin, Brendan. "Theodore Roethke's Proverbs," in *Concerning Poetry.* V (Spring, 1972), pp. 35–47.

Heringman, Bernard. "Roethke's Poetry: The Forms of Meaning," in *Texas Studies in Literature and Language.* XVI (1974), pp. 567–583.

Hoffman, Frederick J. "Theodore Roethke: The Poetic Shape of Death," in *Theodore Roethke: Essays on the Poetry.* Edited by Arnold Stein. Seattle: University of Washington Press, 1965, pp. 94–114. Reprinted in *Modern American Poetry.* Edited by Jerome Mazzaro. New York: David McKay, 1970, pp. 301–320.

Jaffe, Dan. "Theodore Roethke: 'In a Slow Up-Sway,' " in *The Fifties: Fiction, Poetry, Drama.* Edited by Warren French. Deland, Fla.: Everett/ Edwards, 1970, pp. 199–207.

Kunitz, Stanley J. *A Kind of Order, A Kind of Folly: Essays and Conversations.* Boston: Little, Brown, 1975, pp. 96–104.

La Belle, Jenijoy. *The Echoing Wood of Theodore Roethke.* Princeton, N.J.: Princeton University Press, 1976.

Libby, Anthony. "Roethke, Water Father," in *American Literature.* XLVI (1974), pp. 267–288.

McClatchy, J.D. "Sweating Light from a Stone: Identifying Theodore Roethke," in *Modern Poetry Studies.* III (1972), pp. 1–24.

McMichael, James. "The Poetry of Theodore Roethke," in *Southern Review.* V (Winter, 1969), pp. 4–25. Reprinted in *Profile of Theodore Roethke.* Edited by William Heyen. Columbus, Oh.: Merrill, 1971, pp. 78–95.

Martz, Louis L. "A Greenhouse Eden," in *Theodore Roethke: Essays on the Poetry*. Edited by Arnold Stein. Seattle: University of Washington Press, 1965, pp. 14–35. Reprinted in his *The Poem of the Mind: Essays on Poetry—English and American.* New York: Oxford University Press, 1966, pp. 162–182.

Mazzaro, Jerome. "Theodore Roethke and the Failures of Language," in *Modern Poetry Studies.* I (July, 1970), pp. 73–96. Reprinted in *Profile of Theodore Roethke.* Edited by William Heyen. Columbus, Oh.: Merrill, 1971, pp. 47–64.

Mills, Ralph J., Jr.   *Theodore Roethke.* Minneapolis: University of Minnesota Press, 1963.

Pearce, Roy Harvey.   "Theodore Roethke: The Power of Sympathy," in *Theodore Roethke: Essays on the Poetry*. Edited by Arnold Stein. Seattle: University of Washington Press, 1965, pp. 167–199. Reprinted in his *Historicism Once More: Problems and Occasions for the American Scholar.* Princeton, N.J.: Princeton University Press, 1969, pp. 294–326.

Rosenthal, M.L.   *The Modern Poets.* New York: Oxford University Press, 1960, pp. 240–244.

Schwartz, Delmore.   "The Cunning and the Craft of the Unconscious and the Preconscious," in *Poetry.* XCIV (June, 1959), pp. 203–205. Reprinted in *Selected Essays of Delmore Schwartz.* Chicago: University of Chicago Press, 1970, pp. 197–199. Also reprinted in *Profile of Theodore Roethke.* Edited by William Heyen. Columbus, Oh.: Merrill, 1971, pp. 64–66.

Scott, Nathan A., Jr.   *The Wild Prayer of Longing: Poetry and the Sacred.* New Haven, Conn.: Yale University Press, 1971, pp. 76–118.

Snodgrass, W.D.   " 'That Anguish of Concreteness'—Theodore Roethke's Career," in *Theodore Roethke: Essays on the Poetry*. Edited by Arnold Stein. Seattle: University of Washington Press, 1965, pp. 78–93.

Stein, Arnold.   "Introduction," in *Theodore Roethke: Essays on the Poetry*. Edited by Arnold Stein. Seattle: University of Washington Press, 1965, pp. ix–xx.

Sullivan, Rosemary.   *Theodore Roethke: The Garden Master.* Seattle: University of Washington Press, 1975.

Wain, John.   "Theodore Roethke," in *Critical Quarterly.* VI (Winter, 1964), pp. 322–338. Reprinted as "The Monocle of My Sea-Faced Uncle," in *Theodore Roethke: Essays on the Poetry*. Edited by Arnold Stein. Seattle: University of Washington Press, 1965, pp. 54–77.

Praise to the End!

Alvarez, A.   "Art and Isolation," in *Stewards of Excellence.* New York: Scribner's, 1958, pp. 186–188.

Arrowsmith, William. "Five Poets," in *Hudson Review*. IV (Winter, 1952), pp. 619–620.

Bogan, Louise. "Verse," in *New Yorker*. XXVII (February 16, 1952), p. 108. Reprinted as "The Minor Shudder," in *Selected Criticism: Poetry and Prose*. New York: Noonday, 1965, pp. 383–384.

Brantley, Frederick. "Poets and Their Worlds," in *Yale Review*. XLI (Spring, 1952), pp. 476–477.

Chang, Diana. "The Modern Idiom," in *Voices*. CXLVIII (May/August, 1952), pp. 42–43.

Eberhart, Richard. "Deep Lyrical Feelings," in *New York Times Book Review*. (December 16, 1951), p. 4.

Frankenberg, Lloyd. "The Year in Poetry," in *Harper's*. CCV (October, 1952), p. 106.

Humphries, Rolfe. "Verse Chronicle," in *Nation*. CLXXIV (March 22, 1952), p. 284.

Kramer, Hilton. "The Poetry of Theodore Roethke," in *Western Review*. XVIII (Winter, 1954), pp. 131–146.

Kunitz, Stanley. "Roethke: Poet of Transformations," in *New Republic*. CLII (January 23, 1965), pp. 23–29. Reprinted in *Profile of Theodore Roethke*. Edited by William Heyen. Columbus, Oh.: Merrill, 1971, pp. 67–77.

La Belle, Jenijoy. "Theodore Roethke and Tradition: 'The Pure Serene of Memory in One Man,' " in *Northwest Review*. XI (Summer, 1971), pp. 1–18.

Lucas, John. "The Poetry of Theodore Roethke," in *Oxford Review*. VIII (1968), pp. 39–64.

Malkoff, Karl. *Theodore Roethke: An Introduction to the Poetry*. New York: Columbia University Press, 1966, pp. 65–109.

Meredith, William. "A Steady Storm of Correspondences: Theodore Roethke's Long Journey Out of the Self," in *Shenandoah*. XVI (Autumn, 1964), pp. 41–54.

Philips, Robert. "The Inward Journeys of Theodore Roethke," in *The Confessional Poets*. Carbondale: Southern Illinois University Press, 1973, pp. 107–127.

Sawyer, Kenneth B. "Praises and Crutches," in *Hopkins Review*. V (Summer, 1952), pp. 131–132.

Schumacher, Paul J. "The Unity of Being: A Study of Theodore Roethke's Poetry," in *Ohio University Review*. XII (1970), pp. 20–40.

Scott, Nathan A., Jr. *The Wild Prayer of Longing: Poetry and the Sacred*. New Haven, Conn.: Yale University Press, 1971, pp. 76–118.

Shapiro, Harvey. "*Praise to the End!*," in *Furioso*. VII (Fall, 1952), pp. 56–58.

Snodgrass, W.D. " 'That Anguish of Concreteness'—Theodore Roethke's Career," in *Theodore Roethke: Essays on the Poetry*. Edited by Arnold Stein. Seattle: University of Washington Press, 1965, pp. 78–93.

Spender, Stephen. "The Objective Ego," in *Theodore Roethke: Essays on the Poetry*. Edited by Arnold Stein. Seattle: University of Washington Press, 1965, pp. 3–13.

Sullivan, Rosemary. *Theodore Roethke: The Garden Master*. Seattle: University of Washington Press, 1975, pp. 57–89.

Vierick, Peter. "Techniques and Inspiration," in *Atlantic Monthly*. CLXXXIX (January, 1953), p. 81.

Roethke: Collected Poems

Benedikt, Michael. "The Completed Pattern," in *Poetry*. CXIV (January, 1967), pp. 262–266.

Boyers, Robert. "A Very Separate Peace," in *Kenyon Review*. XXVIII (November, 1966), pp. 683–691. Reprinted in *Excursions: Selected Literary Essays*. Port Washington, N.Y.: Kennikat, 1977, pp. 131–138.

Carruth, Hayden. "In Spite of Artifice," in *Hudson Review*. XIX (Winter, 1966–1967), pp. 689–693.

Davison, Peter. "Some Recent Poetry," in *Atlantic Monthly*. CCXVIII (November, 1966), p. 163.

Donoghue, Denis. "Aboriginal Poet," in *New York Review of Books*. VII (September 22, 1966), pp. 14–16.

Ferry, David. "Roethke's Poetry," in *Virginia Quarterly Review*. XLIII (Winter, 1967)) pp. 169–173. Reprinted in *Profile of Theodore Roethke*. Edited by William Heyen. Columbus, Oh.: Merrill, 1971, pp. 96–99.

Hayman, Ronald. "From Hart Crane to Gary Snyder," in *Encounter*. XXXII (February, 1969), pp. 73–76.

Jennings, Elizabeth. "Inspiration and Ideas," in *Twentieth Century* (London). CLXXVII (1968), pp. 52–53.

Lupher, David A. "The Lost Son: Theodore Roethke," in *Yale Literary Magazine*. CXXXV (March, 1967), pp. 9–12.

Malkoff, Karl. "Exploring the Boundaries of Self," in *Sewanee Review*. LXXV (Summer, 1967), pp. 540–542.

Martz, Louis L. "Recent Poetry: Roethke, Warren and Others," in *Yale Review*. LVI (December, 1966), p. 275.

Mills, Ralph J., Jr. "Recognition," in *New York Times Book Review*. (July 17, 1966), pp. 5, 30–31.

Scott, Nathan A., Jr. *The Wild Prayer of Longing: Poetry and the Sacred*. New Haven, Conn.: Yale University Press, 1971, pp. 76–118.

Sergeant, Howard. "Poetry Review," in *English.* XVIII (Spring, 1969), p. 34.

Slater, Joseph. "Immortal Bard and Others," in *Saturday Review.* XLIX (December 31, 1966), p. 24.

Spender, Stephen. "Roethke: The Lost Son," in *New Republic.* CLV (August 27, 1966), pp. 23–25.

Tillinghast, Richard. "Worlds of Their Own," in *Southern Review.* V (Spring, 1969), pp. 594–596.

Vendler, Hellen. "Recent American Poetry," in *Massachusetts Review.* VIII (Summer, 1967), pp. 553–554.

Woodcock, George. "Daring Greatness," in *New Leader.* (September 12, 1967), pp. 21–22.

"The Waking"

Bennett, Joseph. "Recent Verse," in *Hudson Review.* VII (Summer, 1954), pp. 304–305.

Bogan, Louise. "Verse," in *New Yorker.* XXIX (October 24, 1953), pp. 158–159.

Carruth, Hayden. "The Idiom Is Personal," in *New York Times Book Review.* (September 13, 1953), p. 14.

Ciardi, John. "Poets of the Inner Landscape," in *Nation.* CLXXVII (November 14, 1953), p. 410.

————. "Theodore Roethke: A Passion and a Maker," in *Saturday Review.* XLVI (August 31, 1963), p. 13.

Cole, Thomas. "The Poetry of Theodore Roethke," in *Voices.* CLV (September/December, 1954), pp. 37–39.

Davis, William V. "The Escape into Time: Theodore Roethke's *'The Waking'*," in *Notes on Contemporary Literature.* V (1975), pp. 2–10.

Deutsch, Babette. "Poetry Chronicle," in *Yale Review.* XLIII (December, 1953), pp. 280–281.

Husband, John Dillon. "Some Readings in Recent Poetry," in *New Mexico Quarterly.* XXIV (Winter, 1954), pp. 446–447.

Malkoff, Karl. *Theodore Roethke: An Introduction to the Poetry.* New York: Columbia University Press, 1966, pp. 110–123.

Meyer, Gerald Previn. "Logic of the North," in *Saturday Review.* XXXVII (January 16, 1954), pp. 18–19.

Mills, Ralph J., Jr. "Towards a Condition of Joy," in *Tri-Quarterly.* I (Fall, 1958), pp. 25–29.

Nemerov, Howard. "Three in One," in *Kenyon Review.* XVI (Winter, 1954), pp. 144–154. Reprinted in his *Poetry and Fiction.* New Brunswick, N.J.: Rutgers University Press, 1963, pp. 134–142.

Philips, Robert. "The Inward Journeys of Theodore Roethke," in *The Confessional Poets*. Carbondale: Southern Illinois University Press, 1973, pp. 107–127.

Scott, Nathan A., Jr. *The Wild Prayer of Longing: Poetry and the Sacred.* New Haven, Conn.: Yale University Press, 1971, pp. 76–118.

Scott, Winfield Townley. "Makers of Stone Axes," in *Virginia Quarterly Review*. XXX (Autumn, 1954), p. 621.

Seymour-Smith, Martin. "Where Is Mr. Roethke?," in *Black Mountain Review*. I (Spring, 1954), pp. 40–47.

Snodgrass, W.D. " 'That Anguish of Concreteness'—Theodore Roethke's Career," in *Theodore Roethke: Essays on the Poetry*. Edited by Arnold Stein. Seattle: University of Washington Press, 1965, pp. 78–93.

Vernon, John. "Theodore Roethke's *Praise to the End!* Poems," in *Iowa Review*. II (Fall, 1971), pp. 60–79. Slightly revised and reprinted as "Theodore Roethke," in *The Garden and the Map: Schizophrenia in Twentieth-Century Literature and Culture*. Urbana: University of Illinois Press, 1973, pp. 159–190.

"Words for the Wind"

Berryman, John. "From the Middle and Senior Generations," in *American Scholar*. XXVIII (Summer, 1959), pp. 384–385.

Bogan, Louise. "Verse," in *New Yorker*. XXXV (October 24, 1959), pp. 195–196.

Brown, Dennis E. "Theodore Roethke's 'Self-World' and the Modernist Position," in *Journal of Modern Literature*. III (1974), pp. 1239–1254.

Coblentz, Stanton A. "The Reviewer's Quill," in *Wings*. XIV (Spring, 1959), pp. 23–24.

Dickey, James. "Correspondences and Essences," in *Virginia Quarterly Review*. XXXVII (Autumn, 1961), p. 640.

Donnelly, Dorothy. *"Words for the Wind,"* in *Michigan Quarterly Review*. I (Summer, 1962), p. 212.

Eberhart, Richard. "Creative Splendor," in *New York Times Book Review*. (November 9, 1958), p. 34.

Flint, F. Cudworth. "Seeing, Thinking, Saying, Singing," in *Virginia Quarterly Review*. XXXV (Spring, 1959), p. 313.

Freer, Coburn. "Theodore Roethke's Love Poetry," in *Northwest Review*. XI (Summer, 1971), pp. 42–66.

Gunn, Thom. "Poets English and American," in *Yale Review*. XLVIII (June, 1959), pp. 623–625.

Kizer, Carolyn. "Poetry of the Fifties: In America," in *International Literary Annual No. 1*. Edited by John Wain. London: John Calder, 1958, pp. 83–85.

Lupher, David A. "The Lost Son: Theodore Roethke," in *Yale Literary Magazine*. CXXXV (March, 1967), pp. 9–12.

Mills, Ralph J., Jr. "Keeping the Spirit Spare," in *Chicago Review*. XIII (Winter, 1959), pp. 114–122.

Napier, John. "Poetry in the Vernacular and Otherwise," in *Voices*. CLXXVI (September/December, 1961), p. 54.

Pearce, Roy Harvey. "Theodore Roethke: The Power of Sympathy," in *Theodore Roethke: Essays on the Poetry*. Edited by Arnold Stein. Seattle: University of Washington Press, 1965, pp. 167–199. Reprinted in his *Historicism Once More: Problems and Occasions for the American Scholar*. Princeton, N.J.: Princeton University Press, 1969, pp. 294–326.

Rosenthal, M.L. "Closing in on the Self," in *Nation*. CLXXXVIII (March 21, 1959), pp. 258–259.

Ross, Alan. *"Words for the Wind,"* in *London Magazine*. V (March, 1958), pp. 75, 77–79.

Schumacher, Paul J. "The Unity of Being: A Study of Theodore Roethke's Poetry," in *Ohio University Review*. XII (1970), pp. 20–40.

Schwartz, Delmore. *Selected Essays of Delmore Schwartz*. Chicago: University of Chicago Press, 1970, pp. 197–199.

Scott, Winfield Townley. "Has Anyone Seen a Trend?," in *Saturday Review*. XLII (January 3, 1959), p. 13.

Snodgrass, W.D. " 'That Anguish of Concreteness'—Theodore Roethke's Career," in *Theodore Roethke: Essays on the Poetry*. Edited by Arnold Stein. Seattle: University of Washington Press, 1965, pp. 78–93.

Spender, Stephen. *"Words for the Wind,"* in *New Republic*. CXLI (August 10, 1959), pp. 21–22.

Wain, John. "Half-Way to Greatness," in *Encounter*. X (April, 1958), pp. 82, 84.

ROMAIN ROLLAND
(1866–1944)

Jean-Christophe

Backmann, F. "*Jean-Christophe* as a Portrayal of German Character," in *Southwestern Review*. IX (1923), pp. 47–63.

Beiswanger, George W. "Artist, Philosopher, and the Ideal Society," in *Journal of Philosophy*. XXVIII (October 8, 1931), pp. 577–579.

Drake, William A. "Romain Rolland," in *Sewanee Review*. XXXII (October, 1924), pp. 386–404.

Duclaux, Agnes Mary Frances Robinson. *Twentieth Century Writers: Reviews and Reminiscences*. New York: Scribner's, 1919, pp. 34–50.

Harris, Frederick John. *André Gide and Romain Rolland: Two Men Divided*. New Brunswick, N.J.: Rutgers University Press, 1973, pp. 44–52.

Hesse, Hermann. "Romain Rolland," in *My Belief: Essays on Life and Art*. Edited by Theodore Ziolkowski. New York: Farrar, 1974, pp. 331–333.

Marble, Annie Russell. "Romain Rolland and *Jean-Christophe*," in *Nobel Prize Winners in Literature*. New York: Appleton, 1925, pp. 175–188.

March, Harold. *Romain Rolland*. New York: Twayne, 1971, pp. 56–68.

Price, Lucien. "Saga Symphonic of Romain Rolland," in *Atlantic Monthly*. CXXXVII (January, 1926), pp. 71–81.

Rosenfeld, P. "Rolland and the Composers," in his *Musical Chronicle, 1917–1923*. New York: Harcourt, Brace, 1923, pp. 11–19.

Sanborne, Alvan F. "Romain Rolland, Author of *Jean-Christophe*," in *Century*. LXXXVI (August, 1913), pp. 512–518.

Saurat, Denis. *Modern French Literature, 1870–1940*. New York: Putnam's, 1946, pp. 80–88.

Sice, David. "*Jean-Christophe* as a 'Musical' Novel," in *French Review*. XXXIX (May, 1966), pp. 862–874.

Starr, William Thomas. *Romain Rolland and a World at War*. Evanston, Ill.: Northwestern University Press, 1956, pp. 199–213.

_____. *Romain Rolland: One Against All, A Biography*. The Hague: Mouton, 1971, pp. 124–145.

Watson, G. "Socialism and Revolution in *Jean-Christophe*," in *Essays in French Literature*. II (November, 1965), pp. 30–41.

Weinberg, Albert K. "The Dream in *Jean-Christophe*," in *Journal of Abnormal Psychology*. XIII (April, 1918), pp. 12–16.

Whale, Winifred Stephens. *French Novelists of Today*. London: John Lane, 1915, pp. 137–176.

Zweig, Stefan. *Romain Rolland.* New York: Thomas Seltzer, 1921, pp. 172–175, 184–194, 200–210, 229–236.

CHRISTINA ROSSETTI
(1830–1894)

"Goblin Market"

Battiscombe, Georgina. *Christina Rossetti.* London: Longmans, Green, 1965, pp. 28–31.

Bellas, Ralph A. *Christina Rossetti.* New York: Twayne, 1977, pp. 32–37.

Cary, Elisabeth Luther. "Christina Rossetti: Her Poetry," in her *The Rossettis: Dante Gabriel and Christina.* New York: Putnam's, 1900, pp. 254–259.

DeVitas, A.A. " 'Goblin Market': Fairy Tale and Reality," in *Journal of Popular Culture.* I (Spring, 1968), pp. 418–426.

Elton, Oliver. "The Rossettis," in his *A Survey of English Literature, 1780–1880*, Volume IV. New York: Macmillan, 1920, pp. 22–30.

Evans, B. Ifor. "Christina Georgina Rossetti," in his *English Poetry in the Later Nineteenth Century.* London: Methuen, 1933, pp. 69–71.

Golub, Ellen. "Untying Goblin Apron Stings: A Psychoanalytic Reading of 'Goblin Market,' " in *Literature and Psychology.* XXV (1975), pp. 158–165.

Heath-Stubbs, John. "Pre-Raphaelitism and the Aesthetic Withdrawal," in *Pre-Raphaelitism: A Collection of Critical Essays.* Edited by James Sambrook. Chicago: University of Chicago Press, 1974, pp. 174–175.

Johnson, Wendell S. "Some Functions of Poetic Form," in *Journal of Aesthetics and Art Criticism.* XIII (June, 1955), pp. 504–505.

Packer, Lona Mosk. *Christina Rossetti.* Berkeley: University of California Press, 1963, pp. 140–151.

Saintsbury, George. "The Pre-Raphaelite School," in his *A History of English Prosody from the Twelfth Century to the Present Day*, Volume III. London: Macmillan, 1910, pp. 352–359.

Swann, Thomas Burnett. *Wonder and Whimsy: The Fantastic World of Christina Rossetti.* Francestown, N.H.: Marshall Jones, 1960, pp. 92–106.

Thomas, Eleanor Walter. *Christina Georgina Rossetti.* New York: Columbia University Press, 1931, pp. 155–159.

Weathers, Winston. "Christina Rossetti: The Sisterhood of Self," in *Victorian Poetry.* III (Spring, 1965), pp. 82–84.

The Poetry of Christina Rossetti

Battiscombe, Georgina. *Christina Rossetti.* London: Longmans, Green, 1965, pp. 16–36.

Bellas, Ralph A. *Christina Rossetti.* New York: Twayne, 1977, pp. 21–98.

Bowra, C.M. "Christina Rossetti," in his *The Romantic Imagination.* Cambridge, Mass.: Harvard University Press, 1949, pp. 245–270.

Cary, Elisabeth Luther. "Christina Rossetti: Her Poetry," in her *The Rossettis: Dante Gabriel and Christina.* New York: Putnam's, 1900, pp. 251–275.

Curran, Stuart. "The Lyric Voice of Christina Rossetti," in *Victorian Poetry.* IX (Autumn, 1971), pp. 287–299.

de la Mare, Walter. "Christina Rossetti," in *Essays by Divers Hands, Being the Transactions of the Royal Society of Literature of the United Kingdom,* Volume VI. Edited by G.K. Chesterton. London: Milford, 1926, pp. 79–116.

Dombrowski, Theo. "Dualism in the Poetry of Christina Rossetti," in *Victorian Poetry.* XIV (1976), pp. 70–76.

Evans, B. Ifor. "Christina Georgina Rossetti," in his *English Poetry in the Later Nineteenth Century.* London: Methuen, 1933, pp. 65–80.

Fairchild, Hoxie Neale. "Christina Rossetti," in his *Religious Trends in English Poetry, Volume IV: 1830–1880: Christianity and Romanticism in the Victorian Era.* New York: Columbia University Press, 1957, pp. 302–316.

Gosse, Edmund. "Christina Rossetti," in *Century Magazine.* XLVI (June, 1893), pp. 211–217. Reprinted in his *Critical Kit-Kats.* New York: Dodd, Mead, 1903, pp. 135–157.

Hueffer, Ford Madox. "Christina Rossetti," in *Fortnightly Review.* XCV (March, 1911), pp. 422–429. Reprinted as "Christina Rossetti and Pre-Raphaelite Love," in his *Ancient Lights.* London: Chapman and Hall, 1911, pp. 54–69. Also reprinted in his *Memories and Impressions: A Study in Atmospheres.* New York: Harper, 1911, pp. 60–77.

More, Paul Elmer. "Christina Rossetti," in *Atlantic Monthly.* XCIV (December, 1904), pp. 815–821. Reprinted in his *Shelburne Essays.* New York: Putnam's, 1905, pp. 124–142.

Packer, Lona Mosk. *Christina Rossetti.* Berkeley: University of California Press, 1963.

Reilly, Joseph J. "Christina Rossetti: Poet of Renunciation," in his *Dear Prue's Husband and Other People.* New York: Macmillan, 1932, pp. 144–161.

Robb, Nesca Adeline. "Christina Rossetti," in her *Four in Exile.* London: Hutchinson's, 1948, pp. 82–119.

Robson, W.W. "Pre-Raphaelite Poetry," in *British Victorian Literature: Recent Evaluations.* Edited by S.K. Kumar. New York: New York University Press, 1969, pp. 172–191.

Stevenson, Lionel. "Christina Rossetti," in his *The Pre-Raphaelite Poets.* Chapel Hill: University of North Carolina Press, 1972, pp. 78–122.

Stuart, Dorothy Margaret. *Christina Rossetti.* London: Oxford University Press, 1931, pp. 1–18.

Swann, Thomas Burnett. *Wonder and Whimsy: The Fantastic World of Christina Rossetti.* Francestown, N.H.: Marshall Jones, 1960, pp. 32–91.

Symons, Arthur. "Christina G. Rossetti: 1830–1894," in *The Poets and the Poetry of the Nineteenth Century*, Volume IX. Edited by Alfred H. Miles. New York: Dutton, 1907, pp. 1–16.

Thomas, Eleanor Walter. *Christina Georgina Rossetti.* New York: Columbia University Press, 1931, pp. 120–212.

Walker, Hugh. "The Turn of the Century: New Influences," in his *The Literature of the Victorian Era.* Cambridge: Cambridge University Press, 1910, pp. 501–508.

Waugh, Arthur. "Christina Rossetti, December 5, 1830; December 5, 1930," in *Nineteenth Century.* CVIII (December, 1930), pp. 787–798.

Weathers, Winston. "Christina Rossetti: The Sisterhood of Self," in *Victorian Poetry.* III (Spring, 1965), pp. 81–89.

Woolf, Virginia. "I Am Christina Rossetti," in *Nation and Athenaeum.* XLVIII (December 6, 1930), pp. 322–324. Reprinted in her *The Second Common Reader.* New York: Harcourt, Brace, 1932, pp. 257–265.

DANTE GABRIEL ROSSETTI
(1828–1882)

"The Blessed Damozel"

Benson, Arthur C. *Rossetti*. London: Macmillan, 1926, pp. 113–117.

Brown, Thomas H. "The Quest of Dante Gabriel Rossetti in 'The Blessed Damozel,'" in *Victorian Poetry*. X (1972), pp. 273–277.

Cunningham, C.C. *Literature as a Fine Art: Analysis and Interpretation*. New York: Thomas Nelson, 1941, pp. 142–147.

Holberg, Stanley M. "Rossetti and the Trance," in *Victorian Poetry*. VIII (Winter, 1970), pp. 311–314.

Hough, Graham. *The Last Romantics*. London: Duckworth, 1949, pp. 77–78.

Howard, Ronnalie Roper. *The Dark Glass: Vision and Technique in the Poetry of Dante Gabriel Rossetti*. Athens: Ohio University Press, 1972, pp. 40–50.

Johnson, Wendell Stacy. "D.G. Rossetti as Painter and Poet," in *Victorian Poetry*. III (1965), pp. 9–18. Reprinted in *Pre-Raphaelitism: A Collection of Critical Essays*. Edited by James Sambrook. Chicago: University of Chicago Press, 1974, pp. 220–229.

Johnston, Robert D. *Dante Gabriel Rossetti*. New York: Twayne, 1969, pp. 54–61.

Knickerbocker, K.L. "Rossetti's 'The Blessed Damozel,'" in *Studies in Philology*. XXIX (July, 1932), pp. 485–504.

Langford, Thomas A. "Rossetti's 'The Blessed Damozel,'" in *Explicator*. XXX (1971), item 5.

Lauter, Paul. "The Narrator of 'The Blessed Damozel,'" in *Modern Language Notes*. LXXIII (May, 1958), pp. 344–348.

McGann, Jerome J. "Rossetti's Significant Details," in *Victorian Poetry*. VII (1969), pp. 41–54. Reprinted in *Pre-Raphaelitism: A Collection of Critical Essays*. Edited by James Sambrook. Chicago: University of Chicago Press, 1974, pp. 230–242.

Megroz, R.L. *Dante Gabriel Rossetti: Painter Poet of Heaven in Earth*. New York: Scribner's, 1929, pp. 167–169.

Vogel, Joseph F. *Dante Gabriel Rossetti's Versecraft*. Gainesville: University of Florida Press, 1971, pp. 91–111.

The House of Life

Baker, Houston A., Jr. "The Poet's Progress: Rossetti's *The House of Life*," in *Victorian Poetry*. VIII (Spring, 1970), pp. 1–14.

Benson, Arthur C.   *Rossetti.* London: Macmillan, 1926, pp. 129–137.

Bowra, C.M.   *The Romantic Imagination.* New York: Oxford University Press, 1961, pp. 197–220. Reprinted in *Victorian Literature: Modern Essays in Criticism.* Edited by Austin Wright. New York: Oxford University Press, 1961, pp. 248–267.

Harris, Wendell V.   "A Reading of Rossetti's Lyrics," in *Victorian Poetry.* VII (Winter, 1969), pp. 299–308.

Hough, Graham.   *The Last Romantics.* London: Duckworth, 1949, pp. 79–81.

Howard, Ronnalie Roper.   *The Dark Glass: Vision and Technique in the Poetry of Dante Gabriel Rossetti.* Athens: Ohio University Press, 1972, pp. 164–174.

Hume, Robert D.   "Inorganic Structure in *The House of Life,*" in *Papers on Language and Literature.* V (Summer, 1969), pp. 282–295.

Johnston, Robert D.   *Dante Gabriel Rossetti.* New York: Twayne, 1969, pp. 71–108.

Kendall, J.L.   "The Concepts of the Infinite Moment in *The House of Life,*" in *Victorian Newsletter.* XXVIII (Fall, 1965), pp. 4–8.

Robillard, Douglas J.   "Rossetti's 'Willowwood' Sonnets and the Structure of *The House of Life,*" in *Victorian Newsletter.* XXII (Fall, 1962), pp. 5–9.

Ryals, Clyde de L.   "The Narrative Unity of *The House of Life,*" in *Journal of English and Germanic Philology.* LXIX (January, 1970), pp. 241–257.

Tisdel, F.M.   "Rossetti's *House of Life,*" in *Modern Philology.* XV (September, 1917), pp. 65–84.

Trombly, Albert E.   "Rossetti Studies: Craftsmanship," in *South Atlantic Quarterly.* XVIII (July, 1919), pp. 211–221.

Wallerstein, Ruth C.   "Personal Experiences in Rossetti's *House of Life,*" in *PMLA.* XLII (June, 1927), pp. 492–504.

The Poetry of Rossetti

Benson, Arthur C.   *Rossetti.* London: Macmillan, 1926, pp. 78–145.

Buchanan, Robert.   "The Fleshly School of Poetry: Dante Gabriel Rossetti," in *Notorious Literary Attacks.* Edited by Albert Mordell. New York: Boni and Liveright, 1926, pp. 185–213.

Cooper, Robert M.   *Lost on Both Sides: Dante Gabriel Rossetti—Critic and Poet.* Athens: Ohio University Press, 1970.

Doughty, Oswald.   *Dante Gabriel Rossetti.* London: Longmans, Green, 1957.

Hardesty, William H.   "Rossetti's Lusty Women," in *Cimarron Review.* XXXV (1976), pp. 20–24.

Holberg, Stanley M.   "Rossetti and the Trance," in *Victorian Poetry.* VIII (Winter, 1970), pp. 299–314.

Hough, Graham. *The Last Romantics.* London: Duckworth, 1949, pp. 67–82.

Howard, Ronnalie Roper. *The Dark Glass: Vision and Technique in the Poetry of Dante Gabriel Rossetti.* Athens: Ohio University Press, 1972.

Johnson, Wendell Stacy. "D.G. Rossetti as Painter and Poet," in *Victorian Poetry.* III (1965), pp. 9–18. Reprinted in *Pre-Raphaelitism: A Collection of Critical Essays.* Edited by James Sambrook. Chicago: University of Chicago Press, 1974, pp. 220–229.

Johnston, Robert D. *Dante Gabriel Rossetti.* New York: Twayne, 1969.

Lucas, F.L. *Ten Victorian Poets.* Cambridge: Cambridge University Press, 1940, pp. 99–114.

McGann, Jerome J. "Rossetti's Significant Details," in *Victorian Poetry.* VII (1969), pp. 41–54. Reprinted in *Pre-Raphaelitism: A Collection of Critical Essays.* Edited by James Sambrook. Chicago: University of Chicago Press, 1974, pp. 230–242.

Megroz, R.L. *Dante Gabriel Rossetti: Painter Poet of Heaven in Earth.* New York: Scribner's, 1929, pp. 141–318.

Pittman, Philip. "The Strumpet and the Snake: Rossetti's Treatment of Sex as Original Sin," in *Victorian Poetry.* XII (1974), pp. 45–54.

Prince, Jeffrey R. "D.G. Rossetti and the Pre-Raphaelite Conception of the Special Moment," in *Modern Language Quarterly.* XXXVII (1976), pp. 349–369.

Trombly, Albert E. "Rossetti Studies: Craftsmanship," in *South Atlantic Quarterly.* XVIII (July, 1919), pp. 211–221.

Vogel, Joseph F. *Dante Gabriel Rossetti's Versecraft.* Gainesville: University of Florida Press, 1971.

Warner, Janet. "D.G. Rossetti: Love, Death, and Art," in *Hartford Studies in Literature.* IV (1972), pp. 228–240.

Williamson, Audrey. *Artists and Writers in Revolt: The Pre-Raphaelites.* Cranbury, N.J.: Art Alliance Press, 1977, pp. 37–61.

EDMOND ROSTAND
(1868–1918)

Chantecler

Chiari, Joseph. *The Contemporary French Theatre: The Flight from Naturalism.* New York: Macmillan, 1959, pp. 42–44.

Duclaux, Mary. *Twentieth-Century French Writers.* Freeport, N.Y.: Books for Libraries, 1966, pp. 59–66.

Edmonds, Mary Arms. "A Fisher of the Moon," in *Forum.* LI (1914), pp. 592–604.

Frank, G. "Politics and the Cock of Dawn," in *Century.* CIII (February, 1922), pp. 637–640.

Grandgent, C.H. *"Chantecler,"* in *Anniversary Papers, by Colleagues and Pupils of George Lyman Kittredge.* New York: Ginn, 1913, pp. 67–72.

Lamm. Martin. *Modern Drama.* Oxford: Basil Blackwell, 1952, pp. 176–177.

Nicoll, Allardyce. "Neo-Romanticism in the Theatre," in *World Drama from Aeschylus to Anouilh.* New York: Barnes & Noble, 1976, pp. 518–523.

Norman, H.D. "Powers of Darkness and the Cock of Dawn," in *Poet-Lore.* XXXIV (1923), pp. 283–287.

Piggott, F.T. "Season of French Plays: Recollections of *Chantecler*," in *Nineteenth Century.* LXXXVIII (July, 1920), pp. 79–90.

Rosenfeld, Paul. "Rostand," in *New Republic.* XVII (1918), pp. 337–339.

Sheldon, C. "Rostand and *Chantecler*," in *Poet-Lore.* XXIII (January, 1912), pp. 74–78.

Smith, Hugh Allison. *Main Currents of Modern French Drama.* New York: Holt, 1925, pp. 84–93.

Thomas, Eleanor W. "The Romanticism of Rostand," in *Poet-Lore.* XXXII (1921), pp. 64–75.

Cyrano de Bergerac

Beerbohm, Max. *Around Theatres.* Elmsford, N.Y.: British Book Centre, 1953, pp. 4–7, 73–75.

Brenner, C.D. "Rostand's *Cyrano de Bergerac*: An Interpretation," in *Studies in Philology.* XLVI (October, 1949), pp. 603–611.

Brooks, Cleanth and Robert Heilman. *Understanding Drama.* New York: Holt, 1945, pp. 472–473.

Butler, Mildred Allen. "The Historical *Cyrano de Bergerac* as a Basis for Rostand's Play," in *Educational Theatre Journal.* VI (October, 1954), pp. 231–240.

————. "Sources of Plot Ideas in *Cyrano de Bergerac*," in *Western Speech*. XIX (March, 1955), pp. 87–93.

Charnet, P.E. *A Literary History of France*, Volume V. New York: Barnes & Noble, 1967, pp. 144–145.

Chiari, Joseph. *The Contemporary French Theatre: The Flight from Naturalism*. New York: Macmillan, 1959, pp. 36–42.

Duclaux, Mary, *Twentieth Century French Writers*. Freeport, N.Y.: Books for Libraries, 1966, pp. 57–59.

Edmonds, Mary Arms. "A Fisher of the Moon," in *Forum*. LI (1914), pp. 592–604.

Eliot, T.S. " 'Rhetoric' and Poetic Drama," in his *The Sacred Wood: Essays on Poetry and Criticism*. New York: Knopf, 1921, pp. 71–77. Reprinted in his *Selected Essays, 1917–1932*. New York: Holt, 1932, pp. 25–30.

Hamilton, Clayton. *Conversations on Contemporary Drama*. New York: Macmillan, 1924, pp. 33–38.

Jackson, Stoney. *This Is Love?* New York: Pageant Press, 1958, pp. 133–139.

Kilker, J. "Cyrano Without Rostand: An Appraisal," in *Canadian Modern Language Review*. XXI (1965), pp. 21–25.

Lamm, Martin. *Modern Drama*. Oxford: Basil Blackwell, 1952, pp. 171–174.

Miller, Nellie Burget. *The Living Drama, Historical Development and Modern Movement Visualized: A Drama of the Drama*. New York: Century, 1924, pp. 247–250.

Moskowitz, Samuel. "*Cyrano de Bergerac*: Swordsman of Space," in his *Explorers of the Infinite: Shapers of Science Fiction*. New York: World, 1963, pp. 17–32.

Myers, Henry A. *Tragedy: A View of Life*. Ithaca, N.Y.: Cornell University Press, 1956, pp. 146–147.

Nicoll, Allardyce. "Neo-Romanticism in the Theatre," in *World Drama from Aeschylus to Anouilh*. New York: Barnes & Noble, 1976, pp. 518–523.

Parsons, C.O. "The Nose of Cyrano de Bergerac," in *Romanic Review*. XXV (1934), pp. 225–235.

Simon, John. "*Cyrano de Bergerac*," in his *Singularities: Essays on the Theatre, 1964–1973*. New York: Random House, 1975, pp. 17–19.

Smith, Hugh Allison. *Main Currents of Modern French Drama*. New York: Holt, 1925, pp. 76–83, 93–107.

Thomas, Eleanor W. "The Romanticism of Rostand," in *Poet-Lore*. XXXII (1921), pp. 64–75.

Williams, Patricia E. "Some Classical Aspects of *Cyrano de Bergerac*," in *Nineteenth Century Studies*. I (1973), pp. 112–124.

L'Aiglon

Aldrich, Thomas Bailey.   "Note on *L'Aiglon*," in *Ponkapog Papers*, Volume VII. Boston: Houghton Mifflin, 1907, pp. 73–78.

Baring, Maurice.   "Edmond Rostand," in *Punch and Judy and Other Essays*. New York: Heinemann, 1924, pp. 297–301.

Beerbohm, Max.   "Tame Eaglet," in his *Around Theatres*. Elmsford, N.Y.: British Book Centre, 1953, pp. 151–154.

Charnet, P.E.   *A Literary History of France*, Volume V. New York: Barnes & Noble, 1967, pp. 144–145.

Chiari, Joseph.   *The Contemporary French Theatre: The Flight from Naturalism*. New York: Macmillan, 1959, pp. 44–46.

Duclaux, Mary.   *Twentieth Century French Writers*. Freeport, N.Y.: Books for Libraries, 1966, p. 59.

Edmonds, Mary Arms.   "A Fisher of the Moon," in *Forum*. LI (1914), pp. 592–604.

Miller, Nellie Burget.   *The Living Drama, Historical Development and Modern Movement Visualized: A Drama of the Drama*. New York: Century, 1924, p. 246.

Smith, Hugh Allison.   *Main Currents of Modern French Drama*. New York: Holt, 1925, pp. 83–84.

HENRY ROTH
(1907–   )

Call It Sleep

Allen, Walter. *The Modern Novel in Britain and the United States.* New York: Dutton, 1964, pp. 172–175.

————. *The Urgent West; The American Dream and Modern Man.* New York: Dutton, 1969, pp. 101–102.

Fiedler, Leslie. "The Breakthrough: The American Jewish Novelist and the Fictional Image of the Jew," in *Midstream.* IV (Winter, 1958), pp. 23–24.

————. "Henry Roth's Neglected Masterpiece," in *Commentary.* XXX (August, 1960), pp. 102–107.

Freedman, William. "Henry Roth and the Redemptive Imagination," in *The Thirties: Fiction, Poetry, Drama.* Edited by Warren French. Deland, Fla.: Everett/Edwards, 1967, pp. 107–114.

Knowles, A. Sidney, Jr. "The Fiction of Henry Roth," in *Modern Fiction Studies.* XI (Winter, 1965–1966), pp. 393–404.

Ledbetter, Kenneth. "Henry Roth's *Call It Sleep*: The Revival of a Proletarian Novel," in *Twentieth Century Literature.* XII (October, 1966), pp. 123–130.

Lyons, Bonnie. *Henry Roth: The Man and His Work.* New York: Cooper Square, 1976.

————. "The Symbolic Structure of Henry Roth's *Call It Sleep*," in *Contemporary Literature.* XIII (Spring, 1972), pp. 186–203.

Nelson, Kenneth M. "A Religious Metaphor," in *Reconstructionist.* XXXI (1965), pp. 7–16.

Ribalow, Harold U. "Henry Roth and His Novel *Call It Sleep*," in *Wisconsin Studies in Contemporary Literature.* III (Fall, 1962), pp. 5–14.

Rideout, Walter B. *The Radical Novel in the United States, 1900–1955; Some Interrelations of Literature and Society.* Cambridge, Mass.: Harvard University Press, 1956, pp. 186–190.

Samet, Tom. "Henry Roth's Bull Story: Guilt and Betrayal in *Call It Sleep*," in *Studies in the Novel.* VII (1975), pp. 569–583.

Sherman, Bernard. *The Invention of the Jews; Jewish-American Educational Novels (1916–1964).* Cranbury, N.J.: Thomas Yoseloff, 1969, pp. 82–92.

Syrkin, Marie. "Revival of a Classic," in *Midstream.* VII (Winter, 1961), pp. 89–93.

Wirth-Nesher, Hana. "The Modern Jewish Novel and the City: Franz Kafka, Henry Roth, and Amos Oz," in *Modern Fiction Studies.* XXIV (Spring, 1978), pp. 91–109.

PHILIP ROTH
(1933–   )

Goodbye, Columbus

Clerk, Charles. "Goodbye to All That: Theme, Character, and Symbol in *Goodbye, Columbus*," in *Seven Contemporary Short Novels*. Edited by Charles Clerk and Louis Leiter. Glenview, Ill.: Scott, Foresman, 1969, pp. 106–133.

Deer, Irving and Harriet. "Philip Roth and the Crisis in American Fiction," in *Minnesota Review*. VI (1966), pp. 353–360.

Fiedler, Leslie A. *To the Gentiles*. New York: Stein and Day, 1972, pp. 118–123.

Guttmann, Allen. *The Jewish Writer in America: Assimilation and Crises of Identity*. New York: Oxford University Press, 1971, pp. 67–72.

Howe, Irving. "Philip Roth Reconsidered," in *Commentary*. LIV (December, 1972), pp. 69–77. Reprinted in *The Critical Point*. New York: Horizon Press, 1973, pp. 137–157.

———. "The Suburbs of Babylon," in *New Republic*. CXL (June 15, 1959), pp. 17–18.

Isaac, Dan. "In Defense of Philip Roth," in *Chicago Review*. XVII (1964), pp. 84–96.

Israel, Charles M. "The Fractured Hero of Roth's *Goodbye, Columbus*," in *Critique*. XVI (1974), pp. 5–11.

Kazin, Alfred. *Contemporaries*. New York: Atlantic, Little, Brown, 1962, pp. 258–262.

Koch, Eric. "Roth's *Goodbye, Columbus*," in *Tamarack Review*. XIII (1959), pp. 129–132.

Larner, Jeremy. "Conversion of the Jews," in *Partisan Review*. XXVII (Fall, 1960), pp. 760–768.

McDaniel, John N. *The Fiction of Philip Roth*. Haddonfield, N.J.: Haddonfield House, 1974, pp. 68–76.

Malin, Irvin. *Jews and Americans*. Carbondale: Southern Illinois University Press, 1965, pp. 78–79.

Mann, Meryl. "*Goodbye Columbus*, Hello Radcliffe," in *Partisan Review*. XXVIII (January–February, 1961), pp. 154–157.

Meeter, Glenn. *Bernard Malamud and Philip Roth: A Critical Essay*. Grand Rapids, Mich.: William B. Eerdmans, 1968, pp. 30–33.

Nelson, Gerald B. *Ten Versions of America*. New York: Knopf, 1972, pp. 147–162.

Pinsker, Sanford. *The Comedy That "Hoits": An Essay on the Fiction of Philip Roth.* Columbia: University of Missouri Press, 1975, pp. 4–12.

Sherman, Bernard. *The Invention of the Jew: Jewish American Education Novels.* New York: Thomas Yoseloff, 1969, pp. 167–175.

Siegel, Ben. "Jewish Fiction and the Affluent Society," in *Northwest Review.* IV (Spring, 1961), pp. 89–96.

Solotaroff, Theodore. "Philip Roth and the Jewish Moralists," in *Chicago Review.* XIII (Winter, 1959), pp. 87–99. Reprinted in *Contemporary American-Jewish Literature.* Edited by Irving Malin. Bloomington: Indiana University Press, 1973, pp. 13–29.

Trachtenberg, Stanley. "The Hero in Stasis," in *Critique.* VII (Winter, 1964–1965), pp. 5–17.

The Great American Novel

Gilman, Richard. "Ball Five," in *Partisan Review.* XL (Fall, 1973), pp. 467–471.

Leibowitz, Herbert. "Roth Strikes Out," in *New Leader.* LVI (May 14, 1973), pp. 14–16.

Leonard, John. "Cheever to Roth to Malamud," in *Atlantic.* CCXXXI (June, 1973), pp. 114–116.

McDaniel, John N. *The Fiction of Philip Roth.* Haddonfield, N.J.: Haddonfield House, 1974, pp. 161–168.

Maloff, Saul. "Still Room for Badminton," in *New Republic.* CLXVIII (May 19, 1973), pp. 24–25.

Monaghan, David. "*The Great American Novel* and *My Life as a Man*: An Assessment of Philip Roth's Achievement," in *International Fiction Review.* II (1975), pp. 113–120.

Mudrick, Marvin. "Old Pros with News from Nowhere," in *Hudson Review.* XXVI (Autumn, 1973), pp. 545–548.

Pinsker, Sanford. *The Comedy That "Hoits": An Essay on the Fiction of Philip Roth.* Columbia: University of Missouri Press, 1975, pp. 85–101.

Rodgers, Bernard F., Jr. "*The Great American Novel* and 'The Great American Joke,' " in *Critique.* XVI (1974), pp. 12–29.

Siegel, Ben. "The Myths of Summer: Philip Roth's *The Great American Novel*," in *Contemporary Literature.* XVII (1976), pp. 171–190.

Letting Go

Allen, Mary. *The Necessary Blankness: Women in Major American Fiction of the Sixties.* Urbana: University of Illinois Press, 1976, pp. 70–96.

Bellow, Saul. "Some Notes on Recent American Fiction," in *Encounter*. XXI (November, 1963), pp. 22–29. Reprinted in *The American Novel Since World War II*. Edited by Marcus Klein. Greenwich, Conn.: Fawcett, 1969, pp. 159–174.

Deer, Irving and Harriet. "Philip Roth and the Crisis in American Fiction," in *Minnesota Review*. VI (1966), pp. 353–360.

Detweiler, Robert. *Four Spiritual Crises in Mid-Century American Fiction*. Gainesville: University of Florida Press, 1963, pp. 25–35.

Donaldson, Scott. "Philip Roth: The Meanings of *Letting Go*," in *Contemporary Literature*. XI (Winter, 1970), pp. 21–35.

Geismar, Maxwell. "The Shifting Illusion—Dream and Fact," in *American Dreams, American Nightmares*. Edited by David Madden. Carbondale: Southern Illinois University Press, 1970, pp. 45–57.

Guttmann, Allen. *The Jewish Writer in America: Assimilation and the Crisis of Identity*. New York: Oxford University Press, 1971, pp. 72–73.

Hicks, Granville. "Hammer Locks in Wedlock," in *Saturday Review*. XLV (June 16, 1962), p. 16. Reprinted in *Literary Horizons: A Quarter Century of American Fiction*. New York: New York University Press, 1970, pp. 245–255.

Hyman, Stanley Edgar. "A Novelist of Great Promise," in *On Contemporary Literature*. Edited by Richard Kostelanetz. New York: Avon, 1964, pp. 532–536.

McDaniel, John N. *The Fiction of Philip Roth*. Haddonfield, N.J.: Haddonfield House, 1974, pp. 76–89, 116–120.

Mailer, Norman. *Cannibals and Christians*. New York: Dell, 1970, pp. 104–130.

Meeter, Glenn. *Bernard Malamud and Philip Roth: A Critical Essay*. Grand Rapids, Mich.: William B. Eerdmans, 1968, pp. 39–40.

Pinsker, Sanford. *The Comedy That "Hoits": An Essay on the Fiction of Philip Roth*. Columbia: University of Missouri Press, 1975, pp. 28–42.

Podhoretz, Norman. *Doings and Undoings: The Fifties and After in American Writing*. New York: Farrar, Straus, 1964, pp. 236–243.

Weinberg, Helen. *The New Novel in America: The Kafkan Mode in Contemporary Fiction*. Ithaca, N.Y.: Cornell University Press, 1970, pp. 165–199.

White, Robert L. "The English Instructor as Hero: Two Novels by Roth and Malamud," in *Forum*. IV (Winter, 1963), pp. 16–22.

Our Gang

Cooper, Arthur. "*Our Gang*," in *Saturday Review*. LIV (November 6, 1971), p. 53.

Donaldson, Scott. "Family Crises in the Popular Novel of Nixon's Administration," in *Journal of Popular Culture*. VII (Fall, 1972), pp. 374–382.

Kernan, Alvin B. "The Sacred Weapon," in *Yale Review*. LXI (Spring, 1972), pp. 407–410.

McDaniel, John N. *The Fiction of Philip Roth*. Haddonfield, N.J.: Haddonfield House, 1974, pp. 157–161.

Pinsker, Sanford. *The Comedy That "Hoits": An Essay on the Fiction of Philip Roth*. Columbia: University of Missouri Press, 1975, pp. 71–78.

Portnoy's Complaint

Altman, Sig. *The Comic Image of the Jews—Explorations of a Pop Culture Phenomenon*. Rutherford, N.J.: Fairleigh Dickinson University Press, 1971, pp. 102–112.

Amis, Kingsley. *What Became of Jane Austen? And Other Questions*. New York: Harcourt Brace Jovanovich, 1971, pp. 102–108.

Bluestein, Gene. "*Portnoy's Complaint*: The Jew as American," in *Canadian Review of American Studies*. VII (1976), pp. 66–76.

Broyard, Anatole. "A Sort of Moby Dick," in *New Republic*. CLX (March 1, 1969), pp. 21–22. Reprinted in *The Critic as Artist*. Edited by Gilbert A. Harrison. New York: Liveright, 1972, pp. 42–46.

Buchen, Irving H. "*Portnoy's Complaint* of the Rooster's Kvetch," in *Studies in the Twentieth Century*. VI (Fall, 1970), pp. 97–107.

Cohen, Eileen Z. "Alex in Wonderland, or *Portnoy's Complaint*," in *Twentieth Century Literature*. XVII (July, 1971), pp. 161–168.

Friedman, Alan Warren. "The Jew's Complaint in Recent American Fiction: Beyond Exodus and Still in the Wilderness," in *Southern Review*. VIII (1972), pp. 41–59.

Gordon, Lois G. "*Portnoy's Complaint*: Coming of Age in Jersey City," in *Literature and Psychology*. XIX (1969), pp. 57–60.

Guttmann, Allen. *The Jewish Writer in America: Assimilation and the Crisis of Identity*. New York: Oxford University Press, 1971, pp. 74–76.

Harmon, William. " 'Anti-Fiction' in American Humor," in *The Comic Imagination in American Literature*. New Brunswick, N.J.: Rutgers University Press, 1973, pp. 383–384.

Hicks, Granville. "*Portnoy's Complaint*," in *Saturday Review*. LII (February 22, 1969), p. 38. Reprinted in *Literary Horizons: A Quarter Century of American Fiction*. New York: New York University Press, 1970, pp. 245–255.

Howe, Irving. "Philip Roth Reconsidered," in *Commentary*. LIV (December, 1972), pp. 69–77. Reprinted in *The Critical Point*. New York: Horizon Press, 1973, pp. 137–157.

Kliman, Bernice W. "Names in *Portnoy's Complaint*," in *Critique*. XIV (1973), pp. 16–24.

Ludwig, Jack. "Sons and Lovers," in *Partisan Review*. XXXVI (1969), pp. 524–526, 528–534.

McDaniel, John N. *The Fiction of Philip Roth*. Haddonfield, N.J.: Haddonfield House, 1974, pp. 132–148.

Pinsker, Sanford. *The Comedy That "Hoits": An Essay on the Fiction of Philip Roth*. Columbia: University of Missouri Press, 1975, pp. 55–71.

Spacks, Patricia Meyer. "About Portnoy," in *Yale Review*. LVIII (June, 1969), pp. 623–635.

Trilling, Diana. *We Must March My Darlings: A Critical Decade*. New York: Harcourt, 1977, pp. 157–171.

Wisse, Ruth. *The Schlemiel as Modern Hero*. Chicago: University of Chicago Press, 1971, pp. 118–123.

When She Was Good

Allen, Mary. *The Necessary Blankness: Women in Major American Fiction of the Sixties*. Urbana: University of Illinois Press, 1976, pp. 70–96.

Alter, Robert. "When He Is Bad," in *Commentary*. XLIV (November, 1967), pp. 86–87.

Garis, Robert. "Varieties of the Will," in *Hudson Review*. XX (Summer, 1967), pp. 328–329.

Gilman, Richard. "Let's Lynch Lucy," in *New Republic*. CLVI (June 24, 1967), pp. 19–21.

Halio, Jay L. "The Way It Is—And Was," in *Southern Review*. VI (Winter, 1970), pp. 254–256.

Hicks, Granville. "A Bad Little Good Girl," in *Saturday Review*. L (June 17, 1967), pp. 25–26. Reprinted in *Literary Horizons: A Quarter Century of American Fiction*. New York: New York University Press, 1970, pp. 245–255.

McDaniel, John N. *The Fiction of Philip Roth*. Haddonfield, N.J.: Haddonfield House, 1974, pp. 120–132.

Meeter, Glenn. *Bernard Malamud and Philip Roth: A Critical Essay*. Grand Rapids, Mich.: William B. Eerdmans, 1968, pp. 43–44.

Pinsker, Sanford. *The Comedy That "Hoits": An Essay on the Fiction of Philip Roth*. Columbia: University of Missouri Press, 1975, pp. 42–55.

JEAN JACQUES ROUSSEAU
(1712–1778)

Confessions

Corngold, Stanley A. "The Rhythm of Memory: Mood and Imagination in the *Confessions* of Rousseau," in *Mosaic.* V (1972), pp. 215–225.

Green, F.C. *Jean-Jacques Rousseau: A Critical Study of His Life and Writings.* Cambridge: Cambridge University Press, 1955, pp. 43–45.

————. *Literary Ideas in 18th Century France and England: A Critical Survey.* New York: Frederick Ungar, 1966, pp. 409–420.

Havens, George R. *Jean-Jacques Rousseau.* Boston: Twayne, 1978, pp. 109–112.

Huizinga, J.H. *Rousseau: The Self-Made Saint.* New York: Grossman, 1976, pp. 77–79, 108–111, 165–167, 273–276.

MacCannell, Juliet F. "History and Self-Portrait in Rousseau's Autobiography," in *Studies in Romanticism.* XIII (1974), pp. 279–298.

MacDonald, Frederika. *Jean Jacques Rousseau: A New Criticism.* New York: Putnam's, 1906, pp. 19–34.

Scanlan, Timothy M. "An Echo of Marot, Rabelais and Scarron in Rousseau's *Les Confessions*," in *Romance Notes.* XVI (1975), pp. 335–337.

Émile

Blanchard, William H. *Rousseau and the Spirit of Revolt: A Psychological Study.* Ann Arbor: University of Michigan Press, 1967, pp. 147–163.

Brereton, Geoffrey. *A Short History of French Literature.* London: Cassell, 1954, pp. 104–107.

Brooks, Richard A. "Rousseau's Antifeminism in the *Lettre a d'Alembert* and *Émile*," in *Literature and History of the Age of Ideas: Essays on the French Enlightenment Presented to George R. Havens.* Edited by Charles G.S. Williams. Columbus: Ohio State University Press, 1975, pp. 209–227.

Burgelin, Pierre. "The Secondary Education of Émile," in *Yale French Studies.* XXVIII (Fall–Winter, 1961), pp. 106–111.

Compayre, Gabriel. *Jean Jacques Rousseau and Education from Nature.* New York: Burt Franklin, 1971.

Eliassen, R.H. "Rousseau Under the Searchlights of Modern Education," in *American Book Collector.* XII (Summer, 1962), pp. 10–14.

Ellis, Madeleine B. *Rousseau's Socratic Aemilian Myths.* Columbus: Ohio State University Press, 1977.

Green, F.C.   *Jean-Jacques Rousseau: A Critical Study of His Life and Writings.* Cambridge: Cambridge University Press, 1955, pp. 225–264.

Hamilton, James F.   "Literature and the 'Natural Man' in Rousseau's *Émile*," in *Literature and History of the Age of Ideas: Essays on the French Enlightenment Presented to George R. Havens.* Edited by Charles S.G. Williams. Columbus: Ohio State University Press, 1975, pp. 195–206.

Havens, George R.   *Jean-Jacques Rousseau.* Boston: Twayne, 1978, pp. 93–99.

Hudson, William Henry.   *Rousseau and Naturalism in Life and Thought.* New York: Scribner's, 1903, pp. 180–206.

Meyer, Paul H.   "The Individual and Society in Rousseau's *Émile*," in *Modern Language Quarterly.* XIX (June, 1958), pp. 99–114.

Patterson, Sylvia W.   *Rousseau's* Émile *and Early Children's Literature.* Metuchen, N.J.: Scarecrow Press, 1971.

Politzer, Robert L.   "Rousseau on Language Education," in *Modern Language Forum.* XLI (June, 1956), pp. 23–34.

Sahakian, Mabel Lewis and William S. Sahakian.   *Rousseau as Educator.* New York: Twayne, 1974, pp. 78–106.

Scanlan, Timothy M.   "A Biblical Allusion in Rousseau's *Émile*," in *Language Quarterly.* XIV (1975), pp. 12–14.

Sewall, Bronwen D.   "The Similarity Between Rousseau's *Émile* and the Early Poetry of Wordsworth," in *Studies on Voltaire and the Eighteenth Century.* CVI (1973), pp. 157–174.

Warner, James H.   "Émile in Eighteenth-Century England," in *PMLA.* LIX (September, 1944), pp. 773–791.

Winwar, Frances.   *Jean-Jacques Rousseau: Conscience of an Era.* New York: Random House, 1961, pp. 263–265.

The New Héloïse

Anderson, David L.   "Aspects of Motif in *La nouvelle Héloïse*," in *Studies on Voltaire and the Eighteenth Century.* XCIV (1972), pp. 25–72.

Brown, F. Andrew.   "Rousseau's Bomston and Muralt," in *Modern Language Forum.* XXXIX (December, 1954), pp. 126–129.

Cherpack, Clifton.   "Space, Time, and Memory in *La nouvelle Héloïse*," in *L'Esprit Créateur.* III (Winter, 1963), pp. 167–171.

Green, F.C.   *French Novelists, Manners and Ideas: From the Renaissance to the Revolution.* New York: Appleton, 1930, pp. 192–207.

Grimsley, Ronald.   "The Human Problem in *La nouvelle Héloïse*," in *Modern Language Review.* LIII (April, 1958), pp. 171–184.

————. *Jean-Jacques Rousseau: A Study in Self-Awareness.* Cardiff: University of Wales Press, 1961, pp. 116–151.

Hall, H. Gaston. "The Concept of Virtue in *La nouvelle Héloïse*," in *Yale French Studies.* XXVIII (Fall–Winter, 1961), pp. 20–33.

Havens, George R. *Jean-Jacques Rousseau.* Boston: Twayne, 1978, pp. 80–89.

————. "The Theory of 'Natural Goodness' in Rousseau's *Nouvelle Héloïse*," in *Modern Language Notes.* XXXVI (November, 1921), pp. 385–394.

Hoffding, Harald. *Jean Jacques Rousseau and His Philosophy.* New Haven, Conn.: Yale University Press, 1930, pp. 83–89.

Hudson, William Henry. *Rousseau and Naturalism in Life and Thought.* New York: Scribner's, 1903, pp. 153–179.

Lowe, L.F.H. "Saint-Preux's Trip to Sion in the *Nouvelle Héloïse*," in *Romanic Review.* XVIII (April–June, 1927), pp. 134–141.

Macklem, Michael. "Rousseau and the Romantic Ethic," in *French Studies.* IV (October, 1950), pp. 325–332.

Mead, William. "*La nouvelle Héloïse* and the Public of 1761," in *Yale French Studies.* XXVIII (Fall–Winter, 1961), pp. 13–19.

Mille, Pierre. *The French Novel.* Philadelphia: Lippincott, 1930, pp. 49–55.

Mylne, Vivienne. *The Eighteenth-Century French Novel: Techniques of Illusion.* Manchester, England: Manchester University Press, 1965, pp. 166–191.

Sahakian, Mabel Lewis and William S. Sahakian. *Rousseau as Educator.* New York: Twayne, 1974, pp. 61–77.

Scanlan, Timothy M. "The Notion of 'Paradis sur la terre' in Rousseau's *La nouvelle Héloïse*," in *Nottingham French Studies.* XIII (1974), pp. 12–22.

Showalter, English, Jr. *The Evolution of the French Novel, 1641–1782.* Princeton, N.J.: Princeton University Press, 1972, pp. 301–306, 316–322.

Vartanian, Aram. "The Death of Julie: A Psychological Post-mortem," in *L'Esprit Créateur.* VI (Summer, 1966), pp. 77–84.

Webb, Donald P. "Did Rousseau Bungle the nuit d'amour?," in *Kentucky Romance Quarterly.* XVII (1970), pp. 3–8.

————. "Rousseau's *La nouvelle Héloïse*," in *Explicator.* XXX (1972), item 73.

Winwar, Frances. *Jean-Jacques Rousseau: Conscience of an Era.* New York: Random House, 1961, pp. 248–254.

Wolpe, Hans. "Psychological Ambiguity in *La nouvelle Héloïse*," in *University of Toronto Quarterly.* XXVIII (April, 1959), pp. 279–290.

SUSANNA ROWSON
(1762–1824)

Charlotte Temple

Fiedler, Leslie A. *Love and Death in the American Novel.* New York: Stein and Day, 1966, pp. 93–98.

Parker, P.L. "*Charlotte Temple*: America's First Best Seller," in *Studies in Short Fiction.* XIII (Fall, 1976), pp. 518–520.

Sargent, M.E. "Susanna Rowson," in *Medford Historical Review.* (April, 1904), n.p.

Spiller, Robert. *Literary History of the United States.* New York: Macmillan, 1963, pp. 177–178.

Vail, R.W.G. "Foreword: Susanna Haswell Rowson, Author of *Charlotte Temple*: Bibliographical Study," in *American Antiquarian Society Proceedings.* XLII (1932), pp. 62–68.

Van Doren, Carl. *American Novel.* New York: Macmillan, 1922, pp. 7–8.

Wagenknecht, Edward C. *Cavalcade of the American Novel.* New York: Holt, 1952, pp. 4–5.

Whittier, John Greenleaf. "Susanna Rowson," in *Whittier on Writers and Writing.* Syracuse, N.Y.: Syracuse University Press, 1950, pp. 15–18.

JOHN RUSKIN
(1819–1900)

Fors Clavigera

Crow, G. *Ruskin*. London: Duckworth, 1936, pp. 108–121.

Evans, Joan. *John Ruskin*. New York: Oxford University Press, 1955, pp. 324–325, 340–343, 372–374.

Fellows, Jay. *The Failing Distance: The Autobiographical Impulse in John Ruskin*. Baltimore: Johns Hopkins University Press, 1975, pp. 94–126.

Harrison, Frederick. *John Ruskin*. New York: Macmillan, 1902, pp. 181–196.

Hewison, Robert. *John Ruskin: The Argument of the Eye*. London: Thames and Hudson, 1976, pp. 180–182.

Landow, George P. *The Aesthetic and Critical Theories of John Ruskin*. Princeton, N.J.: Princeton University Press, 1971, pp. 281–287.

Mather, Marshall. *John Ruskin: His Life and Teaching*. London: Frederick Warne, 1900, pp. 70–72.

Meynell, Mrs. *John Ruskin*. New York: Dodd, Mead, 1900, pp. 259–272.

Quennell, Peter. *John Ruskin*. London: Longmans, Green, 1956, pp. 23–24.

_____. *John Ruskin: The Portrait of a Prophet*. New York: Viking, 1949, pp. 234–244.

Stein, Richard L. *The Ritual of Interpretation: The Fine Arts as Literature in Ruskin, Rossetti, and Pater*. Cambridge, Mass.: Harvard University Press, 1975, pp. 279–280.

Wilenski, R.H. *John Ruskin: An Introduction to the Further Study of His Life and Work*. London: Faber and Faber, 1933, pp. 131–137.

Wingate, Ashmore. *Life and Writings of John Ruskin*. Folcroft, Pa.: Folcroft, 1973, pp. 147–178.

_____. *Life of John Ruskin*. London: Walker Scott, 1910, pp. 131–136.

Modern Painters

Crow, G. *Ruskin*. London: Duckworth, 1936, pp. 43–54.

Evans, Joan. *John Ruskin*. New York: Oxford University Press, 1955, pp. 85–99, 104–117, 217–223, 246–250.

Fellows, Jay. *The Failing Distance: The Autobiographical Impulse in John Ruskin*. Baltimore: Johns Hopkins University Press, 1975.

Fontana, Ernest L. "Ruskin's *Modern Painters*, II," in *Explicator*. XXIX (1970), item 33.

Goetz, Sister Mary Dorothea. *A Study of Ruskin's Concept of the Imagination*. Washington, D.C.: Catholic University of America, 1947.

Harrison, Frederick. *John Ruskin.* New York: Macmillan, 1902, pp. 41–51.

Hewison, Robert. *John Ruskin: The Argument of the Eye.* London: Thames and Hudson, 1976, pp. 42–46, 54–62.

Ladd, Henry. *The Victorian Morality of Art: An Analysis of Ruskin's Esthetic.* New York: Ray Long and Richard R. Smith, 1932.

Landow, George P. *The Aesthetic and Critical Theories of John Ruskin.* Princeton, N.J.: Princeton University Press, 1971.

Mather, Marshall. *John Ruskin: His Life and Teaching.* London: Frederick Warne, 1900, pp. 48–54.

Meynell, Mrs. *John Ruskin.* New York: Dodd, Mead, 1900, pp. 9–78.

Quennell, Peter. *John Ruskin.* London: Longmans, Green, 1956, pp. 9–11.

————. *John Ruskin: The Portrait of a Prophet.* New York: Viking, 1949, pp. 26–30.

Shapiro, Harold I. "The Poetry of Architecture: Ruskin's Preparation for *Modern Painters*," in *Renaissance and Modern Studies.* XV (1971), pp. 70–84.

Stein, Richard L. *The Ritual of Interpretation: The Fine Arts as Literature in Ruskin, Rossetti, and Pater.* Cambridge, Mass.: Harvard University Press, 1975, pp. 37–67.

Wilenski, R.H. *John Ruskin: An Introduction to the Further Study of His Life and Work.* London: Faber and Faber, 1933, pp. 193–214, 229–244.

Wingate, Ashmore. *Life and Writings of John Ruskin.* Folcroft, Pa.: Folcroft, 1973, pp. 44–70.

————. *Life of John Ruskin.* London: Walker Scott, 1910, pp. 44–60.

Praeterita

Alexander, Edward. "*Praeterita*: Ruskin's Remembrance of Things Past," in *Journal of English and Germanic Philology.* LXXIII (1974), pp. 351–362.

Evans, Joan. *John Ruskin.* New York: Oxford University Press, 1955, pp. 398–399.

Fellows, Jay. *The Failing Distance: The Autobiographical Impulse in John Ruskin.* Baltimore: Johns Hopkins University Press, 1975, pp. 178–187.

Harrison, Frederick. *John Ruskin.* New York: Macmillan, 1902, pp. 197–206.

Hewison, Robert. *John Ruskin: The Argument of the Eye.* London: Thames and Hudson, 1976, pp. 41–42.

Landow, George P. *The Aesthetic and Critical Theories of John Ruskin.* Princeton, N.J.: Princeton University Press, 1971, pp. 281–285.

Meynell, Mrs. *John Ruskin.* New York: Dodd, Mead, 1900, pp. 273–281.

Quennell, Peter. *John Ruskin.* London: Longmans, Green, 1956, pp. 25–26.

————. *John Ruskin: The Portrait of a Prophet.* New York: Viking, 1949, pp. 281–284.

Stein, Richard L.   *The Ritual of Interpretation: The Fine Arts as Literature in Ruskin, Rossetti, and Pater.* Cambridge, Mass.: Harvard University Press, 1975, pp. 279–280.

Wilenski, R.H.   *John Ruskin: An Introduction to the Further Study of His Life and Work.* London: Faber and Faber, 1933, pp. 42–49.

Wingate, Ashmore.   *Life and Writings of John Ruskin.* Folcroft, Pa.: Folcroft, 1973, pp. 178–181.

————.   *Life of John Ruskin.* London: Walker Scott, 1910, pp. 178–181.

The Queen of the Air

Drake, Gertrude.   "Ruskin's Athena, Queen of the Air," in *Classical Bulletin.* LI (1974), pp. 17–24.

Hewison, Robert.   *John Ruskin: The Argument of the Eye.* London: Thames and Hudson, 1976, pp. 154–159.

Landow, George P.   *The Aesthetic and Critical Theories of John Ruskin.* Princeton, N.J.: Princeton University Press, 1971, pp. 399–408, 412–415.

Meynell, Mrs.   *John Ruskin.* New York: Dodd, Mead, 1900, pp. 181–185.

Quennell, Peter.   *John Ruskin: The Portrait of a Prophet.* New York: Viking, 1949, pp. 206–210.

The Seven Lamps of Architecture

Crow, G.   *Ruskin.* London: Duckworth, 1936, pp. 61–67.

Evans, Joan.   *John Ruskin.* New York: Oxford University Press, 1955, pp. 145–156.

Fellows, Jay F.   "Death and Champagnole: A Contribution to the Reading of *The Seven Lamps of Architecture*," in *University of Toronto Quarterly.* XLIII (1974), pp. 132–142.

Harrison, Frederick.   *John Ruskin.* New York: Macmillan, 1902, pp. 52–62.

Ladd, Henry.   *The Victorian Morality of Art: An Analysis of Ruskin's Esthetic.* New York: Ray Long and Richard R. Smith, 1932, pp. 262–263.

Landow, George P.   *The Aesthetic and Critical Theories of John Ruskin.* Princeton, N.J.: Princeton University Press, 1971, pp. 211–222.

Mather, Marshall.   *John Ruskin: His Life and Teaching.* London: Frederick Warne, 1900, pp. 54–57.

Meynell, Mrs.   *John Ruskin.* New York: Dodd, Mead, 1900, pp. 79–97.

Stein, Richard L.   *The Ritual of Interpretation: The Fine Arts as Literature in Ruskin, Rossetti, and Pater.* Cambridge, Mass.: Harvard University Press, 1975, pp. 107–108.

Wilenski, R.H.   *John Ruskin: An Introduction to the Further Study of His Life and Work.* London: Faber and Faber, 1933, pp. 214–217.

Wingate, Ashmore. *Life and Writings of John Ruskin.* Folcroft, Pa.: Folcroft, 1973, pp. 70–77.

————. *Life of John Ruskin.* London: Walker Scott, 1910, pp. 70–77.

The Stones of Venice

Crow, G. *Ruskin.* London: Duckworth, 1936, pp. 67–73.

Evans, Joan. *John Ruskin.* New York: Oxford University Press, 1955, pp. 159–166, 185–189.

Harrison, Frederick. *John Ruskin.* New York: Macmillan, 1902, pp. 65–77.

Hewison, Robert. *John Ruskin: The Argument of the Eye.* London: Thames and Hudson, 1976, pp. 132–137, 176–177.

Landow, George P. *The Aesthetic and Critical Theories of John Ruskin.* Princeton, N.J.: Princeton University Press, 1971, pp. 56–60, 276–280.

Mather, Marshall. *John Ruskin: His Life and Teaching.* London: Frederick Warne, 1900, pp. 57–62.

Meynell, Mrs. *John Ruskin.* New York: Dodd, Mead, 1900, pp. 98–116.

Quennell, Peter. *John Ruskin.* London: Longmans, Green, 1956, pp. 11–14.

————. *John Ruskin: The Portrait of a Prophet.* New York: Viking, 1949, pp. 66–74.

Stein, Richard L. *The Ritual of Interpretation: The Fine Arts as Literature in Ruskin, Rossetti, and Pater.* Cambridge, Mass.: Harvard University Press, 1975, pp. 69–118.

Wilenski, R.H. *John Ruskin: An Introduction to Further Study of His Life and Work.* London: Faber and Faber, 1933, pp. 235–239, 307–310.

Wingate, Ashmore. *Life and Writings of John Ruskin.* Folcroft, Pa.: Folcroft, 1973, pp. 82–89.

————. *Life of John Ruskin.* London: Walker Scott, 1910, pp. 82–89.

Time and Tide

Evans, Joan. *John Ruskin.* New York: Oxford University Press, 1955, pp. 296–297.

Landow, George P. *The Aesthetic and Critical Theories of John Ruskin.* Princeton, N.J.: Princeton University Press, 1971, pp. 298–302.

Meynell, Mrs. *John Ruskin.* New York: Dodd, Mead, 1900, pp. 175–180.

Quennell, Peter. *John Ruskin: The Portrait of a Prophet.* New York: Viking, 1949, pp. 194–196.

Wingate, Ashmore. *Life of John Ruskin.* London: Walker Scott, 1910, pp. 119–120.

Unto This Last

Crow, G. *Ruskin.* London: Duckworth, 1936, pp. 96–99.

Evans, Joan. *John Ruskin.* New York: Oxford University Press, 1955, pp. 260–262.

Harrison, Frederick. *John Ruskin.* New York: Macmillan, 1902, pp. 91–101.

Hewison, Robert. *John Ruskin: The Argument of the Eye.* London: Thames and Hudson, 1976, pp. 138–143.

Meynell, Mrs. *John Ruskin.* New York: Todd, Mead, 1900, pp. 145–157.

Quennell, Peter. *John Ruskin.* London: Longmans, Green, 1956, pp. 19–22.

_____. *John Ruskin: The Portrait of a Prophet.* New York: Viking, 1949, pp. 143–153.

Wingate, Ashmore. *Life and Writings of John Ruskin.* Folcroft, Pa.: Folcroft, 1973, pp. 104–111.

_____. *Life of John Ruskin.* London: Walker Scott, 1910, pp. 109–111.

ANTOINE DE SAINT-EXUPÉRY
(1900–1944)

Flight to Arras

Benet, William Rose. "Flight of the Spirit," in *Saturday Review of Literature.* XXV (February 28, 1942), p. 6.

Burnham, David. "Meditation in Disaster," in *Commonweal.* XXXV (March 27, 1942), pp. 565–566.

Cate, Curtis. *Antoine de Saint-Exupéry.* New York: Putnam's, 1970, pp. 449–456.

Dennis, Nigel. "A Creed for France," in *New Republic.* CVI (March 16, 1942), p. 372.

Fowlie, Wallace. "Masks of the Modern Hero," in his *Love in Literature: Studies in Symbolic Expression.* Bloomington: Indiana University Press, 1965, pp. 80–127.

Frohock, Wilbur M. "Saint-Exupéry: The Poet as Novelist," in his *Style and Temper: Studies in French Fiction, 1925–1960.* Cambridge, Mass.: Harvard University Press, 1967, pp. 31–44.

Jennings, Elizabeth. "Antoine de Saint-Exupéry: A Vision of Space," in her *Seven Men of Vision: An Appreciation.* New York: Barnes & Noble, 1976, pp. 206–223.

Kestner, Joseph A., III. "Pindar and Saint-Exupéry: The Heroic Form of Space," in *Modern Fiction Studies.* XIX (1973–1974), pp. 507–516.

Knight, Everett W. "Saint-Exupéry," in his *Literature Considered as Philosophy: The French Example.* New York: Macmillan, 1958, pp. 160–185.

McKeon, Joseph T. "Saint-Exupéry, the Myth of the Pilot," in *PMLA.* LXXXIX (October, 1974), pp. 1084–1089.

Maurois, André. "Antoine de Saint-Exupéry," in his *From Proust to Camus: Profiles of Modern French Writers.* Garden City, N.Y.: Doubleday, 1966, pp. 201–223.

————. "Meditation of a French Aviator," in *Yale Review.* XXXI (Summer, 1942), pp. 819–821.

Rumbold, Richard and Margaret Stewart. *The Winged Life: A Portrait of Antoine de Saint-Exupéry, Poet and Airman.* London: Weidenfeld and Nicolson, 1953, pp. 166–167, 177–182, 195–197.

Smith, Maxwell A. *Knight of the Air: The Life and Works of Antoine de Saint-Exupéry.* New York: Pageant, 1956, pp. 159–172.

Taffel, Abram. "The Imagery of Confinement and Weight in the Works of Saint-Exupéry," in *Modern Language Quarterly.* XX (March, 1959), pp. 67–73.

Woods, Katherine. "Flight in the Face of Death," in *New York Times Book Review.* (February 22, 1942), pp. 1, 16.

The Little Prince

Breaux, Adele. *Saint-Exupéry in America, 1942–1943, A Memoir.* Cranbury, N.J.: Fairleigh Dickinson University Press, 1971, pp. 74–85, 144–146.

Cate, Curtis. *Antoine de Saint-Exupéry.* New York: Putnam's, 1970, pp. 457–466.

Fay, Eliot G. "The Autobiographical Background of *Le Petit Prince,*" in *Modern Language Journal.* XXXII (November, 1948), pp. 528–529.

Gagnon, Laurence. "Webs of Concern: *The Little Prince* and *Charlotte's Web,*" in *Children's Literature: The Great Excluded*, Volume II. Edited by Francelia Butler. Stavis, Conn.: Children's Literature Association, 1973, pp. 61–66.

Graham, Victor E. "Religion and Saint-Exupéry's *Le Petit Prince,*" in *Canadian Modern Language Review.* III (1959), pp. 9–11.

Maurois, André. "Antoine de Saint-Exupéry," in his *From Proust to Camus: Profiles of Modern French Writers.* Garden City, N.Y.: Doubleday, 1966, pp. 201–223.

Price, Robert H. "Pantagruel et *Le Petit Prince,*" in *Symposium.* XXI (1967), pp. 264–270.

Rumbold, Richard and Margaret Stewart. *The Winged Life: A Portrait of Antoine de Saint-Exupéry, Poet and Airman.* London: Weidenfeld and Nicolson, 1953, pp. 185–187.

Sherman, Beatrice. "A Prince of Lonely Space," in *New York Times Book Review.* (April 11, 1943), p. 9.

Smith, Maxwell A. *Knight of the Air: The Life and Works of Antoine de Saint-Exupéry.* New York: Pageant, 1956, pp. 189–200.

Night Flight

Bree, Germaine and Margaret Guiton. *An Age of Fiction: The French Novel from Gide to Camus.* New Brunswick, N.J.: Rutgers University Press, 1957, pp. 195–197.

Cate, Curtis. *Antoine de Saint-Exupéry.* New York: Putnam's, 1970, pp. 220–232.

Cooper, Frederic Taber. "The Man in the Air," in *Commonweal.* XVII (November 30, 1932), pp. 135–136.

Cov, Laurence W. "Vol de Nuit: The World of Light and Darkness," in *Romance Notes.* XV (1973), pp. 7–9.

Fay, Eliot G. "The Philosophy of Saint-Exupéry," in *Modern Language Journal.* XXXI (February, 1947), pp. 92–93.

Frohock, Wilbur M. "Saint-Exupéry: The Poet as Novelist," in his *Style and Temper: Studies in French Fiction, 1925–1960.* Cambridge, Mass.: Harvard University Press, 1967, pp. 31–44.

Gide, André. "Preface," in *Night Flight*. By Antoine de Saint-Exupéry. New York: Century, 1932, pp. v–xi.

Hill, Frank E. "Portrait of Men as Flyers," in *Saturday Review of Literature.* IX (August 13, 1932), p. 41.

Kestner, Joseph A., III. "Pindar and Saint-Exupéry: The Heroic Form of Space," in *Modern Fiction Studies.* XIX (1973–1974), pp. 507–516.

McKeon, Joseph T. "Saint-Exupéry. The Myth of the Pilot," in *PMLA.* LXXXIX (October, 1974), pp. 1084–1089.

Maurois, André. "Antoine de Saint-Exupéry," in his *From Proust to Camus: Profiles of Modern French Writers.* Garden City, N.Y.: Doubleday, 1966, pp. 201–223.

Peyre, Henri. *The Contemporary French Novel.* New York: Oxford University Press, 1955, pp. 167–169.

Rumbold, Richard and Margaret Stewart. *The Winged Life: A Portrait of Antoine de Saint-Exupéry, Poet and Airman.* London: Weidenfeld and Nicolson, 1953, pp. 109–110, 114–118.

Smith, Maxwell A. *Knight of the Air: The Life and Works of Antoine de Saint-Exupéry.* New York: Pageant, 1956, pp. 81–96.

Taffel, Abram. "The Imagery of Confinement and Weight in the Works of Saint-Exupéry," in *Modern Language Quarterly.* XX (March, 1959), pp. 67–73.

Young, Michael T. *Saint-Exupéry:* Vol de Nuit. London: Edward Arnold, 1971.

Southern Mail

Bree, Germaine and Margaret Guiton. *An Age of Fiction: The French Novel from Gide to Camus.* New Brunswick, N.J.: Rutgers University Press, 1957, pp. 194–195.

Cate, Curtis. *Antoine de Saint-Exupéry.* New York: Putnam's, 1970, pp. 151–159.

Kestner, Joseph A., III. "Pindar and Saint-Exupéry: The Heroic Form of Space," in *Modern Fiction Studies.* XIX (1973–1974), pp. 507–516.

Knight, Everett W. "Saint-Exupéry," in his *Literature Considered as Philosophy: The French Example.* New York: Macmillan, 1958, pp. 162–163.

McKeon, Joseph T. "Saint-Exupéry, the Myth of the Pilot," in *PMLA.* LXXXIX (October, 1974), pp. 1084–1089.

Maurois, André. "Antoine de Saint-Exupéry," in his *From Proust to Camus: Profiles of Modern French Writers.* Garden City, N.Y.: Doubleday, 1966, pp. 201–223.

Mitchell, Bonner. "Mystical Imagery in Saint-Exupéry's First and Last Works," in *Kentucky Foreign Language Quarterly.* VI (1959), pp. 164–166.

Parry, M. "A Symbolic Interpretation of *Courrier Sud,*" in *Modern Language Review.* LXIX (1974), pp. 297–307.

Rumbold, Richard and Margaret Stewart. *The Winged Life: A Portrait of Antoine de Saint-Exupéry, Poet and Airman.* London: Weidenfeld and Nicolson, 1953, pp. 77–82.

Smith, Maxwell A. *Knight of the Air: The Life and Works of Antoine de Saint-Exupéry.* New York: Pageant, 1956, pp. 62–69.

Taffel, Abram. "The Imagery of Confinement and Weight in the Works of Saint-Exupéry," in *Modern Language Quarterly.* XX (March, 1959), pp. 67–73.

Wadsworth, Philip A. "Saint-Exupéry, Artist and Humanist," in *Modern Language Quarterly.* XII (March, 1951), pp. 100–101.

Wind, Sand and Stars

Cate, Curtis. *Antoine de Saint-Exupéry.* New York: Putnam's, 1970, pp. 367–373.

Ferguson, Otis. "The Man at the Wheel," in *New Republic.* XCIX (July 5, 1939), p. 256.

Frohock, Wilbur M. "Saint-Exupéry: The Poet as Novelist," in his *Style and Temper: Studies in French Fiction, 1925–1960.* Cambridge, Mass.: Harvard University Press, 1967, pp. 31–44.

Gould, Bruce. "Pioneers of the Airlanes," in *Saturday Review of Literature.* XX (June 17, 1939), p. 5.

Jennings, Elizabeth. "Antoine de Saint-Exupéry: A Vision of Space," in her *Seven Men of Vision: An Appreciation.* New York: Barnes & Noble, 1976, pp. 173–223.

Knight, Everett W. "Saint-Exupéry," in his *Literature Considered as Philosophy: The French Example.* New York: Macmillan, 1958, pp. 160–185.

Leighton, Clare. "A Poet-Philosopher of the Air," in *New York Times Book Review.* (June 18, 1939), p. 1.

Lindbergh, Anne Morrow. "An Appreciation," in *Wind, Sand and Stars.* By Antoine de Saint-Exupéry. New York: Reynal and Hitchcock, 1939, pp. 1–8.

McKeon, Joseph T. "Saint-Exupéry, the Myth of the Pilot," in *PMLA.* LXXXIX (October, 1974), pp. 1084–1089.

Maurois, André. "Antoine de Saint-Exupéry," in his *From Proust to Camus: Profiles of Modern French Writers.* Garden City, N.Y.: Doubleday, 1966, pp. 201–223.

Peyre, Henri. *The Contemporary French Novel.* New York: Oxford University Press, 1955, pp. 169–173.

Rumbold, Richard and Margaret Stewart. *The Winged Life: A Portrait of Antoine de Saint-Exupéry, Poet and Airman.* London: Weidenfeld and Nicolson, 1953, pp. 10–11, 140–141, 158–161.

Smith, Maxwell A. *Knight of the Air: The Life and Works of Antoine de Saint-Exupéry.* New York: Pageant, 1956, pp. 121–134.

Taffel, Abram. "The Imagery of Confinement and Weight in the Works of Saint-Exupéry," in *Modern Language Quarterly.* XX (March, 1959), pp. 67–73.

The Wisdom of the Sands

Cate, Curtis. *Antoine de Saint-Exupéry.* New York: Putnam's, 1970, pp. 555–571.

Kestner, Joseph A., III. "Pindar and Saint-Exupéry: The Heroic Form of Space," in *Modern Fiction Studies.* XIX (1973–1974), pp. 507–516.

Knight, Everett W. "Saint-Exupéry," in his *Literature Considered as Philosophy: The French Example.* New York: Macmillan, 1958, pp. 173–181.

Maurois, André. "Antoine de Saint-Exupéry," in his *From Proust to Camus: Profiles of Modern French Writers.* Garden City, N.Y.: Doubleday, 1966, pp. 201–223.

Milligan, E.E. "Saint-Exupéry and Language," in *Modern Language Journal.* XXXIX (1955), pp. 249–251.

Mitchell, Bonner. "Mystical Imagery in Saint-Exupéry's First and Last Works," in *Kentucky Foreign Language Quarterly.* VI (1959), pp. 166–167.

————. "*Le Petit Prince* and *Citadelle*: Two Experiments in the Didactic Style," in *French Review.* XXXIII (April, 1960), pp. 454–461.

Price, Robert H. "Saint-Exupéry's Conception of God," in *French Review.* XXXIII (May, 1960), pp. 563–567.

Rumbold, Richard and Margaret Stewart. *The Winged Life: A Portrait of Antoine de Saint-Exupéry, Poet and Airman.* London: Weidenfeld and Nicolson, 1953, pp. 205–208.

Smith, Maxwell A. *Knight of the Air: The Life and Works of Antoine de Saint-Exupéry.* New York: Pageant, 1956, pp. 226–238.

————. "Saint-Exupéry's *Citadelle*," in *French Review.* XXV (October, 1951), pp. 16–22.

Taffel, Abram. "The Imagery of Confinement and Weight in the Works of Saint-Exupéry," in *Modern Language Quarterly*. XX (March, 1959), pp. 67–73.

Wadsworth, Philip A. "Saint-Exupéry, Artist and Humanist," in *Modern Language Quarterly*. XII (March, 1951), pp. 96–99.

SAKI
(1870–1916)

The Short Stories of Saki

Bilton, Peter. "Salute to an N.C.O.," in *English Studies*. XLVII (December, 1966), pp. 439–442.

Drake, Robert. "Saki's Ironic Stories," in *Texas Studies in Literature and Language*. V (Autumn, 1963), pp. 374–388.

————. "The Sauce for the Asparagus," in *The Saturday Book*. Edited by John Hadfield. London: Hutchinson's, 1960, pp. 61–73.

Gillen, Charles H. *H.H. Munro (Saki)*. New York: Twayne, 1969.

Mais, S.P.B. "The Humour of Saki," in *Books and Their Writers*. London: Grant Richards, 1920, pp. 311–330.

Overmyer, Janet. " 'Turn Down an Empty Glass,' " in *Texas Quarterly*. VII (Autumn, 1964), pp. 171–175.

Stevick, Philip. "Saki's Beasts," in *English Literature in Transition*. IX (1966), pp. 33–37.

Thrane, James R. " 'Saki': The Achievement of the Cat," in *Wisconsin Studies in Literature*. II (1965), pp. 46–53.

"Sredni Vashtar"

Cunliffe, W. Gordon. " 'Sredni Vashtar,' " in *Insight II: Analyses of British Literature*. Edited by John V. Hagopian and Martin Dolch. Frankfurt, Germany: Hirschgraben, 1964, pp. 260–263.

Drake, Robert. "Saki's Ironic Stories," in *Texas Studies in Literature and Language*. V (Autumn, 1963), pp. 374–388.

Gillen, Charles H. *H.H. Munro (Saki)*. New York: Twayne, 1969, pp. 86–87.

Spears, George J. *The Satire of Saki: A Study of the Satiric Art of Hector H. Munro*. New York: Exposition, 1963, pp. 48–49.

Stanton, Robert. *The Short Story and the Reader*. New York: Holt, 1960, pp. 49–52.

J.D. SALINGER
(1919–   )

The Catcher in the Rye

Baumbach, Jonathan. "The Saint as Young Man: A Reappraisal of *The Catcher in the Rye*," in *Modern Language Quarterly*. XXV (December, 1964), pp. 461–472.

Bowden, Edwin T. *The Dungeon of the Heart: Human Isolation and the American Novel.* New York: Macmillan, 1961, pp. 54–65.

Branch, Edgar. "Mark Twain and J.D. Salinger: A Study in Literary Continuity," in *American Quarterly*. IX (Summer, 1957), pp. 144–158. Reprinted in *Salinger's* Catcher in the Rye: *Clamor vs. Criticism.* Edited by Harold P. Simonson and Philip E. Hager. Boston: Heath, 1963, pp. 81–91. Also reprinted in *J.D. Salinger and the Critics.* Edited by William F. Belcher and J.W. Lee. Belmont, Calif.: Wadsworth, 1966, pp. 20–34.

Bungert, Hans. "Salinger's *The Catcher in the Rye*: The Isolated Youth and His Struggle to Communicate," in *Studies in J.D. Salinger: Reviews, Essays, and Critiques of* The Catcher in the Rye *and Other Fiction.* Edited by Marvin Laser and Norman Fruman. New York: Odyssey, 1963, pp. 177–185.

Cagle, Charles. "*The Catcher in the Rye* Revisited," in *Midwest Quarterly*. IV (Summer, 1964), pp. 343–351.

Cohen, Humbert I. " 'A Woeful Agony Which Forced Me to Begin My Tale': *The Catcher in the Rye*," in *Modern Fiction Studies*. XII (Autumn, 1966), pp. 355–366.

Creeger, George R. "Treacherous Desertion: Salinger's *The Catcher in the Rye*," in *J.D. Salinger and the Critics.* Edited by William F. Belcher and J.W. Lee. Belmont, Calif.: Wadsworth, 1966, pp. 98–104.

Fogel, Amy. "Where the Ducks Go: *The Catcher in the Rye*," in *Ball State Teachers College Forum*. III (Spring, 1962), pp. 75–79.

Fowler, Albert. "Alien in the Rye," in *Modern Age*. I (Fall, 1957), pp. 193–197. Reprinted in *J.D. Salinger and the Critics.* Edited by William F. Belcher and J.W. Lee. Belmont, Calif.: Wadsworth, 1966, pp. 34–40.

Heiserman, Arthur and James E. Miller, Jr. "J.D. Salinger: Some Crazy Cliff," in *Western Humanities Review*. X (Spring, 1956), pp. 129–132. Reprinted in *Studies in J.D. Salinger: Reviews, Essays, and Critiques of* The Catcher in the Rye *and Other Fiction.* Edited by Marvin Laser and Norman Fruman. New York: Odyssey, 1963, pp. 23–30. Also reprinted in *If You Really Want to Know: A Catcher Casebook.* Edited by Malcolm M. Marsden. Chicago: Scott, Foresman, 1963, pp. 16–22.

Howell, John M. "Salinger in the Waste Land," in *Modern Fiction Studies*. XII (Autumn, 1966), pp. 367–375.

Kaplan, Charles. "Holden and Huck: The Odysseys of Youth," in *College English*. XVIII (November, 1956), pp. 76–80.

Kinney, Arthur F. "J.D. Salinger and the Search for Love," in *Texas Studies in Literature and Language*. V (1963), pp. 111–114.

————. "The Theme of Charity in *The Catcher in the Rye*," in *Michigan Academy of Science, Arts, and Letters. Papers*. XLVIII (1963), pp. 691–702.

Lettis, Richard. *J.D. Salinger:* The Catcher in the Rye. Great Neck, N.Y.: Barrons Education Series, 1964.

Levine, Paul. "J.D. Salinger: The Development of the Misfit Hero," in *Twentieth Century Literature*. IV (October, 1958), pp. 92–99.

Light, James F. "Salinger's *The Catcher in the Rye*," in *Explicator*. XVIII (June, 1960), item 59. Reprinted in *If You Really Want to Know: A Catcher Casebook*. Edited by Malcolm M. Marsden. Chicago: Scott, Foresman, 1963, pp. 98–99.

Maclean, Hugh N. "Conservatism in Modern American Fiction," in *College English*. XV (March, 1954), pp. 315–322.

Marcus, Fred. "*The Catcher in the Rye*: A Live Circuit," in *English Journal*. LII (January, 1963), pp. 1–8.

Moore, Robert P. "The World of Holden," in *English Journal*. LIV (March, 1965), pp. 159–165.

O'Hara, J.D. "No Catcher in the Rye," in *Modern Fiction Studies*. IX (Winter, 1963–64), pp. 370–376.

Pilkington, John. "About This Madman Stuff," in *University of Mississippi Studies in English*. VII (1966), pp. 65–75.

Seng, Peter J. "The Fallen Idol: The Immature World of Holden Caulfield," in *College English*. XXIII (December, 1961), pp. 203–209. Reprinted in *Salinger's* Catcher in the Rye: *Clamor vs. Criticism*. Edited by Harold P. Simonson and Philip E. Hager. Boston: Heath, 1963, pp. 65–71.

Slabey, Robert M. "*The Catcher in the Rye*: Christian Theme and Symbol," in *College Language Association Journal*. VI (March, 1963), pp. 170–183.

Strauch, Carl F. "Kings in the Back Row: Meaning Through Structure—A Reading of J.D. Salinger's *The Catcher in the Rye*," in *Wisconsin Studies in Contemporary Literature*. II (Winter, 1961), pp. 5–30.

Trowbridge, Clinton W. "Hamlet and Holden," in *English Journal*. LVII (January, 1968), pp. 26–29.

"De Daumier-Smith's Blue Period"

Barr, Donald. "Ah, Buddy: Salinger," in *The Creative Present*. Edited by Nona Balakian and Charles Simmons. Garden City, N.Y.: Doubleday, 1963, pp. 48–50.

Elmen, Paul. "Twice-Blessed Enamel Flowers: Reality in Contemporary Fiction," in *The Climate of Faith in Modern Literature.* Edited by Nathan A. Scott. New York: Seabury Press, 1964, pp. 84–87, 100–101.

French, Warren. *J.D. Salinger.* New York: Twayne, 1963, pp. 135–138.

Galloway, David D. *The Absurd Hero in American Fiction.* Austin: University of Texas Press, 1966, pp. 147–149.

Geismar, Maxwell. *American Moderns: From Rebellion to Conformity.* New York: Hill & Wang, 1958, pp. 200–201. Reprinted in *J.D. Salinger and the Critics.* Edited by William F. Belcher and James W. Lee. Belmont, Calif.: Wadsworth, 1962, p. 122.

Goldstein, Bernice and Sanford Goldstein. "Zen and *Nine Stories*," in *Renascence.* XXII (1970), pp. 178–181.

Gwynn, Frederick L. and Joseph L. Blotner. *The Fiction of J.D. Salinger.* Pittsburgh: University of Pittsburgh Press, 1958, pp. 33–40.

Harper, Howard M. *Desperate Faith.* Chicago: University of Chicago Press, 1967, pp. 76–80.

Malin, Irving. *New American Gothic.* Carbondale: Southern Illinois University Press, 1962, pp. 88–89.

Miller, James E. *J.D. Salinger.* Minneapolis: University of Minnesota Press, 1965, pp. 23–25.

Russell, John. "Salinger, from Daumier to Smith," in *Wisconsin Studies in Contemporary Literature.* IV (1963), pp. 70–87.

Stone, Edward. *A Certain Morbidity: A View of American Literature.* Carbondale: Southern Illinois University Press, 1969, pp. 121–139.

Wakefield, Dan. "Salinger and the Search for Love," in *New World Writing.* No. 14. New York: New American Library, 1958, pp. 76–77.

"For Esme—With Love and Squalor"

Antico, John. "The Parody of J.D. Salinger: Esme and the Fat Lady Exposed," in *Modern Fiction Studies.* XII (1966), pp. 326–334.

Barr, Donald. "Ah, Buddy: Salinger," in *The Creative Present.* Edited by Nona Balakian and Charles Simmons. Garden City, N.Y.: Doubleday, 1963, pp. 45–48.

Bostwick, Sally. "Reality, Compassion, and Mysticism in the Works of J.D. Salinger," in *Midwest Review.* V (1963), p. 32.

Browne, Robert M. "In Defense of Esme," in *College English.* XXII (1961), pp. 584–585.

Bryan, James. "A Reading of Salinger's 'For Esme—With Love and Squalor,' " in *Criticism.* IX (1967), pp. 275–288.

Burke, Brother Fidelian. "Salinger's Esme: Some Matters of Balance," in *Modern Fiction Studies.* XII (1966), pp. 341–347.

Davis, Tom. "J.D. Salinger: The Identity of Sergeant X," in *Western Humanities Review.* XVI (1962), pp. 181–183.

————. "J.D. Salinger: 'The Sound of One Hand Clapping,' " in *Wisconsin Studies in Contemporary Literature.* IV (1963), pp. 43–45.

Deer, Irving and John H. Randall. "J.D. Salinger and the Reality Beyond Words," in *Lock Haven Review.* VI (1964), pp. 17–18.

French, Warren. *J.D. Salinger.* New York: Twayne, 1963, pp. 98–101.

Galloway, David D. *The Absurd Hero in American Fiction.* Austin: University of Texas Press, 1966, pp. 152–153.

Goldstein, Bernice and Sanford Goldstein. "Zen and *Nine Stories*," in *Renascence.* XXII (1970), pp. 177–178.

Gwynn, Frederick L. and Joseph L. Blotner. *The Fiction of J.D. Salinger.* Pittsburgh: University of Pittsburgh Press, 1958, pp. 4–8.

Harper, Howard M. *Desperate Faith.* Chicago: University of Chicago Press, 1967, pp. 74–76.

Hassan, Ihab. "J.D. Salinger: Rare Quixotic Gesture," in *Western Review.* XXI (1957), pp. 270–271.

Hermann, John. "J.D. Salinger: Hello Hello Hello," in *College English.* XXII (1961), pp. 262–264.

Malin, Irving. *New American Gothic.* Carbondale: Southern Illinois University Press, 1962, pp. 60–61. Reprinted in *Psychoanalysis and American Fiction.* Edited by Irving Malin. New York: Dutton, 1965, pp. 263–264.

Miller, James E. *J.D. Salinger.* Minneapolis: University of Minnesota Press, 1965, pp. 22–23.

Slabey, Robert M. "Sergeant X and Seymour Glass," in *Western Humanities Review.* XVI (1962), pp. 376–377.

Tosta, Michael. " 'Will the Real Sergeant X Please Stand Up,' " in *Western Humanities Review.* XVI (1962), p. 376.

Wakefield, Dan. "Salinger and the Search for Love," in *New World Writing.* No. 14. New York: New American Library, 1958, pp. 75–76.

Wiegand, William. "J.D. Salinger's Seventy-Eight Bananas," in *Chicago Review.* XI (Winter, 1958), p. 11.

"Franny"

Barr, Donald. "Ah, Buddy: Salinger," in *The Creative Present.* Edited by Nona Balakian and Charles Simmons. Garden City, N.Y.: Doubleday, 1963, p. 59.

Bode, Carl. *The Half-World of American Culture: A Miscellany.* Carbondale: Southern Illinois University Press, 1965, pp. 212–216.

Deer, Irving and John H. Randall. "J.D. Salinger and the Reality Beyond Words," in *Lock Haven Review.* VI (1964), pp. 14–15.

Detweiler, Robert. *Four Spiritual Crises in Mid-Century American Fiction.* Gainesville: University of Florida Press, 1963, pp. 36–43.

Didion, Joan. "Finally (Fashionably) Spurious," in *National Review.* XI (November 18, 1961), pp. 341–342. Reprinted in *Studies in J.D. Salinger.* Edited by Marvin Laser and Norman Fruman. New York: Odyssey, 1963, pp. 232–234.

French, Warren. *J.D. Salinger.* New York: Twayne, 1963, pp. 139–143.

Galloway, David D. *The Absurd Hero in American Fiction.* Austin: University of Texas Press, 1966, pp. 156–159.

Geismar, Maxwell. *American Modern: From Rebellion to Conformity.* New York: Hill & Wang, 1958, pp. 201–203.

Goldstein, Bernice and Sanford Goldstein. "Bunnies and Cobras: Zen Enlightenment in Salinger," in *Discourse.* XIII (1970), pp. 98–106.

Gwynn, Frederick L. and Joseph L. Blotner. *The Fiction of J.D. Salinger.* Pittsburgh: University of Pittsburgh Press, 1958, pp. 46–48.

Levine, Paul. "J.D. Salinger: The Development of the Misfit Hero," in *Twentieth-Century Literature.* IV (1958), p. 95.

Livingston, James T. "J.D. Salinger: The Artist's Struggle to Stand on Holy Ground," in *Adversity and Grace: Studies in Recent American Literature.* Edited by Nathan A. Scott. Chicago: University of Chicago Press, 1968, pp. 123–133.

McCarthy, Mary. "J.D. Salinger's Closed Circuit," in *Harper's.* CCXXV (October, 1962), pp. 46–47. Reprinted in *Studies in J.D. Salinger.* Edited by Marvin Laser and Norman Fruman. New York: Odyssey, 1963, pp. 246–247.

McIntyre, John P. "A Preface for *Franny and Zooey,*" in *Critic.* XX (February, 1962), pp. 25–28.

Marple, Anne. "Salinger's Oasis of Innocence," in *New Republic.* CXLV (September 18, 1961), p. 22. Reprinted in *Studies in J.D. Salinger.* Edited by Marvin Laser and Norman Fruman. New York: Odyssey, 1963, pp. 241–242.

Miller, James E. *J.D. Salinger.* Minneapolis: University of Minnesota Press, 1965, p. 30.

Phillips, Paul. "Salinger's *Franny and Zooey,*" in *Mainstream.* XV (January, 1962), pp. 34–36.

Rees, Richard. "The Salinger Situation," in *Contemporary American Novelists.* Edited by Harry T. Moore. Carbondale: Southern Illinois University Press, pp. 100–103.

Schulz, Max F. *Radical Sophistication: Studies in Contemporary Jewish-American Novelists.* Athens: Ohio University Press, 1969, pp. 198–201.

Seitzman, Daniel. "Salinger's 'Franny': Homoerotic Imagery," in *American Imago.* XXII (1965), pp. 57–76.

Updike, John. " 'Franny' and 'Zooey,' " in *Salinger: A Critical and Personal Portrait.* Edited by Henry Anatole Grunwald. New York: Harper & Row, 1962, pp. 53–56. Reprinted in *Studies in J.D. Salinger.* Edited by Marvin Laser and Norman Fruman. New York: Odyssey, 1963, p. 228.

Wakefield, Dan. "Salinger and the Search for Love," in *New World Writing.* No. 14. New York: New American Library, 1958, pp. 80–81.

Wiegand, William. "Salinger and Kierkegaard," in *Minnesota Review.* V (1965), pp. 141–144.

————. "J.D. Salinger's Seventy-Eight Bananas," in *Chicago Review.* XI (Winter, 1958), p. 14.

"A Perfect Day for Bananafish"

Bryan, James E. "Salinger's Seymour's Suicide," in *College English.* XXIV (1962), pp. 226–229.

Davis, Tom. "J.D. Salinger: The Identity of Sergeant X," in *Western Humanities Review.* XVI (1962), pp. 181–183.

French, Warren. *J.D. Salinger.* New York: Twayne, 1963, pp. 78–85.

————. "Salinger's Seymour: Another Autopsy," in *College English.* XXIV (1963), p. 563.

Galloway, David D. *The Absurd Hero in American Fiction.* Austin: University of Texas Press, 1966, pp. 149–151.

Goldstein, Bernice and Sanford Goldstein. "Zen and *Nine Stories,*" in *Renascence.* XXII (1970), pp. 175–177.

Gwynn, Frederick L. and Joseph L. Blotner. *The Fiction of J.D. Salinger.* Pittsburgh: University of Pittsburgh Press, 1958, pp. 19–21. Reprinted in *J.D. Salinger and the Critics.* Edited by William F. Belcher and James W. Lee. Belmont, Calif.: Wadsworth, 1962, pp. 141–143.

Hamilton, Kenneth. *J.D. Salinger: A Critical Essay.* Grand Rapids, Mich.: Eerdmans, 1967, pp. 28–31.

Harper, Howard M. *Desperate Faith.* Chicago: University of Chicago Press, 1967, pp. 85–87.

Hassan, Ihab. "J.D. Salinger: Rare Quixotic Gesture," in *Western Review.* XXI (1957), pp. 267–268.

Livingston, James T. "J.D. Salinger: The Artist's Struggle to Stand on Holy Ground," in *Adversity and Grace: Studies in Recent American Literature.* Edited by Nathan A. Scott. Chicago: University of Chicago Press, 1968, pp. 110–117.

Malin, Irving. *New American Gothic.* Carbondale: Southern Illinois University Press, 1962, pp. 30–31. Reprinted in *Psychoanalysis and American Fiction.* Edited by Irving Malin. New York: Dutton, 1965, pp. 262–263.

Metcalf, Frank. "The Suicide of Salinger's Seymour Glass," in *Studies in Short Fiction.* IX (1972), pp. 243–246.

Miller, James E. *J.D. Salinger.* Minneapolis: University of Minnesota Press, 1965, pp. 27–29.

Schulz, Max F. *Radical Sophistication: Studies in Contemporary Jewish-American Novelists.* Athens: Ohio University Press, 1969, pp. 199–203.

Wiebe, Dallas E. "Salinger's 'A Perfect Day for Bananafish,' " in *Explicator.* XXIII (1964), item 3.

Wiegand, William. "J.D. Salinger's Seventy-Eight Bananas," in *Chicago Review.* XI (Winter, 1958), pp. 5–7.

"Raise High the Roofbeam, Carpenters"

Barr, Donald. "Ah, Buddy: Salinger," in *The Creative Present.* Edited by Nona Balakian and Charles Simmons. Garden City, N.Y.: Doubleday, 1963, pp. 51, 60.

Baskett, Sam S. "The Splendid/Squalid World of J.D. Salinger," in *Wisconsin Studies in Contemporary Literature.* IV (1963), pp. 54–61.

Chester, Alfred. "Salinger: How to Live Without Love," in *Commentary.* XXXV (1963), pp. 471–472.

French, Warren. *J.D. Salinger.* New York: Twayne, 1963, pp. 148–155.

Gwynn, Frederick L. and Joseph L. Blotner. *The Fiction of J.D. Salinger.* Pittsburgh: University of Pittsburgh Press, 1958, pp. 45–46.

Hassan, Ihab. "Almost the Voice of Silence: The Later Novelettes of J.D. Salinger," in *Wisconsin Studies in Contemporary Literature.* IV (1963), pp. 7–10.

Levine, Paul. "J.D. Salinger: The Development of the Misfit Hero," in *Twentieth-Century Literature.* IV (1958), pp. 95–96.

Malin, Irving. *New American Gothic.* Carbondale: Southern Illinois University Press, 1962, pp. 31–32.

Miller, James E. *J.D. Salinger.* Minneapolis: University of Minnesota Press, 1965, pp. 36–39.

Schwartz, Arthur. "For Seymour—With Love and Judgment," in *Wisconsin Studies in Contemporary Literature.* IV (1963), pp. 88–91.

Wiegand, William. "J.D. Salinger's Seventy-Eight Bananas," in *Chicago Review.* XI (Winter, 1958), pp. 15–16.

————. "Salinger and Kierkegaard," in *Minnesota Review.* V (1965), pp. 151–156.

"Seymour: An Introduction"

Barr, Donald. "Ah, Buddy: Salinger," in *The Creative Present*. Edited by Nona Balakian and Charles Simmons. Garden City, N.Y.: Doubleday, 1963, pp. 60–61.

Baskett, Sam S. "The Splendid/Squalid World of J.D. Salinger," in *Wisconsin Studies in Contemporary Literature*. IV (1963), pp. 54–61.

Chester, Alfred. "Salinger: How to Live Without Love," in *Commentary*. XXXV (1963), p. 474.

French, Warren. *J.D. Salinger*. New York: Twayne, 1963, pp. 57–58, 155–160.

Goldstein, Bernice and Sanford Goldstein. "Bunnies and Cobras: Zen Enlightenment in Salinger," in *Discourse*. XII (1970), pp. 98–106.

————. " 'Seymour: An Introduction'—Writing As Discovery," in *Studies in Short Fiction*. VII (1970), pp. 248–257.

Hassan, Ihab. "Almost the Voice of Silence: The Later Novelettes of J.D. Salinger," in *Wisconsin Studies in Contemporary Literature*. IV (1963), pp. 13–18.

————. "The Dismemberment of Orpheus," in *Learners and Discerners*. Edited by Robert Scholes. Charlottesville: University of Virginia Press, 1964, pp. 161–162.

Lyons, John O. "The Romantic Style of Salinger's 'Seymour: An Introduction,' " in *Wisconsin Studies in Contemporary Literature*. IV (1963), pp. 62–69.

Miller, James E. *J.D. Salinger*. Minneapolis: University of Minnesota Press, 1965, pp. 39–42.

Schulz, Max F. "Epilogue to 'Seymour: An Introduction': Salinger and the Crisis of Consciousness," in *Studies in Short Fiction*. V (1968), pp. 128–138.

————. *Radical Sophistication: Studies in Contemporary Jewish-American Novelists*. Athens: Ohio University Press, 1969, pp. 204–211.

Wiegand, William. "The Knighthood of J.D. Salinger," in *Salinger: A Critical and Personal Portrait*. Edited by Henry A. Grunwald. New York: Harper, 1962, pp. 120–122.

————. "Salinger and Kierkegaard," in *Minnesota Review*. V (1965), pp. 151–156.

"Zooey"

Antico, John. "The Parody of J.D. Salinger: Esme and the Fat Lady Exposed," in *Modern Fiction Studies*. XII (1966), pp. 335–340.

Baskett, Sam S. "The Splendid/Squalid World of J.D. Salinger," in *Wisconsin Studies in Contemporary Literature*. IV (1963), pp. 52–54.

Bode, Carl. *The Half-World of American Culture: A Miscellany.* Carbondale: Southern Illinois University Press, 1965, pp. 216–220.

Bryan, James E. "J.D. Salinger: The Fat Lady and the Chicken Sandwich," in *College English.* XXIII (1961), pp. 226–229.

Chester, Alfred. "Salinger: How to Live Without Love," in *Commentary.* XXXV (1963), pp. 472–473.

Davis, Tom. "J.D. Salinger: 'The Sound of One Hand Clapping,' " in *Wisconsin Studies in Contemporary Literature.* IV (1963), pp. 45–47.

Didion, Joan. "Finally (Fashionably) Spurious," in *National Review.* XI (November 18, 1961), pp. 341–342. Reprinted in *Studies in J.D. Salinger.* Edited by Marvin Laser and Norman Fruman. New York: Odyssey, 1963, pp. 232–234.

Fiedler, Leslie A. "The Breakthrough: The American Jewish Novelist and the Fictional Image of the Jew," in *Midstream.* IV (1958), p. 31. Reprinted in *Recent American Fiction: Some Critical Views.* Edited by Joseph J. Waldmeir. Boston: Houghton Mifflin, 1963, p. 104.

French, Warren. *J.D. Salinger.* New York: Twayne, 1963, pp. 143–148.

Galloway, David D. *The Absurd Hero in American Fiction.* Austin: University of Texas Press, 1966, pp. 159–169.

Geismar, Maxwell. *American Moderns: From Rebellion to Conformity.* New York: Hill & Wang, 1958, pp. 204–208.

Green, Martin. *Some Commonsense Readings in American Literature.* New York: Norton, 1965, pp. 207–210.

Gwynn, Frederick L. and Joseph L. Blotner. *The Fiction of J.D. Salinger.* Pittsburgh: University of Pittsburgh Press, 1958, pp. 48–52.

Hamilton, Kenneth. "One Way to Use the Bible: The Example of J.D. Salinger," in *Christian Scholar.* XLVII (1964), pp. 246–249.

Hassan, Ihab. "Almost the Voice of Silence: The Later Novelettes of J.D. Salinger," in *Wisconsin Studies in Contemporary Literature.* IV (1963), pp. 10–13.

Levine, Paul. "J.D. Salinger: The Development of the Misfit Hero," in *Twentieth-Century Literature.* IV (1958), pp. 97–99.

McCarthy, Mary. "J.D. Salinger's Closed Circuit," in *Harper's.* CCXXV (October, 1962), pp. 47–48. Reprinted in *Studies in J.D. Salinger.* Edited by Marvin Laser and Norman Fruman. New York: Odyssey, 1963, pp. 247–250.

Malin, Irving. *New American Gothic.* Carbondale: Southern Illinois University Press, 1962, pp. 33–34.

Marple, Anne. "Salinger's Oasis of Innocence," in *New Republic.* CXLV (September 18, 1961), p. 22. Reprinted in *Studies in J.D. Salinger.* Edited by Marvin Laser and Norman Fruman. New York: Odyssey, 1963, pp. 242–243.

Miller, James E.   *J.D. Salinger.* Minneapolis: University of Minnesota Press, 1965, pp. 30–36.

Mizener, Arthur.   "The Love Song of J.D. Salinger," in *Harper's.* CCVIII (February, 1959), pp. 86–90.

Phillips, Paul.   "Salinger's *Franny and Zooey,*" in *Mainstream.* XV (January, 1962), pp. 36–38.

Updike, John.   " 'Franny' and 'Zooey,' " in *Studies in J.D. Salinger.* Edited by Marvin Laser and Norman Fruman. New York: Odyssey, 1963, pp. 229–230.

Wakefield, Dan.   "Salinger and the Search for Love," in *New World Writing.* No. 14. New York: New American Library, 1958, pp. 80–84.

Wiegand, William.   "J.D. Salinger's Seventy-Eight Bananas," in *Chicago Review.* XI (Winter, 1958), pp. 16–17.

GEORGE SAND
(1804–1876)

Consuelo

Bradford, Gamaliel. "Eve and the Pen," in *Daughters of Eve*. Boston: Houghton Mifflin, 1930, pp. 226–229.

Cate, Curtis. "Pauline Garcia and Consuelo," in *George Sand: A Biography*. Boston: Houghton Mifflin, 1975, pp. 512–524.

Saintsbury, George. *A History of the French Novel*. London: Macmillan, 1919, pp. 185–191.

Sullivan, Edward D. *"Lelia; Consuelo and La Comtese de Rudolstadt,"* in *Modern Philology*. LIX (November, 1961), pp. 141–143.

Wright, C.D.C. "Fiction," in *A History of French Literature*. New York: Oxford University Press, 1925, p. 718.

Indiana

Cate, Curtis. *"Indiana,"* in *George Sand: A Biography*. Boston: Houghton Mifflin, 1975, pp. 192–206.

Doumic, Rene. *George Sand: Some Aspects of Her Life and Work*. New York: Putnam's, 1910, pp. 76–83.

Grebanier, Frances Winwar. *The Life of the Heart: George Sand and Her Times*. New York: Harper, 1945, pp. 106–108.

Howe, Marie Jenney. *George Sand: The Search for Love*. New York: John Day, 1927, pp. 96–103.

Jordon, Ruth. "Do Not Make Books, Make Children," in *George Sand: A Biographical Portrait*. New York: Taplinger, 1976, pp. 62–63.

Pellissier, George. *Literary Movement in France During the Nineteenth Century*. New York: Putnam's, 1897, p. 299.

Seyd, Felizia. *Romantic Rebel: The Life and Time of George Sand*. New York: Viking, 1940, pp. 71–76.

Wells, Benjamin W. "George Sand," in *A Century of French Fiction*. New York: Dodd Mead, 1903, pp. 223–224.

Wright, C.H.C. "Fiction," in *A History of French Literature*. New York: Oxford University Press, 1925, p. 716.

CARL SANDBURG
(1878–1967)

Abraham Lincoln

Allen, Gay Wilson. *Carl Sandburg.* Minneapolis: University of Minnesota Press, 1972, pp. 28–33.

Callahan, North. *Carl Sandburg: Lincoln of Our Literature.* New York: New York University Press, 1970, pp. 75–106.

Crowder, Richard. *Carl Sandburg.* New York: Twayne, 1964, pp. 95–102, 126–136.

Golden, Harry. *Carl Sandburg.* Cleveland: World, 1961, pp. 239–260.

Haas, Joseph and Gene Lovitz. *Carl Sandburg.* Putnam's, 1967, pp. 108–112, 132–136.

Hicken, Victor. "Sandburg and the Lincoln Biography: A Personal View," in *The Vision of This Land: Studies of Vachel Lindsay, Edgar Lee Masters, and Carl Sandburg.* Edited by John E. Hallwas and Dennis J. Reader. Macomb: Western Illinois University Press, 1976, pp. 105–113.

Wilson, Edmund. *Patriotic Gore: Studies in the Literature of the American Civil War.* New York: Oxford University Press, 1962, pp. 115–117.

Yatron, Michael. *America's Literary Revolt.* New York: Philosophical Library, 1959, pp. 155–160.

Chicago Poems

Alexander, William. "The Limited American, the Great Loneliness, and the Singing Fire: Carl Sandburg's *Chicago Poems,*" in *American Literature.* XLV (1973), pp. 67–83.

Allen, Gay Wilson. *Carl Sandburg.* Minneapolis: University of Minnesota Press, 1972, pp. 12–20.

Crowder, Richard. *Carl Sandburg.* New York: Twayne, 1964, pp. 48–68.

Gregory, Horace and Marya Zaturenska. *A History of American Poetry, 1900–1940.* New York: Harcourt, Brace, 1946, pp. 242–244.

Rubin, Louis D. "Chicago Revisited," in *Hopkins Review.* IV (Winter, 1951), pp. 63–69.

Waggoner, Hyatt H. *American Poets from the Puritans to the Present.* Boston: Houghton Mifflin, 1968, pp. 452–453.

Weirick, Bruce. *From Whitman to Sandburg in American Poetry: A Critical Survey.* New York: Macmillan, 1924, pp. 210–221.

Wood, Clement. *Poets of America.* New York: Dutton, 1925, pp. 249–252.

The People, Yes

Crowder, Richard. *Carl Sandburg.* New York: Twayne, 1964, pp. 117–126.

Haas, Joseph and Gene Lovitz. *Carl Sandburg.* New York: Putnam's, 1967, pp. 130–132.

Hoffman, Daniel G. "Sandburg and 'The People': His Literary Populism Reappraised," in *Antioch Review.* X (1950), pp. 265–278.

Mayer, Charles W. "*The People, Yes*: Sandburg's Dreambook for Today," in *The Vision of This Land: Studies of Vachel Lindsay, Edgar Lee Masters, and Carl Sandburg.* Edited by John E. Hallwas and Dennis J. Reader. Macomb: Western Illinois University Press, 1976, pp. 82–91.

Mieder, Wolfgang. "Proverbs in Carl Sandburg's Poem *The People, Yes*," in *Southern Folklore Quarterly.* XXXVII (1973), pp. 15–36.

Wells, Henry W. *The American Way of Poetry.* New York: Russell & Russell, 1964, pp. 138–143.

Yatron, Michael. *America's Literary Revolt.* New York: Philosophical Library, 1959, pp. 138–154.

Remembrance Rock

Allen, Gay Wilson. *Carl Sandburg.* Minneapolis: University of Minnesota Press, 1972, pp. 33–34.

Crowder, Richard. *Carl Sandburg.* New York: Twayne, 1964, pp. 140–150.

Golden, Harry. *Carl Sandburg.* Cleveland: World Publishing, 1961, pp. 231–235.

Haas, Joseph and Gene Lovitz. *Carl Sandburg.* New York: Putnam's, 1967, pp. 154–155.

Yatron, Michael. *America's Literary Revolt.* New York: Philosophical Library, 1959, pp. 161–164.

SAPPHO
(Unknown, fl. c.600 B.C.)

The Poetry of Sappho

Bagg, R. "Love, Ceremony and Daydream in Sappho's Lyrics," in *Arion*. III (Autumn, 1964), pp. 44–82.

Bonnard, A. "Sappho of Lesbos, Tenth of the Muses," in his *Greek Civilization; From the Iliad to the Parthenon*. New York: Macmillan, 1957, pp. 86–100.

Cameron, A. "Sappho and Aphrodite Again," in *Harvard Theological Review*. LVII (July, 1964), pp. 237–239.

————. "Sappho's Prayer to Aphrodite," in *Harvard Theological Review*. XXXII (January, 1939), pp. 1–17.

Danielewicz, J. "Experience and Its Artistic Aspect in Sappho's Subjective Lyrics," in *Eos*. LVIII (1969–1970), pp. 163–169.

Devereaux, G. "The Nature of Sappho's Seizure in Fragment 31 *LP* as Evidence of Her Inversion," in *Classical Quarterly*. XX (1970), pp. 17–31.

Green, Peter. "The Individual Voice: Archilochus and Sappho," in his *The Shadow of the Parthenon*. Berkeley: University of California Press, 1972, pp. 152–192.

Koxiaris, G.L. "On Sappho, Fragment 31 *L.-P*," in *Philologus*. CXII (1968), pp. 173–186.

Lefkowitz, M.R. "Critical Stereotypes and the Poetry of Sappho," in *Greek, Roman and Byzantine Studies*. XIV (1973), pp. 113–123.

Marcovich, M. "Sappho, Fragment 31: Anxiety Attack or Love Declaration?," in *Classical Quarterly*. XXII (1972), pp. 19–32.

Nagy, G. "Phaethon, Sappho's Phaon, and the White Rock of Leukas," in *Harvard Studies in Classical Philology*. LXXVII (1973), pp. 137–178.

Page, Denry. *Sappho and Aliaeus; an Introduction to the Study of Ancient Lesbian Poetry*. Oxford: Clarendon Press, 1955.

Rexroth, Kenneth. "Sappho: Poems," in *Classics Revisited*. New York: Quadrangle, 1968, pp. 41–46.

Robinson, David Moore. *Sappho and Her Influence*. Boston: Marshall Jones, 1924.

Stanley, K. "The Role of Aphrodite in Sappho, Fragment I," in *Greek, Roman and Byzantine Studies*. XVII (Winter, 1976), pp. 205–225.

Versenyi, Laszlo. "Archilochus and Sappho," in his *Man's Measure; a Study of the Greek Measure of Man from Homer to Sophocles*. Albany: State University of New York Press, 1974, pp. 70–88.

Weigall, A.E.P.B. *Sappho of Lesbos*. Garden City, N.Y.: Garden City Publishing, 1932.

Wyatt, W.F. "Sappho and Aphrodite," in *Classical Philology*. LXIX (July, 1974), pp. 213–214.

WILLIAM SAROYAN
(1908–   )

The Human Comedy

Burgum, Edwin B. "Lonesome Young Man on the Flying Trapeze," in *Virginia Quarterly Review*. XX (Summer, 1944), pp. 392–402. Reprinted in his *The Novel and the World's Dilemma*. New York: Russell and Russell, 1963, pp. 269–271.

Carpenter, Frederick I. "The Time of William Saroyan's Life," in *Pacific Spectator*. I (Winter, 1947), pp. 88–96. Reprinted in his *American Literature and the Dream*. New York: Philosophical Library, 1955, pp. 176–184.

Floan, Howard R. *William Saroyan*. New York: Twayne, 1966, pp. 123–126.

Gray, James. *On Second Thought*. Minneapolis: University of Minnesota Press, 1946, pp. 114–115.

Kazin, Alfred. *"The Human Comedy,"* in *The Critic as Artist: Essays on Books, 1920–1970*. Edited by Gilbert A. Harrison. New York: Liveright, 1972, pp. 217–221.

JEAN-PAUL SARTRE
(1905–   )

The Condemned of Altona

Barnes, Hazel E. *Sartre.* London: Quartet, 1974, pp. 87–97.

Galler, Dieter. "Jean-Paul Sartre's Drama, *Les Séquestrés d'Altona*: Two More Examples of the Schizophrenic Syndrome," in *Language Quarterly.* IX (1970), pp. 55–60.

————. "Jean-Paul Sartre's *Les Séquestrés d'Altona*: Old Von Gerloch, Portrait of a Schizophrenic," in *Language Quarterly.* VIII (1969), pp. 33–38.

————. "The Phases of Schizophrenia in Jean-Paul Sartre's *Les Séquestrés d'Altona*," in *Language Quarterly.* XI (1973), pp. 5–16.

————. "The Relationship Between Soma and Psyche in Jean-Paul Sartre's Drama *Les Séquestrés d'Altona*," in *Language Quarterly.* VI (1967), pp. 35–38.

————. "Stereotyped Characters in Sartre's Play, *Les Séquestrés d'Altona*," in *Kentucky Romance Quarterly.* XV (1968), pp. 57–68.

Lumley, Frederick. *New Trends in Twentieth Century Drama: A Survey Since Ibsen and Shaw.* London: Oxford University Press, 1967, pp. 139–158.

McCall, Dorothy. *The Theatre of Jean-Paul Sartre.* New York: Columbia University Press, 1969, pp. 127–151.

Matthews, Honor. *The Primal Curse, the Myth of Cain and Abel in the Theatre.* New York: Schocken, 1967, pp. 141–147.

Moore, Harry T. *Twentieth Century French Literature Since World War II*, Volume II. New York: Columbia University Press, 1966, pp. 45–51.

Palmer, Jeremy N.J. "*Les Séquestrés d'Altona*: Sartre's Black Tragedy," in *French Studies.* XXIV (1970), pp. 150–162.

Pollmann, Leo. *Sartre and Camus: Literature of Existence.* New York: Frederick Ungar, 1970, pp. 74–81.

Pucciani, Oreste F. "*Les Séquestrés d'Altona* of Jean-Paul Sartre," in *Tulane Drama Review.* V (1961), pp. 19–33.

Simon, John K. "Madness in Sartre: Sequestration and the Room," in *Yale French Studies.* XXX (Fall–Winter, 1962–1963), pp. 63–67.

Tembeck, Robert. "Dialectic and Time in *The Condemned of Altona*," in *Modern Drama.* XII (1969), pp. 10–17.

Thody, Philip. *Jean-Paul Sartre: A Literary and Political Study.* New York: Macmillan, 1961, pp. 122–134.

Williams, John S. "Sartre's Dialectic of History; *Les Séquestrés d'Altona*," in *Renascence.* XXII (1970), pp. 59–68.

The Devil and the Good Lord

Champigny, Robert. *Stages on Sartre's Way: 1938–1952.* Bloomington: Indiana University Press, 1959, pp. 104–132.

Chiari, Joseph. *The Contemporary French Theatre: The Flight from Naturalism.* New York: Macmillan, 1959, pp. 162–169.

Cohn, Ruby. *Currents in Contemporary Drama.* Bloomington: Indiana University Press, 1969, pp. 134–136.

Fauve, Jacques. "A Drama of Essence: Salacrou and Others," in *Yale French Studies.* XIV (Winter, 1954–1955), pp. 30–40.

Frank, Joseph. "God, Man, and Jean-Paul Sartre," in *Partisan Review.* XIX (March, 1952), pp. 202–210.

Hobson, Harold. *The French Theatre of Today.* London: Harrap, 1953, pp. 110–117.

Jones, Robert E. *The Alienated Hero in Modern French Drama.* Athens: University of Georgia Press, 1962, pp. 107–111.

Lewis, Allan. *The Contemporary Theatre.* New York: Crown, 1965, pp. 208–211.

Lumley, Frederick. *New Trends in Twentieth Century Drama: A Survey Since Ibsen and Shaw.* London: Oxford University Press, 1967, pp. 139–158.

Luthy, Herbert. "Jean-Paul Sartre and God," in *Twentieth Century.* CL (September, 1951), pp. 221–230.

McCall, Dorothy. *The Theatre of Jean-Paul Sartre.* New York: Columbia University Press, 1969, pp. 24–42.

Pollmann, Leo. *Sartre and Camus: Literature of Existence.* New York: Frederick Ungar, 1970, pp. 89–96.

Ricoeur, Paul. "Sartre's *Lucifer and the Lord,*" in *Yale French Studies.* XIV (1954–1955), pp. 85–93.

Ridge, George R. "*Le Diable et le bon Dieu*: Sartre's Concept of Freedom," in *Shenandoah.* IX (1958), pp. 35–38.

Thody, Philip. *Jean-Paul Sartre: A Literary and Political Study.* New York: Macmillan, 1961, pp. 102–108.

Dirty Hands

Adereth, Maxwell. *Commitment in Modern French Literature.* London: Gollancz, 1967, pp. 159–164.

Barnes, Hazel E. *Sartre.* London: Quartet, 1974, pp. 77–96.

Brown, John M. "The Boudoir vs. the Kremlin," in *Saturday Review of Literature.* XXXII (January 1, 1940), pp. 24–27.

Chiari, Joseph. *The Contemporary French Theatre: The Flight from Naturalism.* New York: Macmillan, 1959, pp. 155–162.

Clurman, Harold. "Red Faces," in *New Republic*. CXIX (December 20, 1948), pp. 28–29.

Gibbs, Wolcott. "Communism in Graustark," in *New Yorker*. XXIV (December 11, 1948), pp. 57–58.

Glicksberg, Charles I. *The Tragic Vision in Twentieth Century Literature*. Carbondale: Southern Illinois University Press, 1963, pp. 126–136.

Grossvogel, David I. *The Self-conscious Stage in Modern French Drama*. New York: Columbia University Press, 1958, pp. 129–138.

Hobson, Harold. *The French Theatre of Today*. London: Harrap, 1953, pp. 103–110.

Jones, Robert E. *The Alienated Hero in Modern French Drama*. Athens: University of Georgia Press, 1962, pp. 103–107.

Lumley, Frederick. *New Trends in Twentieth Century Drama: A Survey Since Ibsen and Shaw*. London: Oxford University Press, 1967, pp. 139–158.

McCall, Dorothy. *The Theatre of Jean-Paul Sartre*. New York: Columbia University Press, 1969, pp. 53–78.

Mendel, Sydney. "The Ambiguity of the Rebellious Son: Observations of Sartre's Play *Dirty Hands*," in *Forum*. IV (Spring, 1966), pp. 32–36.

Pollmann, Leo. *Sartre and Camus: Literature of Existence*. New York: Frederick Ungar, 1970, pp. 69–74.

Ridge, George R. "Meaningful Choice in Sartre's Drama," in *French Review*. XXX (1956–1957), pp. 435–441.

Sauvage, Leo. "*Red Gloves* and *Dirty Hands*," in *Nation*. CLXVIII (January 1, 1949), p. 19.

The Flies

Adamczewski, Zygmut. *The Tragic Protest*. The Hague: Nijhoff, 1963, pp. 193–225.

Allen, M. "Character Development in *The Oreste* of Voltaire and *Les Mouches* of Jean-Paul Sartre," in *CLA Journal*. XVIII (1974), pp. 1–21.

Artinian, Robert W. "Foul Winds in Argos; Sartre's *Les Mouches*," in *Romance Notes*. XIV (1972), pp. 7–12.

Belli, Angela. *Ancient Greek Myths and Modern Drama: A Study in Continuity*. New York: New York University Press, 1968, pp. 70–87.

Burdick, Dolores M. "Concept of Character in Giraudoux's *Electre* and Sartre's *Les Mouches*," in *French Review*. XXXII (1960), pp. 131–136.

————. "Imagery of the 'Plight' in Sartre's *Les Mouches*," in *French Review*. XXXII (1959), pp. 242–246.

Conacher, D.J. Orestes as Existentialist Hero," in *Philological Quarterly*. XXXIII (October, 1954), pp. 404–417.

Debusscher, Gilbert. "Modern Masks of the Orestes: *The Flies* and *The Prodigal*," in *Modern Drama*. XII (1970), pp. 308–318.

Jones, Robert E. *The Alienated Hero in Modern French Drama*. Athens: University of Georgia Press, 1962, pp. 96–99.

Lerner, Max. *Actions and Passions: Notes on the Multiple Revolution of Our Time*. New York: Simon and Schuster, 1959, pp. 49–51.

Lumley, Frederick. *New Trends in Twentieth Century Drama: A Survey Since Ibsen and Shaw*. London: Oxford University Press, 1967, pp. 139–158.

McCall, Dorothy. *The Theatre of Jean-Paul Sartre*. New York: Columbia University Press, 1969, pp. 9–24.

Pollmann, Leo. *Sartre and Camus: Literature of Existence*. New York: Frederick Ungar, 1970, pp. 44–51.

Thody, Philip. *Jean-Paul Sartre: A Literary and Political Study*. New York: Macmillan, 1961, pp. 71–78.

Zivanovic, Judith. "Sartre's Drama; Key to Understanding His Concept of Freedom," in *Modern Drama*. XIV (September, 1971), pp. 144–154.

Nausea

Arnold, A. James. "*La Nausee* Revisited," in *French Review*. XXXIX (November, 1965), pp. 199–213.

Bree, Germaine and Margaret Guiton. *An Age of Fiction: The French Novel from Gide to Camus*. New Brunswick, N.J.: Rutgers University Press, 1957, pp. 205–210.

Champigny, Robert. *Stages on Sartre's Way: 1938–1952*. Bloomington: Indiana University Press, 1959, pp. 23–45.

Church, Margaret. *Time and Reality*. Chapel Hill: University of North Carolina Press, 1962, pp. 257–263.

Cohn, Robert G. "Sartre's First Novel: *La Nausee*," in *Yale French Studies*. I (Spring–Summer, 1948), pp. 62–65.

Cranston, Maurice. *Jean-Paul Sartre*. New York: Grove, 1962, pp. 13–21.

Grossvogel, David I. *Limits of the Novel*. Ithaca, N.Y.: Cornell University Press, 1967, pp. 226–255.

Grubbs, Henry A. "Sartre's Recapturing of Lost Time," in *Modern Language Notes*. LXXIII (November, 1958), pp. 515–522.

Jameson, Fred. "The Laughter of *Nausea*," in *Yale French Studies*. XXIII (Summer, 1959), pp. 26–32.

Kellman, Steven G. "Sartre's *La Nausee* as Self-Begetting Novel," in *Symposium*. XXVII (Winter, 1974), pp. 303–314.

Magny, Claude-Edmonde. "The Duplicity of Being," in *Sartre: A Collection of Critical Essays.* Edited by Edith Kern. Englewood Cliffs, N.J.: Prentice-Hall, 1962, pp. 21–30.

Mendel, Sydney. "From Solitude to Salvation: A Study in Development," in *Yale French Studies.* XXX (December, 1963), pp. 47–55.

Mueller, William R. *Celebration of Life: Studies in Modern Fiction.* New York: Sheed, 1972, pp. 30–49.

Murdoch, Iris. *Sartre: Romantic Rationalist.* New Haven, Conn.: Yale University Press, 1953, pp. 1–14.

Oxenhandler, Neal. "The Metaphor of Metaphor in *La Nausee,*" in *Chicago Review.* XV (Summer–Autumn, 1962), pp. 47–54.

Walker, Margaret. "The *Nausea* of Sartre," in *Yale Review.* XLII (Winter, 1953), pp. 251–261.

Wilson, Clotilde. "Sartre's Graveyard of Chimeras: *La Nausee* and *Mort de Quelqu'un,*" in *French Review.* XXXVIII (May, 1965), pp. 744–753.

No Exit

Barnes, Hazel E. *Sartre.* London: Quartet, 1974, pp. 73–76.

Blitgen, Sister M.J. Carol. "*No Exit:* The Sartrean Idea of Hell," in *Renascence.* XIX (1967), pp. 59–63.

Bogard, Travis and William I. Oliver. *Modern Drama: Essays in Criticism.* London: Oxford University Press, 1965, pp. 276–289.

Brown, John M. *Seeing More Things.* New York: McGraw-Hill, 1948, pp. 85–91.

————. "The Unbeautiful and the Damned," in *Saturday Review of Literature.* XXIX (December 28, 1946), pp. 26–28.

Cohn, Ruby. *Currents in Contemporary Drama.* Bloomington: Indiana University Press, 1969, pp. 59–64.

————. "Hell on the 20th Century Stage," in *Wisconsin Studies in Contemporary Literature.* V (Winter–Spring, 1964), pp. 48–53.

Falk, Eugene H. "*No Exit* and *Who's Afraid of Virginia Woolf?*: A Thematic Comparison," in *Studies in Philology.* LXVII (1970), pp. 406–417.

Hobson, Harold. *The French Theatre of Today.* London: Harrap, 1953, pp. 96–103.

Kern, E. "Abandon Hope, All Ye . . . ," in *Yale French Studies.* XXX (1964), pp. 56–60.

Lumley, Frederick. *New Trends in Twentieth Century Drama: A Survey Since Ibsen and Shaw.* London: Oxford University Press, 1967, pp. 138–158.

McCall, Dorothy. *The Theatre of Jean-Paul Sartre.* New York: Columbia University Press, 1969, pp. 110–127.

Mendel, Sydney. "The Descent into Solitude," in *Forum*. III (1961), pp. 19–24.

Thody, Philip. *Jean-Paul Sartre: A Literary and Political Study*. New York: Macmillan, 1961, pp. 79–84.

Young, Stark. "Weaknesses," in *New Republic*. CXV (December, 1946), p. 764.

The Respectful Prostitute

Bentley, Eric. "Sartre's Struggle for Existenz," in *Kenyon Review*. X (Spring, 1948), pp. 328–330.

Brown, John M. "Guignal à la Sartre," in *Saturday Review of Literature*. XXXI (March 13, 1948), pp. 26–27.

Clurman, Harold. *Lies Like Truth; Theatre Reviews and Essays*. New York: Macmillan, 1966, pp. 208–211.

Cranston, Maurice. *Jean-Paul Sartre*. New York: Grove, 1962.

Ewing, James M., Jr. "Sartre's Existentialism and *The Respectful Prostitute*," in *Southern Quarterly*. VII (1969), pp. 167–174.

Jack, Homer A. "Censoring Sartre," in *Nation*. CLXVIII (March 12, 1949), p. 305.

Lumley, Frederick. *New Trends in Twentieth Century Drama: A Survey Since Ibsen and Shaw*. London: Oxford University Press, 1967, pp. 139–158.

McCall, Dorothy. *The Theatre of Jean-Paul Sartre*. New York: Columbia University Press, 1969, pp. 79–87.

Mendel, Sydney. "The Descent into Solitude," in *Forum*. III (1961), pp. 19–24.

Moore, Harry T. *Twentieth Century French Literature Since World War II*. Carbondale: Southern Illinois University Press, 1966, pp. 45–51.

Pollmann, Leo. *Sartre and Camus: Literature of Existence*. New York: Frederick Ungar, 1970, pp. 65–69.

Ridge, George R. "Meaningful Choice in Sartre's Drama," in *French Review*. XXX (1956–1957), pp. 435–441.

Shaw, Irwin. "*The Respectful Prostitute*," in *New Republic*. CXVIII (February 23, 1948), pp. 29–30.

Thody, Philip. *Jean-Paul Sartre: A Literary and Political Study*. New York: Macmillan, 1961, pp. 86–88.

Wilson, Edmund. *Classics and Commercials: A Literary Chronicle of the Forties*. New York: Farrar, Straus and Cudahy, 1950, pp. 393–403.

The Roads to Freedom

Beach, Joseph W. "Sartre's *Roads to Freedom* and *The Reprieve*," in *Western Review*. XII (Spring, 1948), pp. 180–191.

Blotner, Joseph L. *The Political Novel.* New York: Doubleday, 1949.

Brombert, Victor. *The Intellectual Hero: Studies in the French Novel, 1880–1955.* Philadelphia: Lippincott, 1961, pp. 181–203.

Church, Margaret. *Time and Reality: Studies in Contemporary Fiction.* Chapel Hill: University of North Carolina Press, 1963, pp. 253–276.

Eoff, Charles A. *The Modern Spanish Novel.* New York: New York University Press, 1961, pp. 213–254.

Fowlie, Wallace. "Existentialist Hero: A Study of *L'Age de Raison*," in *Yale French Studies.* I (Spring–Summer, 1948), pp. 53–61.

Frid, Y. "A Philosophy of Unbelief and Indifference: Sartre and Contemporary Bourgeois Individualism," in *Modern Quarterly.* II (Summer, 1947), pp. 215–223.

Hardwick, Elizabeth. "Fiction Chronicle: *The Age of Reason* by Jean-Paul Sartre," in *Partisan Review.* XIV (September–October, 1947), pp. 533–535.

Matthews, H.J. *The Hard Journey: The Myth of Man's Rebirth.* London: Chatto and Windus, 1968, pp. 97–113.

McLaughlin, Richard. "*The Age of Reason*," in *Saturday Review of Literature.* XXX (December, 1947), p. 13.

O'Brien, Justin. *The French Literary Horizon.* New Brunswick, N.J.: Rutgers University Press, 1967, pp. 313–316.

_____. "*The Reprieve*," in *New York Times Book Review.* (July 13, 1947), p. 4.

Spender, Stephen. "Sartre's Existential Comedy," in *Nation.* CLXVI (February, 1948), pp. 239–241.

Tarbox, R. "Exhaustion Psychology and Sartre's *The Age of Reason*," in *American Imago.* XXX (Spring, 1973), pp. 80–96.

Ullman, Stephen. *Style in the French Novel.* Oxford: Blackwell, 1964, pp. 210–262.

Wilson, Edmund. "*L'Age de Raison*," in *New Yorker.* XXIII (August, 1947), pp. 60–63.

_____. *Classics and Commercials: A Literary Chronicle of the Forties.* New York: Farrar, Straus and Cudahy, 1950, pp. 393–403.

JOHANN CHRISTOPH FRIEDRICH VON SCHILLER
(1759–1805)

The Bride of Messina

Carruth, W.H. "Fate and Guilt in Schiller's *Die Braut von Messina*," in *PMLA*. XVII (1902), pp. 105–124.

Cutting, S.W. "Schiller's Treatment of Fate and Dramatic Guilt in His *Braut von Messina*," in *Modern Philology*. V (1908), pp. 347–360.

Garland, H.B. *Schiller the Dramatic Writer: A Sudy of Style in the Plays.* Oxford: Clarendon Press, 1969, pp. 233–260.

Graham, Ilse. *Schiller's Drama: Talent and Integrity.* London: Methuen, 1974, pp. 67–92.

Hibberd, J.L. "The Patterns of Imagery in Schiller's *Braut von Messina*," in *German Life and Letters*. XX (1967), pp. 306–315.

Mackay, Alexander T. "Fate and 'Hybris' in *Die Braut von Messina*," in *Forum for Modern Language Studies*. VI (1970), pp. 213–225.

Passage, Charles E. *Friedrich Schiller.* New York: Frederick Ungar, 1975, pp. 167–176.

Stahl, E.L. *Friedrich Schiller's Drama: Theory and Practice.* Oxford: Clarendon Press, 1954, pp. 127–137.

Thomas, Calvin. *The Life and Works of Friedrich Schiller.* New York: Holt, 1901, pp. 387–404.

Weigand, Hermann John. *Surveys and Soundings in European Literature.* Princeton, N.J.: Princeton University Press, 1966, pp. 124–163.

Weiser, Ernest L. "The Inner Form of Schiller's *Die Braut von Messina*," in *South Atlantic Bulletin*. XXXIV (1969), pp. 10–12.

Wells, G.A. "Fate-Tragedy and Schiller's *Die Braut von Messina*," in *Journal of English and Germanic Philology*. LXIV (1965), pp. 191–212.

Witte, William. *Schiller.* Oxford: Basil Blackwell, 1949, pp. 180–186.

Don Carlos

Brother Gregory. *Catholicism in Schiller's Dramas.* New York: New York University Press, 1949, pp. 4–6.

Cernyak, Susan E. "A Note on the *Book of Esther* and Schiller's *Don Carlos*," in *Modern Language Notes*. LXXXVII (1972), pp. 758–759.

Ebstein, Frances. "In Defense of Marquis Posa," in *Germanic Review*. XXXVI (1961), pp. 205–220.

Garland, H.B. *Schiller the Dramatic Writer: A Study of Style in the Plays.* Oxford: Clarendon Press, 1969, pp. 96–137.

Graham, Ilse. *Schiller's Drama: Talent and Integrity.* London: Methuen, 1974, pp. 45–66.

Gronicka, Andre von. "Friedrich Schiller's Marquis Posa," in *Germanic Review.* XXVI (1951), pp. 196–214.

Passage, Charles E. *Friedrich Schiller.* New York: Frederick Ungar, 1975, pp. 62–86.

Seidlin, Oskar. *Essays in German and Comparative Literature.* Chapel Hill: University of North Carolina Press, 1961, pp. 92–109.

Simons, John D. "The Nature of Oppression in *Don Carlos*," in *Modern Language Notes.* LXXXIV (1969), pp. 451–457.

————. "The Ritual Execution of Don Carlos," in *Germanic Notes.* III (1972), pp. 53–55.

————. "Schiller's *Don Carlos*," in *Explicator.* XXVII (1969), item 22.

Stahl, E.L. *Friedrich Schiller's Drama: Theory and Practice.* Oxford: Clarendon Press, 1954, pp. 30–44.

Thomas, Calvin. *The Life and Works of Friedrich Schiller.* New York: Holt, 1901, pp. 176–200.

Witte, William. *Schiller.* Oxford: Basil Blackwell, 1949, pp. 135–146.

Love and Intrigue

Garland, H.B. *Schiller the Dramatic Writer: A Study of Style in the Plays.* Oxford: Clarendon Press, 1969, pp. 67–95.

Graham, Ilse. "Passions and Possessions in Schiller's *Kabale und Liebe*," in *German Life and Letters.* VI (1952), pp. 12–20.

————. *Schiller's Drama: Talent and Integrity.* London: Methuen, 1974, pp. 110–120.

Heitner, Robert R. "Luise Millerin and the Shock Motif in Schiller's Early Dramas," in *Germanic Review.* XLI (1966), pp. 27–45.

————. "Neglected Model for *Kabale und Liebe*," in *Journal of English and Germanic Philology.* LVII (1958), pp. 72–85.

Passage, Charles E. *Friedrich Schiller.* New York: Frederick Ungar, 1975, pp. 51–61.

Schwarz, E. "Manuel Tamayo y Baus and Schiller," in *Comparative Literature.* XIII (1961), pp. 123–137.

Seidlin, Oskar. *Essays in German and Comparative Literature.* Chapel Hill: University of North Carolina Press, 1961, pp. 131–140.

————. "Greatness and Decline of the Bourgeoise: Dramas by Schiller and Dumas," in *Comparative Literature.* VI (1954), pp. 123–129.

Stahl, E.L. *Friedrich Schiller's Drama: Theory and Practice.* Oxford: Clarendon Press, 1954, pp. 23–29.

Thomas, Calvin. *The Life and Works of Friedrich Schiller.* New York: Holt, 1901, pp. 112–135.

Witte, William. *Schiller.* Oxford: Basil Blackwell, 1949, pp. 125–134.

The Maid of Orleans

Allison, D.E. "The Spiritual Element in Schiller's *Jungfrau* and Goethe's *Iphigenie*," in *German Quarterly.* XXXII (1959), pp. 16–29.

Blankenagel, John C. "Shaw's *Saint Joan* and Schiller's *Jungfrau von Orleans*," in *Journal of English and Germanic Philology.* XXV (1926), pp. 379–392.

Brother Gregory. *Catholicism in Schiller's Dramas.* New York: New York University Press, 1949, pp. 10–16.

Evans, M. Blakemore. "*Die Jungfrau von Orleans*: A Drama of Philosophical Idealism," in *Monatshefte.* XXXV (1943), pp. 188–194.

Fowler, Frank M. "Sight and Insight in Schiller's *Die Jungfrau von Orleans*," in *Modern Language Review.* LXVIII (1973), pp. 367–379.

————. "Storm and Thunder in Gluck's and Goethe's *Iphigenie auf Taurus* and Schiller's *Die Jungfrau von Orleans*," in *Publications of the English Goethe Society.* XLIII (1973), pp. 1–27.

Garland, H.B. *Schiller the Dramatic Writer: A Study of Style in the Plays.* Oxford: Clarendon Press, 1969, pp. 210–232.

Krumpelmann, John T. "Schiller's Rehabilitation of Jeanne d'Arc," in *American-German Review.* XXVI (1960), pp. 8–9, 38.

Mainland, William F. *Schiller and the Changing Past.* London: Heinemann, 1957, pp. 87–106.

Passage, Charles E. *Friedrich Schiller.* New York: Frederick Ungar, 1975, pp. 150–166.

Richards, David B. "Mesmerism in *Die Jungfrau von Orleans*," in *PMLA.* XCI (1976), pp. 856–870.

Sammons, Jeffrey L. "Mortimer's Conversion and Schiller's Allegiances," in *Journal of English and Germanic Philology.* LXXII (1973), pp. 155–166.

Stahl, E.L. *Friedrich Schiller's Drama: Theory and Practice.* Oxford: Clarendon Press, 1954, pp. 116–125.

Thomas, Calvin. *The Life and Works of Friedrich Schiller.* New York: Holt, 1901, pp. 371–386.

Waterman, John T. "*Die Jungfrau von Orleans* in the Light of Schiller's Essays," in *Germanic Review.* XXV (1952), pp. 230–238.

Willan, J.N. "Schiller's *Jungfrau von Orleans*: Its Point of Contact with Shakespeare," in *Poet-Lore.* VII (1895), pp. 169–183.

Witte, William. *Schiller.* Oxford: Basil Blackwell, 1949, pp. 174–180.

Maria Stuart

Abel, Lionel. *Metatheatre: A New View of Dramatic Form.* New York: Hill and Wang, 1963, pp. 73–74.

Best, Alan. "Schiller's *Maria Stuart*: Masquerade as Tragedy," in *Modern Languages.* LIII (1972), pp. 106–110.

Brother Gregory. *Catholicism in Schiller's Dramas.* New York: New York University Press, 1949, pp. 7–9.

Field, G.S. "Schiller's *Maria Stuart*," in *University of Toronto Quarterly.* XXIX (1960), pp. 326–340.

Garland, H.B. *Schiller the Dramatic Writer: A Study of Style in the Plays.* Oxford: Clarendon Press, 1969, pp. 190–209.

Graham, Ilse. *Schiller's Drama: Talent and Integrity.* London: Methuen, 1974, pp. 149–170.

Mainland, William F. *Schiller and the Changing Past.* London: William Heinemann, 1957, pp. 57–86.

Passage, Charles E. *Friedrich Schiller.* New York: Frederick Ungar, 1975, pp. 131–149.

Sammons, Jeffrey L. "Mortimer's Conversion and Schiller's Allegiances," in *Journal of English and Germanic Philology.* LXXII (1973), pp. 155–166.

Seidlin, Oskar. *Essays in German and Comparative Literature.* Chapel Hill: University of North Carolina Press, 1961, pp. 92–109.

Stahl, E.L. *Friedrich Schiller's Drama: Theory and Practice.* Oxford: Clarendon Press, 1954, pp. 107–116.

Thomas, Calvin. *The Life and Works of Friedrich Schiller.* New York: Holt, 1901, pp. 354–370.

Witte, William. *Schiller.* Oxford: Basil Blackwell, 1949, pp. 167–174.

Zetler, Greta L. " 'Edle Einfalt, stille Grösse': A Comment on Schiller's *Maria Stuart*," in *Language Quarterly.* X (1971), pp. 13–14, 18.

The Robbers

Garland, H.B. *Schiller the Dramatic Writer: A Study of Style in the Plays.* Oxford: Clarendon Press, 1969, pp. 5–39.

Graham, Ilse. "The Structure of the Personality in Schiller's Tragic Poetry," in *Schiller: Bicentenary Lectures.* Edited by F. Norman. London: University of London Institute of Germanic Languages and Literatures, 1960, pp. 105–107.

Heitner, Robert R. "Luise Millerin and the Shock Motif in Schiller's Early Dramas," in *Germanic Review.* XLI (1966), pp. 27–45.

Lambert, J.W. "Highwaymen," in *Plays and Players.* XXII (1975), p. 29.

Passage, Charles E. *Friedrich Schiller.* New York: Frederick Ungar, 1975, pp. 30–40.

Stahl, E.L.   *Friedrich Schiller's Drama: Theory and Practice.* Oxford: Clarendon Press, 1954, pp. 9–17.

Stamm, Israel S.   "The Religious Aspect of *Die Räuber*," in *Germanic Review.* XXVII (1952), pp. 5–9.

Thomas, Calvin.   *The Life and Works of Friedrich Schiller.* New York: Holt, 1901, pp. 31–54.

Veit, Phillip F.   "The Strange Case of Moritz Spiegelberg," in *Germanic Review.* XLIV (1969), pp. 171–186.

Waterhouse, G.   "Schiller's *Rauber* in England Before 1800," in *Modern Language Review.* XXX (1935), pp. 355–357.

Witte, William.   *Schiller.* Oxford: Basil Blackwell, 1949, pp. 105–115.

Wallenstein

Blankenagel, John C.   "*Wallenstein* and Prinz Friedrich von Homburg," in *Germanic Review.* II (1927), pp. 1–11.

Garland, H.B.   *Schiller the Dramatic Writer: A Study of Style in the Plays.* Oxford: Clarendon Press, 1969, pp. 138–189.

Hill, Harold C.   "Astrology and Friendship: The Net of Commitment in *Wallenstein*," in *Modern Language Notes.* XCI (1976), pp. 467–477.

Linn, R.N.   "Wallenstein's Innocence," in *Germanic Review.* XXXIV (1959), pp. 200–208.

Mainland, William F.   *Schiller and the Changing Past.* London: Heinemann, 1957, pp. 32–56.

Marleyn, R.   "*Wallenstein* and the Structure of Schiller's Tragedies," in *Germanic Review.* XXXII (1957), pp. 186–199.

Passage, Charles E.   *Friedrich Schiller.* New York: Frederick Ungar, 1975, pp. 95–130.

Rothman, John.   "Octavio and Buttler in Schiller's *Wallenstein*," in *German Quarterly.* XXVII (1954), pp. 110–115.

Sammons, Jeffrey L.   "Mortimer's Conversion and Schiller's Allegiances," in *Journal of English and Germanic Philology.* LXXII (1973), pp. 155–166.

Seidlin, Oskar.   *Essays in German and Comparative Literature.* Chapel Hill: University of North Carolina Press, 1961, pp. 92–109.

Stahl, E.L.   *Friedrich Schiller's Drama: Theory and Practice.* Oxford: Clarendon Press, 1954, pp. 88–105.

Thomas, Calvin.   *The Life and Works of Friedrich Schiller.* New York: Holt, 1901, pp. 330–353.

Wells, G.A.   "Astrology in Schiller's *Wallenstein*," in *Journal of English and Germanic Philology.* LXVIII (1969), pp. 100–115.

Witte, William. *Schiller*. Oxford: Basil Blackwell, 1949, pp. 147–164.

————. *Schiller and Burns, and Other Essays*. Oxford: Basil Blackwell, 1959, pp. 38–47.

William Tell

Barnstorff, Hermann. "Individualism and Collectivism in Schiller's *Wilhelm Tell*: A Classroom Suggestion," in *Monatshefte*. XLV (1953), pp. 166–170.

Busse, A. "Schiller's *Tell* and the Volksstuck," in *PMLA*. XXXII (1917), pp. 59–67.

Field, G.W. "Schiller's Theory of the Idyl and *Wilhelm Tell*," in *Monatshefte*. XLII (1950), pp. 13–21.

Garland, H.B. *Schiller the Dramatic Writer: A Study of Style in the Plays*. Oxford: Clarendon Press, 1969, pp. 261–286.

Graham, Ilse. *Schiller's Drama: Talent and Integrity*. London: Methuen, 1974, pp. 195–215.

Grotegut, E.K. "Schiller's *Wilhelm Tell*: A Dramatic Triangle," in *Modern Language Notes*. LXXX (1965), pp. 628–634.

Jetter, Marianne R. "*Wilhelm Tell* and Modern Students," in *German Quarterly*. XXX (1957), pp. 45–47.

Jofen, Jean B. "Elements of Homer and the Bible in Schiller's *Wilhelm Tell*," in *Canadian Modern Language Review*. XVI (1960), pp. 27–35.

McKay, G.W. "Three Scenes from *Wilhelm Tell*," in *The Discontinuous Tradition: Studies in German Literature in Honour of Ernest Ludwig Stahl*. Edited by Peter F. Ganz. Oxford: Oxford University Press, 1971, pp. 99–112.

Mainland, William F. *Schiller and the Changing Past*. London: Heinemann, 1957, pp. 107–122.

Mitchell, Roger E. and Joyce P. Mitchell. "Schiller's *William Tell*: a Folkloristic Perspective," in *Journal of American Folklore*. LXXXIII (1970), pp. 44–52.

Passage, Charles E. *Friedrich Schiller*. New York: Frederick Ungar, 1975, pp. 177–191.

Plant, Richard. "Gessler and Tell: Psychological Patterns in Schiller's *Wilhelm Tell*," in *Modern Language Quarterly*. XIX (1958), pp. 60–70.

Richards, David B. "Tell in the Dock: Forensic Rhetoric in the Monologue and Parricida-Scene in *Wilhelm Tell*," in *German Quarterly*. XLVIII (1975), pp. 472–486.

Ryder, Frank G. "Schiller's *Tell* and the Cause of Freedom," in *German Quarterly*. XLVIII (1975), pp. 487–504.

Stahl, E.L.   *Friedrich Schiller's Drama: Theory and Practice*. Oxford: Clarendon Press, 1954, pp. 137–148.

Sumberg, S.L.   "Continuity of Action in Schiller's *Wilhelm Tell*," in *Germanic Review*. VIII (1933), pp. 17–29.

Thomas, Calvin.   *The Life and Works of Friedrich Schiller*. New York: Holt, 1901, pp. 405–422.

Witte, William.   *Schiller*. Oxford: Basil Blackwell, 1949, pp. 187–194.

SIR WALTER SCOTT
(1771–1832)

The Bride of Lammermoor

Beaty, Frederick L. *Light from Heaven: Love in British Romantic Literature.* DeKalb: Northern Illinois University Press, 1971, pp. 104–106.

Brewer, Wilmon. *Shakespeare's Influence on Sir Walter Scott.* Boston: Cornhill, 1925, pp. 281–292, 415–417.

Brooks, Douglas. "Feast and Structure in *The Bride of Lammermoor*," in *Ariel.* II (1971), pp. 66–76.

Cameron, Donald. "The Web of Destiny: The Structure of *The Bride of Lammermoor*," in *Scott's Mind and Art.* Edited by A. Norman Jeffares. London: Oliver and Boyd, 1969, pp. 185–205.

Cusac, Marian H. *Narrative Structure in the Novels of Sir Walter Scott.* The Hague: Mouton, 1969, pp. 49–51, 106–112.

Devlin, David D. *The Author of* Waverley: *A Critical Study of Walter Scott.* Lewisburg, Pa.: Bucknell University Press, 1971, pp. 99–113.

————. "Scott and History," in *Scott's Mind and Art.* Edited by A. Norman Jeffares. London: Oliver and Boyd, 1969, pp. 86–88.

Fiske, Christabel F. *Epic Suggestion in the Imagery of the Waverley Novels.* New Haven, Conn.: Yale University Press, 1940.

Fleishman, Avrom. *The English Historical Novel; Walter Scott to Virginia Woolf.* Baltimore: Johns Hopkins University Press, 1971, pp. 67–69.

Gordon, Robert C. "*The Bride of Lammermoor*: A Novel of Tory Pessimism," in *Nineteenth-Century Fiction.* XII (1957), pp. 110–124.

————. *Under Which King? A Study of the Scottish Waverley Novels.* New York: Barnes & Noble, 1969, pp. 98–109.

Hart, Francis R. *Scott's Novels: The Plotting of Historic Survival.* Charlottesville: University of Virginia Press, 1966.

Hartveit, Lars. *Scott's* The Bride of Lammermoor; *an Assessment of Attitude.* Bergen, Minn.: Norwegian Universities Press, 1962.

Hook, A.D. "*The Bride of Lammermoor*: A Reexamination," in *Nineteenth-Century Fiction.* XXII (September, 1967), pp. 111–126.

Johnson, Edgar. *Sir Walter Scott: The Great Unknown*, Volume I. New York: Macmillan, 1970, pp. 662–670.

Levine, George. "Exorcising the Past: Scott's *The Bride of Lammermoor*," in *Nineteenth-Century Fiction.* XXXII (March, 1978), pp. 379–398.

McCombie, Frank. "Scott, Hamlet, and *The Bride of Lammermoor*," in *Essays in Criticism.* XXV (1975), pp. 419–436.

Millgate, Jane. "Two Versions of Regional Romance: Scott's *The Bride of Lammermoor* and Hardy's *Tess of the d'Urbervilles*," in *Studies in English Literature, 1500–1900*. XVII (Autumn, 1977), pp. 729–738.

Owen, E. "Critics of *The Bride of Lammermoor*," in *Dalhousie Review*. XVIII (October, 1938), pp. 365–371.

Parsons, Coleman O. "The Dalrymple Legend in *The Bride of Lammermoor*," in *Review of English Studies*. XIX (January, 1943), pp. 51–58.

Welsh, Alexander. *The Hero of the Waverley Novels*. New Haven, Conn.: Yale University Press, 1963, pp. 44–45, 216–217.

The Fortunes of Nigel

Brewer, Wilmon. *Shakespeare's Influence on Sir Walter Scott*. Boston: Cornhill, 1925, pp. 196–198, 333–335.

Buchan, John. *Sir Walter Scott*. London: Cassell, 1932, pp. 247–250.

Cusac, Marian H. *Narrative Structure in the Novels of Sir Walter Scott*. The Hague: Mouton, 1969, pp. 54–57, 106–112.

Fiske, Christabel F. *Epic Suggestion in the Imagery of the Waverley Novels*. New Haven, Conn.: Yale University Press, 1940.

Harper, Howard M., Jr. and Charles Edge. *The Classic British Novel*. Athens: University of Georgia Press, 1972, pp. 65–84.

Hart, Francis R. *Scott's Novels: The Plotting of Historic Survival*. Charlottesville: University of Virginia Press, 1966, pp. 198–203.

Hayden, John O. *Scott; The Critical Heritage*. New York: Barnes & Noble, 1970, pp. 261–268.

Johnson, Edgar. *Sir Walter Scott: The Great Unknown*, Volume II. New York: Macmillan, 1970, pp. 822–828.

Rubenstein, Jill. "The Defeat and Triumph of Bourgeois Pacifism: Scott's *Fair Maid of Perth* and *The Fortunes of Nigel*," in *Wordsworth Circle*. II (1971), pp. 136–141.

Welsh, Alexander. *The Hero of the Waverley Novels*. New Haven, Conn.: Yale University Press, 1963.

Guy Mannering

Cusac, Marian H. *Narrative Suggestion in the Novels of Sir Walter Scott*. The Hague: Mouton, 1969.

Devlin, David D. *The Author of Waverley: A Critical Study of Walter Scott*. Lewisburg, Pa.: Bucknell University Press, 1971, pp. 33–62.

Grabo, Carl H. *The Technique of the Novel*. New York: Scribner's, 1928, pp. 11–18.

Gordon, Robert C. *Under Which King? A Study of the Scottish Waverley Novels*. New York: Barnes & Noble, 1969, pp. 26–35.

Hammerton, John A. *Memories of Books and Other Places*. London: Low, 1928, pp. 48–58.

Hart, Francis R. *Scott's Novels: The Plotting of Historic Survival*. Charlottesville: University of Virginia Press, 1966, pp. 259–266, 270–275.

Hartveit, Lars. *Dream Within a Dream, a Thematic Approach to Scott's Vision of Fictional Reality*. New York: Humanities Press, 1974, pp. 119–156.

Hayden, John O. *Scott; The Critical Heritage*. New York: Barnes & Noble, 1970, pp. 86–89.

Johnson, Edgar. *Sir Walter Scott: The Great Unknown*, Volume I. New York: Macmillan, 1970, pp. 530–536.

Lauber, John. *Sir Walter Scott*. New York: Twayne, 1966, pp. 72–79.

Mayhead, Robin. "Scott and the Idea of Justice," in *Scott's Mind and Art*. Edited by A. Norman Jeffares. London: Oliver and Boyd, 1969, pp. 167–184.

Welsh, Alexander. *The Hero of the Waverley Novels*. New Haven, Conn.: Yale University Press, 1963.

The Heart of Midlothian

Clements, Frances M. " 'Queens Love Revenge as Well as Their Subjects': Thematic Unity in *The Heart of Midlothian*," in *Studies in Scottish Literature*. X (1972), pp. 10–17.

Cockshut, A.O.J. *The Achievement of Walter Scott*. New York: New York University Press, 1969, pp. 171–192.

Craig, D. "*The Heart of Midlothian*: Its Religious Basis," in *Essays in Criticism*. VIII (April, 1958), pp. 217–225.

Cusac, Marian H. *Narrative Suggestion in the Novels of Sir Walter Scott*. The Hague: Mouton, 1969, pp. 32–36, 106–112.

Fisher, P.F. "Providence, Fate, and the Historical Imagination in Scott's *The Heart of Midlothian*," in *Nineteenth-Century Fiction*. X (1955), pp. 99–114.

Fiske, Christabel F. *Epic Suggestion in the Imagery of the Waverley Novels*. New Haven, Conn.: Yale University Press, 1940.

Fleishman, Avrom. *The English Historical Novel; Walter Scott to Virginia Woolf*. Baltimore: Johns Hopkins University Press, 1971, pp. 67–69.

Gordon, Robert C. *Under Which King? A Study of the Scottish Waverley Novels*. New York: Barnes & Noble, 1969, pp. 84–97.

Hart, Francis R. *Scott's Novels: The Plotting of Historic Survival*. Charlottesville: University of Virginia Press, 1966, pp. 127–149.

Hartveit, Lars. *Dream Within a Dream, a Thematic Approach to Scott's Vision of Fictional Reality*. New York: Humanities Press, 1974, pp. 22–71.

Hayden, John O.   *Scott; The Critical Heritage.* New York: Barnes & Noble, 1970, pp. 165–176.

Hyde, William J.   "Jeanie Deans and the Queen: Appearance and Reality," in *Nineteenth-Century Fiction.* XXVIII (1973), pp. 86–92.

Johnson, Edgar.   *Sir Walter Scott: The Great Unknown,* Volume I. New York: Macmillan, 1970, pp. 655–662.

Kettle, Arnold.   *An Introduction to the English Novel,* Volume I. London: Hutchinson's, 1951, pp. 105–122.

Lauber, John.   *Sir Walter Scott.* New York: Twayne, 1966, pp. 106–114.

Lynskey, Winifred.   "The Drama of the Elect and the Reprobate in Scott's *Heart of Midlothian,*" in *Boston University Studies in English.* IV (1960), pp. 39–48.

Madden, William A.   "The Search for Forgiveness in Some Nineteenth-Century English Novels," in *Comparative Literature Studies.* III (1966), pp. 139–153.

Marshall, W.H.   "Point of View and Structure in *The Heart of Midlothian,*" in *Nineteenth-Century Fiction.* XVI (1961), pp. 257–262.

Mayhead, Robin.   "*The Heart of Midlothian*: Scott as Artist," in *Essays in Criticism.* VI (July, 1956), pp. 266–277.

Pritchett, Victor S.   *The Living Novel.* New York: Reynal & Hitchcock, 1947, pp. 63–68.

Van Ghent, Dorothy.   *The English Novel.* New York: Rinehart, 1953, pp. 113–124.

Welsh, Alexander.   *The Hero of the Waverley Novels.* New Haven, Conn.: Yale University Press, 1963, pp. 59–62, 127–148, 163–164.

Ivanhoe

Baker, Ernest A.   *History of the English Novel,* Volume VI. London: Witherby, 1929, pp. 176–206.

Brewer, Wilmon.   *Shakespeare's Influence on Sir Walter Scott.* Boston: Cornhill, 1925.

Buchan, John.   *Sir Walter Scott.* London: Cassell, 1932, pp. 180–198.

Chandler, Alice.   "Chivalry and Romance: Scott's Medieval Novels," in *Studies in Romanticism.* XIV (1975), pp. 191–194.

Cockshut, A.O.J.   *The Achievement of Walter Scott.* New York: New York University Press, 1969, pp. 97–100.

Cusac, Marian H.   *Narrative Structure in the Novels of Sir Walter Scott.* The Hague: Mouton, 1969, pp. 106–113, 118–119.

Duncan, Joseph E.   "The Anti-Romantic in *Ivanhoe,*" in *Nineteenth-Century Fiction.* IX (March, 1955), pp. 293–300.

Fisch, Harold. *The Dual Image: The Figure of the Jew in English and American Literature.* New York: Ktav, 1971, pp. 59–62.

Fiske, Christabel F. *Epic Suggestion in the Imagery of the Waverley Novels.* New Haven, Conn.: Yale University Press, 1940.

Hart, Francis R. *Scott's Novels: The Plotting of Historic Survival.* Charlottesville: University of Virginia Press, 1966.

Hayden, John O. *Scott; The Critical Heritage.* New York: Barnes & Noble, 1970, pp. 177–184, 188–255.

Johnson, Edgar. *Sir Walter Scott: The Great Unknown,* Volume I. New York: Macmillan, 1970, pp. 736–746.

Lauber, John. *Sir Walter Scott.* New York: Twayne, 1966, pp. 125–126, 130–131.

Rosenberg, Edgar. "The Jew as Clown and the Jew's Daughter," in *From Shylock to Svengali: Jewish Stereotypes in English Fiction.* Edited by Edgar Rosenberg. Stanford, Calif.: Stanford University Press, 1960, pp. 73–115.

Simeone, William E. "The Robin Hood of *Ivanhoe,*" in *Journal of American Folklore.* LXXIV (1961), pp. 230–234.

Tindall, William Y., Perry Miller and Lyman Bryson. *"Ivanhoe,"* in *Invitation to Learning: English and American Novels.* Edited by George D. Crothers. New York: Basic Books, 1966, pp. 81–88.

Welsh, Alexander. *The Hero of the Waverley Novels.* New Haven, Conn.: Yale University Press, 1963.

Kenilworth

Brewer, Wilmon. *Shakespeare's Influence on Sir Walter Scott.* Boston: Cornhill, 1925, pp. 314–333, 445–447, 456–467.

Buchan, John. *Sir Walter Scott.* London: Cassell, 1932, pp. 231–233.

Cusac, Marian H. *Narrative Structure in the Novels of Sir Walter Scott.* The Hague: Mouton, 1969, pp. 44–45, 106–112.

Fiske, Christabel F. *Epic Suggestion in the Imagery of the Waverley Novels.* New Haven, Conn.: Yale University Press, 1940.

Hart, Francis H. *Scott's Novels: The Plotting of Historic Survival.* Charlottesville: University of Virginia Press, 1966, pp. 196–198, 203–210.

Johnson, Edgar. *Sir Walter Scott: The Great Unknown,* Volume I. New York: Macmillan, 1970, pp. 755–759.

Welsh, Alexander. *The Hero of the Waverley Novels.* New Haven, Conn.: Yale University Press, 1963, pp. 164–165, 220.

Redgauntlet

Buchan, John.   *Sir Walter Scott*. London: Cassell, 1932.

Calder, Angus and Jenni Calder.   *Scott*. New York: Arco, 1971, pp. 141–149.

Cockshut, A.O.J.   *The Achievement of Walter Scott*. New York: New York University Press, 1969, pp. 193–213.

Cusac, Marian H.   *Narrative Structure in the Novels of Sir Walter Scott*. The Hague: Mouton, 1969, pp. 58–60, 106–112, 118–119.

Daiches, David.   "Scott's *Redgauntlet*," in *From Jane Austen to Joseph Conrad*. Edited by Robert C. Rathburn and Martin Steinmann, Jr. Minneapolis: University of Minnesota Press, 1958, pp. 46–59.

Devlin, David D.   *The Author of* Waverley: *A Critical Study of Walter Scott*. Lewisburg, Pa.: Bucknell University Press, 1971, pp. 114–133.

————.   "Scott and History," in *Scott's Mind and Art*. Edited by A. Norman Jeffares. London: Oliver and Boyd, 1969, pp. 75–77.

————.   "Scott and *Redgauntlet*," in *Review of English Literature*. IV (January, 1963), pp. 91–103.

Donovan, Robert A.   *The Shaping Vision: Imagination in the English Novel from DeFoe to Dickens*. Ithaca, N.Y.: Cornell University Press, 1966, pp. 177–192.

Fiske, Christabel F.   *Epic Suggestion in the Imagery of the Waverley Novels*. New Haven, Conn.: Yale University Press, 1940.

Fleishman, Avrom.   *The English Historical Novel; Walter Scott to Virginia Woolf*. Baltimore: Johns Hopkins University Press, 1971, pp. 73–75.

Gordon, Robert C.   *Under Which King? A Study of the Scottish Waverley Novels*. New York: Barnes & Noble, 1969, pp. 149–166.

Hart, Francis R.   *Scott's Novels: The Plotting of Historic Survival*. Charlottesville: University of Virginia Press, 1966, pp. 48–64.

Hartveit, Lars.   *Dream Within a Dream, a Thematic Approach to Scott's Vision of Fictional Reality*. New York: Humanities Press, 1974, pp. 203–247.

Jefferson, D.W.   "The Virtuosity of Scott," in *Scott's Mind and Art*. Edited by A. Norman Jeffares. London: Oliver and Boyd, 1969, pp. 53–61.

Johnson, Edgar.   *Sir Walter Scott: The Great Unknown*, Volume II. New York: Macmillan, 1970, pp. 920–928.

Lauber, John.   *Sir Walter Scott*. New York: Twayne, 1966, pp. 67–71, 117–119.

Mayhead, Robin.   "Scott and the Idea of Justice," in *Scott's Mind and Art*. Edited by A. Norman Jeffares. London: Oliver and Boyd, 1969, pp. 180–184.

Smith, J.A.   "*Redgauntlet*: The Man of Law's Tale," in *Times Literary Supplement*. LXX (July 23, 1971), pp. 863–864.

Welsh, Alexander. *The Hero of the Waverley Novels.* New Haven, Conn.: Yale University Press, 1963, pp. 68–70.

Rob Roy

Brewer, Wilmon. *Shakespeare's Influence on Sir Walter Scott.* Boston: Cornhill, 1925, pp. 262–273.

Buchan, John. *Sir Walter Scott.* London: Cassell, 1932, pp. 181–187.

Cadbury, William. "The Two Structures of *Rob Roy*," in *Modern Language Quarterly.* XXIX (1968), pp. 42–60.

Cockshut, A.O.J. *The Achievement of Walter Scott.* New York: New York University Press, 1969, pp. 152–170.

Cusac, Marian H. *Narrative Structure in the Novels of Sir Walter Scott.* The Hague: Mouton, 1969, pp. 36–39, 106–112, 118–119.

Devlin, David D. *The Author of* Waverley*: A Critical Study of Walter Scott.* Lewisburg, Pa.: Bucknell University Press, 1971, pp. 33–62, 90–98, 122–129.

————. "Character and Narrative in Scott; *A Legend of Montrose* and *Rob Roy*," in *Essays in Criticism.* XVIII (1968), pp. 136–151.

Fiske, Christabel F. *Epic Suggestion in the Imagery of the Waverley Novels.* New Haven, Conn.: Yale University Press, 1940.

Fleishman, Avrom. *The English Historical Novel; Walter Scott to Virginia Woolf.* Baltimore: Johns Hopkins University Press, 1971, pp. 69–71.

Gordon, Robert C. "In Defense of *Rob Roy*," in *Essays in Criticism.* XVIII (1968), pp. 470–475.

————. *Under Which King? A Study of the Scottish Waverley Novels.* New York: Barnes & Noble, 1969, pp. 67–83.

Hart, Francis R. *Scott's Novels: The Plotting of Historic Survival.* Charlottesville: University of Virginia Press, 1966, pp. 31–48.

Hayden, John O. *Scott; The Critical Heritage.* New York: Barnes & Noble, 1970, pp. 146–164.

Johnson, Edgar. *Sir Walter Scott: The Great Unknown*, Volume I. New York: Macmillan, 1970, pp. 600–609.

Lauber, John. *Sir Walter Scott.* New York: Twayne, 1966, pp. 98–101.

Mills, Nicolaus. *American and English Fiction in the Nineteenth Century; an Anti-genre Critique and Comparison.* Bloomington: Indiana University Press, 1973, pp. 32–51.

Tillyard, Eustace M.W. *Epic Strain in the English Novel.* Fair Lawn, N.J.: Essential Books, 1958, pp. 59–116.

Welsh, Alexander. *The Hero of the Waverley Novels.* New Haven, Conn.: Yale University Press, 1963.

Waverley

Baker, Ernest A. *History of the English Novel*, Volume VI. London: Witherby, 1929, pp. 122–143.

Buchan, John. *Sir Walter Scott*. London: Cassell, 1932.

Clipper, Lawrence J. "Edward Waverley's Night Journey," in *South Atlantic Quarterly*. LXXIII (1974), pp. 541–553.

Cockshut, A.O.J. *The Achievement of Walter Scott*. New York: New York University Press, 1969, pp. 107–128, 155–157.

Cusac, Marian H. *Narrative Structure in the Novels of Sir Walter Scott*. The Hague: Mouton, 1969.

Daiches, David. "Scott's Achievement as a Novelist," in *Nineteenth-Century Fiction*. VI (September, 1951), pp. 90–95.

Devlin, David D. *The Author of* Waverley*: A Critical Study of Walter Scott*. Lewisburg, Pa.: Bucknell University Press, 1971, pp. 56–80.

————. "Scott and History," in *Scott's Mind and Art*. Edited by A. Norman Jeffares. London: Oliver and Boyd, 1969, pp. 78–80, 89–91.

Fiske, Christabel F. *Epic Suggestion in the Imagery of the Waverley Novels*. New Haven, Conn.: Yale University Press, 1940.

Gordon, Robert C. *Under Which King? A Study of the Scottish Waverley Novels*. New York: Barnes & Noble, 1969, pp. 11–25.

Gordon, S. Stewart. "*Waverley* and the 'Unified Design,'" in *Journal of English Literary History*. XVIII (June, 1951), pp. 107–122.

Hahn, H.G. "Historiographic and Literary: The Fusion of Two Eighteenth-Century Modes in Scott's *Waverley*," in *Hartford Studies in Literature*. VI (1974), pp. 243–267.

Hart, Francis R. *Scott's Novels: The Plotting of Historic Survival*. Charlottesville: University of Virginia Press, 1966.

Hartveit, Lars. *Dream Within a Dream, a Thematic Approach to Scott's Vision of Fictional Reality*. New York: Humanities Press, 1974, pp. 72–118.

Hayden, John O. *Scott; The Critical Heritage*. New York: Barnes & Noble, 1970, pp. 67–84.

Hennelly, Mark M. "*Waverley* and Romanticism," in *Nineteenth-Century Fiction*. XXVIII (1973), pp. 194–209.

Iser, Wolfgang. *The Implied Reader: Patterns of Communication in Prose Fiction from Bunyan to Beckett*. Baltimore: Johns Hopkins University Press, 1974, pp. 81–100.

Johnson, Edgar. *Sir Walter Scott: The Great Unknown*, Volume I. New York: Macmillan, 1970, pp. 520–530.

Kiely, Robert. *The Romantic Novel in England*. Cambridge, Mass.: Harvard University Press, 1972, pp. 136–154.

Lauber, John. *Sir Walter Scott.* New York: Twayne, 1966, pp. 48–66.

Raleigh, John H. "*Waverley* and *The Fair Maid of Perth*," in *Some British Romantics.* Edited by James V. Logan, John E. Gordon and Northrop Frye. Columbus: Ohio State University Press, 1966, pp. 235–266.

————. "*Waverley* as History; or 'Tis One Hundred and Fifty-Six Years Since,' " in *Novel.* IV (1970), pp. 14–29.

Welsh, Alexander. *The Hero of the Waverley Novels.* New Haven, Conn.: Yale University Press, 1963.

Williams, Ioan. *The Realist Novel in England: A Study in Development.* London: Macmillan, 1974, pp. 25–40.

LUCIUS ANNAEUS SENECA
(c.4 B.C.–A.D. 65)

The Tragedies

Anderson, William Scovil. *Anger in Juvenal and Seneca.* Berkeley: University of California Press, 1964.

Braginton, Mary Victoria. *The Supernatural in Seneca's Tragedies.* Menosha Wis.: Banta, 1933.

Calder, W.M. "Originality in Seneca's *Troades*," in *Classical Philology.* LXV (1970), pp. 75–82.

Canter, Howard Vernon. *Rhetorical Elements in the Tragedies of Seneca.* Urbana: University of Illinois Press, 1925.

Costa, Charles Desmond Nuttall. *Seneca.* London: Routledge and Kegan Paul, 1974.

Cunliffe, John William. *The Influence of Seneca on Elizabethan Tragedy.* Hamden, Conn.: Archon Books, 1965.

Downs, Robert B. "Moral Essayist and Tragic Dramatist: Lucius Annaeus Seneca," in his *Famous Books, Ancient and Medieval.* New York: Barnes & Noble, 1977, pp. 199–203.

Fantham, E. "Virgil's Dido and Seneca's Tragic Heroines," in *Greece and Rome.* XXII (April, 1975), pp. 1–10.

Garton, Charles. "The Background to Character Portrayal in Seneca," in *Classical Philology.* LIV (1959), pp. 1–9.

Hadas, Moses. "The Roman Stamp of Seneca's Tragedies," in *American Journal of Philology.* LX (1939), pp. 220–231.

Harsh, Philip Whaley. *A Handbook of Classical Drama.* Stanford, Calif.: Stanford University Press, 1944, pp. 410–439.

Henry, D. and B. Walker. "Seneca and the *Agamemnon*; Some Thoughts on Tragic Doom," in *Classical Philology.* LVIII (1963), pp. 1–10.

Herington, C.J. "Senecan Tragedy," in *Arion.* V (1966), pp. 422–471.

Hunter, G.K. "Seneca and the Elizabethans: A Case Study in 'Influence,' " in *Shakespeare Survey.* XX (1967), pp. 17–26.

Lucas, Frank L. *Seneca and Elizabethan Tragedy.* Folcroft, Pa.: Folcroft Library Editions, 1972.

Mendell, Clarence W. *Our Seneca.* New Haven, Conn.: Yale University Press, 1941.

Motto, Anna Lydia. *Seneca.* New York: Twayne, 1973.

Motto, Anna Lydia and J.R. Clark. "Senecan Tragedy Patterns of Irony and Art," in *Classical Bulletin.* XLVIII (1972), pp. 69–76.

Nicoll, Allardyce. "From Menander to the Mimes," in his *World Drama; from Aeschylus to Anouilh.* New York: Barnes & Noble, 1965, pp. 74–99.

Poe, Joe P. "An Analysis of Seneca's *Thyestes*," in *Transactions of the American Philological Association.* C (1969), pp. 355–376.

Pratt, N.T. "Major Systems of Figurative Language in Senecan Melodrama," in *Transactions of the American Philological Association.* XCIV (1963), pp. 199–234.

————. "Two Types of Classical Tragedy: The Senecan Revolution," in *Comparative Literature.* Edited by Newton Phelps Stallknecht and Horst Frenz. Carbondale: Southern Illinois University Press, 1971, pp. 218–247.

Sullivan, J.P. "Petronius, Seneca and Lucan; a Neronian Literary Freud?," in *Transactions of the American Philological Association.* XCIX (1968), pp. 453–467.

Tobin, Ronald W. *Racine and Seneca.* Chapel Hill: University of North Carolina Press, 1971, pp. 29–43.

————. "Tragedy and Catastrophe in Seneca's Theater," in *Classical Journal.* LXII (1966), pp. 64–70.

ANNE SEXTON
(1928–1974)

The Poetry of Sexton

Axelrod, Rise B. "The Transforming Art of Anne Sexton," in *Concerning Poetry*. VII (1974), pp. 6–13.

Dickey, William. "A Place in the Country," in *Hudson Review*. XXII (Summer, 1969), pp. 347–349.

Fairfax, John. "More Than Are Dreamt Of," in *Poetry Review*. LV (Winter, 1964), pp. 249–251.

Fein, Richard J. "The Demon of Anne Sexton," in *English Record*. XVIII (October, 1967), pp. 16–21.

Fields, Beverly. "The Poetry of Anne Sexton," in *Poets in Progress*. Edited by Edward Hungerford. Evanston, Ill.: Northwestern University Press, 1967, pp. 250–285.

Howard, Richard. *Alone With America: Essays on the Art of Poetry in the United States Since 1950*. New York: Atheneum, 1969, pp. 442–450.

McClatchy, J.D. "Anne Sexton: Somehow to Endure," in *Centennial Review*. XIX (1975), pp. 1–36.

Meyers, Neil. "The Hungry Sheep Look Up," in *Minnesota Review*. I (October, 1960), pp. 99–104.

Mills, Ralph J. *Contemporary American Poetry*. New York: Random House, 1965, pp. 218–234.

Mizejewski, Linda. "Sappho to Sexton: Woman Uncontained," in *College English*. XXXV (1973), pp. 340–345.

Phillips, Robert. "The Bleeding Rose and the Blooming Mouth," in *Modern Poetry Studies*. I (1970), pp. 41–47.

Rosenthal, M.L. *The New Poets: American and British Poetry Since World War II*. New York: Oxford University Press, 1967, pp. 131–138.